THE 49ers

THE 49ers

THE TRUE STORY

John Warham

Book Guild Publishing
Sussex, England

First published in Great Britain in 2011 by
The Book Guild Ltd
19 New Road
Brighton, BN1 1UF

Typeset in Times New Roman by Ellipsis Books Ltd, Glasgow

Printed in Great Britain by
CPI Antony Rowe

A catalogue record for this book is available from The British Library.

ISBN 978 1 84624 587 9

This book is dedicated to the memories of
Gregory Stephen England
and
Richard David Bennett & Kun
whose young lives were taken so needlessly from
them by an uncaring world

Contents

Permissions

Acknowledgements

My thanks go to all the people who helped me to take this book from a concept to reality. Carol Biss, Ali Hinchliffe, Joanna Bentley, Max Crisfield, Kieran Hood and all of the team at Book Guild Publishing. Andy Tiffany and David Blair for their help with the cover design. Andy Muir and Ho Ting Pong for their help with the proof reading. My special thanks go to Barry Dalton for his patience in helping me to get the words right.

I would also like to thank all the people in our worldwide brotherhood who gave their help, assistance and support to *The 49ers*, whether it be professional, pastoral, financial or just simply a shoulder to cry on sometimes, during our long fight for justice.

In particular, I would like to thank all those who unquestioningly kept the faith and continued to support the 'Band of Brothers' from 2005 onwards either through the Cathay Pilots Union or by any other means.

For the men who continued to believe in us against all the odds and formed the Cathay Pilots Union, especially Nigel Demery, you have my heartfelt thanks.

I would like also to thank Quentin Heron. Without his untiring efforts in dealing with all the administration and paperwork, we would not have succeeded.

Finally, Don, thank you for everything. You are my brother.

1

Taxi

'Oh! I have slipped the surly bonds of earth
And danced the skies on laughter-silvered wings;
Sunward I've climbed, and joined the tumbling mirth
Of sun-split clouds – and done a hundred things
You have not dreamed of – wheeled and soared and swung
High in the sunlit silence. Hov'ring there
I've chased the shouting wind along, and flung
My eager craft through footless halls of air.
Up, up the long delirious, burning blue,
I've topped the windswept heights with easy grace
Where never lark, or even eagle flew –
And, while with silent lifting mind I've trod
The high untresspassed sanctity of space,
Put out my hand and touched the face of God.'
  Pilot Officer John Gillespie Magee Jr., RCAF, *High Flight*

It was the morning of Tuesday 9 May 1989. I had just turned 37 at the end of March and had 8,152 flying hours in my logbook. I walked into the fourth floor office of Mike Hardy, the DFO, in the Cathay Pacific building at Kai Tak. He came round from behind his desk, shook my hand, congratulated me on a job well done and handed me my four bars. I had completed the final check ride on my command course three days before on the previous Saturday night when I arrived back at Kai Tak from Narita via Taipei at 21:05. That was it. The realisation of a boyhood dream. I was now a Captain on the biggest civil jet aircraft in the world. The majestic Boeing 747-200. And not only that: I was a Captain with one of the most prestigious airlines in the world – Cathay Pacific Airways based in Hong Kong.

I had been brought up with aviation. It was in my blood. My father joined the Royal Air Force on 19 December 1939 as a wireless operator. He was recommended for pilot training on 22 April 1940 and gained his wings on 25 September 1942. He flew throughout the Second World War operating the Fairey Battle, Lockheed Hudson, Consolidated PBY Catalina and the B24 Liberator. He served in operational theatres around the globe including Europe, the North Atlantic, Africa and India. He survived the war and was demobbed on 11 April 1946 holding the rank of Warrant Officer.

My father's younger brother, my uncle Arthur, followed his elder brother into the RAF on 21 March 1941, training as a pilot despite the fact that he had a safe job working in the Home Office and was in a reserved occupation. He was killed on active service on 26 September 1944 when his Mosquito crashed. There wasn't much left of him and his remains are interred at Anfield Crematorium in Liverpool. My paternal grand-mother, my Nana, never forgave my father for Arthur's death. She blamed him for encouraging his brother to join up and my father had to live with that for the rest of his life.

The old man didn't talk too much about his experiences during the war but he had some amazing photograph albums that he used to show to me and my sister. He also kept his logbooks and his forage cap, the inside lining of which was stained the colour of verdigris with Brylcreem. They all got lost when I was ten years old when we moved house from Woodhouse in Leeds, where I was born in 1952, to Garforth, West Yorkshire. I've still got his wings from his battledress tunic and the wings that my mother used to have on her handbag to show that she was married to a pilot.

As a kid, my bedroom walls used to be plastered with posters of aircraft. The mighty Lancaster and Halifax, the battle-hardened Spitfire and Hurricane and the beautiful Mosquito. But not just WW2 aircraft. I was a child of the Cold War and loved the new modern generation of jet fighters. The Fairey Delta 2 in which Peter Twiss broke the world speed record on 10 March 1956 and became the first man to travel over 1,000 mph. The English Electric Lightning, the Convair F-102 Dagger, the McDonnell F-101 Voodoo and the Lockheed F-104 Starfighter. Even the names conjured up images of modern day knights streaking through the heavens in their silvery steeds, the sun glittering off their aluminium flanks.

The ceiling of my bedroom was as crowded as the walls. Airfix models of every type hung from the ceiling suspended by fishing line in care-fully choreographed air combat manoeuvres. Everything had to be just right. During construction it was essential to make sure that the propellers, guns, turrets, ailerons, elevators, undercarriage and retractable floats all rotated and pivoted as per the spec. The oft-repeated Airfix instruction, 'ENSURING NO CEMENT COMES INTO CONTACT WITH THE MOVING PARTS', had to be observed meticulously. Paint schemes had to be authentic; roundels and decals placed just so.

My squadron's biggest enemy was its weekly engagement with my mother's duster. As it flicked amongst the formations, battle damage ensued. Propellers shed blades. Guns and turrets were rendered unserviceable (U/S) as their barrels plunged to the carpet. Communications were cut off as aerials and antennae met the same fate. Landings became impossible as undercarriages were rived from their mountings. Eventually further operations became impossible and aircraft were classified as DBR. These were taken to the bottom of the garden for target practice with my .177 air rifle or, until my father caught me one day, doused in lighter fluid, set ablaze and whirled around my head on the end of a piece of string to go down in flaming glory. And then the cycle of reconstruction would begin all over again. I must have built at least seven or eight Catalinas and Lancasters.

My maternal grandfather lived with my grandmother in Southend and worked for Marconi during WW2. One weekend my sister and I were put on the train at Leeds City station bound for Essex with the admonition to behave ourselves and not to talk to any strangers. We were to spend a week with our grandparents, probably to give our parents a much needed rest from our constant bickering. Other than watching a very mediocre performance by Southend United at Roots Hall, the week was uneventful until my grandfather took me to Heathrow to look at some aircraft. He took me into a hangar and it was there that I experienced a revelation that was to map out my future. Inside the hangar was one of the most beautiful sights that I had ever seen in my short life. Standing there was a BOAC Boeing 707. It had been stripped of all its paint, probably prior to repainting. It stood there as naked as when it first left the production line and flaunted its polished aluminium at me like a *Playboy* centrefold. It was mesmerising not only for its glittering lines but also because it grinned at me like a shark does as it senses its prey. The tail fin with its HF aerial looked like a shark's dorsal fin. The forward fuselage looked just like the predator's nose. And it was enormous, huge. It was the first time that I had been up close to a large jet aircraft. Even its wheels were taller than me. It hooked me and landed me there and then. I fell hopelessly in love and resolved that one day I would fly one of these behemoths.

I took the 11 Plus at primary school and won a scholarship to Leeds Grammar School. Although we were not poor, my parents could not afford to send me to a fee-paying school so the scholarship was a godsend. Leeds Grammar School was a prestigious place of learning with many distinguished old boys in fields varying from the arts to engineering, science and sports. It provided a classical, well-rounded education and encouraged competition and excellence, values which are sadly lacking in many of today's institutions. Saturday morning school was compulsory and the school had a Combined Cadet Force (CCF). I joined the RAF section. It was here that I first got into the air and gained my first flying qualification. On some weekends we would go to RAF Church Fenton in the Vale of York for air experience flying in de Havilland Chipmunks. We also used to go away to summer camps during our school holidays and it was during one of these in 1968 at RAF Ouston in Northumberland that I qualified for my British Gliding Association A & B Certificates at the age of 16. It was a first step on the long road towards attaining my dream.

During the 1960s and 70s BOAC & BEA, later BA, ran a cadet scheme to train airline pilots of the future at the College of Air Training, Hamble near Southampton. Competition for places was fierce with tens of thousands of applicants vying for around 200 available places annually. The selection procedure consisted of three rounds of interviews, aptitude and medical tests over a period of months. I applied and was accepted for course number 732 and went to Hamble in June 1973. Even then, acceptance for training did not guarantee graduation. The training consisted of a 21-month full-time residential course with regular examinations and tests on a weekly basis. Failure of any of these tests meant immediate dismissal and the end of one's dreams.

Aviation is a cyclical business and we budding pilots were to learn of this the hard way at first-hand at the very outset of our careers. At the start of our course we were told that we couldn't have arrived at a better time. Airlines were making good profits, expansion plans were in the pipeline and the future looked rosy. We would go straight from successful training to the third seat of a Trident with BA.

Life is fickle and especially so in aviation. In truth the western world was in the middle of an inflationary spiral. US President Nixon had slapped controls on oil in March 1973 as part of his ill-fated price control programme and US oil reserves were at an all-time low. The demand for Middle Eastern oil had been increasing and OPEC was determined to increase its share of the profits. No one was prepared for what happened next.[1]

On 6 October 1973, the Jewish holy day of Yom Kippur, Egyptian forces attacked Israel from across the Suez Canal, while at the same time Syrian troops were flooding the Golan Heights in a surprise offensive. After early losses, Israeli counter-attacks quickly pushed into Syrian territory in the north. As troops outflanked the Egyptian army in the south, Israel, with help from the US, succeeded in reversing the Arab gains and a cease-fire was concluded in November.

But on 17 October OPEC struck back by imposing an oil embargo on the US, while increasing prices by 70 per cent to America's Western European allies. Overnight, the price of a barrel of oil to these nations rose from $3 to $5.11. In January 1974, OPEC raised it further to $11.65.

In our current times of $100 barrels, this seems small potatoes but in net present value terms, $11.65 is equivalent to $90.90 using the UK retail price index or $145 using the average earnings index.[2] The shock waves were immediate. Industrial democracies, accustomed to uninterrupted sources of cheap, imported oil, were suddenly at the mercy of modern Arab nationalism standing up to American oil companies that had once held their countries in a vice-like grip. It was a wake-up call to the West that in the future we could expect to be held hostage to border clashes in what had previously seemed remote parts of the world. OPEC eventually lifted the embargo on 18 March 1974 but the damage had already been done and a severe recession hit much of the western world.

It hit us too at Hamble. Airlines were now in retrenchment rather than expansion including BA. They no longer needed more trainee pilots and we were superfluous to requirements. The normal chop rate of around 25 per cent suddenly increased dramatically and by the time we graduated in March 1975 less than half of us remained on course 732. What was worse, there were no jobs in BA and little chance of employment for us outside of BA. The ink was hardly dry on our brand new licences and we only had a grand total of 225 hours flying time in our logbooks. On top of that, we owed tuition fees of £2,500, which we were supposed to pay back over five years when we took up jobs with BA. It was a small fortune back then. Inflation was spiralling out of control at 24.2 per cent. The average house price for a first-time buyer was £9,549 with interest rates at 11.1 per cent and average annual income at £3,753.[3] BA gave us £600 and told us to go away until they had jobs for us. They waived the £2,500 until then. It was just as well. None of us had any means of paying them.

I was one of the luckier ones. I lived in the north of England and there was more work potentially available up there as the North Sea oil exploration boom gathered pace. I got in my car and drove round all the airfields in the north where there were air taxi companies who might give work to a sprog and knocked on their doors. As so often in aviation, it was a case of right place at the right time. I struck it lucky almost straightaway. An outfit in Liverpool needed a second pilot to sit in the right-hand seat of a Piper PA23 Aztec on contract to the Atomic Energy Authority (AEA) transferring personnel to their facility at Dounreay in Caithness on the north coast of Scotland, where they were conducting fast breeder reactor experiments. Normally the Aztec only needed one pilot but companies like the AEA and ICI required a minimum crew of two pilots after an accident in which some of their personnel were killed. I spent the night of my 23rd birthday huddled in a sleeping bag and jamming newspapers into the gaps in the Portakabin that served as the crew quarters on site at Dounreay, trying to keep out the cold north wind. It wasn't ideal. It was hardly the image I'd conjured up when I imagined being an airline pilot but I wasn't complaining. The Aztec didn't sound quite as romantic as the Voodoo or Concorde but I was on the road to my dream and I was flying!

It was at the airfield at Dounreay that I first came across some of the impractical officialdom that I was to encounter repeatedly throughout my aviation career. The reactor site was built on the disused WW2 Castletown airfield and it was there that we landed. The site was surrounded by fields in which a flock of sheep often grazed. A fence had been erected to stop the sheep encroaching on the airfield since propellers spinning at 2,500 rpm and sheep do not generally make for a good mix. The airfield itself was quite short and some bright spark in the CAA decided that the fence must be frangible in case an aircraft should overrun the field. The trouble was that 4 x 4 Scots pine fence posts aren't frangible. Bright spark's solution to this conundrum was to mandate that the fence posts should be sawn halfway through. His solution satisfied his regulations but the trouble was that the sheep found they could now get through the fence if they pushed hard enough with the result that we often had to make low passes over the field to frighten the sheep away before landing. Whilst aerial sheep herding made for sporting flying, Spark's 'solution' typifies the sort of bureaucratic incompetence we face in the aviation profession from 'managers' who have no practical operational knowledge or experience.

While the job at Liverpool was a start, it was only sporadic and wouldn't pay the bills. Again, fortune favoured the brave, or the persistent Yorkshireman, and I got my next break. There was an air taxi company called Casair Aviation Services based at Teesside airport, formerly RAF

Middleton St George, in County Durham. It was owned by Jack Cassidy, a hard-drinking, no-nonsense Scotsman, and operated two Aztec Ds and a Cessna 337. I had heard they might be looking for a pilot so I got back in my car and knocked on their door. I got the job and on 17 May 1975 I checked out as P1 on the Aztec and flew my first revenue trip on 21 May. I was now a fully fledged commercial pilot albeit with only a toe on the very bottom rung of the ladder.

The Chief Pilot at Casair was Alan Turley. He was ex-RAF and had been on Lightnings based at RAF Leuchars in Fife. He spent a lot of time on QRA launching to intercept Russian Bears sent over to test the UK air defences during the Cold War. He was also a solo display pilot on the Lightning. His logbook contained an assessment: 'An exceptional solo aerobatic pilot'. This was one of the highest accolades that could be given to an RAF pilot. I was in the company of one of the best and was to learn much from him about practical airmanship as I built up hours under his tutelage. During his time in the RAF, Alan also had been a keen air racer and took part in competitions in his Percival Proctor III, a three-seat radio trainer. In 1965 he won the Manx Air Derby Challenge Trophy and the Crockford's Cup both presented to him by long-distance aviation pioneer Sir Alan Cobham. During one of these competitions in the 1960s, when Alan (Turley) was accompanied by his wife Dawn, the engine of the Proctor threw a con-rod through the sump and the aircraft caught fire. He managed to put it down safely but, during their escape, Dawn put her foot through the wing and got trapped. Alan waded back in to get her out but they were both badly burned, particularly Alan's hands. After a long convalescence, he left the RAF and went into civilian flying but his hands never fully recovered. He had a lot of scar tissue and during cold weather this would crack open and blood would ooze out. Sometimes passengers used to request that he not be on their flight because of this. I thought it a shabby way to treat a man who had served his country but an indication of the callousness of human nature of which I was to experience much in later life at the hands of unscrupulous management. On the early morning of 19 October 1987, eight years after I left Casair, Alan was killed when the Beech B200 Super King Air that he was flying crashed two nautical miles (nm) short of the threshold of runway (R/W) 14 at Leeds/Bradford airport during an approach in bad weather. The aircraft hit some trees and was destroyed by fire. Alan was the only occupant. I felt the loss keenly. Alan had put his trust in me and been my mentor in those early days of my career.

All professional pilots face a Catch 22 situation as they climb the aviation ladder. Companies often operate a minimum experience recruitment bar. You need at least 1,500 hours to join our company and you don't have it. Come back when you've got more hours. When you are a low time pilot, how are you supposed to get more hours if you can't get a job? It's the same when transitioning from piston engine straight wing aircraft onto swept wing jets. You've got no jet time, come back and see us when you've got some. How are you supposed to get some jet time if no one will give you a job on jets? The answer is that someone along the line gives you a break. Alan gave me my first break. He gave me a chance even though I was a newly qualified sprog with bare minimum hours. I lost other friends and colleagues during my career and felt their loss just as keenly but Alan was the first. It was a sad end to an illustrious career but at least he died doing what he loved.

It was during the four years that I spent at Casair that I served my apprenticeship and gained the experience needed to climb the next rung of the ladder. The flying was some of the most demanding in civil aviation. Single pilot IFR in crap weather with unreliable equipment and little regulation. In those days commercial operators did not need an Air Operator's Certificate (AOC) if the Maximum All Up Weight (MAUW) of their aircraft was less than 5,000 lb. The MAUW of the Aztec was 5,200 lb but, to get round the regulations, in theory at least, we restricted the Maximum Takeoff Weight (MTOW) to 4,995 lb. The Aztec had six seats, five passengers and one pilot, plus two baggage holds – one forward and one aft. As one of the pilots I knew on the air taxi circuit put it, to keep below the 5,000 lb limit on the loadsheet his company only carried diminutive Japanese businessmen with handbags who had spent some time in Belsen. In truth we spent most of our time carrying bears working on the North Sea oil rigs. These men were big blokes with heavy baggage. Most of the time, not only were we over the 5,000 lb limit, but also we often exceeded the 5,200 lb limit. We flew overweight as a matter of course. If you didn't do it, there were plenty of other out-of-work pilots who would. The trick was to get the weight distribution right and avoid an aft centre of gravity (CG). Put the heaviest baggage in the forward hold and the biggest blokes up the front with the smallest in the back seats. If the CG was too far aft the aircraft would be unstable in pitch in flight and could be a real handful. Instead of pitch disturbances being aerodynamically damped out, they would become increasingly divergent oscillations. The only solution in that event was to jam your knee against the control yoke to stop it moving backwards, hold the nose down and wait for some fuel to burn off and reduce the weight. It led to very bruised knees so we tried to avoid that. We had a rule of thumb. When the aircraft was loaded on the ground sometimes it would sink back on its oleos in a tail-down attitude. If you put your back under the tail and pushed it up to a level attitude and it stayed there after you got out from under, you should be all right. If it sank back again you might want to rethink your loading.

It was the same with flying hours. No AOC so no regulations. A typical flying day would consist of two return trips between Teesside or Aberdeen and Stavanger in Norway. A typical sector time was 2 hr 25 min so we'd log 9 hr 40 min flying in a day. Add to that arriving at the airport before first light to drag the aircraft out of the hangar to cater and prep it for the first flight of the day and then refuelling and cleaning it before putting it back in the hangar at the end of the last flight plus three thirty-minute turnarounds and we were regularly putting in thirteen or fourteen-hour days. We did all the catering, handling, cleaning and refuelling ourselves. We made the coffee and bought the sandwiches, met the passengers, led them in from and out to the aircraft, cleared up the mess they left behind, filed the flight plan, paid the landing fees and sorted out the fuel bowser. It was part of the job. There was no complaining. You just got on with it and did what you had to do to build your hours.

And the weather really was crap. The North Sea in winter is a very unforgiving place. Cold fronts were the norm with the freezing level below 2,000 feet. We had no weather radar and the anti-icing and de-icing equipment was minimal. On a typical climb out the ice would start accumulating soon after takeoff. The electrical propeller anti-icing would sling lumps of ice against the fuselage making a disconcerting banging noise if you didn't know what it was. The wing de-icing was by inflatable pneumatic rubber boots on the wing leading edges. Sometimes they'd have holes in them and wouldn't inflate. Sometimes the shuttle valves in the pneumatic lines would freeze up due to water ingress so a pre-takeoff function check was no guarantee that they'd work in flight. If the wing de-icing didn't work you had two options. Option one was to try to climb above the cloud and get into clear air where the ice would gradually dissipate by sublimation. If that didn't work option two was to descend below the freezing level and it would melt off. That led to a lot of North Sea transits at 500 feet above the waves. It was uncomfortable because you were down in the weather dodging showers, snow and hail but it taught us weather awareness. We learned to read the sky and have an instinct for where the clearest route might lie. That, of course, presupposed that you could see out of the windscreen. There was no windshield de-icing equipment so often you would be flying blind with a covering of ice over the windows until you could get rid of it using option one or two.

Cabin heating was no better. It was provided by a Janitrol heater in the nose compartment that took high-octane Avgas from one of the fuel tanks and burned it to generate hot air. Ignition was provided by a large spark plug that was prone to sooting up. If the previous pilot hadn't followed the correct shut down procedure to clean the plug it wouldn't ignite. In that case you were in for a cold flight, especially if the air vents didn't close properly, which often happened. Sub-zero cold air from outside the aircraft blasting your legs for two hours is not a pleasant experience. On one flight back from Stavanger to Teesside, fortunately empty, I was met by the blood wagons on landing. I tried to get out of the aircraft but couldn't because my legs wouldn't work properly. Air Traffic Control (ATC) approach control had declared an emergency when they heard my voice on the radio. I was in the first stages of hypothermia but didn't know it. As with hypoxia and fatigue, because of their physiological effects, the sufferer is often unable to recognise the symptoms. Another half hour and I'd have been in real trouble.

Despite the long hours, the unreliable equipment and the crap weather, we had a great time. We were young and fit, full of hope and doing what we'd dreamed of and trained for. We were making a living flying aircraft. Jack and Alan were great guys to work for. Jack worked hard himself, expected the same from his employees and we had no problems with that. He also had a private pilot's licence (PPL) so at least he understood the fundamentals. He had sat his commercial pilot's licence (CPL) exams twice but failed them. It gave him an appreciation of the amount of work and effort that goes into obtaining professional qualifications in aviation. He had respect for his pilots and treated them accordingly. There was an *esprit de corps* amongst all members of the team and we looked after each other's backs. If only the same could be said of present day business school trained airline 'managers' with their MBAs and off-the-shelf degrees. At the end of a long day we'd all repair to the pub just outside the main gate of Teesside airport, the Oak Tree, or Twig as it was affectionately known. Pints of Camerons Strongarm were downed with Jack's favourite chaser, a large Famous Grouse with a drop of lemonade. The landlord of the Twig, Peter Goddard, was not averse to a lock-in and the local constabulary turned a blind eye. The traditional nightcap was a pint of Guinness with a barley wine nip in the top. It guaranteed a good night's sleep. The other favoured watering hole was the Cleveland Flying Club at the airport, run by its chief flying instructor (CFI) Mike Cairns who had flown F4 Phantoms when he was in the RAF. BMA had some Viscount crews based at Teesside operating their Heathrow shuttle services. The Rothmans Aerobatic Team was also based there with its Pitts

Specials. It was a party town and we made the most of it. We worked and played hard but made sure the job got done.

It was the same in Aberdeen and Sumburgh, in the Shetland Islands, where I spent a lot of time on night stops. During the North Sea oil boom, these places were cowboy country with people from all around the world in town to cash in. Along with Stavanger and Kristiansand in Norway, they were the main airports where the choppers picked up and dropped off the bears working on the oil rigs. The rigs were dry and the bears usually worked three weeks on and two weeks off. It was hard, dirty and dangerous work and they were usually ready for a drink as soon as their feet touched terra firma. At Dyce airport in Aberdeen, the fixed-wing terminal was on the opposite side of the airport to the helicopter base. It was not unusual for the bears coming off the rigs to have got through a bottle of blue label vodka during the transit between the two. No problems with denied boarding due to 'inappropriate behaviour' in those days. We piled them on and flew them to where they wanted to go, drunk or not. There was no nanny state back then. The bar of the old Skean Dhu hotel at Dyce, and the Bobbin Mill pub just outside the airport, were the watering holes most frequented by the pilots. Some of my compatriots were working for air taxi companies like me and some had got jobs with Dan-Air on the Hawker Siddeley HS748. It didn't matter. We all mucked in together. We were all doing the same thing, climbing the ladder.

In Sumburgh there was only one place to stay, a small hotel a couple of miles from the airfield. When the rigs were fogged in and the choppers couldn't bring the bears off we'd have to stay the night and wait for the weather to clear. With all the crews in the same boat there weren't enough rooms in the hotel so we'd bed down in our sleeping bags on the floor of the dining-room, which had a big open fireplace. We didn't really need an excuse for a party but, if we did, those unscheduled night stops were as good as any. They celebrated the Viking mid-winter feast of Up Helly Aa in the Shetlands on the last Tuesday in January each year and that really was party time.

Sumburgh airfield itself only had pretty basic amenities in the early days. The main runway was 33/15 and it had a hill on the southern tip that obstructed the approach to R/W 33. The only radio navaid was a VOR that was used for a cloud break procedure with a decision height (DH) about 700 feet above ground level (AGL) because of the hill. The cloud base was often well below 700 feet so the published procedure wasn't much help. Instead, we used to home to overhead the VOR, let down over the sea on the 090 radial until we broke cloud, do a 180 degree turn and fly back into the airfield visually at low level. This wasn't without its risks because we didn't have radio altimeters and only had the local QNH as reference, but it worked. The weather up there could be atrocious with snow, hail, sleet and strong gusting winds. It was a miserable experience out on the apron, cold and wet, refuelling the aircraft. If you got wet you stayed that way for the first 35 minutes of the flight until the Janitrol heater did its job, provided it worked. The worst thing was having wet feet so I used to wear polythene bags over my socks inside my shoes.

Later they upgraded runway 09/27 so they could put an instrument landing system (ILS) on it and bring the DH down, but, because it was built on reclaimed land, it was only 3,871 feet long and the eastern end dropped off straight into the sea. On 31 July 1979 at 16:00, a Dan-Air 748 crashed on takeoff from R/W 09 and sank in about one minute in 30 feet of water. The elevator gust-lock had re-engaged and prevented the aircraft from rotating. The Air Accidents Investigation Branch (AAIB) report stated that 'The re-engagement of the gust-lock was made possible by the condition of the gust-lock lever gate plate and gate-stop strip, to which non-standard repairs had been made.'[4] In other words, shoddy maintenance. Fifteen passengers and the two pilots were drowned because somebody had cut corners.

We were taking other risks as well. It was quite routine for us to land at disused airfields with no ATC and no crash rescue facilities. We even did it at night sometimes using a couple of Land Rovers, one to shine its headlights along the landing strip centreline and the other to illuminate across the touchdown point. It was very risky because there was no way to be sure that the strip was clear of obstructions by a precautionary low pass or two as we did during daylight. Also it was very difficult to get any kind of depth perception on the approach and an unexpected contact with the ground short of the touchdown point was a very real possibility.

One of these airfields was Scatsta on Shetland. Nowadays it is a fully licensed airfield serving the Sullom Voe oil terminal but back then it was disused. For me it was something of a homecoming because my father had been stationed there during WW2 when he was flying Catalinas protecting the North Atlantic supply convoys. He once told me how he held his squadron record for the longest duration flight out of Scatsta. He got airborne one day and set out for the rendezvous point (RVP) to meet the convoy. On arrival there was no sign of the convoy so he started a square search procedure. After some hours, still with no sign of the convoy, he asked his navigator for a course home. The nav informed him that he was unable to give him an exact course as he was lost and had been for some time. If you're over the North Atlantic and want to make landfall there are only really two choices, point east or west, so they headed east. After some more time had passed the fuel gauges were knocking on E and things weren't looking good. At least the Cat was a flying boat so it wouldn't sink if they put down on the water but, like the North Sea, the Atlantic can be an inhospitable place and chances of survival in the water are slim. Just when he was preparing to ditch the aircraft, he saw land ahead in the distance. It turned out to be Scatsta right on the nose. Good airmanship, maybe, or complete fluke, maybe. Either way, a lot of beer was downed in the mess that night.

Things couldn't carry on the way they were and the Civil Aviation Authority (CAA) started to take an interest in operations at the lower end of the weight range. They decided that all commercial operations, irrespective of weight, would be required to hold an AOC. This meant tighter regulations, in particular restrictions on maximum flying hours and duty times to cut down on the number of accidents that were being caused primarily by pilot fatigue. In Casair this didn't have a particularly adverse effect on the commercial side of things since we had already started complying with the AOC regulations on duty hours. It meant that we'd had to employ additional pilots but that was the cost of keeping things safe and Jack appreciated that. A very different attitude to many airline managers of today who, all too often, seek to keep blindly cutting costs without any real appreciation of, or even regard for, the effects on safety.

In May 1977 we had started operating a Cessna 421B Golden Eagle owned by William Press & Son, an engineering company heavily involved in the North Sea oil development. They wanted to put it out to charter when it wasn't needed on company business and, as this aircraft had an MTOW of 7,450 lb, for this we needed an AOC. This was a serious step up in equipment from the Aztec. It could carry eight people, had turbocharged engines and was pressurised with a maximum ceiling of 31,000 feet. Although we still had no weather radar, this machine cruised comfortably at 25,000 feet so we could get out of the worst weather. It handled beautifully and the controls were well harmonised. The roll cross coupling was particularly good because of the wingtip fuel tanks that distributed the weight across the aircraft. It was a smooth and stable ride compared with the workhorse Aztec, though I had grown to have a respect for the latter. It had seen me through many tricky situations and brought me safely home. The Golden Eagle confirmed the old adage amongst pilots that if it looks right it'll fly right. It was a good-looking ship and even the name was a step in the right direction.

Casair was expanding and we needed to employ more pilots. I was involved in the interview process with Alan. One day we had an application from a chap called Andrew Newton. I thought his name sounded familiar but couldn't place it. He came for interview and Alan noticed there was a gap in his logbook when he hadn't flown. He asked Mr Newton what had happened to which he replied, 'I was in prison. In case you hadn't realised, I'm the bloke that shot Norman Scott's dog.' The penny dropped. Norman Scott was a former male model who'd claimed that he'd had a homosexual relationship with the leader of the Liberal Party, Jeremy Thorpe, between 1961 and 1963, a time when homosexual acts were still illegal in Britain. An inquiry within the Liberal Party in 1971 exonerated Thorpe but Scott continued to make the allegations. In October 1975, while walking a friend's female Great Dane called 'Rinka' on Exmoor, Scott was confronted by Andrew 'Gino' Newton who was armed with a gun. Newton shot and killed the dog, which had been lent to Scott for protection, then pointed the gun at Scott, but it apparently failed to go off. Gino was convicted of the offence in March 1976 and sent to prison. Upon his release in April 1977, he revived the scandal by claiming that he had been hired by Thorpe and others as a hit-man to kill Norman Scott. Thorpe was eventually acquitted of all charges but it finished his political career. So here was our 'Gino' in front of us asking for a job. Alan and I thought we might give him another chance but Jack vetoed it with the words, 'Unreliable. Send him to kill a bloke and all he does is shoot his dog. Can't trust him to get the job done.' When we told Jack that one of the questions Gino had asked during the interview was, 'Do you get much contract work?' he nearly fell off his bar stool laughing.

As well as the daily milk runs around Scotland, we picked up some interesting ad hoc charters. When we weren't scheduled to fly, we would take it in turns to man the office. We would answer the phone and give quotes for charters. These were calculated using a large map of Europe pinned to the wall, with a piece of string attached at Teesside calibrated in flying hours. When an enquiry was received you simply found the destination on the map, measured the flying time using the string, multiplied that by the hourly rate for the aircraft in question, added a bit for landing fees and gave out the quote. One morning I was rostered for office duty and received a call for a charter to Northolt, in London. This was an RAF airfield that we usually used for charters to London in preference to Heathrow where it was not only difficult to get a landing slot but also very expensive in landing fees. Northolt is famous for a Pan Am B707 that landed there on 25 October 1960, its crew having mistaken it for Heathrow. In the days before navaids like ILS and GPS, and in an effort to prevent a recurrence of such errors, the letters 'NO' (for Northolt) and 'LH' (for Heathrow) were painted on two gas-holders situated on the approach to each airfield. The quote was accepted so I pulled the aircraft out of the hangar, parked it on the apron and waited for the passenger to arrive. A car pulled up and out stepped Jane Fonda. I flew her down to London, dropped her off and was back at Teesside just after lunch. Alan was in the office and asked me what I'd been doing. When I told him I'd just spent a couple of hours with Ms Fonda he turned green. After *Barbarella* and *Klute*, she was something of a heartthrob for Alan. I wasn't so keen myself. The Hanoi Jane rumours were circulating back then after her visit to North Vietnam in July 1972 and, although I agreed with her anti-war stance, I thought her actions betrayed the brave airmen who were being held at the Hanoi Hilton.

Alan picked up an interesting charter one morning just after the Ekofisk Bravo oil rig blow out on 22 April 1977. He was manning the office and got a call to go to London to pick up Red Adair – the renowned US oil well firefighter – who had come from the US to cap the rig. It was to be done under conditions of utmost secrecy as there was a lot of media interest. Alan picked him up and smuggled him into the airport through the baggage bays without attracting any attention. It seemed that the plan had worked well. That is until the girl manning the airport information desk made a PA announcement, 'Would Mr Red Adair please contact the information desk.' The place erupted.

On 30 August 1977 I picked up another ad hoc charter to fly James Hunt to Malaga in the Eagle after he'd been appearing at Croft Racing Circuit in North Yorkshire. I was an avid motor racing fan and Hunt was something of a hero to me after he won the 1976 Formula One (F1) championship in a McLaren. I admired him not only for his racing prowess but also for his gung-ho attitude to life in general. He was a genuinely nice guy, didn't wear any shoes and eschewed the fine wine and canapés that had been catered, being happy instead with a case of beer put on ice in the cabin. We stopped in Le Bourget *en route* to Spain to pick up a female journalist who later wrote a kiss-and-tell piece in one of the tabloids questioning his sexual prowess. Given James's reputation as a ladies man, I doubt he was much bothered by her gutter press.

I met someone else involved in motor racing in a similar fashion. On 4 June 1976 I was on morning office duty and there was a commotion down at the BMA check-in desk. An Australian couple had missed their flight to London and weren't at all happy. I went down to see if I could help. Their names were Bob and Marj Brown and they needed to get to

Heathrow to catch a connecting flight to Bordeaux in southern France. I gave them a quote to take them directly there without the London stop and within 30 minutes we were on our way. On the way down Bob told me that their final destination was actually Pau. The Aztec didn't have the range to make it there in one so we landed at Bordeaux to refuel and then carried on to Pau. Bob asked me if I could stay the weekend and fly him back three days later. I called the office and spoke to Jack. After his initial 'Where the hell are you and where's my plane?' reaction, he saw the commercial sense in my plan. It turned out that Bob and Marj owned a Formula Two (F2) racing team. They had entered a Minos Formula Pacific BDA and we were down there for the race at the Pau street circuit. It was a superb weekend and I was right there in the pits at the centre of the action. Their driver, Bob Muir, and his wife were also Aussies and they were great people. We left Pau on Monday morning and flew up to Le Touquet to clear customs. At this point Marj decided she wasn't quite ready to go home yet and wanted a night on the town. She asked for suggestions. We settled on Amsterdam as a good place for an evening's entertainment and off we went. I finally brought Jack's aircraft back to him at lunchtime on Tuesday. The trip was a great success and I flew Bob and his team to the other European F2 race meetings for the rest of the 1976 season. Some names that would later become famous in F1 were racing in F2 that year. René Arnoux, Vittorio Brambilla, Jean-Pierre Jabouille, Jacques Lafitte, Ronnie Peterson, Keke Rosberg and Patrick Tambay – and I met them all. The other trips that season ran along similar lines with Marj consulting with me to decide on suitable venues for a stopover on the way home. On the way back from Mugello in July, where we had landed at the Borgo San Lorenzo airstrip nearby, we stopped off in Geneva for the night. Marj had asked me previously to recommend a good hotel. I had absolutely no idea as I'd never been to Geneva before. I looked up hotels in the *ABC Travel Guide*, settled on the Hotel de la Paix on the lake and telexed through the reservations. When I saw the bill I expected an adverse reaction from Bob. On the contrary. He actually turned round and thanked me for picking such a good hotel, which, in his words was, 'Just the sort of place me and Marj like to stay.' I was part of an F2 racing team, staying in first-class hotels and getting paid for it. Life was great. I went back to the Hotel de la Paix when I was travelling in Europe years later but it had fallen on hard times and was very down at heel. A shame, but in life things often aren't how you remember them if you try to recapture the moment.

A year after the introduction of the Eagle, things took an even better turn. There was a Cessna Citation I/SP based at Teesside owned by DJB

Engineering, the tractor and engineering manufacturer founded by David J. Brown in 1973 in Peterlee, County Durham. Its owner wanted the same deal as the Golden Eagle owner: to be able to put it out for charter when it wasn't being used on company business. This was another serious step up in equipment. It still only carried eight people but it was a jet! Getting it onto the AOC proved somewhat more troublesome than the Golden Eagle and there were a lot of hurdles to be overcome with the CAA before they gave us approval. Admin is not generally the favourite pastime of pilots. Alan was particularly notable in this department and the job of dealing with the paperwork fell to me as the next most senior pilot. Casair now had eight pilots and I could have delegated the job to one of the more junior men but I chose to do it myself for one reason. With the advent of the Citation came a much sought after jet rating on my licence. There was no way I was going to jeopardise that. It is the most fundamental principle in career progression in civil aviation that there are only three things that count: seniority, seniority and seniority. The bloke who has the highest seniority gets first pick of the goodies, such as when a new type is being introduced. I plugged away at the seemingly interminable obstacles put up by the CAA and successfully got the Citation onto the AOC. More importantly, on 3 July 1978 the Citation type rating was stamped in Part 1 of my licence. I was now a jet pilot.

The Citation was quite an unusual aircraft in terms of executive jets. It was quite slow in comparison with the Learjet 25 or the Hawker Siddeley HS125, its direct competitors. Its maximum cruise speed was 350 knots (kt) compared with the Lear's 473 kt or the HS125's 446 kt. This earned it the nicknames 'Slowtation' and 'Nearjet'. It presented a problem when operating in busy airspace with other commercial jet transports as they would be going that much faster and the Citation would get in the way. It had a trick up its sleeve to overcome this, however. Even at MTOW, it could climb straight to its maximum service ceiling of 41,000 feet. The faster jets couldn't do that and heavy commercial traffic could usually only get to 31,000 feet or so at MTOW. So the technique was to climb out above the rest of the traffic and then the slower cruise speed of the Citation didn't hold anyone up. It had another advantage over its competitors in terms of crewing costs and passenger capacity. All the other jets had a minimum certified crew requirement of two pilots but the Citation was certified for single pilot IFR operations. Not only was I now a jet pilot, I was up there all on my own. At the time it seemed the most glorious thing I could have wished for. With the benefit of experience it is questionable whether such operations in busy air traffic environments around airports such as London Heathrow, Charles De Gaulle and Frankfurt, or any other major hub for that matter, are advisable. However, at the time, that was not a concern to me. I was charging through space with my hair on fire and enjoying every minute.

The advent of the Citation also opened up longer range and more exotic destinations. Not only that but the Italian food company Parmalat had an interest in the aircraft and, because of its association with Niki Lauda, I got to meet another of my heroes. The daily milk runs between Teesside, Aberdeen and Sumburgh were behind me now. I was still doing the occasional one or two but now I was making regular forays around Southern Europe and North Africa, places that I had previously only imagined or read about in books. The ground handling hadn't changed though. I still had to organise the catering, passenger handling, refuelling, landing fees and flight plans by myself. There were also a couple of new variables in the equation, which were to cause me some problems later on. With the operation to more distant destinations came the need to obtain over-flight and diplomatic clearances, which are requirements for some airspace. Not everyone simply welcomes you with open arms just because you've filed a flight plan to tell them you're coming. In places with good communications this generally wasn't too much of a problem. You simply looked up their requirements, took steps to make sure you fulfilled them, sent a telex to the relevant government department and awaited your clearance number in response. Other places where the comms weren't so good, such as Africa, were a different matter and, on more than one occasion, this got me into potentially serious trouble.

In September 1978, we picked up a charter to take some representatives of a German shipping company on a tour round West Africa where they did a lot of business. The routing took us through Senegal, Guinea, Togo, Mali, Niger, Nigeria, Cameroon and Algeria. I set about planning the route but getting the over-flight and dip clearances immediately presented problems. Put simply, many of the listed authorities just didn't bother replying despite repeated telexes, telegrams and phone calls. I was relatively new at this and in a bit of a quandary as to what to do next. There was no one else in the company who had any experience in such matters and I had no contacts to whom I could go for advice. The charter was worth a lot of money to the company and I was under pressure to get the job done. In the end, I succumbed to the pressure and decided to set off with what clearances I had got and try to sort the rest out *en route*. Big mistake! All went relatively smoothly and I managed to talk my way out of trouble until we got to Lomé in Togo. When I tried to get clearance into their airspace they asked for my clearance number. I didn't have one and tried to talk my way in. ATC refused entry permission but I pressed on anyway. As we approached Lomé, ATC again refused landing permission without a clearance number so I told them I was short of fuel and had to land. It was bullshit but I was trying to get the job done. When we taxied in we were surrounded by heavily armed soldiers in armoured personnel carriers with AK47s. We were in serious trouble. We were manhandled off the aircraft and taken into the terminal for questioning. After two or three hours, during which the Togolese government chief of security came to interview us, we managed to convince them that we had arrived on business and were not some sort of expeditionary mercenary force intent on taking over the airport. Things started to look a little better, right up until the chief of security found out that I had a British passport, that is. For some reason the Germans were OK with him but I wasn't. I was taken from the airport under armed guard to the local equivalent of the notorious Kirikiri prison in Lagos for further questioning. This was the most unpleasant and frightening experience of my life both then and since. The fear of physical injury wasn't the worst part. The things that really frightened me were the overwhelming sense that no one knew where I was, that my life was entirely in the hands of these people and that I had no control whatsoever over what happened to me. In the front of a British passport there is a statement that '*Her Britannic Majesty . . . requests and requires . . . all those whom it may concern to allow the bearer to pass freely without let or hindrance and to afford the bearer such assistance and protection as may be necessary.*' Fine words indeed, and perhaps effective during the days of the British Empire, but meaningless to a bunch of thugs armed with AK47s in an African gaol. It turned out all right in the end. The Germans had a Lebanese agent in Togo. The Lebanese were the middlemen in West Africa back then. He found out where I was, came down and got me out. I learned three lessons from that experience. Firstly, I learned about real fear and what my reaction to it was. Nothing in my life since has ever made me experience fear in the same way. I've been scared, yes, even frightened, but not real fear the way I felt then. I learned about my own personal strength and its limits. The ups and downs of life, the problems that we face, the heartbreaks and disappointments are as nothing in comparison. The second lesson I learned is not to succumb to commercial pressure especially when people's lives might be put at risk. It is a lesson that some present day airline management, and indeed pilots, would do well to heed. The third lesson I learned is that, in aviation, if you don't know the answer, go and find someone who does. Don't just go and plunge in headlong and hope for the best. We do not have enough time to make all the mistakes ourselves, even if we might be fortunate enough to survive them. There is a wealth of experience out there and, in the international brotherhood that makes up the worldwide pilot community, there is always someone who has already been there, seen it, done it and got the T-shirt. Do not be afraid to ask for help and advice. Aviation is the safest form of transport because we learn from the mistakes of our brothers who came before us and foster a 'no blame' culture in incident and accident reporting. Well, on the whole, we pilots do, but unfortunately others involved in our profession do not, but more of that later.

It was in the skies over Africa that I first witnessed the power of nature in full force. When you're sitting in your jet at 41,000 feet, feeling like you're the king of the skies, then you see a cumulonimbus cloud formation starting to build below you, come bubbling past you and punch on up through the tropopause to 65,000 feet, it makes you realise really how small you are in the heavens.

All things must pass and so it was with my time at Casair. DJB sold its original Citation and replaced it with a Citation II but the joint user deal wasn't working out and the jet flying was drying up. Air taxi flying is a great way to gain experience. I had learned a lot and had a lot of fun but it doesn't make for a long-term career. I now had 2,873 hours in my logbook and it was time to move on to bigger things. I was sad to say goodbye to Jack and Alan. They were good men to work for and had treated me well. I like to think that I served them well in return but I had to look to the next step up the ladder. After I left, Casair continued to expand and in April 1982 they received licences from the CAA to start operating scheduled services between Teesside, Gatwick, the Isle of Man and Guernsey. Later on Aberdeen, Glasgow and Humberside were added to the route network. Unfortunately, things didn't work out. In March 1988 the banks called in the receiver and the company was dissolved in October 1990. I saw Jack once more after I left Casair when I was travelling in the UK on holiday. It was sad to see him in straitened circumstances.

2

Takeoff

In March 1979 I got a job with British Air Ferries (BAF) based in Southend flying the Handley Page HPR7 Dart Herald. The Herald was a mishmash of an aircraft. It had originally been designed as a four-piston engine aircraft but, part way through the development phase, someone decided to stick two turboprop engines on the wings instead. This buggered up the weight and balance somewhat and so, to compensate for this, it had three pairs of trim tabs on the elevator. The functions of these various tabs made for excellent line check questions. AC electrical power was provided by up to five inverters, which were mounted just below the flight deck and made a terrific racket. They were prone to overheating and it was not unusual to see smoke seeping into the cockpit from beneath the floor. Because it was underpowered, it had water/meth injection to increase takeoff performance. This could lead to a bit of a kerfuffle on takeoff if one or both of the green lights indicating it was working properly didn't come on. It was equipped with a Sperry Zero Reader flight director. This piece of kit didn't compensate for drift, which had to be entered manually. Because of this it wasn't much use really and it was simpler to fly an ILS just using raw data. The BAF aircraft were quite old and there had been problems with the Redux bonding in the keel giving way due to corrosion. One aircraft had actually opened up like a banana skin. To compensate for this the maximum differential pressure had to be limited, which meant that we could only climb to around 17,000 feet instead of the original design service ceiling of 30,000 feet. Other than that though it was an excellent aircraft and it had a very good clock.

I was employed by BAF as a First Officer (F/O) rather than Captain. This was a new situation for me. Up until then, other than during training, I had always operated single crew and made my own decisions. Now I was in a multi-crew environment and I was no longer in charge of the operation. It took a bit of getting used to but the Captains generally were patient with me and helped me to adjust to the situation. They had all been F/Os as well at some time. There was something else that was new. We carried a flight attendant. The BAF ladies knew how to enjoy themselves and the flying club at the airport after work, or the Kursaal in town on a Saturday night, were the scenes of some serious partying.

BAF was owned by Mike Keegan, who started out in the aviation business building Wellington bombers at Vickers and later served in the RAF as a Flight Sergeant, flying in the Berlin airlift. He started his own aviation businesses, including BKS Air Transport and Transmeridian Air Cargo (TMAC), and eventually bought a number of other airlines including BAF. He sold TMAC in June 1977 to the Cunard Shipping Company for £3.4 million. He was one of the pioneers of mass air transport in the UK. His son Rupert raced cars in Formula Ford and there was talk that he would move up to F1 after his father bought the Hawke racing company in 1974. The intention was to build a BAF-sponsored Cosworth F1 car but it never happened. Mike also owned a Cessna Golden Eagle, which he used to travel down to his yacht moored at Marina di Campo in Italy. Since I was type rated on the Eagle I was often seconded to fly him around as his personal pilot on such jaunts. On one trip, whilst returning empty having dropped him off, I stopped in Cannes to refuel. When I went to pay the landing fees I was informed that the aircraft was impounded as security against unpaid mooring charges from the last time Keegan had visited Cannes in his yacht. The only way to get out was to pay the outstanding charges so I used my own plastic and returned to Southend. When Keegan got back and heard what had happened he hit the roof. The discussion was at loud volume. He wasn't averse to the use of Anglo Saxon and neither am I. Apparently, it was all my fault for staging through Cannes. If I'd gone to Nice instead things would have been OK because his credit was good there. Silly me. I should have known that. I got my money back but it was typical of Mike.

He was famous for his blunt approach. The pay at BAF was not very good and there were the usual moans and groans. One day one of the F/Os was walking across the tarmac and the sole of his shoe was flapping up and down where it had come away from the upper. Keegan saw this from the window of his office that overlooked the apron. He opened the window and instructed the F/O in his usual stentorian tones to smarten himself up and get some new shoes before he came to work next time. The F/O responded in kind and informed Keegan equally volubly that he couldn't afford to on what he was paying him. At this, Mike pulled a roll of banknotes from his pocket. The F/O brightened up considerably thinking that his employer was going to give him some money for new shoes. His optimism was short lived. Keegan pulled the thick rubber band that secured his wad from around the roll, threw it down to the F/O and shouted, 'Here then, that should hold it for now.' He was a buccaneer and could be a hard man to work for but, like his pilots, he had aviation in his blood and he knew the business.

The routes we flew with BAF were mainly short haul: cross-Channel trips to Ostend and Le Touquet; night newspaper runs from Rotterdam to Teesside; and European trips to Brussels, Antwerp, Eindhoven and Düsseldorf. In June 1979 we picked up a charter flying scheduled routes on behalf of the French company TAT European Airlines, operating out of Orly. The crews were all based in Paris for the duration and the usual partying ensued. One of BAF's Captains was a female pilot, Caroline Frost. She was great to work with and had what, at that time, might have been considered male interests like rugby, football and cricket. Sometimes when chatting about who had ended up with whom and what they got up to at the previous night's festivities it was easy to forget she was a woman.

It was while I was based in Paris that my father died of a stroke on 16 June 1979. He had been ill for some time so it did not come as a huge surprise but it was a terrible blow nonetheless. Of course it is a rite of passage that most children are destined to go through at some time in their lives but it shook me. At 27, I had reached the age where fathers and sons become closer after the usual teenage rebellious phase. His passing was an awful loss to me. I took some time off and came back to the UK to be with my family.

I was leafing through the jobs section of *Flight International* one day and saw an advert for First Officers on the B707 for a company called Air Transcontinental (Transcon). What was significant about this particular advert was that you didn't need to have a type rating on the 707. They were offering type training. I had heard of Transcon before but these sorts of jobs were in high demand and usually filled by word of mouth by the time the advert appeared in the press. Nonetheless I thought, if you don't ask, you don't get. The question was how to make myself stand out from the hundreds of other applicants chasing the same jobs? I did some research and found out that the Chief Pilot was called Sam Small and his secretary was Gill Bennett. I filled in the application form and wrote a covering letter to Gill, which said:

Dear Gill, if you want someone who will just do as he's told then don't hire me. However, if you want someone who will argue with the bloke in the office at Ouagadougou to get ten quid knocked off the landing fee then I'm your man. And, if you can make sure that my application form gets onto Sam's desk instead of straight into the wastepaper bin, it's worth a large gin and tonic.

I got a phone call a week later asking me to come for an interview at Transcon's offices in Thameside House, Windsor. I turned up with two miniatures of gin and a can of tonic and put them on Gill's desk. She said with a smile, 'Well I know who you are,' and showed me into Sam's office. He looked me up and down and said, 'A bit of cheek can pay off sometimes.' He gave me the 707 flight and tech manuals and told me to come back when I'd passed the Air Registration Board (ARB) exam. That was it. No ground school, no tuition, nothing. Do it yourself. I left and embarked on a home study course on the intricacies of the 707 systems. I had never been on a 707 let alone seen the flight deck. The only time I'd been close to one was with my grandfather. I got in touch with some BMA pilots that I knew from Teesside who had flown the 707 and they gave me some help. When I tried to book the ARB exam at their offices in Huddersfield they were reluctant at first because I hadn't completed a formal ground school training course with a recognised airline. I tried to persuade them that my time at Hamble under BA sponsorship would fit the bill. They rolled and I went to sit the exam. I passed and on 24 August 1979 I was sitting in the BA 707 simulator (sim) at Cranebank with Sam Small doing my type rating training. We did 20 hours in the sim. I sat in the jump seat during a 20-minute delivery flight from Luton to Heathrow, flew four sectors between Tripoli, Sebha and Benghazi in Libya in the right-hand seat, and on 10 September 1979 the 707 was endorsed in Part 1 of my licence. In truth, I hadn't actually managed to land the aircraft properly so far without a lot of help from Sam but what did I care? I was flying the shark and, to prove it, it was stamped on my licence!

The 707 was everything I'd thought it would be and more besides. Transcon had three of them and they were the 100 series. It was a man's aircraft and needed to be treated with respect. Give it a chance and it would turn round and bite you. It was a true swept wing jet and prone to Dutch roll, especially the ones with the series yaw damper, which had to be disengaged on final approach. It was a common sight to see inexperienced pilots like me waving the wings to and fro on finals with PIOs. Unlike the smaller aircraft I had flown up until then, there was quite a bit of hysteresis lag in the controls. Other than the rudder, which was hydraulically assisted, the flying controls were manual. You had to make a control input, wait for the aircraft to respond and then anticipate any needed corrections. The first time I attempted a landing for real in the aircraft was at night in Sebha. It was a black hole approach with no ILS or VASIs and only rudimentary lighting. I was so far behind the aircraft that I might as well have been clinging onto the HF aerial on the tail. Sam nursed me through my first feeble attempts with patience, under-standing and encouragement. During one of my early attempts, after I'd managed to wrestle the thing onto the ground, he pointed out to me that I was running out of runway. With the sweat pouring off me I managed to gasp out something along the lines of, 'I know but it won't stop', at which point he pulled the thrust reversers and helped me apply the brakes. It was a very steep learning curve but I learned fast. Within ten or so sectors I was beginning to get the hang of things and feel more at home in the beast. My fingers stopped aching as I was no longer holding onto the pole with a vice-like grip. Then came cross-wind landings. With under-slung engines, the pods of the 707 were close to the ground and any more than nine degrees of bank in touchdown attitude would lead to a pod strike. It wasn't a particularly exclusive club amongst rookie 707 pilots but one that I had no wish to join. Again, Sam was patient and encouraging. His whole attitude to the job was one of quiet profes-sionalism and he was a role model to me in my future career when I became a Training Captain myself on the big jets.

On the Libyan contract we were chartered by Libyan Arab Airlines based out of Tripoli. Some of the trips consisted of flying African gentlemen dressed in military fatigues to airstrips in the south of the country that weren't actually marked on conventional maps. They were usually accom-panied by two Libyan officers who carried side-arms but the others' firearms were consigned to the holds during flight where they could not be accessed. Some of the pilots were uncomfortable with what we were doing because there was a lot of guerrilla activity going on in Africa at that time and Libya was seen as a sponsor of some of the less savoury groups. In retrospect, mercenary flying is not a part of my career that I'm now particularly proud of but, at the time, with the exuberance of youth, I didn't think too much about it.

The crews all used to live on a Spanish-registered ship moored in the harbour in Tripoli. One day there was a bunch of us out on deck sunbathing and the girls were taking photographs. All of a sudden there was a commotion and some secret police boarded the ship and tried to confis-cate the girls' cameras. We were moored next to a Russian ship that was unloading tanks and military equipment onto the dockside. Apparently we were breaching security regulations by taking photographs. One of the pilots, Pete 'Shagger' Shaw, was having none of it. He had been born in India of colonial parents, brought up with a Raj attitude, and brooked no nonsense from the locals. He refused to hand over the cameras and threw the police off the ship. I heard a few years later that he had been shot dead in a dispute after a traffic accident in Beirut while he was working for Middle East Airlines. He was a character.

After the Libyan deal we picked up a contract with Air Malta based out of Luqa, operating their schedules to Europe and Egypt. Malta is a beautiful place with a lot of history. The people were very friendly even though, at that time, its prime minister, Dom Mintoff, was bosom buddies with Gaddafi and relations with the UK were somewhat strained. It was a fun contract and one that I was to return to later on, albeit with a different company.

Next came a contract with EgyptAir based in Cairo. The crews all lived in the El Salam hotel and it turned into the usual party venue. 'The Slammer' was not without its drawbacks, however. The water supply was unreliable at best and ablutions had to be scheduled to coincide with the daily published hours displayed in the foyer. This led to shower rush and meant the water often ran out sooner than anticipated. I was standing in the bar with Sam having a beer one day when one of the other Captains, Colin Allsop, came in covered in foam and adorned only in the skimpiest of towels. He strolled up to the bar, ordered a beer, turned to Sam and said, 'Water's off again, Sam.' Sam, equally laconically, replied, 'Thanks for letting me know, Colin.' You had to be careful with the beer as well. The only drinkable brew available was bottled Dutch Oranjeboom premium lager. The bottles were well past their sell-by date, if such a thing existed in Egypt, and the caps often were rusty. Careful cleaning was required as well as inspection for snails, which were sometimes found to be in residence at the bottom of the bottle. The same with the peanuts provided on the bar. Always shell them. Never eat the skins. Room service was a permanently active danger area. Down-route health protocol dictates that one should try to stick with the local, rather than western, food. Certainly no salads, no uncooked food and no ice in drinks unless you knew for sure where the water came from. I once made the mistake of succumbing to temptation and ordered a cheeseburger late at night. The result was a bout of amoebic dysentery that lasted several days. It was a most unpleasant experience sitting on the lavatory, head over the bidet with water jetting out at high velocity from both ends. The pills prescribed by the local doctor weren't much help as they didn't stay inside long enough for the plastic coating to dissolve. It was a very quick and effective method of losing weight but not to be recommended as a general strategy. I was better off than one of the other F/Os though. On an early morning departure he projectile-vomited all over the engine instruments on the climb out. He was casevaced out to London, hospitalised and treated for severe dehydration caused by diarrhoea. His Captain, Robbie Robertson, was most put out. He was ex-BOAC and wasn't used to his F/Os behaving in such an unseemly manner on the flight deck. I flew the aircraft later in the day. The sun was streaming in through the side window on the climb and I couldn't read the engine instruments properly because it was reflecting off some dirt on the glass. I was about to clean it with a wet finger but changed my mind when I realised what it was.

One particularly fun route that we operated was from Cairo down to Luxor and Aswan taking tourists to see the Valley of the Kings and the dam. The sector between Luxor and Aswan was only 35 minutes so we took the opportunity to fly it at low level on the pretext of giving the passengers a good view of the Nile. The sight and sound of a 707 emerging from round a bend in the river, roaring along at 1,000 feet banked over at 30 degrees, and trailing smoke, gave one or two Nile boatmen cause for a moment of alarm. It looked good from where we were sitting so it must have looked pretty good from the ground as well.

I flew a lot with a Captain called Mel Bennett on the Cairo contract. He was ex-RAF, flew Short Sunderland flying boats during WW2 and was decorated for a particularly risky operation when he rescued some downed airmen from under the noses of the enemy at great risk to himself and his crew. Like Sam, Mel was a natural trainer and taught me a great deal. He was just happy to pass on his knowledge and experience to the next generation of pilots without any hint of superiority. Some of the other Captains tended to look down on me and three other F/Os who had joined Transcon at the same time. They called us 'the boy pilots' because of our lack of experience, but not so men like Sam and Mel.

There was something else that Mel enjoyed almost as much as flying. He liked to drink, quite a lot. His tipple was whisky and we used to have 'reverse thrust' cocktails on the flight deck at the end of the last flight of the day. In theory the EgyptAir flights were dry but we used to smuggle booze in stashed in the lower 41 equipment compartment under the flight deck floor when we operated in from outside of the state. If the other two crew members shared Mel's penchant for a dram or two, it had been known for Mel, his F/O and Flight Engineer (F/E) to polish off a whole bottle of whisky between them after landing prior to disembarking the aircraft.

Maintenance was always a problem on Transcon's operations. Heavy maintenance and checks were carried out by Monarch Aircraft Engineering at Luton. This was not much help when you were in Cairo. Any down-route rectification cost money as we carried no spares other than wheels, which we became quite adept at changing ourselves under the guidance of the F/E. We had a way of dealing with this inconvenience. We carried an exercise book in the back of the Captain's seat. In this were entered the details of the various defects on the aircraft so each crew was aware of the situation. The aircraft maintenance log or tech log, however, was completed as 'Nil Further' after each sector, otherwise the aircraft would have been grounded pending rectification of the defects. The positioning flight to Luton for maintenance was always a tricky one, however, because after days and weeks of trouble-free flights as certified by the official record, all hell would break loose and the aircraft would arrive in Luton with five or six pages of defects in the tech log that needed rectification. It was odd but it always seemed to happen that way.

There was one aspect of this that gave me cause for concern. The rudder on the 707 has two hydraulic pumps to give power assistance to the manual control. Both of these were turned on for takeoff and landing and then one was turned off during the cruise. The reason for the power assistance was that, in the event of an engine failure at high power, it would be impossible to control the aircraft by manual rudder control alone. Occasionally we had problems with these pumps and sometimes one of them would fail. According to the Minimum Equipment List (MEL) this was a no go situation except in the case of ferrying the aircraft empty for rectification. Because we had no spares and no real engineering backup down-route, we continued to fly the aircraft with one pump U/S until it was scheduled for regular maintenance. Had we lost an engine on takeoff or the one remaining pump had failed as well, we would have been in a serious situation. Fortunately it never happened.

What we were doing was illegal, and in some cases potentially dangerous, but that was the nature of Transcon's operation. You either got on board or looked for another job. There were some other things we did that were a bit shonky. We used to steal fuel. It was quite simple really. Before refuelling, the fuel on board would be recorded from the gauges on the F/E's panel. After refuelling, the fuel on board is recorded again and the difference between the two readings checked against the volume of fuel delivered by the bowser. The volumetric uplift should tally with the increase in tank contents but the refuellers weren't always all that sharp. We used to disconnect the plug from the back of the centre tank gauge on the F/E's panel so that it registered empty. During refuelling the F/E would pop up the gantry, open up the centre tank refuelling valve, pump the odd

1,000 lb or so into the centre and then close the valve off. On the post-refuelling check, the skoshy fuel wouldn't indicate on the disconnected gauge and, if the refueller questioned the volumetric discrepancy, we'd tell him that there must be something wrong with his bowser and only pay for the uplift indicated on the gauges. This little wheeze worked quite well, especially in Libya, and we figured they'd got so much oil anyway they wouldn't miss the odd tonne or two of kerosene.

We pulled other stunts, too. The aircraft were usually painted in the livery of the airline that we were operating on behalf of. This could be a problem when moving from one contract to another. On one occasion I was on Mel's crew and we were in Tripoli. The aircraft needed to be positioned to Cairo but this presented two problems. The Libyans and the Egyptians weren't talking to each other at this point so the livery needed to be changed as we wouldn't be welcomed in Cairo with 'Libyan Arab Airlines' painted down the fuselage. This was easily solved with a coat of white paint to cover up the offending lettering. The second problem was that we couldn't fly directly from Tripoli to Cairo because of the disagreement between the neighbours, but any tech stop in between the two in a neutral country would cost money in fuel and landing fees. The solution to this was also relatively simple. We filed a flight plan from Tripoli to Paris and got airborne. Once we got well into French airspace, we re-filed in the air and diverted to Cairo. We made out another flight plan and fortunately the F/E, one Whacker Payne, had a number of rubber stamps in his nav bag, one of which was a French ATC stamp. He duly endorsed this on the new paperwork by way of proof that we had come from Paris and we landed in Cairo thinking ourselves rather clever. As we taxied in we were met by armed soldiers who surrounded the aircraft. Something was wrong. They boarded the aircraft and subjected Mel, Whacker and me to a somewhat tense 35 minutes of questioning as to where we had come from. We stuck to our story. We had come from Paris and here was our flight plan with a French ATC stamp to prove it. Eventually, the officer in charge gave us all a very old-fashioned look and allowed us to leave. We were a little nonplussed as to how we'd been found out until we looked back at the aircraft from the crew bus. It was night-time and the apron was lit by powerful floodlights. In the glare of the lights, grinning through the new coat of white paint in black lettering were the words 'Libyan Arab Airlines'.

Flying with F/Es was an excellent way to operate. They were experienced men, had intimate knowledge of the aircraft systems and had sat behind all sorts of pilots from the best to the worst. Whilst the Captain was the acknowledged boss and given the respect due to him, they brooked no nonsense if things weren't going to their liking. There is a story, perhaps apocryphal, about an F/E in BOAC during the days when the Captain had his own transport, stayed in a different hotel from the rest of the crew and was considered to be more powerful than God. These men, known colloquially as 'Transatlantic Barons', were notoriously difficult to work with and there was one in particular called Gillette who was the worst of all. During a particular flight, so the story goes, the F/O communicated with Captain Gillette along the following lines: 'OK to set the flaps now, Skipper?', 'Confirm fuel checks OK, boss?', 'Ready to run the checklist, Skip?' and so on. After several such attempts to which no reply was received, the F/E leaned forward, tapped the F/O on the shoulder and said, 'I think the cunt wants you to call him Captain.' These F/Es were great levellers should the situation call for intervention and their technical knowledge was invaluable. I was on a flight one day when the Captain had left the flight deck during cruise to chat to the passengers. The number 3 generator dropped off line. The F/E informed me of this and said, 'I think we're going to lose the number 3 engine as well.' I could see no reason why. Everything else seemed to be normal and, as far as I was concerned, we'd only lost a generator, which was no big deal since we'd got three more. Sure enough, 30 seconds later the number 3 engine started surging and we had to shut it down. It was common for the Pratt & Whitney JT3D engine to dump its generator just before it failed. This was local knowledge that I did not have at the time but the F/E did and gave me some vital seconds to review the engine failure drill so I was fully prepared for what was coming next. I spent a lot of time operating jet transports with F/Es during my career and had cause to thank them for their knowledge and assistance on many occasions. They also had another area of expertise. On unfamiliar night stops they always seemed to know where the best restaurants, bars and knocking shops were located if one was so minded.

There was only one boss on board the aircraft though and that was the Captain. Thankfully the days of the dictatorial Transatlantic Barons had long gone by this time. The British European Airways (BEA) *Papa India* Trident crash on 18 June 1972 had seen to that. The aircraft crashed in a deep stall on the outskirts of Staines two and a half minutes after takeoff from Heathrow killing all 118 people on board. There were many contributing factors in the causal chain leading up to this accident. The Captain, Stanley Key, had undiagnosed severe chronic coronary arteriosclerosis. The pilots were involved in an acrimonious industrial dispute between their trade union BALPA and BEA management, which had split the pilot community. One group of pilots favoured strike action. Captain Key was one of a group of senior pilots opposed to the motion and had been enlisting the support of some of his fellow Senior Captains. When a F/O Flavell questioned his views in the crew room on the afternoon of the accident, Key became 'very angry indeed', leading to what one eyewitness described as 'the most violent argument he had ever heard'. After takeoff a number of mistakes occurred, not least of which was retraction of the leading edge flaps at too low an airspeed, causing the aircraft to stall. Captain Key was handling the aircraft and probably was suffering an incapacitating heart attack but neither of the other two operating pilots, Second Officer (S/O) Jeremy Keighley and S/O Simon Ticehurst, took adequate corrective action to rectify the situation despite various stall warnings being triggered. The inexperience of S/O Keighley was also found to be a contributing factor.[5] The ramifications of this accident resounded throughout the aviation world. It provided many lessons to be learned, some of which seem to have faded with memory in current times. We will revisit and examine some of them later.

When I entered Hamble just a year after the accident, the training was geared to make sure this could not happen again. They used some very effective tools to get the message across. In the propulsion laboratory they had one of the Rolls-Royce Spey engines from *Papa India*. Its casing was broken into three parts and the compressor and turbine blades were smashed and broken. In a locked cupboard they had one of the pilot's headsets. Some hair and dried blood were still attached to it. It was shocking but we all sat up and took notice and I never forgot those lessons. We were taught that the only stupid question is the one that isn't asked. If anything happens on the flight deck that you don't understand, don't just sit there, speak up and ask for clarification, even if you are the most junior and inexperienced man there. We were also told, however, to try to be diplomatic at the same time. Rather than just challenging the boss in aggressive fashion, try to have a pre-prepared form of words such as, 'Excuse me, Captain, are you incapacitated or just flying a spastic ILS?'

We took our training into the outside world and tried to apply it but still we had respect for the Captain's authority. This was not just blind allegiance. We were children of the sixties. We had grown up with the anti-Vietnam war protests and the civil rights movement. Our music was the Rolling Stones, Led Zeppelin and Jimi Hendrix. We questioned everything. Not for us the blind obedience to authority that had sacrificed two generations of young men in two world wars. We believed we could change the world and history shows that we did but, unfortunately, not always for the better. The Captains in Transcon were figures of authority both on and off the flight deck. They had the authority to administer disciplinary action to any members of their crew, both flight deck and cabin crew, who were guilty of misdemeanours whilst away from base down-route. They could even dismiss a crew member if they thought that to be the right course of action. Fortunately these men used their power sparingly and wisely. They were also expected to, and did, look after the commercial interests of the company. On empty sectors, if we could fill the cargo holds with freight, this would make an obvious contribution to the company's revenue. They had contacts in all sorts of unexpected places and sourcing a load of perishable cargo, such as fruit, was particularly lucrative. But it was a two-way street. When we managed to pick up extra revenue, upon return to Windsor the Captain would find a brown envelope full of US dollars in his pigeon hole by way of a thank you and, generally, he would share this largesse amongst his crew. It made for excellent team spirit and *esprit de corps*.

It was the same on other 'special' ops. On one occasion I was despatched with a crew to pick up a 707 that had been parked on the ground in Kuwait for some time. We were directed that we were to fly the aircraft in civvies and on no account to disclose who we were employed by. It took a couple of days to get the aircraft in a serviceable enough state actually to get airborne. When we did, only two of the generators were working properly, the air-conditioning and pressurisation systems were malfunctioning and one of the engines had to be kept throttled back to stop it surging. We gingerly flew it back to Stansted where we parked it in a remote area and left. When we got back to Windsor, all three of us were the recipients of brown envelopes. A year later I happened to transit through Stansted and the aircraft was still there where we had parked it, looking very sorry for itself.

As always, though, life was not perfect. There was one Captain who was a source of acrimony amongst some of the other pilots. He was actually a Captain on the Lockheed L1011 TriStar with BA. The effects of the oil crisis were still being felt in the industry and BA had placed some of its pilots on furlough on half pay. This Captain was one of them. Not satisfied with merely half pay, he had got a job with Transcon whilst awaiting recall to BA but was working for less than the going market rate. Given the number of pilots that were out of work at the time, many of us considered this to be a very selfish stance on his part. Not only was he undercutting his colleagues, but also to have two jobs when many of his brothers had none was considered to be very poor form. It was the first time in my career that I had come across a pilot, motivated by selfishness and greed, acting against the best interests of his fellows but, unfortunately, it was not to be the last.

One of the last contracts I flew with Transcon was taking Muslim pilgrims to and from Jeddah in Saudi Arabia for the Hajj. These operations were organised chaos. The apron in Jeddah was crowded with lines of pilgrims who rushed the aircraft as soon as we parked even though they didn't know whether this was their aircraft or not. The cargo holds were always bulked out with baggage and the ground handlers could never give us accurate weights for the loadsheet. It wasn't unknown for these sorts of passengers to carry a short engine block in their baggage. We were flying overweight and we knew it. Fortunately, having worked for Casair, I had plenty of experience in flying overweight. We got airborne out of Jeddah one day and the aircraft just didn't want to accelerate. The engines were firewalled and all four EGT over-temperature lights were on. There is a maximum takeoff thrust limit of five minutes on the JT3D and only two minutes at over-temp but we had no choice. We just had to keep the levers up and hope we didn't burn the turbines out of the engines. We were in an inversion and if we reduced thrust we'd sink back into the desert. As the curvature of the Earth increased our altitude, slowly we accelerated, cleaned up the flaps and climbed away. If one of those engines had given out, we'd have been in the bundu. Pratt & Whitney's logo includes the motto, 'Dependable Engines'. They lived up to their name that day.

The cabin on these flights was appalling. How the girls used to put up with it amazed me. On one flight the chief purser came to the flight deck to report that she had just stopped a passenger trying to light a primus stove in the cabin to cook some food. Apparently he didn't want to eat the aircraft catering because he considered it unclean. Unclean! We used to lock off the forward lavatory for crew use only because many of the passengers did not know how to use a western style toilet. Instead they'd squat on the seat, or even worse in the wash hand basin, and the results were indescribable. At the end of the season all the crews positioned back to London on one aircraft and went home. The next day I couldn't stop scratching. I came out in a rash in some uncomfortable places and my girlfriend started exhibiting the same symptoms. The doctor diagnosed body lice. We had to shave our body hair, burn our bedding and cover ourselves in permethrin powder. She was very impressed with me. I'd picked them up from the seats in the aircraft and I wasn't the only one. After that we used to fumigate the aircraft with sulphur candles after Hajj flights.

I operated my last flight for Transcon on Christmas Day 1979. We flew up from Luxor to Cairo and returned to the Slammer to find that we'd been thrown out of the hotel because the bill had not been paid. There were three full 707 crews milling about in the foyer and eventually the manager gave us one room gratis to clear us away and stop us from creating a bad impression of his hotel with the other guests. We already knew Transcon was in trouble because, although it was not at all unusual for our salaries to be paid late, at that time we hadn't been paid for three months. We carried on working anyway and lived off the expenses float that was paid to us in cash before we left Windsor on detachment. We all decided to go to the airport and fly the aircraft back to London. They wouldn't let us on board. It had been impounded against unpaid landing fees. *Déjà vu*! We all had one-way FOC tickets on EgyptAir from Cairo to London issued by the company. It was one of the precautions we took on all detachments. Always have an escape route in case of trouble. EgyptAir wouldn't honour them. There was nothing else to do. We used our plastic to buy new tickets and went home.

Transcon was owned by Tony Griffin and Alexander 'Rubber Legs' Rumley, so called because of his lack of tolerance for alcohol. Griffin started out in 1967 with a brokerage company called Templewood Aviation specialising in the sale and lease of transport aircraft. Later, using a subsidiary company called Tempair International Airlines, he moved into the wet lease market providing aircraft complete with crew, maintenance and insurance to other airlines. Here he started operating aircraft as well as buying and selling them. Tempair operated contracts for Union of Burma Airways, Biman Bangladesh, Merpati Nusantara of Indonesia, Somalia Airlines and Air Niugini amongst others. It was a British registered company but did not hold an AOC or any British licences. Its aircraft were registered either in the places they were operating or on the Ghanaian register.[6] Tempair went bust in the late 1970s but Griffin re-emerged with a similar type of wet lease operation under the name of Transasia Airways, which metamorphosed into Air Transcontinental. This time the aircraft were British registered.

On 8 February 1980 the party came to an end. Air Transcontinental went into liquidation and its assets were placed in the hands of accountants Cork, Gully & Co. and Poppleton & Appleby. I had visited the office in Windsor in January and taken the precaution of commandeering a very nice model of a 707 in Somali Airlines livery before the locks were changed, but that was all I got. There was no money left. I was out of a job, out of pocket three months' pay and I was flat broke.

3

Climb

Things looked bad, very bad. The rent on the cottage in Knaresborough in Yorkshire where I was living was due and I couldn't pay it. I'd been to the dole office to see whether I could claim unemployment benefit but there was a snag. They wanted to know where I'd been and what I'd been earning as there was a break in my tax records since I'd left BAF. Transcon had paid us offshore and I hadn't declared any income. I didn't want them poking around there so that was a non-starter. I couldn't even afford to go across the road to the local pub for a few pints to drown my sorrows. At all costs it was essential to keep the telephone working. That was the best point of contact where some work might turn up. There were rumours that Tony Griffin might be starting up again with a new company. Despite what had happened, most of us would have gone back to work for him again at the drop of a hat. He was the kind of man that engendered that sort of loyalty. We all knew he was slightly shady, perhaps a bit of a crook, but he was fun to work for, he looked after his pilots and he shared some of the goodies when they were there to be had. It was the same with Freddie Laker. When Laker Airways went bust on 5 February 1982, as a result of some very dirty pool played by his main competitors – BA, British Caledonian (BCal), Pan Am and Trans World Airlines (TWA) – his pilots were queuing up to go back to work for him if he could get something off the ground. There are some airline managers who can generate that sort of loyalty from their crews and then there are others who either have no idea or don't care.

The liquidator didn't help. When we tried to register as primary creditors, he informed us that he had no records of us ever being employed by Air Transcontinental UK and then followed this up by a demand that we repay the balance of the per diem floats that had been issued to us in Windsor. This begged the obvious question. If we were never employed there, why had they given us money? Examination of my contract paperwork gave the answer. My letter of appointment and other paperwork were all headed Air Transcontinental Hong Kong with an address in Queen's Road, Central. According to the liquidator, it was only the UK company that had gone bust. The Hong Kong company was still in business but was unable to pay us because the UK company was indebted to the Hong Kong company and until the latter received its money from the former it was 'no can do'. Yeah, right! Colin Allsop actually went to the registered address in Hong Kong when he was visiting the colony on business. It was an accommodation address. Well, I did say that Griffin was a bit shady but you had to admire his style. The liquidator threatened us with legal action to recover the supposedly outstanding float money. We told him we'd see him in court and that was the last we heard from him. I came across Griffin again in 1986. He was running a pub called the Prince of Wales in the Makati commercial district of Manila in the Philippines. He sold the bar in June of that year. Two weeks later it closed because of a 'flood' and its staff were locked out. One of the men connected with the bar was alleged to have been named in an Australian Royal Commission into drug trafficking. Griffin and Rumley themselves were under investigation in connection with the sale of two ex-BCal Airbus A310 aircraft to Libya in breach of a US export embargo to what was then considered to be a terrorist stronghold. Griffin's latest company, Service Airlines, registered in Hong Kong, had supposedly acted as a middleman by providing end user certificates to allow the sale of the aircraft through a French company, Europe Aero Services, which turned out to be forged.[7] Whatever the truth of the situation, knowing their track record and their previous Libyan connections, I wouldn't have put it past them.

Just when I was getting really desperate, the phone rang. It was Northair Aviation based at Leeds Bradford Airport (LBA). I knew them quite well because Casair used to get some of its maintenance done there. They were looking for a Cessna 400 rated pilot to do some ad hoc charter work. I jumped at the chance. It wasn't airline flying but it was a job. It was mainly routine stuff on my old Casair stomping ground but I spent an interesting week at the end of January based in Gibraltar working with scientists from GEC-Marconi developing the Sting Ray torpedo project. The Sting Ray had a sophisticated guidance system that allowed the torpedo to be launched in any direction and then guided onto its target without the launch vessel actually being pointed at the target in the first place. The Royal Navy was involved with these tests. The modus operandi (MO) was that they would leave Gibraltar at the crack of sparrow fart and steam out to an RVP in the Mediterranean off the North African coast. I would rise at a gentleman's hour, have a leisurely breakfast, pop down to the airport, fly the 20 minutes to the RVP and the torpedo would be launched. After it had run its course it would surface with a flotation collar and a dye marker. If it surfaced at the pre-programmed position, all well and good. If it didn't my job was to find it and direct the ships onto it for recovery. We filmed the whole operation from the air with a camera mounted in the open cargo door in the rear of the aircraft. This naturally called for some very low flying, buzzing of the various vessels and general good sport. Quite often the guidance system didn't perform to spec so I would set up a square search, just like my father did in his Catalina. During one of these searches I spotted an object floating in the sea and homed in. There, floating in the Mediterranean Sea 30 miles off the North African coast, was a dead, brown and white spotted cow. How on earth it got there God only knows. I had called up the lead ship to let them know that I might have found the target only to have to report my initial sighting was incorrect. I came in for some very ribald ribbing by the Royal Navy chaps that night in the bar. The fish heads thought it most amusing.

I picked up another trip flying the owner of Lotus cars, Colin Chapman, and his wife, Hazel, from their base at Hethel in Norfolk to Basel in Switzerland. Lotus owned two aircraft, a Cessna 414A Chancellor II and a Piper PA31 Navajo. They employed a full-time pilot but he only held a PPL and was not qualified to fly under IFR, which was why my services were required for this trip. The flight went well until we landed at Norwich on the way back home to clear customs. At the time Tissot Watches were sponsors of the Lotus F1 team and, as part of the sponsorship deal, Colin was required to wear a Tissot watch. Hazel had one as well. These were not your run of the mill Tissots, they were encrusted in diamonds. The customs people at Norwich were renowned for being difficult. It was a training station and everything had to be done by the book. When they saw these watches they demanded paperwork, import/export certificates, proof of ownership and all manner of documentation. Of course, Colin hadn't got any and when he told them that they weren't his watches anyway, they were only on loan from Tissot, the jobsworths had a field day. It took us almost two hours eventually to clear customs. They knew very well who Colin was but for some reason known only to themselves they used their powers of petty officialdom to make his life as difficult as possible. Later that year, the Lotus pilot was killed in the Navajo in a crash on 20 August. The accident report concluded that the aircraft broke up in flight while he was attempting to recover from an unauthorised aerobatic manoeuvre.[8] He was 26 years old and left a wife and small baby.

While at Northair, I did some Certificate of Airworthiness (CofA) test flying on aircraft that had completed heavy maintenance. This was to cause some consternation amongst my friends and colleagues. On 4 March 1980, I flew an air test on a Cessna 414 that was scheduled to go to Pakistan on behalf of the World Health Organization. I took along another pilot friend of mine, Norman Rhodes, as observer. I had first met Norman in Teesside when he was flying the Britten-Norman BN2 Islander 'Truck' support aircraft for the Rothmans team. We completed the air test, filled in the post-flight report and went to the flying club for a beer. On 23 March, one of the other Northair pilots took the aircraft on a further air test. It spun and crashed while turning finals onto R/W 15 at LBA killing both men on board. There was a picture of the crash in the *Daily Telegraph* with the aircraft registration clearly visible. Norman couldn't get in touch with me because I'd gone away for a couple of days to celebrate my 28th birthday. He thought it was me in the crash and called round our circle of friends to give them the news. I got back to find a bunch of messages on my answerphone. I was pleased to be able to emulate Mark Twain and let the callers know that the reports of my death had been greatly exaggerated but it was very sad. The pilot and his observer were only 26 and 22 years old.

A charter to Paris on 6 March was also very sad. I flew to Le Bourget to pick up a man and his wife. She was suffering from terminal cancer and had been receiving treatment in France. She was on a stretcher and in great pain. Every movement of the aircraft caused her great discomfort and I tried my best to make the flight as smooth as possible. The weather was good but there was a lot of cumulus cloud overland that was generating turbulence so, instead of taking the direct route, I flew 30 miles out over the North Sea where the air was clear. The route I took added 35 minutes to the scheduled flying time but I thought it well worth it. I had done casevac flights before, mainly bringing men who had been injured on the North Sea rigs home, and had seen some pretty awful injuries, but this was different. The look in this poor man's eyes as he watched his wife suffering was heart-rending. As with all charters, the rate was quoted on expected flying time. Because I had taken longer than anticipated, the trip didn't make a profit. The ops manager questioned me about this in quite aggressive terms asking me what the hell I'd been doing. He didn't get a very polite response.

At the beginning of March I got a phone call from a close friend, Alexander George William Easton, or Sandy to his friends and enemies alike, who was working for Monarch Airlines as an F/O on the BAC 1-11 based at Luton. He advised me to, 'Get your arse down here, Jimmy, they're looking for 707 drivers.'

I had met Sandy on the first day of Course 732 at Hamble. On day one the whole group had been thrown together in a room with some refreshments to get to know one another. It paid to be careful in such situations. We were all about to spend the next two years living and working in close proximity to each other and it is advisable to be selective with whom you team up in the first instance. If you let some plonker latch onto you you're probably going to be stuck with him for the duration. During the get-together I heard someone with a very pukka British accent remarking that the use of profanity merely demonstrated a marked lack of command of the English language, to which the response, in a broad Scottish accent, was, 'Bollocks!' I detached myself from the group I was talking to, approached this other group and enquired as to who had just said 'bollocks'. The mad Scotsman replied, 'Me, what of it?'

I introduced myself, remarked that I completely agreed with his assessment of the debate and offered him my hand. We became friends there and then and have remained so to this day. My father once told me that a man can count himself fortunate if he finds just one true friend in his life. Well on that basis I am a fortunate man because Sandy is that. He is the brother I never had. We have travelled the world of aviation together from those early beginnings in 1973. Sometimes when separated by distance we do not see each other for two or three years but we keep in touch and when we meet up again we take up exactly where we left off.

After his phone call I went down to Luton and knocked on Monarch's door. I got a short-term contract for the summer season, did the base training at Stansted and on 3 April 1980 I was checked out to the line. I was back on the shark but this was the GT version. Monarch had the Boeing 707-720B. This was the smaller version of the 707 produced after the introduction of the larger 100 series and the largest 300 series. The 720B had a MTOW of 235,000 lb compared with 257,000 lb for the 100B and 335,000 lb for the 300B series. They were all, however, powered by the same four Pratt & Whitney JT3D engines producing 18,000 lb of thrust each; so the power to weight ratio of the 720B was much higher than the other variants. It used to climb like a dingbat. On Monarch's bread and butter Inclusive Tour (IT) charters to European holiday destinations, after taking off from Luton we could be at 41,000 feet by the time we crossed the French FIR boundary. It was an absolutely superb aircraft to fly and we pilots loved it.

Monarch was formed in 1968 and is privately owned by the Swiss-Italian Mantegazza family. It started out initially operating two Bristol Britannia aircraft and introduced the first 720B in December 1971. The bulk of the flying was IT work to the Canary Islands, Greece, Israel, Italy, North Africa and Spain. It was seasonal and we would work to maximum hours during the season from March through to the end of October when the flying programme would ease off and we'd get a bit of a respite. We also used to do some very sought after trips to St Lucia in the Caribbean and charters to Wideawake Airbase on Ascension Island, St Helena on behalf of Cable & Wireless who maintained a communications facility down there. Monarch also picked up the Air Malta contract based out of Luqa after Transcon went to the wall, and one of my first jobs for Monarch was back to Malta. We were even flying one of the ex-Transcon aircraft that Monarch had also acquired, albeit under a different registration. The nature of Monarch's operation was markedly different from Transcon's, however. Monarch was fully regulated by the CAA, had full maintenance backup courtesy of Monarch Aircraft Engineering Limited (MAEL) and there was none of the cowboy stuff that had been a feature of my flying career so far. I had joined a proper airline.

The DFO of Monarch when I joined was Jack Burridge. He was ex-RAF and old school. He supported his pilots to the hilt but if you cocked up you'd be invited into the Portakabin that constituted his office for a private dressing down. He commanded great respect from his crews and we admired his leadership style. Joining Monarch was like a Hamsters' reunion. In the old days, Monarch had generally only recruited ex-RAF pilots, mainly from Transport Command. However, after a couple of these pilots joined them on the Britannia, got themselves a type rating on the 707 at Monarch's expense and then immediately departed to Cathay Pacific, they started to look elsewhere and recruited their first Hamster. They obviously liked the product because they employed a lot of us after that. We were all in our late twenties and children of the 1970s oil crisis. We were happy to be in a good job and there was great *esprit de corps*. We all felt that we were a valued part of the company and were helping to build it into a successful organisation. We felt appreciated and it made for an excellent working atmosphere.

The cabin crew were all part of the team as well and the social life was hectic. At the end of the day when we returned to Luton, the girls would go to their crew room, consisting of another Portakabin in the hangar, where they would count the takings from the duty-free bar. We also had another inbound crew room, which was a room off the side of the hangar with some old aircraft seats in it with a couple of tables. When the girls had finished their accounting, they'd join us in there and we'd all share a few post-flight libations, sometimes more than a few. Some of the parties that happened in there, especially at weekends when there was no one in the management offices, became the stuff of legend.

The St Lucia trips were special. We flew there from Luton via Gander, Newfoundland, and the beauty of these trips, from our point of view, was that we got to stay there until the next aircraft was scheduled through, which was usually a minimum of one week but, later in the season, could be anything up to two or three weeks. We had permanent winter suntans, much to the chagrin of the 1-11 crews. The only drawback was that we stayed at the same hotel as the passengers, the Halcyon Days, and this could sometimes give rise to the odd complaint if our antics got out of hand. We had a fix for that. We negotiated a deal with a place up the coast, the Hurricane Hole in Marigot Bay, where *Doctor Doolittle* was filmed in 1967. We swapped our rooms at the Halcyon for ones at the Hole where we could party away from the prying eyes of the paying customers. It was idyllic and I spent Christmas 1980 there. We carried six cabin crew and the girls were always an attraction for local yacht owners who were very keen to invite them out for a cruise. Naturally they would only accept the invitation if the flight deck crew were invited along as well. It was the same when we went down to Wideawake. Ascension Island is very remote in the South Atlantic and was used as a staging point during the Falklands War. There were very few women on the island so we were always popular when we arrived with a Cable & Wireless crew change. We used to take the aircraft down there in 'combi' configuration carrying both equipment and supplies as well as passengers in the main cabin. One of the things we always had on board was a pallet of Batchelor's tinned peas. They were a sought after delicacy in Ascension and in short supply. During the overnight stop we'd be invited to the mess for dinner and treated to the speciality of the house, shepherd's pie with, you guessed it, Batchelor's tinned peas. It was considered to be a gourmet feast. It was the same when I was flying in Africa. Expats would always come up with requests to bring them things that they missed that they couldn't get locally. These would range from Heinz baked beans, HP Brown Sauce and Melton Mowbray pork pies to McVitie's Chocolate Homewheat Digestives, both milk and plain. On one trip to Wideawake with a Scottish captain called Duncan Tamblyn, who became a good friend, one of the passengers on the return trip was a nurse who was being casevaced back to the UK. The Captain was always given details of the patient's condition on casevac flights and, upon receipt of same, Duncan asked me to lock off the forward lavatory for crew use only. Thinking back to my Hajj days I enquired why, to which he replied, 'Because this woman has a severely ulcerated vagina and how am I going to explain it to the wife if I catch something off the toilet seat? She'll never believe it.'

Duncan was a great guy to fly with and we enjoyed each other's company. He had a ribald sense of humour. On another occasion we were sitting on the tarmac in Corfu watching out of the flight deck windows as the return load of passengers was boarding. The procession included a number of very suntanned young women in rather diaphanous, semi-transparent dresses, which were in vogue at that time. After a few minutes Duncan turned to me and asked me to LMC an additional 10 kg on the loadsheet. Reaching for the clipboard I asked him why, to which he responded, 'Because these women are all full of Greek semen and it's bloody dense stuff.'

There were a lot of characters amongst the Monarch Captains in those days and Benny Benson was one of them. I did not get off to a very good start with Benny when I first met him as I committed a cardinal sin. I had been scheduled to fly with him but overslept. This happened very occasionally to almost everyone but the crew controllers were very good. If you didn't turn up on time they would call you at home and, since I only lived 15 minutes away from the airport, I could usually get there in time to avoid a flight delay. If repeated too often, this was a sackable offence, and rightly so. If you don't turn up for your scheduled duty, it means that someone else has to be called out from standby and, on a tight roster, the knock-on effects are very disruptive. You are paid to be there, booted and spurred and on time. On this occasion, however, the crew controllers couldn't get in touch with me as I had spent the night at someone else's place. I missed my flight. I was scheduled to fly with Benny again the next day. I reported for duty to find a not very pleased Captain at flight despatch. Benny was a big man and had a lump under his left eye, which throbbed when he was annoyed. It was throbbing that morning.

'Oh so you've managed to turn up today have you? Good of you to come.'

'Yes, sorry about yesterday but I'm here today,' I replied not very diplomatically. It was all I could think of at the time. We flew to Palma and on the way down he refused to speak to me other than to respond to the checklist. When we got on the ground the F/E was off the flight deck in a shot, and I was left alone with Benny. The silent treatment couldn't go on all the way back to Luton so I turned to him and said, 'Captain, I'm very sorry about yesterday. I fucked up big time. I apologise to you and please be assured that it won't happen again.'

He looked at me and replied, 'Young man, let me tell you something. There are enough people in the management of this company behaving like cunts without the aircrew doing the same thing. Keep that in mind and don't do it again. Your apology is accepted.'

We flew with each other quite a lot after that and got on well but, from then on, he always referred to me as 'That cunt Warham'.

There was another Captain at Monarch whom I admired greatly. His name was Tony Dodd and he had the best pair of hands that I've ever seen in all the different people I have flown with in my career. Not only that, he was a well read, intelligent man and, like Sam and Mel in Transcon, happy to pass on his knowledge and experience to the next generation of pilots. In the 1980s inertial navigation systems (INS) and GPS were becoming standard equipment on most modern aircraft and, instead of flying from beacon to beacon as had previously been the standard operating procedure (SOP), ATC would often give direct routings through their airspace for suitably equipped aircraft. This resulted in a saving in flying time and, therefore, cost. On the 720 we didn't have such equipment but, if offered a direct routing by ATC, being company men, we would accept it. This meant getting out the charts, measuring the mean track between the cleared points and navigating in the old-fashioned way with pencil, eyeball and protractor. One night I was returning from Southern Europe to Luton with Tony. It was around 02:00, there was little other traffic around and, while still in Hungarian airspace, ATC cleared us directly to Abbeville near the French coast. Tony altered heading and I got to work with the protractor. After I'd finished and worked out a course to steer, I checked and found he was already on it. He turned to me and told me he was impressed with my navigational skills but it was all really a waste of time. He gave me the advice, if you're cleared direct in Europe, on all our routes the track's 315 if you're going northbound and 135 if you're going southbound. He was right. There was no need for all the messing around with charts and pencils. Practical airmanship. He also gave me one of the best pieces of advice that I have ever had in my career. I have tried to live by that advice and have passed it on to the next generation of pilots who have flown with me as their Captain. It is this: aviation is a great way to earn a living and we are privileged to be part of this select group. The best we can hope for is to put as much back into it as we derive from it and leave our profession in a better condition than when we entered it. We have a responsibility to our brothers who came before us to ensure that their sacrifices were not in vain.

At the end of the 1980 summer season and, therefore, the end of my initial contract, I was offered a permanent job. I took it. I was offered two options. Option one was to forego the end of contract bonus to which I was entitled and have my seniority backdated to April when I joined. Option two was to take the bonus and have my seniority start with effect from October. I had no option. Given the parlous state of my finances I took the money and dropped the seniority. It was a question of needs must but it was to cost me later on financially when promotion slowed up and I missed out on the last round of commands. I didn't know it at the time but my choice in 1980 was to have a direct bearing on a career decision I was to take almost five years later.

The days of the 707 couldn't last. Fuel was, and still is, a very significant portion of the direct operating costs (DOC) of an aircraft. The JT3D was relatively old technology in terms of the modern high-bypass-ratio fan engines that newer aircraft were fitted with and they were very thirsty in comparison. Monarch started to phase out the 720s and I flew my last flight on the shark on 1 October 1981. It was a 12-minute positioning hop from Gatwick to Luton. I had a total of 4,252 hours in my logbook with 1,274 of them on the 707. I had achieved my boyhood dream that was born all those years before in the BOAC hangar with my grandfather. I had flown the shark, albeit as an F/O not a Captain, but I had done it nonetheless. It was the end of an era.

I had some leave held over from the summer so I took it and went skiing for six weeks with some friends in Les Trois Vallées. When I got back I started conversion training onto the Boeing 737-200, which Monarch had started operating at the end of 1980 as a replacement for the BAC 1-11. I checked out to the line at the end of January 1982 and operated the 737 for a year. Monarch had opened up bases in Birmingham, Gatwick, Glasgow and Manchester as well as their main base at Luton. The pilots were given the opportunity to move to these places on a permanent basis if that was their choice. The company needed a certain number of pilots in each base to meet their commercial goals and, if there weren't enough volunteers, there was a lot of talk about 'compulsory' postings. As the scope of Monarch's operation changed and more and more flights were being operated from places other than Luton, the crews were spending a lot of time in surface transport positioning between the various bases.

As well as the obvious cost involved, this also was having an impact on crew duty hours as positioning before and after flight counted towards total duty times. Things were not always being handled as efficiently as they might have been either. On one occasion I went with a crew by taxi from Luton to Gatwick to operate a flight from there. On arrival, we met a Gatwick-based crew who were just boarding a taxi to position to Luton to operate a flight out of there. It was obvious that, as the nature of the company's operation was changing, we pilots needed to look to see how we could help to accommodate this change. However, there had been a change in management of the company and the new management's initial approach to dealing with the pilots did not endear them to us in the first instance. This led to a certain amount of distrust and resistance by us towards making these changes, but more of that later.

My seniority allowed me to remain based in Luton, which was my preference, but I spent a lot of the remainder of my time with Monarch living in hotels for a week at a time at the various bases, particularly Gatwick. I did not mind this as I enjoyed the lifestyle but for some of the other pilots, particularly those with young children, it was not ideal. We also had a base in West Berlin operating charters out of Tegel to the Mediterranean and Canary Islands on behalf of Flug-Union Berlin. I spent some happy detachments living there. This was before the wall came down and, back then, West Berlin was one of the greatest party towns I have ever had the pleasure of experiencing. The sights and sounds of the Kurfürstendamm on a Saturday night were an eye opener. Sitting on the steps of the Gedaechtniskirche with good company and a case of chilled Sekt from the Lufthansa duty-free stores was a good way to start the evening's entertainment. They even had the shopping sorted out, at least from the male point of view. One of the other pilots, Ken Norman, and I had become friendly with two ladies we met who lived in Berlin. They were called Hanna and Ziggy. Like most women, these girls liked to shop and, like most men, Ken and I didn't. The KaDeWe department store had the answer. On the top floor was a champagne bar with spectacular views over old Berlin. Ken and I would ensconce ourselves in there and indulge ourselves in its delights whilst the girls completed their shopping and joined us at the end of their excursion. Like many things in Berlin, it was an excellent compromise and everyone was happy.

Flying down the Berlin corridor on the way into Tegel was also a unique experience. There were three corridors under the control of the all-Allied Berlin Air Safety Centre. This was manned by US, UK and French controllers who rotated on a monthly basis. The corridors were only 25 miles wide with two-way traffic and a maximum altitude of

10,000 feet. Accurate navigation was essential as any excursion outside the corridors into East German airspace would be met with interception by MiGs. At night, on leaving West German airspace and entering the corridor, we would leave the bright lights of the West behind and enter a dark tunnel. The ground beneath us was the biggest tank range in the world and devoid of all lights except for the occasional muzzle flash. Basically it was a killing ground in case of invasion by the West. We would be surrounded by darkness and then, in the distance, a small light would appear on the horizon shining like a jewel. Gradually it would get bigger until there, in all its decadent glory, laid out before us was West Berlin. It was an oasis of freedom in an otherwise darkened desert. I often thought that if the East Germans invaded the West they probably would not have got far. Having been indoctrinated for years into believing that the average person in the West was poor, had bad housing and was repressed, it wouldn't have taken long for the first tank crews into West Germany – having witnessed first-hand the obvious affluence – to realise that it was all a lie. If I was them, I'd have downed tools there and then. I went on a tour of East Berlin once. The bus was only allowed on a predetermined route where all the flats and houses had a clean façade supposedly showing how nice it was in the workers' paradise. If you looked down the side streets though, it was all concrete and grime. It was like being on a movie set where it all looks great travelling down Main Street but there are no real buildings behind the set. We were invited once to Schönefeld to have drinks and dinner in the mess with our East German counterparts. They were very hospitable and the over-riding impression that I came away with was that they were just like us. They were young pilots who loved flying trying to make their way in the brotherhood of aviation. It seems strange now in the modern world of the Internet, satellite imaging and instant global communications that Erich Honecker and his cronies could have kept their people so much in the dark, but they did. If you want to run a repressive regime, or even just simply control your employees and bend them to your will, control of information and communications is essential.

When I was flying the 737, an incident occurred that demonstrated and reinforced some basic principles of airmanship. On 11 May 1982, I operated a trip from Luton to Ibiza with Captain Charles Arthur Rollo Wells, 'Budge' to his friends. The aircraft had come straight out of heavy maintenance, which was always something to be wary of. After an aircraft has been in the hangar, it is always prudent to double-check everything. Systems, controls and switches that are not normally touched during

routine line operations will have been used by the engineers during maintenance. On such operations normally we would come into work half an
hour earlier than usual to give ourselves extra time to ensure everything
was as it should be before we went flying. On this occasion we didn't
because we hadn't been given prior notice by ops control that the aircraft
was coming off maintenance so we didn't have the extra time for additional checks if we were to depart on schedule. We operated the flight
normally down to Ibiza but, on landing, the thrust reversers wouldn't
work. This was not a big deal from the landing performance point of
view as the runway in Ibiza was over 9,000 feet long and the required
landing distance was well within this, even without thrust reversers. We
stopped the aircraft using the brakes alone and taxied in but now we had
a problem. The MEL stated that it was permissible to despatch with one
reverser inoperable but not both. Unless we could fix at least one of
them we were AOG. The thrust reversers were hydraulically operated
and electrically controlled. There were two circuit breakers (c/bs) on the
panel behind the F/O's seat that protected the electrical circuit. It was a
pre-flight requirement visually to check these and I had done so as part
of the pre-flight checks. It was an obvious solution to check these again
in case they had popped for some reason in flight. We had another look
and everything seemed normal so we searched for other solutions. The
next most obvious was that the ground lock pins had been left in so
locking out the reversers. The ground lock pins are used to prevent inadvertent deployment during maintenance as the buckets can cause serious
injury to personnel in the vicinity. It has been known for people to lose
hands and arms if they are in the wrong place and hydraulically operated components such as undercarriage doors, thrust reversers and the
like are operated without clearance. We checked the pins but, again, all
was normal. Budge called the engineers in Luton but they could offer
no further advice and set about sending a 1-11 with spares and engineers
down to Ibiza to rescue us. I thought I'd check the c/bs one more time.
They were located near the bottom of the panel behind the F/O's seat
and near to the aircraft library stowage. The library wasn't very tidy and
had some papers sticking out partly obscuring the panel. I pushed the
seat to its fully forward position, tidied up the library and squeezed in
behind the seat where I could run my hand over the panel to check all
the c/bs were pushed in. As I did so, I felt an obstruction. Something
was sticking out. I got a torch and shone it down behind the seat for a
better look. Both the thrust reverser c/bs were out. The reason we hadn't
seen them in our previous checks was that not only were they difficult
to get at, but the stems were also coloured grey, the same grey as the

panel itself. Usually the stems on c/bs are a different colour from their panel mount to make them stand out visually when they are popped. For some reason, these weren't and we had missed them despite three visual checks. I told Budge what I had found, pushed the c/bs in, and we checked the reversers. They worked. Fortunately we were just in time to cancel the rescue flight. It was just as well. Had a costly rescue flight been despatched, and all the engineers had to do was remake a couple of c/bs, we would definitely have been on the carpet in front of the DFO upon our return. Like all incidents and accidents, there was a causal chain that led up to the resulting event. The aircraft had been on heavy mainte-nance where systems had been disturbed as part of the process. In the post-maintenance checks, the ground engineers should have ensured that all c/bs were in. I should have ensured the same thing during my pre-flight check. We should have been notified that the aircraft was coming off maintenance to give us additional time but we weren't. An actual functional check of thrust reversers before flight is not carried out because selecting reverse at low airspeed can cause jet engines to surge and damage them. I should have seen the c/bs in my check after landing but I hadn't because they were difficult to get at, the same colour as the panel, and the panel was partly obstructed by an untidy ship's library. The only thing that revealed the actual problem and broke the chain was a tactile check. In this case, had the chain not been broken, the only result would have been financial cost and some very red faces. In most situations in aviation, the cost of an unbroken causal chain is far greater. Some lessons in airmanship that we already knew were reinforced. Just because the aircraft is signed off as fit for flight in the tech log doesn't guarantee it. Do everything you can within the SOPs to double-check. Perform your checks meticulously. Review and repeat everything if neces-sary. Don't be hurried or rushed just to maintain schedule. If you need extra time, take it. When you think you've covered everything and the problem still isn't solved, check again. Better still, try to find a different methodology or a different problem-solving route. Learn from your mistakes and put them in your experience log. Share your experiences with others so that they don't fall into the same traps.

There was another incident that happened on the 737 with similar lessons to be learned. We used to operate into Iraklion in Crete. The main runway was aligned 09/27 with a built-up area and a church off the western end. Because of the prevailing winds, we generally landed and took off on R/W 09. One day the wind favoured R/W 27 and we took off in the westerly direction. As we got airborne, I watched the spire of the church go past the cockpit window and thought it was VFC.

I doubted whether we would have cleared it had we lost an engine on takeoff. When we got back to Luton, I went in to talk to the perform-ance guys to express my concern. The performance charts were gener-ated by computer. The performance people entered all the relevant airport data into the computer and the programme generated Regulated Takeoff Weight (RTOW) charts based on the net takeoff flight path in the one-engine failure case, dominant obstacle clearance and so on. It turned out that the church had been entered into the computer on the wrong end of the runway. All the time we had been operating off R/W 09, we'd been using performance data assuming there was a church where there wasn't. That day when we used R/W 27, the performance data was based on the assumption that there were no obstacles in the flight path and that we were taking off straight over the sea, which was why the church looked big in the windows. Garbage in, garbage out. Obviously, nobody had done this deliberately, it was just human error. It was another good lesson. Just because the computer says so, it doesn't mean it is right. If it doesn't look right or feel right, double-check it. This lesson became particularly relevant in later generations of more automated aircraft where one of the commonest phrases on the flight deck was, 'What's it doing now?'

I operated my last flight on the 737 on 28 January 1983. The day before my 31st birthday, on 24 March 1983, I flew an aircraft from Moses Lake, Washington State, to Boeing Field in Seattle after spending two hours in the circuit. I had just completed two months at the Boeing training facility converting onto one of the first generation of glass cockpit aircraft, the Boeing 757-200. The 757 had a MTOW of 255,000 lb and was powered by two Rolls-Royce RB211-535E4B engines producing 43,500 lb of thrust each. It was similar in size to the 720B, and with a power to weight ratio of 2.93 compared with the 720's 3.26, it was not quite as sporty. Nevertheless, its performance was impressive. It also handled like a dream. Gone was all the 707's hysteresis. This thing had fully powered controls and was very responsive. You could put it exactly where you wanted it. The first time I saw the 757 on the final assembly line at the Boeing plant in Renton, Washington, it reminded me of a praying mantis standing up on its long legs prior to striking. It looked right and it flew right. It was a real pilots' aircraft and we loved it. The assembly line at Renton also was an amazing sight. It was the biggest Airfix kit I'd ever seen.

The routes we flew on the 757 remained the same and I spent much of my time on detachment to the various bases especially Manchester and Gatwick. At the height of the summer season, the IT circus as it took to the air daily was also a sight to behold. Trafford Leigh-Mallory's big wing had nothing on us. Air Europe, Britannia, Dan-Air, Monarch, Orion and others all flying similar aircraft types and all wanting to go to the same destinations in the same piece of airspace. Gatwick and Palma, Majorca were the busiest airports. The night jet ban at Gatwick meant that the earliest permitted departure each morning was 06:00. There would be ten or twelve aircraft all vying for the same slot. Slots were assigned by ground control on a first come first served basis and it was very competitive. Once assigned a takeoff slot you had to be airborne within a seven-minute time window or you lost your position and went back to the end of the queue. For us pilots, it was a balancing act between boarding the passengers and calling up to report doors closed and ready for start. If you actually waited until the doors really were closed, you'd be the last to go. We would liaise with the Redcap and he'd give us a guesstimate of doors closed time. On that basis we'd call for start before we were actually ready to go. We all did it and generally it worked quite well but sometimes things went wrong. The ATC ground control frequency was very busy and often it was difficult just to get a word in. The controllers were under as much pressure as we were and we appreciated the efficient way they handled things but, if someone had called for start but hadn't managed to get their doors closed in time to meet their slot it threw a major spanner in the works. On such occasions the controllers would rightfully get a little tetchy but generally remained calm and professional. But there would be the odd explosion. One particularly busy morning I was sitting on the aircraft playing the usual start-up roulette and a Britannia Airways aircraft on the stand next to us had been given a start-up time. For whatever reason he hadn't managed to board his passengers and his doors were still open when he was due to push back. The woman on ground control had been very harassed and asked him when he would be ready to push back. He responded with something along the lines that he might need another four or five minutes. She pressed the button and went for him.

'I knew you weren't going to be ready when you called for start. You still had the ground equipment attached. You've still got two doors open. You're nowhere near ready. You've completely messed up the flow. I'm going to have to reschedule everything because of you.'

There was a long silence on the R/T. She'd lost it and we all had sympathy for her but you just don't do that on the radio. After six or seven seconds, someone pressed the tit and a male voice said, 'I come to work to get away from that.'

Another, much calmer, voice came back on the ground control frequency and began to get the traffic flowing again. The poor girl had been relieved and probably gone down to the canteen for a cup of tea and a cry. It was a testament to the professionalism of the controllers that it didn't happen more often. The pressure on them was immense.

It was the same, if not worse, in Palma. The airport would be jam-packed with aircraft from all over Europe trying to get out. Three-hour delays on the ground waiting for start clearance were not at all unusual. We played the same game of start-up roulette there as well. It got to the point where we started calling up ground control and asking for start clearance before we'd even landed just to get a place in the queue. The controllers got wise to it and found an effective method of putting a stop to such queue jumping. One day an aircraft on approach called for start and the controller responded, 'Cleared to start, take-off time in twelve minutes, call ready for taxi.'

That was the end of that game.

Having a load of passengers on the aircraft waiting for two or three hours for take-off could be a nightmare for the cabin crew. These passengers were the bucket and spade brigade and not the most patient in the world. The worst were the Club 18-30 lot. After their 'sun, sea and sex' holidays often they would be half cut when they boarded the aircraft. If there was a long delay, the duty free would get cracked open. The crew were very good at handling any disruptive elements but there were occasions when things got out of hand in the cabin. On one Monarch flight, things got so bad that the Captain diverted the aircraft into Bordeaux on the way back from Spain and the flight was met by the French police. They didn't just send the ordinary police. They sent the CRS – the special riot control division. These chaps are not known for their kid glove treatment and the offending passengers were removed from the aircraft in forceful manner to the cheers of the remaining passengers. Some of them tripped and fell down the steps while they were disembarking. They were eventually prosecuted in the French courts and made to pay the costs of diverting the aircraft. So much for a cheap holiday.

By this time, Jack Burridge had retired and the new DFO was a Hamster called Donald 'Mac' McAngus. He was a big bluff sort of bloke who liked a few cold beers on a warm day. I flew with him quite a lot and we got on well. One day we were walking out to our 757 across the tarmac at Manchester and there was a Boeing 747 parked there. As we walked past and marvelled at its size, I caught Mac's eye. We were both thinking the same thing. He just nodded and said, 'One day.'

Things had changed in Monarch and it was no longer the happy company that I'd first joined. In 1979, we acquired a new managing director. His name was Alan Snudden and he joined Monarch from Dan-Air where he had held the same position. His arrival did not have an auspicious start. He brought with him a woman who he installed as head of the personnel department. Prior to this the personnel administration had been handled quite adequately from within the Portakabin office complex but this new woman had to have a 'proper' office. Snudden chose our inbound crew room in the hangar and commandeered it for his 'squeeze'. We were not greatly impressed. One Monday, early in the morning, Sandy and I had returned from our overnight flights and decided to register our protest. We set up a table and chairs and a pub umbrella that we had acquired for the purpose on the floor of the hangar just outside our old crew room and, together with some other crews, proceeded to have our usual inbound landing refreshments. Nine o'clock came and the office bods started arriving for work. Shortly afterwards, a messenger was sent over to inform Sandy and me that Mac would like to see us in his office. We duly paraded in front of the boss to be told, 'Very amusing. You've made your point now clear that fucking mess up and go home.'

Being good company men we did as we were told. It may seem a small point, and our reaction to it somewhat childish, but there was worse to come. The crews worked hard over the summer season. We didn't complain. We were there to work, get the job done and see our company succeed. We had an investment in the company as much as the share-holders. If there's no company then there are no jobs. By way of a thank you for our hard work, each Christmas, pilots and cabin crew alike would receive a Christmas hamper from the company. It was a cardboard box containing a bottle of wine, half a bottle of port, some mince pies, cheese and the like. It was not worth much but it was a token of gratitude that we all appreciated. Often, we would arrange to collect our hampers at the same time, repair to the inbound crew room and have a pre-Christmas party. With the arrival of Snudden came cost-cutting measures and the first thing to go under his axe was our Christmas hampers. The outcry from the crew was immediate and vociferous. For the sake of a few card-board boxes costing less than £20 each he lost our goodwill. Aircrew will put up with a lot of disruption and major change if it's to the benefit of the operation but mess around with the small things for no good reason and you will have a rebellion on your hands. Some airline managers understand this and some either do not or do not care. Snudden didn't and he put us all offside. In the end he relented but the damage was done. He lost our trust. It got even worse. He decided to call all the pilots together for a meeting at which he would address us and map out his plan for the future. Despite the fact that he'd only been in the company two minutes he started his address talking about 'my airline this' and 'my airline that'. This raised the hackles of some of the Senior Captains and one of them said to him, 'With respect, sir, some of the people in this room have been here in Monarch for a lot longer than you and feel that we are much more a part of this company than you are.'

He didn't like this and started to speak whereupon another Captain tried to interrupt him at which Snudden put a finger to his lips and said, 'Shush, Daddy's talking.'

That was it. People started to walk out of the meeting. He'd blown it. His leadership qualities had been found lacking and we didn't like him. From then on, the trust and *esprit de corps* that had been such a feature of working at Monarch were gone. Every time contractual changes were proposed, such as during the negotiations to permanently base some pilots at ports other than Luton, we were sceptical, always looking for the catch or how Snudden was trying to put one over on us. As it turned out our cynicism was well founded. Snudden was one of the first of the modern day bean counter airline managers who view their employees as accounting units to be trimmed and pared at every available opportunity. The future did not look rosy to me and, because of my decision to take the end of contract bonus instead of seniority back in 1980, I had missed out on the last round of promotions in the 1984 summer season. I would have to wait at least another year to get into the left-hand seat.

There was something else that was making me unhappy. Under the Thatcher tax regime, as a single man with no mortgage and no child allowance, I was losing around half of my salary each month in deductions. My colleagues who had a mortgage and 2.4 children were actually financially better off than me in terms of disposable income. Here was the paradox. I could increase my disposable income by taking on some debt but that was the last thing I wanted to do. I had only just managed to wade my way out of the financial quagmire that the Transcon collapse had dumped me in. Also, we had just witnessed Thatcher's emasculation of the power of trade unions in the aftermath of the miners' strike, not that I was then, or am now, a particularly militant trade unionist. Like all things in life, I believe there is a balance to be found. I had grown up in a mining area in Yorkshire and witnessed the National Union of Mineworkers (NUM), under the leadership of Joe Gormley, Mick McGahey and Arthur Scargill, bring down the Heath government in 1974. In my view, there is no way that a trade union should be allowed to have sufficient power to bring down a democratically elected government.

Trade unions do, however, provide a necessary counterbalance to protect workers against unscrupulous and unconscionable management practices. Thatcher's Draconian legislation against the unions moved the scales too far in favour of dictatorial government and did not bode well for the future. History has shown that her monetarist policies destroyed many of the UK's manufacturing industries and ushered in two decades of greed and pursuit of profit for profit's sake with little concern for the effect on society as a whole. In my view, she has much to answer for. She did do one good thing for me, however. She forced me to look abroad and get out of the UK.

Cathay Pacific Airways was advertising for pilots on the Boeing 747 based in Hong Kong. I applied and got accepted. I operated my last flight for Monarch on 4 February 1985. I had a total of 5,620 hours in my logbook with 949 on the 757. I arrived in Hong Kong on 11 March 1985 to climb the next rung on the career ladder.

4

Cruise

Cathay Pacific Airways is part of the Swire Group. The Swire Group's privately owned parent company is John Swire & Sons Ltd, which was originally started as an import/export business based in Liverpool by John Swire (1793–1847), a Yorkshireman born in Halifax. His ancestors had been landowners in the area for more than 150 years before his grandfather went into business as a wool merchant in the late 1750s. By the 1790s the woollen industry was under pressure from imports of cotton from the New World and both his grandfather and his father were declared bankrupt. The Swire Group is now a multinational company that controls a range of wholly owned businesses including shipping, cold storage, road transport and property. Its web stretches around the world and Cathay Pacific is owned through its parent company John Swire & Sons (H.K.) Ltd. The airline was floated on the Hong Kong stock exchange in 1986 but its major shareholder remains the Swire Group.

The airline was founded on 24 September 1946 by American Roy C. Farrell and Australian Sydney H. de Kantzow flying a single Douglas DC3, nicknamed 'Betsy', on routes between Hong Kong, Bangkok, Canton, Manila, Shanghai, Singapore and Sydney. They named it Cathay Pacific because Cathay was the ancient name given to China, and Pacific because Farrell speculated that one day they would fly across the Pacific Ocean. In 1948 Butterfield & Swire, now the Swire Group, bought a 45 per cent share of Cathay Pacific and remains the major shareholder to this day.

When I joined the airline, they only recruited experienced pilots. There was a minimum requirement of 3,000 hours with at least 1,000 hours on jets and, preferably, wide-body time with previous experience on their route network. Employment with Cathay was seen as a premier position within the airline pilot fraternity and competition for jobs was fierce. The interview process was in two stages. The first interview was held in either London or Sydney as, back then, they generally only recruited Brits and Aussies. If you passed that hurdle, you were invited to Hong Kong for four days during which there were a series of interviews, technical examinations, a simulator check ride and a stringent medical. During the visit there was a cocktail party to see whether you were 'one of us'. Many people failed one or more of these tests. As one of the interviewers put it to me, 'We're not recruiting co-pilots, we only recruit potential Captains.' Having succeeded in gaining entry, it didn't end there. On my induction course, we were treated to a welcoming speech by the Chief of Flight Standards, a diminutive Australian chap called Noel Jones, at which he lectured us that we would rise to Cathay's standards, Cathay would not lower its standards to ours, and if we didn't make the grade, we'd be on the first plane out of there, and not on a Cathay flight. To emphasise the point he waved a handful of airline tickets in our faces. There then followed six weeks of ground school and simulator training commencing with the Hong Kong Air Law examination, which was needed to issue us with Hong Kong licences. We were given one day to prepare for the exam and if you failed it you were out. Having completed ground school, there were then 40 sectors of line training. On successful completion of this you were cleared to the line, but only on 12 months' probation. Any infraction or failure to meet the required standards during that period and you were out on your ear. Similarly, if you didn't meet the standard after 40 line sectors, you could be given a further 10 sectors at the discretion of your Check Captain and, after that, if you still couldn't make the grade you were on your way. It was a bit like being back at Hamble. The training actually was very good. My Training Captains, John Lewis-Lloyd and Graham Falkiner, were considerate, helpful and encouraging. Having flown Boeing jets before, the design and philosophy of the 747 was nothing new to me, I just needed a little time to get used to the different handling characteristics. I checked out to the line on 15 August 1985. In truth, the standards at Cathay were no higher than those at Monarch or any other first-tier airline. They were high, as rightly they should be, and there was a strong emphasis on SOPs, again as it should be, but they were nothing out of the ordinary. It was just that Noel had a novel way of putting his message across. In today's politically correct world his approach would probably be consigned to the waste paper bin. Indeed, shortly after I joined, Noel gave his speech to another induction course, one member of which was a very experienced ex-BOAC F/E called David Wales. On having the tickets waved at him, Dave got up and said, 'Give me mine now then. If that's the sort of attitude I can expect I don't want to work here.' Noel must have backed down because I flew with Dave a lot during my time with Cathay and, although I didn't know it then, he was to pay me one of the best compliments that I had in the whole of my flying career.

Where there *was* a difference in Cathay's training, however, was in the simulator. Rather than allot sufficient time for each candidate merely to meet the minimum standard of competency demanded by the regulatory authority, the Hong Kong Civil Aviation Department (CAD), in performing the various required manoeuvres, Cathay went further than that. The simulator was used as a true training tool. Sufficient time was allowed for each candidate to repeat the manoeuvres until he attained a level of expertise where he had full confidence in his own abilities in all flight regimes. The motto in the Training Department was, 'We train for confidence not competence.' It was a very good philosophy but, unfortunately, not one that was maintained in later years.

The 747 was an absolute beauty of an aircraft to fly. It was like a big 707 with all the adverse handling characteristics designed out. It was responsive, relatively light on the lateral controls in comparison to the 707 and did not exhibit Dutch roll. There was no hysteresis, you could put it right where you wanted it; but, instead, there was a lot of inertia. With a MTOW of up to 833,000 lb this was a big, heavy aircraft, more than three times heavier than the 757. If it was going along a particular flight path, it wanted to continue in that direction. If you wanted to change the flight path you could make the control inputs and the aircraft would respond immediately in terms of pitch attitude and roll. Because of the inertia, however, it would take a little time for the actual flight path of the aircraft to change and this requires anticipation. Speed control is similar. A thrust change takes a couple of seconds to start showing its effect on airspeed. Again, anticipation is required. When transitioning from smaller jets onto these heavyweights, there is a learning curve but the required skills are easily mastered given a reasonable background of experience. The 747 is one of Boeing's best and is a pilots' aircraft in every sense of the word. I never met a 747 pilot who had anything but praise for his mount.

The routes we flew in the early years were mainly short and medium haul. Bangkok, Brisbane, Jakarta, Kaohsiung, Manila, Melbourne, Osaka, Singapore, Sydney, Taipei and Tokyo were all on the network. We also flew to Gatwick and Frankfurt with stopovers and crew changes in Abu Dhabi, Bahrain or Dhahran. We operated one long-haul route to Vancouver, inaugurated in 1983, thus fulfilling Roy Farrell's dream. I started travelling extensively in the Far East and, if the Ku'damm on a Saturday night was an eye-opener, there were a number of places I discovered in South East Asia that were even more so.

The career path in Cathay was designed around a duration of 15 to 20 years. We had a provident fund, instead of a pension, to which I contributed ten per cent of my salary each month. This paid out a lump sum on leaving the company and was designed so that it did not give very high returns on investment in the early years. It was not until 12 or more years' service that the big formulaic multipliers kicked in with the maximum returns coming after 17 or more years' service. The obvious intention was to encourage long service. Pilots with sufficient experience to meet the minimum requirements were typically in their thirties and, with a normal retirement age of 55, this allowed for a 20-year career. Like many others, I came to Hong Kong with the intention of serving out my time to retirement age and then returning home with my nest egg. Life has a way of changing things. I reached retirement age three years ago and am still here. Indeed, as we will see later, my employment with Cathay ended in 2001 but here I am. I fell in love with Hong Kong, its lifestyle, its people and its places.

There were some things that took some getting used to in this new culture. The Hong Kongers' predilection for trying to get into a lift before the other passengers have got out was one, as was the need to repeatedly press the lift buttons. Driving in the outside lane no matter what speed you're doing was another. One of my Chinese friends once told me that, as it's called the fast lane, if you drive in it you get there quicker. Indicators on cars seem to be a waste of manufacturing resources as hardly anyone bothers to use them and driving in Hong Kong itself is an acquired skill. If you are on single track road with passing places and the chap coming towards you has overshot by ten yards, you'll be quicker backing up 40 yards to the last passing place on your side as reversing doesn't seem to be included in the Hong Kong School of Motoring's curriculum. Soon after I arrived here, I got conjunctivitis. I went to see a local doctor and, after explaining my symptoms, his first question surprised me.

'Any discharge from the penis?'

'What? No, I've just got conjunctivitis and need some tetracycline.'

'Yes, but any discharge from the penis?'

'No, no I haven't.'

I got my drugs and got out of there. I'd heard that some Chinese medicine treatments could be somewhat different from western ones but I was more than a bit bemused. I found out later that red eye is a common symptom of STDs so he was just being thorough and doing his job.

These are all relatively small niggles compared with the massive advantages of living in Hong Kong, not least of which is the maximum income tax rate of 15 per cent, no matter how much you earn. The restaurants, the bars, the nightlife and the general *laissez-faire* attitude make it a great place to live. There is one major problem that needs to be addressed, however, and that is the air pollution. It has got worse over the years and, on some days when the airflow is coming from the Chinese mainland, you can almost taste it. I live in the New Territories where the air is noticeably cleaner than some of the worst parts of the city, like Causeway Bay. When I first came here in 1985, on descent you would usually enter the haze layer at about 2,500 feet. Nowadays it is common for the haze layer to reach up to 7,000 feet. Our government really needs to ignore the transport lobby and other self-interested groups and start taking positive action to preserve our environment.

Recently I celebrated the 25th anniversary of my arrival and have made my home here. Given the mess that various governments have made of the UK in the intervening years since my departure, I have no intention of returning there to settle. In some ways it is a shame. I am very proud to be British. I am proud of our history, our culture and our heritage but it is sad to see the state to which our once great nation has been reduced by incompetent and self-serving politicians.

I completed my probationary line check on 11 March 1986 with a trip to Tokyo and back via Taipei. One year after joining Cathay Pacific, I was now a fully fledged permanent F/O flying the biggest civil jet with one of the most prestigious airlines in the world. Life was great. Despite Noel's somewhat aggressive introduction to the company, life within the airline couldn't have been more different from that initial impression. The senior management and the board considered its aircrew to be valuable assets who made a significant contribution to the profitability and future of the company. We had regular meetings where we were able to give feedback on operational issues and, similarly, where management could brief us on future plans. There was true two-way communication.

In any service industry, it is the operational people actually at the coalface who have direct contact with the customers, our passengers. We encouraged them to visit the flight deck on trips and it was often there that we would receive feedback from them to be passed on to management through our post-flight admin reports. Like Monarch in the early days, there was great *esprit de corps*. We felt part of a family, indeed we were part of a family. That is not to say that this feeling was only shared amongst the flight crew. It was the same in all departments. An aircraft does not get into the air just because of the pilots. The pilots might be at the pointed end but there is a huge team behind that contributes to the moment when the wheels go up. Without the ground engineers maintaining the aircraft, there would be no aircraft to fly. Without the refuellers the aircraft cannot fly. Without the cabin crew and catering staff, passengers wouldn't fly with us again. Without the ground handling and check-in staff, there would be no passengers boarding the aircraft. Without the sales and ticketing staff, there would be no passengers full stop. Without passengers there is no money and without money there is no airline.

The flight crew is part of a team that starts with the cleaners all the way up to the Captain of the aircraft. Without each part of that machine functioning properly, it will not work. Each part of the machine can have a greater or lesser impact on the overall profitability of the airline. For the aircrew, their contribution can be summarised relatively simply. Their job is to get the aircraft safely from A to B carrying the maximum commercial payload and burning the minimum amount of fuel. It is simply said but sometimes not so simple in practice and we will discuss some of the variables later. However, no matter what other considerations may need to be taken into account in a commercial operation, from the pilots' point of view there are three principles that must be adhered to at all times. Safety, safety and safety. Flight safety is paramount and overrides all other considerations. It should also be the overriding principle of airline management. Passengers who pay premium prices to fly with first-tier airlines expect the highest standards of flight operations; they deserve to have these expectations met. Anything less is fraudulent.

And then there was Kai Tak. The airport got its name from two businessmen, Ho Kai and Au Tak, who started a business in 1922 to reclaim land in Kowloon for development. The business failed and the government acquired their land for use as an airfield. After further reclamation, in 1957 the original runways were replaced by a new runway 31/13 extending into Kowloon Bay. Reclamation continued and the runway was extended further until its completion in 1975. The Kai Tak nullah emptied into the channel alongside the runway on its eastern side and the water was black. The pollution gave off a very unpleasant odour and, after landing, as the air conditioning started to pump this foul air into the cabin, you always knew you were home. It gave rise to a famous story of a high-ranking government official who, upon his first arrival in Hong Kong, turned to his aide and said, 'What is that smell?'

'It's shit, sir,' replied the aide.

'I know it's shit but what have they done to it?'

Kai Tak was classified as a Black Star airport by the International Federation of Air Line Pilots' Associations (IFALPA). This was because of its terrain problems, its reputation for turbulence and windshear on the approach and because the width constraints of the reclaimed land meant that the separation between the runway and the parallel taxiway did not meet international standards. Despite all this, the airport had a comparatively good safety record. During my 13 years of operations into and out of Kai Tak, there were only three accidents.

On 31 August 1988, a Civil Aviation Administration of China (CAAC) Trident hit the approach lights while landing on R/W 31 in rain and fog. The right main landing gear struck a lip and collapsed causing the aircraft to leave the runway and plunge into the nullah. As one wag put it, the only time he managed to get on the glideslope was when he hit the aerial.

On 4 November 1993 a China Airlines B747-400 ran off the end of R/W 13 into the sea while landing during a typhoon. The aircraft's approach was unstable and it touched down more than two thirds of the way down the runway. A go around or missed approach would have saved the situation.

On 23 September 1994 a HeavyLift Cargo Airlines Lockheed L-100-30 Hercules crashed shortly after takeoff from R/W 13 after it suffered an engine failure.

Given the local conditions that could be very sporting on occasions, especially when strong winds were blowing, this is a testament to the professionalism of both pilots and controllers alike. R/W 13 was the preferred runway whenever wind conditions permitted. This was because of the high ground immediately to the north of the airport, which demanded a left turn immediately after take-off when using R/W 31 and restricted the RTOW and, therefore, the commercial payload. The approach onto R/W 13 was via the Instrument Guidance System IGS with a DH of 675 feet followed by a visual segment towards the red and white painted checkerboard with a 47 degree right turn onto finals to line up with the runway. This was usually conducted in crosswind conditions and I was grateful for Sam's patient training back in Libya on the 707. Takeoff from R/W 13 meant a departure through the Lei Yue Mun gap with high ground on both sides, and accurate back tracking of the 31 localiser was essential. For all its problems and foibles, pilots loved Kai Tak. It certainly put the lie to those who say that all pilots do these days is push buttons. There is no autopilot system ever developed that could perform an automatic landing on R/W 13 at Kai Tak. It was real seat of the pants flying. We were sad to see it go when it was finally closed to make way for the new Hong Kong International Airport at Chek Lap Kok (CLK) in 1998. And the words of the controller who finally turned off the lights at 01:28 on 6 July that year echoed our sentiments: 'Goodbye, Kai Tak, and thank you.'

On 3 January 1989, just less than four years after I joined Cathay, I started command training. I had 2,296 hours on the 747 and 7,921 hours total time. With one exception, all the Training Captains I had were very helpful and practical. During the initial simulator phase, my first trainer, Hayden Ashley, gave me a briefing on flying an ILS.

'The sim is just a computer. If you know what it's programmed for it's easy. Get in the landing configuration, cross the needles, set one and a quarter degree pitch attitude and sixty-nine per cent N1, make sure it's trimmed and leave it alone. It'll go down on rails.'

He was right. It worked on the aircraft as well. The command course took four months and I finally checked out to the line on 6 May 1989. This brings us back to where we started. From the humble beginnings of my first solo flight in a Sedburgh Cadet Mark III glider when I was 16 years old, after 21 years of hard work, dedication and sacrifice I now had one of the best jobs in my chosen profession. I was a 747 Captain with Cathay Pacific. To achieve this requires aptitude and talent but these things alone would be of no use without the patience and dedication of the men who had trained me. Men like Dally Purcell and 'Jacko' Jackson who had been my instructors at Hamble, Alan Turley at Casair, Sam Small and Mel Bennett at Transcon, Pete Collins, Spike Kidson, Wally Haggar and Len Amor at Monarch, John Lewis-Lloyd, Graham Falkiner, Hayden Ashley, Martin Willing and Bob Rance at Cathay, and all the other Captains I flew with on the line who shared willingly of their experience as I climbed the ladder. I was now at a point where I could start repaying the debt of gratitude that I owed to all these men.

I had not long been checked out in the left-hand seat when I was making an approach onto R/W 25L at Frankfurt with Dave Wales as my F/E. The wind was blowing from the north, strong and gusty, and it was raining with a cloud base around 1,200 feet. When we broke out, with the crosswind, I was looking at the runway out of the left window. It was very turbulent and I will not deny that the adrenaline was pumping.

Dave leaned forward, put a paternal hand on my shoulder and said, 'You can do this, John.'

'Yes, thanks, I know I can,' I replied exhibiting more confidence verbally than I was really feeling. I guided the aircraft down the approach letting it ride the turbulence, got into the flare, pushed off the drift and it touched down with the wings level, right on the runway centreline like the proverbial cat pissing on velvet. As we were taxiing in, Dave leaned forward again and said to me, 'That was one of the nicest pieces of flying I've seen in all the years I've been sitting in this seat.' Coming from an F/E of his vast experience this was a compliment of the highest order and one that I cherish to this day. Thank you, Dave and thanks again to all the men who helped me to get there.

Just over four years after gaining my command, on 12 November 1993, I checked out as a Training Captain on the 747. Now I could really start to heed the advice that Tony Dodd gave me and start putting back into my profession as much as I had derived from it. I loved training. To be able to take a candidate from his first tentative efforts on the 747, progress him through the training syllabus and see him checked out as a fully qualified, confident line pilot gave me great satisfaction.

Sometimes I would be given candidates who were having trouble and were in danger of being chopped. These were usually low time pilots with little background of experience on other aircraft to fall back on. Their veneer of self-confidence was gossamer thin and easily destroyed. There was one particular candidate who had been given a hard time by his previous Training Captain. He was one of the new breed of cadets that Cathay had started recruiting. There was resistance to this in some quarters in the same way that we 'boy pilots' had met resistance in Transcon. Some of this resistance was justified and some was not. On his last flight, the candidate had flown an IGS approach onto R/W 13 at Kai Tak in weather conditions that were beyond his capabilities. They were beyond F/O landing limits even for a fully qualified line F/O. His Training Captain should have taken it off him but he didn't. During the turn onto finals the aircraft was not lined up correctly with the runway and they had to go around. The Captain took control for the missed approach and then handed the aircraft back to the now completely drained F/O to try again. He never had a chance. He had lost all confidence and the Captain had to take control again and land the aircraft. It was the worst piece of training that I ever encountered in Cathay and was definitely the exception in my time there. Yes, there were some Check Captains who were 'trappers' and took delight in setting up 'gotchas' but they were the exception rather than the rule. You find people like that in all airlines, people who, rather than training, just want to demonstrate their superiority. They are usually just average pilots themselves and feel the need to bolster their own egos.

I had the pleasure of experiencing this particular trainer myself during my command course. I got him because his previous candidate had requested a change of instructor. This was an option that was open to everyone during command training in case of some sort of conflict that couldn't be resolved, but it was only ever used as a last resort. Such requests reflected not only on the candidate but also on the trainer.

On my first sector on the line in the left-hand seat, we were standing in flight dispatch and he made a great show of briefing me in front of all the other crews who were present. He took a piece of paper, wrote something on it, said loudly for the benefit of all present that this was the best piece of advice I would be given in all of my training, that I should keep it for future reference and handed it to me. I unfolded the paper and read it. It said, 'Think ahead'. No! Really? Wow! I wished someone had told me that before.

During the flight he asked me how many '3's there were on the Veeder counter in the heading select window on the autopilot panel. Given that there are three reels it would seem a simple question. It wasn't, however, because the first two reels were fused together so that there were eight rather than the three you might expect at first glimpse. It was a completely pointless question without any operational relevance whatsoever but was typical of this man. He seemed quite upset when I answered him correctly. I didn't tell him that someone had already warned me about his silly questions.

It doesn't matter how good a pilot you are, even the best can be taken into a simulator and loaded with multiple and increasingly complex failures until you reach a point where you make a mistake. That is not the point of training. The point of training is gradually to bring the candidate to the stage where he can confidently deal with all normal, abnormal and emergency situations he might meet out on the line.

I telephoned the candidate who had suffered at the hands of this man and asked him to report an hour earlier than the normal report time for our first flight together so we could sit and chat privately and get to know each other a bit before we went flying. He came into the briefing room and was a complete bag of nerves. His hands were shaking and he kept calling me sir. In Cathay we usually addressed each other on first name terms on the flight deck so I told him my name was John and that it was my job to make sure that he passed the course, not to chop him. He had a CPL so clearly he was capable of flying the aircraft otherwise he wouldn't have gained a licence in the first place. If he failed, I also would have failed in my job as a trainer. 'Yes, sir.' That day we operated to Osaka via Taipei and I flew the first sector to give him a chance to settle down. On the way into Osaka I had to take the aircraft off him low on the approach as it was getting away from him. He just had no confidence at all in his own abilities. He didn't want to come out for a beer that night as he said he wanted to study his manuals. Book work was the last thing he needed. I told him that as part of my training regime he was required to attend beer call. 'Yes, sir.' Over a couple of coldies that evening, he opened up and told me his story.

He had graduated from the cadet training programme in Adelaide, returned to Hong Kong, bought a house on the strength of his new career, and his wife had just had a baby. If he failed, he would lose his house and didn't know how he would be able to support his family. He wasn't just carrying the weight of the world on his shoulders, he had some extra concrete blocks tied to his arms and legs. I told him that now it was even more important to me that I should not fail in my job and that we would start again the next day with a clean piece of paper. On the return trip he was more relaxed and handled the approach and landing into Taipei reasonably competently. On the IGS into Hong Kong on the next sector it started to go wrong again. He was frightened of the approach. There are three dimensions to any approach. One is the side to side to get the aircraft lined up with the runway. One is the up and down to get on the right approach angle. The other is the front and back to get the speed right. I told him to concentrate just on the side to side and I'd do the other two. It worked out OK. On our next IGS, he just handled the up and down and I looked after the other two. The next time he did the side to side and the up and down and I just looked after the speed. Finally he was handling all three dimensions on his own and flying the IGS like a good 'un. He passed his F/O line check and is now a Senior Captain with Cathay. Of all the training that I did, his was one of the most rewarding.

Four months after I gained my command, there was an event that involved some of my ex-colleagues who were still working for Monarch. It left a bad taste in my mouth. On 18 August 1989, after enduring a prolonged period of wage suppression, the Australian Federation of Air Pilots (AFAP) began a work to rule policy. AFAP represented pilots employed by domestic airlines Ansett Australia, East-West, Ipec and Australian Airlines. The pilots imposed a limitation on the hours they were prepared to work, arguing that if they were to be treated in exactly the same way as other employee groups – the edict decreed by the Australian government – then their work conditions should also be the same. Their action initially took the form of making themselves available for flying duties only within the normal office working hours of 09:00 to 17:00. The Labour government supported the employers and brought in the Royal Australian Air Force to combat the pilots' action. The employers also wet leased aircraft and crews from overseas, including Monarch.

Despite the fact that AFAP had not formally requested support from overseas-based pilots' unions, they had a lot of support from their colleagues around the world. Some Monarch pilots made it known to their management that they did not wish to take part in any wet lease operations in Australia. If it came to 'do it or you're fired', then they would go but only under protest. Some others, however, actually went into the office and volunteered for the Australian contract. One of them said to me that he'd never been to Australia before, the allowances were good and it would make a nice holiday. After Transcon, this was the second time in my career that I had encountered this selfish and self-serving attitude amongst my fellow pilots. Again, unfortunately, it was not to be the last by any means. In the end, the dispute was superficially resolved after a significant number of the AFAP pilots resigned *en masse* to avoid litigation from their employers. Their jobs were filled by new recruits from overseas and many of them had to move abroad to find work. This led to a long lasting rift between AFAP and the Australian and International Pilots Association (AIPA), which represented pilots and F/Es employed by Qantas and its subsidiaries. It was not to be resolved until the 1997 annual IFALPA conference held in Cairo almost eight years later.

What happened in Australia in 1989 was a warning sign of what was to happen in the airline industry worldwide in the coming years, but we didn't see it then.

As well as the normal scheduled flights, we picked up some occasional ad hoc charters. During the first Gulf War from August 1990 to February 1991, the British forces were short of transport. The MoD chartered one of Cathay's 747F freighter aircraft as part of Operation Granby to deliver supplies to Dhahran airbase in Saudi Arabia. Only selected crews were asked to volunteer to crew the aircraft as they wanted people who had the reputation for dealing with operational problems and getting the job done. I was invited to take part and agreed. The aircraft was based out of Stansted, operated from there directly to Dhahran returning via Cairo, and was painted all white. Shades of Transcon. I was operating a white-tailed aircraft through Cairo. The loads were mixed consisting of various supplies and equipment but we carried a lot of Chobham armour. It seems that back then, as in the present day in Afghanistan, the blokes on the ground didn't think their vehicles were sufficiently well protected. On each trip we also carried several cold boxes, marked fresh milk, which was one of the things that was in short supply. We emptied out the milk and filled the boxes with cans of McEwans Export, which, given that Saudi Arabia is dry, was in even shorter supply. The RAF regiment and the squaddies were extremely appreciative of this and looked after us very well. There were a lot of RAF Lockheed C130 Hercules aircraft doing the same job as us, albeit with somewhat lower load-carrying capabilities and, as soon as we shut down, their pilots would be straight up to the flight deck asking us how to get a job with Cathay Pacific when they came out of the RAF. On one trip into Dhahran in the early morning of 16 February 1991, whilst we were on the ground unloading, the airbase came under attack by Iraqi SS-1 Scud missiles. We were already wearing most of our nuclear, biological and chemical (NBC) kit but without the hood, mask and gloves. We ran across the tarmac to our assigned bunker, which was built of sandbags, donning the rest of our kit as we went. Once in, the regiment guys checked our kit for us and made sure we were properly sealed. They were very protective of us and they had our appreciation in return. There were a couple of explosions but the missiles fell short and then what I thought was the all clear sounded. As I got up to leave, the NCO in charge growled to me through his mask, 'That was the Saudi all clear, sir. If I was you I'd wait for the British all clear.' I heeded his advice.

My crew – F/O Al Wood, F/E Robbie Gawler and I – got a photograph taken of us on the flight deck of the 747 in full NBC kit as a memento. As well as being a very good F/E, Robbie had one other outstanding attribute. He was quite a small man with a quiet voice and a slight stutter but he was hung like a donkey. I was in a skin bar with him on a layover one night and there was a live show on stage. Having imbibed a couple, Robbie wasn't impressed. He climbed onto the stage and informed the male performer, 'Th-that's not a c-cock, n-now th-this is a c-cock' and pulled his out. The place went quiet as the audience stared open-mouthed. Even the girls on stage just gawped in amazement. The bouncers threw us out shortly afterwards. I wondered how his little body could contain enough blood to inflate this massive dong but he said that he could never remember having sex because he always passed out.

On the return trip from Dhahran we staged in Cairo and checked into the hotel. We looked like chimney sweeps as we were covered in acti-vated charcoal from the inside of the NBC suits. It was more Transcon *déjà vu* as we stayed at the Slammer. It was just over 11 years since I'd last been there. The décor hadn't changed and they were still serving Oranjeboom in the bar. Using my local knowledge I eschewed the room service. A couple of days later we picked up the aircraft again as it tran-sited on its next rotation and set off for Stansted. We were having fun with the aircraft because, since the MoD was paying for it, fuel cost wasn't a consideration. Maximum operating Mach number (MMO) on the 747 is 0.90 but we usually cruised at 0.82 for fuel economy. Not on this trip. We flew it on the barber's pole and, with her nose down and given her head, she was in her element. We could almost hear the airframe singing with delight.

En route to Stansted we were told that a tyre carcase had been found on the runway at Cairo. There were only two aircraft that had taken off since the last runway FOD check: ourselves and a BCal DC10, so it had come from one of us. It was not unusual for tyres occasionally to shed their tread on takeoff, especially when they get close to their retread life. I had experienced this before and it is normally associated with a slight bump and some peripheral damage to the flaps, but nothing to be too concerned about. In this case, though, the whole tyre had come off the rim and they had the side wall as well. It was a Bridgestone. I knew that it was very unlikely to have come from us as the aircraft was quite light on takeoff and there hadn't been any unusual noises. However, we had a ground engineer on board who was rotating from his Cairo detachment and he confirmed that we were fitted with Bridgestone tyres. Better to be safe than sorry. There was only one thing for it, a low pass by the control tower at Stansted before landing to check the condition of the wheels. It is not often in civil aviation that you get the excuse to perform this sort of manoeuvre in a big jet and we made the most of it. We briefed carefully, the F/E was nailed to the rad alt ready to shout if we went below 100 feet and we roared across the airfield. At the end of the runway we poured the coal on and pulled up into a steep climbing turn into the circuit to land. Our tyres were fine. I got something of a bollocking from the station Captain, John Hanson. He demanded to know what I had hoped to achieve with my cowboy stunt. I pointed out that, had our tyres been damaged, I would have diverted to another airfield with multiple runways so as to avoid blocking the single runway at Stansted and thus closing the airfield. Always have a sound operational reason for your decisions. I think he was just a little bit jealous really.

After the Gulf War was over, the DFO, Mike Hardy, held a party for everyone who had taken part in the operation by way of a thank you. During the evening he came up to me and said with a smile, 'I saw your low pass at Stansted, John, it looked very impressive.'

Despite the fact that Mike was no longer operational, he'd had a distinguished career in the RAF graduating from Cranwell in 1954. He initially flew the Gloster Meteor and Hawker Hunter before becoming ADC to Air Commodore Teddy Donaldson and then returning to Cranwell as a QFI in 1961. He commanded the Hull University Air Squadron, became the Deputy Chief Instructor at one of the flying training schools and then attended staff college. After a time in a staff job, by now a Wing Commander, he returned to flying in command of a Lockheed C-130 Hercules squadron and was instrumental in leading the British contribution to the United Nations relief effort in Nepal in 1973 when years of drought followed by torrential rain left thousands of Nepalese people on the verge of starvation. It was a great success and, quoted in the *Daily Telegraph*, Mike summed up the operation by saying, 'We have never worked so hard in our lives, but given half the chance we would go back and do it again tomorrow.' Later he commanded RAF Leeming before leaving the RAF and joining Cathay in 1976. He quickly rose through the ranks and held the position of general staff manager before being promoted to DFO. He retired from Cathay in 1992 and eventually settled in Hamble where he died on 2 February 2007 after a long battle with cancer.

Mike Hardy was old school, appreciated and respected others' points of view and was always prepared to listen. That is not to say that he was a pushover. Far from it. He could be very forthright and expected the same 100 per cent commitment from his team that he displayed, leading by example. In his time as DFO at Cathay he earned the hard-won respect of the pilots and was made an honorary member of their union, the Hong Kong Aircrew Officers Association (HKAOA or AOA for short) upon his retirement. Mike Hardy was the last decent DFO that Cathay Pacific had.

One of the things that struck me during the various 'special ops' that I took part in during my career was how small some of the military aircraft were that I encountered and how young their crews were. I first saw this in Wideawake during the Falklands War. There were some Handley Page Victor tankers on the ground used for air to air refuelling. Together with the Avro Vulcan and the Vickers Valiant, this was one of the trio of mighty V-bombers that protected the UK from the Russian threat during the Cold War. In comparison with the 757 it looked like a roller-skate.

I saw some Boeing B52 strategic bombers up close in U-Tapao in Thailand during circuit training on the Airbus A330 in 1995. They reminded me of Death's-Head Hawkmoths but they were still relatively small in comparison to the A330. Even the United States Air Force's (USAF) heavy lifter, the Lockheed C5 Galaxy, was small potatoes compared with the 747 and, with an MMO of 0.79, its performance was pedestrian.

On a trip out of Dhahran during the first Gulf War, a C5 had got airborne in front of us heading for Europe. We followed ten minutes later and he called us up. He was having trouble with his INS. INS is a great piece of kit provided it's programmed properly on the ground. If it isn't, you've got a bucket of trouble. He asked us to track him to check whether he was on course. We managed to pick him up on our weather radar, caught him up, flew underneath him and then climbed out above, inviting him to follow our contrail. He couldn't stay with us but at least we got him into radar coverage clear of the war zone.

As I said, the military crews that I met during those ops seemed very young to me and they treated me like the old man. Given that I was by then pushing 40, I guess I was the old man to them. We see our young men and women giving their lives in Afghanistan and other conflicts in current times. Many of them are barely out of their teens. My generation was fortunate in that, unlike our fathers and grandfathers, we did not have to go to war. Generation X was even luckier. They grew up after the Cold War and without any real threat. Times have changed and now we are faced with threats around the world from extremist groups of all shades. Those who bemoan the state of the current generation and hold up the ASBO yobs in support of their case need look no further than the example being set by the young men and women who are rising to the current challenges in the same way that their great-grandfathers did. These people are not conscripts, they are volunteers. I have nothing but admiration for them.

Another interesting trip that I operated was a relief flight to Entebbe, Uganda, on behalf of Médecins Sans Frontières (MSF) during the Rwandan genocide in 1994. This was to be operated using one of the freighters from Kai Tak to Entebbe via Jeddah and my crew was to fly the first leg. The aircraft was to be provided gratis by Cathay and the fuel by one of the oil companies. On completion of the return leg from Entebbe to Jeddah we were then to take the aircraft on to Heathrow to insert it back into the normal route network. MSF had only got enough freight to fill the main deck, which meant that the under-floor holds would be empty. In the usual Cathay manner of keeping an eye on the main chance, the planning people suggested filling the under-floor with commercial cargo bound for Heathrow. Prior to the flight, I went for a briefing with the manager line operations (MLO), Jeff Turner, at which he put this idea to me. Having had previous experience of the Saudi authorities carrying Hajj pilgrims through Jeddah, I advanced the view that if we tried to carry anything other than the MSF freight for which we had a one-off dip clearance, we were asking for trouble. If we were found out, the aircraft was likely to be impounded and the crew arrested. Apparently they'd thought of that one. They would seal the under-floor cargo doors with speed tape so they couldn't be opened. I really thought Jeff was joking. I couldn't think of a quicker way to attract the Saudis' attention than having speed tape plastered all around the doors. He wasn't. He was seriously proposing this. I told him that if that was their plan he could include me out. In the event, they dropped the plan and we carried just the MSF load. Even then, the trip was not without its problems. None of us had Saudi visas in our passports but we were told that there was a fixer who would meet us in Jeddah to sort out any immigration problems. Yeah, right! The crew that was to operate the leg into Entebbe positioned to Jeddah the day before we departed Kai Tak. They were held at the airport for five hours. When we arrived, they had their noses pressed up against the window and couldn't wait to get out of the place. We had to overnight in Jeddah awaiting their return and ended up with the same problem, albeit we only had a four-hour wait. It was the same thing on our departure the next day. We had to arrive at the airport three hours before the aircraft was due in to complete yet further immigration formalities. The Saudi jobsworths took great pleasure in making things as difficult for us as possible. Throughout this whole process I kept calm, smiled nicely and was as helpful as possible. My crew were quite surprised by this as I did not have a reputation for suffering fools gladly when faced with petty officialdom. After we got airborne and on our way to London, they asked me how I'd managed to restrain myself. There was one thought that sustained me. I knew that in eight hours' time I'd be sitting outside a pub in Kensington on a warm autumnal evening, sipping a pint of bitter and watching the girls go by in their summer dresses. Those people in Jeddah would still be stuck in their sandpit, with their women in *purdah*, waiting for the cement to arrive. Who was better off?

In the early 1990s, Cathay's route structure started to change. Instead of operating to Gatwick and Frankfurt, via the Middle East, the tech stop was removed and we started operating these flights directly. New destinations were added. Amsterdam Schiphol, Anchorage, Los Angeles, Paris

Charles de Gaulle, Rome Fiumicino, San Francisco and Zurich all came on line. With the introduction of the longer range Boeing 747-400 in 1989, these Ultra Long Range (ULR) routes became commercially feasible. From being an essentially short and medium range operation, Cathay was transforming into a predominantly ULR operation and with this came an increase in average monthly flying hours. The required crewing on ULR ops was three pilots and two F/Es on the 747-200 aircraft and four pilots on the 747-400. The pilots' contract was constructed around a 70 flying hour monthly average and this was difficult to exceed on an essentially regional operation. Any hours flown above 70 each month were subject to overtime, or excess flying pay (EFP) as it was called, which was calculated according to the following formulae:

(i) Over 70 up to and including 80 – 1.50 x standard hourly rate
(ii) Over 80 up to and including 85 – 1.75 x standard hourly rate
(iii) Over 85 up to and including 90 – 2 x standard hourly rate
(iv) Over 90 – 3 x standard hourly rate
Standard hourly rate = annual salary / (12 x 70)

Essentially this meant that if you accumulated more than 90 flying hours in a month it would double your salary. The absolute legal maximum stipulated by the CAD in its safety regulations was 100 hours in any 28-day period. The philosophy behind the formula was that pilots should be rewarded for flying more than their normal contractual hours and that this should become increasingly punitive so that, at a certain point, it became cheaper for the company to employ an additional pilot. On a regional operation, it is not possible to regularly sustain a 90-hour month, have sufficient days off to be properly rested before flight and maintain some semblance of a normal family life. The formula had worked well in the past but, with the change to a predominantly ULR network, we were regularly getting into the 85 hours plus region with associated cost implications to the company. The EFP was very welcome but we knew that it couldn't last. Changes to the contract would need to be made at some point to reflect the change in nature of the company's operation and we were prepared to talk about it in order to come to some new arrangement that satisfied everyone's objectives. Given the past good relationship between management, led by Mike Hardy, and the AOA on behalf of the pilots, we were optimistic that an agreement would be reached. None of us was prepared for, or even imagined, what would happen next.

5

CAT

'When I wrote about "business process redesign" in 1990, I explicitly said that using it for cost reduction alone was not a sensible goal. And consultants Michael Hammer and James Champy, the two names most closely associated with reengineering, have insisted all along that layoffs shouldn't be the point. But the fact is, once out of the bottle, the reengineering genie quickly turned ugly.'

Thomas Davenport

'I wasn't smart enough about that. I was reflecting my engineering background and was insufficiently appreciative of the human dimension. I've learned that's critical.'

Michael Hammer

Clear Air Turbulence (CAT) is usually associated with a jet stream. It is worst when climbing into, or descending out of, the jet where the wind speed gradient between the core and the slower moving surrounding air is the steepest. The most severe CAT I ever experienced was in a 757 over the North Sea one day descending into Luton. ATC gave us an intermediate descent clearance and, just as we levelled off, it was like hitting a brick wall. Our nav bags, manuals, loose articles and dirt and dust from the floor were flying around the cockpit. It was so severe that our eyeballs were bouncing in their sockets and we couldn't read the instruments. Passengers who hadn't strapped in were thrown around the cabin and, when the controller wouldn't give us an immediate further descent clearance, we declared an emergency PAN call to get the hell out of there.

We didn't know it at the time but, in 1992 when Peter Dennis Anthony

Sutch was appointed chairman of Cathay Pacific, we were climbing into a jet stream. Born on 8 April 1945, Sutch was two when his father was posted to Baghdad as a manager of the Ottoman Bank. Over the following decade, the family lived in various cities in the Middle East until they were forced to evacuate from Port Said at the outbreak of the 1956 Suez crisis. He attended Downside, a Catholic co-educational boarding school, where he became head boy, then went on to read history at Exeter College, Oxford, and trained with the University Air Squadron. He joined John Swire & Sons in Hong Kong in 1966. His first posting was to the Swires' shipping division, but in 1970 he moved to Cathay as manager for western Japan. He became passenger sales manager in Hong Kong two years later and returned to Japan as general manager from 1976 to 1981. Three years later, in 1984, he became managing director of the airline and, in 1988, deputy chairman of all the Swires' Hong Kong interests. His appointment as chairman marked a sea change in the relationship between Cathay Pacific and its employees. He brought with him a number of new management appointments.

Roderick Ian Eddington was born in Perth on 2 January 1950 and graduated from the University of Western Australia in 1972 with first class BEng Honours. He was the 1974 Western Australia Rhodes Scholar, obtained a MEng Sci at Oxford and completed his DPhil at its Department of Engineering Science. Eddington joined Cathay Pacific in 1979 and was appointed managing director in 1992 concurrent with Sutch's promotion to chairman.

David Muir Turnbull attended Charterhouse School and joined the Swire Group in 1976 immediately upon graduating from Cambridge University with a MA(Hons) in economics. He served as managing director of the Hong Kong Aircraft Engineering Company (HAECO) from January 1990 to December 1993 and became joint managing director of Cathay Pacific upon Eddington's departure in December 1996.

Gerald Albert Clemmow served with the Royal Navy Fleet Air Arm and worked for East African Airways before joining Cathay Pacific. He was appointed DFO by Sutch in 1992 succeeding Mike Hardy who left when Sutch became chairman. I had first flown with Clemmow in December 1985 on a trip from Kai Tak to Jakarta and return via Singapore. We repeated the same trip in March 1987 on a line check after he had been appointed Check Captain. We spent a very pleasant day off in Jakarta taking in a curry lunch at the Omar Khayyam curry house followed by some beers and margaritas at the Green Pub before returning to the Borobudur Hotel in the late afternoon prior to an early morning departure the next day. His post-flight debrief consisted of:

'Don't put your departure charts away below 20,000 feet, you're supposed to be monitoring me in the climb, don't fill in the CFP below 20,000 feet, you're supposed to be monitoring me in the climb, and don't take the Check Captain out for lunch and make him drink so much tequila that he wakes up with a splitting headache in the middle of the night.'

He passed me with a couple of 'A's for good measure and seemed like a nice bloke. How wrong first impressions can be.

The appointment of Sutch ushered in an era of corporate re-engineering, cost-cutting and depersonalisation. The legacy of Sutch's policies is still with Cathay Pacific today as his successors continued what he started. In the view of many, the airline now enjoys the unenviable reputation in the aviation community of having one of the worst industrial relations with its employees in the business. It can be used as a model of how *not* to implement business process re-engineering. Peter Sutch himself was a very pleasant and personable man socially. He was charming, gregarious and always ready with a word here, a word there. He made you feel completely at home in his company. The same could not always be said of his hatchet men. Sutch presided over his cabal like the Harlequin clown in a three-ring circus. He starts the trouble but when the muck starts flying, he remains clean in his sequinned suit while those around him end up covered in shit.

In 1993, on Turnbull's watch, eleven ground engineers were sacked from HAECO without any prior warning. They were called into the office, handed their letters of dismissal and told to gather their belongings and leave the building. The length of service of these men with HAECO varied from two or three years to some who were only a few months away from retirement. Their provident funds were severely impacted by their sackings. It seemed that the axe was wielded without any compassion or thought for the future well-being of the men and their families. In fact, the larger the family, the greater the risk. The men were selected for dismissal at a meeting held at a hotel in Kowloon. By all accounts, they were categorised by cost of salary and expatriate benefits. If you had four kids at King George V School and a house in the upper end of the rental bracket, it seemed you were for the chop. If you were single and lived in a shoebox, by the same reasoning, you escaped under the radar. If it was intended *pour encourger les autres*, it had exactly the desired effect. The remaining engineers were put in fear of their jobs. It was then a simple matter unilaterally to impose new and more onerous shift patterns and working practices. HAECO was downsized at a stroke.

The next step was to run down the spare parts holding to reduce the amount of capital invested in stock. Engineering budget and manning level cuts were implemented at outports where a lot of maintenance was carried out on the aircraft during overnight stops. The deleterious effect of these cost-cutting measures on engineering standards and aircraft serviceability soon became obvious and we will examine these effects later.

Around the same time, Eddington set about the flight attendants but they were not to be cowed so easily as the ground engineers. The year end negotiations in 1991 between management and the Flight Attendants Union (FAU) had broken down without resolution. One of the FAU's key issues was that, because of staff shortages, senior cabin attendants were regularly being rostered to 'work down' below their normal rank. Attempts to resolve this and other long-standing industrial matters under Eddington's stewardship in 1992 resulted in a 17-day strike by the FAU in January 1993 after three senior cabin attendants were sacked in December 1992 for refusing to work down. Throughout the strike, management took a hard line approach and some commentators were of the view that the sackings were a deliberate ploy to provoke a confrontation. It was Cathay management's first attempted union bust under Sutch's caporegime. The flight attendants gained a lot of public support for their action and were dubbed 'the perfumed picket line' by the press. Not so for Eddington who was likened, in one press report, to 'a Victorian mill owner'.[9] After some unfavourable Eddington TV interviews, Sutch took over as media spokesman.

When the strike ended and the cabin attendants went back to work, the attempted union bust didn't end there. Both the FAU and the HKAOA were issued with eviction notices from their offices in the Cathay building. One of the main sources of income for the FAU was a local light bus crew transport system, which it ran to ferry its members between their homes and work. Cathay set up a rival system and tried to undercut them. At the FAU AGM held in May 1993, a reportedly company-sponsored breakaway group, headed by Rachel Varghese, an ex-union official who had resigned from the FAU executive committee during the strike, attempted to unseat the leadership. It failed. But the most blatant anti-union victimisation was the sacking of Courtney Chong Cheng Lim, the vice chairman of the FAU, on a trumped-up charge of theft of company property.

On 17 May, Courtney operated CX715 from Hong Kong to Singapore. By sheer coincidence, Cathay's chief of security, Frank Laity, was travelling in first class on the same flight. As the aircraft taxied in after landing, Laity asked Courtney for a bag of macadamia nuts. On arrival in Singapore, her bag was searched by customs officers and, by another coincidence, Laity was in attendance. They found a bottle of water and a Chinese gossip magazine that had been given to Courtney by a passenger on the flight. Neither of these items had any markings on them to indicate they were the property of Cathay Pacific but Laity took possession of them. On her return to Hong Kong, Courtney was called into the office and interviewed. She was accused of stealing the magazine, the bottle of water and a packet of macadamia nuts that had now miraculously appeared in Laity's 'evidence'. The bag of nuts had a Cathay logo on it. She was dismissed and given 21 days to claim her repatriation flight to Singapore, her home country. Because of threats made by management during the strike to take disciplinary action against the union leaders, a 14-man Legislative Council (Legco) group had been set up after the strike to monitor Cathay's treatment of the strikers to ensure that there was no witch-hunt. The monitoring group called management representatives to appear before them and investigated Courtney's dismissal. Cheung Man-kwong of the United Democrats and a member of the group reported:

> One of the suspicious points of the evidence provided by the management is that the security officer who caught Miss Chong 'red-handed' did not ask her to sign a form to admit the offence right away. The accusation and the three items were produced only on the following day. A witness to the search, another flight attendant, had only seen Miss Chong handing over the bottle of water and the magazine to the security officer. It was suspicious that the flight attendant had not seen the packet of nuts, which had Cathay's hallmark.[10]

Another member of the monitoring group, Yeung Sum, described the circumstances surrounding Courtney's sacking as 'quite fishy'.[11] Quite fishy? It stank to high heaven. It had all the hallmarks of a set-up but, of course, they denied this. A Cathay spokesman, one Nicholas Peter Rhodes, said the company '. . . had not dismissed any member of staff for their action during the industrial dispute and we have no intention of doing so.'

He flatly denied that Miss Chong's union position or her involvement in the strike had played any part in the decision.[12] This was the first that we had heard of Mr Rhodes and his versions of the truth but we will hear more of him later. Much more. As a result of statements made in a press release and an internal open letter to crew members at the time, in 1995 Courtney filed a libel action against Cathay Pacific. In June 1998, three weeks before the case was due to be heard, Cathay settled out of court for HK$3 million in damages and HK$1.4 million in legal costs. They avoided having their actions examined in the public spotlight of an open court.

In February 1993 Cathay placed adverts to recruit 680 new cabin crew. Management denied that it was a concession to one of the key FAU demands that more staff should be recruited to address the working down issue. They insisted the recruitment initiative had been planned long before the industrial dispute broke out and that no concession had been made.[13] To paraphrase Mandy Rice-Davies, well they would say that wouldn't they?

There were many indications for the future and lessons to be learned from the cabin attendants' strike and the case of Courtney Chong. If only we had been more receptive to them, perhaps much of what happened subsequently to the pilots could have been avoided, or at least dealt with differently.

Frank Laity left Cathay shortly after Courtney's sacking and went to live in Australia. There was another incident that Laity was involved in before his departure that might also be described as 'quite fishy'. In the run up to 1997, many people were emigrating from Hong Kong to settle overseas. These emigrants often bought new electronic equipment, such as TVs and hi-fi equipment, before they left and checked them in with their baggage. Such electronic goods were significantly cheaper in Hong Kong in those days. They were easily identifiable because they were shipped in their original packing. In 1992 Cathay's customer relations manager, Theresa Leung, noticed that she was dealing with a lot of claims for missing baggage on electronic equipment. Missing baggage is nothing new but, with the verification and reconciliation systems in place, it can usually be found and returned to its owner. No trace of these items could be found, however, and the claims were becoming costly to the company. Theresa suspected that there was some kind of scam going on. She reported her suspicions to Laity and to her boss, Paolo Ricciotti, gave them all the relevant details and asked them to investigate. Despite following up her reports with phone calls, she got no response from either of them.

Theresa was a diligent employee with more than 25 years' service in the company. In the past she had been instrumental in catching culprits responsible for stolen ticket scams, illegal immigrants who destroy their documents or exchange identities in the departure hall, and had even caught a bomb hoaxer for which she received a 'Diamond Pin' Outstanding Staff Award by the company as well as a police commendation. She decided to conduct her own investigation. She went down into the baggage loading hall and spoke to the baggage handlers. As this was an all-male preserve it caused some raised eyebrows but she persisted. No one would tell her anything. She found a young man who was new there, gave him her card and asked him to keep an eye out and report anything suspicious directly to her. A couple of months later, with his help, she broke the case. There was a conspiracy involving the baggage handlers and others. It worked like this. When they spotted any electronic equipment, the baggage handlers removed the baggage tags and put the items to one side. They had an accomplice, a Cathay staff member, who would be at the staff check-in counter in the airport terminal with a standby ticket to Bangkok. Once checked in, he would send a message by pager to his accomplices in the baggage hall with his flight number and departure time. They would then re-label the stolen goods with new tags and text the tag numbers to him. Upon arrival in Bangkok, the staff passenger would claim the baggage and clear it through customs to be disposed of locally. Electronic goods normally attract customs import duty and Theresa asked the Cathay security superintendent in Bangkok to check with customs. They had no record of any such items.

She had uncovered an organised network that involved not only Cathay staff in Hong Kong and Bangkok, but also, perhaps, customs officers in Thailand. She immediately reported her findings to Laity and Ricciotti expecting to be commended for her diligence. She could not have been more wrong. She was summoned to the office of her general manager, John Seale, with Laity in attendance. Seale told her: 'Theresa, from now on, you are hands-off on this case. This will be taken over by Frank Laity.'

She responded that there were still a lot of questions needing to be answered. She could work with Frank but, since she had initiated the investigation, she would like to see it through to its conclusion. Seale replied forcefully, 'No, Theresa, you should not do anything more at all and also do not talk to anyone about it. If you do, you will be reprimanded.'

She was astonished and very upset. There were so many unanswered questions. Why was she being taken off the case? What was going on and who was involved? She felt she had to tell her contact in Bangkok that she was no longer on the case, so she sent him a brief private email to let him know. The next day she was summoned by Seale again. He told her that Laity had found a note she had supposedly left by the photocopying machine with details of her email. He said to her, 'I told you not to talk to anyone or do anything about it. Why didn't you listen?'

He spoke to her as if she had committed a serious crime. She told him it was just a quick message to let her contact know she was no longer on the case but Seale told her that even that was not allowed and from now on she should keep her mouth shut. According to Theresa, she had never printed out the message. She found out later that her email was being monitored. The investigation resulted in only a few front-line staff being arrested and charged and the case was closed. The organisers behind the scam were never caught.

With the approach of 1997 and the handover of sovereignty of Hong Kong back to China, many people were nervous. After the Tiananmen Square massacre on 4 June 1989, they were particularly concerned that China might impose a much more repressive regime than the *laissez-faire*, 'benevolent dictatorship' that we enjoyed under British rule. There were also worries about the fiscal system. Would the Chinese seize assets and impose punitive taxation? Some people were not prepared to take the risk and many Hong Kong Chinese residents set about either obtaining foreign passports as insurance or emigrating. One of the requirements of working for Cathay as flight deck crew was that you must live in Hong Kong. Some of the pilots, especially those with long service, also were not prepared to take the risk. The AOA had approached management with a view to permitting aircrew to be based overseas and, under Mike Hardy's leadership, an agreement was reached, which met all parties' objectives. The aircrew were given the right to live overseas and, in return, they gave up some of their expatriate benefits, such as housing allowance. It was a win-win solution. The 'Basings Agreement' alleviated the pilots' concerns for the future and saved the company money. Clemmow attacked it straightaway. Without consultation with the AOA he announced unilaterally that, from now on, there would be no further basings under the terms of the agreement and that it was now subject to renegotiation.

He also announced the introduction of 'B Scales'. With effect from 1 April 1993, all new pilots joining Cathay would be recruited on terms that were significantly inferior to those enjoyed by current employees. Salaries were cut by 40 per cent, expatriate and medical benefits were slashed and leave entitlement was reduced under the new terms. The defined benefit provident fund scheme was closed to new joiners and replaced by a defined contribution scheme.

B Scales were nothing new. The experiment had been tried before in some North American airlines and had been a disaster. Having two men on the flight deck of an aircraft holding the same rank and responsibilities, doing the same job for substantially different remuneration, had proved hugely divisive. It led to bitterness, recrimination and arguments, and it badly affected crew morale. Many American carriers that had tried B Scales acknowledged this and subsequently phased them out. Of course, if your intent is to create division, dissent and discrimination amongst a pilot group without any regard for the potential side effects on the operation, then B Scales are just the ticket. Initially the leadership of the AOA attempted to resist their introduction using just such arguments. Their approaches fell on deaf ears and elicited the stonewall response that we were to hear much of in the future: 'We reserve the right to manage.' The issue threatened to turn into a confrontation and, in light of the recent experience of the FAU, the AOA leadership backed down. The union, in defending its conciliatory position, argued that its duty was to protect its current members and not people who hadn't even joined the company yet. With hindsight, this was a very naïve stance to take. Not only did they back down, they went further than that. They actually wrote a letter to Clemmow, signed by all members of the General Committee (GC), acknowledging the right of the company to recruit new employees on whatever terms they saw fit. It was a terrible mistake and one that was to come back to haunt us in the future.

'Operation Better Shape' was launched and timed to coincide with the 1994 round of contract negotiations. This was a play on words with the Cathay advertising slogan then in vogue, 'Arrive in Better Shape'. A firm of third-party consultants, Towers Perrin, specialising in 'human resources management', was hired and set about analysing the operation. At around the same time, Anne Catterson-Smith, the lady who had run the personnel department with admirable efficiency for some years and was much loved by the pilots, was given her marching orders. She was the sort of personnel manager who actually took an interest in her charges' well-being and in resolving their problems whatever they might be.

On one occasion, whilst on a skiing holiday, I had a bag stolen from a train in Gare du Nord railway station in Paris. Amongst other things it contained my flying licence and my air ticket home. Without my licence I could not fly as it is a legal requirement to carry it whilst operating. It looked like I would have to cut short my holiday and return to Hong Kong to get a replacement issued prior to my next rostered flying duty. I telephoned Anne from France to explain my situation. She saved my holiday. Not only did she go to the CAD and get me a duplicate licence, she also paid for it herself out of her own purse and arranged for a new air ticket to be waiting for me at the check-in desk at Heathrow. Anne was a star. We were all very sorry to see her go.

Her replacement was a surly Australian called Theodore Samios. Under his newly titled 'human resources' department, what had previously been the personnel department very quickly became known amongst the aircrew as the 'anti-personnel department' (APD). Under Samios's new regime, depersonalisation was the order of the day. No longer were company communications addressed to us by our names and titles. Captain John Warham ceased to exist. As far as the APD was concerned I was now 650143H Warham J.S. I became an accounting unit to be analysed, costed, pruned, clipped, trimmed, pared and shaved.

The Towers Perrin benchmarking analysis came up with predictable results. It demonstrated that, when compared with our competitors, the Cathay 'A Scale' crew costs were 'off the scale'. As they put it, if the airline is to succeed in the very competitive market in which it finds itself, the A Scale 'just isn't sustainable'. We had to understand, this wasn't the fault of management. It was simply the result of 'market forces'.

To reinforce the point and ram the message home, we were all required to attend a series of compulsory 'Commitment Days'. At these we were treated to a pre-recorded presentation to demonstrate what a parlous financial state our company was in, how we were contributing to its downfall with our outrageous salaries and, what is more, how we were viewed by other employees in the company as the fat cats that had brought us to the edge of extinction. At the end of the film, what looked like a 17-year-old junior clerk from the typing pool was asked what she thought should be done to get our company back in better shape. Her reply was revealing. 'We should pay our pilots less money', came her knowledgeable response. Clearly if the girl in the typing pool could see that, then intelligent men like us must be able to see the solution as well. The main presenters were Clemmow and his sidekick, Mick Toller, who, in amongst the downsizing, had recently been promoted into a newly created management position of Deputy DFO (DDFO). In the Q&A that followed the presentation we were not permitted to ask questions directly of the presenters but rather we had a chubby bearded chappie, a 'facilitator', puffing enthusiastically around the room with a radio mic paraphrasing everyone's questions.

'Gerry, why is it that you haven't included any of the US airlines like American and Northwest in the study? They get paid a damn sight more than we do and their pensions are better than ours as well,' asked a 'difficult' pilot.

'Yes, thank you for your question, I'm glad you asked that one. Gerry, I think what he's trying to ask is why only our direct competitors are included in our study and not airlines in North America where we don't operate or have any internal route structure,' translated the facilitator.

'Yes thanks for that beardie. You make a very good point. We can only benchmark ourselves against our direct competitors. We have to compare apples with apples and oranges with oranges. If we'd included the US airlines we'd be comparing apples with oranges. It just doesn't work,' explained Clemmow.

'But, Gerry, we do operate to North America. We're in direct competition with Northwest and American on our North Pacific routes,' countered the recalcitrant pilot.

'Yes, thanks again, but I think Gerry's already answered that one. Now who's next?" facilitated beardie.

At the end of the day we'd listened to so many fruit analogies some of the pilots were going bananas. 'Expectation management' was the name of the game. What many of us found insulting at the time was that they really believed we were going to fall for this clap trap. It can best be summarised by a remark made to me by Nick Rhodes some years later after he had risen to prominence in the Flight Ops Department. We were debating some issue or other and I made a point to him.

'No, no, no,' came his reply. 'That's not what we want you to think at all.' The sheer bold-faced arrogance of that statement astounded me. They actually believed that they could control our thought processes.

After we had all been properly 'committed', we were treated to a process with which we were to become very familiar in the years following. Management approached the AOA, looking for concessions to help the company through this very difficult time. After a short period of negotiation during which management simply could not deal with the 'intransigence' of the AOA negotiators who clearly didn't understand the parlous state we were in, they bypassed the union and issued new Conditions of Service (CoS) to all the aircrew. There is no collective bargaining legislation in Hong Kong. The last British governor, Chris Patten, introduced some rudimentary provisions before his departure in 1997. The incoming chief executive of the newly created Hong Kong Special Administrative Region of the People's Republic of China, Tung Chee Hwa, immediately repealed it as one of his first acts upon taking office on 1 July 1997. All employment contracts are between the individual employee and his or her employer. Even if the conditions of the contract are negotiated collectively by the employee's union, each employee has to sign the contract individually for it to become effective. The 1994 CoS issued by Clemmow were presented to the pilots as purely voluntary. It was up to each individual to decide whether or not to 'help out' the company. If you chose not to sign up to the new deal, however, there were certain consequences to that decision. You would not be eligible to go on a basing and, other than annual increments that were listed in the salary scale, you would never receive another salary increase for the rest of your career with Cathay Pacific.

With 1997 fast approaching, the first condition was very persuasive to many. The new CoS contained completely revised rostering practices, which increased contractual flying hours from 70 to 89 per month, whilst, at the same time, drastically cutting EFP or overtime payments. Whilst I could see the need for the company to adjust the EFP thresholds because of the change in the nature of Cathay's operations as described earlier, there were two things that made me reluctant to sign up. The first was that the 'Application of Conditions' section on page 1 was followed by two pages describing how you could be sacked. There was no Disciplinary and Grievance Procedure, as had been promised by Clemmow. Nor was there any provision to ensure fair treatment in such circumstances. The second was that just about every term of the CoS that related to financial benefits contained phrases such as 'in accordance with Company Policy, as the same may be amended from time to time in its discretion'. As far as I could see it was *carte blanche* unilaterally to carve away at my benefits.

Initially the AOA leadership under the then president, Terry Heyes, advised the membership that the solution was simple. If we wanted to ensure a properly negotiated new CoS, all we had to do was refuse to sign the company proposals and they would have no alternative but to come back to the table. If only things had worked out that way. The AOA then took legal advice and was told that, should it adopt that stance, there existed a possibility that the company could sue the union for financial losses sustained as a result of its position. This rattled the AOA leadership. At a meeting held in 1994, Terry apprised the membership of this legal advice and told them that, because of this, the AOA could make no recommendation either way. It was up to each person to make his own decision. In my view, this simply was abrogation of the responsibilities of his office. At a time when resolute leadership was required, he failed to give it. Not that I am critical of the reasons why he came to that decision, however. At the time none of us had any idea what we were up against. We were lambs to the slaughter. After years of existing in a benevolent dictatorship, we didn't realise that the barbarians were at the gates and Rome was about to be sacked.

In retrospect, there were lessons to be learned from what happened between 1992 and 1994. The first is that you should never allow the lawyers to run your strategy. Take advice from them, yes. Listen to their advice, yes. But like all advice, some you heed and some you discount. Lawyers are not industrial negotiators. They simply give you the pros and cons of the situation from a legal standpoint. It is up to the leadership of the union then to decide what strategy to adopt. Sometimes it may be a conciliatory approach, at other times it may be more adversarial but it certainly is not a decision for the lawyers. We also made two mistakes that would come back to bite us. We should have taken a more resolute stance on the introduction of B Scales and, as a group, we should have refused to sign CoS 94. The pressure on us to sign was immense. At 23:30 on the night of the midnight signing deadline, Clemmow telephoned me. He sounded drunk. The conversation went along the following lines:

'You've got to sign. The company's in trouble and needs help. Everyone else is signing. You're not a company man. You don't care about the company.'

'Yes I do, Gerry, I'm happy to help. I can see we need to change the rostering system. The only reason I'm not signing is because of all the "sole discretion of the company" clauses. They mean my contract can be changed any time without my agreement.'

'Oh so you don't trust me then?'

'I didn't say that, Gerry.'

'Yes you did. You said you don't trust me.'

'No I didn't. Even if I trust you, how do I know that whoever comes after you won't rip me off? I didn't say I don't trust you.'

'All right, you didn't say that. I take that back.'

'Thanks, Gerry, but I'm not signing for the reason I just explained.'

'Well, we'll see.'

In the event, without firm leadership, only 57 out of the almost 1,000 aircrew employed by Cathay at that time refused to sign. I was one of them. The champagne corks must have been popping again that night in Swire House. They had rolled us with hardly a fight. That was when Eddington coined a term that later he was to deny he ever said. He called us the 'million dollar morons'.

I got a letter signed by Samios telling me that I was no longer eligible to go on a basing and that I would never get another salary increase. Well I could live with that. I didn't want to go on a basing anyway. 1997 was going to be a piece of history in the making and I wanted to be part of it. And never is a long time. What I couldn't live with, however, was what happened next. I got a letter from the flying training manager (FTM), Geoff Fern, in August 1994 informing me that, since I had failed to sign up to CoS 94, I was no longer productive and that 'it would be impossible to effectively roster me' on the training schedule. I was demoted from Training Captain back to line duties. It meant that I was to lose my training pay increment of 7.5 per cent of salary but that wasn't the worst of it. They took away from me the one thing that I cherished most, the opportunity to put something back into my profession and to leave it in a better state than when I entered it.

I didn't take it lying down. I spent the next couple of months tracking the training rosters and costing them on both the old and new CoS. The results showed clearly that I could be just as productive on the old terms as those who had signed up for the new terms. Because most training took place on regional rather than ULR ops, it was difficult to exceed the 70-hour threshold let alone get anywhere near the new 89-hour EFP cut-off. I sent my results to Clemmow and booked an appointment to see him. I went into his office and he said to me, 'Your figures are very impressive, John, but there's only one solution if you want your training job back, you've got to sign the new contract.'

That was it. Sign or else. If I wanted to follow Tony Dodd's advice the training route was now closed to me. Clemmow left me with only one other option. In June 1994 I joined the General Committee (GC) of the AOA.

6

Rerouting

'*Of mankind we may say in general they are fickle, hypocritical and greedy of gain.*'

Niccolò Machiavelli

My introduction to the General Committee came with an immediate indication of what I could expect from Clemmow in the future now that I had 'changed allegiance', as he saw it. As part of its rearguard action against B Scales, the AOA had put together a cost of living survey comparing Hong Kong with other major cities around the world. It was compiled from data published by the Economist Intelligence Unit and showed that Hong Kong is one of the most expensive cities in the world to live in, especially in terms of property and rental. With the run up to 1997, property prices and rents were spiralling as landlords sought to cash in before the handover. The principle of the A Scale housing allowance formula was that officers should be able to obtain accommodation comparable with what they might expect in their home countries. Using an average family with 2.4 children, this put the target in the top end of the housing market. Space being at a premium, a lot of accommodation in Hong Kong comprises of very small flats with master bedrooms that would only be considered to be box rooms in the UK. In Australia, they wouldn't even be considered as storage space. At that time, in Sterling terms, I was paying the equivalent of £4,500 pcm rental for a 2,100 square foot, three-bedroom village house. In 2010 values, that equates to around £8,380.[2] With the reduction in the B Scale housing allowance, the standard of housing available to new joiners was much lower than had previously been the case unless they were prepared to spend a lot more of their salary on rent. For a man with a couple of kids, he had no alternative. The AOA started receiving complaints from the B Scalers that they were having trouble making ends meet and that the cost of living was far higher than they had been led to believe when they were recruited. The response was in essence, tough, you should have done your research before you came here. Indeed, that was the actual phrase used in one union/management meeting that I attended. When the B Scale representative put the case for an increase in the rental allowance, the response from the leader of the management team was, 'Tough it out.' In response to all this, the AOA put its CoL survey on its website and also sent it to prospective recruits who contacted the union for information when applying for a job.

Clemmow didn't like this but could do little about it as the AOA was only republishing information that was freely available in the public domain. The union then went a little further. It had received letters from some B Scalers explaining and complaining about the financial difficulties they were experiencing in Hong Kong. The union published these as well. The reaction from Clemmow was immediate. He sent every member of the GC a warning letter stating that this was anti-company propaganda deliberately designed to discourage people from joining the company and that any repetition of such crimes would result in summary dismissal. I had only been on the committee for two weeks and had no hand in the preparation or dissemination of the CoL survey but I got one of these letters as well and was now under threat of dismissal.

Welcome to the new world order. Up until then, my personal file had been exemplary with nothing but letters of thanks and commendations. Here was my first black mark. I went to see Clemmow and his response was, 'With responsibility comes accountability.'

I would remember that phrase. It was a standard union-busting tactic. Intimidate the union reps. Of course the letters became common knowledge amongst the membership and achieved another union-busting objective. Discourage others from joining the GC. In the case of the AOA though, it went further than that.

Since 1993, relations between Terry Heyes and Clemmow had been deteriorating. Every time Terry put out an AOA newsletter to the membership, Clemmow would counter it with a Flight Ops newsletter and Terry got drawn into a paper war with tit for tat newsletters going back and forth. Each month, Ops/AOA meetings were scheduled where day-to-day issues were discussed and, hopefully, resolved. As the paper war escalated, Clemmow cancelled all further meetings until the AOA 'came to its senses'. This achieved another objective: control the communications. Terry ended up in the position where he had no direct communication route to management and had to be careful what he wrote to his own membership for fear of reprisals.

Clemmow had another trick up his sleeve on the comms front. All of the AOA reps were line crew and flew a full roster. This meant that their union work had to be done in their spare time. The company refused to roster any time off for union duties other than one day per month for three men to attend the Ops/AOA meeting. The AOA employed a full-time general secretary (gen sec) to provide continuity and oversee the day-to-day running of the office when the union reps weren't available. He also attended the Ops/AOA meetings. Clemmow issued a decree that, henceforth, only employees of the company would be permitted access to Cathay premises and, therefore, that the gen sec would no longer be allowed at such meetings. Another good negotiating tactic. Dictate and define the make-up of the opposition's team. Of course, once he cancelled the Ops/AOA meetings, the point became moot but he went further than that. It was common practice for the gen sec to send letters to the company *per procurationem* on behalf of the president when he was away on duty. Clemmow announced that he would no longer answer any letters from the AOA unless they were signed personally by the president himself and that, additionally, all letters must be addressed only to him. The AOA was not permitted to communicate with any other management officers. That just about gave him complete control on the comms front. Well it did if Terry acceded to Clemmow's edicts. It got to the stage whereby, at the end of Terry's presidency, he had not spoken to or met directly with Clemmow for 15 months. Isolate your opponent.

It didn't go all Clemmow's way though. We aircrew were getting very fed up with our DFO and were supportive of Terry so we started to find ways to express our displeasure. As part of their remuneration package, all DFOs were provided with a residence on Kadoorie Avenue in Kowloon. Back then this was an exclusive area and the DFO's house was quite plush with a swimming pool and extensive gardens. It was traditional for the DFO to host a party for the aircrew every couple of months and invitations were much sought after. People started declining his invitations. It was the same with long service awards. These were in the form of gold pins to be worn on the uniform and were awarded for 10, 15 and 20 years' service. We stopped going to the awards ceremonies. He tried to counter this by putting on a fortnightly 'DFO's Barrel' in the Cathay Club, a bar on the top floor of the building where we used to congregate for a post-flight pint. The idea was that the crew could come and chat to him in an informal atmosphere. Normally if you offer aircrew free beer they will be there in droves. Hardly anyone turned up and he was left to drink his beer on his own. Whilst these were only small tokens of resistance, it was a start.

Clemmow's regime was not only affecting industrial matters: Operation Better Shape impacted on operational matters as well. One of these was fuel policy. Paddy Anderson, a management pilot, was appointed as the fuel czar. His edicts started small with auxiliary power unit (APU) usage.

He issued a Notice to Crew (NTC) that, in future, the APU would only be used at stations where ground power was not available and, even then, should only be started 30 minutes before Scheduled Time of Departure (STD). The APU provides electrical power and air-conditioning (A/C) for the cabin on the ground but ground A/C carts were in short supply and generally unreliable so the effect of the new policy on passenger comfort was immediate. In the tropical climes in which we operated, instead of finding a cool oasis, passengers who had paid premium prices for premium service found themselves entering a cabin that resembled a greenhouse when they boarded the aircraft. The APU used 600 kg of fuel per hour when under full load. The cost saving of 300 kg under the 30 minute rule had to be offset against the handling charges for the ground power unit (GPU) and A/C trucks, not to mention passenger discomfort. The APU policy was an exercise in theoretical number crunching with little or no consideration for the practicalities of large aircraft operations.

Next came fuel uplift. When calculating the required fuel load during pre-flight planning we had hitherto worked in increments of 1,000 kg. The consultants, when looking at cost savings, had calculated that if fuel was loaded in increments of 100 kg there was a potential saving of x dollars per annum. Another NTC was issued stating that, with immediate effect, fuel would be calculated and loaded in 100 kg increments. All well and good in theory, but totally impractical on line operations. A 747-200 holds around 160 tonnes of fuel when fully loaded depending on the specific gravity (SG) of the fuel. The fuel gauges are only guaranteed to be accurate within plus or minus two per cent, or around 3,000 kg at full load. How could we load fuel to within 100 kg when the gauges weren't accurate enough? Even if you calculate the volumetric uplift according to weight, there are still errors because of variation in the SG. Being practical people, we filled in the paperwork in accordance with the new stated policy and just carried on as normal. In any case, a missed approach, circuit and landing in a 747-200 uses around 7,000 kg of fuel. One go around completely wipes out months of fuel savings under the consultants' 'bright ideas' plan.

Next came contingency fuel. Our fuel policy required sufficient fuel to be loaded for the proposed flight with an additional *en route* contingency of five per cent. In addition to this we also had to carry sufficient fuel to divert to an alternate airfield from overhead the original destination and then hold for 30 minutes at 1,500 feet and land. On ULR ops the five per cent contingency could amount to up to 7,000 kg so it was capped at a maximum of 4,000 kg, which made both practical and commercial sense. With the introduction of Operation Better Shape, Paddy put out another NTC stating that, at the Captain's discretion, this 4,000 kg cap could be reduced to 2,500 kg. If forecast weather conditions merited it, some Captains would reduce contingency but it was their choice and led to some interesting exchanges.

I was standing in flight dispatch one day and next to me was a Captain called Steve Holland. Steve was a real character, a rough diamond. He had originally come to Hong Kong when he was doing his national service. He liked it so much that he stayed and set up a used car business. It expanded and he got into high end sports cars. When he found that a lot of his customers were Cathay pilots he got interested in flying, took lessons, got his commercial licence and ended up flying for Cathay. He also diversified his business into property and was a wealthy man. He could have bought and sold most of the senior Cathay pilots three or four times over and some of them resented him for that. He didn't really need the job, it was more of a hobby to him. Steve was doing his flight planning for a trip to Vancouver. In came Paddy to 'explain' to Steve how he could reduce the contingency and get another 1,500 kg of freight on the aircraft instead of carrying all that 'excess' fuel. He ignored Paddy, turned to me and said, 'I'd check your CFP if I was you, John, 'cos mine's wrong. Look, it's got the wrong fucking Captain's name on it.' Paddy left.

Soon after the introduction of the optional reduction to 2,500 kg, it became mandated. All ULR CFPs were now produced with only 2,500 kg of contingency and, if the Captain wanted more, he would have to offload payload in favour of additional fuel. This reversal was a subtle application of commercial pressure. It is one thing to reduce fuel to add payload, it is another to reduce payload to add fuel. Some Captains, like Steve, wouldn't bend to this sort of pressure. Not everyone was like him though. Some felt duty bound to go with what 'they' wanted. The pressure was increased when an extra box was added to the commander's administrative report (CAR). We were supposed to fill this in and give reasons for additional fuel uplifts. I used to annotate this as 'SOR'. My fleet manager (FM) asked me one day what it meant. It was a quote straight out of the fuel policy section of the Ops Manual, which stated that fuel additional to the CFP planned fuel may be uploaded for 'sound operational reasons'. Some of my colleagues were more creative with reasons such as 'grass cutting' and 'swan migration'.

Paddy upped the pressure further. He started running a fuel league table. All Captains' fuel uplifts were monitored and a monthly 'excess' list was produced. Those who starred at the top of the list were invited to his office to 'discuss' fuel policy. It didn't work that well because he found that most of the 'stars' were Check & Training Captains. This was because they generally operated regional routes, encountered the worst weather and, when training, it sometimes pays to have a bit of 'granny fuel' up your sleeve in case of missed approaches or other unforeseen circumstances. The league table did give rise to another amusing exchange between Paddy and another Captain. When invited to the office to discuss fuel policy, in response to Paddy's question as to why he was uploading so much 'excess' fuel, this Captain responded, '145,386.'

'Err . . . what's that?' asked Paddy.

'It's what I get paid every month to make operational decisions. Can I go now?'

Something else happened with the ULR contingency. Contingency fuel is just that. It is there to cater for unforeseen contingencies such as stronger than forecast headwinds. Sometimes you burn it and sometimes you don't. Sometimes if the headwinds are weaker than forecast, you 'make fuel' *en route*. We started to find that we were burning all the contingency fuel on every ULR sector. Statistically this didn't make sense. Either the weather forecasters were getting it wrong every time, which, given the inexact nature of meteorology, could have been the reason, or something else was going on. The more cynical amongst us suspected that the forecast winds were being factored down at the planning stage so that the calculated fuel load would be reduced and the contingency would cover the actual forecast wind. Of course, that couldn't be the case because it would be illegal and a breach of the company's AOC. In any event, we thought it 'quite fishy'.

All these fuel policy changes were obviously intended to save money and, given that fuel cost is a large proportion of the DOCs of an aircraft, it makes very good commercial sense to monitor fuel usage. None of us had a problem with that. We wanted to see the company succeed just as much as anyone. We had our futures invested with Cathay and we all cared greatly about its commercial success. What we did have a problem with was the way these measures were being implemented in a potentially punitive manner. This increasing commercial pressure and blame culture started to permeate all areas of the operation as we shall see later. But, more importantly, the manner of their implementation sought to diminish the authority of the aircraft commander by taking operational decisions away from the Captain and putting them in the hands of the planners and administrators. We will also examine this further at a later point.

The crazy part of this change in culture was that it was counter-productive. Operationally, where we pilots regularly *did* make genuinely big fuel savings was in the selection of optimum flight levels and cruise speeds. If a level was blocked we would liaise with other aircraft on the radio, coordinate our step climbs and push ATC to get clearance to the optimum level for fuel efficiency. We also pushed ATC for direct routings to reduce flight time. These were practical operational measures that had a direct and tangible effect on the financial success of our company. On ULR routes particularly, these measures could result in big fuel savings. As Clemmow's policies began to get us more and more offside, crews no longer bothered pushing for levels and track shortening. After all, why should we put in the extra effort and go the extra mile when all we got in return were more attacks on our conditions and benefits? Squadron morale was dropping and, with it, goodwill. Instead of saving money, his policies were costing money.

There was one final fuel policy change that Paddy brought in that took us into serious 'cowboy country'. He decreed that when one hour flight time from the scheduled destination, or at the top of descent, if the weather was good and the destination airfield had two runways or more, we no longer needed to retain our alternate diversion fuel on arrival at destination. This was a significant change intended to solve a problem on our North Pacific ULR ops. When inbound to HKG, if the contingency had been burned and the in-flight fuel consumption 'howgozit' showed you had burned more fuel than planned and were below the minimum requirement line, the decision point was Taipei (TPE) as this was the last *en route* alternate airfield before arrival. If you were below the line, a diversion to TPE was mandatory. This would mean that another crew would have to be flown to TPE to recover the aircraft as duty hour limitations meant that the operational crew would be out of hours to continue on to HKG. Obviously, such diversions incurred delay and cost and, with the contingency situation, were becoming increasingly common. By coincidence, TPE was one hour out from HKG. The fuel required to divert from HKG to Macao, our fair-weather alternate, was around 7,000 kg. If, overhead TPE, we could now throw away the requirement to be able to divert to an alternate on reaching our destination, this 'extra' 7,000 kg was no longer needed to be kept in reserve. On that basis then we had more than enough to carry on to HKG even if we were below the line. But hang on a minute, HKG hasn't got two runways, has it? Paddy had an answer for that one, too.

'Yes it has. R/W 13 and R/W 31.'

'Yes, well, Paddy, I don't think that's the spirit of what's intended do you? When we say two runways we don't mean the same bit of tarmac. We mean two physically separate runways to cater for one of them being blocked. If there's a blocked runway at Kai Tak that's it, the airport's closed.' He had an answer for that one as well.

'If the runway's blocked you can land on the taxiway.'

Paddy actually put this forward as a viable alternative.

He had yet another bright idea. If you had an engine failure, the fuel policy mandated that you were no longer required to carry alternate fuel. This made sense since, depending on weight, on three engines a 747 burns around ten per cent more fuel than on four, and if you had to carry alternate fuel on top of the increased burn, in the three-engine case it would be unnecessarily restrictive. Paddy's logic went as follows: Let's say we're normal ops on four engines and three hours out from HKG. The fuel burn to destination is around 30,000 kg. Add to this alternate and holding and the fuel required is, say, 45,000 kg. Now let's say we're actually down to 42,000 kg. We're going to have to divert to TPE aren't we? Not if we shut an engine down we don't because although the three-engine fuel burn to HKG is increased to 33,000 kg, we don't need alternate fuel any more. Now we only need holding fuel additional to the burn, say an extra 7,000 kg, giving a total fuel required of 40,000 kg, so we're OK to continue. All we have to do is shut an engine down. Simple really. I actually had a candidate on command training who had listened to Paddy's propaganda and put this forward to me as a viable alternative. I asked him a question:

'What is your minimum bingo fuel for arrival at Kai Tak under normal ops on four engines?'

He said 14 tonnes, which is about right. I posed him a further question.

'So when everything's going fine, you want fourteen tonnes but, just to get the commercial job done, you're prepared, unnecessarily, to put your aircraft and passengers in an abnormal situation on three engines and arrive with less fuel than you'd be comfortable with on four?'

He got the point. There was one Captain who called Paddy's bluff. He was inbound from the Pacific and well below the line but used the 'top of descent, no alternate' policy to carry on to HKG. He landed in Kai Tak with around seven tonnes remaining. The CAD was not impressed and the Captain was called into the office. He stood his ground and insisted it was perfectly legal. He was just following Paddy's fuel policy. We didn't hear too much about throwing away the alternate after that.

Operation Better Shape spread its tentacles into the Check & Training Department. Under the guiding hand of the DDFO, Mick Toller, the cost of aircrew training was analysed and measures implemented to drastically reduce it. The first measure was that newly recruited pilots, instead of receiving 40 sectors of line training, would now get only 20. Simulator training also was chopped back. The old maxim of training for confidence not competence went out of the window. In the new world order the important thing now was to get the pilots through the sausage machine at minimum cost. Instead of having a refresher training session the day before each six-monthly check ride, it was straight into the box and put your licence on the line. It got to the stage at one point where two crews were doing their check rides in the same time slot previously allocated to only one crew.

This was the so-called 'hot seat' checking system. I experienced this myself on one occasion. Where previously I would have been allocated two four-hour sessions to complete my six-monthly licence renewal, I did it in one two-hour session. Instead of continuation training, it was just a box-ticking exercise.

Not only was this a massive reduction in training standards, but also, for some pilots, it put them under enormous pressure. If you fail your check ride you lose your licence and you are out of a job. No one is going to employ a pilot who has lost his job because he failed a check ride. Pilots have to jump through this hoop every six months for the whole of their professional careers. Some pilots find the sim to be something of a nerve-racking experience because of the consequences of potential failure. If you take a man of that disposition and chop his training time by three quarters, the increase in pressure upon him is obvious.

The simulator was also 'reclassified' from being merely a training tool to a 'revenue base'. This meant that because of the time saved in training Cathay crews, the sim could now be rented out to other airlines. But there was more. They started inviting members of the Cathay frequent-flier club to come and spend a couple of hours in the sim to 'try their hand'. It was no longer a training tool, it was a computer game for some privileged passengers to come and have a play with. Of course, they couldn't be expected to come in the early morning hours. No, they would have to be given the plum daytime slots and we could fill the 02:00 and 03:00 slots. Never mind being in the middle of your 'window of circadian low' and feeling very tired. Jump in the box, old son, and put your professional livelihood on the line so that Mr Marco Polo Diamond can have a play around during the day.

Even ground school conversion courses were not exempt from the axe. Out went human lecturers with chalk and talk and open classroom discussion. In came 'carrels' with computer-based training. The standard of technical knowledge deteriorated from 'nice to know' to 'need to know' and only need to know enough to pass the CAD technical exam. It certainly cut costs because ground school conversions that used to take four weeks could now be completed in twelve days. All these changes in the training department caused a huge amount of concern and resentment but complaints to management fell on deaf ears. We had to cut costs, that was that and bugger the reduction in training standards. It wasn't that we wouldn't have been amenable to talking about reducing the training budget and looking for incremental savings where we could. After all it's no use having the safest airline in the world if it doesn't make a profit. In the commercial world there is always a cost benefit analysis (CBA) to be considered and we understood that. It was the way it was done that irked us. Instead of taking an incremental approach and considering cause and effect, they just scythed through the training department wholesale seemingly without any consultation or consideration of the consequences. Consequently our pilot managers became target fixated. We expected better of them but they let us down badly, very badly. To us, the recently promoted flying training manager (FTM), Rick Fry, was one of the most disappointing. He was later to allow his position to be abused and take part in one of the most shameful acts of anti-union victimisation that Clemmow perpetrated before we were finally rid of him when he retired and we will return to this later.

Presumably, Clemmow's sidekick, Mick Toller, thought that when Clemmow went, as DDFO he was a shoo-in for the top job. It didn't work out that way though. The regime that replaced Clemmow cast him aside and he fell from grace. It was the way the Swire system worked. You attach yourself to someone's coat tails on the way up but if your sponsor crashes and burns, you go down in flames with him. Toller left Cathay and later became the director of the Civil Aviation Safety Authority in Australia where he was involved in the grounding of Ansett Australia's Boeing 767 fleet in controversial circumstances.

Operation Better Shape was also used to start recruiting pilots with much lower qualifications and experience levels than had previously been the case. A new rank of Second Officer (S/O) was created by Clemmow. These new recruits were not given the same in-depth training as before. The aircraft rating was only endorsed in Part 2 of their licences and they were not qualified to take off or land the aircraft on the line. They were only allowed in the seat as 'cruise pilots'. Some called them radio operators or 'pilots' assistants'. I personally was not so harsh, having been a 'boy pilot' myself. Some of them, like me, had gone through a BA cadet scheme and, when BA did not immediately have jobs for them, they came to Cathay for two years before being recalled. Cathay had also set up a cadet scheme of its own in Adelaide. Again we had no problem with this and actually thought it a good idea. Where the problems arose was with their experience after initial training. After I came out of Hamble, I had served my apprenticeship before getting into the seat of a big jet. Britannia Airways in the UK used to recruit cadets for operations on their 737s and 767s. However, before being allowed onto the big jets, they served two years with McAlpine Aviation on their HS125 operation to get some sectors in. Flying experience is not just about hours, it is about sectors as well. Takeoff and landing are the two most critical phases of flight and mastery of these only comes with experience. A pilot who flies short haul will experience, say, six sectors in fourteen hours of flying and will actually operate as the handling pilot on three of these. On ULR ops, those same 14 flying hours comprise of only one sector, and the takeoffs and landings have to be shared out amongst the four pilots on the crew. Because of their Part 2 ratings, our S/Os were getting no handling at all in the critical flight phases. This was not their fault. It was the fault of the flying training system. It is a big ask to take a newly qualified pilot out of basic training and stick him in the seat of the biggest, most complex commercial jet in the world. The overall experience level on the flight deck became diluted. Whereas previously we would have had a Captain, a Senior First Officer (SF/O) and two F/Os making up a ULR crew, we now had a Captain, two F/Os and a S/O. Required experience levels for the relief commander – in *loco parentis* whilst the Captain is taking his in-flight rest – were also reduced because of a lack of qualified men. This reduction in experience levels started to manifest itself by an increase in the number of reportable incidents. There were two particular occasions where the inexperience of the 'cruise crew' on the B747-400 resulted in the aircraft entering the stall regime. In both cases, the autothrottle malfunctioned, power was reduced, the aircraft slowed and entered pre-stall buffet without the crew noticing. The first lesson in *ab initio* basic training is primary and secondary effects of flying controls. The second lesson is recognition of, and approach to, the stall and recovery. It is a fundamental principle of flight that you do not stall the aircraft unless you are engaged in aerobatics or air combat manoeuvring (ACM). These crews had not done this on purpose. They became distracted with other operational matters and, because of their lack of experience, did not have sufficient spare capacity to deal with the basics as well. Although they must carry the responsibility for what happened, it was not their fault. It was the fault of a training system that put them in a position for which they had neither the qualifications nor experience to handle. We were right back to *Papa India* and S/O Keighley in 1972. The lessons from that accident had either been forgotten or ignored in the pursuit of commercial gain in the intervening 20 years.

The rot went further than that. Instead of management acknowledging the fault, increasing training and taking steps to make sure it did not happen again, these incidents were swept under the carpet. Rather than being classified as 'inadvertent aircraft stall' (as they should have been) and subjected to a full investigation by the authorities, instead these incidents were listed as 'uncommanded thrust reduction' and reduced to the category of a technical fault on the aircraft. It was a whitewash and demonstrated the malaise that by now affected not only the training system but also the Flight Safety Department under Clemmow's reign.

In October 1995, Clemmow unilaterally announced the formation of a new company called Aircrew Services Limited (ASL), a wholly owned subsidiary of Cathay Pacific. He did this without any prior consultation with the AOA. He simply announced it at an Ops/AOA meeting. From now on, our four freighter aircraft would be crewed by pilots and F/Es employed by ASL. Pilots were to be recruited by ASL on completely new terms and conditions that made B Scales look like untold riches and, what is more, Captains would be recruited directly into ASL rather than be promoted from within Cathay. This was a triple slap in the face for the Cathay aircrew.

Firstly, he was taking away work that had previously been done by us. These aircraft were to remain in Cathay ownership and be operated under Cathay's AOC but he was outsourcing our work to cheap crews to undercut us.

Secondly, with the recruitment of direct entry Captains, this had an immediate and very adverse effect on promotion prospects all the way down the chain from SF/Os to S/Os.

Thirdly, following the formation of ASL, 44 of our F/Es would be made redundant at the end of 1996 as their services would no longer be required – the freighters would be crewed exclusively by ASL personnel. There was a twist to this last turn of the knife. If any of the F/Es scheduled for redundancy wanted to apply for jobs with ASL, they could do so. In other words they were being given an opportunity to apply for their own jobs back flying exactly the same aircraft, but on terms and conditions vastly inferior to those they currently enjoyed. This was a ploy that other Swire-owned companies were to employ in the future with the move from Kai Tak to the new airport at Chek Lap Kok in 1998.

The treatment of these men was unforgivable. Between them they had on average more than ten years' service with Cathay. The excuse offered was that they had originally been recruited on one-year renewable contracts and all that was happening was that their contracts would not be renewed when they expired. It exposed another flaw in employment legislation in Hong Kong. In developed countries, if you employ someone continuously for more than three years, albeit on an annually renewable contract, then his or her employment is deemed to be permanent and brings with it all the protections that that confers. Not in Hong Kong though and Clemmow took full advantage of that. This whole sordid enterprise was presided over by one of his sidekicks, Jeff 'Moshe' Morris, himself a F/E and an erstwhile colleague of those he was helping to axe. Morris added insult to injury.

Some of the F/Es went through Moshe's interview process and he failed them. I asked him about this in a meeting one day and he told me they were using the process to 'weed out' those F/Es who they considered to be 'troublesome'. It was no coincidence that most of these 'troublesome' people had served on the AOA GC at one time or another. After years of loyal service they were simply thrown onto the garbage heap.

The ASL plan didn't work though. It was supposed to be up and running as a self-supporting organisation within one year of its formation. It did not produce the predicted cost savings, it had an adverse effect on the passenger operation and, three and a half years after its formation, it was abandoned as a failure. We will come back to the reasons for this later.

When I joined the AOA GC, my intention was to find ways to help combat the effects of contract changes brought about by CoS 94. As I had remained on the old terms, I had a vested interest in the future of the contract. Self-interest, perhaps, but a good motivator nonetheless. I applied myself to the task with the result that I was appointed vice president professional (VPP) in relatively short order. The chain of command of the AOA was that the president was the boss, his number two i/c was vice president administration (VPA), and VPP was third in charge. VPA had overall responsibility for industrial matters whilst the remit of VPP was generally operational and technical. Under the VPs were a number of principal officers (POs) and GC members responsible to the president via the VPs.

Terry Heyes was coming up for re-election as president towards the end of the year and did not want to serve another term. He approached me and asked me if I would be interested in standing as president. I told him that I was but did not feel qualified as I had not had time to read all the files, get myself familiarised with procedures and generally get to a level of comfort where I felt qualified to pick up the reins. We did a deal. If he would stay on as president for another three or four months after the election, to give me time to get my chairs under the table, then I would be prepared to step up to bat. It was going to be a steep learning curve but I thought I could handle it. I found out quicker than I had planned.

Shortly after we had done the deal, and a couple of months before the elections were due, out of the blue Terry resigned the presidency. Under the rules VPA was now the president. He was a Scotsman called Colin Wright and an old acquaintance. He telephoned me and said, 'John, I don't have the communications skills for the job. I'm out. It's up to you.' Colin holds the record for the shortest serving president of the AOA. Having only served on the GC for two minutes, I was now president and in charge of the whole sorry mess.

7

TCC

'Watch your six.'

I needed a plan but, before that, I needed protection. When engaging in ACM, every formation leader needs a trusted wingman to look after his back. I had no one and this needed to be remedied as a first priority. I looked around at the others on the General Committee but there was no one who fit the bill. Although I had been in the company for almost ten years, I didn't know most of the others all that well as they were mainly on the TriStar fleet, which I'd never flown. Apart from that, they were really Terry's crew and used to his way of working. If we were going to start making any headway in the war we were now fighting on multiple fronts, we were going to need to take a different approach to problem solving and that meant changing the thinking, firstly, of the GC and secondly, of the membership. There was nothing for it, I had to look outside the committee for new blood. I had someone in mind, someone who I'd known from Hamble days, but the question was, would he be prepared to take on the job?

I telephoned Nigel Humphries and asked him whether he fancied meeting me for a beer. Nigel was a Captain on the 747, was not afraid to express his opinion and had a very good head on his shoulders. He was also politically astute, just the sort of man I needed. I explained my predicament over several pints of Carlsberg and asked him whether he would join me on the journey I was about to undertake. He replied that he knew when I called him that it was unlikely to be a social call, had pondered what it was that I was after and already had a good idea of what I was going to ask of him. I pointed out that it was exactly because of his ability to read a situation that I needed him. He gave me something of a wry smile at my pathetic attempt at flattery but accepted the job anyway. Problem one solved, or so I thought.

Wrong! I announced Nigel's appointment as VPA at the next GC meeting and met with an internal power play. There was a TriStar Captain, Nigel Demery, who had joined the committee at about the same time as me. It was his view that the 'promotion', as he saw it, should come from within the current committee and he had in mind a B Scale TriStar F/O, Murray Gardner, for the job. I was not prepared to give the key job to either of them until I got to know them better and time was of the essence. Also, it was Gardner who had been responsible for the B Scalers' letters being included in the AOA CoL package bringing Clemmow's retribution on our heads. I thought it an error of judgment. When I stood my ground, Demery put a notice book in the office asking all the other committee members to signify their assent or otherwise to my decision. It was a challenge to my authority before we had even started trying to address our problems and there was no room for it.

Terry had run his committee in quite a pragmatic manner. Under his management style, in my view, there was a lot of talking and not much action and look where it had got us. What was needed now was a firm hand on the tiller, not more of the same. I convened a meeting of the GC and told them that, under my leadership, things were going to change. If we were going to be successful we needed to take a different approach and I wanted Nigel Humphries by my side. In any case, as president, it was my prerogative to appoint who I saw fit. If they didn't accept that, they could tell me then and there and look elsewhere for a new president. Either it was my rhetoric or the fact that no one else wanted to pick up the poisoned chalice that I'd been handed but, for whatever reason, I won the day, though it did earn me the nickname of 'El Presidente'.

The power challenge didn't end there, however. The annual elections were coming up at the end of the year and Nigel Demery stood against me for the presidency. He lost. In one way he did me a favour. Terry had stood unopposed for the last two years and Clemmow often jibed that he was not representative of the aircrew body as a whole because he had not been 'properly' elected. Thanks to Nigel Demery, Clemmow was never able to use that one against me.

Once the internal politics had been sorted out, the new committee came together as a coordinated team and we each used our talents to best advantage for the good of the whole. That is not to say that we never had disagreements. Far from it. Whilst we both shared a common goal, Demery and I could not have been more dissimilar characters in many respects and, perhaps, therein lay our strength. He was my 'contrarian' and, whatever the subject under discussion, I was always able to rely on him to provide the alternative viewpoint. Consequently this ensured that we explored every angle of a situation. He certainly honed my debating skills and, with his penchant for time-scales and deadlines, helped to ensure that decisions were implemented. He was also largely responsible for helping to formulate a strategic plan for the future, but more of that later.

My new GC was strengthened further when two other Senior Captains, both well respected by their colleagues, volunteered to come aboard. Their names were Don Grange and Barrie Hesketh. These two men were more senior in the company than Humphries, Demery and me. They had been there seven or eight years longer than us and were part of the old school from the days when annual negotiations between the AOA and management were done over a brandy and a handshake in the Hong Kong Club. Despite that, they were both astute men and realised that the company had changed markedly and a different approach was now needed. Many of their colleagues were trying to cling on to the old days and saw my group as the Young Turks, full of enthusiasm but lacking in experience of 'how we do business' with the Swires. Barrie and Don brought gravitas to the committee and rounded out the new team. When Don retired from Cathay, he sent me a letter. In it he wrote, 'I joined your committee because I thought you needed help. It didn't take me long to realise that I was the one that needed help, not you.' Like Dave Wales's compliment, I have cherished Don's words, especially during some of the dark days that I was to endure later on. To have earned the respect of a man like Don Grange was something special.

The next problem that needed sorting out was communications, both with Clemmow and with the membership. Firstly, I needed to open up a line of communication with the management. If you aren't talking, you can't solve your problems. Secondly, I had to get out of the tit for tat newsletter cycle and take back control of our communications with the membership.

I started to receive lots of advice, well meant I am sure, likening the relationship between the AOA and management to a marriage that is heading for the rocks. These self-appointed counsellors suggested employing third party mediation to try to rebuild the relationship. This advice was so far wide of the mark that it told me that the membership really didn't understand what was actually happening and needed to be educated. In a marriage, generally both parties are working to try to make the relationship succeed. Sutch and his cabal didn't care whether it succeeded or not. They were getting what they wanted and that was fine by them. As far as we were concerned, we were the 'battered wives' and, until we started doing something about it, the beatings would continue. This was brought home to me by two incidents that took place shortly after I became president.

The first was when I was operating a sector from TPE to HKG. Sutch was on board the aircraft and came up to the flight deck to say hello. He congratulated me on my new appointment and said to me, 'Of course you do realise that you've just taken on the hardest job in the airline don't you?'

I replied with words to the effect that I'd always thought that his was the hardest job in the airline to which he responded, 'Well what you've got to realise, John, is that all the changes that are being made come from the highest level and they have my full support.'

That was it. A warning. You take us on and you are taking on me and I've got the backing of the Swire board in London. It was delivered in the nicest of terms but it was a warning nonetheless.

The second warning was delivered in a far less subtle manner. I was in the Cathay Club having a post-flight beer. Geoff Fern, the FTM who had taken my training job from me, was in there and he was drunk. He came over to me and slurred, 'I'm gonna tell you something. We've got no need to talk to you cunts in the AOA 'til we've got green an' white tails sittin' on the tarmac with no fucker left to fly 'em.'

This was a reference to the Cathay colour scheme at that time, which comprised a green and white striped tail fin. The vitriol with which he delivered his rant surprised me, especially since Fern had previously served on the AOA GC himself before moving into management. It said it all. Until you people get some backbone, stand up and fight and start hitting us financially by grounding the aircraft, we'll just carry on taking what we want. If I had harboured any illusions that our current problems were going to be resolved by mutual compromise and agreement, these two incidents dispelled them forever. We were in for a fight and the membership needed to understand that as well.

We were discussing the problem of direct communication with Clemmow at a committee meeting in February 1995 and the debate came to a conclusion. The only way to reopen direct communication was a one- on-one approach from me. This went against all the normal protocol which mandates that there is no such thing as an 'off the record' chat. Anything you say can and will be used against you even if it is said in confidence. Never put yourself in the position where there are no witnesses and you can be misrepresented later. Extraordinary times called for extraordinary measures and, there being no time like the present, I telephoned Clemmow and made an appointment to see him later that day. As I was driving to the meeting, I felt like Daniel being thrown into the lions' den. My backside was hanging out in the wind and I had no backup. The adrenaline was up and I wasn't even sure what I was going to say. There were a couple of thoughts that gave me comfort, however. First, I'd been in much worse situations than this in my life and dealt with them. Second, and perhaps more importantly, remember that whoever your opponent may be, they are only human. If you are having doubts before you go into battle, so is your opponent.

OK, in this situation, Clemmow was apparently holding all the cards but he still had to play his hand. If he read me the riot act and I reported back to my troops that he was completely intransigent and simply hell-bent on continuing to hack away at them, where would that leave him? Indeed, where would that leave Sutch? In all likelihood it would lead to another confrontation management weren't yet prepared for, having been through the FAU strike only two years earlier. Whether or not this analysis was correct doesn't really matter. These were the sort of thoughts that were going through my head as I drove to the meeting, and they helped me to prepare for whatever it was that I was about to face. I felt a great responsibility for what I was about to do but, as can often be the case, fear of the unknown is worse than the reality. The meeting went well and Clemmow actually seemed pleased that I'd got in touch. We talked generally and also specifically about getting Ops/AOA meetings back on the agenda, the need to get a Discipline and Grievance Procedure (DGP) sorted out as promised in CoS 94 and concerns that the pilots had for the future.

Clemmow said to me, 'Yes, the crews have had a hard time of it over the last couple of years but there's nothing more to come. Just some fine tuning.'

That last sentence rang alarm bells and I replied, 'That bit worries me, Gerry. It makes me think you've taken an arm and a leg and now you want the fingers and toes off what I've got left.'

He laughed at that and said that he wanted to get things 'back on track' as well. There was some interesting body language while I was in there. His office was on the tenth floor of the Technical Block and had a great view over the apron where he could watch all the aircraft arrivals and departures. His desk was in the centre of the room and, at one point while we were looking out of the window chatting, I strolled over behind his desk. He made as if to come and join me there but I held my ground. He spent the next few minutes strolling to and fro between the window and his desk trying to dislodge me. It was like holding the T on a squash court. I played the game for a few more minutes and then relinquished control.

Later that month there was a long service presentation at Kadoorie Avenue and I was due my ten-year pin. Rather than boycott it, I attended and a picture of me shaking hands with Clemmow appeared in the next management newsletter. I got some flak over that. One of the Australian pilots collared me in the crew room and asked me what I thought I was doing shaking hands with 'that cunt Clemmow'. I replied that I was doing the job that he had elected me to do, trying to fix some of the problems we'd got. How else was I going to do that if I didn't talk to them?

Having got the comms channels open, the next thing was to see whether we could make any progress. One of the big concerns that I had was 'flagging out', that is registering a vessel under a flag of convenience and crewing it with foreign workers not subject to First World regulations. It had become common in Europe for the IT operators to wet lease aircraft and crews during the summer season to cater for the increase in traffic and this was beginning to spread to some of the smaller scheduled operators as well. Basically these operators would bring in cheap foreign aircraft, principally from Eastern Europe, and undercut their British-based crews. There were a number of causes for concern with this arrangement, not least of which was that the aircraft and crews were not maintained and licensed to UK standards. The regulatory authority, the CAA, was complicit in this as it issued these Third World operators with temporary exemptions to operate outside of the normal rules and regulations. I mentioned fraud earlier on. Passengers booked with Air Europe, Britannia, Monarch or whoever had a right to expect to be flown by these carriers and not to turn up at the airport to find a Tupolev or Ilyushin waiting for them with a crew that could hardly speak English.

There are many similarities between the merchant marine and commercial aviation. Much of aviation law derives from maritime law, particularly in respect of the authority of the Captain of the vessel. Flagging out was the downfall of our once mighty merchant marine in the UK. It led to the loss of thousands of jobs. The same thing was starting to happen in commercial aviation and not just in the UK. It was a cause for concern internationally and IFALPA was making representation to the regulatory authorities worldwide because of the impact on standards and flight safety. It was the thin end of the wedge. Locally, in Hong

Kong, we didn't have quite the same level of threat but Dragonair, the local airline in which Cathay had a major stake, was soon to acquire some Airbus A330s. We were also now operating A330s and the last thing we wanted to see was Dragonair being used as a stop gap carrier to fill in when we needed extra capacity, unless we had protections in place to ensure that our crews were not disadvantaged. I put this to Clemmow and he assured me that the company had no intention of doing such a thing, to which I responded, 'Well in that case you should have no objection to formalising that policy in a wet lease agreement to protect our crews.'

As it turned out, he didn't and we signed a Wet Lease Agreement in March 1995. It was the first negotiated agreement that the AOA had signed with the company since the Basings Agreement back in 1992. It looked as though we were making progress and, from small beginnings, who knew what great things might come?

Moshe Morris had become Clemmow's general factotum. He took me aside and told me that Clemmow liked me, that I was a vast improvement on the last president and that I was 'the sort of person they could do business with'. Praise indeed. The honeymoon didn't last long though.

At the annual salary negotiations in June, Clemmow opened the meeting with the words, 'I'm not going to insult your intelligence by pretending that this is a negotiation. It isn't. This is what we are going to do.'

He then announced that they were capping the A Scale salaries and the B Scale increase would be below cost of living. When he said this to me, his mouth was dry, his hands were shaking and he was clearly nervous of my reaction. Unfortunately, because of lack of experience, I blew the opportunity to come back at him. Because of our new found relationship I was not expecting a head on approach. He took me by surprise and it worked. He rolled me at that meeting and I vowed it would never happen again. Later in the year I attended an IFALPA negotiations training course in Frankfurt and got the tools that I needed to be able to look after my troops properly. In October 1995, Clemmow announced the formation of ASL as previously described and the honeymoon was well and truly over. Some 'fine tuning' indeed!

With communications our key priority, in my first newsletter, I addressed the matter of finance. We were being told repeatedly by management that our company was in desperate straits and that, unless we made substantial cost savings, there was little hope for the future. This was underlined by Eddington at a meeting where he addressed the aircrew.

His presentation included various graphs with one in particular that showed income and outgoings crossing over in less than two years' time and we all knew what that meant didn't we? To say that his graphs were simplistic would be an understatement but, then again, he was only talking to his million dollar morons so that should be enough to convince them. At that meeting he also made a statement that was to come back to haunt him. In attempting to justify the formation of ASL, he said, 'There's only one way that freight's headed and that's south.' Freight comprised around 20 per cent of revenue at that time and, in the years following, was one of Cathay's most lucrative profit centres. This had little to do with any reduction in crew costs but rather with the fact that, in connivance with a number of other airlines, Cathay was operating a worldwide price-fixing cartel, for which some were to be convicted of criminal charges, serve prison time and incur multi-million dollar fines in the future.

Around the time of Eddington's 'South' statement, as it came to be known, I happened to be in a lift coming down from the top floor of the Cathay building. Eddington was in there as well so I took the opportunity to ask him a couple of questions. The conversation went along the following lines:

'Rod, could you answer me a question please? How much have these consultants cost us so far?'

'Well it's difficult to put a precise number on it, John.'

'I've heard it's around a million pounds so far.'

'That's probably about right.'

'So, Rod, you know every year we recruit the cream of the Oxbridge graduates into Swire and Cathay, can you tell me how is it that, with all that in-house talent, we have to spend all this money on asking people from outside how to run our company?'

I didn't get an answer. We'd reached the ground floor, the lift doors opened and he walked out.

To counter the 'we're broke, you must help' argument, we analysed the annual reports for the last five years and presented the summary to the membership. This painted a very different picture from the one being force fed to us, particularly in respect of cash reserves. Back then, the accounts used to declare the company's reserves and these showed clearly that Cathay was a very, very cash rich company. The war chest was full. On the basis that in times of recession cash is king, our company was actually in a very strong position to weather the storm, if it actually existed. Now, obviously, it was the responsibility of management to make sure we stayed that way but the purpose of a war chest is that it be used in times of war. The alternative – to pillage the troops to finance the war

– is just plain greedy. Our message was well received by the membership, but not so by Clemmow. He immediately came out with a newsletter in return to try to refute our arguments. This is where we broke out from the tit for tat spiral. Instead of responding to him, our next newsletter changed tack onto a completely different subject. Clemmow responded to that and, again, we changed tack. We continued with the process with the result that Clemmow was put into a responsive posture rather than dictating subject matter to us. We had regained control of our communications with the membership.

There was a spin-off from this comms battle. The accountants changed reporting policy. Cathay's reserves were put in the hands of fund managers – Swire companies, naturally – and, henceforth, only the returns on investment were reported in the annual report rather than the reserves themselves. This made it more difficult for us to state the quantum of the war chest accurately but it was still possible to make an educated estimate. Of necessity, we had begun educating ourselves on the complexities of balance sheets and accounts. Of necessity, because, if you are going to sit across the table from an adversary who is telling you he's broke and needs your money, you'd better be able to speak his language if you're going to be in any sort of position to refute his arguments. For any budding union reps reading this and wanting to start their own education, *Accounting for Growth (Stripping the Camouflage from Company Accounts)* by Terry Smith is recommended reading.

Clemmow went on the attack and started trying to intimidate and victimise members of my GC. On 18 March, Nigel Demery was operating as the Captain of CX508, a TriStar flight out of Kai Tak. One of the doors used for loading catering and other supplies onto the aircraft was unserviceable. Whilst this was not actually a normal passenger door, it was designated as an emergency exit. In such cases, the MEL places constraints on passenger loading and seating. This is to ensure that all passengers can be safely evacuated within the specified minimum time. The exit on Nigel's aircraft had not been properly placarded in accordance with the MEL and, whilst he was checking that the passenger loading was correct, as it was his duty to do, he received a message that he had been taken off the flight by the general manager flight crew (GMFC), Kenneth Roland Barley, and that another Captain would now be operating. On 28 March, he was summoned to the office of the TriStar fleet manager, Colin Pearce, who informed him that he had unnecessarily delayed the flight and that, as a consequence, he was dismissed with immediate effect and given three months' pay in lieu of notice.

To us, it was a total set-up and a deliberate attempt to victimise the principal officers of the AOA. Despite numerous promises dating back to 1994, there was still no formal published DGP but, as president, I contested Nigel's dismissal. He was to be allowed two levels of appeal. The first would be heard by GMFC and the second and last would be heard by the DFO. It was a joke. The GMFC, Barley, had been instrumental in his dismissal in the first place. Nevertheless, I prepared Nigel's appeal, submitted it in writing prior to the first-stage hearing and attending as his 'prisoner's friend'. It was a farce. Barley delivered his verdict within five minutes. The dismissal would stand. If there was to be any hope of success at the final stage, it was no use trying to play it straight; the gloves had to come off.

We had a couple of levers. Firstly, prior to the handover in 1997, the CAD in Hong Kong derived its authority from the CAA in the UK. I had made contact with a Flight Operations Inspector (FOI) in the CAD who was sympathetic to our cause. I took the case to him and told him that, if we were not able to resolve this locally, I would approach the CAA and take it up in the UK. Secondly, the aircraft was registered in the US and was being operated in Hong Kong under a dispensation. This meant that the governing authority in respect of airworthiness issues was actually the Federal Aviation Administration (FAA) in the US. Through our contacts in IFALPA and the Airline Pilots Association in the US (USALPA), I let it be known that we would also take this up with the FAA and the National Transport Safety Board (NTSB). If we were forced to, we would turn this into an international investigation. No one, least of all Clemmow, wanted that, as the spotlight would be shone on Cathay's operation and much dirty linen was likely to be aired in public.

My man in the CAD told me that Clemmow had been advised that, should this matter not be resolved in house, an investigation of Cathay's Flight Operations and Engineering Departments would be conducted, 'as if you have had an accident'. In other words, the CAD would go through everything with a fine-tooth comb. There was no way Clemmow wanted to be exposed to such scrutiny. There had been too many cover-ups, not least in the Engineering Department. The skeletons had to stay locked firmly in their cupboards.

We again submitted our appeal in writing and attended the final-stage hearing chaired by Clemmow with Geoff Fern in attendance. Before I could make my opening remarks, Clemmow said, 'Before you say anything, John, we have reviewed the evidence and have come to the conclusion that a mistake has been made. Captain Demery is reinstated with immediate effect and with no loss of earnings or seniority. Let's get Nigel back where he belongs, on the flight deck.'

He had been forced into a corner and had no alternative but to back down. He carried off the little drama with smiles and handshakes all round, unlike Fern. He had a face like thunder and looked as though he was going to explode. After the extremely unpleasant remarks he'd made to me that night in the Cathay Club, his threats were coming home to roost. This was the first time in some years that the AOA had managed to get a pilot reinstated after being dismissed. It was a huge victory and a lot of beer was drunk that night in the Cathay Club.

I did receive some criticism though. I put out a newsletter praising Clemmow with words to the effect that this proved what could be achieved when the AOA and management worked together. It was a victory for common sense and so on. Some of the pilots didn't like this. They thought I should have crowed it from the rooftops and told everyone how I'd managed to force Clemmow to back down. I took it on the chin. If I'd done what they asked, that would have compromised my contact in the CAD and I knew I might have need of him again.

But we all agreed on one thing: we had had enough and it was time to start fighting back. Our comms campaign to rebuild support and trust with the membership was succeeding. As well as publishing newsletters, we held a series of forum meetings where we explained what corporate re-engineering really meant and what we could do to combat the continuing attack on our contracts of employment. We called these Pendulum Nights. In the balance of power, the pendulum had swung too far in one direction. It needed to be brought back closer to the null position. With each new change we were being nibbled to death by ducks. The theme of our presentations was 'Enough is enough'. No more 'fine tuning'. The question everyone asked was, Yes, that's all well and good but how do we show our resolve and demonstrate our value to the company?

The membership was still reeling from the successive defeats of the last two years and needed to be led gently from their trauma. There had been talk in the past of a 'withdrawal of enthusiasm' or 'woe' campaign, but nothing had come of it. This time we put to the membership that we would adopt a policy of refusing to work on our days off. In the past we had always been more than willing to 'help out' when there was a shortage of pilots and come into work if needed. Because of the increased commercial task, the company was now actually reliant on our goodwill to complete the flying programme so we would take it away and see how they fared. For such a small step, the debate was surprisingly lively and Clemmow's reaction was completely over the top. He put out a newsletter stating that any motion to refuse to work on our days off would be considered by the company to be industrial action and appropriate steps would be taken in response. This put the wind up some of the membership and they were worried that we might provoke an adverse reaction. Adverse reaction? What else could they do to us that they hadn't already done? Sack us for refusing to work on our days off? Even with the very rudimentary employment protection legislation in Hong Kong, it was inconceivable that the courts would uphold a dismissal for insisting on having our statutory days off.

One lesson that these debates did teach me was that we had a long way to go before we would be able to convince the membership to take sterner action. Obviously Clemmow was watching this as well and learning the same lesson. In the end, at the EGM we held a vote on the motion after a lot of debate. A Canadian pilot helped to win the day when he stood up and said, 'Guys, I don't know one way or the other but we've got to do something. Let's just vote this through and see what happens.'

The resolution was carried by an overwhelming majority. In response Clemmow did absolutely nothing. His threats were proven to be empty. It was all posturing and the members were quick to pick up on that lesson. It was a small win after two years of losses but a win nevertheless.

The resolution helped to apply pressure on management because it exacerbated a problem with the new rostering system. Despite the company railroading through an increase in contractual flying hours to 89 per month in CoS 94, that level of productivity wasn't being achieved. The reason for this was simple. Mick Toller's sidekick, Graeme Ogilvie, the architect of the CoS 94 rostering practices, didn't understand the concept of daily hours density. The number 89 was their holy grail. With 89 hours a month you could roster a pilot engaged solely on ULR ops to complete the magic figure of three North Pacific rotations per month. Simple really, except that it's not.

There are 365 days in a year. The contract entitled Captains to 42 days of leave plus 92 Guaranteed Days Off (GDOs) per year. GDOs covered statutory holidays, weekends, and so on, to which employees in 'normal' professions are entitled. This leaves only 231 working days in the year. From this must be deducted a further seven days for annual ground school examinations and simulator check rides, leaving a total of 224. Using an average of 30 days per month, this equates to 7.47 months. Taking the Holy Grail figure of 89 hours per month and multiplying it by 7.47 gives a total flying hours per annum of 664.5. The flying hours for a North Pacific ULR rotation varies according to the season because of changes in winds. A typical Hong Kong – Los Angeles – Hong Kong pattern is 27.83 hours in winter and 28.17 hours in summer. For our purposes we will use an average of 28. Dividing this into the total flying hours per annum of 664.5 gives a total number of rotations of 23.73. At the magic figure of three rotations per month, these 23.73 rotations equate to 7.91 months required. But, of course, we actually only have 7.47 months available. The figures don't work. 89 is the wrong number. And these figures are for pilots engaged solely on ULR ops. Almost no one did that. There were always short haul and medium haul sectors on everyone's rosters intermingled with the ULR ops. Because of the daily hours density on a mixed roster, it was impossible for them actually to achieve the productivity promised by Ogilvie's pie in the sky rostering system. The hours were there in the contract but they were not achievable. Like the goodies on the top shelf in the sweet shop that can't be reached, all you can do is look at them and salivate. They look great, yes, but you can never actually taste them.

There was another factor that made 89 hours unachievable. When we had first started ULR ops, in order to combat cumulative fatigue caused by repeated exposure to jet lag, the AOA and the company had agreed on the 5-4-3 rule. This stipulated that, after completing a ULR rotation, a pilot would have the following:

A minimum of three days off before operating a short haul pattern; or
A minimum of four days off before operating a medium haul pattern; or
A minimum of five days off before operating another ULR pattern.

In addition, for pilots operating mixed eastbound and westbound ULR ops, there would be a minimum of ten days (not days off, just days) between the end of an eastbound pattern and the start of a westbound pattern and vice versa. These rules worked well in practice and had, up until now, protected Cathay's pilots against the debilitating effects of cumulative fatigue. This is not like just being tired in the ordinary sense after a hard day's work. It builds up in the system over a period of time and has all sorts of effects on health and performance. It feels as though you are continually leading your life jet lagged, which indeed you are. Your sleep cycle is disrupted and you can only sleep in fits and starts of three or four hours. You cannot get any REM and deep sleep. Your immune system becomes depressed and you start to suffer from repeated infections, colds and headaches. It also affects your personal life as you become irritable and short-tempered and it can cause loss of libido. From the flight safety point of view, however, the most significant effects of cumulative fatigue are deterioration in motor skills, attention span and concentration.

It is a very serious concern and fatigue has been cited as a causal factor in many aircraft accidents.

The duties and responsibilities of pilots to ensure that they are fit to undertake flying duties are very different from those of 'normal' employees. They are actually legislated in the governing law. Article 20 of the Air Navigation (Hong Kong) Order (ANO) states, in part, that:

(8)(a) A person shall not be entitled to act as a member of the flight crew of an aircraft registered in Hong Kong if he knows or suspects that his physical or mental condition renders him temporarily or permanently unfit to perform such functions or to act in such capacity.

Article 55(1) of the ANO entitled 'Fatigue of crew – responsibilities of crew' states:

A person shall not act as a member of the crew of an aircraft to which this Article applies if he knows or suspects that he is suffering from, or, having regard to the circumstances of the flight to be undertaken, is likely to suffer from, such fatigue as may endanger the safety of the aircraft or of its occupants.

As well as the responsibilities of crew with regard to fatigue, the ANO also places a responsibility upon the operator. Article 54(2) entitled 'Fatigue of crew – operator's responsibilities' states:

The operator of an aircraft to which this Article applies shall not cause or permit any person to fly therein as a member of its crew if he knows or has reason to believe that that person is suffering from, or, having regard to the circumstances of the flight to be undertaken, is likely to suffer from, such fatigue while he is so flying as may endanger the safety of the aircraft or of its occupants.

Thus the responsibility of pilots to ensure they do not fly knowing they are suffering, or are likely to suffer, from cumulative fatigue is mandated in the legislation. Any breach of these regulations renders the pilot liable to criminal prosecution and the loss of his or her flying licence and livelihood. It is equally incumbent upon the operator that it should not coerce its pilots into flying when they are unfit to do so. It is a very serious matter.

The '5-4-3' and '10-day' rules had stood us in good stead up until then in preventing cumulative fatigue, but they restricted the daily hours density. This didn't suit Clemmow any more because it stopped him from getting to the sweets on the top shelf, so he set about dismantling them.

All aspects of commercial aircraft operations are laid out and mandated in the company's Operations Manual. This manual consists of a number of volumes and, in Cathay's case, the administrative aspects of the operation were contained in Volume 1 (Vol 1). Rostering procedures were also contained in Vol 1 and were split into two parts. Rostering practices (RPs) which contained the locally agreed or 'industrial' aspects of the procedures; and the Approved Flight Time Limitations Scheme (AFTLS or FTLs for short), which covered the mandatory aspects. The AFTLS is derived from the governing legislation published by the regulatory authority, the CAD, in document CAD 371 entitled *The Avoidance of Fatigue in Aircrews*. CAD 371 spells out the absolute bottom line regulations below which you must not go. It is the safety net for the prevention of fatigue. Each operator must produce its own AFTLS based on CAD 371 for approval by the CAD. Some slight variation from the basic regulations may occasionally be permitted to suit unusual local conditions but such variations must provide at least as good as or better protection than the original. Thus a company's AFTLS is a legal requirement and must be complied with at all times. It cannot be unilaterally changed without prior approval from the CAD and, supposedly, in consultation with the AOA. The 5-4-3 rule was included as part of our AFTLS.

In September 1994, Clemmow issued an amendment to Vol 1 that removed the 5-4-3 rule from the AFTLS and relocated it into the rostering practices. In other words he took it out of the mandatory section and put it into the industrial section. He did the same thing to the provision that stated that the minimum crew on ULR ops will be four pilots. We didn't need a crystal ball to see what was coming next. Now that he had removed these two provisions from the AFTLS, he could unilaterally change them without approval from the CAD. In 1996, he issued a further amendment, which stated that, under certain conditions, management could request that a ULR op be operated with a crew of only three pilots. This really was the thin end of the wedge.

The flying task that the Flight Ops Department had accepted from the Commercial Department could not be completed because it was based on the unachievable goal of 89 hours. They were relying on pilots volunteering to work on their days off to help them out but even this was not enough. There was a problem in the Training Department because ASL was taking up far more resources than had originally been planned and this was having a knock-on effect on the passenger operation. We couldn't train enough pilots. There was a provision in the rostering practices for pilots to waive the 5-4-3 rule on a voluntary basis and revert to just the basic CAD 371 safety net. In 1995, a NTC came out stating that, with immediate effect, it would be assumed that everyone had waived the 5-4-3 rule unless rostering management heard to the contrary. The 'volunteer out' option. It didn't work. The overwhelming majority of pilots wrote in stating that they wished to continue to be rostered in accordance with the 5-4-3 rule for fatigue protection.

None of Clemmow's attempted fudges solved the problem. The company was suffering from a severe shortage of pilots caused, in our view, by bad management decisions so his solution was simple. Reduce the number of pilots needed on ULR ops and to hell with the flight safety consequences. It got worse.

The AFTLS stated that, other than ULR ops, which required four pilots, any flight over eight and a half hours required a mandatory minimum crew of three pilots. With the introduction of the Boeing 777-200 in May 1996, when a third pilot was required, management started using pilots who were completely unqualified on the B777 to fulfil this requirement. These pilots had received no conversion training, ground instruction or simulator training of any kind on the B777 other than to be made aware of the location of the emergency exits and associated equipment in a similar manner to the way a passenger is briefed by announcements prior to takeoff. Their first experience of operating the aircraft was with passengers on a commercial flight as a legally required member of the crew complement.

The flight deck of the B777 is very different in its layout from the aircraft on which these pilots were normally employed, typically as S/Os on the B747-400. As an example, the fire handles, used to shut down the engines in the event of an engine fire, were located in a completely different place. In the stress of an emergency situation, an unqualified and inexperienced pilot on the flight deck, unfamiliar with the specific procedures applicable to that particular aircraft, has the propensity to exacerbate, rather than assist with, the situation. This latest move was beyond the pale. This wasn't 'fine tuning'. It wasn't even a temporary 'get you home' fix. Flying aircraft with unqualified pilots as part of the legally required crew was worse than anything I'd seen in all the cowboy operations that I'd worked for in the past. This was a lowering of standards to the point where the safety of the operation was being seriously compromised.

It was also severely at odds with the Mission Statement that was plastered seemingly on every vacant piece of wall space in the Cathay building:

We will be the best airline of the decade.
We put safety and security first.

Not to mention:

We will provide rewarding and enjoyable careers for our staff.

All letters and representations by the AOA were rebuffed by a management that 'reserved its right to manage'; and, as far as they were concerned, we were attempting to interfere in matters that were none of our business. The AOA received a letter informing us that all Ops/AOA meetings were cancelled until further notice. Where had we heard that one before? Unless someone stopped Clemmow, there was no knowing what he might do next. We went to the CAD for help but even that was not without its problems.

With the run-up to 1997, many government departments were pursuing a policy of localisation; that is, filling posts that had previously been held by expatriates with local Chinese officers. This was not a problem in many departments, indeed it was to be encouraged. There were many very competent Chinese officers who had been held back from promotion to higher office by colonial attitudes. Unfortunately, it did present us with a problem in the CAD. Aviation is a particularly technical subject that demands detailed and highly specific knowledge; as much of its managers and administrators as of its technical crew. Much of this can only be gained through operational experience, and positions such as FOIs, the 'hands-on' component of the regulatory authority, are usually filled by pilots, either current or retired. There were few local Chinese professional pilots in Hong Kong with the result that, under the localisation policy, some positions were being filled by career civil servants who lacked technical knowledge. As Clemmow made repeated changes to the AFTLS, the AOA had protested these changes to the CAD. Their own document CAD 371 stipulated that there must be 'consultation between operators and crews to agree on basic roster concepts'. Clemmow was unilaterally making changes to fundamental rules without any consultation whatsoever. The CAD's acting assistant director (flight standards), Norman Lo Shung-man, although being one of the few local appointees to have flying qualifications, seemed out of his depth in the cut and thrust of the commercial world. Given that we were all on a very steep learning curve, perhaps it wasn't all that surprising. He had permitted Clemmow to make these changes without the required consultation with the AOA and had breached the terms of the CAD's own document. 'Stormin'

Norman, as he came to be dubbed, now found himself in a difficult position. If he admitted to his error in response to the AOA's repeated letters and protestations, it would be a huge loss of face in front of his superiors. Instead he tried to bury it in paperwork and obfuscation. Rather than answer our questions directly, he tap-danced around the issues. After months of perseverance to no result, we were left with no other option. If the regulatory authority would not do its job and address our flight safety concerns, we would have to force them to do so.

In November 1996, the AOA applied for an order *certiorari* to institute a judicial review of the CAD's decisions. The reaction was immediate.

In response to our complaints about the three-versus four-man ULR ops, we received a letter dated 15 November 1996 from the CAD Chief of Flight Standards in which he stated:

> I agree that a 3 man crew on a flight requiring in-flight rest is outside the provision of the AOC if it is stated in the Operations Manual that the minimum crew shall consist of four pilots. For any flight to operate outside the requirements of the Operations Manual an operation dispensation must first be issued (CPA Operations Manual Vol 1, Appendix A). This has been brought to the attention of the operator.

In other words, he agreed with the AOA view that what Cathay Pacific Airways was doing was illegal and told them to stop it.

On the subject of unqualified pilots on the B777, the AOA received another letter from the CAD dated 13 December 1996, which stated:

> CPA ... have been told that an inappropriately rated pilot ... can in no way be construed as ... having the qualifications necessary to meet the operational duties of either the commander or the co-pilot ... CAD cannot countenance a control seat on a public transport flight being occupied at any time by other than an appropriately licensed and rated pilot.

In other words the CAD again agreed with the AOA view that what the company was doing in its attempt to cut costs was illegal and detrimental to flight safety. The CAD instructed Cathay management to cease the practice and to ensure in the future that all crew members were properly qualified on the aircraft.

We had successfully tackled two of our major concerns about deteriorating flight safety standards, at least for the moment. The reaction from Clemmow was predictable. He had a major foot stamp and tried to victimise another of my principal officers, as he had done with Nigel Demery in April, but this time he dared not go so far. I was away from Hong Kong on duty and my VPP, Murray Gardner, had signed a letter to Clemmow about direct entry commands in ASL, p.p. on my behalf. Clemmow objected to its content and annotated it with a hand-written note that said, 'I will not respond to this rubbish.' He then convened a special meeting of the Command Selection Panel at which there was only one item on the agenda, the assessment of F/O M.A. Gardner's suitability for command. He was assessed as Category C, that is he would never be considered as suitable for promotion to Captain for the rest of his career with Cathay Pacific. Many Captains in the Check & Training Department were absolutely disgusted with this behaviour and one of them leaked the minutes of the meeting to me.

Those present at the meeting were the GMFC, Ken Barley, the FTM, Rick Fry and the B747-400 FM, Mike Lowes. Barley's behaviour was no surprise. He had already been involved in Nigel Demery's case. Fry was a disappointment. He was relatively new to his position but, as far as we were concerned, had allowed it to be used for political ends. The Check & Training Department was generally held in high regard by the pilots for its fairness and objectivity despite the difficult times we were experiencing industrially. Fry completely undermined that confidence. Mike Lowes' participation was very sad for me personally. I knew Mike quite well. He had a reputation for being somewhat abrasive on occasions but I had always found him to be a straight shooter when it came to dealing with professional matters. I was to have a lot more dealings with him in the future and we worked together very well albeit on different sides of the fence. It was sad to see him involved in this squalid affair.

This latest victimisation backfired on Clemmow. We had been continuing our education process with Pendulum Nights and also produced a video that we sent to all of our members as many of them were based overseas and could not easily attend meetings in Hong Kong. At an EGM held on 20 November 1996, the membership voted overwhelmingly to adopt a policy of contract compliance. This involved only working to the terms of our contracts of employment and nothing more. It consisted of:

Refusing to work on GDOs;
Refusing requests to operate ULR ops with only a three-man crew;
Refusing to waive the 5-4-3 rule;

Refusing to work overtime outside of the contract;

Refusing to 'sell back' leave;

Insisting on our statutory right to have one day off in every seven; and,

Not being contactable when not on duty.

Each of these measures was intended to apply further pressure on management to come to the negotiating table and sort out our problems. Yes, they would make it more difficult for the company to complete the commercial task and might lead to delays and cancellations but, as Geoff Fern had so succinctly put it, green and white tails on the tarmac was the only language they understood. Looking back now, these seem like relatively small measures and, as a North American colleague in USALPA said to me, 'Working to your contract, that's what we do anyway. Isn't that what a contract's for?' At the time, however, they seemed like quite large steps to us.

At the same time as these industrial issues, we were also experiencing serious problems with engineering. Because of the budget cut-backs and increased commercial task, there was less down time available for the ground engineers to maintain the aircraft. The run down in the spares holding meant that spare parts now had to be ordered on an 'as needed' basis and the time taken to rectify defects increased whilst waiting for the parts to arrive. Routine overnight maintenance that had previously been performed on night stops in outstations such as Narita (NRT), Singapore (SIN) and Taipei (TPE) was no longer being completed because of man-hour constraints. A typical example was an occasion in NRT when my aircraft had a rotating beacon that was U/S. It was a simple task to rectify the defect but the ground engineers didn't repair it on the overnight stop because it would take them over their budgeted man hours. Before all these cut-backs, Cathay's aircraft were very well maintained and it was unusual to be handed an aircraft for service with more than one or two Acceptable Deferred Defects (ADDs) in accordance with the MEL. Usually the tech log was clean. This now became the exception rather than the norm and the list of unrectified defects got longer and longer to the point that it took 20 minutes or more just to go through the tech log and the MEL before flight to check that everything was legal. As an example of how things had deteriorated, on 27 September 1996 I was offered an Airbus A330 VR-HLA for service on flight CX715 (HKG-SIN) and return CX714 (SIN-HKG) on 28 September with the following entries in the tech log:

2 PADDs, the earliest dating back to 29th August 1996;
6 SADDs, the earliest dating back to 30th July 1996;
17 ADDs, the earliest dating back to 19th March 1996;
7 DDOs, the earliest dating back to 25th March 1996;
1 Maintenance Concession;
1 OEB
5 NTCs relating to technical matters.

When I investigated all these defects I found that three of the DDOs had been rectified but had not been removed from the tech log, one NTC relating to a thrust reverser had also been rectified but not signed off, and because of that, the Maintenance Concession and the OEB were no longer applicable. In addition, one of the SADDs had been incorrectly entered and the required details relating to the defect were incomplete. Even with these corrections, there were still 29 defects on the aircraft, some of which had remained unrectified for more than seven months. I flew the aircraft and during the return flight got a recurring fault indication relating to the operation of the flaps that had occurred on 12 out of the last 15 sectors flown without being rectified. Whilst the errors in the paperwork might seem relatively minor, it was symptomatic of what was happening in the Engineering Department. Lack of attention to detail. The devil is *in* the detail and, in aviation, it is the little things that can kill you. The '6P rule' is important: Piss poor preparation leads to piss poor performance.

Things were no better on the B747 fleet. The rate of in-flight shutdowns and engine failures had gone through the roof with five shutdowns in the six-week period between 3 July and 11 August 1994. When compared with previous performance and the Rolls-Royce claim that, with proper maintenance, an RB211 engine should only need to be shut down every 50,000 flying hours or about once every ten years, this was a serious degradation in engineering standards.[14] It wasn't an isolated case. A shut-down rate of 4.5 per 50,000 hours in the summer of 1996 led to another investigation by the CAD, and on 5 December 1996, during an inspection of one of the freighter aircraft, the torque bulkhead at the rear of the number one engine pylon was found to have a failure crack across the full width of the bulkhead.[15] This was classified as a serious aircraft incident by the CAD and led to an investigation.

Another incident that occurred in 1996 typified the malaise that was affecting HAECO and led to one of the biggest cover-ups of Clemmow's tenure. At 14:20 on 23 June, the second of Cathay's brand new Boeing 777-200s landed at Kai Tak after operating flight CX706 from Bangkok.

On the flight deck, the crew was receiving a cargo fire warning, an indication of a fire in one of the cargo holds. The Captain quite rightly ordered an emergency evacuation of the aircraft. It turned out that the fire warning was false, triggered by excessive moisture in the hold from wet cargo and fruit, but he was not to know that at the time. The smoke detectors in the hold were photoelectric and unable to differentiate between heavy humidity and smoke. During the investigation of the incident, it was found from the maintenance records that, during the overnight stop after its arrival from Hong Kong, a large number of life-jackets had been installed on the aircraft by the ground engineers in Bangkok. These should have been installed on the aircraft in Hong Kong prior to its departure but it had been in the hangar undergoing maintenance. Because of time and manning constraints that were placed upon the engineer in charge of the operation, there was a breakdown in the communication and certification system that resulted in the aircraft being released to service missing these life-jackets. It had flown a revenue service with passengers on board before the error was picked up by the engineers in Bangkok. This was a serious breach of the safety regulations and resulted in another investigation. The engineer was privately interviewed by a CAD inquiry board and he expressed his views as to why the breakdown had occurred. In his opinion the primary factor was the pressure he'd been placed under by his managers. Afterwards he was called into his supervisor's office at HAECO and asked, 'What the hell have you been saying to the CAD? You want to be careful criticising the system.' In so many words he was told to keep his mouth shut if he wanted to keep his job. I met with this engineer personally and he asked me if the AOA could help him and his colleagues to set up a confidential reporting system as they had no effective union in HAECO since Turnbull had wielded his axe. This was the sort of pressure they were working under, continually in fear of their jobs.

Shortly after this incident, a B747 got airborne from HKG bound for Vancouver. After takeoff, the Captain was contacted on the company frequency by Jeff Morris who told him that an engineer who had witnessed the takeoff had seen a fuel leak from one of the engines. It was quite common for fuel to vent from the vent surge tanks in the wing tips on takeoff when fully loaded so the Captain wasn't particularly concerned. Nevertheless, he monitored the fuel state carefully but could find no evidence of a leak. Morris contacted him again and suggested that he should return to Hong Kong. After conducting further fuel checks prior to entering North Pacific (NOPAC) airspace he was happy that there was no sign of a fuel leak and advised Morris accordingly. He received a reply to the effect that 'The DFO orders you to shut down the engine and return to Hong Kong.' He asked to talk to Clemmow directly but was refused. Faced with a direct order there was nothing else for him to do but comply. On arrival in Hong Kong, before he could get down from the flight deck to see what was going on, the ground engineers had the engine cowling opened and then closed again. When he got downstairs and asked to see the fuel leak he was told, 'It's OK, we've fixed it now.' He could get no further details of the supposed problem. Subsequently a ground engineer approached the AOA in confidence and reported that the real reason for Clemmow ordering a turn-back was because the same mistake had been made again. Some life-jackets had not been installed on the aircraft. Had the CAD found out about this so soon after the 777 incident, there would have been very serious implications both for the company's AOC and its senior management.

The victimisation of Gardner by making him Cat C was the last desperate act of a man at the end of his reign of terror. Clemmow retired in December 1996 and we were extremely pleased to be rid of him. In our view, he had presided over one of the worst Flight Operations regimes in living memory and left behind him a department where flight safety had been repeatedly compromised purely in pursuit of financial gain. As one wag reported, his leaving party was held in a telephone kiosk on one of the outlying islands, such was his popularity!

With 1997 approaching, there were management reshuffles scheduled and changes in the Flight Ops Department; what's more, we were to get a new government in July. We were going to be living in interesting times.

8

Crew Change

*'Those whose words are humble while they increase war prepa-
rations are going to advance. Those whose words are strong
and who advance aggressively are going to retreat.'*

Sun Tzu, *The Art of War*

In January 1997, Rod Eddington became chairman of Ansett Australia,
the airline controlled by Rupert Murdoch's News Corporation. His departure from Cathay resulted in a 'cabinet' reshuffle.

Linus Cheung Wing Lam held the position of deputy managing director
of Cathay serving under Eddington. Linus had been present as part of
the management team at the 'Commitment Days' and had impressed me,
at any rate, with his practical approach. Rather than spout rhetoric, he
spoke instead of his optimism for the future of Hong Kong after the
handover, how we should embrace it as our home instead of viewing it
merely as a stopping-off point and do ourselves a favour, learn to speak
Cantonese. I certainly shared his views on the first two points but am
ashamed to say that, even after living here for 25 years, like many *gweilos*,
I still have not mastered the local language. Linus was seen as being
groomed to be the first local Chinese Taipan of Cathay Pacific. It came
as a surprise to Sutch when, after 23 years of service with the company,
he abruptly left in January 1994 to become chief executive of Hong Kong
Telecom. He subsequently went on to become the deputy chairman of
PCCW Limited and the chairman of Asia Television Limited. There was
much speculation at the time that Linus got out when he saw the direction Sutch was taking the company in. His departure prompted the appoint-

ment of Simon Heale as joint deputy managing director (commercial and marketing) working alongside Turnbull as deputy managing director (corporate development). Heale had previously held the post of chief operating officer of Dragonair and was scheduled to leave to become managing director of the Lloyd's of London broking division at Swire Fraser.

Linus's sudden departure forced a change in Sutch's plans. Simon Heale came with a good recommendation from the Dragonair pilots. They had found him to be a fair man to work for with a practical approach. Heale was replaced at Dragonair by Philip Chen Nan Lok of whom we will hear more later.

Late in 1996, I had asked for a meeting with Eddington to discuss the safety matters that were of concern to the pilots since it was pointless persisting any further with Clemmow. Eddington declined my request saying that it would make more sense to speak to Heale and Turnbull since they would be taking over from him soon. I met them both at Swire House shortly afterwards, explained the pilots' concerns and expressed the hope that, with the new management team in place and the departure of Clemmow, we could turn over a new leaf in relations between management and the AOA. After the meeting, Simon Heale walked me to the lift, shook me by the hand, said it had been nice to meet me and then looked me in the eyes and said, 'Good luck, John.' He was sending me a message. Shortly afterwards, he jumped ship and went to work for the Swires' arch rival, Jardine Fleming, first as its finance director and then as chief operating officer. He later went on to become chief executive of the London Metal Exchange. I often thought how different things might have been had Simon Heale become managing director of Cathay instead of Turnbull after Eddington's departure, but then again, he probably would not have gone along with Sutch's plans. He could see where things were heading, which is why he got out.

Eddington stayed at Ansett for three years and on 2 May 2000 moved to BA, taking up the post of CEO, replacing Bob Ayling. On 14 September 2001, after 66 years of operations, Ansett went bust with debts of US$1.8 billion putting more than 16,000 people out of work. There has been speculation that Eddington managed to escape blame for the poor financial state of the airline, apparently aided by his board membership of News Corp, as others were loath to criticise him publicly. The blame for the collapse has tended to be worn by the management of Air New Zealand (ANZ). ANZ, previously a 50 per cent shareholder, acquired full ownership of Ansett in February 2000, buying out News Corp's stake for AU$680 million. This essentially merged Ansett and ANZ into one group, called 'Air New Zealand/Ansett' although both airlines maintained their individual operations. The purchase by ANZ was widely viewed as a mistake. Monash University aviation economics academic Professor Keith Trace commented '. . . by taking it on, they ensured that their own airline was in terrible danger. That was a dreadful mistake. They were taken for a ride.'[16]

At BA in 2002, Eddington launched a cost-cutting programme entitled 'Future Size and Shape'. Now where had we heard that before? On 17 February 2002, the *Sunday Times* ran an article by Dominic O'Connell which asked 'if Rod Eddington, Bob Ayling's successor at BA, is on a mission impossible?' In the article, a BA 747 Captain summed up Eddington's vision for the future as 'Future Shape: pear'. I also wrote a letter to the *Sunday Times* on the subject. An article that appeared in the 28 June 2002 edition of *Private Eye*, quoting extracts from that letter and criticising Eddington's track record at Cathay and Ansett, prompted a somewhat petulant response from him in the letters column of the 12 July issue in which he stated:

John Warham's letter to the *Sunday Times* regarding my tenure at Cathay Pacific actually had BA to do with the truth.

The 'Operation Better Shape' referred to did not involve the loss of a single job at Cathay Pacific. It was a business practice review, not a job axing programme. Many of the 49 Cathay Pacific pilots who sadly lost their jobs last year probably don't know me from Adam – I left Cathay Pacific in 1996. In my book, that doesn't even count as a near miss.

One wonders if the 44 Cathay F/Es who lost their jobs as a result of ASL which was formed in 1995, the year before he left, would share his view.

Eddington took the controversial decision to permanently ground the BA Concorde fleet in 2003 and left BA in September 2005. Since then he has served as a non-executive director of the Rio Tinto Group and on the board of the Allco Finance Group, where he was one of three non-executive directors to approve Allco's ill-fated acquisition of Rubicon Holdings, which led to the company's collapse in 2008. A previously announced plan for Eddington to become chairman of ANZ Banking Group of Australia and New Zealand was first delayed from February 2009 to February 2010 and then finally scuttled on 9 August 2009. It is possible that his directorship of the scandal-plagued Rio Tinto Group made such a position for him at ANZ untenable, as corporate espionage by Rio Tinto against the Chinese government was a hot issue at the time. 'Future Shape: pear', indeed. With responsibility comes accountability.

With the departure of Clemmow in December 1996, Ken Barley was appointed DFO of Cathay and Mike Lowes took over Barley's post as GMFC. With the new team in place, we in the AOA General Committee hoped we could now start making some progress towards resolving some of the outstanding issues that were of concern to us. However, Barley had inherited some problems: the Gardner situation, ASL, CAD and the Airbus. How he handled these would be a good indicator for our future relationship.

Things did not get off to an auspicious start. I went to see him at the end of December and put our cards on the table. If we were going to forge a new relationship and work together, the first thing that I needed was for Gardner's Cat C rating to be removed. My initial approach didn't look too hopeful when he replied, 'That decision is set in stone.'

I quickly learned that Barley's stone was permeable. After the meeting, Mike Lowes took me aside and said, 'Leave it with me, John, we'll sort it.'

Shortly afterwards, Gardner's categorisation was rescinded. At least Mike had done the right thing. Having been part of the original decision, he was also part of its remedy.

Barley also announced at that first meeting that he would no longer be honouring the terms of the Mixed Crew Flying Agreement (MCFA) between the AOA and the company. The terms of the MCFA specified how and under what conditions training of ASL crews could take place. It ensured that there was the absolute minimum of contact between the Cathay crews and ASL crews during their training and that, once it was completed, ASL crews could only operate freighter aircraft. The agreement also specified that ASL crews would have their own, separate flight despatch, planning and crew transport facilities. There was so much resentment amongst the Cathay crews that even Clemmow saw the need to keep them apart. The rationale for Barley's decision was that Clemmow had signed the agreement, not him. I pointed out to him that Clemmow had signed the agreement on behalf of the company and that if he was simply going to dishonour the agreements we already had in place that didn't make for a very trusting relationship, not only with the AOA, but also with the pilots in general who he was now supposed to be leading. However, if that's what he wanted, I'd just let my members know that their new DFO, like his predecessor, was not to be trusted. At that, he threw a bit of a tantrum and started ranting about the right to manage.

Not that old chestnut again! It was odd that when Clemmow had spouted that kind of rhetoric, he almost sounded convincing, but Barley just couldn't carry it off. I was tempted to respond that, given the state our airline was now in, the aircrew would very much like to see some management, but I bit my tongue.

Mike Lowes interceded again after the meeting and asked me to give him some time to talk Barley round to discussing the agreement rather than just ignoring it. Again he was successful and negotiations reopened. We felt that we might now have flown out of the storm clouds into some clear air so, as a gesture of goodwill, in February the General Committee recommended suspending contract compliance and the membership voted to endorse their recommendation on 4 March. When talks resumed, the management team was headed by Mike Lowes and the AOA team consisted of Gardner, the gen sec, John Findlay, and me as the core members. The first item on the agenda was ASL.

ASL was a mess. What was now supposed to be a stand-alone operation with its own Check & Training Department and dedicated crews was nowhere near ready to be independent. The one-year time-scale for completion set in October 1995 was hopelessly optimistic. There were two reasons for this. Firstly, because of the abysmal conditions of employment on offer, they hadn't received anywhere near the number of applications they had anticipated and were having trouble recruiting the requisite staff. We had not helped the situation by letting it be known through our IFALPA connections that we considered ASL to be specifically designed to undercut the mainline operation and disadvantage our pilots. USALPA in particular took a very dim view of this, especially when they found out that Cathay was using UPAS, USALPA's own employment agency, to recruit crews for ASL. Clemmow had crowed about this at the time but stopped very quickly when he received a letter from their president, Randy Babbitt, cancelling the contract and threatening him with legal action if he didn't stop misrepresenting the situation. He might take on the AOA but he certainly didn't have the stomach for a fight with our American cousins. The second reason for their problem was the calibre of recruit they were attracting. The command failure rate was running at 40 per cent. To put this in perspective, the failure rate in Cathay was around 2.5 per cent. At one point, for a very short time, it did rise to almost 10 per cent but that prompted a review of the syllabus to find out where we were going wrong in our training. In the ASL situation, the candidates just weren't up to the job.

We applied a bit more pressure to get Barley to sign a new MCFA. We held some meetings with the Check & Training Captains, explained the situation, and asked them to boycott ASL training. Many of them were very supportive but we couldn't get a consensus for a full boycott. Some of them did offer simply to resign from Check & Training and return to line duties. Rick Fry got wind of this and sent them all letters stating that a resignation from the Check & Training Department would be considered a resignation from the company. This was probably an empty threat but no one was prepared to test it, at least not right then. In that respect our tactic failed but in another way it was successful. It applied sufficient additional pressure that, in March, Barley signed a new MCFA. That was not the end of the ASL story and we will return to it again later.

There was something that happened during the Check & Training initiative that indicated to me just how spineless some of the membership were. One Captain in particular came into my office and explained at great length why he could not support the initiative. The crux of his argument was that his first and overriding responsibility was to his students and he could not possibly jeopardise their future progress and their careers. The fact that he was actually training his Cathay colleagues out of a job seemed to escape him. I didn't mind men who came to me and said they were resigning from the AOA simply because they didn't have the stomach for the fight. This did happen later on when things got confrontational; and, while it was always a matter for regret when a member resigned, I at least admired them for their candour and honesty. What I objected to were people who made lame excuses to cover up their lack of spinal fortitude. They weren't fooling anyone but themselves.

Barley's problems with the CAD started as soon as he got in the DFO's seat. On 9 December I had a private meeting with CAD representatives chaired by Peter Birkett. He had previously held a senior position in the department but had been moved sideways during the localisation manoeuvres. It seemed he'd been called back to sort out the mess that Stormin' Norman had made of the AFTLS amendments. He told me his superiors were very upset by our threatened judicial review as it made them look bad and could we find a way around it? He came as close as any civil servant can to making an apology when I said, 'We didn't really want to go that route but we were left with no alternative.'

Referring to Stormin' Norman's handling of the situation he remarked, 'I would have handled things differently.'

'Yes, it could have been handled better,' I responded.

'It's a sign of the times,' he replied with a smile.

After our meeting he sent a directive to Barley ordering him to change one of the amendments to Vol 1. The effect was that it put a stop to three-man ULR ops. This was a big win for us but there was more to come. We'd been sending the CAD reports on the fatigue issues that were affecting our pilots on sustained ULR ops including medical reports where Cathay's own principal medical officer (PMO) had diagnosed cumulative fatigue. Management's reaction to our complaints was typical of what we'd come to expect. John Nicholls, a Captain based at Heathrow (LHR), started having health problems because of the rosters he was flying. Barley, then GMFC under Clemmow, called him into the office and made him sign a letter to the effect that if his sickness record didn't improve he accepted that either he would relocate himself and his family back to Hong Kong where the rosters would supposedly be more conducive to his health, or he would be dismissed. In our view, the threat of either having to relocate his family halfway back across the world or lose his job was deliberate intimidation. At the time, we had offered to take John's case to the CAD but he wouldn't do it because he was afraid of being subjected to further intimidation.

His was not an isolated case. Peter Birkett announced that he was setting up a Flight Time Limitations Working Group (FTLWG) to review the whole issue of ULR operations as a result of 'diagnosed cases of cumulative fatigue'. This was a massive win for us and got the whole issue out in the open. In return, we suspended our judicial review proceedings. The FTLWG was to comprise representatives from the CAD, airline management (including Cathay, Dragonair and Air Hong Kong), and pilots' representatives including the Hong Kong Airline Pilots Association (HKALPA) and the Guild of Air Pilots & Air Navigators (GAPAN). HKALPA was the umbrella organisation that represented the HKAOA and Dragonair Pilots' Association at the international level through IFALPA. Barley's reaction was typical. He tried to have HKALPA excluded from the group, saying that Cathay did not 'think it appropriate' that pilots' representatives should be included in the working group!

Birkett was having none of it and politely told Barley to wind his neck in. It didn't stop there though. Our nominated representatives on the FTLWG were Terry Heyes, who was now president of HKALPA, and Nigel Demery. Barley refused to roster them for time off to attend the first meeting and actually ensured that they were out of Hong Kong on flying duty. This meant that I had to attend the first meeting on their behalf. To say that Peter Birkett was pissed off by this would be something of an understatement. After that we had no more trouble with rostered time for Terry and Nigel to attend the FTLWG but clearly the storm clouds were gathering again.

While the 'negotiations' were continuing, unbeknown to us management had been working behind the scenes and, in May, Lowes unilaterally put out another amendment to Vol 1, which made three-man ULR ops the norm without any agreement from the Captain. The amendment also extended the eight and a half hour third pilot rule to ten and a half hours. It was an underhand act, especially as we were supposed to be sitting in negotiations with those very issues on the agenda. It just demonstrated their bad faith.

We learned a lesson about dealing with the Swires from that. The slightest hint of compromise in negotiations is taken as a sign of weakness to be exploited. We showed them a small indication of goodwill and they went behind our backs to try and take advantage of it. We would not make the same mistake again, ever. Quite simply, they couldn't be trusted. At an EGM held on 21 May, the AOA membership voted to reinstate contract compliance and the news hit the press the next day.

One of our moles at the Flight Ops midday meeting reported to me that Turnbull was out of town but apparently 'went berserk' when he heard. At the meeting Barley said he was glad Turnbull was out of town and hoped he could sort it out before he got back. So now we knew for sure who was wearing the trousers. I saw Mike Lowes in the Cathay Club that night and he said to me, 'I'm pissed off with the way you've gone. I've been trying very hard to work with you and it doesn't make my job any easier.'

'I appreciate that you've been trying but what pissed me off is the way you punch out yet another amendment to Vol 1 when we're supposed to be in the middle of discussions on that very subject,' was my reply.

'It wasn't intended as an attempt to change them, it was more an admin thing and work had been going on on that before I got the job. I was under pressure to issue it.'

So that confirmed it. It wasn't Lowes – it was coming from higher up; and, with the intel we had, it seemed that it originated from above Barley. It was as Sutch had said to me: It was coming from Turnbull, from Sutch and from the Swire board in London.

In response to the AOA vote, management issued new 'punitive' rosters for June with minimum days off and maximum reserve duty. They also tried to divide us. Barley announced in the press an offer to roster volunteers with: '. . . the maximum possible number of days off, provided they were prepared to work them.'[17] To us, that rather seemed to defeat the object. Cathay's spokesman, Charlie Stewart-Cox, denied that the offer was, 'aggressively designed to split the union'. He stated that 'An aggressive move is the refusal to work one's days off when it's not an onerous task.' [17] Not an onerous task! They just didn't get it. If we had enough pilots, or if Barley did his job and only accepted a commercial task commensurate with the available resources within the Flight Ops Department, we wouldn't have to work on our days off.

Things took a turn for the worse. Three days after the vote to reinstitute contract compliance, the A330 fleet was grounded because of problems with the Rolls-Royce Trent 700 engines.

I had left B747 fleet and converted onto the Airbus A330 at the beginning of 1995. I operated my last flight on the mighty 747 on 26 January 1995 by which time I had accumulated a total of 5,849 hours on the aircraft with a grand total of 11,475 flying hours. I had left the 747 at the invitation of Barley who had written to me asking whether I would like to volunteer to join this 'exciting new fleet'. My initial reaction was to turn down the invitation as my love affair with Boeing aircraft was still ongoing and I knew that the real reason for the request was that not many of the Senior Captains were volunteering to go to the Airbus and there was a concern about a lack of overall experience on the fleet. However, the long-term ULR ops on the 747 were beginning to affect me physically. I was continually tired and run-down and was repeatedly falling ill with colds and flu. With my new AOA commitments, it made sense to move onto a regional fleet. It wasn't brought home to me just how tired I was until three or four months after I'd moved to the Airbus when my wife told me that it was nice to have John back instead of the bear she'd been living with for the last couple of years.

One of the debilitating effects of cumulative fatigue is that, like stress, the person suffering from it often is the last person to recognise the fact.

During my conversion onto the A330, I flew with one of the Airbus test pilots, Harry Clark. Harry had been the Captain of Kuwait Airways flight KU221 from Kuwait City to Karachi that was hijacked on 3 December 1984 by four Lebanese Shi'a hijackers and diverted to Tehran. The stand-off lasted a week and only came to an end when Iranian security forces stormed the aircraft. During the course of the hijack, women, children and Muslims were released but two American officials from the US Agency for International Development, Charles Hegna and William Stanford, were shot dead and their bodies dumped on the tarmac. The few dozen passengers left on board, particularly Americans, were threatened and tortured. At one point the hijackers tied Harry up and wired him with explosives. I asked him about this on an overnight stop in Penang and, remembering my own experience in Togo, remarked that it must have been very frightening. He told me that, at the time, he didn't remember being particularly scared. The reason was that, because the hijackers hadn't allowed the hostages to use the lavatories for some time, while he was tied up he was desperate to empty his bowels and was using all of his concentration not to soil himself. As he put it, 'If I was going to die, I was determined they weren't going to find me with shit in my pants.'

Harry told me an amusing story about an episode that happened when he returned to the UK after his release. The chaps who live at Credenhill near Hereford invited him over to stay a few days for a debriefing. They arranged for a helicopter to pick him up from the grounds of a hospital near his home. Everything was arranged. All he had to do was report to the hospital at the appointed hour and let the receptionist know who he was. Harry followed instructions, went to the reception desk, told the attendant who he was and that he had come to meet his helicopter.

'Really, sir, now why don't you just sit down and we'll have someone attend to you,' came the reply.

'No, I'm here to meet my helicopter. Do you know what time it's landing?'

'Of course you are, sir. I'm sure it'll be here soon, now just take a seat,' insisted the nurse.

Two large men in white coats were approaching holding what looked like a strait-jacket when, just then, the sound of helicopter rotor blades came whomping through the window. It turned out that the facility was a mental hospital and not everyone had been informed of Harry's transport arrangements.

The introduction of the A330 was plagued by a number of problems with both the engines and the hydraulic systems. In all the time that I had flown Boeing aircraft, I only ever had one major hydraulic failure when we got airborne from Luton in a Monarch 720B. While the gear was retracting, a hydraulic line ruptured and sprayed Skydrol in aerosol form into the atmosphere. Vauxhall car works was situated just off the end of R/W 26 at Luton and there were a lot of brand new cars parked in its car park awaiting delivery. The Skydrol cloud descended over them and, since Skydrol in that form replicates the properties of Nitromors, Mr Vauxhall wasn't very pleased.

The A330 had three hydraulic systems nominated blue, yellow and green. In contrast to Mr Boeing's products, during the first nine months of line operations on the A330, I experienced four total hydraulic system losses, one each on the blue and yellow systems and two on the green system. These failures weren't being caused by new technology, they were rather more fundamental. In the drive to keep the weight of the aircraft down to the minimum, the thickness of various components in the hydraulic system had been pared down to the point where some of them were rupturing under pressure. These failures highlighted three other situations that were concerning us. The first was a new company policy that had been introduced called On Time Performance (OTP); the second was the Corporate Safety Department; the third was Extended-range Twin-engine Operational Performance Standards (ETOPS).

The Commercial Department had determined that one of the main causes of passenger dissatisfaction was flight delay. OTP was introduced as a means of monitoring delays, which made good commercial sense. However, the way it was implemented impacted on all aspects of the operation, some to their detriment. Under OTP each flight departure and arrival was timed to the minute and a reason had to be given on the CAR for each and every minute of delay. Regular 'delay' meetings were held at which each department, Flight Ops, Engineering, Traffic, Catering and so on was 'apportioned blame'. OTP became almost an obsession as each department strove to minimise any delays attributed to it. If an aircraft was late in from its previous service, we pilots were put under pressure to rush our pre-flight procedures and checks so as to still depart on time on the next sector. Ground engineers were under the same commercial pressure. Prior to the introduction of OTP, when an aircraft was brought in with an unserviceability, the engineers would do their best to rectify the defect even if it meant that the next service might be delayed. After the introduction of OTP, their first reaction was to reach for the MEL to see whether or not the aircraft could still be legally dispatched with the defect unrectified and signed off in the tech log as an ADD. OTP just exacerbated the problems that were already evident with maintenance.

Eventually the serviceability situation got so bad that engineering delays could not be avoided and it began to have an adverse effect on OTP. The solution was that a 'Get Well' programme was instigated where individual aircraft were taken off the line and scheduled for sufficient hangar time to allow the ground engineers to do their job properly and rectify the defects. It was a good solution but one that should never have been needed in the first place if commercial considerations had not been given priority over safety.

Under Clemmow's regime, the Flight Safety Department (FSD) had been reorganised. Originally it was a dedicated department independent of the Flight Ops Department and its head reported directly to the managing director. This was intended to prevent any potential for 'filtering out' of information by Flight Ops management. The structure was designed as a direct communication route from the FSD to board level to prevent any cover-ups, and it had served us well. As part of the cost savings it was restructured and became the Corporate Safety Department. Rather than being responsible solely for monitoring safety in Flight Ops, this new department had a much wider remit and was now responsible for company-wide safety. Concerns were expressed by many pilots that this would result in a reduction in resources devoted specifically to flight safety and thus dilute the oversight in our own specialised area. In the event of an incident taking place that had a bearing on flight safety, the Captain of the aircraft was required to submit an occurrence report to the company, which, in more serious cases, also had to be forwarded to the CAD. Although the latter was the responsibility of the Captain, his duty was deemed to have been done by sending the report to the company which would then forward it on to the CAD if and when required.

This system had worked well prior to the reorganisation. After this restructuring, however, as president of the AOA, I was approached by two members of the new Corporate Safety Department, Peter Wigens and Dirk Scott. Peter was the head of the Air Safety Department and Dirk was head of the Ground Safety Department, both directly under the manager of the new 'umbrella' department headed by David Mawdsley. Peter reported to me that Mawdsley was filtering occurrence reports that should have been forwarded to the CAD so as to present a rosier picture on in-flight incidents than was actually the case. Peter, Dirk and I held a number of covert meetings over a period of months in a curry house in Kowloon City. At one meeting, they told me they believed that, rather than reporting directly to the managing director as he was supposed to, Mawdsley was colluding with senior Flight Ops Department managers, again to filter information that should have been reported to the CAD.

I had personal experience of this filtration after the double failure of the green hydraulic system I experienced on the Airbus. On 9 April 1996 I operated a flight from Hong Kong to Taipei and onwards to Seoul. On the first sector we had a total loss of the green hydraulic system. As well as operating some of the flight controls, the green system was the sole hydraulic source for extending and retracting the landing gear and for control of the nose wheel steering on the ground. Because of this failure we had to use the abnormal procedure to extend the landing gear on approach into Taipei and the aircraft had to be towed off the runway after landing. The ground engineers in Taipei did not have sufficient time to find and repair the source of the leak if OTP was not going to be compromised. On top of that, there was a night curfew in Seoul and any substantial delay would have meant the aircraft and passengers staying overnight in Taipei and would have cost the company money. The engineers told me they were unable to find any leak, replenished the hydraulic fluid and signed the aircraft off as fit for further flight. On the next sector from Taipei to Seoul, we experienced the same problem on the climb out. As a precaution, and in an attempt to preserve what fluid was left to lower the landing gear on the approach into Seoul, we depressurised the green system. Although this slowed the leak somewhat, ultimately it proved to be of no avail as, when the system was re-pressurised on the approach into Seoul, the whole of the contents were lost again and the same abnormal procedures had to be employed.

During the overnight stop in Seoul the ground engineers were able to find and replace the source of the leak, an aileron actuator that had a cracked casing. As required, I submitted occurrence reports for both sectors to the Corporate Safety Department under the heading of 'Total loss of green hydraulic system'. For such failures it was mandatory for these reports to be forwarded to the CAD. I subsequently found out that Mawdsley had only forwarded the first of my reports to the CAD. When I asked him why, he told me that he had recategorised the second failure as a hydraulic leak, not a total loss of the system and that, as such, the second report was of a less severe nature and did not require forwarding to the CAD. I challenged Mawdsley on this but he remained adamant. As the Captain of the aircraft it was my duty to ensure that my reports were forwarded to the CAD and I requested him to do so.

So why was he doing this? I believe the answer is twofold. Firstly, the CAD was monitoring the problems with the hydraulic systems closely. To have admitted that the same aircraft had the same problem on two consecutive sectors would have caused serious questions to be asked, especially since Taipei had good engineering facilities where the problem could and should have been properly rectified prior to the next flight. Secondly there was ETOPS.

The A330 was intended to replace the B747 on our Australian routes. As the 747 was more expensive to operate than the A330, this would increase profit and made good commercial sense. However, this came with a flight safety proviso. On normal operations, twin-engine aircraft are required always to be within 60 minutes single-engine flying time of a suitable *en route* alternate airfield to cater for diversion in case of an engine failure. When you lose an engine on a twin, the checklist is very clear: 'LAND AT NEAREST SUITABLE AIRPORT.' There should be no exceptions. If the other engine fails, you now have an aluminium glider, which, from cruise altitude, gives you about 20 minutes in the air until you meet terra firma. Aviation is all about 'what ifs'. On a four-engine aircraft, if you lose one and are down to three, once you have the aircraft safely configured your next thought should be, what if we lose another one? What are we going to do then? Always have a contingency plan in place. Always have an escape route. On a twin with an engine failure, there is no real decision to be made. Get it on the ground ASAP.

The 60-minute rule presented a problem on our Australian routes. Because of the long over-water segments and lack of airfields, there is a significant amount of time when the aircraft is much more than 60 minutes away from a suitable diversion. The answer to this conundrum is ETOPS. Under certain strictly controlled circumstances, properly maintained and crewed aircraft are permitted to operate up to 180 minutes single engine flying time from an *en route* alternate. In order to qualify for this, the aircraft must have a demonstrated despatch and in-flight reliability record that is much higher than in non-ETOPS service. With the introduction of the A330, we were undergoing ETOPS certification so that we could put it on the Australian routes. Of course, the more in-flight engine and systems failures we encountered, the less likely it was that the CAD would grant this. Could this be the reason why Mawdsley was filtering our occurrence reports? The cynics amongst the pilot group suspected it might be since any delay to ETOPS certification would incur a significant commercial penalty. During the certification process, there were a number of incidents that happened that heightened our suspicions.

From its introduction into service with Cathay on the A330, the Trent engine was unreliable. There were problems with fuel leaks caused by cracked pipes that fractured under vibration. An engine flamed out in descent for no apparent reason and another one lost power on takeoff when the fuel flow cut back. The C duct on one engine imploded during a ground run and there were 14 precautionary engine changes in the hangar after faults were found during checks. Fortunately, none of these affected ETOPS certification because they were not shut down in the air. On a flight from Indonesia, one of the Airbus management pilots had an engine problem soon after climb out. Instead of shutting the engine down and returning to his departure airfield, he just throttled it back and flew the aircraft all the way back to Hong Kong, effectively on one engine. Passengers reported that there was a lot of vibration throughout the flight coming from the failed, but still running, engine. Again under the ETOPS certification rules it did not count as an unscheduled in-flight engine shut-down and, therefore, did not adversely affect the performance criteria.

There were other fudges going on. Despatch reliability is also a criterion on ETOPS certification. Did the aircraft actually depart on time? On one of our ETOPS proving flights outbound from HKG, the aircraft was AOG on arrival and could not be repaired in time for the departure the next morning. The solution to this was simple. Fly another aircraft down there overnight and operate the return flight with the replacement aircraft. The statistics showed that the despatch reliability met the criterion but it was hardly within the spirit of the rules. It is not general airline practice to have spare aircraft sitting around doing nothing just in case they're needed for backup. That would be an anathema to the accountants because aircraft only make money when they're in the air.

Even when we did get ETOPS certification, the rules got bent. The ink was hardly dry on the approval when a flight from Australia was unable to depart because the weather was below limits at one of the *en route* alternates and there was no other suitable airport. According to the rules, the flight could not depart until the weather cleared at the alternate; otherwise, there would be a route segment where the aircraft would be over the 180-minute single-engine flying time limit. A management pilot told the Captain just to load an extra hour's fuel and come on back anyway. He expressed reservations about this plan since he wasn't sure that simply bunging on some extra fuel and ignoring the 180-minute rule was what he'd been taught on his half-day ETOPS course. His boss ordered him to bring it back so he did as instructed. The trouble was there was a CAD FOI on board who observed all this and was less than impressed. We came very close to having our brand new ETOPS approval withdrawn.

All this was going on at the same time as a spike in the engine failure rate on the 747; there were five engine failures in eleven days. Engineers reported to the AOA that the problem was lack of routine maintenance. One in particular told me, 'We're so short of staff and downtime we've got men burning themselves working on hot engines and blokes working in fuel tanks that haven't been properly ventilated.'

Even when they did get some downtime, there was a shortage of spares. The new Taikoo Aircraft Engineering Co. Ltd (TAECO) facility that had recently been opened in Xiamen using cheap Chinese workers wasn't helping much either. The labour might be nice and cheap but when they drop a jumbo off the jacks the cost savings get offset. An engineer reported to me that the first aircraft they serviced in Xiamen had to go straight into the hangar on its return to Hong Kong to repair the repair.

Matters came to a head on 24 May 1997 when both Cathay's and

Dragonair's A330 fleets were grounded because of engine gearbox bearing problems. I got a telephone call at 06:00 as I was sitting in my study beavering away on some admin. It was Barley. The conversation went along the following lines:

'Good morning, Ken, you're up bright and early.'

'Yes I've been up for some time. I'm calling to tell you that a Dragonair A330 has had an engine failure. We were hoping that it was going to be something else but it's the same problem with the gearbox so the A330 fleet's been grounded. I don't know how long it will take to fix but I would hope that during this period it would be in the company's interest for the chaps to work normally.'

'I'll have to speak to the committee on that, Ken.'

'OK, I'll wait for your call then.'

'OK, thanks for the call, bye.'

'Bye.'

I contacted the GC members that I could get in touch with and asked for opinions. To a man they asked why we should help out now after everything that had been done to us.

'We've got problems and they've refused to help for the last three years, in fact they just go behind our backs and make things worse. Now they've got problems and they expect us to help at the drop of a hat. Fuck them,' was a typical response.

Rather than just dismiss the idea out of hand, I thought we might be able to get something for our cooperation on a quid pro quo basis. Later that morning I called Barley back and said, 'Ken, I may be able to talk the GC into recommending the suspension of contract compliance if you could give me some kind of gesture of goodwill in return, such as withdrawing the latest Vol 1 amendment.'

'I'm not going to do that,' came the response.

'Well, Ken, if you want them to help, I need to show the pilots that you're prepared to give them something in return.'

'We'll manage on our own,' was his reply and he slammed down the phone.

9

PSYOPS 1

'Rationality will not save us.'
Robert S. McNamara, *The Fog of War*

'I was absolutely delighted when they described our report as "absolute garbage". If people haven't got something substantive to say they resort to abuse. Abuse is much the best kind of criticism to receive because it means they haven't got an argument against you.'
Anon, *Private Eye*

If Barley had any misconception that he was a popular choice as the new leader of the Flight Ops Department, or that he had the support of the pilots, he was about to be rudely awakened. Any new leader has an opportunity to stamp his mark on a new command and rally the support of the troops. The first two or three decisions he takes are critical to establishing his power base and determining the future style of his command.

It is the same on the flight deck. The Captain's leadership style determines the atmosphere. Having served as an F/O with different types of Captains, I knew what I wanted on my flight deck when I was promoted. I ran a relaxed operation, by the book and professional, but not too concerned about the nit-picking administrative details. If you wanted to have a look at the newspaper during the cruise, it was fine by me even though Vol 1 said there should be no 'extraneous reading material' on the flight deck. If you wanted to chat about things in general and tell a few jokes when it was quiet, fine by me again. It's a long way across the North Pacific. But it did depend on the other crew members. Some men had plenty of spare capacity and some didn't. I expected everyone to know their job and get on with it without too much direction. If someone made a mistake, my policy was to analyse why and explain what had gone wrong so it wouldn't happen again. As I saw it, it was all part of the learning curve and the Captain's responsibility to pass on his knowledge and experience. That is not to say that I tolerated laziness or incompetence. If you made a mistake through just being slack or not knowing your duties, you deserved a bollocking and you got one.

I had an F/O on my crew on one occasion who kept missing radio calls. I thought perhaps he was having trouble understanding ATC as the accents of some of the controllers on our routes could be difficult to interpret until you got used to them. Then I noticed he had an earpiece in his right ear and was listening to a Walkman hidden in his nav bag. He didn't do it again, not on my flight deck anyway. What I aimed for was a safe, professional operation but saw no reason why we shouldn't have fun and enjoy the job at the same time.

During the introduction of the Airbus A340, we had a number of teething problems with the aircraft, nothing like the A330, but problems nonetheless. The fuel control and monitoring computers (FCMCs) used to manage the fuel system initially were unreliable and subject to failures. On a trip out of Toronto on 25 July 1996, both FCMCs failed and all the fuel quantity indicators just showed yellow crosses. In this condition, the automatics went into a default landing mode, opened some valves in the system and started transferring fuel between the tanks. We had a long way to go and we needed the fuel to be in the right places to manage the trim and balance of the aircraft. The checklist didn't adequately cover this situation so I threw it out. I closed all the fuel cross-feed and transfer valves, established tank to engine configuration and managed the fuel system manually for the rest of the flight. I reasoned that we knew the departure fuel distribution for certain, we could calculate the usage from the 'fuel gone' counters, which were the only part of the system still working, and we could manage the inter-tank transfers ourselves when needed. There was nothing clever about this. All we were really doing was what the F/E used to do on the 747 before he was replaced by computers. The F/O and I each did independent calculations and cross-checked the results for gross errors. I figured that the only thing that could go wrong with the plan was if we sprang a fuel leak because we had no way of checking the actual tank contents against the calculated figures. If that happened, it just wasn't our day and, as a backup plan, we could always dive into an *en route* alternate.

The plan worked and we brought the flight safely home. Afterwards, my F/O said to me, 'I've just learned more about this aircraft flying on one sector with you than I learned in the whole of my line training.' It was a nice compliment. There was no fuss. We just worked together, dealt with the problems, did our jobs and enjoyed a beer together afterwards. That is the way it should be.

Barley decided that with the intransigence of the AOA during the A330 grounding he would simply bypass us and appeal directly to his pilots to help him out in his hour of need. He set up some phone lines and put out a NTC asking people to call in to volunteer their services during the crisis. Mike Lowes told me afterwards it was like being at one of Clemmow's DFO's barrels. If Barley was under any illusion that he had the support of the pilots, the 17 days during which the A330 was grounded should have dispelled that misconception.

He tried another bypass manoeuvre on rostering. Rather than negotiate with the AOA, he set up a Roster Liaison Working Group (RLWG). This was headed by one of Barley's favourites, Colin Pearce. The idea was that the RLWG would communicate directly with the pilots, find out what they really wanted and rewrite the rostering practices accordingly. It was the sort of 'consultation exercise' that we are familiar with in politics and urban planning where a small, carefully selected cross-section of the public is consulted by way of surveys containing questions of the 'When did you stop beating your wife?' type. The results are then used to justify the politicians and planners going ahead and doing whatever it was they intended to do in the first place.

It has been said that 'Those who can, do; and those who can't, teach.' I have never subscribed to this axiom because I believe teachers do an extremely important job and are greatly undervalued by society as a whole. I had some very good teachers when I was at school and one in particular called 'Pug' Wilson. He taught history, which I had always considered to be a dry, boring subject until I met Pug. He walked into the classroom on the first day of term, handed out some mimeographed papers with a list of dates and events and said, 'You are all going to need to know these to pass your end of term exams. I'm not teaching you those. You can learn them yourselves. I'm going to teach you about power, politics and the reasons why things happened. That's what history is really about.'

He had us riveted and also turned me on to English Literature as well.

So, I don't agree with the axiom but, if we were to take it one step further, it should be, '. . . and those who can't even teach become bloody consultants.'

Rather than just be intransigent and disregard Pearce's project, we decided to give it the benefit of the doubt just in case he had something productive to contribute. We arranged for him to brief those members of the GC who were working on rostering. He came into the room, set up his AV aids and opened his briefing with the words, 'Rostering is a very complex subject and there are very few people in the world who actually understand it.'

'Any idea how we can meet these people?' enquired one of our number waggishly.

'You're looking at one of them right now,' came his reply.

We nearly fell off our chairs laughing. Things were made worse when his AV equipment failed because of a faulty Ethernet lead and he didn't have a spare. First rule of presentation, always have a backup. It did give us an opportunity to gain a little intel though. While he was away searching for a new lead, we had a wander around his office, which was close to the briefing room. On his whiteboard were some calculations showing that they could get a ten per cent increase in productivity on ULR ops if they could get rid of the 5-4-3 rule. So now we knew for certain where that attack had originated.

Barley's bypass plan went off like a damp squib. We circulated the membership and asked them to send in a form letter stating that 'The AOA is my authorised representative. Please refer to them on all matters concerned with rostering.' When Barley's office was flooded with more than 850 letters he gave up on that plan and Pearce was 'promoted sideways' to a newly created job of manager special projects.

Barley made another mistake. He described the refusal of the pilots to 'help out' during the A330 grounding as 'contemptible'. Not the refusal of the AOA it should be noted, the refusal of 'his' pilots. If you are trying to gain the respect and loyalty of a body of men it doesn't help your cause if you go around calling them contemptible. In a way, he never really had a chance. His leadership skills were questionable from the outset. It was reported that when he took over from Clemmow, he did so on B Scale terms and that Clemmow was the last DFO actually to have a seat on the board with voting rights. Whilst Barley's title still had the word director in it, it didn't come with a seat on the board. His lack of delegation skills led to complaints when he insisted on attending meetings that were below his pecking order.

Lowes used to complain to me: 'What the fuck's he doing going to that meeting? It's a GM level meeting. I'm his GM, he should be sending me not going himself. He wanders in and all the other GMs wonder why the fuck he's there. He's undermining me. They think I'm not up to the job.'

On one occasion, Mike told me they needed a new coffee machine in the office and he had to get Barley's approval for the expenditure. Now that's micro management. The only time I ever saw him delegate was during negotiations. He didn't have the ability to think quickly on his feet and was lost in the cut and thrust of debate. He was only comfortable reading from a prepared script so he would come in, open the meeting by reading from a piece of paper and then hand over to the rest of his team. The signs were on the wall from early on.

Shortly after he took over I happened to encounter him in a social environment and he confided to me that 'I know I'm probably seen as being attached to the previous DFO but I see things very differently.'

He followed this up by a DFO's introductory newsletter to the pilots in which he stated, 'I am my own man.' He was right in the first respect. He came to the job tainted by his association with Clemmow. However, anyone who feels the need to make a public statement asserting his manhood, well, nothing more needs to be said. At the first Ops/AOA meeting that Barley chaired as DFO, he paused at the door when he entered the conference room. I asked Mike Lowes afterwards what all that was about.

'He expected you all to stand up when he came in the room,' was his reply.

Barley never gained the command or respect of his troops. At a meeting at the Labour Department when we had finalised some negotiations, Barley turned to Nigel Demery, who was the AOA president by that time, and said, 'You'd better let your pilots know.'

Your pilots, not *his*. He ended up as a puppet to the whims of the accountants and the commercial department and, in the opinion of many, did the Flight Ops Department a great disservice in the process.

He hired a psychologist called John Gardner to assist him with 'handling' the pilots. I first met him also on a social occasion. Paul Robinson was there and introduced me to him with the words, 'This is John Warham, he's the boss of the AOA,' to which Gardner replied, 'Yes, I know.'

So apparently he was already one step ahead of me. For some reason the conversation got around to prostate problems. I remarked that I was very disappointed that Frank Zappa had died of prostate cancer. Anyone who could come up with 'Peaches En Regalia' and have a guy called the Mascara Snake in his band deserved at least to die of something spectacular like shotgun wounds or a high-speed car crash and go to Valhalla. Paul looked a bit bemused by this but Gardner nodded sagely and agreed with me. I marked him down there and then as a bullshitter because any 'muso' would know that the Mascara Snake was in Captain Beefheart's Magic Band not the Mothers of Invention. Not quite as far ahead of me as he thought.

With the rostering system in chaos, delays increasing and productivity goals not being met, there was nothing for it. They had to come back to the table even though we still had – or as some would have it *because* we had – contract compliance in force. The AOA team remained the same as before. The company's team was still headed by Mike Lowes but now included Paul Horsting, Dave Roberts, Charles Carlow and Theo Samios. Paul Horsting was an ex-AOA PO now in management. Dave Roberts was a Canadian who had previously worked in industrial relations management for Air Canada. Charlie Carlow was a Swire 'prince' newly appointed to the Flight Ops Department. He always reminded me of Harry Enfield's character, Tim Nice but Dim. He was a thoroughly nice bloke but rather out of his depth. He managed to confirm this on one occasion when, some days into negotiations on rostering practices, he asked me to explain what I meant by ULR ops. Lowes' eyes went to the ceiling and I asked Mike if he might perhaps want to take a break to brief his team. Poor old Charlie put the lie to my maxim that the only stupid question is the one that isn't asked. The last member of their team, Samios, we already know about.

The first item on the agenda was a union recognition agreement. Because of the lack of collective bargaining legislation in Hong Kong, we wanted formal recognition by the company that the AOA was the authorised representative body for the Cathay aircrew. This was polished off in a morning and the signatures went on the first document.

The next item was the DGP, which had never materialised since the original promises three years earlier with the introduction of CoS 94. People were still being subjected to arbitrary disciplinary action with no formalised appeals process. The talks went well and on 20 June 1997, a formal DGP agreement was signed and expressly included as a term of the contract of employment. It had only taken three years but finally we had put that one to bed. So far so good.

After some initial teething problems whilst everyone got used to the new system, the agreement worked extremely well and, indeed, various members of management confided to me that they were as relieved as we were to have a formal process in place as everyone now knew where they stood and there could be no accusations of favouritism or private agendas being pursued.

In fact it worked to the company's advantage as well. Nigel Humphries and I advocated on behalf of a number of pilots who were subject to the DGP and, whilst we would both do our best to defend the 'prisoner at the bar', if we determined that the miscreant had cocked up royally we would say so and just plead for leniency. Indeed, it became known that, in such cases, the offender would get a bigger bollocking from us than they got from their managers. This was appreciated by the B747 fleet manager in particular, Paul Robinson. He would often telephone me to give me a heads up that someone was for the high jump so that we could try to find a way of heading things off before formal charges were laid. He trusted me in the more minor cases to ensure that there would be no repetition by the offender.

In all of the disciplinary cases that I dealt with, there was only one that left a sour taste in my mouth. A Captain on the B747, John Chenery, during a night stop in Australia, was arrested by the police and charged with being drunk in public. His arrest attracted media attention in the Australian press and adverse publicity for the company, particularly as he operated a flight back to Hong Kong the next day. He was subject to disciplinary action and dismissed.

As part of our preparation for an appeal, we would always bring the appellant into the AOA office and, during the briefing, ask him for the full and true story of what really happened. None of us who acted as advocates wanted to find ourselves being blindsided during the appeal hearing. Chenery explained how it was all a misunderstanding after he had accidentally knocked over some drinks, that the police had acted in a heavy handed way and that it was blown up out of all proportion by the media. I had previously spoken to the F/E on Chenery's crew, Max Lollback, who had been drinking with him that day and asked him what sort of condition Chenery was in. Max was a big bloke and I personally had shared a few cool ones with him on a hot day when we'd been down route together. He could hold his ale and if Chenery, who was quite a small man, had tried to keep up with his strike rate I could see how trouble could start. Max's laconic response to my enquiry as to Chenery's condition – 'You'd have to say he was drunk' – did little to allay my fears. However, based on Chenery's assurances that it was a misunderstanding, I went in to advocate on his behalf in front of Barley and succeeded in having his dismissal reduced to demotion to F/O for six months with promotion back to Captain thereafter, subject to good conduct.

When we got into the lift after the appeal, Chenery turned to me with a sly look on his face and said, 'Right, d'you want to know what really happened?'

I resisted the urge to grab him by the throat and throttle him there and then. Instead I told him in not very polite terms that I didn't wish to hear from him ever again. He had lied to me and put my own reputation on the line to save his own skin. He subsequently resigned from Cathay before his demotion had expired. He had put all of his colleagues at risk in any future DGPs, because if the managers who trusted me found out that I'd gone in there and effectively related a pack of lies all of our credibility would have been jeopardised. His behaviour really was contemptible and I was glad to see the back of him.

There were also occasions when management did the right thing for us under the DGP and we always took care to express our gratitude. Terry Heyes got himself into a bit of bother one day when he didn't turn up for a rostered duty and his excuse didn't really hold water. As he was an ex-president of the AOA and one of the movers and shakers on the FTLWG, there were those in the corridors of power who were after his blood. It was an ideal opportunity to take him out. His appeal was heard in front of two management pilots, Andy Maddox and John McCormick, a.k.a. 'The Screaming Skull' on account of his temper, which was quite well known to some of the more junior pilots. I advocated for Terry and managed to get him off with a temporary reduction in seniority and a fine, effectively a slap on the wrist. Half an hour after the hearing, I telephoned Andy and asked him whether he could give me a couple of minutes. He agreed so I went back upstairs and he was sitting in his office with John. They both looked quite worried when I went in. I thanked them for the way they had handled the situation, knowing as I did that they were probably under a lot of pressure from upstairs to chop Terry. The look of relief on their faces was palpable when they realised I'd only come in to say thank you. I don't know what it was they thought I was going up there for but it was an indication that the AOA now had respect in the Flight Ops Department.

At 24:00 on 30 June 1997, a piece of history was made when Hong Kong was handed back to the Chinese after over 150 years of British rule. Because of charitable work that we had been involved in, my wife and I had come to know the 'Last Governor' and his wife, Chris and Lavender Patten. We had attended various social functions at Government House and received an invitation to attend the private handover ceremony there and, later, the main ceremony at the Royal Navy's shore station HMS Tamar. It was a piece of pomp and majesty at which the British excel. During the parade and speeches by Prince Charles and Chris Patten, the heavens opened and the rain came down like stair-rods. Our soldiers ignored the inclement weather and their parade was magnif-icent. Some local Chinese said that God was crying because the British were leaving. We were invited to be in the 'receiving line' at HMY *Britannia* as Chris, Lavender, their daughters and the Prince of Wales said their final goodbyes and boarded the yacht. It was one of the most emotional moments of my life to be part of this historic event. There was a nice touch by Prince Charles, which was not much remarked on in the media coverage. When everyone else had gone up the compan-ionway and only he and Chris Patten remained to board, Charles went up first and let Chris be the last British official to leave the colony. As HMY *Britannia* steamed out of the harbour with the Band of HM Royal Marines on the upper deck playing 'Rule Britannia', 'Land of Hope and Glory' and 'Jerusalem', the tears were streaming down my face. Afterwards, we returned to Kowloon-side where we were attending another party in one of the hotels. As we walked into the foyer, there was Mike Lowes with some friends, beer in hand. He rushed up to me and said, 'Fuck me, John, I just saw you up on the big screen shaking hands with Fat Pang and Charlie. There's two billion people round the world just saw you. Where the fuck were the Swires?'

A very good question indeed. The Swires didn't like Chris Patten's style of government. He was very popular with the people and didn't kowtow either to big business or to the mainland government. The style of his predecessor, David Wilson, and the more toadying approach of the old 'China Hands' like Percy Cradock was more to their liking in dealing with the Chinese government. Cradock was one of the biggest critics of Patten's approach and predicted that, because of him, the Chinese would crack down on Hong Kong after the handover. He was wrong and many believe that Cradock sold Hong Kong too cheaply.

After all the speculation about what China would do once they got their hands on the 'barren rock', as Lord Palmerston dubbed it in 1841, the reality was something of an anticlimax. The People's Liberation Army (PLA) did not come storming into town beating us all with rattan canes, although they did send a small contingent across the border at 21:00 on the night of 30 June three hours ahead of the official handover and the press tried to make much of it. The world's press were in town looking for a story but they couldn't find one. They became so desperate that, outside the Foreign Correspondents' Club on Lower Albert Road one evening, I saw two journalists doing a piece to camera interviewing each other about what might happen. A friend of mine wrote a letter to his sister who lived in Devon. He told her that, after the handover, restaurants in Hong Kong were not allowed to serve English breakfast any more and we all had to wear Mao jackets. Her local paper printed it verbatim. The only time you see the PLA in Hong Kong is if you go on one of the tours round their barracks. The British squaddies used to be much more trouble late at night in the clubs and bars of Wan Chai. The PLA don't go there. They can't afford the prices. Today, Hong Kong remains the free-wheeling place it always was and, most importantly, despite one hiccup when Beijing intervened to 'reinterpret' the Basic Law on immigration issues, the judiciary remains independent from political interference.

Negotiations between the AOA and the company continued. The next three items on the agenda were: CoS, salary and rostering practices. These were the more difficult issues and, whilst the progress was slower than previously, we were actually making progress, or so we thought.

Our objectives on CoS were relatively simple. We wanted to remove the 'at the sole discretion of the company' clauses and make the benefits to which they referred contractual rather than subject to unilateral amendment. We did not think this to be an unreasonable objective. In the background to the talks, Samios's 'APD' had been introducing new benefit policies. A good example was staff travel. My benefits were contractual and couldn't be changed without my agreement. He published a new policy with an invitation to sign up to the new terms. At first blush, the new policy looked better than the old one. Under the old contract, single men could not nominate a 'partner' for staff travel. You could only get such benefits if you were married. The new policy removed this restriction and seemed to be an improvement. There were other such carrots and some people were tempted by them. The downside, however, and it was a big downside, was that instead of being contractual, the new policy was subject to 'amendment from time to time'. The question was, could you trust Samios not to start hacking away at your benefits as soon as you signed up with some more 'fine tuning'?

My assessment was that I wouldn't trust him as far as I could spit. He did the same thing with medical benefits but with a twist. On the A Scale, we had unlimited worldwide medical benefits for ourselves and our families. This was worth a lot. He issued a new 'RightChoice' scheme, which greatly restricted these benefits. The carrot was that the new scheme included dental coverage whereas the old scheme didn't, but the decision for me was obvious. His trick was to introduce it as an 'opt out' scheme. It was presented as a *fait accompli* that everyone would be moved across to the new scheme unless you wrote in and specifically stated that you wished to retain your original coverage. We didn't fall for it and, naturally, it became known as 'WrongChoice'.

The roster was in complete chaos. The first underlying problem was that we simply didn't have enough pilots to complete the commercial task under the current rules. One of the issues exacerbating the problem was ASL. It was taking up so much training capacity that there was insufficient left to train enough pilots for the mainline passenger operation. The second fundamental problem was Ogilvie's 89 hours. It was flawed and unobtainable as discussed previously. Without an overhaul of the whole rostering system we were never going to be able to complete the commercial task under the existing rules unless we employed more pilots. The AOA and the company had a common objective in that we both understood the need to reform the rostering system. Where we differed was that the company just saw it as a productivity issue. Whilst we were prepared to look at productivity, we had three other overriding objectives. Firstly, any new system must provide our pilots with protection against cumulative fatigue. Secondly, we needed roster stability. Thirdly, we must put a stop to the repeated breaches of the AFTLS rules that were now commonplace.

Roster stability is recognised by regulatory authorities and aviation medical specialists alike as an essential requirement to any rostering system. Simply to be able to plan your month ahead so as to be able to have some kind of 'normal' family life is very important. Pilots often work when the general public is enjoying time off. Holidays, such as Christmas, Easter, New Year, Thanksgiving, school holidays and so on are the times that the general public wants to travel, so someone has to fly them, and that's the pilots. Weekends are the same. Pilots tend to get their 'weekends' in the middle of the week. Not that we are complaining about this. It goes with the turf. If you go into professional aviation as a career, that's what you have to expect and if you don't like it, pick another way of making a living.

What we do complain about, and with justification, is completely chaotic rostering and the inevitable consequences. If you are rostered for a duty starting at 06:00 and finishing at 17:00 and then arrive at the airport and find that your trip has changed and you won't now be back until 21:00, no one is going to complain too much so long as it doesn't happen too often. If you work in an office, it's a bit like your boss occasionally asking you to work late at short notice when something comes up unexpectedly. Your partner might complain a bit because the dinner's burnt but it's just part of working life. But what if this happened just about every working day? It wouldn't make for a very stable and harmonious home life. Take it further. On Friday morning, your boss doesn't just tell you you're working late, you're also being sent away to a conference for the weekend and you won't be back until Monday night. You might have a kid's birthday party planned for the weekend and you were supposed to be taking your son to a rugby match but, bugger that, the boss says you've got to work or else. When this goes on week in and week out, it won't be long before your partner is telling you to choose between the job and your family, and rightly so. Well that was the state of Cathay's rosters but it got even worse. Crew Control used to cheat.

GDOs on the roster were supposed to be sacrosanct. If you were in Hong Kong and you reported for duty and were given a roster change that would infringe on a GDO, you were entitled to refuse the new duty. Down route was a different matter. If you were at an outport and a roster change came through that infringed on a GDO, you had to do the duty irrespective. This provision was in place to cater for unforeseen emergencies and contingencies such as a typhoon hitting Hong Kong, an aircraft going AOG or other acts of God. Again, we considered the provision fair enough so long as it was used in the manner in which it was intended. We put it under the military term of 'exigencies of the service'. The crew controllers were abusing the system.

You would depart Hong Kong on, say, a four-day pattern. As soon as you reached your first stopover, there would be a telex waiting that completely revised your pattern to six or seven days and infringed your rostered GDOs. The cheat was that they knew about this change before you even left Hong Kong but didn't tell you at flight despatch because you would have had the right to refuse the new duty. Again, if this just happened on the odd occasion we would have just accepted it as part of the job but it didn't. It happened all the time and it stank. Pilots always complain about rosters. If you find a bunch of pilots in a bar having a beer, you can guarantee at some point the subject of rostering will come up and there'll be the usual moans and groans. No matter how good the system, there will always be something to grouch about. It's just human nature. At some time in the future there'll be a couple of intergalactic freighter pilots standing in a *Star Wars*-style bar complaining that they've pulled the long Jupiter rotation with the double Ganymede/Io shuttle again. It wasn't like that. It was much, much worse.

Cathay's rosters were in total chaos with no immediate solution on the horizon. The pilots' complaints were fully justified. The situation was also having an impact on the legality of the operation and putting our licences at risk.

The rules in the AFTLS are there as the absolute bottom line safety net to ensure that pilots have sufficient rest before their flying duties and to restrict their maximum duty times to protect them against fatigue. Crew Control – in trying to deal with the pilot shortage – started to apply 'flexible' interpretations of these rules. Pilots should be able to trust their schedulers only to roster them for legal duties in compliance with the AFTLS. They should not have to check each duty to ensure that it is legal. We could no longer trust them to do so and it led to friction. If we pointed out to a crew controller that the duty was illegal, we would be referred to a supervisor who would then try pressuring us to do the duty anyway with coercion and threats of disciplinary action. The manager in charge of Crew Control was a man called Chris Hoyland and, as a fellow Yorkshireman, I expected better of his department. Whilst it is true to say that he derived his authority from the DFO, nonetheless it was his responsibility to ensure that the rosters were legal. Instead, he permitted an attitude to develop in Crew Control that, rather than regarding the AFTLS as sacrosanct, seemed to view the rules as little more than inconvenient impediments to achieving greater efficiency and commercial gain.

In one typical incident I had operated a series of three consecutive night flights, which was the maximum permissible under the rules. After such a series of duties, the AFTLS specified that the subsequent rest period should be a minimum of 48 hours' duration and should include two 'local nights'. Crew Control contacted me during my rest period and attempted to schedule me for a further flying duty that was in breach of the 48 hours regulation. When I pointed this out and refused the duty, Hoyland telephoned me back and tried to argue the toss with one of his 'flexible' interpretations. Supposedly my interpretation of the rule, which had been followed by custom and practice during my entire tenure at Cathay, was now wrong. I resisted his pressure and suggested if he wanted to take it further we could discuss it with the CAD. He backed down. It was OK for me with my position and seniority to take him on but some of the other pilots, particularly the more junior chaps, were easier meat and they gave in. The result was that flights were being operated in breach of the AFTLS. This made them not only illegal and in breach of the company's AOC, but also put the pilots' licences at risk. Had they been investigated by the CAD, the 'Nuremberg Defence' would not have saved them.

We took these problems to Mawdsley in the Corporate Safety

Department but he was no help. At a meeting he actually stated to me that, in his opinion, the AFTLS had nothing to do with flight safety. Mawdsley came with apparently good credentials, being a graduate of the RAF College of Aeronautics and the RAF Staff College. He held the post of Engineering Inspector of Flight Safety in the RAF before joining Cathay but therein lay the problem as we saw it. His essentially military engineering background meant that he had no real appreciation of the operational problems that we were experiencing or the rules that apply in civil aviation. In the military, you just followed orders or else.

In contrast, Mike Lowes had a good appreciation of the rostering problems and from July through to September both parties put in a lot of work developing new RPs. We got to the point where we produced 'ghost' rosters, which replicated the flying task actually performed in June under the current rules for comparison with our new proposals. Obviously, in any commercial operation, cost is an important factor and a CBA was essential if we were to come to agreement. We were very careful, therefore, at the outset to agree on the costing methodology that would be applied to our new rostering proposals so that we did not fall foul of the situation where one party comes up with one set of numbers and the other, another. Down that road lies failure if you can't even agree the dollars. It seemed that we were making significant progress and we were all optimistic that our work would bear fruit, right up until the time when Samios stuck his oar in, that is.

Simultaneously with the negotiations on CoS and RPs, the 1997 annual salary negotiations were being conducted. The first meeting was held on 22 April where the AOA submitted its opening position. We included a cost comparison of nine competitor airlines produced by Towers Perrin for KLM, which demonstrated that Cathay had the third lowest crew costs, based on flying hours. These figures were in contrast to a similar survey of the exact same nine airlines also produced by Towers Perrin for Cathay as part of Operation Better Shape in 1994. These showed that our A Scales were 'off the scale'. Some mistake surely? Two days later, after receiving up-to-date crew data from the 'APD', we submitted a formal proposal, which costed at HK$111.3 million, an increase of 6.12 per cent of the 1996/7 total aircrew payroll.

We smelled a rat when, on 27 May, we received a letter from Towers Perrin's solicitors alleging that, during the meeting with management on 22 April, we had falsely claimed that Towers Perrin were acting on our behalf and that we had published certain tables and charts in one of our newsletters that were subject to copyright. This letter made various demands including a public apology to Towers Perrin and all their clients, and destruction and/or return of all Towers Perrin data. On 10 June, the AOA's solicitors replied that no such misrepresentation had been made, that the meeting was in any case confidential, that all information used was in the public domain, that the allegations were untrue and that certain of their allegations were libellous.

Our solicitors requested information as to Towers Perrin's sources so that we could proceed with an action for damages. It was a complete try-on and we heard nothing further. However, it was an indication of what Barley was up to. At a meeting on 25 June, I asked him whether he was aware that we had received a letter from Towers Perrin's solicitors and he replied that he was. He didn't like it that we'd put the lie to the data they had used during Operation Better Shape to show how 'off the scale' we were. At that same meeting, Samios produced a costing of our proposal that showed it would cost HK$164.2 million, or 9.02 per cent of payroll instead of the figures that we'd arrived at. We went through their costing together and found they had made a number of incorrect assumptions. We reviewed and agreed the costing methodology, recalculated the figures together and came up with an agreed number of HK$137.5 million or 7.56 per cent of payroll. As with the RPs costing, at least we had the salary costing methodology agreed, which was a start.

At the next meeting, on 7 July, management tabled its first proposal, which costed out at HK$16.5 million. It was derisory. One of our big concerns was to protect the value of the Provident Fund, our retirement benefit. The proposal did not address any of our objectives, let alone the Provident Fund, Clearly we were a long way apart. At the next meeting, held on 23 July, we restated our concerns, especially on the Provident Fund, and asked Barley to go back and have a rethink.

The next meeting was held on 5 August where they tabled a new proposal, which they had costed at HK$60.8 million or 4.18 per cent of payroll. On checking their figures, we found that Samios had got the dollar figure wrong, in fact their proposal would have cost more than he had calculated but at least it showed that they were prepared to accept a 4.18 per cent increase in payroll. It seemed we were making progress.

On 11 August, we tabled the AOA's second proposal, which costed out at 5.92 per cent of payroll. We were moving towards each other, always a good sign in negotiations.

On 12 September, Turnbull, the managing director, invited me and my two VPs for lunch at the Hong Kong Club. He was accompanied by Barley. What took place at that lunch was like watching a ventriloquist and his dummy with Barley parroting the last few words of Turnbull's sentences.

'There's no doubt that our First Class product is second to none.'

'. . . second to none.'

'You won't like what I've got to say but I'm going to say it anyway.'

'. . . say it anyway.'

'Load factors on some of our high yield routes are down and we need to make savings.'

'. . . make savings.'

'We're cutting the catering budget but there'll be no reduction in standards.'

'. . . in standards.'

If the subject wasn't so serious, it would have made a good comedy act. I asked Turnbull how he was going to cut the catering budget without a reduction in standards. After all, if you buy a piece of steak for $10 and then buy another one for $7, you aren't going to get the same cut of meat and the passengers will be able to taste the difference. He didn't like that question much.

Despite the fact that we'd heard all the poverty pleading before, we decided to at least make it look as if we were listening. On 25 September we submitted the AOA's third proposal, which costed out slightly below management's last offer with a rider for a further percentage increase should turnover improve.

The response to this was that on 30 September Barley sent the AOA a letter that stated bluntly that he was imposing a further freeze on the A Scales, would not now be offering anything to protect the Provident Fund and would be imposing a derisory award on the B Scales. In other words he reneged on all previous offers despite all his previous undertakings that he intended to work with the AOA this year and have a 'proper negotiation'. The 'negotiation' has just been window dressing.

On 1 October, Samios came into a meeting on CoS with a completely new document that had clearly been cobbled together at the last moment. It was full of typos, errors and mistakes. The document we had been working on together was now in its ninth draft but he just threw that out and insisted that, from now on, we would be working from his version. It was a deliberate strategy designed to break the negotiations. He had been acting in bad faith the whole way through the process.

The last nail in the coffin of the 1997 negotiations was when Barley told me he had been advised that he would 'have to have rocks in his head' to accept our rostering proposals. Apparently they were 'unworkable' and the potential cost would be 'astronomical'. When we looked at the costings, we soon discovered that his 'advisors' had not used the agreed methodology; there were numerous simple arithmetical errors and, again, it was very clear that the whole thing had been cobbled together at short notice. It was just another ploy designed to break the negotiations. More bad faith. After more than four months of hard work they had deliberately scuppered the whole project.

I met Mike Lowes privately for a beer away from prying eyes and asked him what was going on. His reply was illuminating.

'I'm really sorry, John. I've been doing my best but it's that cunt Samios. Him and Barley have just pulled the rug on me. I don't even know how much longer I'm going to be in my job.'

That was it then. But they had one more card to play. The MCFA only ran to the end of the year. After that, ASL had to be a stand-alone entity and do its own training. It was still nowhere near ready. Barley wrote and asked for an extension to the agreement. This time around I adopted the same position as the General Committee during the A330 grounding. Fuck them! At an EGM held on 4 November, the membership passed a resolution that, with effect from 31 December 1997, there would be no further mixed crew flying or training with ASL crews. In addition, until further notice, no pilot would accept a new Check & Training appointment.

10

PSYOPS 2

'Those who come seeking peace without a treaty are plotting.'
Sun Tzu, *The Art of War*

'Get the data.'
Robert S. McNamara, *The Fog of War*

The Asian financial crisis hit the markets on 2 July 1997 with the collapse of the Thai baht. It was only 24 hours after the handover of Hong Kong and, although the two events were totally unconnected, it prompted much speculation by the Chinese astrologers and *feng shui* practitioners. By the time it was over in August 1998, the other kind of speculators had had a field day on the currency markets. As well as the Thai baht, other Asian currencies like the Malaysian ringgit, Philippine peso and the South Korean won had depreciated by around 40 per cent against the US dollar. The Indonesian rupiah was particularly hard hit, falling by 83 per cent. In US dollar terms, these countries' GNPs fell by similar amounts. Many businesses collapsed and people were thrown out of work but when George Soros and his pals came looking for a killing in Hong Kong in October 1997, they were in for a big surprise. The Hong Kong dollar had been pegged to the US dollar at a nominal rate of 7.80 since 1983 and, because Hong Kong's inflation rate had been significantly higher than that of the US for some years, the Hong Kong dollar was a tempting target. The Hong Kong Monetary Authority (HKMA), effectively our central bank, had more than US$80 billion in foreign reserves at its disposal. This was equivalent to 700 per cent of our M1 money supply and 45 per cent of our M3 supply. During the whole crisis, our markets came under attack four times and the HKMA spent more than US$1 billion to defend the peg.

The first attack was in October 1997. The sharks took large short positions against the Hong Kong dollar expecting to break the peg. They failed when the interbank interest rate soared automatically under the currency board mechanism, reaching 300 per cent on 23 October, forcing them to unwind their positions. The sharks tried again in January and June 1998 but were beaten off with similar results.

They had one last go in August 1998 but this time they tried a double play against the currency and equity markets at the same time. They pre-funded themselves with Hong Kong dollars in the debt market and, at the same time, took a large short position in the stock futures index market. They dumped their dollars in the 'spot' and 'forward' markets causing a huge interest rate hike, at one point up to 500 per cent, which prompted a corresponding collapse in the Hang Seng Index with panic selling of shares. The sharks figured they could then make big profits by closing their short positions in both the money and equity markets. They hadn't figured on the reaction of Donald Tsang, Hong Kong's Financial Secretary, who declared war on them. The HKMA entered into the stock and futures markets and, on 14 August, spent an estimated US$517 million to buy stocks and futures contracts, which resulted in an increase in the Hang Seng Index (HSI) of almost 9 per cent. Donald intervened again on 18 and 28 August with the result that at the end of the month the HKMA had accumulated US$15 billion, or around 7 per cent of the total stock market capitalisation. The speculators were forced to close out their short positions with heavy losses and were sent home with their tails between their legs. In 1999, the government launched the Hong Kong Tracker Fund, started selling its shares and made a profit of around US$5 billion.

The Asian financial crisis sent the markets, and Cathay management, into a tailspin. The crisis was unprecedented and would tax the capacity of any financial manager, but when you have been accustomed to operating with a market monopoly, as Cathay had for years, it came as a double whammy. The onset of the crisis prompted Turnbull's ventriloquist luncheon invitation in September 1997 and directly affected what happened in 1998.

This time around we were ready. At the beginning of 1996, we had formulated a multi-path strategic plan to defend ourselves. The first stage was to get the communications sorted out. We'd done that. The next stage was to educate and unify the membership. We'd done that. The next step was to demonstrate that we were firm in our resolve and that the membership was prepared to take action. We'd done that with contract compliance. Now we filed a legal action against the company to get a judicial ruling on the terms of our contract of employment. Even under Hong Kong's rudimentary employment legislation, we had certain protections. An employer cannot unilaterally cut an employee's wages without his or her agreement. On that there was no dispute.

We then say that protection similarly extends to any form of benefit that is financial in nature. Samios disagrees. He says that benefits are subject to unilateral amendment. We say, OK, let's ask the courts. We also say that protection extends further to any amendment of the contract that fundamentally changes the hours we have to work and, therefore, directly affects the effective hourly rate of pay we receive. On that argument, therefore, any change to rostering practices that affects our contractual flying hours, or the way we do that work, can only be done by agreement. Samios says no. We say, OK, let's ask the courts that one as well.

It took them by surprise. Strangely, the first thing they were concerned about was that this did not end up in the public arena. We assured them that it was not our intention to turn this into a trial by media, rather we had some points of disagreement that we'd been working on for some time and had been unable to resolve by negotiation, so the best thing to do was get a definitive ruling. That way, hopefully, we would be able to progress the negotiation once everyone was in agreement about where we stood legally. They couldn't really argue with the logic of that if they were genuinely negotiating in good faith.

Other than the judicial review we'd filed against the CAD, this was one of our first forays into the legal jungle. Contract law is a relatively complex subject and, because what we were doing had never been tried before in Hong Kong, getting advice was a problem. It is a fact of life that you will never get a lawyer to give you a definitive yes or no answer. We learned that very quickly. A barrister will give you his opinion and may be prepared to estimate your chances of success, but to get him to give you a categorical 'Yes you'll win this one'? Not a chance. There is an added complication. It is a common maxim in aviation that if you have 100 pilots in a room, there will be 100 ways to descend an aircraft. Similarly, as we found out, if you have five barristers in a room, there will be five different opinions, especially if there is no local precedent as in our case. We shopped around but could not get an opinion that made us confident of success. Because this was going to be a test case, we could not find a barrister in Hong Kong who had any hands-on experience in a case like ours.

There was nothing for it. We went abroad and found a barrister in London whose specific area of expertise was employment and contract law. There was a problem with this though. The Bar in Hong Kong is a closed shop. You cannot bring in a 'silk' from overseas to advocate on your behalf without first obtaining the permission of the court and this is not readily given. Permission is only usually granted in cases involving specialised matters where there is insufficient local expertise to deal with the case. We could argue that ours was such a case but there was no guarantee that we would win even that argument. Our London silk was not even permitted to come to Hong Kong just to give us advice without breaching the rules. We got around that one. We went to Macau for a week and held our conference there.

We learned some other lessons as well that were to stand us in good stead for the future. Do not just accept your barristers' opinion as gospel. If you disagree with them, argue and debate the point until either you have convinced them of your view or they have convinced you of theirs. If at the end of this process you are still not happy, get a second or third opinion. If a doctor tells you that you have bone cancer in your arm and the only solution is amputation, you would not accept this diagnosis without question. You would get at least a second opinion before submitting yourself to radical surgery. This actually happened to a friend of mine. Had she accepted the first diagnosis she would now be an amputee. As it is, she had a bone graft instead and five years on has both her arms and is in remission.

It is the same with barristers. Do not be afraid to shop around and find someone who not only gives you confidence in their opinion and abilities, but also is someone you can work with. If you can find someone who believes in your cause, then so much the better. Do not be afraid to change legal counsel if you are not getting the service you need. When dealing with relatively complex and specialised matters as we were, it can be a pain to have to start the process all over again, explaining the ins and outs of things like rostering practices. It causes delay and increases cost but it is worth it in the end. Always strive to give yourself the best chance of success. We sacked one Hong Kong barrister because he was too slow and, we believed, actually incompetent. He couldn't make up his mind about anything. If you ask a pilot what is the worst kind of Captain to have on your crew, other than the overbearing 'Gillette' type, the most common answer will be one who won't make a decision. This man was a ditherer so we got rid of him.

Similarly, don't just sit back and expect your instructing solicitor to get on with the job. You are not his only client. He will have other cases to work on as well as yours. Make sure you get regular updates on progress and, if things are not going to your liking, be prepared to apply pressure to get what you need. Don't just leave the drafting of technical documents to your solicitor. He may not have the necessary specialised knowledge until you have completed his education process. Get involved in the drafting yourself. It is much easier to draft an outline argument yourself in the first place rather than correct someone else's draft. Similarly, go online and research precedent yourself. You might find something that your counsel has overlooked and, as we will see later, barristers can and do make mistakes.

The most important lesson of all that we learned from our experience in the legal jungle, though, is this: DO NOT ALLOW YOUR LAWYERS TO RUN YOUR STRATEGY. It cannot be emphasised strongly enough. Your lawyers are there to give you legal advice and that is all. It is up to you to make strategic and tactical decisions based on that advice. If the advice is that there are three possible options, the lawyer will always recommend the path of least risk. Sometimes you may want to favour that option but sometimes, if it suits your strategy, you might opt to take the high risk road. It is up to you to make that decision and instruct your legal team accordingly. It is rather like dealing with accountants if you are in business. They are not there to run your business for you. Rather they are there to give you financial advice on which to base your business decisions. At least, that is the way it should be. Unfortunately, too often these days, the accountants have been allowed to get sole control of running the business, which to my mind was precisely why we were experiencing the problems we had in Cathay Pacific.

In the face of the Asian financial crisis, management knee-jerked. The most expensive aircraft in our fleet in terms of DOCs were the B747-200 Classics. They used more fuel and were more expensive in terms of maintenance costs than the newer aircraft. The fact that they were already bought and paid for didn't seem to come into the equation. The radical surgery solution was to get rid of them and that's what they set about doing. Things didn't go all their way though. They thought they were going to be able to offload them on Virgin until they were gazumped by Air New Zealand doing the same thing. Then there was talk about simply parking them in the desert. In the end they went to Pakistan International Airlines on a lease purchase arrangement. The decision caused a major furore though because it meant that more of our F/Es, already badly hit by ASL, would be made redundant. This wasn't the main issue though; it was the way it was handled that really irked us. ASL had been recruiting F/Es on the market and now we were placed in a position where our F/Es who had ten or more years' service were being thrown out of jobs while people who had only been with ASL for two minutes were being kept on. One of the ASL F/Es was still in ground school and hadn't even begun his flying conversion training. Admittedly, our men were being offered a 'voluntary' redundancy package but if there weren't enough volunteers then it would be pressed men in reverse seniority order. We proposed a revised package to the company that would help to protect their Provident Funds but they wouldn't even move on that. We pressed very hard to have the ASL F/Es made redundant first but they weren't having it. Their argument was that ASL was a separate company. The fact that ASL was a wholly owned subsidiary of Cathay Pacific, that many of its directors also held senior posts in Cathay Pacific, that its DFO was employed by Cathay and that its aircrew flew Cathay aircraft under the Cathay AOC using Cathay route licences held no water according to them. The troops were incensed.

I wrote personally to Sutch asking him to intervene but he refused. I even wrote to Sir Adrian Swire in London asking him to intervene, or at least give me an appointment so that I could explain the situation to him personally, but all I got back was a form letter saying that he had 'every confidence in his senior managers'. The whole thing stank to high heaven and just demonstrated to us that, despite the overtures they were now making about coming back to the table to try to resolve our differences, nothing really had changed. They were focused on the bottom line, and loyalty was a term that seemed to have been dropped from the Swires' vocabulary.

Mike Lowes' assessment of his job security was right. He lost his job as general manager aircrew (GMA) and went back to the line. His replacement was someone of whom we have only heard fleetingly so far, Nicholas Peter Rhodes. He attended Lawnswood Secondary School in Leeds, obtained a degree in Zoology from Leeds University and joined the Swire Group in 1980 at the age of 22. He came into the senior post of GMA in the Flight Ops Department in 1998 with little or no qualifications or operational experience in professional aviation. This was to cause serious problems in the future. We had a good indication of where we were headed after a conversation between the AOA gen sec and Rhodes during Mike Lowes' leaving party held on 19 February at the Dickens Bar in the Excelsior Hotel.

Rhodes started off by saying that he couldn't believe this party was going on without, seemingly, a care in the world. The rest of the company staff were going around with long faces and working all the hours under the sun to get business in. He added that he hoped Lowes was paying the bill for the party and not Cathay. Next he said the company was losing $1 million a day. The financial crisis was hitting us hard. The Japanese, Thai and Indonesian markets had collapsed and it was only because we were a global airline that some of our other routes were just about keeping the company from collapsing. In global terms, Hong Kong had the highest cost base, even higher than Japan, and it cost more to have a reservations clerk in HKG than anywhere else. The move to the new airport at CLK was hugely expensive and even the injection of new shareholders' cash didn't cover it. Company results for 1998 would go into the red and he just couldn't understand why the aircrew alone seemed blissfully unaware of how serious it all was. He went on to say that recent AOA newsletters had pissed him off, and many of his colleagues. Two things in particular he didn't like. One was the AOA claim that the aircrew had already given more, and done more for the company than any other employee group. The other was our claim that management salaries and bonuses continued to go up while ours had been capped.

He went on to give examples of Cathay staff around the world who worked in dreadful conditions, in Bombay for example, for low pay, in freight sheds with rats running around. When the gen sec suggested that the Swires should pay them more and treat them better his answer was that they treated them as well or better than other employers! Next he got onto salaries and asked whether we had any idea how much House Staff like him earned. He volunteered that his salary was HK$66,000 per month, he had quite a nice gratis house but his bonus was based on profit share on the Swire results. He maintained that Cathay staff did not earn bonuses except for profit share and his last pay increase was only 3.9 per cent. He said that even directors like Turnbull and John Slosar didn't earn huge salaries. They were, however, very good at using their own money to make more money, he added, clearly a fan.

When the subject got on to pilots' salaries, he trotted out the standard line that we'd been hearing for the last four years. He said that the A Scale was off the scale, pointing at the ceiling, and the B Scale was there in the top handful. He based that view on his reading of the most detailed comparison exercise in the business, which took all factors into account and resolved the numbers to a cost per hour flown. This was the best, most comprehensive survey and it was right. Unfortunately they couldn't release the figures to us because of confidentiality agreements. It was the survey compiled annually by Emirates, the middle eastern airline. There were a number of such surveys in the business but management tended to like the Emirates one because, unlike some of the others such as the South African Airways survey, it was compiled without any input from pilots. He insisted that the Emirates' figures were correct because they had checked them themselves. That really filled us with confidence!

He let slip another choice piece of intel when he remarked that 'David would like the next DFO not to be a pilot.' That was ominous. Shortly after that he made another comment about the cost of the party and left. When the gen sec warned the 744 fleet manager, Dick Marsh, that the cost of Flight Ops parties was about to come under scrutiny he received the concise reply, 'Fuck them! We have a budget and, as long as we have, we'll spend it.' As for Turnbull's salary, the Cathay annual reports showed that his remuneration was HK$5-5.5 million in 1997. It went up to HK$5.5-6 million in 1998 despite the financial crisis. Slosar was in the same league.

So that was it then. We were in for another round of cost cutting and attacks on our terms and conditions under the pretext of the financial crisis. As we were to find out though, rather than coming down on us with the proverbial iron fist, this time around they would bring in a couple of trick cyclists, Gardner and Pendleton, and would try the 'velvet glove' approach to give us 'ownership' of the problem.

The opening gambit came with a suggestion from Barley that he would like to have a meeting 'to thrash things out behind closed doors'. I went to his office on the morning of 4 March and the meeting lasted just over an hour and a half. The best way of describing what took place is simply to reproduce my note of the meeting written immediately afterwards:

KB: What can I do for you?
JW: You asked to meet so here I am, no time like the present.
   [He spoke about the F/E situation.]
KB: The formal written package should be out by this afternoon. I will fax you a copy to the office. We have now extended voluntary redundancy to F/Es who have less than two years to go to retirement. It's a very difficult situation. We'll try to cater for individual needs, e.g. if people have specific dates such as Provident Fund qualification, we can do a deal so that instead of three months' pay in lieu of notice and six months' redundancy we'd give them six months' in lieu and three months' redundancy.
JW: Do you think our alternative proposals have merit and that the emphasis should be on voluntary redundancy as far as possible?
KB: Yes but we didn't feel that we needed to offer a quite so generous package as you proposed. We feel that we can get sufficient volunteers on our package.

JW: What, you think you'll get 40 volunteers on your package do you?

KB: Well we can't be sure can we? Anyway the rest will be done in seniority order but we couldn't go with your idea of merging the seniority lists.

JW: Why not?

KB: Because ASL is a separate company and I can't ask Graham Keddie to make his people redundant. He wouldn't wear it and I don't have jurisdiction over ASL.

[Graham Keddie was the chief operating officer of ASL.]

JW: They're flying our aircraft on our AOC with your name on it. What answer do I give to an F/E who asks me why he's being made redundant after ten years' loyal service when an ASL recruit who isn't even out of ground school is being kept on?

KB: There isn't an answer is there?

JW: Yes there is, it's wrong. It's not even as if it would cost the company anything. The Cathay blokes would go across on ASL terms.

KB: There's nothing I can do about it.

JW: Have you asked Keddie?

KB: <look of surprise> No.

JW: What about offering voluntary redundancy to ASL blokes and see if there are any takers? Even if it saves just one or two of our blokes it's worth it.

KB: <surprised again> Well I can ask but I don't hold out much hope.

JW: Well will you ask?

KB: Well I can ask.

JW: This is causing a lot of resentment. The blokes are very, very angry. Anything that can be done to help them would be worth it. This isn't going to go away.

KB: There's nothing I can do.

JW: What about future ASL jobs, will they be held open for our blokes?

KB: Yes.

JW: Are there any available ASL jobs open now? Have they got a full complement of F/Es or are they going to recruit some more?

KB: No, they've got all they need. I don't know how many will become available through wastage but they'll be offered to Cathay engineers.

JW: What about retraining?

KB: We've been down that route and we don't think it's very successful.

JW: Well there are two guys who were accepted for pilot training last time, what about them?

KB: We're not going to offer that.

JW: Well that's not what it said in the papers at the weekend and that's caused a lot of ill feeling.

KB: <shortly (if he could get any shorter)> We did not release any press statements.

JW: Well Mr Kwan was quoted as saying retraining was offered.

KB: <still short> That was in response to a press enquiry and we were misquoted.

JW: Another thing that's upset the guys is that some of them have read your letter to mean that redundancies will start on 27th March and all 40 will have gone by 30 June.

KB: That's not what it says. We're not even sure when the aircraft are going yet.

JW: Well that's how it's been interpreted so maybe it needs clarifying. So you don't know when the aircraft are going?

KB: No, two will go in April but we're not sure about the rest yet.

JW: Have the two been sold?

KB: No, Air Pacific have expressed interest but we're not sure yet.

JW: So you don't know if they're going to be parked or sold or what?

KB: No.

JW: So if two go in April, when will the first guys be made redundant?

KB: The first date is 1st May. It's difficult because the roster comes out before the decision on dates will have been made. We don't think it's a good idea to have them flying when they've got a date so we'll keep them on the payroll but give them a minimum hours roster.

JW: I agree. They shouldn't be flying with redundancy hanging over them. <KB flinches slightly> Anyway, I should tell you that the Association will be working independently to try and find them jobs. The reason being that the last time we went through this as a joint effort it took three months just to agree the advert.

KB: That's understood. I've already had a call from BA's chief F/E making enquiries.

JW: Yes, I've been in touch with BALPA and they're very short at the moment.

KB: Yes, but I understand it's only a one year contract and the terms aren't very good.

JW: Yes, BALPA are in talks with them at the moment. Luckily there are plenty of other jobs around.

KB: Virgin may be interested if they pick up the Air New Zealand aircraft.

JW: Yes, we've heard that as well. By the way, we've had an enquiry from USALPA asking our opinion on Cathay's freighter work being farmed out to Atlas or Polar. Is that where we're going next?

KB: *<breaks eye contact and looks out of the window but doesn't look like he usually does when you've really caught him by surprise>* Not to my knowledge. No I haven't heard anything about that.

JW: Well do you think it's a possibility that's being looked at?

KB: I don't know, John. Between you and me and these four walls, I don't even know if we'll still have any Classics in two or three years' time. There's a lot of uncertainty, even at the MD level. Well *<picking himself up from the incipient dropped bollock>* not that the MD is uncertain of his actions but the future's very uncertain.

JW: Yes, these are very difficult times but it doesn't help with people making blanket statements like we're losing a million dollars a day. I mean, what currency are we talking? Does that mean we've lost $60 million since 1st January?

KB: Well I don't know where that number came from but it depends what you're looking at. If you're comparing against budget we're well behind and if you're comparing against the first half of last year we're also well down but then the first half of last year was a bumper time.

JW: So we're not actually making a loss. The report is due out on the 11th, isn't it? So we'll be able to see how we did in the second half of last year.

KB: No, we're not making a loss but we're getting pretty close.

JW: Yes it's just that some of these figures can come across as scare-mongering. There are a lot of us who've seen all of this before in our careers.

KB: There's no doubt that different sections of the workforce view this in different ways. *<looks at me in an old-fashioned manner>* For many employees this is the first time they've seen a situation like this and they do find it frightening. I have a meeting with the MD this afternoon and one of the points is how we get across the reality of the situation to all employee groups.

JW: Well, Ken, I'd like to talk about the contractual issues. I believe we've got to a point now where we can't move any further forward because we have different positions. We've talked about this for six months and we can't seem to find any common ground.

KB: Well we've taken our advice and we believe your stated position is wrong.

JW: Yes, well obviously the feeling is reciprocated. That's why we've decided to go for a judicial ruling so that everyone knows where they stand. If you like we're taking it to the referee for a decision so we can then try and move on. It's not our intent that this will be a high profile event in the media. We're just trying to find a solution.

KB: OK well I'll pass that on to the MD.

JW: Well I'll be writing to the MD as well in reply to his letter. Can we talk about S/O seniority Ken?

KB: Yes.

[S/Os in the company did not receive a seniority number until they were promoted to F/O. This was a concern because it undermined their job security and meant that some of them were being promoted out of seniority order depending on which fleet they were on.]

JW: Is there any further movement on this? It's one of the areas that we came very close to agreement on.

KB: Well we won't be recruiting any F/Os now. We will still be recruiting S/Os but not as many and there'll still be some command training but not as much. If I knew that we weren't going to be recruiting F/Os for the next couple of years I don't think I'd have too much of a problem with it.

JW: Well in these uncertain times, if that issue was sorted out it would certainly give the S/Os a boost. We'd actually agreed the principle; it was just the time to getting a number. Our last proposal was at the completion of their probation and I still think they'd buy that.

KB: Well I can look at it again.

JW: When?

KB: I should be able to give you an answer within two or three months.

JW: OK I'll look forward to that. Another area where we have a lot of common ground is rostering. I believe that we should still be working together on this; what do you think?

KB: Yes, it's a good idea. I think we should keep the team small; say just two from your side. *<note those last two words>*

JW: Yes, small teams are good so what, shall I get Murray to give Mike a call or do you want him to call you?

KB: No, ask him to call Mike direct.

JW: OK can you tell me what these consultants are doing on rostering?

[They had recently brought in yet more consultants to advise them on rostering.]

KB: They're part of the FOCC integrated system plan. They're looking at systems, processes ... *<then goes into a lot of 'yuckspeak' that would fit very well in Pseuds Corner in* Private Eye*>*

JW: So they're working in parallel rather than doing the same thing?

KB: Yes. A lot of the problem in rostering is educating the people who write the rosters. Showing them the problems and the solutions to use. *<more waffle about processes>*

JW: What sort of timescale have they got?

KB: They're tasked to produce their recommendations by July.

JW: So it's a fixed-term contract?

KB: Yes, it's a consultancy contract.

JW: OK, well I'll ask Murray to get in touch with Mike and see if we can move forward on that. Is there anything else you'd like to talk about?

KB: No, I don't think so, thanks for coming in.

JW: Thanks for your time, Ken.

KB: Not at all.

NOTES TO GC: My impression is that this was not the sort of meeting he had originally envisaged when he suggested we should meet to 'thrash out some issues behind closed doors'. He seemed at times on his guard and at other times distracted. I believe that he is under great pressure and has so many balls in the air that he's in danger of dropping some. The F/E situation certainly was uppermost in his mind and was preoccupying him. He didn't have much to say on anything else except when he started rambling about systems, processes and all that stuff that I find absolutely riveting. I left it wide open a couple of times for him to have a go about contract compliance, etc. He didn't bite and even went on the defensive regarding the press quotes when he could have easily fired back about the engine failure stories. All in all, not a great deal of progress made; he's going to do nothing about the F/E seniority vs ASL issue so we'll have to push it elsewhere. Might get the S/Os sorted out soon though. That'd be a win for them. Why is it always like pulling teeth trying to get these people to do anything?

So, something had changed between his initial approach to me for a meeting to 'thrash things out behind closed doors' and the actual meeting taking place. What was it? We were to find out very soon. They were trying another bypass manoeuvre.

Turnbull started holding some seminars with the aircrew to explain to them personally how difficult things were financially. Unlike the 'Commitment Days', these were voluntary. He had tried this before with the ASL crews but had to cancel them when hardly anyone turned up. Significantly, only A Scale Captains were invited to his new seminars. So now we knew who he was targeting. Rhodes started running a 'hearts and minds' campaign as well to convince the aircrew that we were all doomed unless something drastic was done and soon. It wasn't as easy as he thought it was going to be. We'd had four years to educate the troops and they were somewhat cynical of this new suit. Despite the fact that Barley had said in our meeting we should start talking rostering again, bringing in outside consultants was not a good sign. From previous experience, they would come up with a new plan and present it as another *fait accompli*.

If we were going to have any chance of concluding a successful nego-tiation, we were going to have to address their concerns as well as them addressing ours. There was no doubt that the Asian economy was in crisis and that we needed to plan to help to make savings. Rather than going the easy route of just chopping pay, we looked to find other areas where significant savings could be made.

The first was ASL. It was costing a lot of money and had come nowhere near to achieving its target, neither was it likely to do so in the short or medium term. The main reason was economy of scale. It was too small to be self-supporting, there was duplication of overheads and administration and its routes were too thin for its crews to be anywhere near as productive as the mainline operation. They had another problem with ASL. After the AOA resolution in December 1997 to end the MCFA, although they had managed to browbeat some of the Check & Training Captains into continuing to train ASL crews under threat of dismissal, the training was now taking place on the freighter aircraft only. We had managed to get the ASL pilots who were under training off the passenger aircraft. They had to concede this after a fight almost broke out on the crew transport. Having pilots engaging in fisticuffs before going flying is not a good way to enhance flight safety. The resolution that no one would accept a new Check & Training appointment also was having an effect. They needed to expand the Check & Training Department to cope with the increased training task and they couldn't. The boys held firm.

There was an easy and cost-effective way of solving the problem. ASL was a failed experiment and we put together a plan to reintegrate the freighters into the passenger operation.

Basings was another area where we identified significant cost savings. Their basings costings showed that, because the pilots no longer received expatriate allowances on a base, they were saving HK$1.2 million per Captain per year. Whilst we did not necessarily agree with that figure, we took it as read. If you have the right number of pilots on a base to accomplish the task, then the savings can be realised. The problem is that, when you have too many people on the base and there is not enough work for them, the only solution is to 'duty travel' (DT) them around the network. This has two effects. Firstly, it chops into their productivity. To DT a pilot from Europe to Hong Kong and back each month takes up 48 duty hours in travel time and required rest periods before he can even undertake any productive flying duty. Under the AFTLS, the absolute maximum permitted duty hours, as opposed to flying hours, in any 28-day period is 190. By having a pilot on the wrong base with not enough work available out of his home port, you have just lost 25 per cent productivity right away. Secondly, all this DT incurs costs in air tickets, accommodation and allowances. Company figures showed that in 1997 it cost HK$94 million in hotel bills and allowances for Europe-based crews that had to be duty travelled into Hong Kong. That wiped out the cost savings made by 79 individual basings at a stroke. It is obvious that having the right number of people in the right places is fundamental to actually realising projected cost savings on a based hub and spoke operation such as ours. We developed a mathematical formula to calculate the required pilot numbers on each base, given certain variables, and put together a revised basings proposal to ensure that those cost savings could be realised.

Despite the rejection of our last proposal on rostering, because of Samios' poor mathematics, we constructed an analysis to demonstrate the costing process in steps that even a nine-year-old would be able to understand. We also revised our rostering proposal. By integrating the short- and medium-haul patterns to be more efficiently rostered, we were able to meet two objectives. Firstly, we could provide more days off to improve the pilots' lifestyle and, secondly, we could secure a productivity increase of around 5 per cent to the company. Our proposal was a 'win-win' for both parties.

We thought we were well prepared to restart negotiations. If the other party had been equally willing to enter into the talks in good faith, we would have been. Unfortunately, as usual, this was not the case.

Rhodes first proposed that negotiations should re-open at an informal 'clear the air' meeting with Ted Pleavin and me in late May. Ted was a Canadian who had a lot of experience in negotiations from his time in Air

Canada and I was looking to him to take over as president when I stepped down at the end of the year. At the meeting, Rhodes asked who we would like to see on his negotiating team. Good ploy that one. Try to find out who the opposition doesn't want there. He said that Barley wanted to be at the opening meeting but, thereafter, he, Rhodes, would lead their team. He also asked my opinion of Barley being on the team. I replied that, because of his conservative attitude and reluctance to make decisions, he would slow the process down. Rhodes said he tended to agree. Another good ploy. He's my boss but, between you and me, he's not up to much. We'll do much better just between us. The 'we can be mates' approach.

The first meeting took place on 25 June and started with Barley reading from a prepared statement in which he requested confidentiality on the talks and that any press statements be issued jointly. We agreed with the proviso that we reserved the right to issue independent statements to our membership if the situation warranted it, as one of the complaints we'd received the previous year was lack of information. Rhodes got quite hot under the collar over this point and came back to it later in the meeting. We found out why very soon after. His 'hearts and minds' campaign wasn't working the way he thought it would and he needed to shut our comms down. Despite agreeing to confidentiality in principle, within hours of the meeting, members were phoning in and telling us virtually verbatim what had taken place. They got the information directly from Rhodes himself. It was pure expectation management. So now we knew for sure. Despite his matey approach, we couldn't trust him as far as we could throw him. Nothing new there then.

There was a difference though. Unlike Barley, Rhodes was glib and might fool the unwary to begin with until his true colours revealed themselves. He had one big fault, which was to be his downfall much later on as we shall see. When faced with a difficult point or question during negotiations for which he lacked the knowledge or adequate preparation, instead of parrying the question he would waffle and try to play it off the cuff. This would send him off at tangents and lead him into making statements that he would later either come to regret or deny he ever made. When he couldn't then remember which story he'd told last, he frequently contradicted himself and talked himself into trouble. He just didn't know when to keep his mouth shut.

Rhodes then tabled an agenda that consisted entirely of salary, allowances and benefits issues with seniority and freighter crewing tagged on the end. He said that if we could come to agreement on salary then perhaps he could do something about the latter two points. His salary proposals were vague but the gist of it was that they were looking to cut the based A Scales, 'to be in alignment with local conditions', and 'narrow the gap' between the A and B Scales. This narrowing would, naturally, be brought about by reducing A Scales rather than uplifting B Scales.

After a break we asked where they saw all the other issues on our agenda such as CoS, rostering and basings. Barley replied that they were prepared to discuss these as long as we had moved from our previous position. I asked Rhodes whether he had seen any of our papers from the previous talks or our latest proposals, and Barley butted in to say, 'No, he hasn't.'

This was significant and showed us the way. Rhodes had no intention of addressing the other issues. He didn't know anything about them. The technical aspects of our proposals were beyond his understanding anyway as we were to find out later. He was just coming after pay. They added a couple of carrots by trying to link seniority and ASL to pay, but we weren't falling for that one.

When we suggested first looking for cost savings in rostering and basings as per our proposals, Barley said, 'We've already got that, we're keeping it and the new target is based on a clean sheet of paper.'

In other words, thank you for doing all the work for us in identifying where we can make substantial savings. We'll take that but we're not going to give you anything at all in return and, actually, we want more. Their greed rather pissed off one of my team members who had done a lot of work on our proposals and he had a few choice words to say in return. This was no real negotiation on any of the issues that concerned us. It was neatly summarised when Barley said, 'Everything is on the table but we are not prepared to talk about anything unless you agree first to salary concessions.'

Some negotiation! It was already doomed to failure. In any negotiation, if at least some of the needs of both parties are not addressed there will be no deal. Even if you can get to a deal in those circumstances, it will not last because one of the parties will feel shafted and will come back later to try to redress the balance. The barbarians were at the gates again.

Our response to their position was simple and followed advice I had received from Rob McInnes, the IFALPA president. If you just say to me you *want* concessions, you won't get them. If you say to me you *need* concessions, then I am prepared to consider it but first you have to prove to me that you really do *need* them. You have to open your books to me and show me the data. The information presented so far by Rhodes was neither sufficiently detailed for us to make an objective assessment, nor did we possess the necessary expertise to make such an assessment. What was needed was not just an audit of the accounts, but an in-depth analysis of our company's overall financial position.

USALPA had conducted many such analyses in the past in situations such as we were facing and we enlisted its help. Airline managements that had previously agreed to a USALPA analysis included Northwest, United, KLM, Aer Lingus and Air France. USALPA agreed to conduct an analysis for us, with a projected completion date of the end of September.

Our reasoning was that it would be foolhardy to enter into concessionary bargaining without the data. Whilst there was no doubt that the Asian economic situation was bad, the question of whether concessions, from any employee group, were warranted was complex. In our cyclic industry, company profitability varies from year to year. A period of reduced return does not necessarily indicate that the labour force should accept reduced reward, whether temporary or permanent. What may be warranted is to accept a short-term reduction, with appropriate recompense and spring-back mechanisms when things improve, in order to assist a company through short-term difficulties. Alternatively, it may be that no concessions are needed at all. I sent Barley a letter stating that:

> In order to be convinced that there is a genuine need for any further concessions from the aircrew of the type that you have suggested, the Association will require that the ALPA Economic and Financial Analysis Department conducts a financial analysis of the Company. Until such time as management agrees to this, and the results are available, it would be irresponsible of me to recommend to the Membership of the Association that there is a genuine need for further concessions and I will not do so.

A second meeting was held on 24 July, at which Barley stated: We are not prepared to let that organisation conduct an analysis.' We restated our position and told them if they were looking for concessions, for us this was a 'show-stopper'. Barley agreed to take it back to the Executive and, to help him, we sent him a list of referees provided by USALPA, which was made up of the CEOs of several major North American and European carriers. In response, on 31 July we received a letter from Barley informing us that:

> . . . following consultation with the managing director and members of the Management Committee, management remain unwilling either to allow the [US]ALPA Economic and Financial Analysis Department

access to financial documents or to interview senior members of management.

He gave no reasons for the rejection but merely restated that the company's accounts are publicly recorded and audited and that they were '... unwilling to allow the USALPA Economic and Financial Analysis Department to perform an additional audit of our books.'

They were deliberately missing the point. The USALPA analysis that we required was NOT an audit; rather it would look at issues NOT covered in an audit, such as disposition of crew, assignment of aircraft types to particular routes, the likely impact of cost-saving measures already implemented and the overall financial situation of the company. There were some possible reasons for their attitude and we put these to our membership in a newsletter.

We haven't done anything like that before. Well, it's time we did. This technique has been acknowledged internationally to be very successful and it is now common practice in enlightened companies to allow employee groups full access to information in situations such as this. In that way they can be convinced of the need, or otherwise, for concessions to safeguard the well-being of the company.

Management is concerned that confidential data may be leaked to the public or to our competitors. So should they be, but the reality is that ALPA sign legally binding confidentiality agreements and would never consider breaking confidentiality. Management has been provided with a list of ALPA referees that includes the CEOs of Northwest, United and KLM. ALPA is completely beyond reproach in this area and is highly respected.

The reality may be that management *want* concessions but don't *need* concessions. If this was indeed the case, they would be concerned that an analysis would show that concessions are not warranted. It may simply be a negotiating tactic to attempt to use the current down-turn to attempt to wring further concessions out of employee groups. We require to be convinced of there being a genuine need before considering concessionary proposals.

In the end, no agreement was reached and the negotiations resulted in what Barley chose to call 'an impasse'. This was significant for us. We had successfully resisted a further assault on our terms and conditions. Unlike 1994, we had stood together and just said no. We were prepared to talk, yes, we were prepared to look at proposals, yes, but we were not just going to take their word for it and, more importantly, we were not going to let them bully us any more. They could have tried to complete their bypass manoeuvre by simply putting new contracts in our mailboxes but they didn't. They knew the boys would reject them this time around and they couldn't risk losing face. If they had done, their power would have been diluted. Power generally is only a perception. Use it and lose it. We were prepared in case they took that route. We had the comms ready, the support groups and all that would be needed to resist them. They weren't needed but the '6P' rule is essential in contingency planning.

We had won this round and all the time and effort that we'd spent rebuilding the AOA over the last four years had been worthwhile. Of course, that wouldn't be the end of it. The barbarians would be back.

11

Brotherhood

'Brotherhood is the very price and condition of man's survival.'
Carlos P. Romulo

The International Federation of Air Line Pilots' Associations (IFALPA) is the overall brotherhood of professional airline pilots around the world. It was created during a conference of pilots' associations held in London in April 1948 for the express purpose of providing a formal means for the airline pilots of the world to interact with the then newly formed UN body, the International Civil Aviation Organization (ICAO). The belief then was that the unique perspective of pilots operating in scheduled flying would be of critical benefit to the creation and adaptation of ICAO Standards and Recommended Practices through which ICAO regulates international civil aviation. This belief holds true today, is backed up by over 60 years of experience and the association holds permanent observer status on the ICAO Air Navigation Committee. From its origins, membership of IFALPA has now grown to over 100 member associations representing in excess of 120,000 airline pilots worldwide. The member associations, in their turn comprise representatives from all the pilots' associations in their respective countries. Thus, the HKALPA board consisted of representatives from the HKAOA, Dragonair Pilots' Association and the ASL Flight Crew Association, until it was disbanded with the demise of ASL.

IFALPA was originally set up with a technical focus to have input into such areas as 'accident analysis and prevention', 'aircraft design and operation', 'airport and ground environment' and 'air traffic services'.

179

Much of its work is still technically focused and, through its offices, pilots have made an enormous contribution to the safety of air transport over the years. In our own case in Hong Kong, the HKALPA team, headed by Captain Brian Greeves, was one of the founder members of the New Airport Safety Committee, which was instrumental in the design and operation of the airport at CLK. Through IFALPA training and support programmes, we also maintained a team of fully qualified and internationally accredited accident investigators (AIs).

In mature civil aviation environments, it has long been accepted by regulatory authorities, aircraft manufacturers and airline managements alike that line pilots can make a significant contribution to accident investigations and that their representatives should be included in the inquiry team formed subsequent to an accident. One reason for this is that, because of potential litigation in the aftermath of an accident, management pilots may be gagged and not as forthcoming as they might otherwise be with information relevant to the inquiry. This enlightened attitude was demonstrated admirably in the accident investigation into Swissair flight SR111, a McDonnell Douglas MD-11, which crashed south of Halifax, Nova Scotia, on 2 September 1998. From the outset, the Swiss Airline Pilots' Association, Aeropers, and the Canadian Airline Pilots' Association were invited to be part of the investigation. The manner of the deliberations and the objectivity of the conclusions can be used as a model of how a free and open accident investigation should be conducted.

Unfortunately, the same cannot be said of the accident investigation into the crash of China Airlines flight CI642, also an MD-11, on 22 August 1999 at CLK. At the time of the accident the airport was under the influence of a typhoon with strong crosswinds, heavy rain, turbulence and windshear. After touchdown the right main gear collapsed, the right wing broke off, fire broke out and the aircraft overturned. The fuselage came to rest beside the runway, upside down and facing the landing threshold. Two people were killed in the accident and another person died later in hospital. The Hong Kong CAD convened an accident inquiry panel, which included representatives from China Airlines management, the Taiwanese Civil Aviation Authority, NTSB and Boeing. The UK AAIB was used for assistance in analysis of the cockpit voice recorder (CVR) and flight data recorder (FDR). HKALPA offered assistance and asked to be involved in the inquiry but was cursorily rebuffed by the CAD. Approaches by USALPA, the Association of Airline Pilots of Taiwan and the Italian Airline Pilots' Association were similarly rebuffed. USALPA was particularly interested in the accident because it had many similarities to two other DC10/MD11 accidents at Faro, Portugal in December

1992 and Newark, New Jersey in July 1997. By coincidence, at the time of the accident, a member of the AOA was filming aircraft approaching CLK. He had a video of the crash, which he provided to HKALPA. Our accident investigators examined the tape and offered it to the inquiry. When they delivered it to the inquiry team, the CAD ushered our AI into a room at the far end of the building, refused point-blank to discuss its content and would not even permit him to meet the investigation team.

The treatment of the crew of the aircraft was much worse; in fact it was shameful. The Captain of the aircraft was an Italian national, Gerrardo Lettich. Immediately after the accident, the first interview with Captain Lettich and his F/O, Liu Cheng-Hsi, was conducted by the CAD in the coffee shop at the airport hotel in the presence of the general public and passengers from the flight. Both pilots were soaking wet, wrapped in blankets, smelling of aviation fuel and in shock. We contacted the pilots to offer assistance and they both requested to be accompanied by representatives from HKALPA at any subsequent interviews. This request was refused by the CAD. We also arranged for legal representation to be provided but the CAD also refused them access, calling one of the solicitors 'impertinent' when he put his head round the door to introduce himself. The F/O eventually agreed to be interviewed alone after a management pilot from China Airlines had spoken to him but the Captain refused further interviews without representation. After some written exchanges between him and the CAD, he was informed that he was no longer required for interview. The Captain's personal belongings were later returned to him by a representative of China Airlines. Why the CAD had passed his personal belongings to China Airlines rather than direct to their owner was a cause for concern. Significantly the only thing missing from his belongings was his passport and it was made clear to him that China Airlines management wanted him to return to Taipei for further investigation. We had seen this kind of treatment before in other places where, instead of conducting a proper investigation, the first action is to bring criminal charges against the crew and put them in jail. People involved in traffic accidents in Hong Kong receive better treatment than the CAD afforded these pilots.

We obtained a replacement passport for Captain Lettich and, with the help of some of our overseas colleagues, got him out of Hong Kong on a flight to Europe that night.

During the course of the investigation, information that could only have come from inside the investigation was leaked to the press leading to a lot of media speculation. These leaks concentrated on the actions of the crew and there were various attempts to apportion blame to the pilots and, in particular, the Captain. The CAD did nothing to refute the claims but, instead, on 17 September 1999, less than four weeks after the accident, published an 'Interim Accident Bulletin'. This bulletin contained a lot of subjective language, which, rather than putting a stop to the speculation, merely added fuel to the fire. The official CAD report into the accident was published in December 2004. It blamed the pilots, in particular the Captain, stating that 'The cause of the accident was the commander's inability to arrest the high rate of descent existing at 50 ft RA'.[20] The bulletin also made seven recommendations for China Airlines to change its training and procedures. It totally exonerated Hong Kong's shiny new airport and made only passing mention of the weather conditions in its conclusions, saying that 'variations in wind direction and speed below 50 ft RA may have resulted in a momentary loss of headwind component.'[20] This is in contrast to a statement made by a government spokesman on 24 August in which he said that in the previous two hours before the accident there were six missed approaches and two diversions. The CAD contradicted these numbers in its Interim Bulletin saying there were four missed approaches and five diversions. Whatever the correct figures, surely the weather conditions must have played a significant part. China Airlines contested the findings prior to the report's publication but a review board held before a magistrate in Hong Kong dismissed the objections almost in their entirety. It was an astonishing report and led many to conclude that one of the prime motivations of the inquiry was to ensure that no fault would be found with the facilities, location or anything else to do with CLK. Much easier just to blame the pilots. In stark contrast to the way the investigation into the SR111 crash was handled, this was an object lesson in how not to do things. It led to a serious loss of confidence in the objectivity of the Hong Kong CAD in the eyes of the international pilot community.

In response to incidents of this type in the past, pilots' associations through IFALPA had set up mutual aid networks to assist colleagues who might find themselves in trouble in far-flung corners of the world. IFALPA also supports member association pilots in such circumstances through its Legal Committee. In less enlightened places, it was commonplace that the first step in any investigation would be for the crew to be placed under arrest and detained by the local law enforcement authorities. One of the most notorious examples of this kind of behaviour occurred after a Swissair McDonnell Douglas DC8 overran the runway while landing on R/W 15L at Athens airport on 7 October 1979. The weather conditions at the time were poor with windshear and heavy rain. The runway was known for braking action problems because of contamination with deposits of rubber and oil. The pilots were charged with manslaughter, criminal negligence and interruption of air traffic. Their trial was held on 25-27 April 1983 in the full glare of a media circus. It was reported that the court was composed of three judges, one state prosecutor and one secretary. The first morning session started at 09:30 with cases dealing with prostitution, theft, swindling and other similar crimes. Without any recess, the same court then proceeded with hearing the prosecution of the pilots' case. The hearing was adjourned at 14:00 and then reconvened at 18:00, continuing until 03:00 the next day. The final day's session started at 18:00 and the verdict was rendered at 01:30.

At numerous times during the trial, the main judge was seen sleeping while the secretary doodled instead of taking minutes. The Swissair pilots' lawyers presented an excellent defence and everyone was confident they would be acquitted. At the end of the hearing the judges came back after only a ten-minute recess, delivered a guilty verdict and sentenced them each to five years and two months' imprisonment.

IFALPA also has an Industrial Committee set up to offer assistance to member associations that need help and advice in dealing with their local industrial problems. In Hong Kong, in the future, we were to be very grateful for its help. Whilst IFALPA cannot fight individual member associations' industrial battles for them, it does offer mutual assistance policies in the form of a recruitment ban, denial of capacity, maximum competition, denial of training facilities and assistance to pilots stranded away from home base.

With a recruitment ban in place, pilots in IFALPA member associations will not join the subject airline thus restricting any attempts to hire replacement crews. Denial of capacity involves member associations refusing to operate charters and wet leases on behalf of the subject airline thereby curtailing its operations. Maximum competition involves member associations operating as many flights as possible on behalf of the subject airline. At first sight these two policies appear to be in opposition to one another and, obviously, they cannot operate in parallel. In fact, maximum competition can impose a commercial penalty not only because of loss of loyalty from passengers in the future, but also because airlines, ever ready to take commercial advantage of a situation, often charge each other usurious rates on wet lease deals. It is up to the member association concerned to decide which strategy to adopt. Denial of training facilities involves member associations refusing to train pilots from the subject airline in third-party training establishments, thus making it difficult for the airline to maintain currency amongst its crew. Finally, assistance to pilots stranded away from home base is self-explanatory.

Whilst these policies may seem to be relatively low key when compared with more aggressive industrial options, they are designed to take account of the widely differing conditions that prevail among member associations around the world. These were nowhere more apparent than at annual conference.

IFALPA holds a conference every year at different locations around the world. During my time working with HKALPA, I attended annual conferences in Dublin in 1996, Cairo in 1997, Montreal in 1998, Pattaya in 1999 and Madeira in 2002. I also attended meetings in Islamabad, Johannesburg, Kuala Lumpur, Madrid, Seoul and Tokyo. At these meetings we would hear stories of the sort of challenges that our colleagues were facing worldwide. With 'code sharing', 'flagging out', alliances and the advent of the mega-carriers transcending national boundaries, airline managements are working globally in coordination to cut costs and lever down not only the terms and conditions of pilots but also flight time limitations and safety regulations. To do this, they are using everything at their disposal including local laws to try to impose their will.

In Cairo in 1997, we heard from pilots in Kenya who were being prosecuted by their national authorities because of their union activities. Being a small association with few resources, this placed a severe financial strain on them, and other member associations clubbed together to contribute to their legal defence costs. We heard a similar story the year before in Dublin from some Venezuelan pilots; and, locally, that same year, it was only with assistance provided by IFALPA member associations from the UK and US that we were able to get Nigel Demery reinstated. When faced with difficulties in your own locality, one of the things that can help to provide the strength to face such challenges and follow them through to their conclusion is to know that you are not alone. The knowledge that your colleagues around the world are prepared to come to your assistance is a great fillip. Extracts from a speech made at IFALPA's 50th-anniversary conference in Montreal in 1998 by the president, Captain Rob McInnis, illustrate some of these points admirably.

Message from Captain Rob McInnis, President of IFALPA

Learning from the Past – Looking to the Future

Despite the tremendous technological advances and improved reliability of aircraft over the last 50 years, the infrastructure necessary to support our industry has not kept up. Many developing countries cry poverty while skimming the income from aviation and using it for other purposes. Wealthier countries often fail to recognise the importance of air transport to their national economies. Rather than nurture the industry they squeeze the golden goose for everything they can get [and] practise cost recovery on a scale that does not exist in other modes of transportation.

Some of the reasons that IFALPA, and indeed most of our member associations, were formed many years ago are as valid now as they were then. Unfortunately, criminal liability, the inability to speak up on professional issues or participate in investigations and even the absence of fundamental human rights, such as freedom of association, continue to plague our profession.

In the early days of aviation, pilots not only flew the aircraft, but they usually provided the marketing, sold the tickets, loaded the baggage and even provided maintenance. The early airlines were run by pilots. Regulations were very limited in their number and scope. Today the pilot is often only an interested observer of corporate decisions made by accountants, lawyers or politicians. Regulations are a necessary part of a complex industry, but we need to be vigilant when powerful groups lobby for regulations that are operationally unsafe or detrimental to the health of our industry. As our individual influence diminishes, our collective influence takes on new importance.

At the same conference in Montreal, we heard a report from pilots in Japan Airlines, the country's biggest carrier, that their management had unilaterally imposed new rostering practices, which resulted in them operating trans-Pacific flights from San Francisco with only two pilots on board. They reported that it was common on these flights for the pilots to fall asleep at the controls and one pilot stated that he personally had been unable to execute a missed approach from decision height at NRT because of his inability to cope mentally with a go-around or diversion. He ended up busting minimums. This report was in stark contrast to a statement made by Akira Kondo, the president of Japan Airlines, in a 1996 Boeing-produced Flight Safety Foundation training video on 'Controlled Flight into Terrain', in which he said, 'Safety will always be the key element in our planning. All of Japan Airlines people are dedicated to safety. That is our mission.'

Put bluntly, what Japan Airlines was doing was dangerous and we decided to do something about it. In 1999, a number of airlines joined forces to form the **one**world® alliance. These included American Airlines, British Airways, Canadian Airlines, Cathay Pacific, Finnair, Iberia, Japan Airlines,

LanChile and Qantas. Knowing what was to take place, pilots' associations from each of these airlines formed the OneWorld Cockpit Crew Coalition (OCCC). A 'Memorandum of Understanding' was signed at a meeting in Tokyo in September 1998 and, at a press conference held afterwards, the chief delegates from the American Airlines, British Airways and Cathay representative associations, Richard Lavoy, Mike Oldham and I expressed the view in public that what Japanese Airlines was doing was unsafe. Up until then, cultural sensitivities had prevented the Japanese pilots from making such a statement in public. On 1 November, the AOA received the following message from the Japan Airlines Flight Crew Union:

> We are pleased to inform you that for a limited period of November 1 to the end of the year, the controversial San Francisco to Tokyo flight will have augmented crew for the first time in five years after the abrogation of the work agreement (three pilots for two-man aircraft and three pilots and two flight engineers for three-man aircraft). Japan Airlines management says it is just a seasonal adjustment and they have not indicated any intention to change the company-imposed work rules.

It was a good demonstration of what can be done to protect the travelling public in the face of managements that pay lip service to flight safety but continue to degrade standards with commercially inspired imperatives. If pilots as a group work together internationally they *can* make a difference.

After the formation of the OCCC, we received a petulant letter informing us that our name breached the **one**world® trade mark. Silly us! We had called ourselves the 'oneworld CCC'. We had to change the name to the 'OneWorld CCC'. This type of pettiness would be laughable except that it demonstrated the lengths these sorts of management were prepared to go to in order to try to stifle union representation. Internationally, victimisation of union officers was commonplace. At the Montreal conference, a pilot from Cyprus reported that he had received a notice of suspension by his company. The reason given was that, on a recent flight, he had declined to extend his flying duty period above that normally permitted by the regulations and operate into 'commander's discretion'. Fortunately, after direct intervention by IFALPA, he was reinstated within 24 hours. At the same conference, Captain Duane Woerth, the president of USALPA, reported being subjected to similar intimidation with the result that he had to insist his check rides were conducted with an FAA observer present to ensure impartiality. At one point he was suspended from duty as a result of an operational incident in which he was involved. Once again, with the support of IFALPA, he successfully resisted the pressures put on him and emerged with his reputation and professional status intact. The question has to be asked, however, what of the managers who initiate such attacks? Are they discredited, removed from office and made to apologise? Are they made to accept responsibility for their actions as aircrew must do every day of their working lives? Experience teaches us the answers to these questions.

One of the worst examples of victimisation I witnessed was with pilots working for Korean Air (KAL) and Asiana Airlines. They had never had any formal union representation but were faced with the same problems as the rest of us and realised that this needed to change if they were to have any hope of protecting their profession. This was particularly important since Korean Air had a very poor safety record at that time. HKALPA was seen as a relatively strong association in the Asia Pacific region so the Korean pilots came to us for help in starting their fledgling union. At a meeting I attended in Seoul on 5 December 1998, the Air Line Pilots' Association of Korea (ALPA-K) was formally inaugurated headed by Captain Chung Hui Yi of Asiana as president. On 8 December Captain Yi received a letter from Asiana informing him that he was dismissed from the company with effect from 3 December. The reason given for the dismissal was his involvement in a very minor in-flight incident that took place a month earlier on 6 November, for which he had already been cleared of blame. This was also despite the fact that he had just completed his simulator renewal on 2 and 3 December to the complete satisfaction of the Check Captain. To us, it was deliberate victimisation. The situation was no better at Korean Air.

An organisation called the Hang-Woo-Hueh had existed in Korean Air since the airline's inception. It was a fraternal association of KAL flight crew, which collected money for the celebration and/or commemoration of members' (and their families') births, marriages and deaths. It had nothing to do with safety or industrial representation. All previous attempts to form a true professional labour union, including the last one in 1989, were met with immediate and severe retribution by management. In June 1999, Captain Lee Sung-Jae, a Captain on the 747 with KAL who had been with the company for 25 years was elected president of the Hang-Woo-Hueh by a three to one majority. Captain Lee had also been appointed vice president of ALPA-K at its formation six months earlier. In July 1999, IFALPA held a meeting of its principal officers in Seoul where they met with representatives of the Korean Civil Aviation Bureau, KAL's CEO Shim Yi-Taik and Asiana's vice president Hur Cha-Dong. At this meeting the POs lobbied for recognition of ALPA-K by the regulator and the two airlines. Also in July, Captain Lee surveyed the membership of the Hang-Woo-Hueh for the formation of a labour union. As a result of this survey, on 30 August 1999, 112 pilots met to formally inaugurate the Korean Air Flight Crew Union (KAL FCU). The company sent non-pilot employees to the meeting to photograph those taking part and threaten the participants with dismissal. Captain Lee was elected unanimously as president with ten other board members, Captains Baek S.I., Choo M.Y., Chun D.J., Han C.S., Kim H.S., Kim H.Y., Lee S.C., and F/Os Ha H.Y., Kim J.O. and Lee K.I. I make no apology for listing their names. These were brave men to stand up and be counted in the face of certain retribution.

On 31 August the KAL FCU submitted a request for certification with the Korean Ministry of Labour. On the same day, KAL suspended Captain Lee and F/Os Lee K.I., Ha H.Y. and a Hang-Woo-Hueh staff member F/O Choi Jae-Hoon from flying duty and instructed them to report for desk duty at company premises. In the ensuing week, the KAL FCU membership quickly swelled to 1,150 out of a total pilot force of around 1,500. On 7 September the Labour Ministry formally rejected the request for union certification citing the status of the pilots as 'special detail police' and representatives of management and, therefore, disqualified from forming a union.

The term 'special detail police' was normally applied to armed private security officers deployed in banks and the like. Their freedom to organise is limited by the Korean National Government Employee (Public Servant) Ordinance. The KAL FCU filed a legal action to have this designation of their pilot members overturned by the courts but that could take years. In an attempt to circumvent their unilateral designation as security guards, the union also circulated a request for cancellation of this status, and the first day saw over 400 pilots signing the petition. KAL management's response to this tactic is perhaps best described by reproducing extracts from a Kafkaesque letter from CEO Shim Yi-Taik dated 9 September 1999.

Regarding the Formation of an Unlawful Flight Crew Union

Just when we were finally becoming stabilized in recovering the fallen honour of our company from a series of accidents . . . a minority of crew members have caused severe detriment to flight safety by agitating the majority in the effort to set up a labour union which as yet is not recognized by law, and I cannot hide from you my exasperation.

Therefore, I intend to clearly spell out the company's stance regarding the insistence by the board members of Hang-Woo-Hueh regarding designation as 'special detail police'.

A flight crew member is empowered to execute the authority of law enforcement on board an aircraft by the 'Aircraft Operation Safety Law', and is delegated the use of weaponry by the 'Aviation Act', while an airline operator is required to place an armed security guard or a 'special detail police' on its aircraft according to the 'Security Duty Regulation' . . . and the 'Security Objective Management Policy' and 'Airport & Port Security Duty Detailed Operating Policy' established under Article 28 of the Presidential Order.

Accordingly, . . . the company is fulfilling the execution of law enforcement authority and use of weapons by designating flight crew members as 'special detail police'.

However, a group of flight crew members have been distributing forms for requesting cancellation of their designation as 'special detail police' and have been initiating unlawful group activity in violation of the Special Detail Police Law . . . which prohibits group activity for purposes of labour coalition . . . [and] it is hereby made known that these actions which are clearly in contempt of not only the company regulations but also the national laws in full force, must be punished.

Even if a flight crew member were not designated as 'special detail police', the Ministry of Labour has repeatedly notified . . . that a Captain of an aircraft cannot participate in a labour union as the de facto manager in the place of the operator to have substitute authority for enforcement of common law . . . and has also lately clarified . . . that an aircraft crew member who is a 'special detail police' is not entitled to the qualifications of labour union membership. What is more, the recent application for approval of the Flight Crew Labour Union forwarded by the central leadership of the Hang-Woo-Hueh was denied by the government authority on September 11, 1999, giving undeniable proof that the formation of a flight crew labour union is an unconstitutional activity which cannot be recognized by current laws.

Disregarding its unquestionable illegality and inappropriateness, some crew members have opted not on the honing of their flight skills and in the reinforcement of safe practices, but rather on the agitation of the many superior flight crew members, unrestrained in group activities both within and without, adversely influencing the very survival of the company; such malignant behaviour against the company certainly cannot be tolerated, and shall be dealt with severely.

Those crew members who interfere against company business and threaten flight safety through unlawful activities are forewarned that they will not only be severely punished according to company regulations . . . but may be criminally prosecuted for violations of related ordinances when necessary.

In addition, it is noted that those employees who fall in line with these agitators and sign the so-called 'Application for Cancellation of Designation as Special Detail Police' will be considered to be voluntarily abdicating their duties as flight crew members, and will certainly be dealt with accordingly through personnel actions.

Flight safety is the foundation for our survival which cannot be compromised. Safety stems from compliance with procedures and regulations, and precious lives of passengers cannot be entrusted to those flight crew members who flagrantly break rules and act as lawbreakers.

Despite the threats, intimidation, rhetoric, misuse of labour laws and blatant misrepresentation of the flight safety situation by a man who was the CEO of an airline with one of the worst safety records in the business, the Korean pilots ultimately prevailed and the KAL FCU was granted certification by the Korean authorities.

No story about civil aviation in the Asia Pacific region in the 1990s can be complete without relating what happened to Philippine Airlines (PAL), one of the region's oldest carriers. Included in Appendix 1 to this book is a copy of an article on the subject that was first published in the September 1998 edition of the AOA's quarterly magazine *The Flyleaf*. It is a story of corruption, cronyism, asset stripping and union busting. Through my work with HKALPA and IFALPA, I was directly involved in trying to help the Airline Pilots' Association of the Philippines (ALPAP) and its president, Captain Sotico Lloren, with their problems. Sotico is one of the most honourable and principled men that have I met in my aviation career. He and his colleagues faced insuperable odds but he did not flinch from the fight. At a meeting in Manila with him and his legal counsel (a very brave young woman), they both told me that they had received death threats against themselves and their families. In a country like the Philippines, which has an active organised crime and gun culture, such threats are to be taken seriously. Despite this, Sotico did his duty. He tried to leave his profession in a better condition than when he entered it. When asked by a journalist whether it had all been worth it after PAL went into receivership in 1998, Sotico replied, 'Yes, most definitely. With no contract and no collective bargaining agreement, it is better not to work at all than to work as a slave.'

In 2001, in recognition of his efforts, he was awarded an IFALPA presidential citation.

At the IFALPA annual conference held in Madeira on 5 April 2003, I was fortunate to receive a similar award from the president, Ted Murphy. It read:

FOR INSPIRATIONAL LEADERSHIP
AND MOTIVATION OF THE MEMBERS OF
HIS HOME ASSOCIATION
AND TO IFALPA MEMBER ASSOCIATIONS
IN THE ASIA AND PACIFIC REGIONS

DEDICATED TO THE 49ERS

12

Is It Safe?

Szell: *Is it safe?*

Levy: *I don't know what you mean. I can't tell you something's safe or not, unless I know specifically what you're talking about.*

Szell: *Is it safe?*

Levy: *Tell me what the 'it' refers to.*

Szell: *Is it safe?*

Levy: *Yes, it's safe, it's very safe, it's so safe you wouldn't believe it.*

Szell: *Is it safe?*

Levy: *No. It's not safe, it's . . . very dangerous, be careful.*

John Schlesinger's *Marathon Man*

What is 'safe', what is 'unsafe' and what is 'dangerous'? In aviation we have to be very careful in using these terms, so how do we define them? Definitions from *thefreedictionary.com* include:

Safe: Secure from danger, harm, or evil.
Unsafe: Not safe; perilous.
Dangerous: Involving exposure or vulnerability to harm or risk; perilous. Being able or likely to do harm.

Pilots are often accused by management of 'playing the safety card' in industrial relations. Equally, pilots often accuse management of doing the same thing in pursuit of commercial gain. So who is right or is it all posturing?

In 1992, Cathay Pacific's original rostering practices provided extra protections against pilot fatigue over and above the basic safety net of CAD 371. They were safe. The basic provisions of CAD 371 are also safe. It can be said, however, that in downgrading from the rostering practices merely to CAD 371, the additional safety margin has been eroded and the operation is now less safe than it was, albeit that it is still inherently safe. Conversely, we can say that CAD 371 is safe, but Cathay's rostering practices were safer.

CAD 371 contains some inviolate rules as well as some recommendations. The essentials are identified by use of the words 'shall' or 'must'; desirable features are introduced by the words 'should' or 'may'. An example of a desirable feature is to avoid scheduling rest periods of between 18 and 30 hours when constructing crew rosters. The reason for this is that it is very difficult to complete two sleep cycles in such a period and you will end up reporting for duty just at the time when your body is telling you to go to sleep. If a monthly roster contains one 18-30 rest period, is it unsafe? Probably not. What if it contains five such rest periods? It is certainly less safe but is it unsafe? If it only happens once a year, maybe not. However, if rosters are produced like this month in and month out then, yes, it becomes unsafe because pilots are now being routinely exposed to rosters that will make them more likely to suffer from cumulative fatigue. Having said that, is it dangerous? In the strict dictionary definition of the term, the answer is yes. In comparative terms, however, maybe not, because dangerous is an emotive word; that is up until there is a crash caused by pilot fatigue at which point it most definitely is dangerous.

What we can say categorically *is* dangerous is flying aircraft with unlicensed pilots on board as part of the legally required crew. Flying trans-Pacific operations with only two pilots on board who are falling asleep at the controls, as certain Japanese airlines were doing, is dangerous. It is not just unsafe. It is an unacceptably high level of risk and it is dangerous. Allowing aircraft maintenance to deteriorate to the point where an engine mounting bulkhead is cracked across the whole of its width is dangerous. It could be argued that the system worked because the crack was found before it caused separation of the engine in the air. I would argue that the crack should have been found much sooner, before it had spread so far.

An airline management will point to its accident record to show that its airline is safe. In many cases this is true, but statistics alone do not prove the case. At a safety meeting I attended, pilots from a Nigerian carrier reported that they had serious safety concerns about their operation.

Their airline had a very high rate of incident reports and the pilots asked for help. Pressure was brought to bear on their management with the result that, the next year, the incident report rate had dropped to zero. The pilots had received instructions from their management that, hence-forth, no further incident reports should be filed because it was impacting on the reputation of their airline. So that fixed it. Zero incident reports equals zero safety problems. Problem solved? Of course not. There is a maxim in cricket that you are only as good as your last innings. It doesn't matter how many centuries you might have in the score-book, if you put up a pair in the next match, that's what counts. Similarly, if we just use statistics, on the face of it you have a safe airline up until the point when you crash. Flight safety is a matter of degrees. Pilots are responsible people and they do not use the safety card for industrial leverage. There may be very occasional exceptions to this that management will hold up, but one swallow does not make a summer. Crying wolf is not what we do.

In any business, CBA is part of the decision-making process. Unpalatable though it may seem, airlines routinely run a CBA on acci-dent scenarios as part of their contingency planning. It's too late to start planning after the event. You need an accident contingency plan in place just in case it happens. It's another example of 'what if' thinking that is essential in aviation and is an entirely responsible approach. Let us take this one step further. I was present at a meeting where Turnbull said, 'We've done the CBA on accidents and we can afford a hull loss every three years.'

I was flabbergasted. It is one thing to run a CBA as part of contin-gency planning. It is another thing entirely actually to envisage a scenario where a hull loss every three years could be considered in any way to be acceptable. Just the expression of a potential reality in those terms shocked me. It is clear by now, no doubt, that I am no fan of the Turnbull school of management. Perhaps I misunderstood the intent of his state-ment and took away the wrong impression. I find it very hard to believe that anyone in a senior management position in an airline could ever hold such a view. If they did, then their suitability for the job should be seriously questioned. There is no doubt that an accident will affect an airline financially. The cost of hull insurance goes up. Passenger confi-dence is damaged and they will choose to fly with other airlines for a while until memories fade. Then there is the asset value of the aircraft itself and the cost of compensation claims. However, it is this concen-tration solely on the financial aspects of safety that is of concern.

The tragic events of 11 September 2001 reverberated throughout the airline industry. The loss of life was horrendous. For me, personally, seeing something that I had spent my professional life trying to make as safe as possible turned into a weapon was absolutely sickening. When I first heard the news, I was in my local pub. A friend came in and said, 'You've got to look at CNN.' We turned on the television and saw what we saw. I went home, woke up my wife to tell her what had happened, sat on the bed and cried. Through my professional life and my work with IFALPA and the OCCC, I had many friends and colleagues in America. Although I didn't know any of the pilots involved personally, I felt very deeply for them, their families and their loved ones. If ever there was a time when the brotherhood needed to come together to give one another succour and support, it was then. The next day, Turnbull put out a letter to all the employees in Cathay. It consisted of five paragraphs. The first four concentrated on the potential financial impact of the tragedy. He talked about the financial downturn, the cost of fuel and declining share prices. Only in the last paragraph, consisting of three lines, did he make any mention of our colleagues and their families. Could we have not at least been given some time to grieve before considering the damned dollars and cents? I found the content and timing of his letter in particularly poor taste.

As I have said, safety is a matter of degrees and, despite all the probability calculations in the world, to some extent will always remain subjective; a matter of judgment. There are many rules, regulations and limitations in aviation designed to ensure safety. They have been developed over the years as a result of lessons learned the hard way. Limitations are fixed points that we must not pass, for beyond here be dragons. However, just because a limitation is there, it does not mean that we should routinely operate right up to that limit. As an example, there are a number of variables that affect the landing performance of an aircraft. These include:

V_{REF} Target touchdown speed;
V_{AT} Speed of aircraft over runway threshold – nominally V_{REF} +5 to V_{REF} +15;
Wheel height over the runway threshold – nominally 30 ft;
Glideslope angle – nominally 3 °;
Touchdown point – nominally 1500 ± 500 ft;
Weight – up to MLW for the particular runway;
Brake application time – nominally 1.44 seconds after main wheel touchdown;
Level of brake pressure applied – up to 3,000 psi;

Reverse thrust application time – nominally three seconds after
main wheel touchdown;

Level of reverse thrust applied – nominally 90 per cent N1;

Runway slope – nominally ≤ 0.8 per cent;

Mean braking coefficient of friction – nominally 0.2242 µ.

At 12:27 on 27 May 1985, a British Airtours Lockheed L1011 TriStar
landed on R/W 14 at Leeds Bradford airport. It failed to stop within the
runway length and ran off the end at a speed of 30 kt. The aircraft came
to a stop with the main wheels half buried in soft ground 35 feet beyond
the end of the paved surface. All the passengers and crew evacuated from
the aircraft and there were no injuries. The aircraft accident investigation concluded the following:[18]

$V_{AT} - V_{REF}$ +13;

Wheel height over the runway threshold – 27 ft;

Glideslope angle – $3\frac{1}{2}°$;

Touchdown point – left main wheels 1,476 ft. right main wheels
1,640 ft;

Weight – MLW 162,400 kg, Actual LW 159,929 kg;

Brake application time – 4 seconds after main wheel touchdown

Level of brake pressure applied – 3,000 psi;

Reverse thrust application time – without delay after main wheel
touchdown;

Level of reverse thrust applied – 90% N1 increasing to
maximum;

Runway slope – 0.25% down-slope overall, but 0.83% over the
first 1,876 ft.

So, the aircraft speed was within limits albeit on the higher end of the
range. The wheel height was within limits. The glideslope angle was
slightly steeper than normal, because of obstacles on the approach to the
runway, but still within limits. The touchdown point was right on the
button. The aircraft was 2,471 kg below its MLW. The brakes were
applied slightly later than scheduled but still within the parameters specified in the BA Operations Manual. This was more than compensated
for by immediate application of reverse thrust up to maximum. The
runway slope was within limits albeit that the down-slope on the first
part of the runway was slightly greater than scheduled. Everything was
within limits, so why did the aircraft not stop in time? The answer is
that the achieved braking coefficient was far lower than scheduled. This

was caused by degradation of the runway surface. It was also wet from a rain shower that had passed through earlier, but that should not have been a contributing factor because the actual landing performance was scheduled on a wet runway condition. Additionally, wet runway landing performance is scheduled on a condition of one thrust reverser inoperative. All three thrust reversers on the aircraft were working so it had 'one extra' over and above the schedule. It should have stopped safely but it didn't. The accident report exonerated the crew from all blame and concluded that 'The accident was caused by the failure of the aircraft to achieve the expected level of braking effectiveness on the wet runway.' Various recommendations were made to ensure that this would not happen again and that, in the future, wet runways would provide the required level of braking coefficient of friction.

The point is that it only took one out of eleven parameters to be outside limits for the accident to happen. Had the runway slope been level or uphill instead of just above the downhill limit for the first 1,876 feet, the accident might not have happened. Had V_{AT} been V_{REF} +5 instead of +13, it might have helped. Had the glideslope been 3° instead of 3½° it might have made a difference. Had the aircraft been 10 or 15 tonnes lighter, it might have stopped before the end of the runway. Had all these parameters been below the limits, with some extra 'padding' instead of right on the margins, the accident might have been prevented even given the low braking coefficient caused by the runway surface condition. So, we return to the original premise that, just because there is a limitation, it does not mean that we should routinely operate right up to that limit when it is not necessary.

Sometimes we have no choice. On ULR ops, we routinely take off at MTOW. We have to. As Captains, one of our responsibilities is to carry the maximum commercial payload so we load the aircraft to the limit. It's one of the things we are paid to do. The same does not hold true for MLW. We have much more control over this. It is commercial policy in many airlines to 'tanker' fuel. Cathay operates a number of routes to Japan. Because of import costs, fuel in Japan is considerably more expensive than fuel in Hong Kong. On those routes, therefore, we would carry more fuel on the outbound sector than we actually needed to complete the flight with the result that we would have to pick up less fuel in Japan for the return flight. It saved money. In theory then, the biggest cost saving can be achieved if we tanker right up to the MLW for arrival at our destination, but should we always do this? The accountants run their numbers and say yes because, to them, it is purely a numerical calculation. If the arrival runway is 11,000 feet long and there are no landing distance considerations, I might agree with them. However, if I am going to land on R/W 14 at Leeds Bradford in a rain shower then I most certainly do not. In this case, in terms of the variables, I am going to make sure that I have as much going for me as possible. If that means not tankering any fuel at all to keep the landing weight as low as possible, then so be it. Safety should always override cost considerations.

Whilst the purpose here is only to examine safety considerations, there is also an environmental argument against tankering that is worth a mention. On a typical four or five hour sector, if we carry an extra 10 tonnes of fuel for tankering purposes, at the end of the flight we will only have around 8.5 tonnes of our 'extra' fuel remaining. This is because of the increased weight of the aircraft. Higher aircraft weight equals higher *en route* fuel burn. There is an argument to say, therefore, that we have burned off an additional 1.5 tonnes of a non-renewable natural resource purely in the pursuit of commercial gain.

Airlines and oil companies these days are all very keen to jump on the green bandwagon and it is a source of amusement to me to listen to the spin doctors trying to establish their green credentials. As one who used routinely to burn around 650 tonnes of Jet A-1 fuel per month in following my chosen profession, I guess I can hardly talk. Air travel is here to stay and modern jet engines are much cleaner and more efficient than their predecessors, but the tankering issue is one that the environmental lobby would do well to address. Airlines will argue that their competitors do it and, if they don't do it, they give them a commercial advantage. It's the classic child's plea, 'He can do it, why can't I?'

As my mother used to reply, 'If he stuck his hand in a fire, would you do it as well?'

If all airlines together took the initiative and, as a group, abandoned fuel tankering, that truly would be a genuine contribution to the environmental agenda. They manage to operate in concert when running their price-fixing cartels so there should be no reason why they couldn't apply the same level of consensus to saving our planet. Of course, there would be no way to monitor that everyone was sticking to the policy and not cheating to gain a commercial edge. They'd just have to trust one another.

The overriding authority of the aircraft commander in respect of certain aspects of the AFTLS is a safety issue worthy of examination. Maximum allowable flight duty periods (FDP) and minimum allowable rest periods on normal operations are specified in the AFTLS. These are the basic ground rules used to prevent pilot fatigue. Of course, things sometimes go wrong so we need to have some 'what if' provisions to cater for unforeseen circumstances. These extra provisions are contained in a section entitled Service Disruption. In certain defined circumstances, the Captain of the aircraft may increase the normally permitted FDP by up to three hours. Similarly, he may also reduce a rest period. It is worthwhile quoting some extracts of CAD 371 in respect of 'Commanders' Discretion'. On service disruption generally it states:

> This provision is to cover unforeseen circumstances which occur during operations. It is not intended for use in regular practice, cannot be rostered and shall only apply once the flight crew member has commenced a rostered FDP.

On the method of use, it states:

> In the case of service disruption the operator may request the aircraft Commander to implement the provisions of this Section in order to extend an FDP, **or exceptionally**, to reduce a Rest Period, or the aircraft commander may at his own initiative decide to do so.

On the decision-making process, it states:

> After receiving a request the aircraft Commander, taking into consideration all relevant factors including the circumstances of the other crew members, and the overriding consideration of safety, shall inform the operator of his decision. The aircraft Commander may elect to work less than, and not necessarily to the full extent of, the provisions. **His decision in such matters shall be final and unquestioned**.

On extension of an FDP, it states:

> In the case of service disruption the maximum FDP shall be calculated by adding 3 hours to the FDP otherwise available using the appropriate standard provisions. In the event that the standard FDP has already been extended by use of an augmented crew, or split duty, or follows upon a reduced rest period, then the maximum that can be added is 2 hours. These 3 and 2 hour extensions may only be exceeded in an emergency. In this respect, **an emergency is a situation which in the judgement of the aircraft Commander presents a serious risk to the health or safety of crew and passengers, or endangers the lives of others**.

On reduction of a rest period, it states:

> An aircraft Commander may, at his discretion, and after taking note
> of the circumstances of other members of the crew, reduce a rest
> period but only insofar as the room allocated to the crew member
> must be available for occupation for a minimum of 10 hours. **The
> exercise of such discretion shall be considered exceptional** and
> must not be used to reduce successive rest periods.

It would seem that the regulations are clear cut. Not so to some. Before
the issue of CAD 371 in 1998, the previous CAD AFTLS document did
not even allow the operator to request a Captain to exercise his discretion. In fact it specifically prohibited any such requests. Cathay managers
used to get round this by leaving messages to the Captain on arrival,
which stated something along the lines of: 'Captain x [usually a duty
manager] wants you to know that he will have no objections if you
choose to exercise Commanders' Discretion.'

Very subtle. During the proceedings of the FTLWG, management
lobbied to have this restriction loosened. We felt it would be a small
concession that we could live with. The introduction of the revised CAD
371 permitted them now to actually make direct requests. We thought
that this loosening of the regulations would be enough, but no. As always,
they wanted more. The ducks carried on nibbling. Despite the fact that
the Captain's decision was supposed to be 'final and unquestioned', they
started calling people into the office to 'discuss' such decisions when
Captains declined to exercise discretion. These were actions in direct
breach of the regulations and typified the sort of attitude we faced in the
Flight Ops Department under Barley's watch.

The use of Commanders' Discretion most often came into play when
a typhoon hit Hong Kong. Aircraft would be unable to land and the
squadron dispersed to various alternates such as Manila, Taipei and
Shenzhen. The whole recovery process could take three or four days to
return to normal operations. The pressure would be on to reduce rest
periods so as to get the aircraft back ASAP once Hong Kong reopened.
Unfortunately for the Commercial Department, from the safety standpoint this is just the time when you may NOT want to reduce a rest
period. A diversion would generally, of necessity, involve a very long
duty day with possibly two attempted approaches into Hong Kong in
very poor flying conditions at the limits of controllability of the aircraft
prior to diverting. To reduce a rest period after such a duty and then
return to Hong Kong again with a tired crew in continuing adverse

weather conditions at best poses an increased risk to the safety of the aircraft and at worst is asking for trouble.

During negotiations on rostering practices in 2000/1, which we will cover in more detail later, Commanders' Discretion became a show-stopper and was one of the issues that ultimately led to a breakdown in the talks. Rhodes was leading the management team and his stated objective was to be able to *order* the aircraft Captain to exercise Commanders' Discretion. In other words, he wanted to take away the authority of the Captain. He wanted some unqualified clerk sitting in FOCC to have the authority to order the Captain to use provisions that are supposed to be reserved for 'exceptional' circumstances. It demonstrated to us his complete lack of understanding of operational matters. This was confirmed when he stated, 'Well we just see Commanders' Discretion as an industrial tool used by the pilots to disrupt the operation.'

His remark was crass in the extreme.

Throughout the whole process we had tried to educate Rhodes in the duties and legal responsibilities of the aircraft Captain. It is mandated in the various legal statutes and instruments relating to civil aviation: there is only one person who carries the can in the event of an accident and that is the man wearing the four bars. The other crew members may come in for criticism but in the end the Captain is held responsible and 'pilot error' is such an easy and convenient way to close the book. This was demonstrated very clearly in the BEA Munich air disaster of 6 February 1958 and the Air New Zealand Mount Erebus crash on 28 November 1979 where Captains James Thain and Jim Collins were held to be solely responsible by the initial accident enquiries. It took their relatives and colleagues many years to unearth the true causes of the accidents and finally clear their names.

With the similarities in maritime and aviation law, the inquiry into the *Herald of Free Enterprise* roll-on-roll-off ferry disaster on 6 March 1987 at Zeebrugge was a good example of everything we were trying to convey to Rhodes. In his report, the chairman of the inquiry, Lord Justice Sir Barry Sheen, castigated Townsend Thoresen, the ship's owners, and identified a 'disease of sloppiness' and negligence at every level of the corporation's hierarchy. The report also remarked on equipment deficiencies on board the ship. Despite all this, however, ultimately the Captain of the vessel, his First Officer and a deck-hand were found to be responsible for the accident. In October 1987, a coroner's inquest jury into the capsizing returned verdicts of unlawful killing. Seven individuals involved at the company were charged with gross negligence manslaughter, and the operating company, P&O European Ferries (Dover) Ltd, was charged with corporate manslaughter. The case collapsed after the judge directed the jury to acquit the company and the five most senior individual defendants.[19] We prepared an extensive dossier of the accident inquiry for Rhodes to read and, hopefully, gain some understanding of what it was we were talking about. A couple of weeks later, during another meeting, I asked him some questions designed to see whether he had grasped any of the concepts that we were trying to convey. It was obvious from his answers that either he had not even looked at our dossier, or he simply didn't understand, or care.

If we accept the premise that the ultimate extension of aviation is space travel, then the Challenger and Columbia space shuttle accidents provide many lessons when confronted by this type of management ethos. The Challenger exploded 73 seconds after liftoff on 28 January 1986. The explosion was caused by the failure of an O-ring seal in the right solid rocket booster. The O-ring failure caused a breach in the joint it sealed, allowing pressurised hot gas from within the solid rocket motor to reach the outside and impinge upon the adjacent attachment hardware and external fuel tank. This led to the separation of the booster's aft attachment and structural failure of the external tank. Aerodynamic forces then broke up the orbiter.

The Rogers Commission, which investigated the accident, found that NASA's organisational culture and decision-making processes had been a key contributing factor to the accident. NASA managers had known that contractor Morton Thiokol's design of the solid rocket boosters contained a potentially catastrophic flaw in the O-rings since 1977, but they failed to address it properly. Rather than redesigning the joint, they came to define the problem as an acceptable flight risk. Even when it became more apparent how serious the flaw was, no one considered grounding the shuttles until a fix could be implemented. They also disregarded warnings from engineers about the dangers of launching posed by the low temperatures that morning and had failed adequately to report these technical concerns to their superiors. The report also strongly criticised the decision-making process that led to the launch of Challenger, saying that it was seriously flawed. One of the commission's most well-known members was theoretical physicist Richard Feynman. He was so critical of flaws in NASA's 'safety culture' that he threatened to remove his name from the report unless it included his personal observations on the reliability of the shuttle. These appeared as an appendix to the report in which he argued that the estimates of reliability offered by NASA management were wildly unrealistic, differing as much as a thousand-fold from those of working engineers. 'For a successful technology,' he concluded, 'reality must take precedence over public relations, for nature cannot be fooled.' The Challenger disaster has been used as a case study in many discussions of engineering safety and workplace ethics.

The Rogers Commission offered nine recommendations on improving safety in the space shuttle programme and NASA was directed by President Reagan to report back within 30 days as to how it planned to implement those recommendations. Although significant changes were made by NASA after the Challenger accident, many commentators argued that the changes in its management structure and organisational culture were neither deep nor long lasting.

After the space shuttle Columbia disaster on 1 February 2003, attention focused once again on the attitude of NASA management towards safety issues. The Columbia Accident Investigation Board concluded that NASA had failed to learn many of the lessons of Challenger. In particular, the agency had not set up a truly independent office for safety oversight and 'NASA's response to the Rogers Commission did not meet the Commission's intent.' The Board also believed that 'the causes of the institutional failure responsible for Challenger have not been fixed,' saying that the same 'flawed decision-making process' that had resulted in the Challenger accident was responsible for Columbia's destruction 17 years later.

In civil aviation we MUST take heed of these lessons. In the face of management failures, the ultimate responsibility for protecting our profession and ensuring that we leave it in a better state than when we entered remains with us, the pilots. The operational safety envelope is there and if we push it in two or three directions at the same time it will normally hold but the probability that it will break increases. Such matters are command decisions. They should neither be influenced nor made by people who lack the qualifications, the knowledge, the expertise or the experience to do so. The authority of the Captain in this respect should be inviolate. If professional aviation is to maintain its hard won safety record, every effort must be made to resist those who seek to undermine this principle in the pursuit of financial gain, no matter how it is dressed up.

13

Why Things Happen

'Anything that can go wrong will go wrong.'

Murphy's Law

'Shit happens.'

Anon

In April 1997, I was scheduled to operate a flight out of Kai Tak on the A330. Whilst in flight despatch, I was notified of an aircraft change because the original aircraft was U/S. The replacement aircraft was parked on a remote nullah bay and, after completing the pre-flight planning, I went out there with my crew. When we boarded the aircraft, there was no engineer in attendance, which was unusual, but the tech log was sitting on the control pedestal and the aircraft had been signed off as fit for flight. We completed our pre-flight checks and ten minutes before STD the ground engineer who had signed the tech log boarded the aircraft to despatch the flight. All seemed normal until a couple of minutes later when a mechanic, who was looking very sweaty and harassed, came onto the flight deck and asked me to move my seat so that he could get access to the trapdoor into the avionics bay underneath the floor. He was carrying a spare part. After he had been down into the bay and re-emerged, I asked the ground engineer what the mechanic had been doing. Everyone was now looking a bit sheepish. It transpired that the mechanic had been refitting the electrical emergency power contactor, which he had previously removed to troubleshoot a problem on another aircraft. He had removed this part without making an entry in the tech log, which was a no-no.

Because he had not made an appropriate entry, the ground engineer didn't know that this component had been removed and had signed off the aircraft as fit for flight when, in fact, a safety-critical part of the electrical system was missing. Had we got airborne and lost normal electrical power, the emergency generator would not have been able to take over to power the AC system and we would have been down to battery power only. The A330 is an electric aircraft and it doesn't work very well without AC power. Clearly a case of someone not doing his job properly and he should be for the high jump. Rather than pilot error, it was engineer error. How did this happen when there are supposed to be specific procedures in place to prevent exactly this sort of mistake? The first link in the causal chain was that the aircraft was not originally scheduled for the flight so the mechanic thought it was 'spare'. The comms system failed to notify him that it had been rescheduled. The next link was a lack of spare parts. Another aircraft had an electrical fault and he needed an emergency power contactor to troubleshoot the problem. There wasn't one in stock so, using his initiative, he cannibalised one from my aircraft to try to sort it out. He was under a lot of time and workload pressure because of OTP and staff cut-backs so he cut a corner by neglecting the tech log entry, thinking that it would be OK. The last link was that the despatching engineer was unaware of any of this when he signed the aircraft off because he was trying to despatch four or five other aircraft at the same time. He was under just as much workload pressure as the mechanic. Because it was a potential serious hazard to flight safety, I was duty bound to fill in an air safety report. I was reluctant to do so because I knew it would get the engineer and the mechanic in trouble but, if I didn't, what was to stop the same thing happening again? Systemic failures needed to be reported so that Mawdsley's department could, hopefully, do something about it. Yes, the mechanic made a mistake and did not follow proper procedures. Yes, the engineer signed off the aircraft when it was not fit for flight. But the root cause of the problem was not these two men. They were diligent and responsible employees. The root cause was a systemic failure that put excessive demands and pressure on them to the point where they made the mistake. If there had been enough spare parts, if they had more staff and if their managers weren't so obsessed about OTP, it would probably never have happened. I heard later that the mechanic had been disciplined for his part in the incident. Instead of addressing the systemic failure, they just kicked the cat.

On 17 January 2000, B747-400 B-HOX got airborne from Xiamen under the command of Captain Ken Carver. It had been at the TAECO engineering facility to receive a new 'Spirit of Hong Kong' paint job as part of a public relations campaign by Cathay. The livery had originally been applied to a 747-200, VR-HIB, back in July 1997 to commemorate the handover. There was a reception committee of government officials and Cathay directors waiting in Hong Kong for Ken's arrival as part of a PR fanfare before the aircraft departed for London that night. The aircraft was very light, only 200 tonnes for the ferry flight, and with maximum TOGA power for takeoff, the V1/VR speed of 116 kt arrived in the twinkling of an eye. As soon as he rotated, Ken knew he was in trouble. The stall warning stick shaker activated, the F/O's ASI was decreasing, Ken's ASI was increasing towards 250 kt and the standby ASI was fluctuating like a pendulum around 80 kt. On top of that, because of the pollution haze, he was in IMC with no external visual reference. There were no checklists or procedures to cover this situation. The probability calculations said it would never happen so there was no need for a checklist or a procedure. Ken was left with nothing but to revert to basic airmanship and flying skills learned over his years of experience. He brought the aircraft back to Hong Kong, flying by the seat of his pants, and landed safely with no airspeed or vertical speed information available to him. He flew the approach using his knowledge and experience of aircraft configuration, attitude and power settings. As a substitute for airspeed he used the groundspeed readout from the INS and corrected it mentally for the prevailing wind. The whole transit was flown in IMC and Ken didn't get visual contact with the runway until 500 feet. It was a superb piece of airmanship. Two B757s crashed in 1996 because of exactly the same problem.

What had gone wrong here? It was very simple. During the repainting process, the mechanics in Turnbull's 'economical' engineering facility hadn't masked the static ports and pitot heads that provide information to the aircraft's pressure instruments. Because of carelessness, lax standards and abysmal quality control, the static ports and the pitot heads were blocked by paint and debris. It was the most basic of blunders that could be made. The PR reception committee was somewhat more subdued than the Cathay managers had anticipated. The aircraft was parked at the HAECO hangar and the investigation got under way. At least this time there was no question of pilot error. Rather the reverse. Ken should have been highly commended for his outstanding airmanship. Instead of that, on 9 July 2001, by way of thanks for his achievement, Ken was sacked along with 48 other pilots and became one of *The 49ers*.

All airlines have the occasional incident in the normal course of events. Things do go wrong from time to time and the system is supposed to have enough checks and balances to protect against the unforeseen. No one expects everything to be perfect all the time. But these sorts of engineering problems were avoidable incidents and, in our company, they were becoming more frequent. Like NASA at the time of Challenger and Columbia, it had got to the point in Cathay where there were serious flaws in the safety culture and, like Townsend Thorensen's 'disease of sloppiness' and negligence at the time of the *Herald of Free Enterprise* disaster, the responsibility for this went up the hierarchy right the way to the top.

Similar problems were occurring in the Flight Ops Department. One morning, a Cathay B777 got airborne from Penang (PEN) bound for Kuala Lumpur (KUL). When the Captain tried to retract the gear after takeoff, one of the main wheels stayed down and refused to budge. The distance between the two airports is only 175 nm, a flying time of around 25 minutes. Rather than land back at Penang to determine the cause of the problem, the Captain decided to continue on to Kuala Lumpur and landed there normally. So what had happened? On inspection on the ground, it was found that the gear pin had been left in. Gear pins are used to physically lock the gear down on the ground and prevent inadvertent retraction when ground engineers are working on the aircraft. The pins are cylindrical metal rods around half an inch in diameter which fit through holes in the gear down lock arm that are aligned when the gear is extended. They are supposed to be removed before flight otherwise the gear cannot be retracted as had happened in this case. To make this clear, gear pins have long, high visibility red flags attached to them with the words 'REMOVE BEFORE FLIGHT' stencilled on in white lettering. There are two people who are supposed to check that the pins have been removed before flight. The first is the ground engineer. Part of his pre-flight check is to ensure that the gear pins have been removed. The second is the Captain. During his external inspection of the aircraft prior to flight, or walk round, the Captain is supposed to check that the pins have been removed. So, quite clearly then, neither performed their pre-flight checks properly. They were derelict in their most basic of duties, fucked up royally and deserved a severe bollocking, not to mention disciplinary action. A clear example of pilot error; case closed.

But wait a minute. How is it that two professional men could both make such a basic mistake? Why did it happen? As in most aircraft accidents and incidents, to find the answer to this question we have to look in the most unlikely of places. The scheduled time of arrival (STA) of the aircraft into Penang the night before was 20:40. Under the AFTLS, the minimum rest period that the crew should have on arrival is ten hours physically in the hotel. With a travelling time of 15 minutes each way from the hotel to the airport, this gives a total of 10 hr 30 min. The rest period commences 30 minutes after blocks on; that is, in this case, at 21:10 if the aircraft is on schedule. Therefore, the earliest that they can report for duty the next day is 07:40. Again, under the AFTLS, the minimum permissible report time before flight is one hour before STD, making the earliest possible departure time 08:40. The actual STD was 08:45 so the whole duty was right on the limits of the AFTLS with no slack or margin for error. This worked, just, when the aircraft maintained schedule. Here, the total flight rotation consisted of HKG-KUL-PEN-KUL-HKG. Unfortunately, on the leg from HKG to KUL, it was very common to experience arrival delays because of the weather. At the STA in KUL, there were often evening thunderstorms in the vicinity of the airport. There were two choices if the storm was right over the airport. Land in the thunderstorm or hold off for 20 minutes and wait for it to pass through. Holding off was the obvious choice as no pilot will deliberately fly into a thunderstorm if he can avoid it. It is the safe option but, as in this case, this now put the aircraft behind schedule for its departure from PEN the next morning. A 20-minute knock-on delay meant that the aircraft would not arrive in PEN until 21:30. Therefore, to comply with the AFTLS, the earliest departure time would be 09:00; 15 minutes behind schedule. Remember, OTP was the prime directive at that time. Every minute of delay had to be accounted for and every effort made to pick up time wherever possible.

Being good company men, the crew arrived at the airport in PEN in the morning and did their best to get the aircraft out on schedule. Instead of taking the full 60 minutes to conduct their pre-flight checks, they rushed them. On top of that, the big red flag on the gear pin had come off. The gear pins were actually quite difficult to see inside the undercarriage bay unless you looked carefully. It is an old maxim that you should look for the holes, not the pin when checking the gear. In his hurry, the Captain didn't do this and missed the fact that the pin was installed. It is arguable from all of this that the aircraft got airborne with the gear pin still installed primarily because the crew was trying to maintain OTP.

In terms of flight safety risk, they were lucky. The single engine takeoff performance of all twin-engine aircraft is calculated assuming that the gear is retracted at the normal time. If an engine had failed on takeoff at MTOW, the aircraft would not have been able to meet its scheduled climb performance. There is high ground to the north of Penang and a hill immediately to the north east of the airport. When taking off on R/W

04 in IMC with an engine failure, there is an emergency turn required to avoid the hill. With the gear down, it is questionable whether the aircraft could maintain adequate terrain clearance in the engine out case. Fortunately, the aircraft was well below MTOW so they probably would have got away with it had an engine failed.

Because of the increased drag, an aircraft with the gear down uses a lot more fuel than when it is 'clean'. Typically, the fuel burn increases by around 50 per cent. They were lucky it was only a short flight to KUL from PEN. They had enough fuel to make it. Had it been a longer flight, they would have had to return to PEN or land somewhere else *en route*.

During my command training on the 747, I flew with a Training Captain who gave me some good advice. We were getting ready for departure, it was looking like we were going to be delayed and I was trying my best to get things moving. The flight deck was full with people from engineering, traffic and catering asking whether it was OK to board the passengers, was the fuel load right? what time did we expect to depart? and a host of other questions. In attempting to demonstrate my outstanding command qualities I was trying to deal with all this while also completing my own pre-departure duties. I was getting snowed under when the Training Captain tapped me on the shoulder and motioned for me to get out of my seat and come with him. He took me to the galley in the upper deck, put on the hot cup and made us a cup of tea. He was a broad Aussie and asked me in 'Strine', 'Mate, d'you think it'll matter in three months' time if this aircraft's delayed?'

'No, I don't suppose so,' was my reply.

'D'you think it'll matter in three weeks' time?'

'Probably not.'

'D'you think it'll matter in three days' time?'

'No, not really.'

'Right, drink your tea, calm down, let the others do their jobs and we'll go when we're ready,' was his advice.

It was very good advice and a principle that I adopted and passed on to my candidates not only when I was a Training Captain but also on line operations. When things are mounting up and the pressure is on, that is the time to slow everything down rather than rush, because that is when you are most likely to miss something and make mistakes. The safety ethos that prevailed in the Flight Ops Department back then had long since gone with OTP and all the other commercial pressures that had been allowed to build under Barley's watch.

So now not only do we know what happened but we also know why it happened. The crew made a mistake because they allowed themselves to be rushed under commercial pressure. Even so, they are paid not to make mistakes and, presumably, they would have been subject to some form of disciplinary action? Well, no, actually. A bit like landing with the wheels up, there is one school of thought that says you only make that sort of mistake once. Do it once and you will never do it again. That wasn't the reason though. The reason was that the Captain on the flight was Rick Fry, the flying training manager. The rest of us received some extra training though when he put out a NTC cautioning us not to make the same mistake that he had. As one wag commented, 'Which mistake? Leave the pin in or give in to commercial pressure?'

Another management pilot had a similar 'careless' incident. Andy Maddox was the Captain of a 747-200 that pushed back in TPE with the L1 passenger door still open and the air bridge attached. The door was pulled off its hinges and badly damaged. Why would an experienced man make such a basic mistake? The reason can be found in triggers. On normal operations, everything happens in a pre-planned sequence of events in accordance with the checklist. The completion of each sequence of checks triggers the start of the next sequence. Under normal circumstances on departure, the aircraft engines are not started until after the pushback has commenced. One of the final checklist items before pushback is 'doors closed' and this is verified by indicator lights on the F/E's panel. On this occasion, however, the crew had begun starting the engines before pushback while still on the stand. This meant that the normal sequence of events had been disturbed and the 'before start' checklist had not actually been completed. It is always a trap for the unwary to leave a checklist before it has been completed or to have more than one checklist in progress at the same time. So, normal procedure is that the doors are closed before the engines are running. Ergo, it is an easy assumption to make that if the engines are already running then the doors must be closed. Whilst patently false logic, it can still act as a trigger when procedures are being rushed as in this case.

The crew made a mistake because they varied normal procedures that had been ingrained over years of operations. Any analysis of this incident is going to come to the conclusion of 'pilot error' in that the crew did not complete the checklists in accordance with the specified procedures. But these are experienced professional men. They definitely did not do it on purpose. No pilot deliberately makes mistakes. We can look at the causal chain, determine the contributing factors that led the crew into making such a basic mistake and list the extenuating circumstances.

On the record though, it is still going to go down as pilot error, case closed.

There is, however, an alternative analysis for the cause of the incident. 'OTP error'. Although the Captain always has to carry the can because, as the commander, that is one of his responsibilities, it was also part of the F/E's duties to ensure the doors were closed. In any event, another cat got kicked as a result of this incident. They disciplined the pushback tug driver.

Around the same time, a more serious incident occurred that serves to demonstrate why we were so concerned with the direction in which the Flight Ops Department was headed. On 30 November 1995, a Cathay Airbus A330 was *en route* from Bali to Hong Kong. The aircraft was in IMC about two hours into the flight when it flew straight into a cumulonimbus (Cb) thunderstorm cloud. The resulting turbulence threw passengers, crew and equipment around the cabin. On arrival in HKG, 26 people were taken to hospital including six cabin attendants, some of whom had hit the ceiling of the cabin during the upset. As well as experiencing control problems during the encounter, the Captain also reported having difficulty controlling the aircraft on the approach into HKG. Analysis of the FDR during the subsequent investigation indicated that the aircraft had exceeded MMO during the upset with the result that it may have suffered substantial damage. The Captain was suspended from duty and the initial inquiry pointed the finger directly at him. Another case of pilot error. But this was an experienced man who was not just a line Captain, he was a Training Captain. What on earth was he doing flying his aircraft straight into a Cb? No pilot would do this on purpose. There had to be a reason for his action but what was it?

When the A330 was introduced into service, it was fitted with a flat plate antenna weather radar, which was supposed to be state of the art. It was also rumoured to be the cheapest on the market. There had been a number of complaints about the performance of this equipment but they had been dismissed as 'finger trouble'. The truth was that it wasn't up to the job. It didn't function the way it was supposed to. You could sit there in VMC with a Cb right in front of you and it wouldn't paint a return on the radar screen unless the antenna was tilted right down into the lower levels of the cloud. Further investigation revealed that the combination of the chosen radar frequency and the size of the water droplets in the upper levels of Cbs in tropical regions meant that it didn't paint weather returns the way that it should. It worked fine in more temperate regions where the water droplets were of a smaller diameter, but not in the tropics. The aircraft flew into the Cb because the crew could neither see it visually, nor did it paint on their radar screen. The equipment failed them.

So now we know the immediate cause of the accident, but, having got into the situation, how was it that this experienced crew so mishandled the aircraft that they managed to overspeed it? The FDR readout showed conclusively that the aircraft had exceeded MMO. There was a clue as to what might have happened in the pilots' reports. During the recovery from the upset, they reported that not only were they receiving overspeed warnings but also low speed warnings with a discrepancy between the readings on the Captain's and F/O's ASIs. They were in severe turbulence, faced with contradictory aural and visual warnings whilst attempting to recover from the upset.

There was another clue in the FDR readout. It showed that both pilots were trying to control the aircraft and, at some points, they had used opposite control inputs during the recovery. This was significant. The A330 is controlled by the pilot using a sidestick situated beside his thigh. There is one on the left side of the aircraft for the Captain and one on the right side for the F/O. Unlike aircraft with a conventional central control column, it is difficult for one pilot to see what the other one is doing with their control inputs unless they lean forward and look across the cockpit. There is another difference between the two systems. On conventional aircraft, when one pilot moves his control column, the other one moves as well, reflecting the original input. If both pilots attempted to make control inputs at the same time, it would be immediately obvious and they would have to 'fight' against one another to make opposite inputs. With the Airbus sidestick, if one pilot makes a control input, the other's stick stays in the neutral position. It does not give a tactile feedback indicating what the other pilot is doing. There is a further difference. If both pilots make control inputs at the same time, the flight control computers algebraically sum the inputs from the two sidesticks and the resultant signal is sent to the control surfaces. Thus if one pilot demands a nose-up pitch and, at the same time, the other pilot demands a nose-down pitch of the same acceleration, the result will be that nothing happens. This applies in both pitch and roll. This is exactly what happened. During the recovery from the upset, both pilots were making inputs on their sidesticks, sometimes in concert and sometimes working against each other. But why would the pilots be making opposite control inputs? The answer lay in the flight data being displayed to them on their instruments. One pilot's ASI told him they were flying too fast so he made a nose-up pitch demand and the other pilot's ASI told him he was flying too slow so he made a nose-down pitch demand. But surely, only one pilot should be flying the aircraft at a time? Why were they both trying to fly it? The answer to that one is instinct. In the confusion of the situation, faced with severe turbulence, the noise of contradictory aural warnings and visual information telling them they were in a critical part of the flight envelope, they did what any pilot would naturally do: they tried to recover.

There was one thing that they could have done to prevent opposing control inputs, but didn't. There is a red button on each pilot's sidestick. In manual flight, if one pilot presses this button, it disconnects the other pilot's sidestick for as long as it is held down. If this is done for more than 40 seconds, it will 'latch out' the other sidestick and prevent any control input from the other pilot until such time as either button is pressed again. There are various modes and combinations in which these takeover priority buttons can be employed and there are also visual and aural indications associated with their use. In fairness, when the process is demonstrated and the various modes are practised in the simulator, it is much easier to understand than the written word. But the point is that we had NOT been given proper training on the use of these buttons during our conversion training. They had only been demonstrated cursorily and no particular emphasis had been put on their use. After this incident, the next time I got into the simulator for recurrent training, part of the module was devoted to the use of the takeover buttons and practising various different scenarios. That fixed the problem after the event but, at the time, the pilots of the flight were criticised by the inquiry for incorrect use (or, rather, lack of use) of the takeover buttons. The truth was that they had been let down by their initial conversion training.

As for overspeeding the aircraft, the FDR showed it had exceeded MMO so it must be right surely? Well, the FDR receives its data from the same sources as the pilot's instruments and these were giving erroneous and conflicting indications, so might not the FDR readout be in error as well? There was one way to find out. On the A330 there are three accelerometers that record acceleration in the vertical, horizontal and lateral axes. Their readings are not modified by any type of processing or integration. Their output is simply raw data sampled at regular intervals. The AOA was helping the Captain with the investigation and, on this occasion, Rick Fry did the right thing. He allowed us access to the data and for this we were grateful. Having got the data readout, we were able to apply some basic physics to the situation. Newton's three equations of motion state that:

$$v = u + ft$$
$$v^2 = u^2 + 2fs$$
$$s = ut + \tfrac{1}{2}ft^2$$

We knew f (the acceleration), and t (the time) from the data readout and we could also calculate s (the distance) from the navigation information. If we could determine u (the initial velocity) it should be a simple matter to calculate v (the final velocity) in each axis and then integrate the results for the whole period of the upset and thus determine the actual speed of the aircraft. We took u to be the initial velocity in stable flight at the time when both the ASIs were in agreement and worked from there. Our boffins' results showed that the aircraft had not actually exceeded MMO and, in fact, it had remained within the certified flight envelope during the whole of the upset. This was borne out by the engineers' examination of the aircraft; they could find no sign of the sort of damage that would normally be expected to be evident in the event of an over-speed. So why were the instruments and the FDR indicating that there had been an overspeed? The answer the inquiry finally came up with was icing. During the upset, the Rosemount probe that measures total air temperature (TAT) had iced up and sent erroneous signals to the data-processing units. There was also the possibility that the pitot probes, too, might have iced up, further degrading the data. Pitot icing has been suggested as a factor in other Airbus incidents that have occurred since. So, garbage in, garbage out. Equipment failure again.

This left the last issue. Why did the Captain have trouble controlling the aircraft on approach into HKG? He reported that the aircraft had behaved as if the flight control logic had reverted from Normal Law into either ALT 1 or ALT 2 Alternate Law, a degraded form of flight control logic. He was told that he must be mistaken as, according to the technical manuals, this could not have happened. All very well but he knew how the aircraft handled. Some weeks after the incident, he received a letter from Airbus. They had investigated the incident and found that, in the combination of circumstances he had experienced, the flight control logic could indeed degrade as he had reported. The manuals were wrong.

For the Captain of the aircraft this whole episode was a terrible time personally. He was an experienced professional Training Captain with an unblemished record. People had been injured on board an aircraft of which he was the commander. Forget cost benefit analysis and 'what the company can afford'. The finger of suspicion was pointed at him, pilot error was assumed and he felt the responsibility deeply and personally. The truth of the matter was that he and his F/O had been let down by

equipment failure, inadequate training and incorrect technical information. In the end he was exonerated and should have been commended
for the way he and his crew handled a very difficult and confusing situation. The trouble is that life doesn't work like that. He would always
now be known as 'the bloke who had that upset'. *The 49ers* were to be
similarly stigmatised.

The whole episode left a bad taste in the mouth. Instead of taking a
cautious, objective view of the incident, the knee-jerk reaction was to
blame the pilots, and an attitude prevailed that 'There can't possibly be
anything wrong with our brand new shiny aircraft.' Even the initial remedy
for the radar problem pointed the finger at the pilots. We were all issued
with a handbook on how to operate weather radar, the inference being
that it was our fault for not using the kit properly. To tell a pilot with
thousands of hours of incident-free flying in the tropics that all this time
he hasn't been using the tilt control on the weather radar correctly was
not just insulting, it smelled of cover-up. What was actually needed was
to spend some money on equipment that worked as advertised and it
was eventually upgraded.

There were a lot of things wrong with the A330 when it was first introduced into service with Cathay. Even something as basic as the in-flight
entertainment (IFE) system didn't work properly and the first aircraft
delivery was delayed ten days while the engineers tried to get it sorted
out. It took a number of software revisions before it finally started working
as advertised. As pilots, we understood these initial teething problems
and were quite prepared to work through them. Any new aircraft when
it is first introduced into line operations will have some problems; it was
just that the A330 seemed to have more than its fair share. Even so, as
professional pilots we would deal with them provided we got support
from our pilot managers. Unfortunately we didn't get it. Instead, an insid-
ious culture of blame pervaded the Flight Ops Department, exactly the
opposite of what is needed to promote flight safety.

14

Fatigue

'*My mind clicks on and off. I try letting one eyelid close at a time while I prop the other with my will. But the effect is too much, sleep is winning, my whole body argues dully that nothing, nothing life can attain is quite so desirable as sleep. My mind is losing resolution and control.*'
  Charles Lindbergh (about his 1927 transatlantic flight)

With all the flight safety issues in Cathay that the AOA was concerned about, we at least felt we were making significant progress on pilot fatigue. The FTLWG completed its deliberations and, in August 1998, the CAD published a completely revised edition of CAD 371. It was a ground-breaking document. It was the first set of FTLs designed specifically to address the issue of cumulative fatigue caused by long-term ULR ops. It introduced two new concepts: duty cycles and recovery periods. Previously, the duration of required rest periods was determined only by the length of the duty immediately preceding the rest. Duty cycles introduced the concept of using the total time spent away from home base to determine the required amount of time off once the pilot returned home. The introduction of recovery periods also took into account the amount of time zone displacement, or jet lag, that the pilot had been subjected to during the duty cycle to determine the minimum time off required for his body clock to return to normal. The following extract from CAD 371 demonstrates the principles involved.

22.3. **Length of Recovery Period between Duty Cycles**

22.3.1. The duration of the recovery period which must be given to a flight crew member following return to home base is given by Table 'X' below.

22.3.2. The intent of Table 'X' – is to ensure that a flight crew member's body clock is recovered to home base local time before the commencement of the next duty cycle.

22.3.3. The table is constructed using following assumptions:

- the body clock moves at one hour per day when its circadian rhythm is disrupted;

- the body clock moves at one hour per day when it resynchronises to local time;

- maximum circadian disruption (12 hours) requires 7 nights recovery;

- no account is taken for gradual time zone displacement or a gradual recovery to home base.

22.4. **Table X – Instructions for Use**

- Enter Table 'X' below at the row which gives the length in hours of the completed duty cycle;

- Move across to the column which gives the maximum time zone displacement achieved during the duty cycle;

- The figure in italics shows the required length of recovery period in DDOs.

22.5. Table 'X'

Length of Completed Duty Cycle (hours)	Maximum Time Zone Displacement during Duty Cycle				
	4 Zones	5 Zones	6 Zones	7 Zones	8-12 Zones
48+ to 72	1 DDO	1 DDO	2 DDOs	2 DDOs	2 DDOs
72+ to 96	3 DDOs	3 DDOs	3 DDOs	3 DDOs	3 DDOs
96+ to 120	3 DDOs	4 DDOs	4 DDOs	4 DDOs	4 DDOs
120+ to 144	3 DDOs	4 DDOs	5 DDOs	5 DDOs	5 DDOs
144+	3 DDOs	4 DDOs	5 DDOs	6 DDOs	6 DDOs

This was a major step forward in protecting our pilots against cumulative fatigue. It wasn't the 5-4-3 rule that we'd hoped for, rather it was more like a 4-3-2 rule, but it did provide extra protection for longer duty cycles. What was also very important to us was that, whereas Cathay management saw the 5-4-3 rule as an industrial agreement and, therefore, open to unilateral amendment, Table X was now legislated by the regulator and there was no way for them to get round that, or so we thought.

The CAD issued a Notice to AOC holders informing them that they must submit a revised AFTLS in compliance with CAD 371 by 30 November 1998. These would be subject to approval by 15 December 1998 and the new schemes would come into effect on 1 March 1999. There were two clauses to accommodate situations in which an operator might apply for a variation to the standard provisions. These were:

6. Variations to the Standard Provisions

6.1. While operators are required to construct their schemes in accordance with the standard provisions, it is recognised that these provisions will not necessarily interact sensibly with every type of operation. In such circumstances operators may apply to incorporate variations from the standard provisions in their FTL

Scheme. **Approval to do so will only be given where an operator can show that, despite the variation, the level of protection against fatigue will, at least, be equivalent to that provided by the standard provision.**

6.2. Variations from the standard provisions may be permanent in nature or temporary, and applicable only to a certain aircraft fleet, schedule, route, flight or series of flights. Any variation of a permanent nature must be incorporated in the approved scheme. Those of a temporary nature must be brought to the attention of crew members by incorporation in the operations manual, or other suitable operating instructions (e.g. 'Notices to Crew').

6.3. Operators requesting permanent incorporation into their scheme of any significant variation from the standard provisions **will be required to show that consultation has taken place between the operator and their crews** regarding the implementation of the variation(s).

These provisions are quite clear in their intent and most people reading them will appreciate exactly what is required to show compliance. Not so with Flight Ops management. Their attempts to have us excluded from the FTLWG had failed and the CAD had listened to the pilots for a change. The new CAD 371 was not at all to management's liking because it got in the way of their plans to make the pilots fly even more hours. I got an inkling of what was to happen next at a meeting with Sutch in September. He was far from his usual charming self. In fact he was quite surly when he remarked to me, 'Why should we have the most restrictive FTLs in the world?'

'Peter, the AOA's been trying to address the fatigue problem with Flight Ops management for two years now but we can't get anywhere. In fact it's got worse. Gerry took 5-4-3 out of the FTLs and Ken's tried to do away with it altogether. We were happy with 5-4-3 but what do you expect us to do when all we see are unilateral changes and no one takes any notice of what we're saying? We're the guys out on the line dealing with these problems month in, month out, not the blokes in the office. We were left with no option but to go to the CAD.'

'Well it's no good having the safest airline in the world if we can't make a profit.'

'I agree, Peter, but we've got to find a balance on the fatigue issue. Even CAD's acknowledged that there's a problem,' I responded.

'Well we'll see about that,' was his ominous reply.

It didn't take long to find out what he meant by that. Rhodes tried another of his bypass manoeuvres. He put out a rostering survey to the pilots. To say it was simplistic in the extreme is something of an under-statement. In coming to its conclusions, the FTLWG had considered evidence from experts in the field of pilot fatigue including a study conducted by the NASA Ames Research Centre considered at that time to be one of the definitive works on the subject. However, Rhodes and Hoyland thought they knew better. Their survey consisted of a series of sample roster patterns with the searching question, Which do you like best? It was designed to elicit replies along the lines that the pilots would much rather cram all their ULR ops into three-week periods of high density flying and then have ten days off instead of using the very incon-venient Table X. This suited their latest plan to use roster stacking to try to squeeze out more productivity. It demonstrated yet again that either they did not understand or simply did not care about the fatigue issues that were of so much concern to us. All they were interested in was getting more hours out of us. The AOA circulated a notice to the pilots, explaining what Rhodes was trying to do, and advised them not to respond to the survey. We then suggested that if they felt they must respond, they should forward their answers to the AOA and we would pass them on to Rhodes after we had entered the results into our database. That nipped his little plan in the bud.

Soon after, the CAD informed us that Cathay had submitted its AFTLS scheme for approval and asked whether we had any comments. Comments? Too damn right we had comments. This was the first we had heard of their new draft scheme. They had gone behind our backs and tried to pull a fast one as usual. We told the CAD that Cathay had breached the regulations by not consulting with its crews. You can guess the response to that one by now. Rhodes' survey was held up as evidence of consul-tation. It was a joke. The number of responses he received to his survey did not even constitute a statistically significant sample of the aircrew body and we pointed that out. He had a solution to that one too. He refused to disclose the actual number of replies he'd received but assured the CAD that it was a significant number.

That was the least of it though. Their draft AFTLS had so many vari-ations to CAD 371 that it drove a coach and horses right through the intent of the new rules. To go into the implications of all of their attempted changes would take another book, but one in particular stood out. For freighter operations, they cut one DDO off each of the figures in Table X. We knew the reason why. It was because the ASL operation with its thin route network was so inefficient in crew utilisation that any further degradation would make it financially unviable. How they intended to demonstrate that their variations met the 'equivalent protection' provision was yet to be revealed. We waited with bated breath to see their 'scientific' evidence demonstrating that freighter pilots don't need as much rest as passenger pilots. Presumably freighter pilots are more expendable than passenger pilots since they don't take another 400 people with them when they crash, just a load of freight that isn't likely to sue. On the other hand, I doubt whether Ah Wing and his wife and kids would be likely to differentiate between a freighter and a passenger aircraft when 285 tonnes of aluminium and kerosene arrive unexpectedly in the front room of his flat in Kowloon City because the pilot was suffering from cumulative fatigue.

We faced a further problem. Peter Birkett, the instigator and chairman of the FTLWG, had by this time retired from his post in the CAD. His replacement, Jim Adams, or Slick as he came to be known, was not as sympathetic to our cause as Peter had been. He granted Cathay all its variations to CAD 371 in its AFTLS and effectively destroyed two years of work. Neither he nor Rhodes were able to provide any scientific evidence whatsoever to demonstrate that the scheme would provide at least an equivalent level of protection, a clear breach of the new rules. Slick's response to our protestations was that the variations had been granted only temporarily and would be reviewed again in September after a trial period. Now where had we heard that one before? If we allowed this to go through unchallenged we would be fighting yet another rearguard action. With the departure of Birkett our relationship with the CAD was deteriorating and we could not take the chance. Once again we were left with no alternative.

In April 1999 we resorted to legal action and the AOA filed for a judicial review of the CAD's decision. Slick's reaction was immediate. We were at the 1999 IFALPA Annual Conference in Pattaya and he was attending at HKALPA's invitation as an observer. He stormed off home and left me a letter in which he accused me of being 'disrespectful'. The CAD refused to engage in any further dialogue and filed an application to have the judicial review set aside. Its application failed, the court granted the AOA leave for the review to be heard and a date was set.

The hearing was held on 28 and 29 October before Mr Justice Frank Stock in the Court of First Instance. The first day of the hearing was taken up with legal arguments. To start with Cathay's lawyers tried to have the case stopped on technical grounds. They made no representations either on the content of CAD 371 or the variations; rather they just argued that the court had no jurisdiction to hear the matter. They failed. Next the CAD argued that CAD 371 was only a guideline document and not a policy and, therefore, was not binding. The judge disagreed and ruled that it was indeed a policy and, therefore, that all parties were bound to abide by its provisions. He opened the second day of proceedings by remarking that he believed the matter should have been resolved by negotiation in the intervening time period between the action being filed and the actual hearing. He was not particularly complimentary towards the CAD regarding its refusal to engage in further dialogue. He pointed out that if he ruled in favour of the pilots it would mean that Cathay would have to suspend all its flights. In his words, 'I quash the decision, Cathay does not fly.' The CAD's barrister immediately conceded three of the eight points on which we were arguing our case and several hours of out of court negotiations then took place. It was agreed that meetings of the FTLWG would recommence with immediate effect and that the director of the CAD would ensure that the provisions for consultation contained within CAD 371 would be properly complied with. We also received a number of written undertakings on transparency and other associated issues and a proviso that any proposed variations would have to demonstrate 'at least equal or better protection against fatigue' to the satisfaction of all parties concerned before being granted. In return the AOA agreed to withdraw its application. The CAD applied to the court for costs and this was denied. In essence the judge instructed the CAD to return to the table and ensure that it complied with its own regulations.

It was a major victory for us and finally put a stop to the behind-the-scenes lobbying and secret deals. Having heard the assurances given by the CAD and our agreement to withdraw the judicial review having received those assurances, the judge asked Cathay's barrister for his view. He was most put out and replied, 'I and my client have been treated as an unwelcome excrescence by both parties.' For once, we were in agreement.

While this was all going on, a document came into our possession that had very serious flight safety implications. It was forwarded to the AOA by a member of Flight Ops management who was equally concerned about its consequences. The document was a copy of the minutes of a meeting held at 10:00 on 29 September 1998. It was chaired by Rhodes and entitled 'Sick Leave' Meeting. Others in attendance included Corinne Aldis, Paddy Cavanagh, K.M. Chan, K.Y. Chong, Greg Gibbins, Richard Hall, Denly Hau, Hoyland, Dennis Leung, Dave Roberts and Nelsson Wu.

Aldis and Cavanagh were involved in administration duties. Gibbins was the 747 Classic fleet manager and Hall, similarly, was a management pilot. Messrs Chan, Chong, Hau, Leung and Wu worked in the rostering department. Hoyland and Roberts we have already met.

The minutes showed that a 'blacklist' of pilots who were deemed to be taking 'too much' sick leave had been compiled and that a series of 'incentives' and 'disincentives' had been implemented to encourage an improvement in such anti-company behaviour.

These 'incentives' included:

- *'request G days'*, i.e. only granting requests for specific days off to non-blacklisted pilots;
- *'request trips'*, i.e. only granting requests for specific flight patterns to non-blacklisted pilots;
- *'temp bases/swaps'*, i.e. only granting requests for temporary basings or base swaps to non-blacklisted pilots;
- *'more reserves/less G'*, i.e. scheduling blacklisted pilots for more reserve duty instead of days off, making it more difficult for them to plan ahead;
- *'roster "in bin"'*, i.e. deliberately disrupting a blacklisted pilot's scheduled roster, causing more instability;
- *'O days after ULH vs G days'*, i.e. instead of rostering a blacklisted pilot in accordance with the 5-4-3 rule after a ULR op, only rostering him the absolute legal minimum under the AFTLS and then calling him out for a further duty earlier than normal;
- *'repeat rosters – including Xmas'*, i.e. deliberately rostering blacklisted pilots repeatedly for flights to the less desirable destinations on the route network or with the more onerous and fatiguing work patterns. Also, rostering a blacklisted pilot for repeated duties over public holidays such as Christmas so that he will be away from his family;
- *'staff travel (annual FOC, UGSA)'*, i.e. making life difficult for blacklisted pilots and their families when on staff travel and making sure that they do not get upgraded in accordance with the terms of their contract even when space is available.

The 'disincentives' included:

- *'loss of training'*, i.e. returning blacklisted pilots who hold training positions back to line flying duties so imposing a financial penalty as well as reducing their professional standing;

- '*loss of job*', i.e. firing blacklisted pilots;
- '*loss of increment*', i.e. refusing to award a blacklisted pilot his annual incremental pay award;
- '*loss of base*', i.e. forcing a blacklisted pilot based overseas to return to Hong Kong with the consequence of disrupting his family life;
- '*loss of command/delay in promotion*', i.e. demoting blacklisted Captains or delaying the promotion of blacklisted pilots to higher rank to impose a financial and professional penalty;
- '*full body check by PMO*', i.e. subjecting blacklisted pilots to unnecessary, intrusive and embarrassing medical procedures by the principal medical officer.

If we needed any further proof that they had no intention of addressing our concerns over fatigue, here it was in black and white. There was no doubt that sickness levels had been increasing and the reason was obvious: the rosters that we'd been flying for the last four years. But they weren't going to acknowledge that there was a fundamental systemic problem, oh no. They couldn't possibly admit that the rostering system they had imposed in 1994 was a mess and that they didn't have enough pilots to complete the commercial task. Instead they decided that we were all just malingering so the obvious answer was to institute a system of coercion, intimidation and victimisation. The result of their sickness blacklist, or the 'Absence Management Programme' as they later renamed it, was that pilots started reporting for flying duty when they weren't physically fit to do so. If that isn't a clear and present danger to flight safety I don't know what is. The increase in sickness levels wasn't just occurring amongst the pilots; the same thing was happening to cabin crew, and their own departmental management introduced similar practices to penalise those who were deemed to be taking 'too much' sick leave.

On 2 November 1998, Ted Pleavin, who was now president of the AOA, wrote to both Sutch and the CAD protesting about the blacklist policy. He received a reply from Sutch dated 10 November in which he stated:

I have checked with Flight Operations Department management who have confirmed that this issue has been discussed **but that no policy changes have been formulated, let alone implemented.**

Ted got a similar reply from Stormin' Norman at the CAD dated 19 November in which he stated:

In the interest of an unbiased and balanced view, we have requested Cathay Pacific Airways to comment on this issue. In their response, they stated that they have been reviewing and monitoring sickness absence levels amongst Cathay Pacific crew, **but at the time of writing, had not implemented any new measures in this area.**

They were caught out, both Sutch and the CAD. Ted had not forwarded a copy of the minutes of the meeting with his letters. He kept them in reserve to see what the responses would be. Predictably they lied. Ted's next letters enclosed a copy of the minutes and forced Rhodes out into the open to admit what they were doing. It also earned him a bollocking from Sutch as he told me later. The correspondence between the AOA, the CAD and Cathay management on the subject of the sickness black-list continued on through into 2001 until after *The 49ers* were sacked. A copy of the full correspondence is included in Appendix 2 to this book.

We have already discussed the legal responsibilities placed on both pilots and operators by the ANO to ensure that pilots do not undertake flying duties when they are suffering from fatigue or have reason to believe that they are likely to suffer from fatigue during the flight duty. Any breach of those regulations by either the pilot or the operator is a criminal offence. It is sad to say that, ultimately, the CAD failed in its duty to take action to prevent Cathay pilots from being coerced and intimidated into reporting for flying duty when they were unfit to do so. Instead they abnegated their responsibility and left it to the pilots to shoulder the full burden of that responsibility alone.

So exactly why were sickness levels increasing? One of the effects of cumulative fatigue is to lower the body's immune system. A lowered immune system equals greater susceptibility to everyday infections. Even a mild illness such as a common cold stops a pilot from undertaking flying duty because of the possibility of ear damage caused by air pressure changes. We are taught from the outset in basic training not to fly with a cold. We can't even use drugs such as decongestants contained in common cold remedies because of their possible side-effects. The use of prescription drugs is also strictly controlled by regulation.

Because we travel for a living, we are exposed to far more infections than the general population. It is a medically acknowledged fact when people travel they are more likely to develop illness than when they stay at home because they are exposed to infections for which they have little developed immunity. Continual ULR ops don't help. The aircraft cabin air is devoid of moisture and dries out the mucous membranes, one of the body's first lines of defence against airborne infection. Being routinely confined in an aircraft cabin for 90 hours a month with 400 other people increases infection risk and this is not helped by recirculation of the cabin air to save fuel. Whatever the PR people might have us believe, the cabin air filters do not filter out micro-organisms.

Cumulative fatigue causes disruption of sleep patterns and insomnia. We are not allowed to use drugs such as melatonin to combat jet lag or sleeping pills unless they are specifically prescribed by an authorised medical examiner. And, of course, why should we be reliant on drugs simply in order that we can do our jobs effectively?

A simple stomach upset or diarrhoea can preclude pilots from undertaking flying duty. In a study published by the Australian Transport Safety Bureau in January 2007, it was reported that, 'The majority of in-flight medical and incapacitation events in Australian civil pilots for the study period were due to acute gastrointestinal illness (usually food poisoning), a finding consistent with other published studies.' In the event of in-flight pilot incapacitation, Cathay's Operations Manuals stipulate that the remaining pilot(s) must declare an emergency situation to Air Traffic Control so it is a very serious matter. Whereas most people can continue to work with such a complaint provided that they can remain near to a lavatory, pilots, for obvious reasons, cannot.

It was of extremely serious concern to the AOA that Cathay management were acting in direct breach of the ANO and seemed to think that they could do so with total impunity. Given the lack of action by the CAD, it seemed that their assumption was correct.

15

1999

Don Corleone: *Santino, come here. What's the matter with you? I think your brain is going soft with all that comedy you are playing with that young girl. Never tell anyone outside the Family what you are thinking again.*

Francis Ford Coppola's *The Godfather*

At the 1998 AGM in September, I stood down as president of the AOA and Ted Pleavin was elected to take over the position. There were three reasons for my decision. Firstly, I knew what was coming next. After the pay negotiations that year had reached an impasse, there was no way that was going to be the end of it. They were bound to come back and try again especially in view of the state of the economy. The Asian financial crisis had ended in August but it was going to affect the year end results and they were bound to use that as a reason for seeking more pay concessions. All the best advice on negotiating strategy says that you should not hold the positions of union boss and chief negotiator at the same time. If you do, you forfeit a tactical advantage. As chief negotiator, you can say, 'Well I'll take your offer back to my boss and see whether I can sell it to him and the GC, but I don't hold out much hope. If you can give me something more I'll have a much better chance.'

When the boss says it's not good enough, you can come back to the table and say, 'I tried my best but my boss just isn't having it. Personally I think your offer is quite a good one and we're almost there but the final decision's not up to me. If you can just concede on a couple more minor points, I think I can sell the deal for you.'

229

If you are the boss as well as the chief negotiator, you can't do that because you effectively hold plenipotentiary power sitting right there in the room with your opponents. They can put you on the spot and ask you to make the decision then and there. You can try to give yourself manoeuvring room by saying you have to take it back to the membership to vote but it's a pretty weak position. If your membership votes you down on a deal that you recommend to them what does that say about your leadership? Similarly, if you take the deal back and recommend they turn it down, you open yourself up to accusations of bad faith. Either way, you're snookered. No, by far the best strategy is to separate the two jobs. I had previously held both jobs because we didn't have enough people with the training and experience to field a full team. Now we did. With the help of IFALPA we now had four trained negotiators and enough experience on the General Committee to fill the other support roles. I had discussed this with Ted and we agreed that I would take on the job as chief negotiator after I stood down as president.

The second reason for my decision was that my work with IFALPA was taking up more of my time especially in the FTL and industrial arenas. With the introduction of the new CAD 371 in Hong Kong, other member associations were using it as a model for what they wanted to achieve in their own countries and I was being asked to give presentations to different groups around the world. I was also working with Cathy Bill, Rick Brennan and Stan Clayton-Smith, who were on the IFALPA Industrial Committee, to try to encourage IFALPA to devote more resources to industrial issues. One of the problems that I'd had to deal with in rebuilding the AOA was lack of knowledge. If there had been a library or central repository where we could have gone for research information, it would have made the task of educating ourselves so much easier. It is a problem that all of the smaller, less well funded, member associations faced. Of course the big boys like BALPA and USALPA didn't need this. They already had the knowledge and experience. It was the little fish that needed help and, whilst the IFALPA Industrial Committee assisted as much as it could, it was short of resources. We were in a catch-22 situation. The minnows needed the information but they didn't have the money to set up a library. The big fish had the money but they didn't need the library.

We were also up against some of the 'purists' who believed that IFALPA should restrict itself to technical matters and not dirty its hands in the industrial cesspool. Some of the techies could be quite vocal in their opposition. It was always a source of amusement if we could turn one of them to our side because they would then apply the same zeal to industrial matters as they had previously to their technical work and become far more radical than their mentors. Cathy had previously worked for the South African Airways pilots' union and was a staunch ally as were Rick and Stan who both came from BA. In Hong Kong we were to have much to thank them for during 1999. At the 2003 IFALPA Annual Conference, Cathy was awarded a Presidential Citation for her work in professional aviation.

The last reason for my decision was that I was tired. After three and a half years on the General Committee and almost three years as president, I needed a rest. It is not until you actually do the job that you realise the demands that are placed upon you as the leader. Sutch's remark back in 1996 had been right. It was the hardest job in the airline. It is a 24/7 job with the membership expecting you to have all the answers all the time. And you have to be prepared to listen to everyone, no matter how much you sympathise or otherwise with their views and problems.

On one occasion a member telephoned me to say that he needed to speak to me urgently on a matter of flight safety. He came into the office and told me that he had identified a serious problem amongst our flight crews. Apparently he had just come back from a trip to Paris and had witnessed a pilot consuming two litres of beer at one sitting. I personally considered this to be par for the course but kept my views to myself. He then went on to tell me that he was a practitioner of transcendental meditation, was shortly going to be setting up a course in Yogic Flying and would appreciate it if the AOA could provide him some free advertising. Since it was going to be a commercial venture, the terms of his contract required him to inform the company of his intentions and he was going from this meeting to see Barley and brief him as well. I resisted the temptation to suggest he might like to rethink his plan and perhaps seek professional help first, thanked him for his time, shook his hand and he left. I do not know what happened at the meeting with Barley. Perhaps he embraced the idea as well since Yogic Flying would certainly involve much lower fuel costs than the more conventional form of aviation.

When I stepped down from the presidency, the next time I walked into a bar, in answer to the usual greeting of, 'Oh hello, John, just a quick question,' I was looking forward to being able to reply, 'Ask Ted.'

As predicted, the 1998 annual report showed a significant loss after taxation: US$65 million on a turnover of US$3,422 million and predictably, they came after us for salary concessions, screaming poverty. The fact that in 1997 we had reported a profit after tax of $222 million on a turnover of

$3,929 million had nothing to do with it. That was then and now was now. The world had changed fundamentally and we were all doomed, again. The 1997 results rather proved our point that we were not prepared to talk about concessions without seeing the data. This time, though, there was no arguing the results. We had made a loss and we had to go back to the table at least to discuss the situation otherwise we'd just look like a bunch of hard-liners with no concern for our company. We didn't know it at the time, of course, but in the following years we were to make massive profits as the following table compiled from the annual reports shows:

Year	Profit/(Loss) USD million			
	Turnover	Operating	Before Tax	After Tax
1997	3,929	221	260	222
1998	3,422	(100)	(78)	(65)
1999	3,680	360	318	290
2000	4,426	678	667	653
2001	3,902	107	116	90
2002	4,242	609	556	514
2003	3,792	285	225	173
2004	5,482	673	636	579
2005	6,527	531	509	445
2006	7,793	669	648	548
2007	9,661	992	1,027	924
2008	11,098	(1,029)	(1,257)	(1,086)
2009	8,587	735	659	623

Other than 1998, the only glitch in the figures is for 2008 when we took a massive hit because the accountants bet the wrong way big time on the fuel-hedging policy, and we will return to that later. Based on these figures, there was no arguing the fact that the Asian financial crisis had hit us hard in terms of both turnover and profit. However, turnover had only dropped by 13 per cent so why had profits been hit so hard, dropping by 132 per cent? On a pro rata basis, with a drop in turnover of 13 per cent, surely we should only expect a similar drop in profits, giving an expected operating profit of $192 million. Instead of that we made an operating loss of $100 million. Where had $292 million disappeared to? That's a chunk of change to disappear down the Asian financial crisis black hole. Perhaps we'd better find out where it went before getting into negotiations. After all, if we help them out by giving them some of our hard earned cash, the least we should do is make sure they don't just throw it down the same hole and then come back for more next year. So it's off to the 1998 annual report and the consolidated profit/loss account to see whether that gives us any clues . . .

Consolidated Profit and Loss Account

	Note	1998 US$M	1997 US$M
Turnover	*1*	**3,422**	3,929
Operating profit	*2*	**51**	308
Exceptional items	*3*	**(111)**	(44)
Net finance charges	*4*	**(40)**	(43)
Net operating (loss)/profit		**(100)**	221
Share of profits of associated companies	*12*	**22**	39
(Loss)/profit before taxation		**(78)**	260
Taxation	*5*	**13**	(38)
(Loss)/profit after taxation		**(65)**	222
Minority interests		**(4)**	(5)
(Loss)/profit attributable to shareholders	*6*	**(69)**	217
Dividends	*7*	**(44)**	(126)
(Loss)/retained profit for the year	*8*	**(113)**	91
(Loss)/earnings per share	*9*	**(2.1¢)**	6.3¢

There seem to be a couple of clues here. Operating profit dropped by 257 million and exceptional items took another 67 million. That's 324 million. We're looking for 292 million so we're in the right ballpark, give or take the odd 30 million or so. Let's look for exceptional items first and check out note 3.

3. Exceptional Items	**1998**	1997
	US$M	US$M
The exceptional items consist of the following:		
Net profit arising from the sale of investments	**(24)**	–
Provision for severance payments arising from staff retrenchments	**27**	44
Provision for the impairment in value of the B747-200 and B747-300 aircraft and related equipment arising from decisions to remove them from service	**79**	–
Provision to write down the B747-200 and B747-300 aircraft spare parts to net realisable value	**29**	–
	111	44

The net profit arising from the sale of investments mainly relates to the sale of a 4.5 per cent shareholding in a company operating a computerised reservation system business in Asia. The Group still maintains an 8.4 per cent shareholding in this business.

The provision for severance payments arising from staff retrenchments in 1998 is in connection with staff redundancies undertaken or to be undertaken as a result of the decisions to remove the B747-200 and B747-300 aircraft from service.

The provision for the impairment in value of the B747-200 and B747-300 aircraft and related equipment arises from decisions to remove these aircraft from service. The carrying value of these aircraft and related equipment has been written down to estimated net recoverable amount. Provision has also been made to write down the related aircraft spare parts to net realisable value. The net realisable value of the spare parts has been determined based on market resale price.

So let me just get this right. We sold some shares in a reservation system and made 24 million. OK, I'm cool with that. We made a profit so let's share in some of that. Then you've written down the value of the Classics and the spares holdings to the value of 108 million because you decided to get rid of them. Now hold on a bit. That's just an accounting exercise to save tax and, anyway, it's only a provision. You haven't actually sold them yet, Ken told me. The latest intel is that they're going to PIA on a lease purchase so they'll still be a capital asset and an income source for the next two or three years. We'll have to talk about that one and we'll need some convincing. Now what's this 27 million from this year and 44 million from last year? Oh, I see, it covers redundancy payments to the F/Es you got rid of when you ditched the Classics, the same F/Es that were replaced by new ASL recruits, the ones that Adrian Swire wouldn't even talk to me about. And now you want me to pay for that out of my pocket! I don't think so!! Let's see what else we can find that's caused such a big drop in the operating profit. Let's check out the direct operating costs.

Operating Costs	1998	1997	
	US$M	US$M	Change
Staff	970	989	-1.9%
Route	824	856	-3.7%
Fuel	463	604	-23.3%
Aircraft maintenance	341	397	-14.2%
Aircraft depreciation and operating leases	352	299	+17.7%
Other depreciation and operating leases	121	130	-7.5%
Exchange losses	11	58	-80.5%
Commissions	92	112	-17.8%
Others	197	177	+11.6%
Total operating costs	3,372	3,621	-6.9%

- Staff costs decreased by HK$143 million, as a result of reduced headcounts.
- Route costs, which include costs such as meal costs, landing and parking charges, decreased primarily due to cost efficiencies and the effect of weaker foreign currencies.
- Fuel costs fell by HK$1,097 million as a result of lower fuel prices and the increased use of more fuel-efficient aircraft.

- Aircraft maintenance costs reduced significantly as a result of the retirement of the B747-200 aircraft.
- Aircraft depreciation and operating lease costs increased, reflecting deliveries during the year.
- Exchange losses realised on repayment of borrowings reduced as the Japanese yen was weaker than in 1997.
- Commissions paid to agents decreased due to lower turnover.
- The increase in other operating costs was mainly due to higher provision for doubtful debts and the costs associated with the airport move.
- Cathay Pacific's cost per ATK fell by 12.5 per cent to HK$2.25 reflecting successful cost management.

So let's see then. All things that I have some degree of control over such as staff costs, route costs and fuel costs dropped. In fact everything went down from last year except for aircraft depreciation and leases and 'others'. So why is that?

'Aircraft depreciation and operating lease costs increased, reflecting deliveries during the year.' Oh, I see. You bought some new aircraft and so that went up by $153 million. Well that's what happens when you buy new stuff. Surely you're not asking the pilots to pay for your new aircraft with salary concessions are you?

'The increase in other operating costs was mainly due to higher provision for doubtful debts and the costs associated with the airport move.' What? You lent some money to some people who aren't going to pay you back or you gave credit to some shady operator who's done a runner. We're supposed to pay for that as well are we? And as for the move to the new airport, that's just a cost of doing business. Hopefully you planned for that; you've known about it for long enough. And, in any case, you've got more than enough in your war chest from years of making fat profits to cover that. 1998 was the first full year loss reported in 35 years. So let's see, 'others' comes to an additional 20 million over last year.

So, in summary then, you want your employees to pay for the cost of buying some new aircraft, the cost of moving to CLK, writing down the cost of the Classics for tax purposes, some bad debts and very suspect redundancies? I definitely don't think so!!

But they did expect us to pay. They came at us looking for cuts of up to 28 per cent on the A Scales. We had a couple of choices. We could front them off again as we'd done the previous year and just say no. Or we could look at their proposals and see what we could get back in return. This time around, they knew they weren't going to get what they wanted without some quid pro quo, so they came to the table with a different approach.

We started off with ASL. We re-tabled our previous proposal to shut it down and reintegrate the freighters into the mainline operation. This time we had some very compelling statistics and costings to show it hadn't worked when they first set it up, it wasn't working now and it wouldn't work in the future. They couldn't refute our figures and agreed to our proposal. Not only that: Rhodes threw in the two Air Hong Kong B747 freighters as well.

Air Hong Kong (AHK) was set up in November 1986 by three local businessmen. It started off operating a B707-320C freighter and by March 1993 had acquired two B747-100SF freighters. In June 1994 Cathay bought 75 per cent of AHK's shares for HK$200 million We hadn't asked for AHK to be included in the ASL deal but Rhodes threw it in without our asking. When he offered it across the table we were a bit taken aback but Rhodes just carried on as if it had been intended to be part of the deal all along. We maintained poker faces and went along with his assumption. Result! That was two more aircraft in our freight network and we'd shut down ASL.

We managed to look after the ASL pilots while we were at it. Some of the General Committee members had adopted the view that we shouldn't do anything for them because they were 'scabs'. I didn't see it that way. They didn't know what they were getting into when they joined ASL but they soon found out. Also I'd been working with the ASL Flight Crew Association through HKALPA and saw it as a way to bring these guys back into the brotherhood. Our deal offered them a chance to come across into Cathay mainline and get a number on the seniority list. It offered a permanent job with a chance to move onto the passenger operation as well. Most of them took it. A few stayed on their ASL contracts but the company itself was to wither on the vine. The deal stipulated that ASL would not recruit any more pilots. Some of the GC members saw this as a big win but I was more circumspect. Yes, we'd finally managed to get rid of ASL but all we'd really done was to get back what was ours in the first place. The real answer to ASL, or any other such alter ego operation, was to strangle it at birth. We couldn't do that because the Check & Trainers wouldn't stand up and be counted. It was a victory, yes, but it came at a price. Forty-four of our F/Es had lost their jobs and management were still asking us to foot the bill for their redundancy payouts. It was their failed plan. Why should we pay for it? It was a start but only a start. There was a long way to go yet.

Next we got onto CoS. All the work that we'd done previously with Mike Lowes, before Samios stuck his nose in, stood us in good stead. We rattled through the contract with almost indecent haste. Rhodes knew he wasn't going to get anywhere with his pay cuts unless he came to agreement on CoS. Again, some saw this as a victory. I didn't. It was just another case of getting back what had been taken away from us in 1994. We got rid of all the 'as may be varied from time to time at the discretion of the company' clauses but, really, so what? We had an ongoing court case to establish the legal terms of our contract and we would win that, albeit it would take time. Yes, agreeing the terms of the new CoS obviated the need to spend any more money on the legal action but, again, it wasn't really an improvement over what we'd had in the first place. Of course management would spin it as, 'Look, we're making massive concessions here. We've shut down ASL and we've agreed to a new CoS using your words. What more do you want? And now we've agreed to that, we want pay concessions.'

We got onto rostering and that's where things started getting difficult. They wanted to link a rostering deal to pay concessions and we could see why. In their position, I'd have done exactly the same thing. We had a counter to that. Our position was that rostering and pay were separate issues but if you want to start talking pay cuts, we want something in return. If our company really is in a bad way financially, we're prepared to consider pay cuts but we want a spring back mechanism so that we get our money back when times are good again.

We'd proposed a deal based on turnover and profit before but there's a problem with such deals. As we've already seen, money can be shifted round the balance sheet, especially with a conglomerate like the Swire Group, and the numbers can be made to tell any story you want. No, this time we had a better plan, one that reflected what the *market* rather than the accountants valued the company at. We wanted a share option scheme and we had our proposal all ready. We had employed the services of Arthur Andersen to construct our proposal and it took the opposition somewhat by surprise. We brought our AA chaps in and they brought their treasury chaps. We sat back and watched a few rounds of 'expert jousting'. Of course, the whole thing came down to valuing the shares at some point in the future and, on this point, there was severe disagreement. We used the Black-Scholes mathematical model, an industry standard used for the pricing of European-style share options. Their treasury people didn't agree with this model. They had their own figures. Of course they would. Never mind what the rest of the world uses, we're going to do it the Cathay way.

While the argument over numbers was going on though, it was significant to note one point in particular. Rather than take the approach that 'we're taking it and not giving you anything back', they had accepted the principle that there had to be a quid pro quo. This was a huge step forward. Well in that case, as well as financial recompense, we wanted something more. We wanted job security. After all, if we weren't around to reap the benefits of a share option scheme, what was the point? No, we needed some assurance that our jobs were going to be secure during the lean times and that they weren't going to just set up another low cost operation to undercut us. We wanted a scope clause in our contracts.

Scope is an American term. It refers to contractual clauses that dictate which pilots can fly the company's aircraft. Some scope clauses run to numerous pages of legalese and are virtually indecipherable without a team of lawyers. Our proposal was simple. Only pilots who were on the Cathay seniority list could fly Cathay aircraft. With globalisation, alliances and code-sharing, this would prevent them from, say, using pilots from another airline to fly our aircraft on a shared route and thereby taking our work away from us. Scope is very common in US pilot contracts but was a new concept to Cathay. It proved to be a major stumbling block and was a show-stopper for them, or so they said. Rhodes reported that Turnbull's reaction to our proposal was, 'There'll be no scope in the contract as long as my arse points towards the ground.'

That would seem to be it then. Well, no actually. You want pay cuts, well we want share options and scope in return. That's the deal. Take it or leave it. They left it and negotiations broke down. Predictably, they tried a bypass manoeuvre but this time with a difference.

On 15 March, Barley sent a letter to all the A Scale pilots with a package containing their proposals for pay cuts together with a request for a reply by 9 April. The package was very comprehensive and had obviously been in preparation for some time. So, as usual, while they'd been sitting in meetings with us going through the motions of negotiation, behind the scenes they'd been secretly putting all this together, painting us, yet again, as the intransigent hard-liners who refused to accept the commercial realities of life. *We are appealing to you directly to help out your company in its time of need because we've tried our best but we just can't work with your union.* Same old claptrap, same old tactics.

They got a shock though. If they thought the pilots were going to roll over just like they did in 1994, they were sadly mistaken. Virtually to a man the pilots refused to sign. Barley's attempt to impose a deadline of 9 April didn't work either. All the good negotiating courses teach that there's only one thing to do with unilaterally imposed deadlines. Simply ignore them. That's what we did and it worked. Their next move was a ball-buster though, or so they thought. On 24 May Barley sent out another 'appeal for help' to all the A Scale pilots. In it he offered them two options. The first was to accept the new CoS package. The second was to accept a voluntary redundancy package that was included with the letter. But what if the pilots didn't want to accept either option? The next bit was a beauty and is quoted verbatim:

> A notice to terminate current employment contracts will be issued on 11th June to all 'A' scale crew members who have not elected to accept the new Conditions of Service or who have not applied for the Voluntary Separation Scheme.

So that was to be the 'negotiated' settlement. Sign or be fired. Now they had really stirred up the hornets' nest. We knew they might have something like this up their sleeves and we had some plans in place. It was time to activate them.

The first thing was to look after safety. To put pilots who had devoted their careers to the company in such a position was intolerable. They had families, children in school, houses, mortgages and other financial commitments. The stress that was being placed on them by Barley's actions was unacceptable and would inevitably impact upon safe aircraft operations. Anyone who felt unfit to continue to perform his duties under such circumstances was advised to report to the company's PMO, Dr John Merritt. Many did and he placed them on stress leave. It is to John's eternal credit that he resisted the pressure that was put upon him by senior management and did his professional duty. We have already discussed the symptoms of cumulative fatigue. Add to that insomnia and other ailments caused by stress and you have a recipe for disaster. Because of his actions, John lost favour with the board and he was later to be pushed out of his job under the guise of reorganisation and outsourcing of the Medical Department. He did an excellent job and is a credit to his profession.

Afterwards, management tried to characterise this as a 'sick-out'. It was rubbish. There was no sick-out then or later. The responsibility for the increase in sickness levels lay fairly and squarely at their own door. Their actions were unconscionable and led to a clear and present threat to flight safety. The sickness levels resulted in flights being cancelled and they had to start bringing in outside charters. They also stopped taking forward bookings. It was during the press coverage of what happened in 1999 that Cathay's corporate development director, one

Anthony Nigel Tyler, first came to prominence as the company's public mouthpiece. We shall hear much more of him later.

We instigated the IFALPA Mutual Assistance clauses with 'recruitment ban', 'maximum competition' and 'assistance to pilots stranded away from home base' in full effect. The IFALPA president, Ted Murphy, wrote to the Swire board, the chief executive of Hong Kong, Tung Chee Hwa, and the director of the CAD, asking them to intervene and instruct management to return to the negotiating table. The presidents of many other member associations did the same thing. We had also been in touch with the International Brotherhood of Teamsters (IBT) in the US who pledged us their support. The Swire Group has a lot of shipping interests as well as cold storage and road freight facilities in the US. It would be costly to them if their ships remained unloaded at the dockside or their trucks stopped running. Of course, outside help and support is always welcome and it is good to know that you are not facing the enemy alone but the real fight is on the front lines at home.

We held a lot of seminars and meetings with the pilots and their families where we could let them know what was going on, answer their questions and bolster their resolve. It is very important in such situations to make sure that families are included. Family support groups are an essential component to a successful outcome. Of course, management did the same thing. They held meetings to explain their 'very reasonable' proposals to the troops. It got quite silly at one point. They had hired a conference facility at a hotel right next door to the ballroom where we were holding one of our meetings. Pilots were nipping into their room to come back and report what they were saying about us and give us numbers. We were certainly winning the attendance figures and when one came back and reported that they were making personally abusive statements about me, I knew we had them on the back foot. Rick Fry reportedly said, 'No one had heard of scope before John Warham brought it up. The only reason he wants scope in the contract is because he wants to be president of IFALPA.'

If they were resorting to personal attack, it meant that they weren't succeeding with their arguments. I considered it pretty rich for them to be questioning my integrity, given the way they routinely behaved, and I said as much to the assembled throng. They also sent their own moles into our meetings to try to challenge us. One pilot stood up and asked me about scope.

'I never gave you a mandate to put scope in my contract. You're holding up the whole deal because of some crusade you're on. David's already said he won't entertain scope. Why can't you just accept what he says? You're putting my job at risk because of some personal bee in your bonnet.'

'Did you give me a mandate to protect your contract?' I enquired in response.

'Well yes.'

'Good, well do you want employment protection as part of your contract or are you happy to see another ASL pop up after you've given salary concessions?'

'Well obviously I don't like ASL but . . .'

'No you don't and neither do any of us. It was your mate David who brought in ASL and there's nothing to stop him from doing it again if you don't get scope in return for salary concessions. Scope's not a bee in my bonnet as you call it. I'm pursuing the mandate that you gave me to protect your contract. Ask yourself why they're so resistant to scope. If Turnbull isn't planning another ASL why would he be bothered? The only reason he'd want to keep scope out is if he's going to try to undercut you again just like last time. Wake up. Now, next question.'

They gave up after a while.

Then we played our trump card. We went to the Hong Kong Labour Department and asked them to provide mediation services to help resolve our dispute. Management weren't expecting that and their first reaction was a typical knee-jerk. They refused to attend the meetings, saying that it was an internal matter. That put them in a bad spot though. With all the pressure being applied at governmental level by third parties such as IFALPA, how could they possibly come off as a caring employer acting in the best interests of the company, not to mention Hong Kong, if they refused to avail themselves of a government department deliberately set up to assist in such cases? They gave in and on 5 June talks started again at the Labour Department's offices in Sheung Wan.

Behind the scenes, we weren't as sure of support from the membership as we were making out. If it came to the sign or be fired deadline, we knew a lot of people would probably cave. We had stated that we would call a strike ballot if anyone was fired but we had to give them some sort of collective will to support one another. If we all said no, there was nothing Turnbull could do. He couldn't sack all the A Scalers because that would mean he would have no Captains and it would ground the airline quicker than any strike. Yes, he could offer them their jobs back the next day on new B Scale contracts but, again, if everyone held firm, there was no way he could hire enough new pilots, train them and get them out on the line without incurring massive cost. The shareholders would be really impressed!

We'd all heard threats before that 'If you don't agree, he'll just shut the airline down and open up the next day under a different name.'

Yes, sure he would. He'd get a new AOC, new route licences and new ATC slots overnight! We'd heard it all before and I had had enough of it so when one of their go-betweens came into my office one day to whisper it in my ear, I told him to go back with the response, 'Good. Let's see you do it then.'

He asked me whether that was really what I wanted him to say and I confirmed it. I never heard that one again until Rhodes came up with a new variation.

'David will just downsize Cathay and turn it into a boutique airline.'

'Yes of course he will. That's why we've just spent billions on moving to CLK and made enormous investment in buildings and infrastructure so we can turn into a flying club. I'm sure Sir Adrian will be impressed with that. Not much chance of Tung giving Peter the Grand Bauhinia Medal when he leaves either.'

Rhodes never tried that one again. The fact still remained, though, that the pilots might crumple under pressure. It only takes a few to cross the line and then the floodgates open. That's what management were relying on and we needed a strategy to deal with it. We came up with a 'critical mass' mechanism. All the pilots were issued election forms to be completed and sent confidentially to our lawyers. On this form the pilots stated their intent as to whether or not they would hold out on the deadline of 11 June. Once the critical mass of 380 of the 600 pilots under threat was reached, that would be conveyed to management by the lawyers. It was a compromise but we needed to give the troops some level of comfort. I personally didn't favour this tactic because it demonstrated potential weakness in our resolve. However, it had to be done to appease some of the weaker members.

Negotiations continued in the Labour Department and, after a meeting lasting eleven hours on 10 June, we had moved closer but they still wouldn't agree to scope. That evening in the debrief with my own team, something happened that was an indicator of what was to come within the AOA in the future. My core negotiating team consisted of myself, Murray Gardner and John Findlay, the general secretary. That night Gardner advanced the view, as he had done all the way through the talks, that they weren't going to agree to scope so we'd have to concede the point to close the deal. His view was that 'management just don't want to go there.'

I totally disagreed with his viewpoint. To me, scope was essential to protect us from another ASL after they'd taken our money. Yes we'd got rid of ASL, fixed the CoS and agreed a new basings deal but, as mentioned earlier, these improvements were only regaining what we had lost. They weren't 'wins' as such. To my thinking, they were separate from the money issues. Management wanted to link them so that they could say that they had made these concessions to as a trade-off for pay cuts. In my view, in return for salary concessions, so far all we had really got in return was the share option deal, and the recouping of our money was contingent on the share price increasing to HK$24 in the next five years. That was the figure their treasury people were predicting and I didn't believe them. The Black-Scholes model put the price nearer to HK$17, which meant that we weren't going to recover a significant percentage of our concessions. In terms of career earnings, we were losing out. Therefore, scope was essential to protect our jobs and would go some way to recompensing for the shortfall, otherwise the deal was too one-sided. History shows that the share price did get above HK$20 in 2007 and peaked at HK$23.10 on 26 October, but over the ten-year period post-1999, at the end of which the options lapsed, it averaged at around HK$14.50. Clearly the Cathay treasury people either knew less about finance than Messrs Black & Scholes or they were trying to screw us.

Gardner and I had attended the same IFALPA negotiations training course in Frankfurt. The course included a simulated negotiation. There were 24 of us on the course from different member associations. We were split into four groups of six for the simulation and each group was divided into two teams of three, one representing the pilots and one management. Each team was given a set of objectives to be achieved from the negotiation and, naturally, these differed. The ensuing negotiation was videotaped and all teams were debriefed together after the simulation. It was very effective and an excellent learning tool. In my own simulation, I was cast in the role of team leader of the management side. We let the pilots' team start talking for 30 seconds and then I interrupted them with a four-minute speech about how everything was on the table, we were fully prepared to address their concerns but first they must agree to salary concessions because our company was in a desperate financial state, the forecasts for the future looked very bleak, blah, blah, blah. In the debrief, the moderator said to me, 'That was very good, John. Where did it come from?'

'It's simple really. I've been listening to this shit across the table for so long that I'm almost word perfect now,' was my reply.

During the simulation, Gardner's team was the only one of the four that failed to reach an agreement and, afterwards, during the debrief, he became quite agitated about this. He saw it as a failure. In retrospect, this was a warning sign. He had flown F18s in the RAAF before coming into civil aviation and was a classic over-achiever. After Clemmow made him Cat C, I went through his personal records to see whether there was anything in there possibly to justify such categorisation. Typically he had kept all his records going right the way back to his school days and they were exemplary; in fact more than exemplary. They were perfect. He had never failed at anything. He was totally goal oriented. Complete the mission at all costs. This is not a bad thing provided that you have selected the correct goal.

It is a fact of life that the hardest negotiation is often with your own team. This was true of the relationship between Gardner and me. The reason we made a good team is that we approached the problems from different points of view. In our discussions prior to meeting management, we would have to find consensus between us, and the compromises we made meant that the position we took into the actual negotiations was balanced. Because of this, we made a successful partnership.

One of the objectives that we were taught in our training was to try to get to the next meeting. Gardner was always very driven by this. He disliked the thought of talks breaking down with no deal being struck. Whilst this is a good objective, it must always be viewed in context. Another key point we learned was knowing when to walk away from the table. In other words, do the deal if you can live with it, but not at any cost. Know when to say no as well when to say yes. To my mind, scope was a show-stopper. Without it, we should walk away from the table and deal with whatever happened next. No scope, no deal. Ted had discussed this with me previously. Indeed it was his decision as president, and my stance simply mirrored his own view. We went into the meeting at the Labour Department on the morning of 11 June with the deadline of 12:00 only three hours away. Before we went in, Gardner tried one last time to get me to agree to drop scope but I refused to move. Ted had given me authority as team leader and made it my call on the day. I made my decision and Gardner didn't like it. We were not a particularly happy team that morning, though we showed a united front.

Our team was small, just the three of us. Management had come in mob-handed all the way through the talks. There were nine or ten of them and it worked to their disadvantage. Discipline is essential in any negotiating team. There should be only one person doing the talking with the others listening and taking notes. If one of the other team members has something to say or wants to make a point, he should do so by passing a written note to the speaker. Under no circumstances should anyone speak ad lib unless it has been agreed as a tactic beforehand. Having said that, any team member can call a break at any time by passing a note in case things are not going according to plan. When 'blooding' new negotiators, I would always brief them before their first meeting that their role was to observe and take notes and that under no circumstances should they say anything. In my time as a negotiator, there was only ever one man who managed to adhere to that rule. Everyone else just had to open his trap and say something. The temptation was just too much. They had waited so long to get in front of management and tell them what they thought that they just couldn't keep their mouths closed.

Communication, which is the crux of negotiation, should be more about listening than speaking. You have two ears and one mouth, use them in equal proportions. Know when to just shut the fuck up. If your opponent makes a statement to which a response is expected and either you don't like it or it's taken you by surprise and you don't know how to respond, just sit there and say nothing. Sit there for as long as it takes, two, three or four minutes if necessary. Pass notes between your team. Shuffle some papers. Do something on your laptop. People do not like silence in a conversation. It makes them uncomfortable and they feel it necessary to fill the void with words. Rhodes was always a sucker for this tactic. He could never last more than 30 seconds without having to open his mouth again. It was a great way to get him to talk himself into a corner. If you're up against a professional who uses the same tactic on you, wait them out for as long as you can and, if they don't break silence, call time out to defuse them, then come back in with, 'I'm sorry, what were you saying?'

Management's team was ill-disciplined. Because they were there, they all had to show how clever they were by trying to score points. They all had to have a speaking part. It was very easy to deal with them. Barley was designated as their team leader but, because he couldn't think on his feet, he would open the meeting and then hand over to Rhodes as the mouthpiece. At some point one of the clever dicks would try to have his say with some convoluted question that he'd dreamed up the night before to demonstrate his skills. I'd simply listen to what he had to say and then turn to Barley and say, 'I'm sorry, Ken, I thought Nick is supposed to be your spokesman. Was that question directed through the chair or not?'

That would leave Barley waffling and Rhodes trying to talk over him. On some occasions, they actually ended up having a group discussion and arguing a point amongst themselves in front of us. That is an absolute no-no in negotiations. Never, never, never disagree in front of your opponents.

When we went into the meeting on the morning of 11 June, I felt a very heavy responsibility. There was a group of the pilots and their wives assembled in the ballroom at the Excelsior Hotel waiting to find out whether Sutch was going to go through with the threat to sack them if there was no deal. We also had video conferencing links set up with the UK, Australia and Canada so that our based pilots and their families were in the loop as well. The burden on Ted as the president was also huge but he had put his trust in my judgment. I was going into battle with a team where one person disagreed with my position and Findlay, as usual, was sitting on the fence. I felt very isolated and alone. This was it. My actions that morning were going to affect the lives of hundreds of people and, if I called it wrong, the Monday morning quarterbacks would have a field day. The strategy I had chosen and the direction in which I had led the AOA and its members since joining the General Committee in 1996 were about to be crystallised. At that moment, I truly felt the burden of command. I decided to follow best practice, keep my mouth shut and make them do the talking.

After the normal exchange of greetings, Barley opened proceedings with the words, 'Will you accept your scope provisions if they apply only to wide-bodies?'

I responded, 'I'll have to check with my president, Ken, but I think I can say that we could live with that.'

We went into breakout and I phoned Ted to give him the news. We had to resist the temptation to cheer, scream and shout because the breakout room wasn't soundproofed. We'd done it! They'd rolled! We'd got scope! Turnbull's arse must have been getting a suntan as we spoke!

We waited 15 minutes before going back in to make it look as though I was having trouble convincing Ted that we could make the compromise. We didn't give a toss about narrow-body aircraft. Cathay was an all wide-body fleet and there was no way they were ever going to start using narrow-bodies. Dragonair had some but that wasn't a concern to us. There was relief all round in the meeting. We had been down to the wire and looked over the precipice but, finally, common sense had prevailed.

The relief was short lived. When we had finished tying up the loose ends of what had been agreed and what had not been agreed, Barley pushed a piece of paper across the table and said, 'There's one other thing, as part of the deal you have to sign this.'

I read it. It was a statement saying that, during the course of the negotiations, the AOA had been running a sick-out campaign and that it agreed to pay reparations for the resultant losses and damage caused to the company. Throughout all of the negotiations I had been involved with during my time in the AOA, I had never lost my temper. In my opinion, it is not how negotiations should be conducted. Scenes of table thumping and shouting that are portrayed in fictional movies are just that. I lost it then though.

This was typical. This item was never on the agenda, had never been mentioned and it proved what we knew all along. Sutch and Turnbull were trying to break the union. If we signed that piece of paper, they would come after the AOA for all its assets and break us financially. My language became somewhat choice and it surprised everyone in the room, not least Mrs Siu who was the leader of the Labour Department mediation team. Even Rhodes looked surprised. He'd never seen me blow my top before.

We left the room and I called Ted to tell him what had happened. I asked for authority to tell them to go fuck themselves and the horse they came in on and he gave it to me. We went back into the room to find Barley was missing. He was outside speaking to his boss. He came back in and said, 'My managing director has instructed me to inform you that unless you sign that paper there is no deal.'

'In that case, Ken, you do not have a deal.'

The meeting broke up again. Barley left the room but I stayed there along with Rhodes, Mrs Siu and my team. She was beside herself. Just when she thought she'd averted a shut-down of the airline it seemed that all was lost. She implored me to just agree to it for the sake of Hong Kong. I pointed out to her that this was the sort of shit that we had to put up with all the time from these people. They didn't negotiate in good faith, they couldn't be trusted with their own grannies and they were just out to bust the union. She was a bit taken aback by my vehemence and looked as if she might cry. For once, Rhodes did something right. He said they could live without the reparation part and couldn't we come to some other form of words that we'd be able to sign. I left it to him, Findlay and Gardner to draft something. They came up with a statement saying that it was not AOA policy to encourage its members to report unfit for duty when in fact they were fit so to do, that it would not adopt such a policy in the future and that it does not and would not condone any such type of action by its membership. Barley returned to the room and we gave him our counter-proposal. He scuttled off again to consult with his boss.

At 11:55 I was standing outside the room in the corridor and Barley was still on the phone a few feet away from me. I told him I needed his decision now as, with the deadline approaching, I had to give instructions to the lawyers on the critical mass mechanism. If they didn't receive my instructions by 12:00 the rejection letters would be going in and that would be that. The airline would be shut down. He rolled. They accepted our revised draft.

Under the terms of the deal, we had got rid of ASL and agreed a revised CoS and basings agreement. They got their salary concessions but considerably reduced from their original proposals and spread over three years. In return we got a share option scheme and scope in the contract. We also protected the defined benefit Provident Fund scheme by ghosting the salaries used in the formula to their original pre-concession levels. There was one outstanding matter that we hadn't had time to finalise and that was rostering practices. However, it was agreed as part of the deal that negotiations would continue with the aim of completing an agreement by 31 October. As with all things, however, the devil is in the detail. There were a couple of glitches that had to be sorted out.

One of their team members was Ronald Benjamin Davies. His position was manager bases and he was detailed to send out the share option scheme documents to the pilots. He sent out the wrong draft. It was either incompetence or deliberately done because the earlier draft he distributed was less advantageous to us. When it was pointed out to him what he had done he tried to stand on his position. It took intervention by his boss, Dave Roberts, to put that right.

Barley tried to pull another one. After the meetings at the Labour Department were over, at a subsequent admin meeting, Rhodes turned round and said to me, 'Of course the new deal doesn't apply to the 1994 non-signers, they're still on their old contracts.'

That was the second time I lost my temper. There had been no such exclusion ever mentioned and it was another try-on. Barley just didn't like it because, under the new terms, the non-signers, including me, would actually receive a pay increase rather than a cut because we'd been on frozen scales since 1994. After we came to an accommodation to account for Provident Fund contribution shortfalls in the intervening years, that got sorted out as well. It was notable, however, that when management came in with their calculations, they were full of errors. They used some wrong formulae, incorrect salary levels and some wrong assumptions. They brought their Provident Fund 'expert' into the meeting to try to justify their figures. We took him through his spreadsheets, pointed out his errors one after the other and he lost serious face when Rhodes conceded the point and said, 'I think we'll just use the AOA's figures.'

There had been an enormous amount of media interest in the Labour Department proceedings and a photo opportunity was held there after the talks had concluded. As Barley and I were standing there shaking hands and smiling, I said to him through gritted teeth, 'If only they knew, eh, Ken?' He didn't respond.

After that, one of the management team, Augustus Tang, came up to me and said, 'You remind me of someone.'

'Really, and who might that be?' I enquired.

'You remind me of a very good negotiator.'

I thanked him and took it as a great compliment coming from one of my opponents.

There was one last incident that happened that day. In the evening we held a full briefing at the Excelsior for the pilots and their families. Coincidentally, the 44 F/Es that had been made redundant were having a farewell bash in one of the function rooms upstairs. They invited me to attend for a couple of drinks before it started by way of a thank you for all the effort that I'd put in on their behalf, albeit to little result. They emphasised that they didn't want it to turn into a political event, rather it was a social occasion. Ted and I went up there at 19:00 and the men and their wives formed two receiving lines. I felt very privileged to be accorded such courtesy. When we were nearing the end of the first line, the door opened and in walked Sutch. He refused to acknowledge Ted and me and made a particular point of ignoring us as he passed by in the line. Mindful of what the F/Es had requested, we moved on quickly and left. I was completely taken aback by his attitude after all the dealings we'd had with each other over the years. He was also leaving Hong Kong that month for good and returning to the UK, presumably to take up a place on the Swire board in London, which was the usual progression for the Cathay Taipan. I went downstairs and met Nigel Demery. I was quite upset by what had just happened and, rather than go straight back into the pilots' meeting, we went across the road to a quiet bar for a beer until I calmed down a bit.

When I related what had happened, Nigel said, 'Well what did you expect?'

'What do you mean?'

'Don't you realise what you've done?'

'No. What have I done?'

'Sutch was supposed to be leaving here in a blaze of glory having sorted out the pilots once and for all and go back to the UK with his seat on the board. Instead of that, he's had to delay his departure until this was sorted out and he's leaving Cathay at the height of the worst industrial confrontation they've had in years.'

When Nigel explained it that way, I saw his point. Despite my personal feelings about the whole management ethos under Sutch's regime, I still tried to look at the negotiations as business. It seemed that Sutch had taken it personally. With responsibility comes accountability.

16

Descent

'*The ponderous machinery took so long to set itself in motion; the great wheels and levers, once started, revolved with such a laborious, such a painful deliberation, that at last their work was accomplished – surely, firmly, completely, in the best English manner, and too late.*'

Lytton Strachey, 'The End of General Gordon' in *Eminent Victorians*

'*If you wanted nothing done at all, Balfour was the man for the job.*'

Winston Churchill

There was one matter still outstanding from the 1999 negotiations. We had not finalised a deal on rostering practices. A lot of work had been done in the last two years and agreement was close, or so we thought. The compromise we reached to sign the 1999 deal was an agreement that talks would continue with the intent of finalising a deal by 31 October. To protect both our positions, the following clause was included in the new 1999 CoS:

The Company and the Officer hereby agree and acknowledge that no agreement has been reached with regard to Rostering Practices and that the Company and the Hong Kong Aircrew Officers' Association will continue negotiations with a view to reaching such agreement. The Company and the Officer further agree that rostering will continue to be in accordance with the Rostering Practices & Procedures for Cockpit Crew (1994) pending further agreement on Rostering Practices

251

or final resolution of HCMP No. 1679 of 1999, whichever is the earlier. The Company and the Officer further acknowledge that the agreement of the Officer to the matters referred to in this clause is without prejudice to the assertions about Rostering Practices made by all the parties in HCMP No. 1679 of 1999 and similar assertions made by the Hong Kong Aircrew Officers' Association.

This clause protected our legal position on contractual determination and was drafted on the assumption that both parties would now continue to negotiate in good faith to get new rostering practices agreed once and for all. After everything that had happened since 1994, the question might be asked: Were we being naive? Well, after we'd both looked over the edge into the abyss, there was optimism that common sense might now prevail over corporate greed. After all, they'd got their salary concessions so that should be enough shouldn't it? If Mike Lowes was still involved, or if we had a DFO who was capable of making a decision, then maybe so. If we weren't dealing with Turnbull and the Swires, maybe so. A lot of 'ifs' really, but there was reason for optimism.

If Turnbull had been hoping to step into Sutch's shoes, when the latter departed, it didn't happen. Instead, James Hughes-Hallett was appointed chairman. Born in 1949, Hughes-Hallett graduated from Oxford University in 1970 with a degree in English Literature and joined the Swire Group in 1976. He held various positions in Asia and Australia, and was managing director of John Swire & Sons in Australia until January 1993 when he transferred back to Hong Kong as director responsible for the group's ship-owning and consumer trading interests. Perhaps his arrival might herald a new approach to staff relations.

During two weeks in June more than 600 flights had to be cancelled and estimates of lost revenue over the period varied from HK$455 to $700 million which would put a sizeable dent in the cost savings made by the pilots' salary concessions. Perhaps they'd come to the conclusion that the Turnbull scythe style wasn't actually as efficient as advertised and Hughes-Hallett was brought in to adopt a more pragmatic approach. A degree in English Literature might indicate a more open mind than your average number cruncher.

There were also personnel changes in the AOA. Gardner had stood down from the General Committee after the 1999 talks so I needed to put together a new negotiating team. I recruited Don Fraser and Drew Searle. Both were Australian and ex-RAAF but from the Air Lift Group rather than the Air Combat Group. They were both very astute men with good political antennae but weren't quite so goal-oriented as Gardner.

Target fixation was not now going to be a problem. Don in particular was a good man to have on the team as he was good at cultivating allies in the opposition's camp. As well as holding Bachelor of Science and Bachelor of Business degrees, he had also completed an MBA under Cathay sponsorship and had maintained the contacts he made during the course. I didn't know it at the time but Don and I were going to end up working together for many years into the future and would become firm friends; in fact more than just friends. Like Sandy Easton, I count Don Fraser on the very short list of people I have met in my life who are *true* friends.

We put the team together, got our proposals ready and looked forward to getting things sorted out by 31 October. It was going to be hard work but it would be worth it.

We were met with a new tactic to which we assigned the acronym DPGFD. Delay, prevarication and general foot dragging. We were to encounter much of this over the next nine years. Despite the 31 October deadline, the first meeting wasn't held until 1 November and only then because we went back to the Labour Department to tell them that management wasn't honouring its side of the bargain. The first part of the talks centred on them trying to get us to agree to their variations to CAD 371. Why on earth would we want to do that? Good try but a non-starter given that the result of the judicial review had dealt us a strong hand. Our objective was to agree a complete set of rostering practices that would form part of the CoS and be contractually binding. This would put a stop to any further 'flexible' interpretations of the rules and, more significantly, it would mean that there could be no further 'back door' variations without prior agreement. It would form a stable base from which everyone could be clear about exactly what was and wasn't permitted. By December, it seemed that we were making progress and before the Christmas holiday break we were optimistic that we would manage to reach an agreement. There was a warning sign, however. Some of the issues that were relatively simple to deal with were agreed without too much debate. Some others were more contentious and required negotiation to come to an agreement that both sides could live with. Then there were the show-stoppers. For us, these included 'commander's discretion', which we discussed earlier, and reserve or standby duty rules, which had previously been open to abuse.

Reserve is a particularly onerous form of duty from the lifestyle point of view because it is virtually impossible to plan anything ahead. Typically, reserve would be scheduled in 8- or 12-hour periods during which you could be called out for any duty ranging from a quick Taipei out and back and home in time for dinner to a five-day trans-Pacific ULR op. In theory, at least, reserve should be scheduled to the absolute minimum to cover for unforeseen events such as an in-flight turn back or a crew member reporting sick. Any more than minimum coverage is wasteful because reserve still counts towards cumulative duty hour totals irrespective of whether or not the pilot is called out for a flying duty. Thus a pilot on a 12-hour reserve block who is not called out still logs some duty hours, which count towards his mandated cumulative totals.

With a stable roster and historical data available, it is a relatively simple matter to schedule the minimum 'right amount' of reserve to cover unforeseen glitches in the operation. With an unstable roster it is a different matter. When things are continually being changed at short notice, such as switching aircraft types to cater for varying passenger loads, as the Commercial Department would love to be able to do, then we are in a different ball game. In these circumstances it is not possible to roster reserve efficiently and the knee-jerk reaction is to put as many people as you have available on reserve. This, of course, has a knock-on effect with the rest of the roster. If a pilot is on reserve on day one and scheduled to operate a specific flight on day two, if you call him out from reserve on day one for a ULR op, he cannot now operate his scheduled flight on day two so you have to call out someone else to operate that flight. If this second pilot is in the same position as the first, now he cannot operate his day-two flight and you have to call out a third pilot. And so on and so on. In this way, roster instability ripples all the way down the chain and, with 2,000 or so pilots on the roster, the disruption can be enormous.

It is an acknowledged fact in aero-medicine that roster instability is a contributory cause of pilot fatigue, both short term and cumulative. The ability to properly plan rest periods before flying duties, especially on ULR ops, is a critical factor in avoiding cumulative fatigue. Similarly, the inability to properly plan your home life because of roster instability leads to domestic stress, a disrupted family life and an increase in risk exposure. For these reasons, CAD 371 specifically mandates that:

> It is the responsibility of the operator to prepare duty rosters sufficiently in advance to provide the opportunity for crews to plan adequate pre-duty rest.

Implicit in this statement is the intention that crews should actually operate their rosters as notified and not be subject to repeated changes at short notice. The rosters in Cathay were constructed on a monthly basis and were supposed to be notified to the crews by the 15th of the previous month. Reserve duty was also supposed to be rostered on a 'fair share' basis, i.e. the total amount of reserve required would be shared out equally amongst all the pilots over a 12-month period. With the advent of basings, this was no longer happening and the Hong Kong-based pilots were shouldering far more than their fair share of reserve duty. This was a cause of friction and was one of the issues that we wanted to address in the rostering practices talks.

The warning bell that started ringing at the end of 1999 was that each time we tried to address one of these show-stoppers, Rhodes and his team would avoid the issue and put it aside to be dealt with later. Their approach was, 'Let's deal with the easier issues first and get those out of the way and we can come back to the difficult stuff later.' Whilst agreeing the easy issues gave an illusion of progress, in reality no progress was being made at all on the stuff that would make or break the deal. It wasn't even being addressed and this would come back to bite us later.

In these talks, instead of the mob-handed approach, the management team consisted of Rhodes, Hoyland, Phil Walker, who was a management pilot, and Geoff Cole, who worked in the rostering section as their number cruncher and computer boffin. We held the talks on neutral ground in the Josey Room of the Hong Kong Aviation Club at Kai Tak. When the airport had been operational, there were strict building height limits to prevent obstruction of the approach flight path. With the closure of the airport, these restrictions had been lifted and a lot of construction was in progress. Right on the dot of 12:00 each day, multiple pile drivers would start up and their reports would shake the foundations of the room and rattle the windows. Given that they had luxurious meeting rooms in Cathay City at CLK, it was a source of some irritation to Rhodes and his team that they were sequestered with us in the middle of a construction site. It is one of the principles of good negotiating practice that you should try to choose a venue that is to your advantage. Certainly the Aviation Club was advantageous to my team in that it saved us from driving out to CLK every day. If the noise and vibration interrupted our opponents' concentration then that was an added bonus. The club also had a bar, which was very handy for a couple of beers at the end of the day when business was over.

Geoff Cole was partial to the occasional beer and often would stay on with us after the rest of his team had left for home. During some of these evenings we would gain valuable intel on what was going on within his own team dynamic. He was basically a numbers man, had no axe to grind and so didn't take up a 'management speak' attitude. Phil Walker also took a practical approach. Being a pilot, he had a very good grasp of the problems we were trying to solve and, in private conversation, told me that he had a deal of sympathy for our position. The problem was that the decision was not his. It wasn't even Rhodes' decision. It came from higher up. As Rhodes lamented to me one day, some of the people on the board, his 'grown-ups' as he called them, believed that the only good result of a meeting with the union is when the union men come crawling out on their bellies. This was the real Swire mentality and illustrated to me what we were up against.

The talks continued in the new year after the Christmas break and we got onto one of the nitty-gritty issues: monthly credit hour thresholds. These numbers are at the core of any rostering practices no matter what the actual rostering system. From the management point of view they directly affect productivity and operating cost. From the pilots' point of view they directly affect the structure of the roster and therefore lifestyle as well as overtime payments for extra flying above the contract. The mathematics of credit hour calculations are not especially complex although some of the formulae used in the spreadsheets we constructed could appear a little confusing at first glance. Walker and Cole understood exactly how these worked and were not at all fazed. Spreadsheets were not Rhodes' forte and we could see the discomfort in his face when a number he proposed didn't work out the way he thought it would. We were back to the same old problem of the sweets on the top shelf. He couldn't understand why he couldn't reach them just by putting the number in the contract, and no matter how hard we tried, we couldn't get him to grasp the concept. He didn't believe the maths because he didn't understand the principles.

Sickness credits was one of the issues that seemed completely beyond him. If a pilot is contracted for 80 flying hours in a month but is unfit for duty for seven days of that month, Rhodes saw no reason why you could not cram the 80 hours into the remaining three weeks. This was particularly important to us because of the high amount of ULR ops on the rosters. If a pilot is suffering from cumulative fatigue and his fitness level drops because of that, it is no good loading him up with work when he returns to duty because all it will do is exacerbate his condition and cause him to fall ill again. Our solution was to apply a daily hour credit for pilots' sick days to prevent roster stacking and give them a chance to recover properly. You simply have to accept that the productivity lost when a pilot is sick is exactly that. It is lost and cannot be recovered by stacking. Pilots are human beings, not automatons. Rhodes couldn't accept this principle because it got in the way of his Holy Grail number, a theoretical figure derived from another of Turnbull's ATK targets.

Despite all these problems and in order to try to reach agreement, on 3 July we tabled a proposal that would allow 84.5 credit hours per month without triggering EFP. The proposal allowed three trans-Pacific rotations in any one month and an average of five over two months. This was as close to their theoretical goal of three ULR rotations every month that was sustainable and was as good as it was going to get. When we tabled the proposal, Phil Walker actually said to me with incredulity, 'Are you offering eighty-four and a half flying hours a month without EFP?'

When I confirmed this he gave me a very old-fashioned look. There were some constraints in the proposal to prevent such a level of workload being sustained over three or more months but we were offering Rhodes what he had asked for. Rhodes then made a very basic negotiating mistake.

It is one of the fundamental principles of negotiation that, as well as knowing when to walk away from the table if there isn't a deal to be done, you also need to know when to say yes. Know when to *do* the deal. Rhodes just couldn't help himself. Instead of taking us up on our offer, he just had to try to get more. It wasn't negotiation; it was either greed or ignorance. Greed because, no matter what you give to the barbarians, they always come back for more. Ignorance because he didn't understand the principles well enough to realise what was on offer. Either way he blew it. This round of talks ended without agreement and, when we returned to the table later in the year, the offer was off the table. The sweets had been there for the taking and he'd missed his chance.

The roster continued to be in chaos because of the pilot shortage. We simply didn't have enough pilots to complete the commercial task. One of the terms of the CAD Air Operators Certificate Requirements document states that an operator must have sufficient staff to undertake the envisaged operations. The fact was that Cathay was acting in breach of that requirement. When we drew this to the attention of the CAD, Rhodes' reaction was typical. Rather than acknowledging the problem and working with us to find solutions, he commissioned an in-house audit of roster disruption. The terms of reference of this audit were deliberately designed to show that little roster disruption was taking place. They were contrived to cover up rather than address the problem. The definitions used for roster disruption were so wide that, provided a pilot operated any flight to anywhere within a five-day period of his originally assigned duty, it would not be classified as a roster disruption. Not surprisingly, given its terms of reference, the in-house audit concluded that there was minimal disruption to the roster. It was a purely cosmetic exercise and did not even attempt to acknowledge or address the underlying fundamentals.

The AOA managed to get its hands on some of the raw data from this exercise. It showed that, in November 2000 alone, there were more than 14,000 notified roster changes. Given the pilot complement at the time this meant that each pilot, on average, received over nine changes to his flying roster that month. For a pilot flying exclusively ULR ops with three rotations per month, it meant that each of his trips was changed three times. That is the sort of level of disruption you'd expect to see in some tin-pot, cowboy operation, not a supposedly well-managed, first-tier, international airline.

The pilot shortage led to yet another reduction in flight safety standards when they started putting two S/Os on ULR ops. There were two reasons for this. Firstly, an S/O training course is not as long as a full F/O course so you can push more candidates through the sausage machine in a shorter time. The second reason was cost. A detailed training cost analysis for all ranks and aircraft types had recently been completed. One of the people involved in the analysis had supplied the AOA with the results and the figures made interesting reading. The data showed that the cost of S/O induction training on the B747-400 and the A340, the two aircraft types that S/Os operated, was HK$560,782 and $573,313 respectively. F/O upgrade training on these two types added a further HK$503,151 and $531,214 to the bill, so clearly it's cheaper just to train S/Os. The result was that, instead of having one Captain, two F/Os and one S/O, we now only had one F/O to fly the aircraft with the Captain on our ULR ops. S/Os were not qualified to occupy a control seat during the takeoff, descent, approach or landing; nor were two S/Os permitted to occupy control seats at the same time in the cruise. This meant that the Captain's capacity to schedule the in-flight rest to ensure that the handling pilots were fresh during the approach and landing was significantly diminished. As a consequence, one of the pilots was going to be tired and unable to operate at peak efficiency. Not only was this yet another reduction in the overall experience levels on the flight decks of our ULR ops, but also it was a definite degradation in flight safety standards. Our data showed that no other airline we knew of carried two S/Os on its ULR ops. Even the second- and third-tier operators carried two F/Os.

I brought this up with Phil Walker during an annual performance review interview. After he had looked at my training file and informed me that I had 'absolutely no problems', he asked me whether there was anything I'd like to discuss. When I voiced my concerns about the deteriorating standards caused by the reductions in experience levels, he said to me, 'I agree with you, John, but with my management hat on, I'm never going to admit as much in public.'

I thought it a terrible indictment of where the Flight Ops Department now found itself on Barley's watch. It wasn't just the line pilots who were being intimidated by the prevailing ethos. Even Barley's own pilot managers were worried about the situation but were afraid to speak out.

17

Approach

Absent (adj) – *away or not present; missing.*
Absenteeism (n) – *habitual failure to appear, especially for work or other duty.*
Sick (adj) – *suffering from or affected with a physical illness; ailing.*
Sickness (n) – *the condition of being sick; illness.*

www.thefreedictionary.com

Because of the workload and roster instability, sickness levels started to increase again. The 'Sickness Management Programme' or the 'Absence Management Programme' as it had now been renamed, (or the 'Sickness Punishment Programme' as the pilots dubbed it), swung into operation. Pilots on management's blacklist who were deemed to be taking 'too much' sick leave started receiving a series of letters from the personnel manager flight crew, Dave Roberts. The first letter stated:

Dear Bloggs,
A recent review of attendance records of all Flight Crew shows that you have been absent from work on <N> occasions in the twelve months [sic] period from <DATE> to <DATE>. This level of absence is higher than the norm and is, understandably, a cause for concern.
Initially, we wish to confirm that our records are correct and a copy is attached for your perusal. If you feel that the data is inaccurate please let me know as soon as possible.
In additional [sic] we would like to see if there is anything we

can do to assist your return to full flying duties. Please do not hesitate to contact me, your Manager Flying, Crew Personnel Manager or a Company Medical Officer if there is anything we can do to help or if you simple [sic] want to discuss the situation. Sometimes a quiet informal chat can help.

In the meantime, we will continue to monitor the situation.

A relatively benign communication from a caring employer one might think at first glance. Perhaps so, except for the implied threat that 'We are watching you', and the fact that we had conclusive evidence that they were planning punitive measures against pilots on their sickness blacklist. The AOA drafted some form letters to use in response. The first one stated:

Dear Mr Roberts,
    I refer to your letter of <DATE>.
    In this letter you point out that I have been absent from work on <N> occasions during a twelve-month period.
    According to my records I have not been absent from work on any occasions. I have been unable to undertake flying duties for medical reasons on <N> occasions in the aforementioned period.
    In accordance with my contract of employment I have supplied a Medical Certificate when required.
    I would be happy to discuss my 'medical' history with the Company Principal Medical Officer. As a matter of course similar discussions take place every licence renewal medical.
Yours sincerely,
Bloggs

The second letter from Roberts stated:

Dear Bloggs,
    With reference to my letter dated <DATE>, regarding your attendance, I note that you have been absent on <N> occasions since that letter was sent.
    This level of absence continues to be of concern to the company. Please contact myself or Paddy Cavanagh at your earliest convenience to arrange a mutually convenient time to discuss your attendance. We would like to have this discussion in private and in confidence to explore any options to assist your return to full flying duties.

Not quite so benign this time around. We knew what their options were going to be. Another Barleyesque sign or resign letter. The AOA's suggested response was:

Dear Mr Roberts,

I refer you to my previous correspondence regarding sickness.

I have mentioned previously that according to my records I have not been 'absent' from work on any occasions. Please would you confirm that the absence occasions that you refer to are actually the periods when I was legally unfit to report for duty.

My inability to attend work for medical reasons is obviously of concern to both the Company and me. I would certainly be prepared to discuss my sickness with the Principal Medical Officer.

I would reiterate that these discussions frequently take place whenever I undertake an aircrew medical. Furthermore I am only reporting sick as per the ANO.

Yours sincerely,

Bloggs

Roberts' third letter in the series varied according to circumstances but was much more threatening in tone. As far as we were concerned the Absence Management Programme was an intimidation tool intended to coerce pilots into reporting for duty in breach of their legal duties and responsibilities under the ANO. It was typical of the prevailing management attitude. Instead of addressing the root causes of the problem, shortage of pilots and a broken rostering system, they sought to impose punitive measures on the pilots as a sop to their own failures. A letter that one of the pilots wrote to Roberts in response to one of his letters neatly summarises the concerns that we all had (further correspondence on the subject can be read in Appendix 2). The pilot wrote:

Dear Dave,

I hope you won't mind if I stray a bit from the AOA response form letter. Hopefully you will find the change refreshing.

I have known yourself and Paddy Cavanagh for some time and I have been the fortunate recipient of fairness, professionalism and respect from both of you. Although you and I have not always agreed, it has always been a pleasure to work with you. From our dealings, I'm sure you will not be surprised to know that the concept of management's Sickness Management Program [sic] troubles me greatly.

I noted with concern that a request to visit the Principal Medical Officer was 'absent' from your letter of 28 May. This makes it very difficult for me to sway my belief that this Sickness Management Program [sic] is indeed not for my benefit, but rather a method of intimidation. Although I am sure you will insist that intimidation is not the purpose, I can assure you that such is the result. Indeed, since the Sickness Management Program [sic] has begun, concern of management repercussion has entered my mind each time I have judged my fitness for duty. Although I have yet to operate when unfit, the temptation is now there. The last time I was about to advise the company that I was unfit, my wife's initial reaction was to query 'how it would look'. **This is not safe.** As I am copying this letter to the CAD, I must mention that I am less convinced of their own commitment to safety in not severing this dangerous program[sic] from the start.

I also noticed with disappointment in your letter that management's stated concern was not for my health, but for my lack of productivity. Due to my own health concerns, I have just yesterday visited the company medical officer. We discussed the issue of my sickness record and the possible catalysts. We discussed how the company's endless poor labour relations have contributed to increasing stress and fleet wide health problems. We discussed how aggressive and unstable rosters have further contributed to the level of illness amongst my peers. We also discussed the company's lack of good judgment in launching a Sickness Management Program[sic].

I must reiterate at this point that I have never been 'absent' from my professional duties at Cathay Pacific. To report sick when unwell is my legal obligation and each time I have been medically unfit for duty, I have followed the policy set out in our Operations Manual providing a doctor's certificate as required.

As I close, may I repeat that I have always enjoyed our professional relationship. As such I would be delighted to sit down with yourself or Paddy Cavanagh to discuss the issue of Sickness Management. As I am a veteran in the battle to receive properly credited time for Union duties, I am sure you will understand my insistence that such an interview be properly rostered and credited as an office day. It is also only fair of me to point out that I do not feel it appropriate to discuss any issues of a medical nature with non-medical personnel.

I trust this will satisfy all your concerns and I look forward to our dealings in the future. Please do not hesitate to contact me any time.

While this was happening, management adopted other 'intimidation' tactics. With the rostering system in chaos, it became increasingly common for pilots to report for duty expecting to operate, say, a TPE turnaround only to be told that they were now operating to Australia, the Middle East or, even worse, a ULR op. Ignoring the disruption caused to any domestic arrangements that the pilot may have planned, the problem with this was planning pre-flight rest. We adopted different rest strategies depending on the type of operation. If it was a daytime out and back flight, you could stay on your normal sleep cycle. With ULR ops it was very different. These were usually late-night departures so, if you were scheduled to take the first in-flight rest period once airborne, you would plan to arrive at work having not slept in the previous eight or so hours, the objective being to be able to get some sleep in the bunk during your in-flight rest period. On the day of the flight, therefore, you would have a lie-in and get up after midday. If you were scheduled for the second in-flight rest period, however, your pre-flight rest strategy would be different. In this case you would go to bed and sleep in the afternoon prior to reporting for work so that you would be more able to stay awake for the first six or seven hours of the flight.

Crews scheduled for a ULR op often contacted the Captain the day before the flight to check which in-flight rest period they would be assigned so that they could plan their pre-flight rest accordingly. The most difficult time to stay awake is during the 'window of circadian low' (WOCL), the period between 02:00 and 05:59 body clock time. This is the time when your body is telling you that you should be asleep and employs strategies to send you to the land of nod. Therefore, to report for a short-haul duty only to find that you were now operating ULR was not in the best interests of flight safety, and some pilots declined such roster changes on the basis that they were not sufficiently rested to undertake the proposed duty. They weren't being difficult, they were just complying with the requirements of the ANO.

Of course, that's not how Barley and his managers saw it. They just considered the pilots were being difficult and started subjecting them to disciplinary proceedings. Another example of management failure to address the root cause of the problem – in this case the rostering system – and, instead, simply wielding the big stick.

One of the worst cases of this type happened on 9 November 2000.

Dave Clapson, an SF/O on the B747, and also, coincidentally, a previous serving member on the AOA General Committee, was scheduled for a simulator duty. Shortly before it was due to start, he was told that he was now required for a flying duty to operate CX271, a ULR op to Amsterdam. When he refused the duty because he was not properly rested, the duty operations manager, one Jonathan Legat, tried to intimidate Dave into accepting the duty, saying that 'The last person who refused a duty like this had disciplinary proceedings taken against him.' When Dave still resisted, Legat sent him a fax actually ordering him to undertake the duty despite the fact that he knew full well he was not fit for it. This was a flagrant breach of the operator's responsibilities under the ANO. It is to Dave's credit that he resisted the pressure and still declined to operate the flight. The consequences of this were just as Legat had threatened. Dave was charged with 'Wilful neglect of the companies [sic] interests' and 'Conduct considered to be a breach of trust'. At a disciplinary hearing held on 17 November chaired by his fleet manager, Andrew Maddox, he was found guilty as charged and dismissed. I was present as Dave's work colleague at the first stage appeal held on 8 January in front of Rick Fry and Phil Walker. We submitted a comprehensive document prior to the appeal, which contested these charges.

In summarising our responses to the first charge, 'Wilful neglect of the company's interests', we stated:

Rather than being subjected to disciplinary action, Mr Clapson should be commended for his dedication in discharging his duties in accordance with the law, the regulations and in the best interests of Flight Safety when faced with a situation where he was subjected to extreme pressure to act otherwise.

The document went on to conclude as follows in this regard:

1.4 Summary
1.4.1 Company representatives failed in their responsibility to inform Mr Clapson sufficiently in advance of his duty so as to provide him the opportunity to plan adequate pre-flight rest.
1.4.2 Under the circumstances, it was not reasonable for the Company to expect Mr Clapson to have been adequately rested to undertake a ULR operation at short notice.
1.4.3 The Duty Operations Manager failed both in his duty of care to Mr Clapson as a subordinate Officer and in his responsibilities under the Air Navigation (Hong Kong) Order 1995 in

attempting to coerce Mr Clapson to act in breach of the regulations.

When faced with a very difficult situation, Mr Clapson acted entirely correctly in accordance with the applicable laws and regulations, in best interests of Flight Safety and, therefore, in the Company's best interests.

The charge of '*Wilful neglect of the Companies[sic] interests*', therefore, should be dismissed.

With regard to the second accusation of 'Conduct considered to be a breach of trust', the report concluded as follows:

Rather than being '*deliberately misleading*', Mr Clapson's actions present classic symptoms of an individual reacting to a very stressful situation. Such reactions are typical 'human factors' issues and to classify them as a deliberate breach of trust would be to ignore not only those issues but also the principles of natural justice.

Therefore, the charge of '*Conduct considered to be a breach of trust*' should also be dismissed.

On 11 January Dave received a letter from Rick Fry notifying him of the outcome of the appeal. The charge of 'Wilful neglect of the company's interests' was dismissed but the second charge of 'Conduct considered to be a breach of trust' was upheld. However, his punishment was reduced from dismissal to a warning letter placed on his personal file. We thought that to be a victory albeit it was just another example of having something given back that should never have been taken away in the first place. Of course, just like the Demery and Gardner incidents, Dave's work for the AOA had nothing to do with him being targeted by Barley!

The victimisation of Dave Clapson didn't end there. On 5 July 2001 he had further disciplinary charges levelled against him as a result of a minor incident that had occurred on a flight from Vancouver. At the disciplinary hearing he was cleared of all charges and exonerated. As he was leaving the hearing, he was asked to step into the office next door. Barley was in there waiting for him. He handed him a letter of dismissal with three months' pay in lieu of notice. Dave Clapson had become the first of *The 49ers*.

18

Landing

'*Proportionality should be a guideline in war*'
Robert S. McNamara, *The Fog of War*

After the failure of the rostering practices negotiations to reach agreement in July 2000, the AOA reintroduced contract compliance. It seemed that after everything we'd been through in 1999, management either had learned nothing or simply refused to acknowledge our concerns. The only way to bring them to the table to address our problems was to apply pressure. It worked, but in a way we weren't immediately expecting. This time around, they went to the Labour Department and complained that they couldn't get agreement on rostering practices because of the AOA's obstinacy. As far as I and my team were concerned, it was all to the good. Let's get back in there under mediation and finally get things sorted out. So in December 2000 we found ourselves back in the same room in Sheung Wan with Mrs Siu. It was then that Rhodes showed his cards.

Throughout the talks earlier in the year, we had been working on drafting a comprehensive document to be included in the CoS as a contractually binding rostering practices agreement. When we got into the Labour Department, Rhodes produced two completely new documents, one printed on pink paper and the other on green. His pink document was a proposed AFTLS, which he wanted to put into the Operations Manual only; the green document was a bare bones rostering practices proposal, which consisted of what he called the 'industrial issues'. It was this second document that he proposed would be attached to the CoS but only as a

267

policy. It was just the same old shit all over again. They had no intention of including the rostering practices into the contract. They wanted the guts of the rules, the AFTLS, to be in the Ops Manual where they could again be subject to back door amendment just as in the past, and the rest of their very watered down rostering rules in the form of company policy. At least this time he didn't include the phrase 'As the same may be varied from time to time at the sole discretion of the company'. Even he didn't have the barefaced cheek to try that one. It demonstrated yet again what we should have known all along. We had spent the best part of seven months in negotiation since November 1999 and all that time they were planning a back door move. Good faith and negotiation with these people was an oxymoron.

We had a response to their tactic. We tabled the document that we had been working on and said to Mrs Siu, 'This is where we had got to previously, now they're trying to change the rules again. They're trying to throw away all that work and start from scratch. We don't see how that progresses the negotiation do you? It seems to us that they're just trying to use your good offices to railroad through another one-sided deal that doesn't address any of our concerns.' Being the pragmatist, and not really understanding the issues anyway, she suggested that we look at their documents to see whether there was any common ground. We agreed to do so because we knew that Rhodes wouldn't have done his preparation. The 6P rule would trip him up. We went to page one of the first document and started going through it. OK, line one, third word should be capitalised, fifth word there is a double space, eighth word is a spelling mistake, last word, first letter should be lower case. Line two, second word is a typo, fourth word also a typo. Line three, double space after the fifth word and there should be a full stop at the end. Line four, typo on the ninth word. Line five and so on. We didn't even get to the end of the first page before they called a break. As usual, they'd cobbled together some toilet paper using a last minute cut and paste job.

It wasn't the first time we'd seen this. During previous talks on rostering, when we were working on sample rosters in their department, we discovered they were using three different computer programmes. They were producing some data using Microsoft Excel, some using Lotus and some using software written in-house. Each little group jealously guarded their own way of doing things and none of the three systems could easily exchange data without a lot of debugging and error checking. There was a lot of empire building going on and the result was amateurish, just like Rhodes' pink and green documents.

Barley tried to impose a deadline on us in the talks, insisting that agreement must be reached by the end of December. It suited us and backfired on him. Instead of working on the draft documents, regarding which we were clearly far from agreement, and which couldn't possibly be completed in time for his deadline, we proposed an alternative solution. Currently there were two sets of rostering rules. There were the new rules brought in with CAD 371 and the old rules contained in the pre-371 rostering practices. These were at odds with each other in some areas so to progress things we should compile a set of rules, using the most restrictive from each set, and produce an interim composite table to clear up the confusion. Fortunately, by sheer coincidence, we had a table that we had prepared earlier in the *Blue Peter* studios and we put it forward. This was not at all to Barley's liking as it wasn't what he had planned and he protested in his strongest voice to Mrs Siu. According to him our table was very confusing, difficult to understand and wouldn't help the situation at all. Mrs Siu didn't agree. She grasped the idea as a quick fix to what was becoming another confrontation and could turn into a potential PR nightmare for her department, as before. Things weren't going at all well for poor old Ken but he persevered with his 'confusing' line. To help him out, we brought in a copy of the MEL with all its tables and cross-references to demonstrate to Mrs Siu that pilots were well used to using tables and charts in the normal course of their work and wouldn't find our table at all confusing. Whether or not she really understood the issues didn't matter. She just liked the fact that there appeared to be a solution that could be agreed quickly. There were 121 rows in our table that covered all the issues. Because of their variations for the freighter operation, there were an additional 55 entries in the 'freighter differences' column, a total of 176 entries in all. They simply couldn't mount a decent argument against our logic and within a short space of time we had agreed everything apart from two outstanding issues, one of which was our old friend, commander's discretion.

On the morning of 19 December we went into the meeting, with Don and me as the negotiators and the AOA president, Nigel Demery, as our chairman. When Barley tried again to hold out on commander's discretion, Don and I held a short muttered conversation, closed our laptops, packed our briefcases and got up to leave. Mrs Siu looked panicked and everyone started rhubarbing. Nigel interrupted and said words to the effect that unfortunately his team was leaving and the deal was going to fail because it was one of the most important issues to us and had been the main stumbling block all along. He was sorry but . . . And at that point Barley rolled. We signed an interim agreement that was effective from 1 January 2001 for a period of three months with an extension of one further month if final agreement still had not been reached by the end of March. Even then, Barley's deadline worked against him. We had offered a period of validity of up to six months to ensure that we had time to come to final agreement given the history of the negotiations so far. No. He insisted it should only be a short-term agreement to give us an incentive to get the final deal done. That was just fine by us. He was only putting pressure on his own team. His deadline had forced him into agreeing to our table when he had expected it to railroad us into agreeing to Rhodes' pink and green toilet paper, and now he was persisting with the tactic. It seemed to us to be a tactical error on his part.

There was a further proviso. Future talks on rostering practices would be monitored by the Labour Department and we would have to report back on progress on a monthly basis. That suited us just fine as well. It would put a stop to any DPGFD from them. As a final attempt to make a point, Barley turned to me and said, 'I still find your table very confusing, John.'

I resisted the temptation to reply, 'Why doesn't that surprise me, Ken?'

It was the most successful negotiation that Don and I had taken part in. We won 176 points out of 176. It doesn't get better than that. Of course we had stage-managed the walkout. We knew they were going to try to hold out on commander's discretion. There was no way we were going to concede that point and we figured the best way to get them to roll was to do what we did. We didn't let Nigel into our plan, however, so the surprise he showed was genuine. After the meeting ended, Augustus Tang came up to me and said, 'I feel like I could punch you in the stomach.'

'Why would you want to do that, Augustus?' I enquired.

'Because after we were here in 1999, I thought you got everything you wanted.'

'No, Augustus, we didn't. We never got a deal on rostering. We've been trying to get an agreement ever since but it's your side that's the problem. If you want to punch anyone, go and punch Nick and Ken.'

Talks started again back at the Aviation Club in 2001 but they were nothing like what they had promised in the Labour Department meetings. DPGFD was again the order of the day. They had agreed to roster my team for office duties with sufficient preparation time so that we could do the necessary work. They didn't do it. I was rostered for only six days of office duty in January and flew a full roster for the rest of the month including two ULR ops. They gave me another full roster in February with no office duty scheduled. It was the same with Don and

Drew. It was clear to us they were deliberately making sure that we wouldn't have time to get together to prepare, especially as Drew was based in Australia. They even lied to the Labour Department about how many meetings had taken place. We went into one of our monthly update report meetings with Mrs Siu, and Rhodes sat there and told her barefaced lies. We called a break as I was more than a little annoyed by this. After I had calmed down, we went back in, I called Rhodes for the liar that he was and told Mrs Siu that, rather than trying to facilitate the negotiations, they were actually trying to sabotage them by punitive rostering. Hoyland got quite hot under the collar at my accusation as he was responsible for constructing the rosters, but the point was made.

I was scheduled only for sufficient flying to keep my landing recency current in March and April and we got back to work. Again, it seemed we were making progress but, as before, it was an illusion. The showstoppers, commander's discretion and reserve, were still on the back burner.

It was during one of the meetings in March that Geoff Cole did us a great favour. We had been discussing sickness credits and Rhodes put up a graph on the screen showing actual sickness levels for all the pilots in the company for the previous 18 months. Although the pilots' names had been removed from the data, it was very illuminating and proved our point. Generally the sickness levels were highest amongst pilots who were operating predominantly ULR ops. Now why would that be? During a break, they left the room and Geoff left a floppy disk on the table. We plugged it in and there was all their data along with draft documents and meeting notes. It found its way onto our laptops and, when they came back into the room, the disk was still on the table where they had left it. We gave it back to Geoff with a comment along the lines of, 'Is that yours, Geoff? We think it must be because it's not one of ours.'

To this day, I do not know whether Geoff left it there on purpose or not. He left Cathay some time later and ran a bar in Wanchai called Chinatown. A band that I play in used to do some gigs there and over a few late-night beers I asked him about it but he always remained tight-lipped. Whether or not it was done 'accidentally on purpose', it was certainly very useful.

I flew another full roster in May, logging over 80 hours and things came to a head in June. The interim agreement had expired at the end of April so the pressure was now on. It was time for them to piss or get off the pot. No more putting the show-stoppers on the back burner. We went into a meeting and posed them the straightforward question, 'Do you agree to the wording of our commander's discretion provisions or not?'

'Well we want to be able to order Captains to use commander's discretion. We think it should be up to the company to be able to tell . . .'

'Never mind what you think. You don't have the right to do it. You've never had the right to do it. Even CAD 371 doesn't give you the right to do it; in fact it specifically prohibits you from doing so. You can ask and that's it. That's a big concession in itself. Can you read? The Captain's decision will be final and unquestioned.'

That's when Rhodes came out with his most crass statement of all: 'Well, we just see commander's discretion as an industrial tool used by the pilots to disrupt the operation.'

That really pissed me off and for only the third time in all the negotiations I'd been in I lost my temper.

'You might be the Deputy DFO but you haven't got any qualifications at all even to be part of making an operational decision. None of you have on your side of the table except for Phil because you haven't got any operational experience whatsoever. You're not pilots, never have been and never will be. Even Phil isn't qualified to make a decision on someone else's aircraft as he'll be the first to admit. Now answer this question, "yes" or "no"! Do you agree to our proposals on commander's discretion or not?'

'Well we think . . .'

'Yes or fucking no.'

'No.'

'In that case this negotiation is over.' And it was.

I reported back to Nigel that the negotiation had concluded without agreement and that I could not see any point in meeting again until they changed their position. With all the other ongoing flight safety issues that management were refusing to address all the way up the chain of command to board level, this just put the cap on it. Nigel called an EGM of the AOA. At the meeting held on 20 June 2001, the membership voted by a majority of 92 per cent in favour of the following motion:

Be it resolved that following Cathay Pacific Airways' management's failure to resolve long outstanding issues on Rostering, Remuneration and Benefits, all Full Members of the Hong Kong Aircrew Officers Association will undertake limited industrial action with effect from 1 July 2001, until further notice.

Nigel was upping the ante with an incremental increase in pressure from basic contract compliance. The timing of the vote and actual implementation of limited industrial action (LIA) was designed to allow a breathing space where a last-minute resolution might be found. Also, it wasn't specified what form the LIA would take. None of the membership knew. They just trusted their leadership to take them wherever they needed to go. Even though I was in the thick of things on the negotiating side, I had no idea what was planned as I wasn't part of the industrial team. There was a flurry of activity with meetings back in the Labour Department but I wasn't part of that either. As far as I was concerned, I had done my job as far as I could go and, like the rest of the membership, I trusted our leadership.

We started hearing ominous noises coming from the other side. Barley put out some letters to the pilots with the usual appeal to common sense and veiled threats if we didn't toe the line. Rhodes was running a spin campaign in the cafes and restaurants in Cathay City and it was there that he came out with a classic statement that he was later to deny he ever said.

'If the union takes industrial action we'll just fire 20 to 30 pilots and the rest will fall into line.'

As in all industrial confrontations, there was a lot of bluff, counter-bluff and posturing going on through the media. I was never a great supporter of trying to fight the war in the media. The PR people and spin merchants will disagree, but to me the deal gets done across the negotiating table, not in the public arena. I subscribe to the school of smoke-filled rooms rather than the glare of the spotlight. Pilots never win in a PR war because it is so easy just to portray us as overpaid play-boys. *Look at them. They fly around the world for free going to exotic places with a planeload of stewardesses at their beck and call. All that and they get paid shed loads of money for doing it as well. What have they got to complain about? They're just spoiled prima donnas.*

Lenin is attributed as having said, 'A lie told often enough becomes the truth.' Proof by assertion. 'Cathay pilots are the highest paid in the world.' If I had a dollar for every time I heard that one I would indeed be a rich man. Even government officials parroted that line. It simply is not true. Yes, Barley's salary and allowances as DFO put him right up there amongst some of the highest earners, but the average A Scale line pilots were quite a way behind a lot of the US and European carriers, especially where pensions are concerned. As for the B Scalers, they aren't even in the picture. In the public perception, unfortunately, that doesn't matter. We can go on about how long it took us to get to where we are, the dedication, the sacrifices, the days spent at Sumburgh with plastic bags in our shoes. None of that matters. It doesn't even matter that our dispute in 2001 was not about money, it was about rostering and flight safety. In a world of sound bites, true or not, relevant or not, 'Cathay pilots are the highest paid in the world' wins every time. So why engage in a battle that we have no hope of winning?

During 1999, the AOA did employ the services of a PR company. Because of the technical nature of aviation and the precise form of its language, their draft press releases were a nightmare and had to be carefully edited for factual accuracy. It was actually easier to write them ourselves rather than correct their stuff. I have always found it an easier task to compose a draft with a clean sheet of paper rather than edit someone else's work. In my view, they charged us a lot of money and achieved very little.

A good example of this is the accident investigation that is currently taking place (at time of writing) into a Cathay A330 flight, CX780, from Surabaya that landed at CLK on 13 April 2010 with a double engine failure. Initial reports and data indicate that there were problems with the engines on the climb out from Surabaya and this has led to a lot of speculation in the press that the aircraft should have returned to Surabaya and landed immediately upon first indication of these problems rather than continue with the four-hour flight to Hong Kong. Just like the CI642 investigation, no doubt we can rely on the CAD to carry out an objective accident analysis and get to the truth, provided there are no vested interests at work, that is. In the meantime, in their rush to say something, anything to show that there couldn't possibly be anything wrong with their aircraft, the next day in the *South China Morning Post* a Cathay Pacific flight quality controller, whatever one of those is, was quoted as saying, 'Even with both engines dead, our planes still have a backup power supply that should allow it to glide for up to an hour, with the help of flaps and spoilers.'

This is, of course, total horse shit. In the words of Mark Twain, 'It is better to keep your mouth shut and appear stupid than to open it and remove all doubt.'

As the rhetoric and propaganda escalated, the rumour mill was working overtime. It was difficult to separate fact from fiction or even discern what form the LIA was likely to take until on 29 June, just before the deadline of 1 July, the AOA published a document to the membership entitled 'Maximum Safety Strategy' (MSS). The MSS was simply a distillation of flight safety related procedures contained in the various volumes of the Cathay Operations Manual. This quick reference handbook highlighted where it had become common practice to cut corners and circumvent procedures in pursuit of OTP and other supposed 'efficiencies'. It advised that, in view of the highly stressful situation we now found ourselves in yet again, our first duty should be to ensure the safety of the operation and not allow ourselves to be rushed. It was good advice at any time, but particularly so now. Of course, there was an element of threat contained in its pages in that it suggested that, should we strictly adhere to all relevant procedures, this was going to start causing delays to our flights and so impact the operation. Again, there was a lot of bluff and posturing going on as there always is in any industrial confrontation.

We were all well aware of a ruling handed down by Lord Denning in the case of the *Secretary of State for Employment v ASLEF* (no. 2 [1972] 2 QB 455 CA) in the UK. In his ruling he held that a worker who sticks rigidly to his contract of employment with the object of disrupting his employer's business is taking part in industrial action and that, furthermore, in certain circumstances he might be acting in breach of his contract. He used the analogy of a driver taking his employer by car to the train station each morning to catch a train to work. If he normally drove there at 40 mph that would be his custom and practice. If the speed limit was actually 30 mph and, because of his dissatisfaction, he reverted to driving at 30 mph there was little his employer could say since all the driver was now doing was complying with the law. If he missed his train as a result of the slower speed, it would be up to the employer to set out from home earlier in order to be sure of catching the train. If, however, the driver drove at 20 mph even though the road conditions would allow a speed of 30 mph, with the deliberate intention of making his employer miss the train, he could now be held to be acting in breach of his contract and, therefore, liable to dismissal.

This case law has since been overtaken by other events but the principle still holds good in the case of a work to rule. If MSS was going to be characterised thus then we had to be careful. If our pre-flight preparation normally took 60 minutes, then that was our custom and practice and we could not start taking 80 minutes with the deliberate intent to delay the flight unless there were valid operational reasons for doing so. What we could do, however, was if the inbound aircraft was late, instead of rushing our pre-flight checks and cutting corners for the sake of OTP, just take the normal preparation time. Similarly, if called out from reserve to operate a flight, instead of jumping on the flight deck and getting the show on the road as soon as possible, as had become the habit under OTP (a bad habit at that), we could take the full prep time to perform the pre-flight checks. Given that the roster was in chaos, such operations were commonplace. It was not unusual to be called out from reserve and, instead of going to flight dispatch to complete the pre-flight planning, being asked to go straight out to the aircraft with a message along the lines of, 'The rest of the crew's already on board, the fuel's on, the passengers are loaded, all you've got to do is light the fires and go.' This would mean trusting that the other crew members had got it right and sorting the rest out in the air. It meant that a lot of cross-checking during the pre-flight was cut short and you took some things on trust. Thinking about it now, we should never have allowed the operation to deteriorate to that level but, under the stress of the times and with OTP as the prime objective, it happened. Well no more. MSS was going to get the operation back to where it should be and a good thing too.

Upon a direct request from the government after further talks in the Labour Department failed to come to a resolution, the implementation of MSS was delayed until 3 July to avoid disrupting the annual 1 July handover celebrations. After that, MSS became official AOA policy. Did MSS cause or would it have caused the predicted delays? We will never know. Typhoon Utor hit Hong Kong on 5 July and the whole operation was disrupted. The squadron was spread to the four winds and took some days to recover. On 6 July I operated CX785, an A330 flight to Denpassar (DPS) in Bali. On the return leg to HKG we couldn't land because of the weather conditions and diverted to Manila (MNL). We didn't recover to HKG until the evening of the 7th. The next day I operated CX502 to Kansai (KIX), arriving 1 hr 6 min late because of the disruption caused by Utor. On 9 July 2001, I operated CX503 back to HKG, arriving 47 minutes ahead of schedule, hardly the actions of someone intent on disrupting the operation. By coincidence that day my F/O was John Sweetman. He had also been my F/O on 5 May 1989, the day I first checked out as a Captain on the B747. I didn't know it at the time, but CX503 was to be the last flight I would ever operate as a professional pilot.

After landing back in HKG, I stopped off for a beer in Sai Kung on my way home. While I was enjoying a cool one, my phone went. It was John Findlay, the AOA general secretary. He told me that they were getting reports in from a number of pilots who'd received dismissal notices from the company delivered by courier. My wife was away so I telephoned my amah to ask whether there had been any courier deliveries to the house that day. She assured me there hadn't so I breathed a sigh of relief and went back to my Carlsberg. I got home a couple of hours later to find a DHL packet sitting on the kitchen worktop. My amah was Sri Lankan and there was a language problem. I opened up the packet and found a letter signed by Barley dismissing me from Cathay Pacific Airways and giving me three months' pay in lieu of notice. I was one of *The 49ers*.

19

Shock

'If you're going through Hell, keep going.'
Winston Churchill

It took a few days to complete the battle damage assessment and compile a casualty list. It turned out that, as well as firing Dave Clapson on 5 July, on the same day they had also dismissed two other pilots on trumped-up disciplinary charges. On 9 July they sent dismissal letters to 49 other pilots. We weren't able to confirm the final figures immediately because some of the pilots were away on leave and weren't aware of what had happened until they returned home. Two of the pilots, Brian Keene and Phil Yiasoumi, were actually on sick leave on 9 July. The Hong Kong Employment Ordinance prohibits dismissing employees while they are on sick leave. With Brian they waited until his sick leave finished on the 10th and sacked him on the 11th. With Phil they just went ahead and sacked him anyway. Of the total of 52 pilots, all but one were members of the AOA. The one who was not a member was called Lawrence Wong. There were two Lawrence Wongs in Cathay. It looked like they had picked the wrong Wong by mistake. Given their usual lack of attention to detail and general administrative incompetence, it came as no surprise.

There were 21 people on the 2001 AOA General Committee. Five of them were dismissed. There was a total of 31 people on the combined 2000 and 2001 AOA General Committees, some serving on both. Nine of them were dismissed. The AOA had seven trained negotiators in 2001. Four of them were dismissed. These selections were not random, they were deliberate. Over the ensuing years, Barley, Rhodes and others would insist repeatedly, both in sworn statements and in verbal testimony under oath, that AOA membership was never considered when *The 49ers* were selected for dismissal. They even went so far as to say that they had no way of knowing which pilots were AOA members and which were not. This statement was an outright lie. They continued with this line until a man who had been present at the selection meeting eventually came clean and told the truth. One of their own colleagues filed a witness statement that refuted their story.

The truth was that the company deducted AOA dues directly from the pilots' salaries each month and paid them to the AOA as a monthly lump sum. It was a simple matter to look at the standing order deductions in their database to compile a list of AOA members. Also, after each annual election, the president wrote to the DFO to give him a list of names of the newly elected General Committee. This was supposed to facilitate the rostering of time off for AOA duties. We did the same thing whenever a new member was seconded onto the General Committee between elections. So they knew all right!

We commissioned a probability analysis of *The 49ers'* selection to see whether the make-up of the group could have been by random chance. Was it just sheer coincidence that they happened to pick exclusively AOA members, past and present General Committee members and negotiators? The study was conducted by Dr Paul Yip, senior lecturer in the Department of Statistics and Actuarial Science at the University of Hong Kong, an expert pre-eminent in his field. He compared the probability results with the chances of winning the Mark 6 lottery in Hong Kong, which has 49 numbers; to win the jackpot, you need to pick all six winning numbers with second and third prizes being awarded for picking five or four numbers. He concluded that:

> The probability that [all] of *The 49ers* were HKAOA trade union members is 1 in 833. It is **unlikely** that this outcome is the result of random selection.

> The probability that 5 or more of the 20 members of the Year 2001 HKAOA General Committee were in *The 49er* group is 1 in 3,333. It is **very unlikely** that this outcome is the result of random selection.

> The probability that 4 or more of the 7 members of the HKAOA Negotiating Committee were in *The 49er* group is 1 in 32,258. This is a similar probability to that of selecting 5 winning numbers out of the 49 numbers in the Mark 6 lottery. It is **exceedingly unlikely** that this outcome is the result of random selection.

My father, Sergeant James Stanley Warham, 25 September 1942.

My mother and father on their wedding day, 2 January 1945.

Above: My father and my maternal grandfather, Peter William Hill, who introduced me to the Boeing 707 and changed my life.

Below: Leeds Grammar School CCF summer camp 1967. Author front row, first on left.

Above: Leeds Grammar School CCF summer camp 1968 with the mighty English Electric Lightning. Author back row, fourth from right.

Below: College of Air Training, Piper PA 28-180 Cherokee, 29 January 1974.

Above: College of Air Training, de Havilland Chipmunk, 1 March 1974.

Below: College of Air Training, Beechcraft D55 Baron G-AWAD, 14 January 1975.

Above: Bob & Marj Brown Formula 2 team, Borgo San Lorenzo, 11 July 1976. Bob Muir (driver) top, Marj second from left.

Below: If it looks right, it'll fly right. Casair Cessna 421B Golden Eagle, Teesside Airport, 20 July 1977.

Casair Piper PA23-250D Aztec G-AYZC. Engine failure, 21 May 1977.

Above: Monarch days, 1983. Charity cricket match in aid of the NSPCC at the Geoff Banks-Smith memorial cricket ground, Hertfordshire. Lilley CC vs England Ladies XI captained by Rachael Heyhoe-Flint (front row centre). Author back row fourth from left.

Below: 'Steely-eyed ace'. Command party poster, June 1989.

Above: Bright eyed and bushy tailed. Author on arrival in Hong Kong, March 1985.

Below: White tail B747-236F VR-HVY. Operation Granby, 1991.

Operation Granby. B747-236F VR-HVY, Dharhan A/B, 02:15LT 16 February 1991.
Iraqi SS1 Scud attack. L-R: Author, F/O Al Wood, F/E Robbie Gawler.

Above: Airbus A330 conversion training, U Tapao, Thailand, 1 April 1995. Author fourth from right.

Below: Standing room only. AOA meeting, Mariners Club, 30 June 2001. Doug Gage second row, second from right.

Author and Nigel Demery at the House of Lords, 15 November 2005.

Cathay Pilots Union celebration after House of Lords victory.
L-R: Nigel Demery, Don Fraser, Chris Lawrence, Author, Quentin Heron.

Above: VFL. Boeing Field, 30 January 2008.

Below: Don and me in the Captain's Bar, 5 May 2008 – the day we found the smoking gun.

Hong Kong High Court, 5 October 2009. L-R: Kevin Hoban, Matt Rogers, Angela Carver, Ken Carver, Don Fraser, Richard Warham, Priscilla Leung, Author, Steve Shaw, Mike Fitz-Costa, Chris Lawrence, Cam Blakeney-Williams, Anne Lawrence, Nigel Demery, Tracey Wu, Kelly Neal.

Above: On the way to a record bar bill in the Captain's Bar, Mandarin Oriental Hotel, 23 October 2009. Foreground L-R: Becky Kwan (second from left), Author, Ken Carver, Brian Keene, Henry Van Keulen, John Dickie.

Below: Hong Kong High Court, 23 October 2009. L-R: Doug Gage, Author, Ken Carver, Don Fraser.

The probability that 9 or more of the 31 members of the combined Year 2000 and 2001 HKAOA General Committees were in *The 49er* group is 1 in 4,761,905. It **borders on the impossibility** [sic]that this outcome is the result of random selection.

The suggestion that the four events were the result of random selection are [sic] **very unlikely** and **the probability value is extremely small.**

The following table of probability of being in *The 49er* group as compared with the chances of winning the Mark 6 lottery summarises Dr Yip's conclusions.

Selecting 49 AOA members	0.12%	1 in 833
Choosing four winning Mark 6 lottery numbers	0.097%	1 in 1,031
Selecting five or more 2001 GC members	0.030%	1 in 3,333
Selecting four or more AOA negotiators	0.0031%	1 in 32,258
Choosing five winning Mark 6 lottery numbers	0.0018%	1 in 55,556
Selecting nine or more 2000 or 2001 GC members	0.000021%	1 in 4,761,905
Choosing six winning Mark 6 lottery numbers	0.0000072%	1 in 13,983,816

Since pilots like pictures, the following chart shows the conclusions of Dr Yip's analysis in pictorial form.

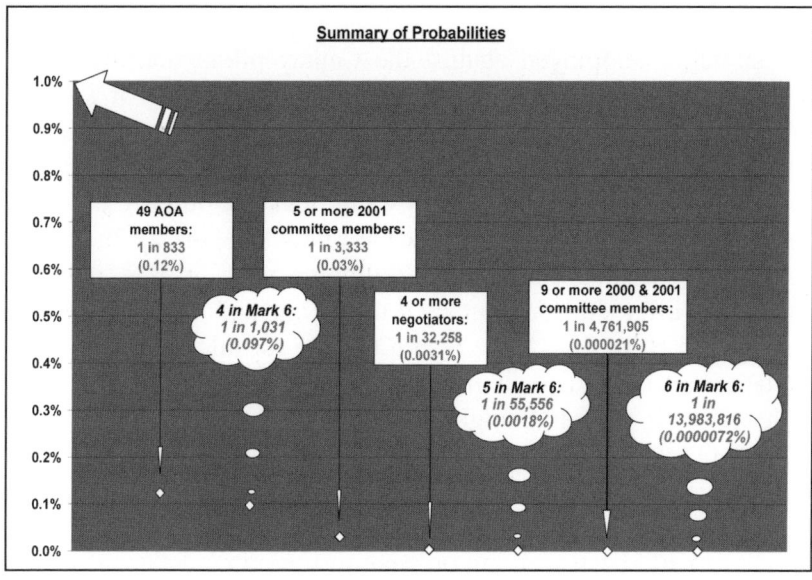

This was extremely powerful evidence against their testimony and, inevitably, they sought to keep our analysis out of court.

Another persuasive indicator of the truth of the matter was that none of the 100 or so pilots still employed by the remnants of ASL were members of the AOA and none of them were selected for dismissal. Another coincidence?

Another remarkable feature of the make-up of *The 49ers* was that the group was spread across the entire seniority spectrum so that every pilot in Cathay – from the most junior S/O to Senior Captains of my vintage – had a member of his peer group dismissed. The implication was obvious. It doesn't matter who you are, you're under threat and unless you toe the line you're next.

We knew they were being advised by Freehills, an Australian-based law firm that specialises in labour law. It acted for the Melbourne Port Corporation during the 1998 Australian waterfront dispute between the stevedores, represented by the Maritime Union of Australia, and the Patrick Corporation. The dispute was severe and protracted and was the most contentious industrial relations confrontation in Australia for many years.

During 2000, the AOA invited Martin Jay Levitt to Hong Kong to come and hold some seminars with the pilots. His book, *Confessions of a Union Buster,* published in 1993, is required reading for anyone involved in trade union activities. It describes in detail the strategies and tactics, both legal and illegal, that he used when he worked as a union buster in the US.

The strategies employed against the Cathay pilots, starting in 1993 with Operation Better Shape and leading up to the sacking of *The 49ers* in 2001, were classic union-busting tactics. Our analysis of the situation was that, with the sackings in July 2001, they were hoping either to provoke a strike by the pilots so they could lock the others out and then re-hire them on B Scales or to break the pilots' support for their union. Having seen what happened to the Philippine pilots in PAL only three years earlier, after the lock-out by Lucio Tan, and with the toothless labour laws in Hong Kong, we weren't going to fall for that one.

Management showed their true colours yet again when Barley sent out a letter to all the remaining pilots dated 19 July 2001 together with a new set of rostering practices, which they intended to implement unilaterally. Needless to say, three-man ULR ops would become the norm and the 5-4-3 rule was abolished in their new document. All the supposed negotiations we'd been working on were just window-dressing. As usual they had been working behind the scenes to their own agenda. It proved yet again that they couldn't be trusted. With his normal administrative incompetence, Barley sent out the new rostering practices to *The 49ers* as well, inviting them to sign up to the new deal, despite the fact that he had purported to terminate our employment ten days earlier. In fact their plan failed when one of the pilots, in a test case, won a ruling in the High Court of Hong Kong that the rostering practices are not open to substantial unilateral amendment. It took him until April 2003 to get the judgment but it put a stop to their back-door plans.

When they sacked us, they immediately cancelled our security passes so that we couldn't get into Cathay City to collect our personal effects unless we were accompanied by security guards. But that wasn't the end of it.

To add insult to injury, they wrote to the Inland Revenue Department (IRD) informing them that we were leaving Hong Kong so that we all received substantial tax bills that had to be paid immediately. They also misreported our taxable income with the result that our tax bills were much higher than they should have been. We applied for a time extension and it was granted; until the IRD found out who we were, that is. When they realised we were *The 49ers*, we were told, 'No, no. No extension. You must pay now. You must pay now.'

It seemed someone had put the fix in to cause us maximum financial hardship. Even when we wrote to Cathay and pointed out that they had wrongly declared our income, they refused to change their figures and persisted with their vindictive stance. In my own case, I got a tax bill for HK$201,124 which I had to pay within seven days of receiving the demand. In fact the correct bill was $78,331 and it took me four months to get the overpayment refunded. One of *The 49ers* who lived in Canada thought he'd got away with his tax bill as he didn't receive one. When he got in touch with the IRD he found out that his bill had been sent to his crew room mail box, which was his registered address. It had been returned marked 'Not known at this address' despite the fact that they'd known his address only a week earlier when they'd sent him his dismissal papers. It was sheer coincidence that the tax bills started accumulating penalty charges if they were not paid on time.

Some of *The 49ers* had Staff Visa cards with Citibank. They received letters informing them that their cards were cancelled. They even went so far as to terminate the housing leases of *The 49ers* which had been signed by Cathay on behalf of the employee. It was a shameless act and they even followed up on it to make sure that the pilots were evicted. One of *The 49ers*, Nick Lee, was friendly with his landlord who came to tell him that his lease had been terminated by Cathay. Nick made arrangements to stay in his home but subsequently received a phone call from Dave Roberts telling him that he had to get out of his house. When Nick told him that he would not be leaving his home despite his best efforts, Roberts put the phone down on him.

The treatment of *The 49ers* was not just vindictive, it was malicious. There was extensive media coverage of *The 49ers* sackings and Cathay put out a number of press releases and interviews. They used two mouthpieces in this exercise – Anthony Nigel Tyler and Philip Chen Nan Lok – both of whom we have mentioned previously, but only briefly.

Tyler graduated from Oxford University and joined the Swire Group in 1977. He joined Cathay in 1978 and in 2001 was director corporate development, a post he had held since November 1996, so he was one of Sutch's boys.

Chen also joined the Swire Group in 1977 and became deputy managing director of Cathay in 1997. A year later he became chief operating officer, a post he still held in 2001.

The pair of them carried out an orchestrated campaign against *The 49ers*. They said that we 'deliberately intended to disrupt operations'. It wasn't true. They said that we actually did disrupt 'the airline, [its] customers [and] the reputation of Hong Kong'. It wasn't true. They said that we were 'holding Hong Kong to ransom'. It wasn't true. They said that 'the sackings had nothing to do with the labour action'. It wasn't true.

They denied 'that the sacking was specifically related to the union's industrial action'. It wasn't true. They said that we 'cannot be relied upon to act in the best interests of the company'. It wasn't true. They said that we were 'unprofessional'. It wasn't true.

None of these statements were true but they made them anyway knowing full well that they would spread rapidly around the world via the news media, as indeed happened. They continued to repeat similar statements about us for the next eight years until they were finally brought to account for their actions.

The world of professional aviation is a small one. As the IFALPA membership numbers show, there are only around 120,000 professional airline pilots worldwide. It is a very small brotherhood and word spreads like wildfire. By their actions, the Swires made us pariahs in the profession that we had all worked so hard to become a part of. We were made unemployable overnight and our careers were destroyed. And they did it deliberately. The shock of being fired was bad enough but to be subjected to such viciousness was doubly shocking.

Well if it was shock they wanted, they'd get it. If they thought they'd just run us out of Hong Kong and we would all be forgotten in three months, they had another think coming. If they thought we'd just lie down and take it, like most of us did in 1994, we would show them otherwise. Some of *The 49ers* were based in Australia, some in Hong Kong, some in the UK and some in the US. We filed legal actions against Cathay and its subsidiary companies, Veta Limited and USA Basing Limited, in Hong Kong, London, Los Angeles and Sydney. They weren't expecting that. They thought that they'd simply be able to use Hong Kong's archaic and one-sided labour laws to run roughshod over us. Well, if you want unrestricted trade across international boundaries, if you want globalisation, and if you want mobility of labour, expect to be subject to some of the downsides that come with those policies. You don't get to just cherry pick what suits you and then go on your merry way. Their blitzkrieg wasn't going to be as easy as they thought. Welcome to the New World Order.

20

Anger and Pain

'In depression . . . faith in deliverance, in ultimate restoration, is absent. The pain is unrelenting, and what makes the condition intolerable is the foreknowledge that no remedy will come – not in a day, an hour, a month, or a minute. It is hopelessness even more than pain that crushes the soul.'

William Styron

On 29 January 2002 Gregory Stephen England, one of *The 49ers*, was found dead on the ground below the bathroom window of his third-floor apartment in Kennedy Road, Wanchai. He was only 31 years old. I firmly believe that if Greg had not been fired six months earlier, he would not have died in the way he did. I also believe that at least some, if not most, of the responsibility for his death lies squarely at the door of those who took part in his dismissal. On Monday 4 February, we held a memorial service for Greg in St John's Cathedral in Hong Kong. All the pilots turned up in uniform and there was not a spare seat in the house. A close friend, Corey Bousen, delivered a very moving eulogy, which is reproduced in Appendix 3 to this book together with a letter written by Greg's mother in 2006 in memoriam to her son.

Not one single member of the Cathay Flight Ops Department management had the common decency to attend the service and pay their respects. Not one. Had they sent even one representative to stand alone, out of respect for Greg's memory, there wasn't a single pilot at that service who would have caused trouble, I am sure. Perhaps they hadn't got the guts to face Greg's family. They went even further than that. A picture of the pilots leaving the service was published the next day in the press. At the head of the group in the picture was Kai Chung, another of *The*

285

49ers. Two days later we all received letters from Cathay's lawyers, Johnson Stokes & Master, demanding that we return our uniforms and other 'company property' with immediate effect or face legal action to recover the same.

We were already in the anger stage of our grief and if they wanted to do anything to fan the flames of that anger further, they couldn't have picked a better method.

Greg wasn't the only one to lose his life in the aftermath of our sackings. On 15 October 2005, I received an email from Richard David Bennett, another of *The 49ers*. It said, 'I am very sad to inform you that my beautiful Kung took her own life early yesterday morning.'

His partner hanged herself in the garage of their house in Thailand. Two months later, on 17 December 2005, Richard died of a heart attack. He was only 35 years old and left a young daughter.

On the morning of Saturday 13 July 2002, I was lying on my bed doing *The Times* crossword in that day's edition of the *South China Morning Post*. My left arm started aching and nothing I could do would make it go away. I tried walking around the room, swinging it back and forth, moving it around, holding it above my head but nothing worked. I had had an operation on my left shoulder in April 2000 to repair torn ligaments from some old sports injuries. The post-operative physiotherapy had been quite uncomfortable at times but this was something different. It wasn't an acute shooting pain, rather it felt like a deep-rooted ache and it wouldn't go away. I called my wife from her office upstairs, told her what was happening and suggested it might be a good plan to nip up to the hospital at Tseung Kwan O near to where we lived and get it checked out.

'OK but don't panic, you're not having a heart attack,' was her advice.

'I'm not panicking but actually I think I am having a heart attack,' was my response.

We got into the car and drove to the hospital. We called ahead on the phone and they were waiting for us at the A&E department. I had suffered a myocardial infarction (MI) and was diagnosed with unstable angina. I subsequently underwent angioplasty to install two stents in my coronary arteries. After years of passing my aircrew licence medicals, annual ECGs and other tests with no sign of any problems, why had it happened to me now? Certain risk factors predisposed me to potential cardiovascular problems but why had it only manifested itself now? I was only 50. One of the acknowledged causal factors in MI is stress and I had certainly been placed under enormous stress by the Swires' union bust. Clever lawyers and their medical experts could argue in court that my condition had nothing to do with me being sacked. I could provide other medical experts who would testify the opposite. Whichever side you care to take, one fact was irrefutable. I carried loss of licence and permanent health insurance to the value of the equivalent of five years' salary in the event that I lost my licence on medical grounds. There was only one problem with that. It is only valid if you are in employment at the time of the onset of the medical condition. Since I was not, the insurance had lapsed.

Let's say the MI would have happened anyway. If I had still been employed by Cathay in July 2002, I would still have lost my flying licence but I would have picked up around HK$10 million in insurance payments. As it was I got nothing. Like all *The 49ers*, I was already in a difficult financial situation and this didn't help. It wasn't just the money though. If I had still been employed, I could have got my licence back. It would have taken me about a year do it with a lot of post-operative medical testing, stress ECGs and so on, but it can be done. Many pilots have been through what I experienced and subsequently returned to flying. In my situation, I just couldn't face it. Again, like all *The 49ers*, I was already unemployable because of the lies spread about us in the media, so even after a year of jumping through the doctors' hoops there was little chance that I could get back in the seat of a jet. If my health was to improve, I needed to reduce the stress I was under, not increase it. I had to make a decision. In fact, it was forced on me. After more than 28 years in the profession that I had dedicated my life to, it was the end of my aviation career. They had done that to me.

Something else happened to me two years after my illness. In July 2004 my wife came home from a trip to China and told me she wanted to separate. I am firmly convinced that had I not been sacked as part of the Swires' union bust, my wife and I would still be together. With all of our other commitments, the enormous amount of additional stress that I was put under was just too much for us to survive. Mine wasn't the only *49ers* marriage to fail and at least some of the blame for the break up of these families must lie with those who took part in our dismissal. Our separation plunged me into a black pit of despair. It was the most difficult period of my life that I ever experienced, both before or since. I disappeared into a gin bottle and worse. I could not have survived that time alone. Five friends in particular deserve mentioning by name. Pete Bissell, Jason Corr, Steve Dullard, Andy Maxwell and Tony White. Between them they sat with me, listened to me, nursed me through my pain, gave me a place to stay and helped me to climb back out of the darkness. I will be forever grateful to them as well as all the other friends who rallied round and gave me their support.

Because of my financial situation, I was forced to sell my house. It was a beautiful beachfront property in Clearwater Bay, Sai Kung. Although it was only a 2,100 square foot village house, it had a small swimming pool and garden with steps down onto the beach at the end. Our eight dogs used to run out on the beach every morning at seven o'clock sharp. By Hong Kong standards it was spacious and my wife and I had lived there since 1986. We had built our home and our lives together there. It held so many wonderful memories for us both. It was a happy place and the last refuge of my previous life. It broke my heart to sell it. I was by no means the only *49er* to lose my home because of the Swires' union bust.

Some time after our separation, my wife was at a social function that was also attended by Tyler. Someone who was a bit of a stirrer introduced her to him by saying, 'This is John Warham's wife. I think you know John Warham don't you?'

'Yes, I know John Warham. He's some kind of amateur musician now isn't he?' he replied in a supercilious manner. This was a reference to the band I play in and was presumably intended to be a clever dick remark to show how low I'd now sunk after we'd tried to face off him and his Swire mates. My wife walked away fuming. A few minutes later he was standing by the bar. She walked up behind him, tapped him on the shoulder and, when he turned round, said, 'Whatever John Warham is now, he's still more of a man than you'll ever be.'

According to my wife Tyler's jaw hit the floor, the blood drained from his cheeks and he spent the rest of the evening looking ashen-faced. We were already suing him for defamation and here he was slagging me off again in public. Perhaps, because of his own experience, he couldn't understand how two people could separate but still remain good friends and be supportive of each other.

Just as my friends supported me in my personal hour of need, *The 49ers* stood together as a group to help one another through our problems. We set up family support groups and had regular meetings where we could get together and talk. Sometimes talking is all it takes. Like with the brotherhood of IFALPA, it's just good to know that you're not alone in facing your problems. The AOA was also providing us with financial support. As well as picking up the bills for all the legal fees, it had set up a subsistence fund to provide each *49er* who needed it with a monthly payment to help with the household bills.

All of these different types of support together make an excellent case study of how people can stand together in adversity, face what seem to be insurmountable problems but still come through because they look after each other. The Swires had tried to run us out of Hong Kong and failed. The frustration this caused them is exemplified by a conversation that took place between Turnbull and two of *The 49ers*, Craig Van Poelgeest and Steve Shaw, during a chance encounter at 00:30 on 10 October 2002 at the Alibi Restaurant in Hollywood Road, Central. It is reproduced verbatim from their notes.

<As we sat downstairs we noticed DT (and a Chinese lady) coming down the stairs from the restaurant above. Recognising him, we said, 'Hello Mr Turnbull'*, and a brief conversation ensued>*

DT: Do I know you?

SS: No, but we work for you.

DT: Oh! Are you pilots?

SS: Yes.

DT: What do you fly?

SS: 747-400.

CVP: That is not altogether correct, we used to fly the 400 for you. Up to July of last year.

<Seeming very agitated at this point he took a step back from the conversation, but not as to leave. His friend also removes herself from the direct conversation but not out of earshot, off his left shoulder perhaps five feet away>

SS: Our positions aside, can you see any way of moving forward and solving the current problems?

DT: There is no problem, we are fine, we make lots of profit.

SS: David, do you not think there are some fundamental problems within flight operations that need addressing?

DT: What problems? You tell me what the problems are! We don't have any problems. The only problems are created by Nigel Demery, John Findlay and the union. We are the best managed company in the world and our profits show it. You must know why you were fired!

SS/CVP: No we don't actually.

DT: Probably your sickness/attendance record. Have you been sick?

SS: Yes flying ULH for seven years is hard on your body and I have been sick more than I would like.

DT: Well I fly a lot too!

SS: Yes, in first class.

DT: Can you say that you love this company and would do anything for this company? Why are you still here? Why do you want to work for a company that doesn't want you? Some of the other guys have jobs, go and get another job!

CVP: It's not that easy, many companies seem to have a problem with hiring us.

DT: The company hasn't done anything to hurt your employment prospects; you're good pilots and should find work.

CVP: Yes, with China Airlines? They don't seem to have a problem with us but that's not the point.

DT: Where would you like to work? British Airways? Qantas?

SS: Air Canada? Yes I would, but I can't right now, it is very difficult to find employment right now as a *49er*.

DT: Yes I know and you have just blown the best airline job you'll see in the world. Maybe you should have thought of that earlier.

SS: We want our jobs back at CX, we have time and a career invested here.

DT: Maybe you should have thought about that before your union tried to hurt the company with sick-outs, MSS, LIA!

CVP: So we were fired for our union activities?

DT: Uh . . . no, but you followed union directives didn't you? Were sick a lot? Didn't demonstrate to us that you love this company!

<During this tirade DT brought up sick-outs and the 1999 pilots' dispute>

DT: Why can't you guys move on? We have!

CVP: It is very difficult to move on when you don't know what we did to deserve this type of treatment. Many of *The 49ers* have clean personal files so why were we singled out?

DT: You must know. There must be something. You're in the union right?

SS/CVP: Yes.

DT: *<mumbling>* But . . . well . . . there's nothing wrong with that. But you followed union directives like MSS and LIA, *et cetera*.

CVP: We were actually fired before MSS got going! Many of us didn't even fly a sector under MSS.

DT: What are your last names again and I'll look at your file tomorrow.

CVP: Please do, I would very much appreciate that. I know that I did not participate in these alleged union activities you speak of.

DT: Do you know how much Demery, Findlay and the union have hurt me over the last six years? Every day I read something bad about myself in the press. I get phone calls at night at two and three in the morning, some wishing cancer upon me! And I have to answer the phone in case there's a crash. I may come down with cancer one day and for people to wish it on someone is not very nice and just last night someone spray-painted my house.

SS: Nigel and the union do not condone that sort of behaviour.

DT: Yes but they don't do anything to stop it!

CVP: It's not fair to victimise fifty pilots and their families due to certain individuals' immature behaviour.

<Now seeming very agitated, with a raised voice and almost screaming>

DT: Do you know how hard it is to run a company with twenty-nine thousand employees? What makes you think you're so special?

SS: I don't think I'm special. I realise that it is hard to run a company of this size but do you still not think there are fundamental problems in Flight Ops that need addressing?

DT: Like what?

SS: Like rostering. Do you think it is unreasonable to be able to get time off for important things such as a wedding or anniversary? Because it seems very difficult to do that with our current system.

DT: I never get any time off. I haven't had any leave for a long time either.

SS: Maybe you should take some time off then.

DT: I'm leaving now.

<Leaves abruptly and gets into silver Volvo with girlfriend>

So now we knew. There were no problems with the company because it's the best managed in the world as demonstrated by its profits. Bit of a change from them screaming financial ruin three years earlier. Our problems were all of our own making for supporting those pesky union people even though under Hong Kong's employment legislation, it's an offence to discriminate against union members. There was nothing wrong with the rostering system. We should have just stopped being sick so much and, instead, demonstrated our undying love for our company.

Edmund Burke is often quoted as saying, 'All that is necessary for the triumph of evil is that good men do nothing.' Cliché or not, we were good men and we were not going to do nothing. We had the support of each other, the support of our union and the financial backing to take the fight back to them. We had the resources and the resolution and thought ourselves well placed. We didn't know it at the time but their attempted union bust wasn't over yet. They still had another card to play.

21

Legals 1

*'(though the) mills of God grind slowly, yet they grind
exceeding small.'*

Longfellow

We formed a legal liaison team consisting of Quentin Heron, Nick Lee,
Kai Chung and me with others of *The 49ers* contributing to the effort
when needed. Our job was to coordinate the various legal actions and
report back to the General Committee. The AOA provided funding for
the actions by means of loans to *The 49ers,* which would be repaid from
the costs awarded by the courts at the conclusion of each case. The
primary objective of our legal strategy at the outset was to get our jobs
back and, failing that, to seek compensation to redress the damage that
had been done to us. In Australia and the UK, the courts have the power
to order reinstatement. The courts in Hong Kong have the same power
but only if the employer agrees to reinstatement, so in reality the court
is toothless. We faced a similar problem with respect to compensation.
The employment protection legislation in Hong Kong is very basic and
the remedies are capped at low levels. For example, the maximum compensation that can be awarded for breach of employment contract is three
months' pay or HK$100,000, whichever is the lower. Similarly, the
maximum compensation that can be awarded for anti-union discrimination is HK$150,000 Compared with the remedies that are available for
similar offences in other jurisdictions, these numbers are piffling and
would hardly address the damage done to us.

We picked the plaintiffs for each jurisdiction according to whether or

293

not they had a 'connection' to that place. For people who were living there it was simple. If you were based in the UK, lived there, paid tax there, were on the electoral roll, etc. you went on the UK case. The same applied to Australia and the US. Of course, because of the low level of employment protection legislation in Hong Kong, the chaps wanted to be on the cases filed outside of Hong Kong if at all possible. We had some guys who were British passport holders and owned a house back in the UK but were based in Hong Kong. They wanted to be on the UK case if they could so we tried it. Also, because of the massive damages that can be awarded by the American courts, anyone who had the slightest connection to the US wanted to be on the case in Los Angeles. Given that our primary objective at this point was to get our jobs back, this approach might seem to be mercenary but money was always going to come into the equation at some point and this is where it first raised its head.

Then we had to decide on the causes of action in each jurisdiction. Because of the differences in employment legislation in each place, the causes of action had to be selected appropriately. In Hong Kong we used the services of Haldanes, one of the legal firms that the AOA had been using for some time, and the solicitor in charge of the case was David Hoare. In the UK we used Simpson Millar, a company recommended to us by BALPA, with Tony Hows as point man. In Australia we hired Abbott Tout with Bryan Belling as lead. In the US we used Christensen, Miller, Fink, Jacobs, Glaser, Weil & Shapiro with Skip Miller in charge.

In Hong Kong we filed actions for breach of the Employment Ordinance S.21B(2)(b), which relates to anti-union discrimination and for breach of contract. We considered also filing an action for defamation but were advised by Haldanes that 'it would be difficult to pursue', so we left it on the back burner for the moment. It was bad advice that we would remedy at a later date.

In the UK we filed actions under Section 94(1) of the Employment Rights Act 1996 for unfair dismissal, failure to provide written reasons for dismissal and breach of contract.

In Australia, we filed an action under the New South Wales Industrial Relations Act 1996, 'unfair contracts' provisions that were designed to provide remedy for unconscionable conduct. The main thrust of this cause of action is that any contract that facilitates conduct that is harsh, unfair and/or unconscionable can be declared to be an unfair contract. If a contract is declared unfair, the Industrial Court has extremely broad remedial power. It can declare the contract void, rewrite the contract to render it fair and make an order for compensation, typically for up to 60 months' salary.

In the US we filed an action for wrongful termination in violation of California public safety policy and libel. Tyler and Chen were named specifically as defendants in this action, which claimed damages of US$100 million.

Our multi-path approach presented some problems for our opponents. Firstly, it took them by surprise and they didn't have a prepared strategy in place. They were just expecting to be dealing with the pro-employer biased labour legislation in Hong Kong, not the sort of protections that are available to employees elsewhere in the world. Secondly, the remedies available in these other jurisdictions were far greater than that which they might have to shell out in Hong Kong. Thirdly, and this was their main problem, because of the different causes of action, the defences that they would have to mount in each jurisdiction would contradict each other and, indeed, this proved to be the case.

Their initial solution to this dilemma was to challenge the right of the courts to hear the cases rather than defend the causes of action *per se*. From their point of view, this made sense of course. If you are caught in a position where whatever you say in one place is going to undermine your position in another, then the obvious solution is to try to stop the debate happening in either of those places. By this tactic, you can hope to suppress the details of what actually took place. It is one thing to be dealing with a little local matter in Hong Kong where it is considered 'normal' for the employer to just about do anything it wants. It is a different matter to have your dealings exposed in countries such as Australia, the UK and US, where you have significant business interests and where bully boy tactics are viewed with a more jaundiced eye. With modern communications, however, just as the Chinese government found out with the Tiananmen Square massacre, the Swires were going to have problems keeping this one quiet and avoiding international repercussions.

One of the vehicles they used to try to shut down the overseas cases was *forum non conveniens* (FNC). This is common law legal doctrine whereby courts may refuse to take jurisdiction over matters where there is a more appropriate forum available to the parties. As a doctrine of the conflict of laws, it applies between courts in different countries and between courts in different jurisdictions in the same country. A concern often raised in applications for FNC is forum shopping, or picking a court merely to gain an advantage in the proceeding. Their position was that some of the pilots were filing an action in Hong Kong for the same cause of action as those in the UK and the only reason that some had filed in the UK was that the remedies were higher. We were ready for that one.

We were careful to ensure that the causes of action that we filed in each country were different.

In the UK we filed for unfair dismissal. In Hong Kong, as mentioned earlier, it was unlawful dismissal by way of a breach of the EO S21B. Unfair and unlawful. Whilst these two terms might seem to be almost synonymous in common parlance, in legal terms they have quite different meanings. One of the things that we were to learn in our eight years of litigation is that, like aviation, the language and terminology is very precise. Attention to detail and the 6P rule are just as important in legal proceedings as they are in aviation. There is no unfair dismissal legislation in Hong Kong and that was why the UK-based pilots filed their action in London. Similarly there is neither 'unfair contract' nor 'breach of public policy' legislation in Hong Kong, which is why the Australian and US-based pilots filed their actions in Sydney and Los Angeles. It was a good plan and effectively countered the forum shopping argument. The opposition was left with one other argument on FNC: that of connection.

Their stance was that Cathay Pacific is a company registered in Hong Kong, its main place of business is Hong Kong, its senior management is located in Hong Kong and that the pilots' contracts were constructed under Hong Kong employment law. Furthermore, since Cathay only has a minimal presence in the various overseas jurisdictions, clearly it would be very costly to be forced to make its personnel travel to these far-flung places for the court hearings. This defence was to lead to some interesting exchanges in the UK in particular.

Like all businesses these days, courts are much more 'cost aware' and more amenable to arguments that will keep costs down. However, for an international airline that has two daily return flights to London to argue that it would be very costly to transport its personnel there never was going to hold much water. Worth a try, I suppose. Anything's worth a try when you're grasping at straws. However, you have to be careful about fielding frivolous or vexatious arguments. The people who preside over the various courts are not idiots, far from it in fact, and they don't like to have their time wasted with arguments that have no chance of success from the outset. This principle is more important the further up the chain of command you progress. What you might get away with in an Employment Tribunal (ET) will not be tolerated in the High Court. What might be acceptable in the High Court won't cut the mustard in the Court of Appeal and, if you get to the House of Lords in the UK, the highest court in the land equivalent to the Supreme Court in the US, expect no mercy from their Lordships if you try it on with them. The principle can be summed up in five words. Don't piss the judge off.

Management's tactic of jurisdictional challenge gave them another advantage. It enables a lot of costly DPGFD to take place. Arguing legal semantics requires just as much preparation and court time as addressing the factual matrix surrounding the cause of action. It is costly and time consuming. Given that Turnbull was reported to have said at one point that whatever we did, they would just delay things and, in his words, 'Run us out of money', it was something we had to be prepared for and have plans in place in order to counter.

The first hearing in the UK action took place from 7 to 11 October 2002 in the Employment Tribunal in Croydon, South London. The bench consisted of a chairman with a legal background, a gentleman from the 'union side' who was a retired general secretary of Unison and a lady from the 'business side' who had previously worked for the Confederation of British Industry. The structure of the hearing consisted of opening skeleton arguments by each side. This was followed by witness statements, testimony and cross-examination. Finally, each side's barrister made detailed submissions to the tribunal. Present as witnesses for the opposition were Barley and Ronald Benjamin Davies, the Cathay basings manager responsible for the administration of Veta and USAB. They were in attendance for the whole four days whilst Rhodes attended only for the first day. The demeanour of Barley and Davies was interesting. They were clearly very uncomfortable to be there. They avoided eye contact with any of us throughout the proceedings even when on the witness stand. When, either by accident or by design, they were unable to avoid being in close proximity with us, they were obviously ill at ease. Rhodes tried to put a brave face on it but it was clear from his body language that he also was very uncomfortable. When he tried to invite some of us to join him for a drink at the end of the first day, the offer was declined with one of our number remarking that he was selective about his drinking companions.

The opposition opened first and their stated position was that our complaints should be struck out or stayed on the basis that:

- Cathay, Veta and USAB are Hong Kong companies;
- Veta and USAB have no corporate presence in the UK;
- The contracts of employment were constructed under Hong Kong law;
- The ERA (Employment Rights Act) does not extend beyond England and Wales;

- Avenues exist for the complainants to take action in Hong Kong with remedies available to them similar to those in the UK;
- The ET does not have jurisdiction to hear the case or, in the alternative, should decline jurisdiction under the principle of FNC.

They did not file a defence against the substantive claims for unfair dismissal. To have done so would have defeated their object of keeping the factual matrix out of the public arena and it would be tantamount to admitting that the ET had jurisdiction to hear the complaints.

Our response to their arguments was that:

- The Cathay, Veta and USAB structure is just a smokescreen to avoid paying tax and other costs of employment;
- The substantial shareholder in Cathay is John Swire & Sons in London via its shareholding in Swire Pacific;
- Cathay has a corporate presence in the UK and can be served there;
- Veta and USAB 'carry on business' in the UK and, therefore, can be served there;
- The dismissals took place in the UK in the case of the Veta and USAB complainants;
- The CPA complainants have retained sufficient connection with the UK to permit them to bring their complaints;
- Section 196 of the ERA, which previously excluded employees who ordinarily worked abroad, has been repealed absolutely and now covers the complainants;
- The causes of action available in Hong Kong are different, much more limited in scope and their remedies are toothless;
- The jurisdictional challenges fail on a number of legal principles.

It was interesting to listen to some of the arguments put forward by the opposition's counsel in his opening remarks in support of their position. He attempted to make much of the fact that pilots often started what he called their 'active flying cycle' from ports other than London Heathrow. By that he meant that these pilots were often positioned to ports other than Heathrow. This was an attempt to suggest that the pilots only occasionally 'did an actual takeoff' from Heathrow and that they spent most of their time abroad. He failed to make the point that positioning at the behest of the company constitutes duty and that for the Veta and USAB complainants, at least, it usually, if not exclusively, commenced in the UK. He also stated that the 'actual take-off' was only a very small part of the flight and that for most of their working lives the pilots were out of the UK in the air.

He also argued that Veta and USAB have formal service agreements with Cathay to supply pilots to operate its aircraft in return for payment. He tried to make much of the fact that these are constructed under Hong Kong law. The fact that the pilots have no knowledge of, and are not party to, such agreements seemed to escape his notice.

Much was made about where the pilots reported for duty at Heathrow, whether or not they went straight out to the aircraft or to a designated reporting point. He stated that they routinely went straight to the aircraft as they do at most ports around the world. This wasn't true and his arguments were strongly refuted during cross-examination.

It was stated that the normal way for pilots to pick up their rosters was from their mail boxes in Hong Kong. The fact that, for based pilots, their rosters were routinely sent to their home addresses by mail as the primary means of notification seemed to have slipped his mind.

It was also represented that, when on reserve duty, there was no limitation placed on where pilots actually lived in relation to their home base. This was again refuted during cross-examination.

He pointed out that some of *The 49ers* were taking action in Hong Kong in relation to their purported dismissal. He argued that their cause of action was very similar, if not identical, to the action being taken by the UK complainants. He maintained that the remedies available in Hong Kong were very similar to those in the UK. Our counsel in response pointed out that the causes of action were in fact very different in that the pilots taking action in HKG contended that the purported dismissals were either in breach of the Employment Ordinance and therefore unlawful or that they were in breach of the terms of the contract and as such the contract still subsisted and had not been terminated. Conversely, the pilots taking action in the UK accepted that the contract had been terminated and were seeking compensation for unfair dismissal. During a comparison of possible remedies, the severe limitations in Hong Kong were pointed out and when it was shown that the remedy of reinstatement was only effective if both parties agreed to it, this caused some merriment on the bench.

Their counsel also argued that some of the complainants were already involved in legal action against the company in Hong Kong in relation to rostering. This was true with respect to HCMP 1679, the contractual determination case, but was an entirely separate matter. He then said that *The 49ers* who were taking action in Hong Kong with respect to their purported dismissal had recently amalgamated their case with HCMP

1679. This was blatantly untrue and the fact was pointed out to the bench by our counsel.

They then argued that our position with respect to the applicability of the ERA subsequent to the repeal of section 196 in 1999 would mean that the floodgates would be opened and that any person anywhere in the world would then be able to take action in the UK irrespective of where they resided and/or where their employer was situated. This became known as his Pitcairn scenario. Thus an aggrieved employee living in Pitcairn Island working for a Saudi Arabian bank would be able to take action in the UK simply because the bank had a branch in London. This was clearly a rather poorly constructed attempt to portray the complainants as forum shoppers and their position as one that would subject the UK courts to a deluge of similar cases should the ET agree to hear this one. He also failed to explain why a Saudi bank would open a branch in Pitcairn Island. The argument was refuted by our counsel in his response.

It was put forward that, because all of Cathay's aircraft are registered in Hong Kong, the applicable law should be Hong Kong law. He skated over the fact that, irrespective of the state of registry, aircraft are required to comply with the laws of the airspace in which they are flying. This came up again during oral evidence.

Barley was the first to take the stand. His evidence consisted of him reading out his witness statement with counsel interrupting him at various points to ask him questions by way of expansion on his written statement. This is Barley's forte when it comes to public speaking, negotiation and the general cut and thrust of debate: reading from a prepared script.

To say that Barley, and later Davies for that matter, had been thoroughly rehearsed prior to the hearing would be an understatement. His responses to questions from his own counsel were wooden and almost parrot fashion. The questions were, naturally, designed to support their counsel's opening remarks.

His responses to certain questions under cross-examination were interesting. For example, he was asked whether he had taken legal advice before dismissing the complainants. He replied that he had. It should be noted that it is not permissible in the ET to ask what that legal advice actually was. Some questions later our counsel, David Griffiths-Jones, asked him, 'So you decided to dismiss them because, under Hong Kong law, you thought you could get away with it?' to which Barley replied, 'Yes.'

Quite a clanger! His response ran somewhat counter to his own counsel's argument that the complainants enjoyed equal if not better protection under the laws of Hong Kong and should, therefore, be taking action there.

In his witness statement, Barley had described a meeting that had been held to select the pilots for dismissal. He admitted under cross-examination that he chaired this 'Star Chamber' meeting. He stated that there were 25 other people present but no one at executive director level or above, other than himself. Davies was one of those present. Barley was asked, 'Presumably a record or minutes of the meeting were kept?' to which he replied, 'No.'

There was then a deathly silence as the assembled throng was asked to believe that, at a meeting of such importance chaired by a senior manager where the careers of 49 men were to be destroyed, no records were kept. They also marvelled at Barley's remarkable feat of memory in being able to recall 49 names without keeping any records, especially when, as he stated later in his evidence, he couldn't even remember the names of the main Cathay shareholders. The members of the ET had what can best be described as quizzical expressions on their faces. It should also be remembered that this evidence was given under oath.

He was then asked for the reason for the dismissal of the pilots, and a vigorous debate ensued between counsel. The opposition counsel obviously did not want Barley to go anywhere near this one and came up with a number of arguments along the lines of it being 'not relevant' to the current proceedings, which were concerned solely with jurisdiction. In response, our counsel made a very good case that, since the opposition were saying that the complainants enjoyed equal if not better protection under Hong Kong law, we would need to know the reason for their dismissal if the tribunal was to be able to compare like with like when looking at causes of action, remedies, etc. The reason given for the dismissal is critical when considering causes of action in the UK.

Led by his counsel, Barley was coaxed into making a statement that he had nothing further to add to his witness statement on the subject. This debate between counsel lasted for some 10 or 15 minutes. This was an obvious minefield for the opposition in the light of the contradictory statements that had been made by various people in written form, in the media and under oath. It was also very revealing that they did not want the ET to hear any of the supposed reasons for dismissal given so far, as they would be laughed out of the place under UK legislation. The chairman also made an interesting aside at the end of this exchange. In commenting on Barley's statement where it mentions that they had a problem with the pilots' attitude, he remarked, 'Not that I'm suggesting that a supposed poor attitude would in any way constitute an adequate reason for dismissal.'

Both Barley and Davies under cross-examination on the issue of reserve duty tried to give the impression that there were no restrictions on where pilots had to live and that the 'two-hour rule' was not enforced. This was obvious rubbish and shown to be so when Paul Robinson in his evidence stated to the contrary. Counsel also pointed out that there had been a crew notice issued to the effect that pilots would be expected to comply with the two-hour rule and that disciplinary action had been taken against at least one individual for non-compliance. Counsel for the opposition rather tetchily countered that no such exhibit (the crew notice) had been entered and also attempted to make a rather poor joke about Paul's speed on the M4 when driving in to Heathrow from his home in Gloucestershire. Paul did not rise to the bait.

Under questioning regarding the reporting arrangements at Heathrow, Barley stated that he had no knowledge of them as he had never operated into or out of there. Davies stated that pilots are routinely taken straight out to the aircraft at Heathrow, as is common (so he said) at most ports. Again this was countered when our witness Paul Robinson testified that crew based in the UK were required to report to a designated reporting point in an office to pick up passes, paperwork, etc. This stumped the opposition's attempt to demonstrate that Veta and/or USAB do not have a corporate presence in the UK.

Barley dropped another clanger when he let slip under questioning that the local Veta coordinator in the UK reported to the manager Europe who is a level D or E employee. Prior to this they had argued that Cathay had no senior level staff in Europe and that the whole operation was managed remotely from Hong Kong. Unfortunately, this hearing was the last we were to see of Barley on the stand in any of our cases. It was a shame because he made a very good witness for us, the plaintiffs.

When Davies took the stand, he adopted a somewhat aggressive posture under cross-examination. Under questioning by his own counsel, he argued that basings were purely voluntary, were solely for the benefit of the pilots, that the company got nothing out of it of any significance and that they were also financially advantageous to the pilots. In support of his last position, he stated that pilots received their provident funds tax free upon taking up a basing. When it was pointed out that this was the norm anyway for all Cathay pilots he then attempted to defend his statement by saying that it was to their advantage because they received their fund earlier than would be normal. Again when it was pointed out to him that taking the funds out early is less advantageous than leaving them to mature and increase in value, his only response was to state petulantly, 'Or go down.' The bench and almost everyone in the room, including some of his own people, laughed at him.

Davies suggested that the 'two-hour rule' for reserve was not enforced. Again this was refuted. Interestingly, he also stated that, until recently, i.e. 1999 (after what he described as the unfortunate industrial events of that time), reserve was not rostered for based crew. This, technically, was correct but painted the wrong picture. Reserve was not put on the printed roster but based crew were routinely assigned reserve duty when their roster was changed, as inevitably it was, given the appalling state of the rostering system. This was clarified by our witnesses, and again Davies' assertions were put to the sword.

Davies also had the temerity to suggest that allowing Steve Parrock, the USAB plaintiff, to undertake reserve duty in the UK when his home base was actually New York was 'the company being nice to him'. This brought guffaws from the assembly.

The next source of amusement was Davies stating under questioning by his own counsel that 'as far as he is aware' the only law that applies to Cathay aircraft is that of their state of registry and that the laws of the airspace through which they are flying have no applicability or relevance. Presumably counsel for the opposition chose to ask this question of Davies rather than Barley because the latter, even with his seemingly limited knowledge of international aviation, would have known the true situation. As it was, the tribunal was treated to a demonstration of Davies' expansive knowledge on such subjects.

Davies was also questioned by his own counsel on the subject of the shareholdings of the various companies. Barley had earlier declined to comment further on the basis that 'he didn't know'. Davies stated that John Swire & Sons had a minority shareholding in Swire Pacific, which in turn had a minority interest in Cathay so that, really, John Swire & Sons didn't have all that much of an interest in Cathay. Ergo their link was a bit tenuous and they shouldn't be held accountable for the actions of a bunch of managers on that barren rock so far away from London. When the shareholding numbers were revealed under cross-examination to be somewhat more than the minimal amounts portrayed earlier, Davies suffered from amnesia with respect to the actual numbers other than that they were 'minority'.

Questioning of our witnesses was confined generally to refuting the erroneous statements made by the opposition. Their counsel adopted a somewhat aggressive tone when cross-examining our men. This did not really do him any favours in the popularity stakes and actually elicited some interesting answers. When he asked Steve Lang, 'Why aren't you suing in Hong Kong?' his response was 'I'm here in England, they threw me and my family out of my house in Hong Kong.' This ensured that the line of questioning ceased immediately.

When he asked Paul Robinson, 'The two-hour rule wasn't really an issue for you where you were living was it?' Paul quite rightly responded that it was an issue and that his inference was incorrect. This led counsel to try to extricate himself from that mess with the rather poor joke referred to earlier. His very aggressive treatment of Steve Parrock under cross-examination eventually led to the tribunal chairman intervening.

During final submissions, the opposition changed their emphasis from their opening skeleton. Whereas formerly they had focused equally on the matters of whether or not Veta and USAB could be served in the UK, Section 244 of the ERA and its applicability, Article 3 of the Extension of Jurisdiction Order, and, finally, FNC, during final submissions much more emphasis was placed on the latter with the majority of time being devoted to it. This was clearly because our counsel had done such an excellent job of showing that the structure of John Swire & Sons, Swire Pacific, Cathay, Veta and USAB is purely smoke and mirrors and a vehicle designed to avoid their responsibilities to their employees.

This argument was put forward under the 'Super Wheeze' concept by Mr Griffiths-Jones. If a UK company wanted to avoid such responsibilities, what a 'Super Wheeze' it would be to set up an offshore company with no assets, no management structure and no employees other than the target employees, write their contracts of employment under the auspices of the offshore law, fire them at will, giving no reasons and no justification and then hold that they have no protection under UK law. Why doesn't everyone do it? Well if the opposition had their way and the court declined jurisdiction, that's exactly what would happen with unscrupulous employers.

As a means of demonstrating that equal protection and remedies under Hong Kong law were available to the complainants, the opposition also attempted to use a case in Hong Kong involving a journalist who sued the *South China Morning Post* as a result of him being dismissed for alleged plagiarism. This backfired badly as it demonstrated once again that adequate remedies are NOT available in Hong Kong. Our counsel did an extremely good job of demonstrating the accepted principle that such evidence from a foreign court should not be admitted or relied upon without the benefit of expert testimony and opinion, which the opposition had signally failed to provide.

It was mentioned repeatedly during the hearing that the case was likely to go further. By this it was meant that, whichever party the judgment went against was likely to appeal. There was currently another case, *Serco v Lawson*, already in the appeal process dealing with very similar matters to ours. It was likely, therefore, that the Employment Appeal Tribunal (EAT) would prefer to hear both cases together. This was good news for us as it meant that our own case would be accelerated through the appeal process to catch up with *Serco*, thus serving our aims of curtailing their DPGFD.

There was another implication as well. A judgment handed down in the ET does not form case law although such judgments may still be referred to. A judgment made in the EAT becomes case law. Thus, any appeal was fraught with danger for Cathay *et al*. If they lost, it would have far reaching implications for their employment cost avoidance strategy. The attendant publicity would mean that the Swires' name would be in the spotlight. It would be brought to the attention of the authorities, not only in the UK but elsewhere, that companies in the Swire Group routinely employ people in their jurisdictions but avoid paying the local costs of employment, such as national insurance, social security contributions, etc. by use of offshore brass plate companies such as Veta and USAB. It would also be demonstrated that they seek to evade their local responsibilities to their employees by the use of such subterfuge. Labour organisations in other countries would take a very dim view of this as would the International Labour Organisation and similar international groups. The lack of legislation in Hong Kong and the pro-business stance of the government would once again be highlighted, this time in a more international context.

The ET handed down its verdict on 10 March 2003. It held that:

- The tribunal had jurisdiction to entertain complaints brought under the ERA by the five Veta pilots, but not those of the six Cathay pilots, or the USAB pilot;
- It had jurisdiction to entertain breaches of contract claims brought by the Veta pilots, but not that of the USAB pilot; and that
- Whilst it had jurisdiction to entertain breach of contract claims by the Cathay pilots, it declined to hear those claims on *forum non conveniens* grounds and stayed them.

This was a double-edged sword for us. We had won the jurisdictional aspect of the case for the UK-based Veta *49ers* outright. Similarly we had won the breach of contract aspect of the case for the Hong Kong-based Cathay *49ers* but the tribunal declined to hear them and we had lost the case for the USAB *49er*. Predictably, the opposition filed an appeal against this decision and we filed a counter-appeal. The appeals were heard by the Employment Appeal Tribunal on 13 and 14 May

2004 and their ruling was handed down on 24 June 2004. The EAT dismissed our appeals and allowed Veta's appeal holding that the original ruling by the ET in accepting jurisdiction in the Veta cases was wrong because of developments in the *Serco v Lawson* case where it had been subsequently ruled in the High Court that the ET had no jurisdiction to hear that case. The EAT referred our Veta case back to the original ET inviting it to revise its decision in light of the *Serco* developments. It seemed like a total loss for us. We were not to be defeated that easily, however.

The *Serco* High Court judgment was going forward to the Court of Appeal and, rather than having our case remitted back to the ET, we petitioned that the sensible and most cost-effective method of deciding our case was to remit it to the Court of Appeal alongside the *Serco* case since the issues were very similar and both could be heard at the same time. Our petition was accepted and our case was sent straight to the Court of Appeal. This was a significant 'leapfrog' of the system for us and cut through the opposition's DPGFD tactics. Naturally, they had petitioned that they'd much rather just go back to the ET. It was set down to be heard in February 2005 before Lord Phillips of Worth Matravers, the Master of the Rolls, the most senior Court of Appeal judge in the UK. When you've got the boss hearing your case, you know you've attracted someone's attention. That was where our UK case sat at the end of 2004.

22

Legals 2

*'Never forget that everything Hitler did in Germany was
legal.'*

Martin Luther King, Jr.

Things weren't going quite so well for us in the US. In fact they were
going badly. I had travelled to Los Angeles to visit Skip Miller and his
team in his offices on the Avenue of the Stars just after the 9/11 attacks
and security was intense. We had discussed the case at length and the
thrust of the action in the US was that *The 49ers* based there had been
dismissed for questioning flight safety issues. There is legislation in
California that protects employee 'whistle-blowers' from dismissal where
their complaints relate to public safety, and Skip was very confident that
we had a strong case. In fact, in his words, 'It was a slam dunk.' A team
got together back at the AOA office in Hong Kong and pulled all the
correspondence and records that we had pertaining to flight safety since
1993. These were all collated and four boxes of documents were sent to
LA. The submissions were all prepared and the case set down for hearing
on 14 December 2001 before LA Superior Court Judge Frances Rothschild.
We lost. The judge ruled orally from the bench that part of our action
be stayed and part dismissed on the grounds of FNC. Given the assurances we'd received prior to the hearing, I was gobsmacked. This was
a major blow to our strategy especially given the level of remedies available in the US. In a letter summarising the judgment, Skip stated that:

> . . . at its core, the ruling means that while an American carrier such
> as UAL or American or Delta cannot terminate an employee for

voicing concerns over safety issues without legal exposure, never-theless, a foreign-based carrier that flies in and out of California's largest airports (in Cathay's case at least 28 times a week) can retaliate against an employee and be immune from legal recourse.

It made no sense. I didn't attend the hearing myself but one of *The 49ers* who did, Henry Van Keulen, sent me the following report:

The judge reminded me of Judge Judy (on TV). I watched her handle a half a dozen cases before ours, and soon got the impression that she was pretty 'flaky'. She didn't make one decision herself, always asking counsel what they wanted to do and then making that her ruling. She tried her (bad) sense of humour on the audience as often as possible. She had written a preliminary ruling as we had anticipated and then forgot to give it to counsel until our case was called. It was apparent from her 'ramblings' that she didn't want to have our case in her courtroom, citing reasons including the cost to the taxpayer of what would be a huge trial. She never seemed to address the point of the motion, but kept on about off-topic ideas such as how to make the company fix its flight safety issues that we were complaining about. It was one of those times when you had to be there to believe it. The other side never really had to prove their case, since the judge was off on such a tangent.

Skip did an excellent job of arguing our case, and at one point seemed to have her swayed to at least reconsider her preliminary ruling, however, she got back into her own line of thinking and stayed with it. Another attorney who was present in the courtroom during this introduced himself to us afterwards. He apparently does a lot of aviation law, and he congratulated Skip on his argument stating that it could not have been made any better, and that he thought the judge was wrong in her ruling.

I have discussed this with George Milman [another attorney who we had been consulting] and he was also dumbstruck. He also feels very strongly that the judge made an error and that we should have a good chance at appeal. I am getting a copy of the ruling and transcript of the hearing when it is available.

Skip feels strongly that we should appeal. The cost will not be that significant (relatively speaking), but the downside is it will take eight months to a year to resolve.

I know this is very discouraging at the moment, but, I hope we are able to get our spirits back up, and focus on the end result so we can keep fighting.

Henry was right. It was a big blow to team morale but you can't expect to win every battle in a war. We had to pick ourselves up and get back into the fight. There was one light on the horizon. The judge had not granted the opposition's motion to dismiss the case in its entirety for the three *49ers* who were actually residents of California; rather she had only stayed their case. The two terms might be similar in effect but are different in recourse. We decided to appeal the judgment and our opening brief was filed on 26 February 2002. At a hearing held on 14 November, the Court of Appeal upheld the Rothschild stay ruling but again declined to dismiss the case in its entirety. Although we continued to be stayed, we still had three active plaintiffs in the US and this is how our action in the US stood at the end of 2004.

Of course the opposition crowed about this and Barley stated in a newsletter that we had been 'kicked out' of the courts in the US. Well he could spin it any way he liked as far as we were concerned. We knew the truth and, although our case there was now on the back burner pending developments in Hong Kong, we weren't dead yet. On top of that, Skip was so incensed about what had happened there he agreed to act for us *pro bono* from now on.

Things were going a lot better for us in Australia. On 17 September 2001 a hearing was held before Justice Heylen in the Industrial Relations Commission (IRC) of New South Wales in court session. The opposition had filed motions to strike out our cases on jurisdictional grounds and this hearing was purely for directions. When Ms Morris, the solicitor appearing for Cathay, attempted to raise some jurisdictional objections, she was rebuked by the judge to the effect that it was inappropriate to raise jurisdictional objections as a preliminary matter, thereby incurring unnecessary costs. His Honour stated that such objections are properly raised and dealt with during the substantive hearing. It was only a minor point but a good start. She also asked for an adjournment because she needed further instructions on the Veta plaintiffs. The case was stood over until 18 October for further directions. It seemed our opponents hadn't prepared very well.

As Bryan Belling, the leader of our team of Australian layers, put it, their next move was 'extraordinary'. At the hearing on 18 October they informed the judge that they had, that day, filed a summons in the High Court and, therefore, the proceedings in the IRC should be stood over. In deference to the superior court, Justice Heylen agreed to do so for 14 days to 1 November. The High Court is Australia's superior court in which constitutional challenges are heard and determined. Cathay's new High Court action sought four orders.

Firstly, an order that a claim under the unfair contracts provisions of the Industrial Relations Act 1996 (NSW) could not be brought or maintained because, in matters involving airline pilots, there was a Federal or Commonwealth statute, namely the Air Navigation Act 1920, that was inconsistent with the State law and therefore rendered the State law inoperative.

Secondly, an order declaring that no part of the international air transport industry operating within the limits of Australia was an 'industry' within the meaning of section 106 of the Industrial Relations Act 1996, in as much as no part of that industry was 'in or of' the State of New South Wales.

Thirdly, an order that the Industrial Relations Commission of New South Wales had no jurisdiction in relation to the contracts between Veta and the applicants unless such contract was a contract effectively made in New South Wales.

By means of these first three applications, they sought a declaration that the IRC had no jurisdiction to entertain our claims. Employment protection law in Australia is very well developed and the courts are not sympathetic to bully boy tactics by employers. Quite clearly, they didn't want to be anywhere near the IRC where they would get found out.

They went further than that. They sought a fourth order declaring that Cathay, as an airline designated by Australia under a bilateral agreement for the purpose of the Air Navigation Act 1920, was entitled to engage pilots for the provision of air services between Australia and Hong Kong without regard to the provisions of the Industrial Relations Act. In other words they wanted to be able to carry on business in Australia but exempt from its employment laws.

This High Court challenge was an attempt to keep the factual matrix out of the public arena; the advice given to us was that it was unlikely to succeed and, rather, was part of a strategy to 'burn off' our applications by point-taking and delay. In the words of our written advice:

> There is no doubt that the strategy adopted by the respondents in mounting the High Court challenge is designed to do one of two things:
> (i) Either defeat the litigation altogether on the basis that the constitutional challenge has merit, or alternatively;
> (ii) As part of a strategy of delay and obfuscation with a view to

creating sufficient difficulty and delay to oblige you to incur such cost and expense and to suffer such frustration as you will 'give up and go away'.

Our understanding of the merits of the constitutional challenge are such that we suspect the true motive is (ii).

To date, there had been no actual findings of fact in the proceedings and the High Court is usually reluctant to take on such cases. It does not like to sit as a tribunal of fact. The High Court is essentially a constitutional court or an ultimate appeals court only. Because of this, there existed the possibility that we could get the case remitted back to the IRC by the High Court to first determine and rule on the factual issues. That would suit us because it would be the quickest route but, clearly, it wouldn't suit our opponents. Their delaying tactics worked. Before we could even apply for the case to be remitted back, we needed to see their stated case and they took their time about preparing it. Australian law firm Freehills were acting for the opposition and were pass masters at DPGFD. By April 2002 we still had not had a hearing in the High Court nor was a date set on calendar. We had asked Freehills in January 2002 to provide us with their draft pleadings of the stated case but so far they had not responded. Therefore, on 25 April, Anzac Day, we filed a motion seeking the following orders in the alternative:

(a) That the High Court challenge be dismissed and that the respondents pay our costs; or
(b) That the whole of the proceedings be remitted back to the Industrial Commission to determine all issues including the Federal Constitutional issues; or
(c) In the alternative, to oblige Freehills to state a case as a matter of expedition.

We thought this might light a fire under them and get things moving. No such luck. We didn't manage to get a hearing until over a year later when on 12 May 2003 our application to have the case referred back to the IRC was heard in the High Court before His Honour Justice McHugh.

The opposition's senior counsel at the hearing was Bob Ellicott. It is worthwhile quickly reviewing his CV. Robert James 'Bob' Ellicott was born on 15 April 1927 and admitted to the New South Wales Bar in 1950. He was solicitor general from 1969 to 1973 and was attorney-general in the Fraser Ministry from 1975 to 1977. He resigned as attorney-general as a result of a dispute with Malcolm Fraser over the payment of costs in the *Sankey v Whitlam and Others* case. Ellicott was reappointed as Minister for Home Affairs and Minister for Capital Territory from 1977 to 1980. He was Minister for Home Affairs and the Environment from November 1980 until his resignation on 17 February 1981 to become a judge on the Federal Court of Australia. Ellicott resigned from the court in February 1983. Later he became an arbitrator on the Court of Arbitration for Sport, and on 20 November 2007, he was named as chair of the tribunal to investigate allegations of misbehaviour against the suspended Chief Justice of Fiji, Daniel Fatiaki. Clearly no lightweight then. They had brought out their big guns.

To our advantage, however, the attorney-general for New South Wales took an interest in our case and appeared at the hearing as a third party represented by the solicitor general, Mr M.G. Sexton. We were involved in seriously high-stakes poker with constitutional repercussions hanging on the outcome of the proceedings.

One of the thrusts of our argument to have the case referred back to the IRC was that all issues, including those of jurisdiction and the actual merits of the case, could be dealt with without fragmentation. Being very busy, the courts do not like to see cases being duplicated and/or different parts being heard in different venues. Of course, our opponents wanted to separate the two parts of the case leading to yet more delay.

Ellicott went first and began to speak but was interrupted by the judge who said he had read all the papers and there were nine clear points in their submissions. He dealt with each in turn in summary fashion, saying that seven of them had little merit and suggesting they concentrate on the other two. Ellicott proceeded down the suggested line.

Their first point was that the matter should be settled in the form of a 'stated case'. This is a vehicle whereby the two sides agree a 'raft of facts' where there is no dispute between the parties. The remaining outstanding disagreements are then decided by the judge on the basis of the written submissions made by both parties and oral submissions by counsel with no witnesses called. In essence, this is similar to the difference between an action by originating summons in Hong Kong, where the evidence is given by affidavit and then argued by counsel without witnesses being called, and a writ action where there is a full court hearing with witnesses giving oral evidence, cross-examination, etc. The stated case option was likely to lead to the greatest delay and we pointed this out. Freehills still had not adequately responded to our requests for pleadings and they were just trying to cause us maximum inconvenience. Ellicott, in return, attempted to paint a picture that it was us who had been unresponsive and difficult and that we had only recently raised our objection that the stated case was not a suitable vehicle for our proceedings because of the complexity of the issues at hand. This wasn't correct. We had expressed our reservations about the stated case route at the outset.

At this point, the judge intervened and said that, in his 15 plus years of experience of similar 'industrial type' cases, he found that very few of them could be adequately dealt with via the stated case route and that it was not a suitable vehicle for dealing with such matters. He also remarked that it was his experience in such cases that the employers always wanted to have such cases heard in the High Court rather than the IRC with words to the effect that 'we all know why that is'. This raised something of a titter amongst the assembled throng. He was alluding to the reputation of the IRC for taking a very dim view, perhaps more so than the High Court, of employers who abuse their employees by unconscionable conduct; exactly what we were accusing Cathay and Veta of doing.

There was then some debate about the stated case issues and the judge questioned whether or not some of the facts could be agreed. This, in part, centred on operational matters such as reporting arrangements, etc. It didn't really address the core question that was in dispute: that of connectedness, i.e. do the parties have sufficient connectedness with NSW for the courts to accept jurisdiction?

We argued that the IRC had the power to decide all such issues as well as the actual merits of the case. If the High Court merely ruled on the jurisdictional issues, then the merits would remain outstanding to be dealt with by the IRC and, therefore, to avoid fragmentation, the best course of action would be to refer the whole matter to the IRC immediately. Should the opposition be unhappy with the IRC's ruling on the jurisdictional issues, they would still have the option open to them of appealing the judgment to the High Court.

It was during this debate that the judge suggested that it might save the court's time if the parties could have one more attempt to see whether or not they could agree on a stated case. The opposition jumped on this suggestion with alacrity. As the judge had suggested it, we had little to gain by refusing to take his path. He did, however, impose a deadline. The parties were to meet again to report to the court on progress down this route on 23 May. The judge said one more thing. He said forcefully that '. . . the matter *will* be decided by the end of June.' In other words, no more messing around by Freehills.

The opposition tried one more tack, questioning the judge's power to refer the case back to the IRC. Ellicott indicated to the judge that, should he decide to refer the matter to the IRC, they would appeal that decision based on a hitherto untested question. The unresolved argument goes as follows. The rules state that the High Court may refer matters to another court. There had been some debate as to whether or not the IRC constitutes a 'court' in the strictly legal sense of the word. There are those that have argued that the IRC sometimes acts like a court but often more like a tribunal. The rules governing the conduct of the two are different. If the term 'court' is to be defined in its narrowest context, then the argument is that the IRC is not a court *per se* and, therefore, the High Court does not have the power to refer cases thereto. If, on the other hand, the term 'court' is to be interpreted in its wider sense, then clearly the High Court does have power to refer matters to the IRC. This is a matter that had been raised in previous cases but left unanswered. If you want to clutch at straws, there was one floating by right now.

Over a few debriefing beers that night, I was told that the judge had a long and experienced background in labour matters, both when he was practising and on the bench. He came to the bench 'the hard way' by originally being a solicitor and was described to me as a 'black bag' judge. I had not heard this term before but it refers to a method of adjudication designed to prevent the sort of tactics our opponents were using. The black bag theory goes as follows: Parties who disagree about a claim must fully air the arguments and facts that divide them before it can be said that a dispute has crystallised. Only then can a claim be referred to adjudication, bundling up all those arguments and facts into a black bag and passing it to the adjudicator. The adjudicator reaches his decision based on what he finds in the black bag. Neither the adjudicator, nor either party, can put anything more into that bag.

Justice McHugh had had some very sardonic expressions on his face at times when Ellicott was speaking and he was very aware of what the opposition were trying to do. They were trying to leave the bag open so they could throw some more spanners in there whenever they felt like it. Also, should he decide to refer the case to the IRC, the opposition's threat was just another spoiling tactic to appeal his decision on an untested point of law. This would take even more time before we got to the merits hearing and was a very strong pointer to their tactics. As one member of our legal team said to me:

> They're absolutely shit scared of having the merits of the case heard in open court because they know they're going to get trashed when the court hears what they've done and they'll try anything to avoid it. This is very dirty pool.

The further attempts at agreeing a 'stated facts' case ordered by the judge came to nothing. Justice McHugh handed down his judgment on 2 July. He ordered that our case be remitted back to the IRC and awarded full costs in our favour. It was a massive win for us. The opposition didn't follow through on their threat to appeal his judgment but they had managed to delay everything by 18 months with their DPGFD tactics.

The next step was that we were ordered to go for mandatory conciliation. This was obviously going to be a complete waste of time given our opponents' attitude but a required step. It failed with no resolution. At the conciliation hearing the opposition actually tried to characterise *The 49ers'* dismissals as redundancies. When we showed the chairman the 'last in, first out' redundancy clause in the CoS, together with the pilots' seniority numbers, he just dismissed their argument as rubbish, which is exactly what it was. Another straw floating by.

We had to wait another year before we got to the next hearing in front of the IRC, presided over by Justice Staunton, on 15 July 2004. The opposition persisted with their argument that the jurisdictional and constitutional issues should be heard separately from the factual matters. Another attempt to cover up what they had done and keep their actions out of the public spotlight. Justice Staunton disagreed with their arguments and, in her judgment delivered on 20 July, ordered that the case be re-listed as soon as possible for directions where all matters would be heard together. Freehills responded to this ruling with what Bryan termed 'more bastardry'.

On 29 July 2004, they filed an appeal against the judgment, their main argument being that:

> ... Her Honour (allegedly) erred in direction that the matters be joined and heard in their totality in that such process impermissibly combines an exercise of New South Wales legislative power with federal judicial power.

What happened next is perhaps most easily described by copying verbatim some incoming emails that we received from our legal team in Australia over the next five months:

Mention before Justice Staunton on 30 July 2004

Bryan appeared before her Honour for a mention of the matters on 30 July 2004. Her Honour's hands were basically tied because of the Application for Leave to Appeal and Appeal filed by Veta/CX and accordingly the matters have been stood over pending the outcome of the Application. The Application will be referred to the President of the Commission for allocation to a Full Bench. As previously indicated we hope that the matter will be listed before a Full Bench for mention/programming in the next month or so. We have filed a Notice of Appearance in relation to the Application for Leave to Appeal and Appeal and need take no other steps at this stage.

Appeal to a Full Bench of the IRC, 3 August 2004

Good news. The appeal has been listed for directions/hearing at 11am on Friday 6 August 2004, before one of the judges who will be on the Full Bench (who are to hear the appeal). Veta/CX will apply for a stay of the IRC proceedings (i.e. your substantive claims) pending outcome of the appeal. They are likely to be successful with this application, particularly as our argument is that the IRC proceedings and the remitted matters should be heard together. The judge is likely to set a timetable regarding exchange of arguments between the parties, and hopefully a date for the appeal.

Mention before Justice Walton today, 6 August 2004

Bryan and I appeared before Justice Walton (one of the judges on the Full Bench) this morning. The matter was listed to discuss a stay of the proceedings pending the outcome of the application to appeal. Veta/CX rolled out Bob Ellicott QC. He was up to his usual malarkey, attempting to delay the matter as much as possible. We indicated that we would agree to a stay on the condition that the appeal be prosecuted by Veta/CX with alacrity. Justice Walton accepted this and has programmed the matter as follows:

Veta/CX to file and serve its submissions on or before 10 September 2004;

We are to file and serve our submissions on or before 15 October 2004; and Veta/CX are to file and serve submissions in reply by 22 October 2004.

Justice Walton indicated a preference for a hearing day in either of October or November (however these were dependant [sic] upon the availability of the Full Bench).

Appeal to be heard on 18 October 2004

The Full Bench of the IRC has set 18 October 2004 to hear the appeal by Veta/CX against the decision of her Honour Justice Staunton that the proceedings remitted by the High Court and the substantive proceedings (i.e. your unfair contract claims) should be heard together. Amended directions have been made regarding filing the submissions from the parties (the NSW Attorney-General is going to intervene in the matter as he did in the High Court proceedings). We should receive a detailed outline of the Veta/CX submissions this Friday, or at the latest, next Monday. Richard Kenzie QC and Shane Prince will continue to represent your interests at the appeal. The dark side will be briefing Robert Ellicott QC and Garry Hatcher SC.

Appeal to the Full Bench of the Industrial Relations Commission,
18 October 2004

Today we appeared before a Full Bench of the Industrial Relations Commission for the appeal against Staunton J's decision to hear together the proceedings remitted from the High Court and the substantive section 106 proceedings. Richard Kenzie QC and Shane Prince appeared on behalf of the pilots. Bob Ellicott QC and Garry Hatcher SC appeared on behalf of Veta/CX. Naomi Sharp (Counsel) appeared for the NSW Attorney-General who intervened in the matter.

The basis argument propounded by Veta was that the remitted proceedings should be determined first as if the pilots were unable to establish the requisite jurisdictional link (i.e. that they participated in an industry in and of NSW or that their contracts required them to work in an industry in and of NSW) then the matter would be determined with finality. This would obviate the need to determine the difficult (their submission) constitutional issues.

We submitted that the two proceedings should be determined together so that it was not necessary to have two hearings which would basically cover the same factual scenario. The constitutional issue, in a nutshell, revolves around whether the Commission, when exercising its powers under s[ection] 106 (i.e. the unfair contract provisions), is exercising judicial or arbitral (i.e. non-judicial) power. Veta claim that the Commission is not able to hear and determine at the same time proceedings involving judicial power (i.e. the remitted proceedings which involve the exercise of Commonwealth judicial power) and arbitral power (i.e. the s[ection] 106 proceedings which, they argue, are arbitral in nature). We argued, amongst other things, that the s[ection] 106 proceedings were not in fact arbitral in nature. The Attorney-General supported the position propounded by us.

The Full Bench reserved its decision.

Full Bench decision, 15 December 2004

Leave to appeal granted but appeal dismissed (i.e. we won) the Dark Side to pay our costs. Matter should now proceed to a merits hearing some time later next year.

So here we were then, almost three and a half years on from our dismissals and back in the same court where we had started. But we had defeated all of their technical challenges. We had navigated all their road blocks, bastardry, malarkey and DPGFD and were set fair to have our day in court to show them up for what they were. Despite the delays, we had made good progress in the last six months and we were pleased with our position.

23

Betrayal

> *'An appeaser is one who feeds a crocodile – hoping it will eat him last.'*
>
> Winston Churchill

> *'Betrayal is the only truth that sticks.'*
>
> Arthur Miller

Nigel Demery stood down as president of the AOA at the end of September 2003 and Murray Gardner took over the position. He had returned, having taken a rest after the 1999 negotiations. Shortly after he took over the post, he came to see me at home and asked for a briefing on the last state of play of the rostering practices negotiations in 2001. Clearly he was going to have another try at getting to an agreement. At that meeting, some warning bells started ringing. I asked him who was going to lead his negotiating team and he replied that he was. I pointed out to him that best practice says that the jobs of president and chief negotiator should be kept separate but this didn't seem to concern him.

The next thing that happened was that the subsistence payments being made to *The 49ers* by the AOA came under 'review'. In order to receive subsistence above a basic level, everyone was required to fill out a means test questionnaire that was very detailed and intrusive. Many of *The 49ers* objected to this and did not want to reveal such intimate details of their personal finances without any proper guarantees of confidentiality.

A whispering campaign began and we started hearing rumours along the lines of, 'So and so got his A Scale Provident Fund payout but he's still claiming his mortgage payments. Why should we be paying for his house?'

I was subject to one of these rumours after I'd been seen with my wife in the front row seats at an Elton John concert. The rumour went, 'What's Warham doing in the most expensive seats in the house when he's taking money from the AOA?'

I actually had to stand up and defend myself in front of the membership at an AOA meeting. My response was simple.

'Yes, I was at the concert and I was in the most expensive seats. But I haven't taken a red cent, not one penny, from the AOA in subsistence payments since I was sacked. I figure there are other *49ers* and their families who are worse off than me financially so I've always left the money I could have claimed in the pot for them to use. So, it's my own money and I'll spend it how I like. Any other questions?'

It was true. I hadn't taken a cent. Rather the reverse. I'd actually lent money personally to a couple of my colleagues who were in financial trouble and needed some short-term help. Something didn't smell right.

There was another warning sign. Gardner started clearing out people from the General Committee who didn't agree with his views. Two of these were Chris Lawrence and Nigel Demery. Nigel didn't agree with some of the new policies being adopted and voiced his objections in his position as immediate past president. Chris had worked tirelessly helping *The 49ers* both with pastoral care and on the subsistence side of things. He was also very active at IFALPA in promoting our cause.

Then we started getting reports that Gardner was having private one-on-one meetings with Hughes-Hallett and Turnbull. This did not bode well. Quite apart from the danger involved in these sorts of meetings with no witnesses present, something was going on behind the scenes and *The 49ers* weren't being included in whatever he was planning. We soon found out. On 15 December 2004 I received information that he had been negotiating a deal behind our backs. He and Findlay also had broken with protocol and gone to each of our sets of lawyers and asked them some very loaded questions designed to undermine the confidence of *The 49ers* and the membership as a whole with regard to the potential success of our legal strategy. They excluded us from any of these meetings apparently with the intent of presenting the whole thing as a *fait accompli* and railroading 'the offer' through. I was told that a meeting of the General Committee was to take place the next day and immediately telephoned Findlay with the intention of attending the meeting as an observer. Findlay informed me that the meeting had actually taken place the previous day. I asked him what had been discussed at that meeting and he replied that he would not disclose that to me. When I asked why not, he said that it was because the minutes of the meeting had not yet been published.

I asked, 'Is that as good as it gets then?'

He replied, 'Yes.'

It stank to high heaven. But now they knew I had found out what they were up to, they had to start some damage limitation. Findlay called me back and asked to arrange a private meeting between me, him and Gardner. Yeah, I was really going to fall for that one. The meeting took place on the 17th and I took Kai Chung along with me.

Gardner opened the meeting by apologising for the lack of consultation on 'the offer'. He stated that they had intended to publicise the offer to the members on Monday 20 December and to meet with me to discuss it on the previous Friday. Apparently, however, there had been a 'security breach', details of the offer had got into the public domain and that necessitated formal publication of the document on the 16th without prior consultation. Of course it did. He then gave an executive summary of 'the offer'.

- An *ex-gratia* payment of ten months' salary would be made. This would be capped for anyone who had reached normal retirement age within ten months of their dismissal;
- *The 49ers* would be allowed to submit an application for employment. This was not an offer of reinstatement; it was simply an application for a new job just like anyone on the street could do;
- Applicants would have to undergo psychological evaluation by the company.
- Successful applicants would be employed on 12 months' probation, i.e. one month's notice, as F/Os on the freighter fleet.
- Salary would commence at year one based on a new date of joining;
- Seniority would 'snap back' after a three-year period of employment;
- Salary would not 'snap back';
- Staff travel would not 'snap back'.
- There were no job security provisions in the offer.
- Prior to being eligible to accept the offer, each *49er* would have to withdraw permanently from all legal actions relating to the dismissals and accept the offer as 'full and final settlement', prior to actually participating in the offer.

• The AOA would cease funding all legal actions related to the dismissals.

So, in summary, the great negotiator had come up with a deal where, before receiving any money, offer of employment, or anything else, *The 49ers* would have to relinquish all legal claims of any nature relating to our sackings. We would then have to take it on trust that we would either receive ten months' salary only, not salary and allowances, or we could apply for a job as a new joiner on Freighter Scales that were even lower than B Scales, but be forced to undergo some special psychological testing that no other 'normal' job applicant was subject to.

The AOA had previously stated its objectives in coming to any form of settlement with the company. These were:

• Fair treatment of *The 49ers* with reinstatement in their previous jobs and/or proper financial compensation for the damage they had suffered.
• Employment protection for the membership as a whole to ensure that this could never happen again.

We asked the president a few questions:

Q. Under the terms of the offer, who will pay the legal costs?
A. Each party will be responsible for their own legal costs.
Q. What about the loans to *The 49ers*?
A. The subsistence loans would be waived but those who have outstanding tax loans would be required to repay them.
Q. Yes but what about the loans to *The 49ers* for legal costs?
A. *<After some confusion>* 'That's money that's been spent.'
Q. Would *The 49ers* who wish to apply for employment be required to drop their legal actions prior to going through the psychological assessment and/or interview process?
A. Yes.
Q. Does the possibility not exist that some *49ers* who wish to apply for employment might drop their legal actions and then subsequently be unsuccessful in the selection process?
A. Yes but then they would receive the financial offer instead.
Q. What if the membership reject the offer?
A. Then we would continue on our current course with the legal actions. Further, the General Committee would take such a

rejection as a positive direction from the membership to continue on our current course.

Q. What if the membership vote to accept the offer but the 49ers reject it?

A. Then the loans to *The 49ers* for legal funding would be withdrawn.

Q. Will the members be told which way *The 49ers* vote on the offer prior to the membership vote?

A. Yes.

Q. Will the AOA comms channels be made available to *The 49ers* for them to put their views to the membership?

A. Probably.

Q. Will the subsistence payments to *The 49ers* continue?

A. *<There was some confusion on this issue and he undertook to respond at a later date>*

Q. Do you believe that the objectives agreed upon prior to entering into negotiations have been met by this offer?

A. 'No.' *<Both the president and general secretary answered>*

Some deal. He was recommending an offer to the membership that achieved none of the stated objectives. None at all. Some negotiator. What was worse, the pair of them had gone behind our backs to the lawyers to get skewed opinions that would support their recommendation of the offer. I asked Findlay for copies of all the relevant correspondence to which I and the other plaintiffs had not been party. He refused, saying it was privileged. Privileged? These cases belonged to us, *The 49ers*, not to Findlay, Gardner or the AOA. Our names were on the summonses and writs not theirs. The only interest they had in these cases was that the AOA was providing the funding by means of loans to *The 49ers*. Findlay relented after some pressure was applied and we subsequently received copies of the lawyer's answers to his questions but he still refused to give me a copy of his original letter requesting the advice. Now why would he want to hide that from me?

Gardner had included excerpts from these legal opinions with 'the offer' paperwork that he sent to *The 49ers*. They differed considerably in emphasis from those that we had previously received, especially from AOA's legal firm Haldanes, and I wanted to know why. I arranged a meeting with Haldanes' David Hoare and, on 21 December 2004, five of us went along to his office.

Throughout the legal process in Hong Kong, our solicitors had repeatedly stated to us that our chances of success in the case were 'good'. In Hoare's advice in response to Findlay's letter he had revised this to 'reasonable'. I asked him why he had downgraded his assessment. After some waffling, Hoare stated that when he'd originally drafted the advice to the General Committee he'd written 'good' but that this was subsequently amended to 'reasonable' on suggestion from counsel. But why? On the basis of advice we had previously received from Australia and the UK, the term 'good' means 75-80 per cent chance of success. Hoare was now saying our chances were only 'better than even'. Previously he had repeatedly stated to us, 'They cannot possibly mean to go to court with this.' He now subtly changed emphasis from his previous position, saying, '. . . the evidence . . . in the case of the defendants is in our view weak.'

Even in the conservative language of lawyers, this still indicated to us chances that were better than 'reasonable'. He also repeated his advice on defamation in response to Findlay's request for an opinion: 'Theoretically, there could be an action for defamation but this would be difficult to pursue . . .'

We had taken the trouble to obtain further independent advice on this matter from another senior counsel in which he opined on the issue of identification, one of the core issues in any defamation case. His view was much less pessimistic than Hoare's. He advised us that '[Plaintiff 1] may therefore have a good cause of action in defamation . . .' and '[Plaintiff 2] could therefore sue in defamation without facing the difficulties which others might encounter.' He also advised that success in the case with respect to breach of the Employment Ordinance and/or breach of contract could add weight to a possible defamation suit. So, again, why had the emphasis of the advice contained with 'the offer' shifted? We were unable to elicit a satisfactory reply to that question. However, we saw a copy of Findlay's letter asking for advice and in it were the words, 'In replying please be as realistic, or stark, as you feel you can be . . .'

So that was why Findlay didn't want to show it to me. He was trying to skew the advice to paint a pessimistic view of our legal strategy and so make Gardner's 'offer' appear more attractive.

A lot of backpedalling went on at the meeting with Hoare. I asked him why he hadn't consulted me or any member of the legal liaison team when preparing his advice as had been the standard custom and practice over more than three years. He replied that he had been 'sworn to secrecy' by those requesting the advice because, should it get out, it might jeopardise the negotiations. Mike Fitz-Costa, one of *The 49ers* who attended the meeting with me, almost exploded at that point. These were our actions not the AOA's and certainly not Gardner's or Findlay's. Hoare tried to say that since the AOA was a long-standing client and since it was 'paying the bills' on this action, the AOA was the client. We pointed out to him that, actually, *The 49ers* were paying the bills by means of loans from the AOA and that Haldanes had drafted the letters of agreement on this at the inception of the actions. I asked him the question, had *The 49ers* borrowed the money from a bank, which was also a client of Haldanes on other matters, and the bank asked for advice or gave directions on the case, would they then give such advice or accept such directions? His answer was no, they would not. The whole thing was a set-up.

He backpedalled even further when he went to great pains to point out that the advice given on whether or not to accept the offer was based solely on the financial and other remedies available under the law. It took absolutely no account of issues of principle or of industrial and political considerations. So that's all right then. I was told later that Hoare said that particular meeting was the most uncomfortable he had ever had with clients in the whole of his career. And so it should have been. We were getting sold out and, whether unwittingly or otherwise, he was part of the sell-out.

Gardner didn't get it quite so easy with our Australian lawyers. They maintained that our chances of success there for the three *49ers* based in Sydney were 75 per cent. Considerably better than 'better than even'. 'Good' in fact. He and Findlay started telephoning people and running some roadshows to sell 'the offer'. Findlay organised a meeting with the lawyers in Sydney on 3 January 2005. He tried to keep it quiet but Seamus Burke, Bryan Belling's second-in-command, was having none of it. Unlike Haldanes, he had no problem at all identifying who was the client and kept us fully in the loop. I flew down to Sydney to attend the meeting under my own steam and the look on Findlay's face when he walked into the room and saw me sitting there was a picture. It got worse for him. Bryan stated to the assembled *49ers* that there was no way he could recommend 'the offer' to his clients as it stood because it had not been submitted in proper written form and that, under its terms, he could not recommend forgoing the legal actions without proper written guarantees of both compensation and/or interviews. Also, part of the offer constrained the AOA in any further action by the following clauses:

In particular, the Association is required under the Agreement to:
(i)   immediately cease assisting (directly or indirectly) any of the Terminated Pilots in any existing Legal Action against Cathay, Veta Limited or USA Basing Limited or any Relevant Person;

(ii)   not assist (directly or indirectly) any of the Terminated Pilots in any future Legal Action against any Relevant Person; and

(iii) not assist any other person (being an individual, corporation or any unincorporated organisation, society or union) in assisting, whether directly or indirectly, any Legal Action (whether an existing Legal Action or a future Legal Action) by any of the Terminated Pilots against any Relevant Person.

Bryan was not happy about those terms. As he put it:

> The question which has been raised is how the Association proposes to assist *The 49ers* where the membership votes to accept the offer and one, or more, of *The 49ers* chooses not to. The provisions in the Agreement go beyond what we initially anticipated was the cessation of financial assistance by the Association to now include under the definition of 'assist' the following:
>
> • The provision of advice or facilities which operate to facilitate any person in bringing or continuing a Legal Action; or
> • Any act which would encourage any person to bring or continue a Legal Action.
>
>   This is likely to have a very detrimental impact on *The 49ers* doing such things as gathering evidence, calling winesses for further legal action in circumstances where *The 49ers* wish to continue using alternative sources of funding.

He was exactly right. Gardner's 'offer' not only closed the door on *The 49ers* who chose to take the deal but would also make life extremely difficult for those who chose to continue the fight for justice with other means of funding. The debate in the meeting in Sydney was robust. Findlay had brought along a member of the General Committee with him to answer questions. When he didn't spout the right mouth music in response to questions from some of *The 49ers*, Findlay tried to shut him up. In response to a question, Findlay jumped in with, 'Don't answer that.'

'What do you mean, don't answer that? I've asked him a question and I want an answer. He's the General Committee member, not you. You're the hired help. You can't tell him not to answer.'

'Yes, I can. I just have.'

It wasn't going at all according to plan and he lost it completely when, in answer to another question, he suddenly exploded and shouted, 'And as for that fucking cunt sitting there, no one told me he'd be here.' He was referring to me.

He blew it. It was at that point that I realised truly what we were up against. It was a wholesale sell-out on the shabbiest of terms and we were being betrayed by the leadership of our own union.

Back in the time when I was president and Findlay worked for me as my general secretary, we had become close. We were from similar educational backgrounds and held similar views on a lot of topics, or so I thought. One evening I was sitting in the office and my wife came in to meet me as we were going out for dinner that night. Findlay and I were finishing off a discussion on some topic or other. My wife said to me later, 'You and John are really close with each other aren't you? You're both on the same wavelength.'

'Why do you say that?' I asked.

'Because you finish off each other's sentences when you're talking.'

I hadn't thought of it that way before but she was right. We did have a close working relationship, so much so that when he got married he asked me to be his best man, a job I undertook willingly. By 2005, we had moved on a long way from those days. Of all the things that I was forced to endure in the long fight to get justice for *The 49ers*, Findlay's betrayal was one of the hardest to bear. It wasn't just that he supported Gardner's sell-out offer, he actually worked against me and the others who chose to carry on with the fight. He worked through IFALPA to stop us raising funding from other organisations that might help us financially. When asked at a meeting of the OCCC whether or not *The 49ers* were seeking funding assistance, he replied, 'No.' He actively worked to stop Nigel Demery attending an IFALPA meeting to press our case.

He showed his true turncoat colours during 2008 when it was becoming obvious who was going to be on the winning side. He telephoned me out of the blue to ask for details of where he might make a personal donation towards our legal costs. This after all the years that we had fought on alone despite his best efforts to undermine us. I gave him a bank account number and he put HK$5,000 into it. If that was all it took to salve his conscience then he was cheaper than even I had assumed.

The Gardner/Findlay roadshow to sell the offer failed. They had originally wanted to put the offer to the membership as a whole to vote on without them first being made aware of the views of *The 49ers*. There was such an outcry that they were forced to allow a vote amongst *The 49ers* first with the outcome made public to the membership before they voted. We voted the offer down by 41 votes against (with four to accept and four undecided). The membership voted with *The 49ers* against acceptance of the offer. So that was it then presumably. Panic over. Given Gardner's undertaking to me on 17 December that should the membership reject the offer, 'Then we would continue on our current course with the legal actions,' and that, 'Further, the General Committee would take such a rejection as a positive direction from the membership to continue on our current course,' then presumably we would do exactly that.

Not a chance. Gardner hadn't finished trying to railroad through his deal yet. He broke his word to me and set about a scare campaign amongst the membership, attempting to demonstrate how much the legal costs were likely to amount to in the future. He predicted that they could potentially run into tens of millions of dollars. He even went so far as to tell the General Committee that there was a possibility that they could be held personally responsible for the legal fees should we lose and have costs awarded against us. It was complete bullshit. As an exercise in spin and scare tactics it really plumbed the depths.

I called another meeting with Haldanes in March and, with Findlay in attendance, asked the direct question, 'In the event that we lose the court case and have costs awarded against us, is there any possibility that the members of the General Committee could be held personally liable for those costs?' The answer was as straightforward as you can get from a lawyer.

'It is exceedingly unlikely.'

Disregarding all this and the previous way that we had successfully funded the legal costs so far from the normal monthly income of the AOA, Gardner decided that money that might or might not be required some years into the future had to be raised right now. He called another EGM to be held in April where the membership would have to vote on swingeing fee increases and also be given the opportunity to vote again on his 'offer'.

Since the crux of his argument was now money, some of us had been making approaches in various quarters to seek alternative sources of funding and had had some success. I wrote to the committee to inform them that we had secured alternative funding that might help to allay their fears. I asked for a postponement of the EGM and the setting up of an independent panel to reassess the financial situation. Instead of taking it as a positive initiative, Gardner put it about that I hadn't actually sourced any funding and it was just a 'hollow delaying tactic'. As the EGM approached, at the beginning of April 2005, I sent the following newsletter to *The 49ers* to summarise the situation:

Gentlemen,

As the April EGM approaches, we find ourselves in a situation that none of us could have envisioned 12 months ago. For the last 44 months we have pursued our dual goals of fair and equitable treatment for the group of us that were victimised by the management of Cathay Pacific and to ensure that such treatment cannot be meted out to any of our colleagues again. Throughout that time we have had the support of our colleagues in our fight. One of the key weapons that we have employed in that fight is use of the legal process. The road has been hard with our opponents using every means available to them to prevaricate and delay their appearance on the witness stand where they will be required to justify their actions. Despite that, we have remained together as a cohesive group and the end is now in sight.

In Australia, a firm trial date has been set which is now only 11 months away. Between now and then, there is an extensive and definitive timetable that has been set by the court that must be met by our opponents. A significant date is 8 April 2005 by which time the defendants must file their defence on both the substantive and jurisdictional issues. This is the first time that they will be compelled to reveal their justification for the treatment to which they have subjected us. Our lawyers in Australia tell us that we have a very good chance of prevailing there. The remedies available to us under law are also the most favourable in that jurisdiction. The cost estimate from our lawyers for this part of the process is AU$550,000 with $250,000 being the cost of the preparatory process to the end of November and $300,000 for the hearing itself scheduled for four weeks commencing on 6 March 2006.

In the UK, we are awaiting the judgment from the Court of Appeal. This judgment will set precedent and form case law. **If we are successful, it will mean that all Veta employees based in the UK will enjoy the protection of UK employment legislation**. The only further avenue of appeal is to the highest court in the land, the House of Lords. The cost estimate from our lawyers is that a further appeal to the Lords would cost £45,000 to £60,000 depending on how many barristers we employ.

Until recently, this process has been managed by your Legal Liaison Team (LLT) working in conjunction with the General Committee of our Association and our legal advisers. This process worked well for three years.

Towards the end of last year, the President entered into negotiations with a view to finding a resolution to the situation. Some of our group did not wish him to pursue such a path at that time and informed him accordingly. Prior to entering negotiations, he agreed certain objectives namely:

1. To ensure that Cathay Pacific pilots can never again be put in the position in which we have found ourselves.

2. To ensure full reinstatement and proper compensation for *49ers* who are qualified and wish to return to work for CX and to ensure proper compensation for those who are not now qualified or do not wish to return to work for CX.

These were communicated to you in a newsletter dated 14 October 2004. Nothing further was then heard until the announcement was made of 'the offer' on 16 December. This was accompanied by 'advice' from our various legal representatives by way of answers to certain questions that had been posed to them by the General Secretary. This was the first that your LLT had heard of this and took place in deliberate secrecy behind our backs. Subsequent to this, the General Secretary initially refused to disclose the full text of this 'advice' under the cloak of privilege and also attempted to prevent your LLT from obtaining a hard copy of the letter of enquiry. The nature of the questions and the manner in which they were posed resulted in a much more gloomy forecast of the efficacy of our various legal actions than had previously been the case. This was used to support the case for acceptance of 'the offer'.

At a meeting on 17 December, both the President and the General Secretary agreed that 'the offer' failed to meet the two stated objectives that had previously been agreed. In answer to the question, 'What if the membership reject the offer?' the response was received that, '**Then we would continue on our current course with the legal actions. Further, the GC would take such a rejection as a positive direction from the Membership to continue on our current course.**'

Initially, our leadership put us in a position where we were deadlined [sic] and would have to decide on 'the offer' before we knew the result of the vote by the Membership. This was seen by many of us as trying to force us into making a career-threatening decision with incomplete information being made available to us. After considerable lobbying, the order of events was reversed. In a poll conducted by the Association, *The 49ers* voted 41 to 4 against accepting the offer.

In the lead-up to that poll, a number of *49ers* received personal telephone calls in which they were told that they were definitely on the list of those who would be accepted back into CX should they avail themselves of the job application process. At the same time, the spectre of massive financial costs being awarded against us in the event that we should lose was raised. Other spins and sales pitches were used by our leadership in an attempt to persuade us and the Membership into accepting an offer that is wholly inadequate and fails to meet the previously agreed objectives.

In the event, in accordance with the rules of our Association, the resolution to accept 'the offer' failed to be carried by the Membership vote.

In accordance with the undertaking given by the President on 17 December, that should have been the end of the matter. However, our leadership has now decided to take a second bite at the cherry and attempt to use the unlikely prospect of massive costs awards as an excuse to levy greatly increased dues on the Membership.

No proper justification for such increases has been provided. Certain qualified individuals who have analysed the Association's finances are unable to agree with the Committee's assessment. Initially these individuals were denied access to our Association's accounts. Our leadership has decided to depart from a budgeting strategy that has carried us through more than three years and now to budget for a worst case catastrophic scenario as a justification for their latest actions.

They have also stated that the GC could 'probably' be held personally responsible for those costs. At a meeting with our lawyers in Hong Kong with the General Secretary present held at the beginning of March, a question was posed regarding possible liability for costs of our Association, the GC and/or the Membership as a whole. The response was received that, '**It is exceedingly unlikely that either the AOA or individual GC members could be held liable for any costs award made against the plaintiffs**.' This advice was confirmed in writing on 10 March. Thus, the assertion made previously was simply not true.

Much has also been made of the 'paid into court' scenario increasing our costs risk exposure. No such action has been taken by the defendants. Under the terms of 'the offer', each party would bear its own legal costs. In other words, none of our costs to date, other than those already received in Australia, would be recoverable. If we pursue our current course and are successful, then much of these could be recovered irrespective of whether or not an offer is paid into court at a later date.

In an attempt to assist with the potential financial crisis as being painted by our leadership, some *49ers* have been looking for sources outside of our Membership to provide supplementary funding. One such possible avenue was mooted to the GC in a letter dated 10 March. At a membership meeting held on 11 March, before any formal response or enquiry was received to that letter, the President described the initiative as a 'hollow delaying tactic'.

The IFALPA Annual Conference takes place this week. It was intended that a former President of our Association would attend and use the opportunity to lobby other fellow Member Associations for financial assistance should it be required. Our leadership took active steps to have him barred from attending the conference even in the capacity of observer. Why would our leadership do such a thing? If there truly does exist a potential financial crisis, should we not be pursuing every available source for supplementary funding rather than just attempting to tax our own Membership? Why actively thwart others who are trying to provide alternative solutions?

Rather than raise subscriptions, an alternative of placing a cap on the amount of funding assistance supplied by the Membership has been suggested with our own group being responsible for finding any shortfall in requirements from other sources. Apparently, this solution is not considered to be acceptable. Why not?

Also, why the hurry? The unlikely doomsday scenario of losing multiple appeals in multiple jurisdictions that is being painted is just that: unlikely. On the one hand we are being told by our leadership that results from the legal process are too far in the future to bring any immediate pressure to bear on the defendants yet, at the same time, so close that they must be funded now. There exists ample time to investigate other sources of funding should it become necessary. This is all being done with indecent haste but for what reason?

One possible conclusion is that our current leadership is hell bent on railroading through an offer that is wholly unacceptable to the vast majority of our group before the end of its term of tenure. The terms of 'the offer' will effectively preclude any future GC from representing or supporting *The 49ers* in pursuit of our objectives. One can only speculate on the reasons for adopting such a course of action.

The result of this turn of events is that, if we wish to continue to pursue our stated objectives, then we must be prepared to act on our own behalf in spite of the leadership of our Association. Should the Membership vote against the subscription increases proposed at the EGM and vote in favour of accepting 'the offer' at the second time around, then we must be prepared to deal with that situation. To the end, the following actions have been taken.

1. In accordance with the Association Rules, a petition has been presented to the GC to have the EGM postponed in order that a sub-committee can be formed to properly analyse the financial position and construct a realistic business plan and cash flow. The Labour Department has been briefed and is taking an active interest in the situation.

2. A supplementary income stream has been identified from a sponsor in Hong Kong to be used to assist *The 49ers* in their legal costs. This funding would be in the form of a loan repayable in part or in whole only in the event that costs are awarded to us. This fund will be managed and administered by *The 49ers* themselves in conjunction with the sponsor. For business reasons, the sponsor wishes to remain anonymous.

3. An alternative union is being set up in Hong Kong. Initially, its main objective will be to support those *49ers* who wish to continue to pursue our stated objectives. We have received many calls from Members of the AOA who have stated that, should our funding be removed by the current leadership, they will either leave the AOA and/or pay their subscriptions directly to *The 49ers*. This union will not be bound by the terms of 'the offer' which, should it be accepted by our current leadership, would remove the right to legal recourse in the event of contractual dispute and bar the AOA from providing assistance to such members, either financial or otherwise.

4. We will continue to focus on our legal actions with emphasis being placed initially on those in Australia and the UK followed by HKG.

Gentlemen, it is likely that each of us is going to be faced with making a personal decision by the middle of May. I am aware that many of you are reliant on the subsistence provided by our colleagues to keep your heads above water pending a properly negotiated settlement that meets our objectives. Despite claims to be merely wanting to maintain the status quo, the current leadership of our Association has chosen to put that in jeopardy as well as [seeking] a means of coercing you into taking 'the offer'.

We are currently unable to make any commitment on continued subsistence from other sources although it is planned to set up a benevolent fund. However, there is no guaranteed income stream for this purpose that has been identified as yet. What we *can* provide is alternate [sic] legal funding assistance.

Only each of us individually can decide what to do under the current circumstances. For those who wish to continue with our current strategy, the vehicle is in place for you to do so. For those who feel that they can no longer continue down this path, for whatever reasons, then that is your choice.

Bear in mind, however, that if you accept 'the offer' as it stands, you will forfeit all right to any improved offer that is negotiated at a later date. Also, if your sole reason for accepting 'the offer' is to avail yourself of the job application process, be aware that, should you be unsuccessful in that application, all you will receive is a lump sum payment that goes nowhere near addressing the loss that you have suffered. Your reputation will not have been restored and your career prospects will remain poor. In fact it could be argued that they will have been damaged further.

In our current situation, the optimum result that we could hope for at the forthcoming EGM, if it is held as proposed by our current leadership, is that the Membership votes in favour of the subscription increases and against acceptance of 'the offer'. **Even if the Membership votes against the subscription increases then, irrespective of the way in which the resolutions have been worded, if we believe that our current path is the way to go, we should urge the Membership to continue to vote *against* resolution 4, acceptance of 'the offer', and use all available communication channels to urge our colleagues to do so.**

The fact is that 'the offer' does not meet our objectives and is not acceptable to the majority of us. Forty-one of our group have already stated that clearly. Irrespective of the increased pressure that is being applied to our group and the Membership as a whole by our current leadership, that situation has not changed.

John Warham

5 April 2005

Gardner ignored the petition to postpone the EGM and the meeting went ahead as planned on 13 April 2005. In the face of his scare tactics and swingeing increases in fees, the membership voted to accept his miserable 'offer'. That day, Gardner and Findlay became the architects and prosecutors of what many consider to be one of the worst betrayals in modern union history.

24

Rebuilding

'Never give in – never, never, never, never, in nothing great or small, large or petty, never give in except to convictions of honour and good sense.'

Winston Churchill

Gardner might have bullied the membership into accepting his shabby deal, but *The 49ers* weren't going to be such pushovers. With his private meetings and back door deals he'd stirred up a hornets' nest and some of us weren't going to let him get away with it that easily. We were now on a fresh green wicket and there were quite a few fast bowlers demanding to be given the ball off a long run up. He started another campaign phoning round *The 49ers* trying to get them to accept his 'offer'. He let them know in confidence that he had it on good authority that, if they applied for a job, they would definitely be on the list of people who would be accepted. He intimated that even though they would start on the freighters, they would have a command on the passenger fleet within three years. He tried to persuade them that it was great deal and they should just 'give it a go mate'. He also tried to convince them that we didn't know what we were talking about, that we didn't have any funding in place, and that it was all just bluff.

Things didn't quite go according to plan for him, however, and this led to some memorable quotes:

Gardner to Steve Shaw – 'You had better take the deal, Steve; I guarantee you will never have your day in court.'

335

Steve Shaw to Gardner – 'Go fuck yourself, Murray.'

George Crofts' wife to her spouse – 'If you take that deal, you'll never have sex with me again.'

In a draft message from Brian Keene to Gardner on the subject of *The 49ers* repaying AOA loans, Brian didn't hold back on his incredulity at the latter's temerity:

How dare you? You broker an admittedly crap deal and then plan to pick my pocket for almost 30 per cent of a lousy ten months' salary? How dare you?

My wife and family have suffered enough don't you think? Paying back a loan to the very union that horribly let us down? How dare you? What the fuck is 30 grand to you anyway? Six weeks pay? You could write a cheque for that! How dare you? How fucking dare you???

This employment offer of yours is bad enough and by the way I would appreciate it if you stop calling it re-employment, it's anything but that. That job is open to anyone off the street and I can't afford to take it. Then you come after me for a few bucks because you think I owe it, that is reprehensible, how dare you? You want me to lose my home to refill union coffers?? Are you fucking nuts?

Give your fucking head a shake for Christ's sake!! How fucking dare you????

My wife and I are on the verge of losing everything every month and it's been that way for over three years waiting for the big resolution. Now you come to us with this piece of shit and then have the nerve to take money from me????? How fucking dare you????

Trust me pal, if you and I were in the same room right now you would be in a lot of pain.

One of the most enlightening exchanges took place between Gardner and Findlay and Becky Kwan, the chairwoman of the Flight Attendants Union. A group of pilots headed by Nigel Demery was incensed with the AOA's abandonment of *The 49ers* and set up an alternative union, the Cathay Pilots Union (CPU), with the prime objective of continuing to raise funds to support *The 49ers'* legal cases. The CPU was registered with the Registrar of Trade Unions on 1 May 2005 and needed some temporary banking facilities. Becky and the FAU agreed to provide these. Findlay was livid and telephoned her. During their conversation, Becky told him,

'Your members are selfish and balls-less. If the AOA won't help *The 49ers*, the FAU can and will.'

Gardner was most put out by this. He wrote a letter to the FAU dated 9 May 2005, which can only be described as Clemmowesque in its arrogance and pomposity. He even used Clemmow's phraseology, describing the CPU as 'a breakaway group of disgruntled members of the AOA' and saying that Nigel Demery '. . . was specifically not selected by the Membership of this Association in any representative capacity', presumably a reference to the fact that he was elected as president unopposed. He went on to say that, 'I find your remarks offensive and impertinent; they are not at all what I would expect from a fellow union leader.' Now where had we heard that sort of language before? He finished off by informing Becky that all forms of cooperation between the AOA and the FAU were 'suspended with immediate effect' and requesting 'an opportunity for my General Secretary to address the FAU EXCO [Executive Committee] as soon as possible in order to try to repair the damage that has been done'.

Becky wrote back to him and described his letter as '. . . high-handed, colonial and grossly inappropriate'. She also informed him that, 'We are of the opinion that your small Hitlerian [sic] rhetoric is a failed attempt at managerial posturing.'

Maybe Becky had hit the nail on the head. Why was Gardner so incensed about the new union, the CPU? He even went so far as to bring in new rules in the AOA that prohibited the Cathay pilots from being members of both unions at the same time and supporting *The 49ers* who chose to continue their fight for justice. Why would he want to do that? Why would he try to shut down all forms of funding for their legal cases? One theory stood head and shoulders above the others. If he had done a dirty deal with Turnbull to make the legal cases go away and deliver the *The 49ers* trussed up like chickens in return for a position in management, that would explain his actions.

It wouldn't be the first time that a pilot had used a position in the AOA as a stepping stone to management. I myself had been approached by emissaries during my time as president promising me that I could be a Senior Check & Training Captain in no time if I stood down from the AOA. I didn't take their 30 pieces of silver but maybe Gardner had. The circumstantial evidence all fitted. He'd been off the roster for more than a year on office duties and spent a lot of his time rubbing shoulders with those people. Even one of the secretaries was reported to have said, 'Oh yes, Murray Gardner, he's one of the management team.' From personal experience, we all knew that he was very ambitious and saw himself as DFO material.

Whatever the truth of the matter, if he did do a deal he failed, and failed spectacularly, to deliver on his side of the bargain. The Swires are not tolerant of failure. Whilst his erstwhile colleague on my General Committee and former squadron mate Phil Elliott is now the B777 fleet manager, Gardner remains on the line on a base in North America. If he had management aspirations, they have not been fulfilled and those of us who were so badly let down by him can take comfort from that fact.

The last time I saw Gardner was Christmas 2006. I was in Pacific Place shopping mall buying some Christmas presents. I was going down an escalator and he was coming up in the opposite direction. He was carrying a cup of coffee and saw me on his way up. He went bright red and looked away. They were long escalators and crossed in the middle. As we neared each other, he kept his back turned and refused to acknowledge me. He didn't even have the common courtesy to say hello or wish me Merry Christmas. Now where had I received that kind of treatment before? Oh yes, Peter Sutch just before he left Hong Kong for good.

In the meantime, things were not going all our way. The rhetoric and threats had taken their toll. We had 41 men who had indicated that they would not accept 'the offer'. We had hoped to maintain that level of support but it was not to be. It was important to us to maintain at least one plaintiff in each jurisdiction. That way we could keep our cases alive and use the overseas ones to gather more evidence and conflicting statements to be used in our Hong Kong case. The actions in Australia and the UK were much further advanced. We had a specific court date for the trial in Australia and a fixed timetable laid down for pre-trial procedures albeit that the actual court date was still over a year away. The Court of Appeal in the Strand in London had heard our case on 15 March and we were awaiting its judgment. We were very optimistic of a good result. After all the time and effort we had expended, it would be a crying shame if our overseas cases went begging for lack of plaintiffs.

We needn't have worried about London. George Crofts was one of the plaintiffs on the action and his wife's threat regarding future conjugal relations should he take 'the offer' was enough to keep him on the team. Here, clearly, was a man who did have balls and he wanted to keep them. It was a close run thing though. George was the only plaintiff in the UK to stay the course. The rest of them rolled and took the deal.

We thought we were going to be OK in Australia as well. We had two 'hard men' down there who we thought we could rely on to continue the action. Unfortunately we had reckoned without Drew Searle. After all his work with me on the General Committee, on my negotiating team and on the legal team itself, we thought he was safe. In the first week of May I started getting phone calls from him arguing why he should take 'the offer'. Despite my best efforts to persuade him otherwise, he did a 180 and pulled out. This was a serious blow to the confidence of the other *49ers* in Australia and I started getting phone calls from them as well. It seemed that Searle wasn't content just to roll himself and keep quiet about it; he had to call everyone else down there to explain his reasons and persuade them of his logic.

We still had one more hope, Dave Spong. He had been a stalwart all the way along the road and we thought he would stay with us. It wasn't to be. The supposed threat of massive legal fees in the event that we failed caused him to have second thoughts. He wanted to know details of where the money was coming from but I couldn't give him the reassurance he sought because of a confidentiality clause with the sponsor. Failing that, he wanted us to deposit AU$500,000 in an escrow account as proof of funding. We couldn't do that either. The funding wasn't a lump sum. It was a cash flow on an as needed basis. I argued that, in the past, he had never required the AOA to do such a thing so why should he insist on this now? It wasn't enough to give him the confidence he needed. He pulled out and accepted 'the offer'. With the loss of Dave, we lost all of our Australia-based plaintiffs and the case there was at an end. It was a bitter blow.

I got many other phone calls during the first two weeks of May as the deadline to accept 'the offer' approached. These were coming in at all hours of the day and night and some of them were very harrowing. I had men's wives calling me up crying their hearts out down the phone and asking what they should do. I had some very poignant conversations with Greg England's mother Terry and his younger brother Brad. It was heart-wrenching. Once more I felt the terrible burden of leadership and the black dog came to visit me on more than a few nights. In the end, everyone had to make their own decision. I couldn't make it for them no matter how much advice or opinion I gave. I was under immense pressure and, eventually, I had to crystallise the debate and hand it back to *The 49ers*.

Ken Carver called me one night and said, 'The AOA is saying that you haven't got the funding for the legals and you're saying that you have. You can't or won't give us details of where the money's coming from and I don't know what to do.'

My response was simple. 'Well, Ken, one of us is telling the truth and one of us is lying. You decide which is which.' He did. He stayed with the team.

In the end when the dust had settled, out of the original *49ers* there were 18 of us who kept the faith and remained standing. I had hoped for more but, given the odds that we had faced, it wasn't a bad result. At least it wasn't a rout. George Crofts summed it up when he said to me, 'Well now it's just the 18 hard bastards.' He was right. It also made my job a lot easier. It's much simpler to lead a small team of hard men than a large group with doubters undermining their colleagues' resolve. At least now I knew that each and every man on the team could be relied upon to stand his ground and support his brothers.

That was when I came up with a new name for our group. The Band of Brothers. Some of our chaps thought I was referring to the TV series about the 101st Airborne. With his classical education, Quentin corrected their misapprehension and pointed out that it came from Henry V's address to his army before the Battle of Agincourt on 25 October 1415. A bit of posturing perhaps but we needed a new flag to rally round. The roll of honour of the Band of Brothers is listed at the end of this chapter.

Neither then nor today have I felt any malice towards those who succumbed to the pressure and accepted 'the offer'. Each man had to make a decision based on his own personal and family circumstances. As with everything in life there was risk involved and each person had to make his own assessment. Yes, time has shown that had they stayed the course, many would have been much better off than they were from accepting 'the offer'. Of the 19 people who applied for new jobs, only 12 were accepted. I know that some of them were bitterly disappointed to be rejected but that's what happens when you trust people who have a track record of lying and vindictive behaviour. And then again, hindsight is a marvellous thing. I was saddened at what Drew Searle did though. His U-turn was instrumental in bringing our action to an end in Australia. We had previously worked closely together and had been friends. I cannot say that is the case now. Another casualty of war.

We got on with the rebuilding process. We sacked Haldanes, and Becky Kwan introduced us to a new firm of solicitors, Chiu, Szeto & Cheng, and their senior partner Benedict Chiu. He recommended new counsel, Clive Grossman and Kam Cheung. Priscilla Leung also came on board the team.

Clive Stephen Grossman QC, SC, FCI, ARB was born in London in 1940 and lived in Rhodesia from 1947 to 1983. He graduated and obtained his BA/LLB from the University of Cape Town in 1966 and was a member of the Rhodesian, later Zimbabwean, Bar from 1967 to 1983. In August 1983, he joined the Legal Department in Hong Kong where he attained the rank of Deputy Director of Public Prosecutions and Head of the Commercial Crime Unit. In 1993 he 'took silk' and, in 1994, left the Legal Department for private practice. He is the general editor of *Archbold Hong Kong*, an authoritative criminal law reference book and one of the most frequently cited texts in the criminal court. He is also a fellow of the Chartered Institute of Arbitrators, an accredited mediator, an executive member of the International Criminal Bar Association, a World Court listed counsel and former vice chairman of the Hong Kong Bar Association. He is also an honorary lecturer of Law at the University of Hong Kong.

Dr Hon Priscilla Leung Mei-fun, as well as holding the position of associate professor at the City University of Hong Kong School of Law, is an elected member of the Legislative Council of Hong Kong representing the geographical constituency of Kowloon West. She is also a highly respected arbitrator and labour advocate. Her inclusion in our team brought a political aspect to our case that would throw into focus the lack of labour protection legislation in Hong Kong.

One of the first things that our new team of advisers asked was, 'Why on earth haven't you filed an action for defamation?'

When we explained the previous advice we'd received it was quickly dismissed and we amended the action in Hong Kong to add a claim for defamation. That immediately upped the ante and got over the problem of the poor financial remedies available in Hong Kong for the other two causes of action.

On 19 May 2005, the Court of Appeal in the UK handed down its judgment on George Crofts' case. By a majority verdict of two to one they ruled in our favour, the dissenting voice being Lord Phillips, the Master of the Rolls. We were also awarded costs. Predictably the opposition lodged an appeal against the judgment but permission to appeal initially was denied them. After further petitioning to the House of Lords permission to appeal was granted and the case was set down to be heard on 14 and 15 November 2005. We were going to the highest court in the land and very happy we were about it too. Now we'd see who was lying and who was telling the truth.

The Band of Brothers

Campbell Richard Blakeney-Williams
Kenneth Gordon Carver
George Andrew Crofts
John Wallace Dickie
Terry England for Gregory Stephen England
Michael John Fitz-Costa
Douglas Gage
Quentin James Lee Heron
Brian David Keene
Pierre Joseph Roger Morissette
Damon Neich-Buckley
Mathew David Rogers
Michael Steven Shaw
Christopher Leo Sweeney
Hendrik Van Keulen
John Simpson Warham
Brett Alexander Wilson
Craig Michael Young

'*This story shall the good man teach his son;*
And Crispin Crispian shall ne'er go by,
From this day to the ending of the world,
But we in it shall be remembered;
We few, we happy few, we band of brothers;
For he to-day that sheds his blood with me
Shall be my brother; be he ne'er so vile
This day shall gentle his condition:
And gentlemen in England, now a-bed
Shall think themselves accurs'd they were not
here,
And hold their manhoods cheap whiles any
speaks
That fought with us upon Saint Crispin's day.'

William Shakespeare – *King Henry V*

25

Here Comes the Sun

> *'Remember that the darkest hour of all, is the hour before day.'*
> Samuel Lover, *Songs and Ballads*

The Sunday before we were due to appear before the House of Lords was Remembrance Sunday. I went to Westminster Abbey and placed a cross of remembrance in the grounds with my Uncle Arthur's name and squadron number on it. It was the first time that anyone from my family had done that and it was a very moving moment. Although I stood alone, I felt that Arthur and my father were there with me. Our case started the following day and was held in Committee Room 1 in the Palace of Westminster, just across the road from the Abbey. The appeal committee consisted of the following five Law Lords: Lord Hoffman (chairman); Lord Woolf (recently retired Lord Chief Justice, the highest judge in the land); Lord Rodger of Earlsferry; Lord Walker of Gestingthorpe; and Baroness Hale of Richmond.

Two other cases were to be heard at the same time as ours because the issues raised therein were similar in nature to our own, although the factual matrix and construction were distinctly dissimilar.

The first of these cases was *Serco v Lawson*. In this case, Mr Lawson was an employee of Serco Ltd. working in Ascension Island on a contract on behalf of the UK government and he was suing Serco for unfair dismissal. Serco had been awarded a number of UK government contracts as part of Tony Blair's policy to contract out what were previously government undertakings to the private sector.

The second of these cases was *Botham v Ministry of Defence* (MoD).

343

Mr Botham was an employee of the MoD working in Germany on a government contract and was also claiming that he was unfairly dismissed.

Whilst there were similarities in these cases to our own, there were also significant differences in that:

1. Messrs Lawson and Botham were based wholly overseas in the course of their employment but were employed by UK entities that have their main place of business in the UK.

2. The Veta *49ers* were based in the UK working for an overseas-based company that has a place of business in the UK. They were also on wholly civilian contracts.

3. Mr Botham was employed by the UK government and, as such, might be subject to different contractual entitlements than those enjoyed in the private sector.

4. Mr Lawson, although also working on a government contract, was actually employed by a private contractor, i.e. Serco.

5. Messrs Lawson and Botham had originally been awarded a ruling in their favour by the Employment Tribunal but this was overturned by the Employment Appeal Tribunal. Therefore it was the employees that had lodged the appeal in the House of Lords rather than the employer as in our case.

Each of the appellants and respondents were represented by their various barristers and each of them made their submissions to their Lordships, making six submissions in all. The batting order was that the appellants went first in the order of Lawson, Botham and Veta followed by Serco, MoD (represented by the Foreign & Commonwealth Office) and ourselves. The appellants were then afforded a short right of reply. This order of play was seen as favourable to us because, whilst the issue at law was the same in all the cases, i.e. the applicability of the Employment Relations Act to peripatetic employees, it served to throw in marked relief the differences between the three cases.

All parties had previously made extensive written submissions to their Lordships prior to the actual hearing and the purpose of the oral submissions was to allow the barristers to expand on those arguments and afford their Lordships the opportunity to question the various representatives.

The prime objective of the hearing was for their Lordships to pronounce upon how the Employment Rights Act (ERA), as amended by Parliament in 1999, should be interpreted by the courts in circumstances similar to those now before them. This would form case law, set precedent and be used by courts and tribunals to decide how they should deal with such cases in the future. It was, therefore, very significant. Whilst we had already set such precedent by the judgment we had received in the Court of Appeal, the current hearing would serve either to confirm or overturn that precedent.

Rather than being an 'adversarial' process as such, the hearing was more in the form of a debate between counsel and their Lordships as to the consequences of interpreting the applicability of the ERA in various circumstances.

It was clear from the outset that their Lordships had a very firm grasp of the issues involved and cut straight to the heart of the matter. They brooked no bullshit, which put the counsel for Veta at a distinct disadvantage since his case was mainly composed of the same. Whilst all of the barristers had to field questions from the panel during the course of their submissions, our own included, the barrister representing Veta came in for some particularly probing bowling.

Lord Woolf especially noted that, surely, if a company such as Veta was to benefit from the significant financial savings that it made by basing its employees in the UK, should it not then also be subject to the downside (from its point of view) that those employees be afforded the protection of the ERA?

In response to this, counsel for Veta continued to bang on about Veta being a Hong Kong company, that management control was exercised from Hong Kong, etc. Lord Hoffman intervened to point out that Veta is a wholly owned subsidiary of Cathay Pacific, is merely a service company and that Cathay is ultimately owned and controlled by the Swires in London.

After further banging on from counsel, Baroness Hale intervened to liken Veta to a 'brass plate' company based in the Cayman Islands set up purely to attempt to get round UK employment protection and health and safety legislation. Clearly she had been reading her *Private Eye*.

Further debate then ensued and when it was pointed out that Veta does not have any management structure and only employs pilots, the question was directed, 'Well what actually is the purpose of Veta?' Counsel for Veta was forced to concede that it exists solely to supply pilots to Cathay at its overseas bases. This was all quite entertaining and engendered some most amusing exchanges as counsel for Veta tried to waffle his way out of his predicament. Their Lordships were having none of it and their rapiers flashed in the sunlight that streamed in through the leaded windows.

We came out of the hearing very pleased with the overall conduct. As always our counsel, David Griffiths-Jones, was both eloquent and erudite and his manner of delivery served to keep the court attentive and entertained when deliberating on what were some very dry points of jurisprudence.

His style contrasted markedly with the lumpen plodding of Veta's counsel.

The Law Lords handed down their verdict on 26 January 2006 under [2006] UKHL3. They found unanimously in favour of the employees in each of the three cases, ruled that the UK courts had jurisdiction and that the employees were entitled to protection under the Employment Rights Act 1999. They also awarded us full costs. It was a massive victory for us and an ignominious defeat for our opponents. With all their money, power and influence, they had lost and lost big time. In his judgment, Lord Hoffman also remarked upon Lord Phillips of Worth Matravers' findings in the Court of Appeal when he stated:

> Like the majority in the Court of Appeal, I think that Lord Denning's approach in *Todd v British Midland Airways Ltd* points the way to the answer in *Crofts v Veta Ltd* . . . employees of a foreign airline can also be based in Great Britain and in my opinion this was the situation of Mr Crofts. Unless, like Lord Phillips of Worth Matravers MR, one regards airline pilots as the flying Dutchmen of labour law, condemned to fly without any jurisdiction in which they can seek redress, I think there is no sensible alternative to asking where they are based. And the same is true of other peripatetic employees.

This was a very significant point. It meant that the precedent did not just apply to airline pilots as in George's case. It applies to any employee of an overseas registered company who is based in the UK. It closed down the 'brass plate' option. By taking the case to the House of Lords, the Swires had opened up a huge can of worms with repercussions that would affect many other companies worldwide who were also using the 'Super Wheeze' scenario to avoid their responsibilities to their UK-based employees. *Crofts v Veta* became precedent and is now widely quoted.

Private Eye had been following our case in the UK. It had published a report on the judgment from the Court of Appeal and now did a follow up on the House of Lords' judgment. This *Private Eye* piece was to have far reaching consequences.

George's case was remitted back to the Employment Tribunal for a hearing on the factual matrix of the case and dates were fixed for 25 and 26 July 2006 under case number 2304383/2001. Barley had retired from the position of DFO in January 2003 and Rhodes had taken his place, although Barley still held the post of chairman of the Board Safety Review Committee. It was a shame as it meant that he would not now be appearing as a witness at the ET hearing and dropping some more clangers. Here we were five years on from our dismissals back in the same tribunal that we had started out from. The situation was very different this time around though. This time the court was going to hear the facts of what they had done to us.

Before the hearing, the opposition conceded two of the three legs of our case. Firstly, that George's dismissal was unfair and secondly, that they had failed to give written reasons for his dismissal. They did not concede, however, that they had acted in breach of contract. This was significant because it reflected directly on our proceedings in Hong Kong. They held that, irrespective of the fact that the Disciplinary and Grievance Procedures were expressly included in the contract of employment, they had an overriding right to be able to dismiss an employee under the terms of Clause 34.3 of the Veta contract, which dealt with period of notice. We held that they did not have such a right.

Ron Davies appeared as their main witness with George and me as witnesses for our side. Davies' witness statement and his testimony were very revealing. He was forced to give more details of the conduct of the 'Star Chamber' meeting that was held to decide on which pilots to dismiss. He said that they had reviewed the employment records of all of the more than 1,700 pilots in Cathay during a meeting that lasted two days. Unfortunately though, no written records or minutes of the meeting were kept so it was impossible to verify the truth of what went on. Presumably we'd just have to take Davies' word for it and trust him to tell the truth. After all, he was under oath so he couldn't possibly be lying could he? Under cross-examination he spent most of his time trying to avoid answering the questions. In particular, when repeatedly asked who had instructed him to take part in the 'Star Chamber' meeting, he replied that it was 'Cathay management' but was unable to remember the names of anyone in that organisation who had given him specific direction.

From the evidence presented, it became obvious that the only person at that meeting who had proposed George for dismissal was Davies himself. Despite Davies' attempts to try to spin things to the contrary, none of George's superiors in Cathay's freighter division with whom he had direct contact in the day-to-day completion of his duties had been at the meeting. Indeed, subsequent approaches by George's managers to try to have the decision reversed were either rebuffed or simply ignored completely by Davies. It seems that Davies had a personal grudge against George and had used the opportunity to get rid of him. As the cross-examination proceeded, Davies' responses became almost 'Clintonesque' in nature. He did not actually resort to debating the meaning of the word 'is', but when asked how they had managed supposedly to '. . . consider in depth. . .' the contents of more than 1,700 personal files in the space of only two days, the best he could muster in response was that '. . . they were very long days'.

There were some law students in attendance at the hearing. Towards the end of Davies' testimony, they could be heard chuckling aloud at his responses. The following excerpts from a contemporaneous note of the hearing demonstrate Davies' slipperiness.

Q. Is it correct that you never expected to be judged under UK law?

A. Yes.

Q. I want to focus on some of the aspects of the CoS D&GP [Disciplinary and Grievance Procedure]. Under General Principles it mentions the principles of natural justice and common sense should be followed. Did those standards not apply?

A. The Company decided they didn't apply.

Q. Did you take the view that these principles went out of the window?

A. Circumstances, events occurred that Cathay decided they didn't apply in these circumstances but normally apply to Officers otherwise.

Q. I don't mean the Company, what about you?

A. I applied the instructions given to me by the Company. We terminated 49 Officers' employment.

Q. Were you under instruction that the D&GP didn't apply?

A. I followed instructions. I was instructed not to follow the D&GP.

Q. Who gave you those instructions?

A. The management of CPA.

Q. Who in management?

A. Nobody in particular. It was specified in the review meeting.

Q. You mentioned the dismissals were not deemed to be disciplinary dismissals.

A. The terminations were to be carried out in accordance with Para 34.3 of Veta CoS. That's the premise the Company were applying.

Q. Did you think it might be Disciplinary?

A. No I did not.

Q. Looking at the D&GP, there are different levels of Disciplinary action leading up to dismissal. In Para 8.5 b) 'dismissal after appropriate notice'; in c) 'not normally dismissed for the first offence', e.g. gross misconduct. And then examples of gross misconduct, e.g. viii) 'conduct considered given by the Company to be prejudicial to its interests'. How did these apply to Mr Crofts?

A. Statements in D&GP were considered not applicable. Didn't need to consider D&GP.

Q. I'm asking a factual question. You were judging Mr Crofts to be guilty of conduct prejudicial to the Company's best interests.

A. Not acting in the Company's best interests.

Q. Isn't that prejudicial?

A. I'm not sure I know how to answer that question. The reasons given are not in D&GP and there was no need to refer to them. My interpretation is they didn't refer.

Q. To be clear, you said 'Not acting in the Company's best interests'.

A. That's what I said.

Q. All this resulted from Industrial Action by the union?

A. That's what's in my statement, as a result of industrial action.

Q. So if there had been no Industrial Action then none of this would have happened?

A. If everything in Cathay was perfect there would be no need for a review team.

Q. So the Review Team was convened as a consequence of industrial action?

A. Yes indeed.

Q. You have described Mr Crofts as prickly and difficult.

A. That's true.

Q. You mention you had one or two heated discussions with him, remonstrating with him to show more consideration for other members of staff. Do you recall these occasions?

A. I recall some occasions, I was contacted by staff, Mr Crofts was over-zealous. I saw Mr Crofts later and had a discussion on what went wrong with a view to resolving the matter. It was not successful.

Q. You did not regard any of these matters of great consequence?

A. I was concerned and I had to attempt to resolve them.

Q. None of these incidents received any formal process?

A. D&GP – no.

Q. Did you make any record, note or correspondence?

A. I haven't written to Mr Crofts. No I didn't. They were verbal exchanges. I hoped to resolve the issues.

Q   So there was no correspondence – not even a note on his file in case of repetition?

A.   True.

Q.   We know there were two incidents recorded on file. [193 last para] 'no further action will be taken. D&G will be considered in the event of repetition'. Did you see that?

A.   That may be my signature. I probably would have seen it.

Q.   Was there any subsequent reoccurrence later than November 2000?

A.   The incidents I had with Mr Crofts were not singularly of great importance. My memory cannot say the dates.

Q.   [194] culminated with the decision at [200] 'matter considered to be closed'. These two incidents are the only two adverse comments on Mr Crofts' file?

A.   True.

Q.   By contrast, there are several letters of commendation – eight or nine?

A.   True. The letters shown in the bundle were issued to all pilots whose lives were disrupted. They were generally issued for flying aeroplanes and resuming schedules, for going the extra mile.

Q.   Are you aware Mr Reynolds protested his dismissal?

A.   I was not aware of that.

Q.   Did you know that Mr Keddie, Reynolds and Dyball all protested his dismissal?

A.   I have been told that's what happened.

Q.   The Review Team. Who was responsible for initiating that?

A.   I don't know.

Q.   Who was the senior person?

A.   The DFO – Captain Barley.

Q.   Had he received instructions as to what should happen re the D&GP?

A.   Yes.

Q.   Was the whole team under that instruction?

A.   I assume yes.

Q.   There was nobody but you from Cathay Freighters on that team?

A.   I can't remember the names. There were 20. I would have been surprised if they weren't. My memory fails me.

Q.   You state that there was a comprehensive review of the employment histories of each aircrew officer. Was it just CPA and Veta?

A. It was all pilots, not just CPA and Veta.

Q. Presumably you had all the personnel and training files?

A. We had information drawn from those two documents. The files were available.

Q. Were files on the desk?

A. Not on the desk as there were 1,700 pilots employed by the Group. The procedure was that each individual name was considered from the Aircrew Seniority List. Where there was concern we referred to the document drawn from the files.

Q. All this was done over two days?

A. Yes.

Q. That's not much time for each individual is it?

A. They were long days.

Q. 1,700 people reviewed. If one assumes ten hours per day that's still less than one minute per person.

A. Even if the maths are correct, we went through the names. If there was a comment then we held a discussion. No comment meant no discussion.

Q. It seems the only comment was from you.

A. I mentioned Mr Crofts' behaviour and suggested he should be considered. The review team would be able to draw down info about commendations.

Q. There was no one else there from Cathay Freighters?

A. I can't confirm or deny that.

Q. This was a comprehensive review?

A. Yes.

Q. Was it only union members?

A. Every single pilot was reviewed. I had no way of knowing who was a union member.

Q. But Cathay knew who were union members didn't they?

A. The airline did not know who were AOA members. Either an individual declared himself or admin knew the AOA dues were deducted.

Q. On any view, you cast aspersions on Mr Crofts' conduct at the Review didn't you?

A. Yes. The occasions concerned ground staff working for Cathay. I didn't bring specifics onto his file.

Q. At the Review, was anybody interested in specifics?

A. I suggested he should be considered for termination as not acting in Cathay's best interests.

Q. Who would have known him?

A. Management pilots.

Q. Who?

A. I don't know if those were there.

Q. In your Para 41 you say that there was no dissent from anyone else in the room some of whom would have known Mr Crofts. Who?

A. I don't have a list.

Q. You don't have a clue if anyone knew him?

A. There should have been someone.

Q. Were there documents, notes or minutes that we could refer to?

A. Not that I'm aware of.

Q. 1,700 names – how did anyone remember? You said it was a long day one and you finished after another long day.

A. Captain Barley chaired the meeting and confirmed the recommendations.

Q. Nobody was taking any notes?

A. Not that I can recollect.

Q. The intention was to target members of the union wasn't it?

A. It was a review of all Cathay pilots. I didn't know the union members.

Q. The ASL pilots were not subject to review?

A. No.

Q. Are ASL pilots union members?

A. I don't know.

Q. Why were ASL pilots excluded?

A. I don't know.

Q. Were all those pilots terminated union members?

A. I don't know although I believe one was not.

Q. Was Mr Crofts on leave from the announcement of industrial action until his dismissal?

A. I don't know. I cannot remember.

Q. The theme of Cathay publicity at the time was to castigate those terminated wasn't it?

A. There was a lot of publicity on both sides.

Q. The Cathay publicity would not help would it?

A. The press statements of Cathay were to explain rather than to victimise.

Q. It did not help, they were castigated as causing trouble weren't they?

A. The publicity was not specific, the identities were not known.
   <much loud merriment from the public gallery>
Q. Oh come on, Mr Davies, are you seriously suggesting that Singapore Airlines does not know?
A. Most certainly.

So they were sticking with the story that they reviewed the personal files of 1,700 pilots during a meeting that lasted two days, but they didn't keep records, they simply remembered the names of the 49 pilots selected even though Davies couldn't actually remember the names of the 20 or so people who were at the meeting. It was remarkable that he could remember several interactions with George so vividly but yet was unable to recall who instructed him to completely disregard the Disciplinary and Grievance Procedure. And, of course, they didn't know which pilots were union members. Yeah, right! Davies was to be found out later for what he was when one of the other people who was present at the 'Star Chamber' meeting came forward and not only told the truth but also had a copy of the agenda used at the meeting.

When George took the stand, he was subjected to 90 minutes of cross-examination by Veta's counsel that was aggressive and hostile in tone. It focused mainly on the fact that George had very few financial records to support his claims of loss. He had been forced to sell or abandon many of his personal possessions when he had moved from the UK back to Australia because he was broke and could only afford one shipping container. This included disposing of a lot of paperwork. Throughout the whole of this tirade, George acquitted himself extremely well. Veta's counsel kept trying to goad George into becoming annoyed in an attempt to demonstrate to the tribunal that he was, as Davies had stated, '. . . a prickly person . . .' He was unsuccessful and his approach backfired on him.

One of the remedies we were asking for from the tribunal was an order for reinstatement. Counsel suggested that this would be to the detriment of George's daughter's education since he would have to now 'drag her halfway across the world from Australia back to the UK'. George replied that he was fortunate that both his wife and daughter had supported him wholeheartedly throughout the five years of trials and tribulations he had been forced to endure and would continue to do so. This brought sympathetic nods from the panel and showed counsel, as in the rest of his defence, to be clutching at straws.

The ET handed down its judgment on 16 October 2006. It found in favour of George on all counts and awarded him £70,291 in damages.

The tribunal did not accept Veta's defence that they could simply dismiss George under the terms of Clause 34.3 of the Veta CoS. Rather they were compelled by UK legislation to provide written reasons for dismissal. This was very significant. It meant that for UK-based pilots at least, 34.3 would now be effectively null and void in cases of this nature. Cathay and its subsidiaries would no longer be able to subject its UK-based pilots to its 'fire at will' management policy. One of our prime objectives all along had been to ensure that what happened to *The 49ers* could never again happen to another Cathay pilot. In the UK at least we had achieved that objective.

In its judgment, the tribunal also made comment on George's refusal to accept 'the offer'. The opposition had tried to make much of this as a means of showing that he was 'difficult' and could have settled much earlier without wasting the court's time. It stated:

> We heard much evidence in relation to the settlement offer and were invited to draw the inference that the Claimant was not keen to be reinstated because he did not accept it. The Claimant was entitled to decline the settlement offer. It did not guarantee re-employment, any such re-employment would be at first officer level . . . was on a reduced salary and did not acknowledge unfair dismissal.

In other words, they agreed with us. 'The offer' was entirely insubstantial. Immediately upon receipt of the ET's verdict, George filed an action for defamation in Hong Kong.

Shortly afterwards, on 24 October 2006, Phil Walker, who was now GMA, put out the following notice to crew:

The Crofts case and consequences for UK-based crew

As many of you will be aware, the UK Employment Tribunal recently handed down its judgment in the Crofts case (see DFO Update 20 October 2006). This case has been proceeding through the courts since 2001 and during this time has generated press interest both in Hong Kong and the UK.

As a result of an article on the Crofts case published in the UK satirical magazine *Private Eye* late last year, the UK HM Revenue and Customs (HMRC) launched an expatriate employer review of Veta. HMRC has concluded that Veta (and any other CX subsidiary companies basing employees in the UK) is required to operate a PAYE system. This conclusion is contrary to the advice that the

Company has received from both its financial and legal advisors since early 1992.

The Company is now actively working with its UK advisors to assess the implications of the HMRC review. While further legal advice is being sought, it is possible that in the near future the Company may need to establish a PAYE system.

Indeed they did have to start paying PAYE and other costs of employment such as National Insurance. HMRC didn't just investigate Cathay's operations with respect to the pilots, it looked at other employees as well. Reliable sources reported that it claimed £125 million in back taxes and £40 million in penalties from the company. Cathay came to a settlement with HMRC in 2008 but refused to divulge the terms of that settlement. At the Cathay AGM in 2008, and again in 2009, I attended as a shareholder and asked for details of the terms to be publicised as the shareholders had a right to know how much money had been wasted by management's actions. The board refused to disclose the terms at either meeting and, in a written reply from the chairman of Cathay, Christopher Pratt, in 2009 in response to a further formal enquiry, he again refused to disclose the terms of the settlement. Given that settlement in such cases is usually reached at around 66 per cent of the amount claimed, it probably cost around £110 million. Now why would they want to hide that from the shareholders? Perhaps because it wiped out all of the savings made by basings and opened our company up to greatly increased costs for all of our overseas-based employees in the future. And all because management insisted on pursuing its course of action regarding *The 49ers* and the union bust. Surely someone's head would have to roll over that one?

In January 2005, David Turnbull had been promoted to chairman of Cathay Pacific succeeding James Hughes-Hallett who went back to London at the end of 2004 to take up the position of chairman of John Swire & Sons. On 25 November 2005, after only 11 months in the job, it was reported that Turnbull had decided to step down as chairman of Cathay and take up a position as the non-executive chairman of HAECO with effect from January 2006 as he 'had decided that he wanted to resume a more active operational role'. As one report put it, 'Swire's public statement, issued late yesterday afternoon, offered no statement of thanks for Mr Turnbull's 11 month tenure at the top. Executives close to the group who are in regular contact with senior management said they had no inkling of his imminent departure.' Turnbull subsequently resigned the position of non-executive chairman of HAECO with effect from 9

August 2006. It ended a 30-year career with the Swire Group. With responsibility comes accountability.

In March 2006 Turnbull joined Australia's Allco Finance Group, a privately owned investment bank based in Sydney, as an executive director. Also on the Allco board was his old mate Rod Eddington. In late 2006 a group called Airline Partners Australia, consisting of a consortium involving Macquarie Bank, Allco and others, made a highly leveraged takeover bid for Qantas. Under the terms of the deal three Allco directors, including Eddington and Turnbull, were poised to take seats on the Qantas board. The deal fell through after a shareholder revolt that resulted in the Qantas chairman, Margaret Jackson, not standing for re-election when her term expired. By 2008 Allco was in serious financial trouble and went into administration in November with debts of more than AU$650 million leaving its shareholders cleaned out and, like Ansett seven years earlier, its employees looking at the dole queue.

26

Smoking Gun

'The mighty words of the proud are paid in full with mighty blows of fate, and at long last those blows will teach us wisdom.'
Sophocles, *Antigone*

On 30 January 2008 the Cathay B777 fleet manager, Captain Ian Wilkinson, got airborne from Boeing Field, Seattle in a brand new B777-300 on its delivery flight to Hong Kong. On board was a party of VIPs including Christopher Pratt, the chairman of Cathay, on the flight deck. After takeoff, Wilkinson flew round the circuit and performed a low level flyby over the runway before setting course for Hong Kong. It wasn't the first time this had happened on delivery flights. Some onlookers videoed the manoeuvre and posted the results of their efforts on YouTube. It generated a lot of publicity and discussion on the Internet, and the Cathay PR team swung into action announcing that an investigation was now taking place. From that moment on Ian was toast. If they had just dismissed it along the lines of, 'Yes, impressive wasn't it, our pilots are very well trained', it would have quickly become yesterday's news. Instead, with the usual foot-in-the-mouth approach, they turned it into a media frenzy. There is no doubt that the flyby was VFL, the aircraft crossing the runway at 28 feet by some estimates, but the video shows the approach to be stable and well executed. In any event, whatever view one may hold on the safety or otherwise of the manoeuvre, the inquiry resulted in Wilkinson being fired. In the words of a company spokesman, 'The pilot in command of the flight was dismissed as he had neither sought nor obtained the necessary company approval to undertake such a flyby.'

357

When it was revealed in the press that Pratt had been on the flight deck during the manoeuvre, a Cathay spokeswoman managed to put the other boot in her mouth when she stated that, 'The chairman is not an aviator and was purely there in a ceremonial role.'

So the chairman of the company knows nothing about aviation then. We had long suspected that about the DFO but to have it confirmed about the chairman as well was somewhat disconcerting. Wilkinson went through the two stages of appeal as provided for in the Disciplinary and Grievance Procedure and his dismissal was confirmed.

I had known Ian for a long time as he was a Hamster, had joined Cathay at about the same time as me and got his first command on the TriStar around the same time as I got promoted on the B747. Having been sacked myself, I knew what he would be going through so I got in touch with him to see whether I could be of any help. We had lunch at Dan Ryan's Chicago Grill in Ocean Terminal on 5 May 2008 together with his wife Dim. We talked about the similarities between his treatment by Cathay and that of *The 49ers*. Like with us, his employment was terminated abruptly and Cathay's actions caused him maximum inconvenience and disruption. He was fired via a telephone call to his home without the courtesy of inviting him into the office.

Cathay reported to the Inland Revenue Department that he was leaving Hong Kong resulting in a tax demand for immediate payment. His taxable income had been misreported resulting in a higher than necessary tax bill. His Cathay ID card was immediately cancelled so that he could not gain access to the building without prior permission and under escort. When he tried to gain access to his office to retrieve personal belongings it was made as difficult as possible and the person who eventually allowed him in was later given a dressing down by Sten Kroutil, the personnel & industrial manager, for leaving him in his office alone.

Ian was also having difficulty extricating himself from his rental lease as the Cathay housing department had conducted the negotiations and neglected to put a break clause in the lease with the result that he might be liable for up to two years' rental if he vacated his apartment before the lease expired. Just like *The 49ers*, the guillotine came down and he was summarily excluded from the life he had known for more than 30 years. He was going through exactly the same kind of emotional turmoil that we had all suffered and was having similar reactions. We discussed these at some length together with coping strategies, methods of stress alleviation and the importance of familial support in such circumstances.

Ian related the circumstances of his two appeal procedures. The first was chaired by Rhodes and lasted over an hour. The second was chaired by Tyler and lasted less than ten minutes. As Ian put it, Tyler had already made his decision before he had even listened to the advocacy.

Our discussion then turned to *The 49ers* and the conduct of the 'Star Chamber' meeting. We knew that Ian had taken part in the meeting and he confirmed that he had, albeit reluctantly. He revealed that he had been telephoned at home by Barley and told to report to the office. One of the intended members of the meeting had reported sick so Ian was summoned to replace him. Barley briefed him outside the door, told him that nothing that took place inside the room was to leave the room and he was then plunged into the meeting. He was not allowed home and was made to stay the night in Cathay City. He was incredulous to find out what he was part of as he had only been promoted to a management position a couple of weeks previously. During our conversation, Ian confirmed that they did not go through all 1,700 pilots' personal files as claimed. Instead, they had a prepared 'hit list' agenda and only the pilots on this list were considered. As our luncheon came to an end, we were standing adjacent to the lavatories and Dim went to go inside. Ian grasped my hand strongly as we were shaking hands to say goodbye, pulled me to one side out of earshot of his wife and said, 'I can tell you how you were sacked. At the meeting Rhodes said, "You can have Warham or you can have Demery but you can't have them both".'

Ian had related earlier how Barley had personal animosity towards me because of the circumstances surrounding the grounding of the A330 during its introduction and the AOA's response to that situation. So Barley picked me. Ian told me something else as well. When we stood up to the victimisation and bullying and filed our legal cases around the world with me as one of the leaders of the legal team, Rhodes subsequently said to him, 'When I said you can have Warham or Demery, we picked the wrong one.'

It was confirmation of exactly what we knew all along. They picked union members deliberately to intimidate everyone else. The only logical reason for Rhodes' 'Warham or Demery' remark was that, if they had sacked us both, it would have shown beyond doubt that they were targeting the union leadership. Ian had one more revelation for me. He said, 'I've got the original document. I shoved it down the back of my trousers when I left the meeting.'

I was speechless. Throughout all the legal proceedings, we had made repeated requests to discover any and all documents or records relating to the 'Star Chamber' meeting. They had responded to all our requests by saying that 'no records were ever kept', 'no such documents exist or ever existed' and similar assertions. In an affidavit sworn under oath by Rhodes before the Hong Kong court on 21 June 2007, he stated that:

> On behalf of the Defendants and as a member of the review team (in my then capacity as General Manager Aircrew), I confirm the Defendants have never produced any documents such as agendas, circulars, memoranda, notices, notes, minutes or a transcript **for and/or during** the review meeting.

Ian confirmed that Rhodes had handed the hit list to him when he entered the room. It caught Rhodes out in a lie made under oath. He had perjured himself. Ian subsequently gave me a copy of the hit list and then the original document, which we entered into evidence in our case in Hong Kong. It also caught out Davies in a lie in his evidence to the Employment Tribunal in the UK. They had not undertaken an in-depth review of all 1,700 pilots' records in the 'Star Chamber' meeting as he had testified. There were no personal files in the room and neither were they all consulted. Instead they just had a hit list with a total of 184 names on it. By sheer coincidence, my name was number 180 on the list and I was the last person to be selected for dismissal.

The Cathay PR department helpfully came to our aid. The hit list got into the public domain and, in an article in the *South China Morning Post* on 8 October 2008, a Cathay spokeswoman 'confirmed the list was believed to be genuine'. We had found the smoking gun and they admitted it. A copy of the hit list is included in Appendix 4 to this book. Ian provided me with an explanation of the columns and his hand-written notations on the list. The column codes are:

Letter on file – this refers to whether or not the pilot had any disciplinary letters recorded on his personal file.

Attnd Ltr 1 – this refers to the first 'attendance letters' that were sent to pilots under the 'Sickness Punishment Programme'.

Attnd Ltr 2 – this refers to the second attendance letters that were sent to pilots under the same programme.

No rep to Ltr 2 – this column is marked with an X if the pilot had failed to reply to Attnd Ltr 2.

Attnd Ltr 3 – the third letter in the Sickness Punishment Programme.

No rep to Ltr 3 – failure to respond to Attnd Ltr 3.

No AEP – once every 12 months, pilots were required to undergo Annual Emergency Procedures training (AEP). This was a one-day training course to do with emergency equipment stored aboard the aircraft such as fire extinguishers, dinghies, etc. and their location and use. It had become practice for participants in AEP courses to be invited to lunch by members of management. Such luncheons were used by management representatives to push the company position on matters that were under dispute with the AOA. These lunches were advertised as voluntary and, because of their nature, some pilots declined the invitation. If a pilot decided not to accept the invitation, then he earned an X in this column.

High RSV bk-off – this refers to pilots who were considered to be reporting unfit for reserve duty 'too much'.

Notice bk-off – this refers to pilots who were considered to have reported unfit for duty 'at short notice'.

Control Assist – this refers to whether or not crew control considered the pilot to be 'helpful' or not. If you were considered 'unhelpful' you received an X in this column.

Total – the total number of Xs that each pilot had 'earned' according to these criteria.

The notes can be interpreted as follows:

The *A & B* note on the left-hand side denotes Airbus or Boeing, i.e. which fleet the pilot was on.

The *Crew Control List* note on the third page is a list of pilots who did not make it onto the original list of 184 because they had not 'earned' sufficient Xs. These additional pilots were nominated for dismissal by Hoyland and Davies. According to Ian, these were people for whom Hoyland and Davies had a particular disliking.

The tabulated notes are attempts to classify the selected pilots by rank and fleet, i.e. Captain, First Officer, Airbus and Boeing.

The hit list revealed further lies. The only documents the opposition had 'discovered' (or disclosed) to us during the litigation process were copies of our personal files They maintained that these were the only documents that were ever considered during the selection process. Of the information on the hit list, only that detailed in the first six columns after the Total was recorded on the personal files. The data held in the last four columns was not. Therefore, they must have consulted information in documents other than the personal files but had not disclosed these in contravention of the court's directions during discovery.

A further examination of the records revealed that, of the 184 names plus the Hoyland/Davies eleven, only eight were non-union members at that time and, of these, only one was selected for dismissal: the wrong Wong. It is statistically untenable to suggest that such odds are a consequence of chance rather than a deliberate correlation to union membership. This further supported our statistical analysis and proved beyond doubt that this was a union bust.

According to their 'non-union' argument, in my own case I had been selected for dismissal because I didn't go to a supposedly voluntary AEP lunch and Crew Control considered me to be 'unhelpful'. I had no letters on my personal file nor any letters issued under the Sickness Punishment Programme. The only reason I didn't go to the AEP lunch was because I had spent so much time sitting across the negotiating table from Rhodes listening to his bullshit that I didn't need to listen to him regurgitate it all again over lunch. As for being unhelpful to Crew Control, if they meant that I refused to undertake duties that were in breach of the AFTLS regulations, pointed out their potentially dangerous mistakes and filed air safety reports as required by their own regulations, then yes, *mea culpa*. Apart from anything else, if they weren't targeting AOA General Committee members and negotiators, why didn't they just pick the top 49 pilots on the hit list who had earned the most Xs? Why did they go all the way down to 180 to get me?

We also knew now who had been present at the 'Star Chamber' meeting because Rhodes had been forced to give us a list of the participants under a discovery request. Their names are listed at the end of this chapter.

As an aside, during one of our meetings Ian reminded me of an exchange that had taken place between us back in 1985 when we both joined Cathay. We had been given some company freebies and, as he was walking to the Cathay building one morning to attend ground school, apparently I came up behind him and said, 'Bloody hell, Ian. Cathay bag, Cathay umbrella, Cathay jacket. Have you got Cathay tattooed on your arse as well?'

If he had, he'd need some laser surgery now.

Ian's new evidence left the opposition with further problems. In their statements made in the various jurisdictions, they had told different stories depending on which cause of action they were trying to defend.

In a letter dated 24 July 2001, Barley stated that my dismissal '. . . was not as a result of any particular offence'. He used this approach to attempt to justify the fact that they had not used the Disciplinary and Grievance Procedure before dismissing us. Of course, had we committed a disciplinary offence and been sacked without implementing the DGP, that would constitute a breach of contract, one of the legs of our case. He repeated this in another letter dated 13 August 2001, when he stated that my dismissal '. . . was neither as the result of any particular offence nor was it in violation of the Conditions of Service, and that for those reasons the Disciplinary and Grievance Procedures do not apply'.

Unfortunately, in a letter dated 14 August 2001, Bob Nipperess, the employee services manager, wrote to the partners of two of *The 49ers* denying them staff spouse travel benefits stating that '. . . the rules of the travel policy states that an employee who has been terminated for misconduct is not entitled to travel benefits . . .'

This seemed to be at odds with Barley's position. We were either dismissed for misconduct or we weren't. Which was it? The situation was even more confusing when a Cathay spokesman in a CNN report dated 10 July 2001 insisted that '. . . the sackings had nothing to do with the labor [sic] action, that they would have happened anyway because of an examination of the pilots' records.' Let's just be clear here. It was nothing to do with the union action. OK, got that. And it was nothing to do with misconduct, so the DGP didn't apply, but it was to do with an examination of our records that showed we weren't acting in the best interests of the company. But wouldn't that be misconduct? It got even more confusing. In a statement made on 7 November 2001 in the US case, they stated that:

> . . . the nine plaintiffs in this case are part of a group of 51 pilots terminated by CPA . . . in July 2001 as a result of and in response to industrial action by the pilots' union . . . All nine plaintiffs were terminated in the context of a long-standing dispute in Hong Kong between CPA, Veta . . . and the . . . union.
>
> As a consequence of this CPA, Veta and Basings undertook an assessment of all their aircrew . . . and resulted in the identification by them of 51 pilots for termination because they were not working in the interests of CPA . . . The dispute at the core of this lawsuit revolves around the HKAOA's industrial action and CPA's response to it.

So, in the US we were sacked because of our involvement in the union but in Hong Kong it was nothing to do with the union and it wasn't misconduct either, it would have happened anyway but we can't have our staff travel because staff who have been dismissed for misconduct aren't entitled. But Davies said in the UK that if there had been no industrial action there would have been no need to convene the 'Star Chamber' so isn't that to do with the union again? Yes, but not in Hong Kong. I see, well what about the redundancy argument that they tried to field in Australia? Let's not even go there. And what about Ian Wilkinson's new evidence; where does that fit in with all these different stories? I'm getting very confused now, probably even more confused than Barley was with my rostering practices table last time we were in the Labour Department with Mrs Siu. I've got a good idea. Let's go to court in Hong Kong and see whether the judge can work out who is telling the truth and who is telling a lot of big fat porky pies.

The Star Chamber

Captain Kenneth Roland Barley – Director Flight Operations
Nicholas Peter Rhodes – General Manager Aircrew
Captain Richard Fry – General Manager Flying
Captain Jeff Turner – General Manager Operations
Captain Philip Walker – Manager Flying (Airbus)
Captain Andrew David Maddox – Manager Flying (Boeing)
Captain Gary Sampson – Manager Training (Airbus)
Captain Henry Craig – Manager Training (Boeing)
Captain Richard John Hall – Chief Pilot (Airbus)
Captain John McCormick – Chief Pilot (Boeing)
Captain Roger Marin – Deputy Chief Pilot (Airbus)
Captain Ian Rodwell
Captain Ian Wilkinson
Patrick Cavanagh – Crew Personnel Manager (Airbus)
Denly Hau Ho Ki – Crew Personnel Manager (Boeing)
Zdenek Kroutil – Industrial Relations Manager Flight Crew
Ronald Benjamin Davies – Manager Basing Companies
Christopher Hoyland – Manager Integrated Crew Management
Dennis Leung Wai Hung – ICM Scheduling Manager

27

Trial 1

'The day may dawn when fair play, love for one's fellow men, respect for justice and freedom, will enable tormented generations to march forth triumphant from the hideous epoch in which we have to dwell. Meanwhile, never flinch, never weary, never despair.'

Winston Churchill

In Hong Kong they had tried every form of bastardry, malarkey, shenanigans and DPGFD in the book to stay out of court. One thing they couldn't contest though was jurisdiction. Instead, they pursued Turnbull's tactic and tried to run us out of money. We joined all the plaintiffs who had originally filed overseas actions to the Hong Kong action. Cathay had to agree to this because, if they didn't, we'd be able to get the stay lifted on the case in the US on the basis that those men couldn't get justice in the Hong Kong courts because our opponents wouldn't agree to them filing here. They were forced to concede the point unless they wanted to reopen the can of worms in California. But they had a comeback.

They applied for an order for security of costs for the plaintiffs who were no longer resident in Hong Kong, citing as their reason that it might be difficult to recover said costs in the event that our actions were unsuccessful. This is a mechanism often used by large companies that are being sued by smaller companies with few assets and is intended to deter vexatious litigation. It is less commonly awarded in personal cases. We argued that they had never asked for security for costs previously when the AOA was lending us the money to fund the cases, so why should they be granted an order now? We also argued that the defendants had made a payment into court in respect of potential damages in both the EO S21B and breach of contract legs of our case. This payment into court was another 'run us out of money' tactic.

If a party makes a payment into court prior to a case being heard, it puts the other party at risk of losing their costs even if they win the case because, in the event that the damages awarded are lower than the 'payment in', they will be held liable for not only their own costs, but also those of their opponent. It is a common tactic used to try to pressure the other party into settling out of court. Had we not had our defamation claim in place as well, it might have caused us pause for thought. As it was, we were confident that the defamation damages would be far in excess of their payment in. There is one other point about payments into court. They are only usually made by parties that are not confident of their chances of success. For this reason, the judge hearing a case is not permitted to know that a party has made such a payment. If it comes into his (or her) knowledge, then they must recuse themselves from hearing the case.

Their first application for security for costs was heard on 10 October 2006. They asked for HK$560,000 per head in respect of four plaintiffs, a total of $2.24 million. Instead, the Master who heard the application made an order for $180,000 per head, a total of $720,000. We paid it. They tried some more financial loading. Instead of agreeing to costs in the cause, which would mean that all costs would be reckoned at the end of the case, they asked for an order for costs for the application, which meant that we would have to pay them straightaway. They were successful and it cost us another HK$75,000. We paid it. They made another application for security for costs in March 2009 after we had joined the remaining overseas plaintiffs. The court made an order for a further HK$1.2 million. We paid it. So we now had HK$1.92 million sitting in court as security for costs but their tactic failed. They had not run us out of money. It gave us confirmation of what we already knew. They thought that, with all their money, they could overpower us. They were wrong. If anyone needed proof that my funding arguments back in 2005 were not just bluff, well now they had it.

They tried another tactic. It had previously been agreed that the trial in Hong Kong would take place in two stages. The first stage would be determination of the substantive issues, i.e. whether or not they had acted in breach of contract, whether or not they had acted in breach of S21B and whether or not they had defamed us. Once those issues were determined, a second stage of the trial would take place to determine the quantum of damages. The idea behind this was to bring the action to court more quickly and save time and cost, because if we were unsuccessful, the quantum hearing would not be needed. They changed position and demanded that the substantive issues and quantum be heard together. They also requested that we should forgo our right to trial by jury and have the case heard by judge, 'in order to expedite matters'. We were somewhat bemused by their second request. If they thought it would delay things while we argued the toss, they were wrong. Given the very technical nature of some of the issues, we much preferred to have our case heard by a judge who would be able to grasp those issues rather than a panel of lay people who might not be quite so capable. Also, given that we were never going to win a PR war, again we would much rather have the damages assessed by a judge who would not be subject to prejudice against us. We agreed with their proposals and, from the tone of their letter we received in reply, it seemed we had rather taken the wind out of their sails.

They tried to delay things further by making numerous requests for discovery with our additional action for defamation. They also threatened that they were going to make an application to have substantial parts of my various witness statements struck out as being, in their view, 'irrelevant'. They were trying to litigate by letter and so keep the case out of court. We weren't falling for that one.

By consolidating the cases and joining the liability and quantum issues, they had shot themselves in the foot. In long and complicated cases there is an avenue available for either party to apply to have a trial judge assigned to the case. The advantage of this is that, once the trial judge is appointed, he will hear all interrogatory applications and oversee the progress of the proceedings. If any party tries to delay the proceedings or acts unreasonably, the trial judge will restrain it from doing so by making an order. Also, even if the judge were to grant an order to strike out parts of my witness statements, he would at least have to have read them first and would thereby gain an overall impression of the case, even though the struck out portions would be disregarded in coming to final judgment. We suggested to the opposition that we should apply to have a trial judge assigned to the case in March 2008. They didn't like it much and tried to raise objections because of incomplete discovery and other outstanding interrogatory matters. We went ahead anyway and there was nothing they could do to stop us.

On 7 July 2008, the Honourable Mr Justice William Duncan Stone was assigned as the trial judge to our case. It was almost seven years to the day since we had been sacked. Like the 'mills of God', the legal wheels also grind slowly. Shortly afterwards we were informed that the judge had removed himself from the case because he was well acquainted with one of the key witnesses and the Honourable Mr Justice Anselmo Francisco Trinidad Reyes had been assigned in his stead.

Mr Justice Reyes was born in 1959 in Manila. He obtained his BA (Law), LLM and PhD (Law) from Cambridge University, England in 1982, 1983 and 1987 respectively. He was called to the Bar in England (Inner Temple) in 1985 and the Bar in Hong Kong in 1986. He was admitted as advocate and solicitor of the Supreme Court of Singapore in 1995 and was appointed as senior counsel in 2001. He was a Law lecturer at the University of Hong Kong from 1986 to 1988 and went into private practice in 1989. He was appointed by the Hong Kong Judiciary as deputy judge of the court of first instance of the High Court in 2002. He has a reputation as a very shrewd judge and extremely hard working. As one commentator put it to me, 'He is very robust in court and never allows any rubbish.' We were very pleased with his appointment.

On 5 August 2008 a preliminary hearing was held before Judge Reyes and he set a date of 8 September for a directions hearing where all the outstanding interlocutory matters would be dealt with. We also made it known that we would be applying for a trial date to be set at that hearing. The hearing on the 8th proved to be an interesting couple of hours in court and set the scene for the way in which the judge would deal with the case in the future. As my commentator had said, he didn't put up with any rubbish. The opposition fielded Mr Hunsworth, a solicitor with JSM. We went in with Kam and Benedict. Mr Hunsworth made five submissions.

Firstly, that a direction be given to amend the pleadings after the consolidation of the overseas plaintiffs' cases. He wanted them to be more 'user friendly' so that the plaintiffs would be identified by name rather than Plaintiff 1, Plaintiff 2, etc. He also requested that the pleadings themselves be amended to 'clarify' the various causes of action. The judge declined the request. He opined that there was no need for such amendments as he believed that he had the intellectual capacity to deal with the pleadings as they stood and that, as the trial progressed, the names of the plaintiffs would become familiar to him, in his words, 'like old friends'.

Secondly, that the plaintiffs provide further discovery of documents within 14 days. We readily agreed to this and the judge seemed pleasantly surprised with our inferred efficiency. Actually, we already had the documents ready in anticipation of their delaying tactics and could have handed them over right then and there.

Thirdly, that their summons to strike out part of my witness statements be scheduled with a hearing time of one day. The judge opined that one day was far too long a time for such a relatively simple matter to be dealt with and that, rather, two hours of his time would suffice. He ordered that this be scheduled as soon as possible. When Mr Hunsworth pointed out that their lead counsel was quite busy and might not be available at such short notice, Judge Reyes asked whether or not they had a follower or junior counsel. When he was told that they did, he instructed that he would suffice and that, as he put it, 'any counsel will do'. He was insistent that this hearing be held with as little delay as possible and gave Mr Hunsworth a very old-fashioned look.

Fourthly, that the defendants be given 42 days to file a supplemental witness statement in reply subsequent to the hearing above. Again the judge opined that 42 days seemed to be an inordinate length of time in which to prepare a witness statement and 28 days would be quite sufficient. Another delaying tactic thwarted.

Lastly, that contrary to the plaintiffs' assertion in our submission to the court, 'This consolidated action is nowhere near ready for trial.' Particularly since there was so much discovery still outstanding. In response, the judge did not agree at all with Mr Hunsworth. He saw no reason for the trial to be delayed for lack of discovery since this would merely provide 'fertile ground for counsel during cross-examination'. On the contrary, he was very sympathetic to our submission and ordered that the matter immediately be set down for trial.

There then followed something of a bidding process as to when the actual trial date should be. We were constrained by the judge's diary and he said that the currently available bid was 'as soon as possible after 1 January 2009'. It was something of a reversal for us that, after all the delaying tactics we had seen from our opponents, we ourselves had to submit a bid of 'as soon as possible after 1 April 2009', the reason being that our lead counsel, Clive Grossman, was scheduled to be involved in a lengthy trial in the first quarter of 2009 and would not be available to us. We would either have to change counsel or go to trial without our lead counsel if we were to bid for an earlier date. We had already waited eight years so what was another three months to us? We were going to field our full team.

At the end of the hearing we almost split our sides laughing when Mr Hunsworth thanked the judge for his wisdom in setting the matter down for trial as, in his words, 'We have been waiting for this since 2001.'

It was a good day for us and a bad day for our opponents and there was more where that came from. We achieved all of our objectives at the hearing and the opposition achieved none of theirs. We had reached a major milestone in having the case ordered to be set down for trial. Predictably though, they persisted with their DPGFD. Having stated before Judge Reyes at the hearing on 8 September that they would be ready for trial in early 2009, they then contrarily argued to the listing clerk not three weeks later that they could not secure the services of a barrister until October 2009; a year away. On that basis the listing clerk scheduled the trial to commence on the 5th of that month. It was just more of the same. In response we arranged for a short hearing before Judge Reyes on 13 November to express our concerns to him that our opponents were deliberately trying to delay proceedings further and to ask him to order that the trial date be brought forward as a matter of priority. Unfortunately we were unsuccessful because the trial was scheduled to last six weeks and, if we didn't take the date as already set, there was a chance that we would lose that date as well. He understood our concerns though and was sympathetic. Oh well, October 2009 it was.

He gave one other direction that was interesting. He ordered that there would be a pre-trial determination hearing to decide whether or not our opponents had the right to dismiss us on three months' notice in accordance with Clause 35.3 of the CoS but with complete disregard for the DGP as they held in their defence, or whether they were constrained from doing so by that DGP as we held. Both sides were to submit draft questions to the court to form the basis of this pre-trial determination. It was an interesting development since, if the court ruled in our favour, it virtually blew their defence out of the water on the breach of contract leg. To date, they had been relying on winning this part of the argument virtually to the exclusion of all else. We had let them continue down that road and led them to believe that breach of contract was our main point of attack. Far from it. They were in big trouble with the S21B leg of the case because, under this cause of action, the burden of proof lies with the defendant not the plaintiff. This means that the court assumes the plaintiffs *were* dismissed because of their union activities and it is up to the defendants to prove otherwise. To do this they would have to show the court other valid reasons for our dismissals. That dropped them between two stools. In providing such reasons, they could only really argue misconduct, which means that they then fall foul of the breach of contract claim because they failed to invoke the DGP. It was a circular argument they couldn't win. On top of that, they had failed to file any defence whatsoever to our defamation claims. Events were overtaking them and the next hearing before Judge Reyes on 4 December 2008 revealed that they might finally have woken up to their predicament. There were three matters to be dealt with.

The first was the hearing of the pre-trial determination questions. The judge set a time of one day for the hearing and ordered that it be scheduled as soon as possible. Both parties had submitted two questions for determination. Of course, both sets of questions were skewed to get the result that each party wanted. Mr Adrian Huggins SC, appearing as counsel for the opposition tried very hard to have the hearing limited to determination of their two questions only and pressed the judge quite strongly on this point. Judge Reyes was having none of it and ruled that he would consider all four questions in his determination.

The second matter was the application to strike out all witness statements relating to the hit list. Four days prior to the hearing, our opponents had filed a surprise summons to strike out my second supplementary witness statement and that of Ian Wilkinson, both of which dealt with the revelations about the hit list. We proposed that, despite the very late timing of their summons, in order to save the court's time we should hear this new summons concurrently. Judge Reyes was very forthright on the matter and informed our opponents that, should they proceed with their application at this hearing, they would fail. After a short debate, the matter was adjourned *sine die*, meaning until some date in the future as yet to be determined. In other words, their attempt to have the hit list evidence excluded from the trial failed.

The third matter at hand was the application to strike parts of my original witness statement and first supplementary witness statement. They wanted to get rid of all the background information in my various witness statements that related to flight safety issues, the Sickness Punishment Programme, the history of AOA/management relations and like matters. Of course they would. They didn't want that sort of information getting into the public arena. Perish the thought that Joe Public should find out what really went on. Submissions were made by both sides at the end of which the judge reserved his decision. However, during the submissions we learned more of our opponents' strategy or, more correctly, their change in strategy. During their submissions, they informed the court that they intended to apply for leave to amend their pleadings to include a defence of 'justification', i.e. they intended to put forward a defence that they had valid reasons for dismissing us and, therefore, were justified in making the defamatory remarks about us in the public arena. This was significant because it was the first time that they had attempted to launch any kind of defence against our defamation claim. Up until now they had studiously avoided the topic.

Of course, their new tactic left them with a number of problems. If they changed their story yet again, given that this would be their fourth or fifth version of the 'facts', it would call into serious question the veracity of their evidence. In addition, if they now contended they had valid reasons for dismissing us, they would fall foul of our breach of contract claim in that, in such circumstances, they should first have invoked the DGP. It also meant that, at trial, they would have to produce evidence of misconduct justifying dismissal by each and every one of us to sustain their defence. That, in itself, should prove to be an interesting exercise in creative writing.

We were also treated to a performance from their counsel, Mr Huggins, in which he attempted to assert that we had never made any pleadings in respect of our S21B claim. Clearly they had woken up to the fact that the burden of proof was upon them to prove that they had not dismissed us for our union activities. Our tactic of seemingly concentrating on the breach of contract issue had worked and drawn them into a contrary defence. Our S21B claim was pleaded in the first instance with the breach of contract claim being argued in the alternative. It had been there for all to see from the outset, hiding in plain view, but they missed its significance.

Judge Reyes handed down his verdict on the motion to strike parts of my witness statements on 10 December. He allowed their application and was very succinct in his ruling. He ruled that some of the information was, in his words, 'irrelevant to the factual issues which [he had] to determine at trial'. It was not what we wanted but we understood and accepted the reasons for his decision. He had at least considered our submissions and must now better appreciate the background to our dismissals. What was more significant in his decision, however, was the following statement in which he neatly crystallised the issues to be determined at trial:

Those factual issues are essentially as follows:
  a) Whether, contrary to Employment Ordinance (Cap. 57) s. 21B(2)(b) and despite its denials, Cathay in fact terminated the Plaintiffs' employment (including that of Mr. Warham) on account of the Plaintiffs' participation in trade union activities.
  b) Whether, despite its denials, Cathay in fact terminated the Plaintiffs' employment on the basis of perceived misconduct on the part of the Plaintiffs.
  c) Whether, around the time when Cathay terminated the Plaintiffs' employment, Cathay was justified in making statements to the effect that the Plaintiffs were:
    i) unprofessional pilots;

  ii) uncaring about Cathay's interests as employer; and,
  iii) bad employees.
 d) Whether the Plaintiffs' have suffered loss and damage (and if
 so what) as a result of any breach by Cathay.

We couldn't have put it better ourselves. This is precisely what we, as
plaintiffs, wanted to have determined by the court. In particular, we liked
the words 'despite its denials'.

As in previous hearings, our opponents asked for costs for the application so that we would be liable to pay their costs immediately. Instead the
judge gave them an *order nisi,* which meant that we would not have to pay
their costs until the end of the main trial itself. He also ruled that, despite
the fact that they fielded both senior and junior counsel, he did not believe
that this was a matter that called for the instruction of two counsel and only
issued a certificate for their junior counsel's costs. Another blow to their
'run us out of money' strategy. Subsequent to that hearing, the pre-trial
hearing date for determination of the preliminary issues was set for 2 March
2009 and scheduled for one day. Finally we were going to get to grips with
some of the substantive issues. This hearing would effectively dispose of
one third of the trial and resolve one leg of the three causes of action.

The hearing took place in Court 19 at the High Court, Queensway. It
started at 10:00 and was adjourned at 11:45 until 16:30 when Justice
Reyes handed down his judgment. It was initially listed as a hearing in
chambers but was changed to an open court hearing. This was significant because the press are precluded from reporting directly on a hearing
in chambers whereas at an open court hearing there are no such restrictions and all documents, evidence and the actual proceedings themselves
become a matter of public record. The press was now taking quite an
interest in our case and we received several enquiries asking for interviews and comment.

The crux of the matter to be decided was, under the terms of the contract
of employment and in the event of dismissal for disciplinary reasons, could
Cathay simply bypass the DGP and give us three months' notice of termination under Clause 35.3? Put another way, could 35.3 be read as a stand-
alone term or was it modified by the DGP provisions in the case of dismissal
for misconduct?

For the purposes of the pre-trial determination, and for this hearing
only, Judge Reyes made the assumption that our dismissals were for
misconduct. As he put it in his judgment, 'I stress that this is merely a
working assumption. It remains an unresolved factual issue whether the
defendants actually had any such underlying motivation.'

The arguments that our opponents put forward in support of their position were interesting to say the least.

First, they argued that they were entitled under the Employment Ordinance and under the contract of employment to give us notice of termination without giving any reasons. This argument failed because this hearing was about breach of the contract, not about their rights under the Employment Ordinance. Their 35.3 argument was unlikely to be successful given the numerous statements both in their pleadings to the court and in the media regarding our purported misconduct. In any case, for the purposes of this determination, it was being assumed that we were dismissed for misconduct so, again, the argument failed.

Then, they put forward a proposition that our dismissals were for no reason whatsoever, i.e. just because they could under 35.3, and that the later statements were after the event and, therefore, did not relate to the condition of the actual dismissals. Whilst this might seem an outlandish proposal, many of their arguments were characterised by such straw grasping. This argument fell foul of the principle of 'improper collateral purpose' in that you cannot use one provision of a contract to bypass another and thereby obtain an advantage.

Then came the 'soft way' and 'hard way' propositions. Under the 'soft way' they could simply dismiss us under 35.3. Under the 'hard way' they would have to go through the DGP but still end up with the same result as, irrespective of the outcome of the DGP, they would then just dismiss us under 35.3 anyway. In effect they were arguing that going through the DGP would just be a waste of time. They then took this argument a step further. In order to shorten the DGP they proposed that they would simply commence the DGP, immediately find that there was no case to answer under the first step of the process, dismiss the charges and then sack us anyway under 35.3.

This particular argument was one of their most repulsive propositions and a damning indictment of the corporate ethos that prevailed in Cathay. In his judgment Judge Reyes characterised this as coming 'close to positing bad faith on the defendants' part'. This is very polite. Put more directly, what they were saying was: it doesn't matter what provisions you put in the contract of employment, we will find a way to get around them, worm out of our responsibilities to our employees and sack them anyway. This total lack of good faith towards its employees stands in stark contrast to the Cathay vision statement that 'We are a socially . . . responsible company'.

It was sickening to listen to them actually proposing this argument as a justification for destroying our careers. Rhodes, Kroutil and Richard

Hall, the GMA, were in the public gallery listening to all this. As Cathay representatives, presumably they endorsed such arguments.

At this stage it became obvious that their arguments were failing and that the DGP *does* modify 35.3 in the case of dismissal for misconduct. There then followed some legal debate on the actual interaction between the DGP and 35.3. Our opponents argued that, had it been the intention that the DGP should modify 35.3 to such an extent that it could not be used in the manner they proposed, then the contract should specifically state this. Justice Reyes opined the opposite view that under the principle of *contra proferentem*, where there is such an ambiguity, the contract should be interpreted in favour of the weaker party and that, if their proposal was to stand, then it would have had to have been specifically stated in the contract that 35.3 could be read in isolation. Their argument also failed.

When Judge Reyes handed down his judgment he ruled that, in the event of dismissal for misconduct, Cathay must first follow the DGP and that, if they do not, they are in breach of contract. We were also awarded 80 per cent of our costs for the hearing including two barristers' fees. The judge then directed that, given his judgment on this issue, both parties should now consider what steps should be taken next to deal with further issues that may be settled before the trial proper with a view to shortening the actual trial. He directed that this should be completed within 14 days ('and I *mean* fourteen days') and be returned to him for further directions.

This was an enormous step forward for us. We had won the second leg of our claim. Despite our opponents' best efforts over the last eight years to stay out of court, we had finally succeeded in forcing them into the ring and they had comprehensively lost the first round. Additionally, the submissions they put forward during the hearing substantially undermined their defence of the other two legs of the case. It was going to be interesting to see which version of 'the truth' they were going to attempt to trot out in subsequent hearings.

They hadn't finished with their underhand tactics just yet though. They waited until the last possible day and filed an appeal against Judge Reyes' judgment on the pre-trial determination. Our advice was that it was wholly without merit, contained no new arguments or evidence, effectively just said that 'the judge was wrong' and was just another attempted delaying tactic designed to increase costs. As one of our team remarked, 'I can't believe that a senior counsel would put his name to such rubbish.' Nevertheless, we had to deal with it and a date for the Court of Appeal hearing was set for 5 December; *after* the main trial was due to commence.

Initially we had hoped to have the appeal heard at an earlier date but this was not possible because of counsels' diaries and available court dates. Our only concern was that our opponents might attempt to use this as an excuse to try to delay the trial proper. We initially thought this might be a possibility but, after proper consideration and analysis, we came to the conclusion that, actually, it would work to our advantage. The logic of our reasoning went as follows:

The defendants had trapped themselves in the arguments supporting the appeal and those to be advanced at the trial.

The only outstanding matter for the appeal on the preliminary issues was DGP. Their arguments were mainly that the plaintiffs had not been dismissed for disciplinary reasons, and even if they had, the defendants were entitled to dismiss them without giving reasons and hence didn't need to invoke the DGP.

At the trial on 5 October, the defendants would have to stick to such arguments pending the appeal in December. That would aggravate the contradictions in their defence: on the one hand, they were alleging that we were not dismissed for disciplinary reasons, yet on the other, they would have to justify their defamatory remarks. If we *had* been unprofessional and had *not* worked in the best interests of the company, how could they say that there were no disciplinary reasons? To act unprofessionally and against the interests of the company must be misconduct liable to disciplinary action. Because of the defence they had filed in their witness statements and affidavits, the submissions their counsel made at the hearing on preliminary issues and the arguments raised in their notice of appeal, they could not change their stance in respect of DGP and discipline. Therefore, they would be bound to contradict themselves at trial when they tried to justify the defamatory remarks.

If, on the other hand, the appeal was heard *before* the trial in October and the Court of Appeal upheld Justice Reyes' decision, they could say at the trial that they now agreed with the decision of the Court of Appeal, and try to minimise the contradictions in their arguments. As it now stood, they were stuck and it was to *our* advantage.

As for any attempts by our opponents to use the appeal as a means to try to delay the trial, we were very confident that any such attempts would be firmly rejected by the judge and recognised for what they would be: DPGFD.

At the next directions hearing before Justice Reyes, our opponents' counsel ventured the view that he did not see how determination of the preliminary issues had really moved the case any further forward, since the crux of the case was the factual matrix of the reasons for dismissal, and until that was determined no real progress could be made. Presumably if he appeared again before the judge to try to delay the main trial pending the outcome of the appeal hearing, he would have to reverse his arguments and contradict himself again.

They had shot themselves in the foot yet again. We had initially thought that, as bipeds, they would only have two shots. It just shows you should never underestimate the enemy!

28

Trial 2

'I pass with relief from the tossing sea of Cause and Theory to the firm ground of Result and Fact.'

Winston Churchill

On 9 July 2009, eight years to the day after our dismissals, I sent out a newsletter to the BoBs titled, 'IT'S ONLY 3 MONTHS TO GO'. Finally, after everything we had been through together, we were going to get our day in court and there was nothing more the opposition could do to stop it happening. I was having a beer with Mike Fitz-Costa shortly after the newsletter went out. We were talking about the CPU website which had a Tiananmen Square style countdown clock of the days, hours, minutes and seconds to go to the start of our court case. I remarked that we'd all come a long way together and that now there were only three months to go. He said to me,

'Yes John, but you've been telling me that it's only three months to go for the last eight years.'

In one way he was, of course, quite right. The Chinese philosopher Lao-tzu said, 'A journey of a thousand miles begins with a single step.' Had we known back in July 2001 where the road that we chose would take us, and how long the journey would be, how many of us would have taken the first step? The fact is though that we did take that first step. We came to many crossroads along the way and all of us sacrificed much that is dear to us in completing the journey. We had island-hopped across the ocean, enduring good weather and bad during our voyage, but we had made it to the other side and left no one behind along the way. I summarised my emotions to the team in the following words:

'Ladies and gentlemen, it has been an honour and a privilege to have you, your families and loved ones as travelling companions along the way. Without each others' help and support as a group I doubt that some of us would have made it this far. When we reach our destination it will be as a complete team. We will have left no one by the wayside and, whatever the results that we achieve, it will not be for the want of trying.'

I could not ask for more.

As a result of the pre-trial determination, the opposition were now in disarray and, yet again, had amended their defence to two strategies.

Their first strategy was that they were now saying that they fired us in July 2001 in accordance with Clause 35.3 but, in their new words, 'without cause'. This abrupt 180 was doomed to fail on at least two counts. Firstly, they were still required to answer the primary leg of our case that they dismissed us for our union activities. It was incumbent upon them to prove that they did not do so and a simple denial would not cut it. They had another problem with this. In April 2009 there had been some changes to court procedures in Hong Kong under the Civil Justice Reforms designed to put a stop to vexatious litigation and time-wasting tactics. One of the provisions of these reforms states that:

'Bare denials will no longer be possible under the new court rules. A party who denies any allegation in the statement of claim or counter-claim will have to (a) state the reasons for the denial; and (b) state any version of events that he wishes to put forward.'

Secondly, of course, their media statements put the lie to their 'without cause' defence.

Their second strategy was to try to mount a justification defence to our defamation claims, i.e. that the statements they made about us were true. Given that, at this point, they had failed to provide any evidence to support such a position, our advice was that their defence could not possibly succeed. However, in mounting their defence, our opponents asked us to particularise, both in content and location, the statements that we say are defamatory. This gave us an ideal opportunity to submit to the court examples of the statements made and the media in which they were reported. A trawl of the Internet garnered a plethora of reports ranging from high profile publications such as the *New York Times* and the *Wall Street Journal* all the way down to regional newspapers such as the *St. Petersburg Times* and the *Kashmir Times*. Prompted by their request, our research also revealed that the Cathay website still had copies, available for reading and download, of the original public statements that they made about us in their press releases back in July 2001.

This amounted to continued and continuing repetition of their original defamatory statements and supported our claim for aggravated, as well as ordinary, damages. We pointed this out to our opponents in our response to their request for particulars and awaited their response with interest. They could either take the reports off their website, which might be interpreted as an admission that they are defamatory, or they could leave them there in which case they ran the risk of increasing aggravated damages. The phrases, 'horns of a dilemma', or more colloquially, 'they're fucked either way', came to mind. Whoops, there goes another foot.

They continued with their bastardry and their next tactic was to try to drown us in paperwork starting with a 72 page tabulated request for further discovery for each Plaintiff in the minutest of detail. There was one final pre-trial review hearing held on 9 September before the trial proper began. This was to deal with administrative matters relating to the conduct of the case and for both parties to bring up any issues that they considered to be outstanding. It lasted 35 minutes. They used it as an opportunity once again to bang on about discovery and how they considered our discovery of various documents to be incomplete. Judge Reyes was having none of it. He told them directly that, should they consider that we had not supplied sufficient documentary evidence then they could make that point during the trial and the court would take it into account accordingly. When they tried to press this further, the judge said that he had already reviewed the very extensive trial bundles that had been submitted to date and there comes a point where you have to say 'enough is enough' and get on with the trial. We agreed. At 18:00 on the night before this hearing, we had received yet another bundle of papers from our opponents amounting to around 250 pages. The main part of this was a further witness statement by Rhodes together with a covering letter stating that he would be their 'main witness' although they would, 'also be providing copies of further witness statements in the near future'.

We were only three weeks away from the start of the trial and they still had not provided us with a witness list. This was in breach of the court procedures and we could have objected and demanded an order that they disclose a full and final witness list. We didn't bother to press the point too hard though. We didn't really care who they called. We could deal with whatever they tried to throw at us and their malarkey just served to cast them in a poor light in front of the judge. He was well aware of what they were up to. If they weren't calling Tyler and Chen, as it appeared from their latest paperwork, their defamation defence was in severe jeopardy since, if the people who made the defamatory statements did not appear in court, they would effectively be offering no defence. Rhodes could not defend their statements, even if he was their main witness, because that would be hearsay and carry little weight. What we did was to ask the judge to rule that any further witness statements should be completed within the next seven days and that our opponents supply us with a witness list also in the same timescale. This he declined to do but said instead that further witness statements may be submitted but that, 'the closer the trial date approached, the greater was the likelihood that he would rule them inadmissible'. So, they'd better get a move on then. Their solicitors must have been burning the midnight oil to produce the amount of paperwork they had over the last four weeks and they didn't come cheap. As one of our team remarked, given that their case was so weak, perhaps they were just taking the opportunity to milk the cow one last time.

The content of Rhodes' latest witness statement is best described by quoting verbatim from an assessment by one of our legal team.

> 'Excellent. Some quick observations for you having perused the opposition's latest. Leopards don't change their spots. 234 pages; impressive. My usual anger when reading this stuff subsided faster than usual . . . this looks very good for us. They're worried about defamation and no surprises with their arguments.
>
> 1. They're still trying to say they could have run 49 DGPs in quick time.
> 2. They're still saying that having run a DGP, successful or not, they would have terminated the Plaintiffs anyway. Shows them for what they are and ignores JR's remark in his ruling of "positing bad faith".
> 3. They try to blame the inability of the Plaintiffs to secure equivalent employment on seniority lists, 9/11, SARS and the 2008 economic tsunami! This is scrabbling around and easily refuted. This stands in contrast to what they testified in the UK and the fact that Cathay has gone from 1500 to over 2600 pilots in the same period.'

Rhodes' statement also went on at some length about what the union was doing at the time and gave background to the dispute between the AOA and management. This was a total 180 from their application to have all of the similar material in my own witness statements struck out as being irrelevant. It re-opened that particular door. I do wish they would make up their minds. I filed a couple of supplementary witness statements by way of reply which reintroduced a lot of the background material that they had had struck out and also included all the Sickness Punishment Programme correspondence by way of an exhibit. Bang went another foot.

Our assessment was that they had finally woken up to the fact that their run us out of money and delaying tactics had failed, they could not now avoid a trial and that they hadn't constructed any kind of tangible defence. They were now faced with scrabbling around at the last minute to try to cobble something together. Now what were we taught in basic training about last minute planning and deviating from the flight plan? The 6P rule.

We weren't without problems ourselves, however, the main one being the logistics of getting all 18 Plaintiffs into Hong Kong at the right time to give evidence. Given that the trial was scheduled to last for six weeks, we couldn't possibly have everyone here for the full time as, disregarding work, family and other commitments, the cost would be prohibitive. We drew up a batting order and our admin team got to work. They did an absolutely outstanding job of coordinating everything especially when, once the trial started, it became obvious very quickly that Judge Reyes was going to live up to his reputation and run the case very efficiently. Instead of taking six weeks, all of the evidence including direct and cross examination of witness from both sides was completed in nine working days. After the first day, when we realised how things were going to be conducted, we had to completely re-jig the travel arrangements and timing of the batting order. Again, our team did a superb job of reorganising things and making sure that the right people were in the right places at the right time. It was an object lesson in man management and one that Cathay crew control could learn a lot from.

At last, after more than eight years of waiting, the morning of 5 October 2009 dawned bright and clear and at 10:00 the court came into session with Honourable Mr Justice Reyes presiding. The public gallery was full to overflowing with our supporters all wearing yellow ribbons. These were a token that we had used back in 2001 when we were first fired. All the pilots wore yellow ribbons on their uniforms when they went to work as a sign of their missing colleagues. Barley didn't like this so, in one of his foot stamps, he issued a NTC that no additional unauthorised regalia should be worn with the uniform. The boys got round that. They got yellow neckbands for the security passes that were required to be worn when in the building. They got yellow nav bags or anything else that they could think of to stick it up Barley's nose. He went as far as to write a petulant letter to one Senior Captain, dated 12 October 2001, in which he stated:

'On 9 October, 2001, a number of women came to Cathay City and carried out what was assumed at the time to be a protest appearance. This assumption was subsequently confirmed through other sources. Your wife was identified as one of the protesters.

In my Notice to Crew dated 28 September, 2001, I pointed out that the wearing of yellow ribbons as a form of protest within Company premises was being interpreted very negatively by other Cathay Pacific staff . . .

. . . The Company therefore believes the activity conducted to be totally inappropriate.'

It was a good job he wasn't in court; he'd have probably burst a blood vessel. But then again, given his past performance on the stand, they wouldn't want to let him anywhere near the place. Rhodes had said in his last witness statement that Barley had now retired and implied that, as a result, he could no longer be called as a witness in the trial. It was the usual half truth and designed to try to suppress contradictory statements made by Barley in two affidavits he had filed in Hong Kong. I filed a witness statement in response to Rhodes' porkies in which I stated:

'Whilst it is true that Captain Barley has retired from the post of Director Flight Operations with CPA, he currently holds the post of Chairman of CPA's Board Safety Review Committee (BSRC). The BSRC is the most senior safety review committee within CPA and includes at least three directors of the Main Board. The position of Chairman of the BSRC is a senior appointment and is made by the Chairman of the CPA Main Board.

The BSRC meets in Hong Kong every six months with the last meeting being held on 13 May 2009 and the next scheduled for November 2009. It should, therefore, present no logistical problem for Captain Barley to appear in court for examination on his affidavits, some parts of which are at considerable variance with the version of events now being related by Mr Rhodes in his Supplemental Witness Statement.'

They carried on with their tactic of trying to suppress all previous statements prior to the final one made by Rhodes dated 7 September 2009. The first part of the morning of the first day of the trial was taken up by Mr Huggins making submissions to try to have my witness statements in response to Rhodes' latest stories excluded from evidence. He also tried to have all previous statements by Barley and others made prior to Rhodes' statement taken out of the trial bundles. He had another go at getting Ian Wilkinson's statement excluded as well. They had twigged to the fact that they had re-opened the door on the Sickness Punishment Programme and the flight safety issues. In Mr Huggins' words, if these documents were not excluded, we would, 'be free to give it to the press, who will then be free, under the cloak of privilege, to publish all kind of wild, scandalous and irrelevant, inadmissible matters'.

Clearly they were rattled. Well they should have thought about that before Rhodes put together his latest pack of porkies at the last moment. Perhaps they thought we wouldn't have the time to respond in kind under the weight of all the other last minute paperwork they were using to try to drown us. If that is what they thought, they were wrong. Bang goes another foot. Unfortunately for them, the judge was against them and he responded:

HIS LORDSHIP: Thank you very much Mr Huggins, I still am against you. I am not persuaded by the submission . . . I think we will proceed in the way we agreed at the pre-trial review. I think it's far too late now to do things wholesale; that would simply delay the substantive trial unnecessarily. That is not to say that I am unsympathetic. People say all sorts of things at trial. That doesn't mean it's a finding of the court; that doesn't make it true; that doesn't mean that it necessarily can be reported, because anyone reporting has to, under the laws of contempt of court, make a fair and accurate account of what has been said, and just because something is said in court doesn't mean that it is true. It has to wait until the court makes certain findings, and the court will only make findings on what it relevant. In terms of guiding your cross-examination, Mr Huggins, you are an experienced counsel who has been in these courts for a long time. I think one can rely on your judgment on the matter; that's what you are paid for by your clients, to make judgments on what is or is not necessary. You are here to assist the court, not take up the court's time under the underlying objectives of the CJR. If I think that something is inadmissible or irrelevant or whatever, and you are embarking on it out of an abundance of caution or whatever, I shall simply say so.

So that was that then. Their plan had backfired. After dealing with some more housekeeping, the trial got under way. I was scheduled to open the batting. I checked my pads to make sure there were no loose straps that might tempt a bad LBW decision, made sure my box was comfy and my inners weren't wrinkled inside my gloves, picked up my Duncan Fearnley Magnum, strode out to the crease, took middle and leg and prepared to face the first delivery.

To say that I was nervous would be an understatement. After more than eight years of preparation and training, the test match was finally on. I needed to get our innings off to a good start and put some runs on the board for the team. If I fucked this up as the team Captain, what would the rest of the order do? OK John, just get the golden duck out of the way, play a straight bat, get your eye in and put a few singles up before you start looking for boundaries. Have a good look around the field and do a bit of gardening. Don't let them see you're nervous. Don't start flashing outside the off stump until your feet are moving and you're comfortable. Leave the wide stuff alone and let the bowler tire himself. I had been through this mental litany so many times when I played cricket but this was different. I was at Headingley now about to open the batting in an Ashes test or, even worse, against Lancashire.

The first ball came down and it was nothing like I was expecting. Not particularly quick, no swing and no movement off the seam. I played a forward defensive stroke and waited for the next one. It was more of the same and continued like that for the next couple of overs. Where the hell was he going with this? What was he trying to achieve? He kept asking me about the content of a lot of AOA newsletters, what was my reaction to them, what I thought they were meant to achieve and did I support the union view and act on them. Of course I supported the . . . whoa just a minute. It's spinning the wrong way. The googly. Adjust quickly and play it off the back foot. What the hell is this? I'm expecting a pace attack with some bouncers and the odd Yorker and he's bowling the wrong 'un at me. I'm expecting Lillie and Thomson and they've brought on Shane Bloody Warne. Now I saw where he was going with his questions. You were a member of the union weren't you? You supported the union didn't you? You acted on the union's instructions didn't you? They were trying to disrupt the operation and you went along with that didn't you? In fact you were a bad employee weren't you, deliberately trying to cause trouble? You couldn't be trusted. You see, just as they've said all along, you weren't acting in the company's best interests. That's why they lost confidence in you and sacked you. You deserved it.

Right, now I had the measure of the bowling and I knew how to play it.

MR HUGGINS: Mr Warham, may I summarise your status and relationship with the union: long-term member since 1986?

A. That's correct.

Q. Member of the general committee in 1995?

A. Correct.

Q. Elected president in 1997 and held that position for two years?

A. That's correct, yes.

Q. And did you support the actions which the union was taking in furtherance of its aims and objectives?

A. I wasn't actually part of that decision-making process at the time, but I was a member and I voted at the union meetings.

Q. So is the answer 'yes'; did you support the actions which the union was taking in furtherance of its aims and objectives, whether or not you were party to the creation of those policies?

A. I voted in favour of the motion, yes.

Q. In particular in relation to both contract compliance and subsequent limited industrial action?

A. Yes, I voted in favour of those motions.

Q. On the subject of contract compliance, in the couple of years prior to the dismissal of the 49ers, did 95 per cent of the union membership vote in favour of a resolution to implement the so-called contract compliance campaign?

A. I can't remember, Mr Huggins. Is it in this bundle here?

Q. Yes. If this bundle of documents, containing such things as the newsletters from the union, says 95 per cent, does that accord with your understanding, your general understanding of the ...

A. If the union newsletter says that, I believe it would be true.

Q. Very good. In addition to the terms of the resolution itself, did the union go on, to use its own words, beyond the motion, by encouraging its members to comply with a number of specific tactics designed to make it more difficult for the management to run the operation of the airline smoothly and effectively?

A. If this is in the union newsletter, then I believe it's true.

Q. Let's just glance at pages 101 and 102. 'Aircrew are not required to be contactable on any other day except reserve days'. Was it your understanding that the union was encouraging its members to make themselves uncontactable as far as the management of the airline was concerned, so that if they needed assistance but it didn't happen to be the member's duty day, they would not be contactable by the airline?

HIS LORDSHIP: When you say 'member's duty day', you mean a reserve day?

MR HUGGINS: Or reserve day.

HIS LORDSHIP: So apart from duty or reserve days, they were being encouraged not to be contactable?

MR HUGGINS: You are absolutely right, my Lord. That's exactly how I should have put it. Do you understand the question?

A. I understand the question, Mr Huggins, the point being this was published in the year 2000. I wasn't at that point a member of the general committee anymore, I was merely the chief negotiator. So whatever the intent of the union was, I can't really comment on that.

Q. Did you understand that you were being encouraged to follow what is set out at page 102?

A. I merely read what the union produced. I don't know what the union were asking me to do. I don't know what the intent of the union was. But I read this and if it says that I'm not required to be contactable on any other date except a reserve day, that was already in my contract of employment anyway.

Q. Mr Warham, let's not fence. You understood, did you not, that the purpose of this document and the contents of it were to identify what should be done in furtherance of the so-called contract compliance campaign, the purpose of which was to pressurise the airline. Do you seriously disagree with that?

A. I was not the author of this. Anybody can read it, Mr Huggins, and put an interpretation on it.

Q. I am asking you your state of mind and what you intended to do and what you did not intend to do yourself.

A. I intended to continue working for the company and carrying out my duties as required by the company.

Q. Did you feel encouraged by the union to take measures to make it more difficult for the airline to contact you directly when you were not either on duty or on a reserve day?

A. I was always contactable when I was required to be contactable, and I was often contactable when I wasn't required to be contactable.

Q. If you can, to help me meet the deadline I have set for myself, try and focus on the question, and if it is capable of a 'yes' or 'no' answer, give it. If it's not, of course, you must elaborate. More specifically, were members encouraged by the union to designate a separate phone line for Cathay Pacific that either would remain unanswered when you were on off-duty or reserve day, or which was connected to an answering machine so you wouldn't have to answer it?

A. That is one interpretation you could put on this document, yes.

Q. Was that your understanding that that was what you were being encouraged to do and members were being encouraged to by the union?

A. That is one interpretation you could put on that, yes.

Q. I am asking you, Mr Warham, what was your understanding?

A. I would say that yes, that was my understanding of it.

Q. It was designed, was it not, and you understood it to be so designed, to make it impossible for the airline to seek assistance from pilots when they weren't on duty or on reserve?

A. No, when you are on reserve day you have to be contactable.

Q. Or not on a reserve day, I'm sorry.
A. So when off duty, to be not contactable.
Q. That is what you were being encouraged to do?
A. That is an interpretation you could put on this, yes.
Q. Do you agree that the contract compliance campaign and the additional measures set out in this document were intended to put pressure on the commercial operations of the airline? Are you able to answer that 'yes' or 'no'?
A. I believe they were intended to put pressure on management to come back to the table to talk about the issues that we needed to resolve.

And so it went on for the next few overs. Right arm leg spin but generally readable. Nothing much in the pitch for him and he started to get a bit frustrated.

Q. 'CONTRACT COMPLIANCE. For avoidance of doubt, management has not made significant progress towards our remuneration and rostering concerns and therefore contract compliance remains in full effect.' Did you understand that to be the union's position?
A. Yes, I did.
Q. So as long as they didn't come back to talk turkey with you over remuneration and rostering, you were going to continue to apply this form of pressure?
A. This was in January 2001. At that point the main focus was the rostering practices which had not been finalised after 1999, and the ongoing negotiations had taken two years.
Q. Mr Warham, what I really am trying to do is get, if possible, a 'yes' or 'no' answer, without going into the history of anything. Is that position set out there a position which you supported and understood?
A. That was the union's position as at January 2001.
Q. And you supported it?
A. I am a member of the union. I voted for that, yes.
Q. So the answer is yes.
A. Yes.
Q. Quite simple. Let's try and keep it that way.

Tetchy. He tried a different line and length with what might happen to AOA members who didn't comply with the resolutions.

Q. Could you go to page 119, under the heading 'Current Misconduct of Members' – misconduct, please note – 'We have three members under investigation for breaches of contract compliance. We also have two members who have been confirmed to have been in breach and have been suspended for a period of 12 months.' Do you see that?

A. Yes, I do.

Q. You would have known about it at the time, would you not?

A. This was again in 2000. I was not a member of the general committee at that point. I would have read the newsletter . . .

Q. The point I am making to you, which I respectfully suggest to you is inescapable, is that you knew that any member, including yourself, who did not comply with the union's campaign of contract compliance would be branded, to use your union jargon, as a scab. You knew that, did you not?

A. I don't agree with the term, Mr Huggins.

Q. What term would you prefer?

A. Well, I certainly wouldn't use the term 'scab'.

Q. What term would you have used, Mr Warham?

A. Well, the terms here are 'members who are in breach'. I think 'scab' is a very emotive term. It's not the way we conducted business.

Just keep knocking them straight back to the bowler. He sent down a couple of quicker deliveries.

Q. Could you help us a wee bit with pages 178 and 179. 'Contract compliance is definitely working, but it can always work better. Ask yourself if you are rigidly adhering to these numbers each and every time they are applicable', the numbers being 45, 80 and 120. You see that, do you?

A. Yes, I do.

Q. Number 45, you can see what that says: 'If you are on reserve duty, you are entitled to 45 minutes' preparation before you leave your home.' It is then saying, the last sentence: 'Doing so will compromise safety and weaken contract compliance.' Right?

A. Yes, that's what it says.

Q. That was your understanding?

A. That's what it says.

Q. And that was your understanding? Why are you fencing with me, Mr Warham?

A. If I read this paragraph, Mr Huggins, I will put the same interpretation on it as you. Yes, that's what the union was saying to its membership.

Q. And you supported the union in this regard?

A. I supported the union, yes, I did.

Q. Over the page, 80 and 120: 'Management require you to sign on for flights at CLK 80 minutes prior to departure time. Do not sign on or make yourself available before this time. Doing so makes you available for poaching onto other flights. If your flight preparation needs longer than the 120 minutes given – take that time', and so on. You see 80?

A. Yes, I see 80.

Q. And you supported that?

A. As I said earlier . . .

Q. Did you support that?

A. I didn't actually comply with that particular . . .

Q. Did you support that policy?

MR GROSSMAN: If my learned friend were to let him answer, it might help.

HIS LORDSHIP: I'm not very much helped by overly aggressive cross-examination, Mr Huggins.

MR HUGGINS: Your Lordship is entirely right.

HIS LORDSHIP: At the moment it seems to me to be fast going to the point of being overly aggressive. Sometimes I just like to hear what he has to say. He may not answer your question necessarily, but that is usually is manna from heaven for counsel because you then say the witness is evasive and therefore he was not credible, but I would like to at least hear the sentence, where it is going.

A timely intervention by the umpire. The bowler's been running all over the pitch in his follow through trying to scuff it up. First warning. The umpire's giving the batsman the benefit of the doubt just as he should. Could be Dickie Bird standing. Concentrate and don't lose your momentum.

MR HUGGINS: Your Lordship is entitled to an apology, and if you will forgive me for saying so, Mr Warham perhaps, even before I apologise to your Lordship, is entitled to an apology, certainly if your Lordship thinks I was being aggressive. I was trying to get on fast. I will now . . .

HIS LORDSHIP: It's not necessarily getting on at all costs. I think what Mr Warham is saying is that's the union's position, we can all read it, we can all draw our conclusions as to what the union is saying. He is an ex-president of the union, he supported the union's position. He did not necessarily follow every little bit down to the letter . . .

MR HUGGINS: Thank you, my Lord. Out of interest, these particular items here, 45, 80 and 120, does that mean there was a document where a fuller, more comprehensive account would have been given and this just happens to be three of the paragraphs taken from that document?

A. Those times were actually specified in the conditions of service and the rostering practices, so actually, when the rostering practices talked about standby duty, there was a time constraint in the rostering practice saying if you are called out on standby you have to be able to leave your place of residence within 45 minutes. And similarly, there were reporting times specified in the rostering practice for when you come in for duty, and the same with reserve, when you are home base and on overseas reserve. Those times were specified in the contract.

HIS LORDSHIP: Let's take one of them, for instance the first one, 45 minutes. It says: 'If you are on reserve duty, you are entitled to 45 minutes' preparation time before you leave home.' In the normal course of events, you may have a discretion. You are entitled to 45 minutes, but let's say you are ready after 15 minutes, you are all set and ready to go. Would you have gone right there and then or would you have waited until 45 minutes, contract compliance, so I will wait until the full 45 minutes elapses, even though I am now ready to go after 15 minutes? How did you actually act on this 45-minute period contract compliance suggestion?

A. As it happened, I was scheduled for very little reserve, but had I been on reserve I wouldn't necessarily have done this the 45 minute thing. Basically the 45 minutes is there for you to get a shower, get your uniform, pack an overnight bag and leave the house . . .

MR HUGGINS. Can we look at page 179, under the words '120': 'I'll do my best.' That is the answer you should give to any and all questions regarding your travel time to Cathay City after a Hong Kong reserve call-out. 'When will you arrive?' 'I'll do my best.' 'How long will it take you once you're ready?' 'I'll do my best.' 'Can you catch the next bus?' 'I'll do my best.' 'Can you make it in time for scheduled sign-on?' 'I'll do my best.' That's what the union was encouraging members to do, and you supported that, did you?

A. That is certainly what it says here, that is what the union were advising.

Q. Did you support the policy, were you ready and willing to do it, and were you ready and willing to encourage others to do it?

A. I was a member of the union. I voted for the resolution . . .

HIS LORDSHIP: What about Mr Huggins' other question: did you encourage other members?

A. No, I didn't encourage other members, because at this point I was not on the general committee of the association, I was merely the chief negotiator. So I wasn't part of the sort of policy formulation group, if you like.

HIS LORDSHIP: Were you part of the editorial committee that produced these Between the Leaves, these newsletters?

A. No, I wasn't.

HIS LORDSHIP: Did you have any say on the production of these newsletters?

A. No, I didn't.

And so it continued for a few more overs. The occasional attempted googly and a few late cuts in reply. The scoreboard was ticking over nicely and then he came round the wicket with a new line.

Q. You were aware, weren't you, of another form of industrial action known as sick-outs?

A. I know that Mr Rhodes has put some information in his witness state- ment. As far as I am aware, in all my time in the union, the union never adopted a sick-out policy and I certainly never took part in a sick-out.

Q. I'm not asking you, nor is the airline accusing you, nor has it ever accused you in this context of this case, of personally having done that. They have no evidence of that and have never accused you.

Oh really? That should come back to bite them later because Rhodes has been accusing us of exactly that. I hope our bowler heard that one. Should be able to send him a bouncer right under his chin when it's our turn in the field.

HIS LORDSHIP: Perhaps we can define what we mean by 'sick-out' because I'm not necessarily sure I understand what you mean by that. Deliberately saying you are sick when you are not, is that what you define it as?

MR HUGGINS: My Lord, there are, as it were, gradations of it, because if the union orchestrates . . .

HIS LORDSHIP: All I need at the moment, Mr Huggins, is when you say to Mr Warham that there was a sick-out policy, which gradation, which definition are you adopting, so we all clear what the extent of your question is.

MR HUGGINS: My Lord, that's very helpful. Perhaps we can go to pages 157 and 158 in this bundle for a moment. Here we see, Mr Warham, an email which – I think if you go to page 158 you will see who this email from John Findlay was sent to. NJD, who would have been Nigel Demery, the president, do you agree?

A. That is correct, Nigel Demery.

Q. JSW, John Simpson Warham, that's you.

A. That's correct, yes.

Q. Would you just go back to page 157. This is John Findlay of the union, sending an email saying: 'Hi Guys Appended is a self-explanatory email from GMA.' GMA being?

A. General manager aircrew.

Q. 'I've just put the phone down on him so I may have your concurrence (or not as the case may be) to the following: Before that, some of you may remember me saying last Monday that Rhodes had the shits when he spoke to me. Reason being that 87 officers, including 3 GC', that's general committee, 'members & JSW', that's John Simpson Warham, 'were off sick last Sunday. He half hinted that the [union] had arranged it. This is twice the average and I am told today by a good source that IOC', integrated operations control, 'nearly imploded in trying to keep the operation going', and then these word which I will read out more slowly, 'So we now know the target to aim for.' Do you see that?

A. Yes, I do see that.

Q. This email fell into the hands of Cathay, did it not?

A. Yes, it did, yes.

Q. You weren't expecting it to, were you? It wasn't intended that it should go to Cathay?

A. I would assume not.

Q. But it did go to Cathay, and here Cathay, when they see this email, on the face of it, I hope you will agree, it appears to be the like of John Simpson Warham, Nigel Demery . . . and others all receiving this indication from John Findlay that 'we now know the target to aim for', that is by how many people off sick at once is likely to cause implosion in the operations of the company. That's what it says on the face of it, isn't it?

HIS LORDSHIP: We can read it, Mr Huggins. That's what it seems to say.

MR HUGGINS: Was that your understanding?

A. Firstly, I was certainly sick at that point but . . . I wasn't partaking in any form of sick-out. I had a proper doctor's note . . . There was no AOA policy adopting a sick-out. At that point I was still not on the committee at that time, I was just chief negotiator, which is actually what the main body of the email is about, about scheduling talks on rostering, which is why it was copied to me.

HIS LORDSHIP: We still haven't gotten a clear answer from you, Mr Huggins, on what you actually mean when you say sick-out policy. You said there were many gradations. What gradation were you focusing on?

MR HUGGINS: I will confine myself to the evidence adduced by the defendants in this case. I don't think it would be appropriate for me to go beyond that.

HIS LORDSHIP: You asked him the question. Just to know, when you say 'sick-out policy', when you refer to 'sick-out policy' in your questions, what am I to understand by your question?

MR HUGGINS: The union encouraging its members to call off sick.

HIS LORDSHIP: Even though not sick.

MR HUGGINS: My Lord, as the witness has said, he is saying it is not the policy, but if they are calling people to come off sick on a chosen day so that you achieve the target referred to here, you are in effect orchestrating, you are orchestrating a sick-out to put pressure on the management.

HIS LORDSHIP: We will leave it at that. I'm not quite sure you have answered my question, Mr Huggins. I am no clearer on what the thrust of your question is, but let me put a question to Mr Warham instead.

MR HUGGINS: Of course.

HIS LORDSHIP: Let's look at it this way, Mr Warham. You talk about there being no official or unofficial policy of the union to direct members to call in sick when they are not sick, but there is a whole gradation of sicknesses: there is very minor sickness, very, very minor, which doesn't really prevent you from flying, or there are more serious ones that do clearly prevent you from flying. There's a whole range. Are you saying that the union didn't have a policy – let's say I just had a very, very minor sickness – was the union encouraging me, 'Well, however minor your sickness might be, even if in the normal course of events you would fly, you should exercise your discretion not to fly?'

A. No, my Lord. Not to my knowledge.

HIS LORDSHIP: There was no such policy?

A. Not to my knowledge, my Lord. I was never encouraged by any union officials. I have no knowledge of the union adopting that policy or encouraging its members to do so.

HIS LORDSHIP: That may be the suggestion. Maybe you have some minor sickness, you go to the medical officer, let's say Discovery Bay medical doctor; you say, 'I've got this sickness' – it might be a slight illness, very, very slight, nothing that would prevent you in the normal course from flying – you get the certificate and then you don't report for duty because you are sick; is that what the union was encouraging you to do, in your understanding?

A. No, they weren't, and I have no knowledge of the union doing that at all.

HIS LORDSHIP: Thank you . . .

MR HUGGINS: I will move on. Maximum safety strategy. Now, you were aware of negotiations between the union and the airline breaking down in June 2001?

He's coming over the wicket again. Didn't get anywhere with the sickness thing. Couple of boundaries there and he's upset the umpire again. Concentrate. Watch out for wrong un again.

A. Yes, I was.

Q. And that on 3 July the union launched a new campaign of industrial action?

A. They adopted a policy of MSS, yes.

Q. Are you quibbling with the expression 'they launched a new form of industrial action'?

A. They called it limited industrial action, yes, that's what they called it.

Q. So it is industrial action?

A. That's what they called it, limited industrial action.

HIS LORDSHIP: I think he has given his evidence. You can make submissions accordingly. I decide what as a matter of law constitutes industrial action so far as relevant here.

Whoops. Running on the pitch again. Second warning.

MR HUGGINS: As your Lordship pleases. Pages 217 to 220 in this bundle, Mr Warham. 15 June, just before the resolution, 'Open letter from Hong Kong Aircrew Officers Association', that's the union, 'to Hong Kong's travelling public': 'As professional aircrew of Hong Kong's flag carrier, Cathay Pacific Airways, we regret sincerely the need to take 'limited industrial action' and the inconvenience this will cause to you, our passengers.' Not just 'may cause'; 'this is going to cause you inconvenience'. Do you see that?

A. Yes, I see it.

Q. That was what it was designed to do, was it not?

A. Are you talking about MSS?

Q. This limited industrial action that is being referred to . . .

A. MSS was simply extracts from the company's own operations manuals, and in my opinion there was a lot of bluff going on. All you are doing is taking extracts from the company's own manuals and saying operate to normal company procedures, and that's what we did anyway. As airline pilots we operate to very specific procedures, so in effect this MSS did not have the effect that it says here, but yes, they were threatening that.

HIS LORDSHIP: And that would cause inconvenience to the passengers?

A. Yes. The threat of inconvenience . . .

MR HUGGINS: The letter goes on in the next paragraph to refer to: 'An unhelpful approach', that is by the management, 'and a refusal to negotiate constructively has led to this committee proposing the "limited industrial action" to our members.' . . . So far, not specifying what form that will take, but saying that there will be limited industrial action, and it's going to cause, it will cause, inconvenience to the passengers.

HIS LORDSHIP: I think he has said yes to that already.

MR HUGGINS: Thank you. I am trying to take it slowly so I don't muddle it all up.

HIS LORDSHIP: That's fine, Mr Huggins. I am just indicating that he has already agreed with that.

Good. The umpire's not liking the new bowling line.

MR HUGGINS: Thank you, my Lord. The reality is that on 3 July, the only limited industrial action was the MSS, was it not?

A. The publication of the MSS, yes, that's correct.

Q. And the limited industrial action that was being referred to here was referring to the implementation on 3 July of the campaign using MSS, was it not?

A. That's correct.

Q. And it was, in effect, a go-slow, was it not?

A. It didn't work that way, Mr Huggins.

Q. But that was what it was intended to do.

A. But it didn't work that way.

Q. We will look at whether it did or not as a separate issue. It was intended, was it not?

397

A. There was an implied threat there, yes, that it would slow down operations.

Q. If it did not slow down operations, or threaten to slow down operations, it wouldn't be any value at all as pressure, would it?

A. As I say, I believe a lot of that was bluff, and management reacted very strongly to it.

Q. The MSS was to be implemented by the members on a go-slow basis, without any flexibility whatever, and by the members taking it slow, taking their time, in a markedly different way from the carrying out of their normal procedures. That is the reality, is it not, Mr Warham?

A. That is the implication, but the actual effects – it didn't have that effect.

Q. That was the intention. Do you agree?

A. It was the implication.

HIS LORDSHIP: By 'implication' you mean intention?

A. I mean implication to management to say, 'Right, we need you back at the table, and until you come back we're going to do this and it has potential to slow down the operations'. In practical terms, it didn't work.

HIS LORDSHIP: I think Mr Huggins wishes to take what the actual effect was, put that to one side, but the intention of the union was to threaten a go-slow that would further disrupt the commercial management of the airline. You step it up a gear. Contract compliance hasn't brought them to the negotiating table, so you step it up, go to limited industrial action, MSS, and that, in effect, the intention there, in effect, go slow and that will bring them to the negotiating table?

A. That's correct, apply further pressure to bring them back to the table.

HIS LORDSHIP: By effectively going slow.

A. Yes, my Lord.

MR HUGGINS: There can be no doubt about this, because if one goes to the letter on page 221, which is a letter of 20 June from the president, headed 'Limited Industrial Action': 'Today, you the membership voted to take limited industrial action to protect your contract . . .' That was the purpose, wasn't it, to protect their contract?

A. That's what the president says, yes.

Q. And that's what you understood yourself?

A. Well, yes, that's what the president said, that's what I read, and that's how I interpreted it.

Q. I'm far more interested in you than the president, Mr Warham, at the moment. Was that your understanding, that that was the purpose of it? When you voted?

A. I voted in favour of the motion.

Q. And when you did, you would want to know what the purpose of it was, would you not?

A. The purpose was, as I've stated, to put more pressure on management to come back to the table and negotiate with us.

Q. About your contracts, your rights, your benefits?

A. The rostering practices in the contract, yes.

HIS LORDSHIP: I think he has made it clear, Mr Huggins.

OK the bowler's rattled now. He's getting tired. Look for the loose ones and bang them back over his head.

MR HUGGINS: 'The industrial subcommittee has been working hard to refine a strategy that will maximise pressure on management to address your concerns, while working within the bounds of your contract. The full details of that strategy will be released to you by email on 29 June, backed up by a hard copy in your mailbox.' Right?

A. Yes, that's what it says.

Q. Did that happen and was it all related to the implementation of the MSS?

A. I don't actually remember getting an email and I must have got a copy of the MSS, hard copy, yes.

Q. The third paragraph, after the first sentence, reads: 'This next logical step of incremental pressure can be performed without placing undue risk on any union member.' You saw that?

A. Yes.

Q. In assessing whether or not to pass the resolution you would have taken account of what was being said here?

A. No. This was published after the vote. So this was a newsletter after the vote was taken at the meeting.

Q. We will check that.

A. It says 'Today the membership voted to take', so this is . . .

Q. Are you saying that this came as a surprise to you, then, that this was not your understanding when you voted in favour of the resolution?

A. Actually we didn't know what form limited industrial action was going to take, so we only voted at the meeting to undertake limited industrial action and it wasn't until after the meeting that the MSS was released to the membership.

Q. But it was clearly your understanding that, certainly within a matter of days, the limited industrial action that was being talked about was a go-slow on the MSS?

A. No. We didn't know that it was going to be MSS. MSS was not revealed until after the votes had been taken.

Q. I just said, within a few days, it was your understanding that that was the form the limited industrial action was going to take?

A. After the MSS was published, yes.

Q. Yes, 'within a few days' is the expression I used. This letter goes on: 'It is crucially important that you do not endanger the careers of your peers by sticking your head in the sand and not following the full spirit and intent of this industrial action.' All right? Now, you would have been interested, wouldn't you, in that?

A. Yes.

Q. Because you want to get the full benefit for the membership of following the full spirit and intent of this industrial action, which was to cause disruption to the airline, or threaten to cause disruption to the airline, to bring them to heel; that was the purpose of it?

A. Not to bring them to heel, Mr Huggins. To bring them back to the table to talk about rostering practices. I was the head of rostering practices negotiating team and I wanted to bring them back to the table to talk rostering practices. That was the intent as I saw it.

Q. Sorry, I interrupted you. That's my fault. It was very rude of me and I ask your forgiveness. Page 222: 'You deserve a fair contract. Limited industrial action was instituted to accelerate the process of achieving that contract.' So that, again, is the purpose, I suggest to you. It's for your benefits, contractual entitlements is what we are talking about.

A. Yes, to get management back to the table to resolve the issues of difference between us.

Q. Can I just ask you this: the original date for the launch of this limited industrial action was to be 1 July, wasn't it?

A. Yes.

Q. It was then changed to 3 July 2001, was it not?

A. That's correct.

Q. Let me help your recollection as to how that came about. 1 July 2001 was a Sunday, was it not? You don't remember?

A. I don't remember.

Q. I will go on and see whether this prompts a recollection. 2 July, the Monday, was a public holiday, and so it was Tuesday 3 July that was the amended date for the start of the operation? Factually we can see that's right, can we not?

A. Yes. It was changed to 3 July.

Q. Let me see whether you recall this; maybe you don't. Had the Governor, the then Governor CH Tung, not asked the union to put off the proposed

400

industrial action, and the inevitable disruption that everybody knew would accompany it, until after the holiday weekend, and the union obliged? Does that fit with your recollection?

Watch this one. This is the 'holding Hong Kong to ransom' justification line.

A. I don't know, Mr Huggins. I wasn't part of the decision-making process at the time. All I was was the chief negotiator. I wasn't on the general committee. I wasn't part of the decision-making process. I don't remember. I didn't take part in that decision. But certainly it was delayed until 3 July.

Q. Of course, not only was Sunday the 1st a holiday, 2 July was a holiday, but it was at a time when all the children in the UK would be coming out from school for their holidays and a lot of families would be going back from Hong Kong to Europe on their holidays, so disruption over that weekend would have been particularly onerous on them, would it not; would you agree with that observation?

A. Mr Huggins, I don't know, I took no part in the decision-making process. I don't – if you are asking me, was it designed to cause maximum disruption to the schoolchildren, I don't know. I didn't take part in this decision.

Q. Forgive me. I was rather saying the opposite. I was saying because it was going to and everyone knew it was going to, the authorities asked the union to put it off until later, and they said, 'All right, we won't cause disruption over this weekend, this holiday weekend, when all the kids are coming and going; we will do it on the 3rd.' Are you seriously saying you didn't know that?

A. I didn't know that. I took no part in the decision. If you say that's what happened, I will take your word. I didn't take part in that and I don't know.

HIS LORDSHIP: In fact there's a document in the bundle where I think the union say that because 1 July is the anniversary of the return of Hong Kong to the mainland, therefore, for patriotic reasons, because a lot of people are travelling between Hong Kong and China particularly, it was moved to 3 July.

MR HUGGINS: Exactly. That was the Governor's interest. I wasn't going, if I may respectfully say so, suggest that his interest descended to the level at which I was talking about, the kids coming and going, but it was that important weekend, the reunification weekend which I was essentially talking about.

HIS LORDSHIP: Mr Warham says he was not aware of the reasoning for delaying it, and it may be for a variety of reasons. We have some evidence within the bundle itself.

MR HUGGINS: My Lord, in relation to what I had said earlier, your Lordship may or may not have got to the point of making a ruling yet, but what I was saying in relation to these non-agreed bundles, until such time . . .

HIS LORDSHIP: I think the document I am referring to is actually in your own bundle.

MR HUGGINS: If your Lordship is allowing us to get it in in that way, then fine. Anyway, I will press on. Can we look, please, at the minutes of the EGM on 20 June, where the motion was passed. You will see that the president was saying that 100 per cent support was vital. Was that your understanding, having been at the meeting?

A. Yes. If the president said 100 per cent support is vital, that's my understanding.

Q. At the bottom of the page, the president asks rhetorically, 'What is limited industrial action?', and then he answers that question in this way: 'The first thing is that it is not voluntary. If we vote for this today, on 1st July you have to go on 100 per cent committed, 100 per cent AOA. Limited industrial action is not a strike. Your committee's view is not "all on or all off", it is incrementally increasing pressure.' Again, was that your understanding, that you really had no choice as a union member but to give it full 100 per cent support?

A. It's certainly a rallying speech by a president to his members, Mr Huggins, yes.

He's getting nowhere with this. If he carries on this way he's bound to send a couple of loose ones down. Look to play some strokes.

MR HUGGINS: Can we go back to bundle X, page 160. Again, another president's letter to you all. If you look at the right-hand column: 'The focus discussions were another clear indication that the membership want to apply further pressure in the near future to encourage management to meet our financial needs. In other words, we may have to cross the boundary between simple contract compliance and limited industrial action.' Are you able to help us on that? What was the distinction as far as you are concerned between simple contract compliance and limited industrial action?

A. Again, as the president is saying, under contract compliance we still haven't got the management to come back to the table to resolve the issues so we need to apply further pressure.

Q. You've got to cross the line?

A. Going to apply further pressure.

HIS LORDSHIP: The suggestion being made by Mr Huggins is probably that you have tried complying with your contract so you may have to try breaching your contract.

A. No, my Lord. Actually I believe we were extremely careful to make sure we didn't breach our contract.

HIS LORDSHIP: Even under limited industrial action, you didn't understand that to mean breaching one's contract?

A. No. We didn't understand it to be breaching our contract at all. In fact, as I understood it, we were very cautious to make sure that we didn't do that.

Thank you, umpire. Cover drive to the boundary.

MR HUGGINS: One thing is for sure, and I want to get this absolutely clear, that the limited industrial action which was launched on 3 July was the MSS go-slow?

A. The limited industrial action was the MSS, yes, it was.

Q. But it's not just the MSS, because you are saying, 'Oh, well, these are all procedures which we would have had to carry out anyway under our contract'?

A. Well, they are. The whole point of MSS was that it was just extracts from the company's own operations manuals.

Four more. Keep 'em coming just like that, bowler.

Q. Let's get real, Mr Warham. If you had done nothing different in the weeks before 3 July to what you were doing on 3 July, where is the limited industrial action, where is the pressure?

A. It's a very good question. In fact, as I said earlier, I believe there was a lot of bluff going on. I actually operated six flights while MSS was in effect, three of them I brought in early, they arrived early, they weren't delayed at all, and in fact the last flight I operated, on 9 July, I arrived back 42 minutes ahead of schedule. This is while MSS was in effect.

First six of the innings. Right over his head. It's his own fault. Shouldn't have bowled me a long hop.

HIS LORDSHIP: Mr Warham, let's just return to Mr Huggins' point, which is that it's a little puzzling, here we are going an extra gear, we are moving from contract compliance, fulfilling the terms of the contract, to limited industrial action, and that limited industrial action was going to be MSS. What's the difference between MSS and contract compliance? The way you are putting it, there's no real difference.

A. Well, my Lord, I would say the potential threat of MSS was there, it could disrupt the operation, but in real terms it didn't have the effect that was threatened. In fact we couldn't really tell whether it had that effect because Typhoon Utor hit the day after MSS was brought in and the whole operation went into chaos anyway, so you couldn't really say whether MSS was having that effect, until the last flight I flew after recovery and we were back 42 minutes early. So I think there was – I believe, my personal view, is that there was a lot of bluff going on with MSS.

MR HUGGINS: Let's see whether this helps. Go to page 266 in the same bundle ... In large capital letters: 'WE ANTICIPATE THAT FLIGHTS WILL COMMONLY INCUR DELAYS OF 15 [to] 60 MINUTES OR MORE. The actual extent of each delay will depend on the nature of the flight. ULH and ETOPS flights have considerably more pre-flight briefing material and will necessarily incur longer delays. If you are departing without incurring delays, it is most likely that you are subconsciously acting at your previously abbreviated pace and not maximising safety.' Wasn't that a rather disingenuous piece of window dressing, Mr Warham?

HIS LORDSHIP: I think you can make that submission, Mr Huggins. I can read it.

No ball. Extras are mounting up nicely now.

MR HUGGINS: As your Lordship pleases. Mr Warham, I am interested in your understanding of all this. You are not suggesting, are you, that you personally, with all your years in the union, somehow did not understand that what was really going on here was a go-slow to cause, if only incidentally, whatever other purposes you were seeking to achieve, delays?

A. Certainly the threat was there, Mr Huggins, I agree.

HIS LORDSHIP: Shall we take that as a convenient pause, Mr Huggins?

MR HUGGINS: I think it would be fine for everyone, my Lord.

Drinks break. Just sit in the pavilion and keep your concentration. The shine's off the ball now and he's straying well off the line. Time to pick off a few more before lunch. We resumed.

MR HUGGINS: Mr Warham, you will be pleased to know that I only have a couple more questions on this topic before I move on to something completely different. while we are on bundle X, page 227, the middle of the page, 'Maximising Safety In Flight': 'Maximising safety is not limited to pre-flight preparation. In flight, do not be tempted to rush the aircraft to return to schedule.' I appreciate what you are saying, that 'Oh, well, of course this is all standard procedure, what we do all the time. Safety, safety, safety', but what you cannot, I suggest, get away from is that there had to have been a substantial and material difference in the way the pilots were being encouraged to behave after 3 July as compared to the period prior to that date, otherwise this whole thing is a nonsense. Do you really not agree with that?

A. The operation had been – the pilots had been under pressure for quite some time. Corners were being cut to meet on-time performance. It became the mantra that we needed on-time performance, and basically what this is saying is forget on-time performance, let's stop cutting corners and let's operate the way we should be operating.

Q. Can you help me, please, with the sentence that begins at the bottom of page 227, in the last two words: 'We remind . . .' And if you turn over the page: '. . . you that operations are no longer normal', in bold print. What did that convey to you?

A. I don't know, really, Mr Huggins. I can't put an interpretation on that.

Q. You see, I am suggesting to you that this is the clearest of indications that it wasn't a question of simply following out normal safety procedures, which any responsible pilot can be taken to have been following. It is saying, 'We are not in the normal procedure game anymore, we are in the go-slow game, boys. Slow it all down. Let's get some delays and pressure going.' That, in a nutshell, is what this is about; do you agree or disagree?

A. That is an interpretation that could be put on it, Mr Huggins, yes.

HIS LORDSHIP: But do you agree or disagree with that, personally, your interpretation?

A. Personally, as I've said, my Lord, I believe there was a lot of bluff going on here. There was a lot of posturing.

HIS LORDSHIP: I've got that point, Mr Warham, but you understood this to be an instruction from the union down to members like yourself, to take your time. If in the past, using your discretion as a captain, you would feel, 'It's okay, the plane is ready', because of this limited industrial action, you would say, 'Got to double-check, triple-check', et cetera, even though in the normal course of events you would be satisfied as the captain that you could fly?

A. We certainly wouldn't be doing some of the things we used to do to get the operation back to schedule, if there was a delay.

HIS LORDSHIP: Can you just elaborate what you mean by that, Mr Warham?

A. As an example would be pre-flight preparation, pre-flight briefing, where you are required to report 80 minutes before departure. If we got called out on reserve, let's say, and we arrived 30 minutes before departure, it means the aircraft was going to be delayed, and quite often what we would do is go straight out to the aircraft and cut short the pre-flight preparation. To me, what this is saying is in that event, don't cut corners like that; go through the full process.

HIS LORDSHIP: Did you believe that cutting corners in the situation that you just described was okay or was unsafe, or did you have any views on that?

A. I have to be careful what I say here, my Lord. I never operated an aircraft unsafely. I am a professional pilot and I always make sure all my operations are safe. So if I went out with 30 minutes' notice and operated that aircraft, then yes, I believe it was safe, but I was cutting corners.

HIS LORDSHIP: You believed it was safe but you were cutting corners?

A. Yes.

HIS LORDSHIP: What do you mean then by cutting corners?

A. I wasn't taking the full amount of time — for instance, in pre-flight preparation there are some documents called NOTAMs, notice to air men, and they list on your route all the various unserviceabilities; for instance, if a radio navigation beacon is unserviceable, it will be listed in the NOTAMs. Prior to flight you are supposed to read all of the NOTAMs applicable to your route. What we would do is, at short notice like this, I wouldn't read all the NOTAMs. I would read them once I am airborne.

HIS LORDSHIP: Right. And that's cutting corners?

A. It is cutting corners, sir, yes. In the procedures it says you are supposed to read all the NOTAMs before you go flying.

HIS LORDSHIP: Thank you. Mr Huggins, I'm sorry again to have interrupted.

Bloody hell, Warham. NOTAMS. Is that the best you could come up with? That one should have gone right out of the ground and you only managed a dodgy single. What about not checking the fuel calculations, the Tech Log, the weather? What about not doing the walk round? What about carrying a list of defects as long as your arm? What about just jumping on board, firing it up and going in 10 minutes without cross checking anything because of OTP? He gave you an opportunity to air all the flight safety stuff and you just came up with bloody NOTAMS. Concentrate you idiot.

MR HUGGINS: My Lord, as always, it's very helpful to clarify. Let me move away from all of that. One of the complaints that you have in this case, which the learned judge will decide in due course, is that the company dismissed you without having followed the DGP, the disciplinary and grievance procedures.

Right. Change of direction again. Now keep your eye on the fucking ball and put some to the boundary.

A. That's the second leg of our case, yes.

Q. Forgive me, that's how it all began, did it not?

HIS LORDSHIP: I don't think we have to argue about that. I can read the pleadings. Whether it's the first leg, second leg or the third leg.

MR HUGGINS: I was merely surprised at the answer, my Lord. I will go on.

HIS LORDSHIP: I don't think it really matters to me. Shall we carry on, Mr Huggins?

MR HUGGINS: Yes, my Lord. If Cathay had carried out a DGP hearing and as a result of it you had been cleared of any misconduct, and if at that stage Cathay had terminated you anyway by three months' notice or payment in lieu, whatever the result if the DGP had been, as his Lordship has held it was entitled to do, do you say that the distress and loss to you would have been any less?

A. Yes, it would have been. Had they not defamed me, I would have been able to go and get another job. But as a result of the statements they made in the media about me and my group of peers and colleagues, we were effectively pariahs in the business and we were unable to get jobs.

That's more like it. Straight down the ground for four.

Q. I know you say that now, but that is not something you began to say in these proceedings until 2005, is it?

A. That's correct.

Q. So you let 2001 go by, relying on breach of contract, 2002, 2003, 2004, and then in 2005 suddenly up comes this complaint, 'Oh, but we've been defamed'. Why did it take so long for this complaint to come into the . . .

HIS LORDSHIP: I'm not really helped by that question, Mr Huggins, because whether it came earlier or later I have to deal with the matter whether the statements are or are not.

MR HUGGINS: On liability, yes, my Lord, but in terms of damages, one is entitled to ask, with respect, whether it be a truthful sugges-tion that all this distress was being caused if no one even complains about it until 2005.

HIS LORDSHIP: Right. I think one can make that submission, Mr Huggins. I'm not sure I'm really helped by whatever answer he might give on this.

Thank you, umpire. We'll take that as four byes.

MR HUGGINS: As your Lordship pleases. Let us look then at objective facts in terms of consequences to you. If you will forgive me, I'm only going to ask you to tell us about consequences to you, because all the other plaintiffs will be entitled to tell his Lordship what the consequences were to them. Is that fair enough? It will keep things short.

A. Yes, that's understood.

Q. In fact you personally did not apply to any other airlines for a job as a pilot for health reasons, is that right, according to your state-ments?

A. To start with, the solicitors we were using at the time in 2001 firstly advised us not to apply for any jobs, in the initial stages, because the position they were taking was that the contract was still in full effect and force and had not been repudiated, and if we were – this was the advice we were given, Mr Huggins; whether it is correct or not legally, I don't know.

Q. You can say what you like, Mr Warham. I am listening.

Careful now, almost edged that one.

HIS LORDSHIP: Normally it's not a good idea to say what solicitors' advice to you is, because that is subject to legal and professional privi-lege, so that's a matter of privilege. So I wouldn't, if I were you, be saying what solicitors have advised. From your point of view, what you are saying is you did not look for a job in the initial stages because, as far as you are concerned, you were wrongfully terminated and therefore you were still employed, unless you accepted the wrongful termination, by Cathay Pacific. Whether solicitors advised you on that, rightly or wrongly, that's irrelevant. If I were you, I wouldn't disclose what solicitors advised you because that's not normally a wise thing to do. That unravels legal and professional privilege, and that's usually very unwise.

A. Thank you, my Lord.

HIS LORDSHIP: So I think the answer so Mr Huggins' question is probably 'yes', from what I gather – 'yes', and now you are saying why you haven't applied to any other airlines. Is that the way we would perceive it?

A. That is correct, yes, my Lord.

HIS LORDSHIP: You were saying in the initial stages it is because you were wrongfully terminated; you were effectively still employed. Then?

A. Subsequent to that I had a medical problem and lost my flying licence.

The next few overs were sparring about my medical problems and lack of discovery of my records. No advantage either way really. The occasional quick single and a couple of dodgy appeals turned down by the umpire. The bowler tried a new line.

MR HUGGINS: Can you help me with this? You made a statement which I will remind you of – and if you can't remember it we can go to the document itself – in your affidavit, which although you have referred to at the start of these proceedings, I'm not sure it is actually a document in evidence in these proceedings because it is your witness statements that are, but my Lord and I can sort that out at the appropriate time, but one of the things that you did say there is: '. . . I will not seek alternative employment unless and until [Cathay Pacific] confirms that I have a clear record or it conducts and completes the disciplinary procedure necessary before a finding against me might lawfully be made.' Do you remember saying that?

A. It doesn't immediately come to mind, Mr Huggins. It was in an affidavit, was it?

Q. It was.

A. That would be early on in the proceedings, would it?

Q. Indeed. But you were expressing your intentions in the future.

HIS LORDSHIP: Let's assume he made the statement, Mr Huggins. Then what?

409

MR HUGGINS: Cathay Pacific did offer to give, did it not, just such a letter of confirmation, but you did not take them up on that?

A. A letter of confirmation of what, Mr Huggins, sorry?

Q. The very thing you refer to in your affidavit. I will read it to you again, and if you want to actually see it in print just say so and we will get it up for you: '. . . I will not seek alternative employment unless and until [Cathay Pacific] confirms that I have a clear record or it conducts and completes the disciplinary procedure necessary before a finding against me might lawfully be made.'

HIS LORDSHIP: So it gave a certificate of a clear record?

MR HUGGINS: The offer was made by Cathay to give you a letter confirming to the world that you were not terminated for any kind of misconduct. That was the offer that was made to you, was it not?

A. I don't remember that, Mr Huggins.

Q. Do you really not?

A. No, I don't, honestly.

Q. Because you actually responded to that. It was Mr Barley, whose affidavit, for some inexplicable reason, has been put in the bundle by your solicitors, who we are told they are going to be applying at some time or other to cross-examine him, although we are not calling him as a witness, but your own affirmation addressed the offer that was being made by Mr Barley and it was in response to that that you say, 'I am not going to seek alternative employment'; is that not right or have I got that wrong?

A. I would need to look at the documents, Mr Huggins.

Q. Fair enough. Let's go to bundle III, page 471, paragraph 20. This is Mr Barley's affidavit.

A. I remember this now, yes.

Q. 'In so far as Mr Warham claims in paragraph 23 of the Warham Affidavit to be concerned that any other airline whom he might approach for a new job would regard him as someone who had been dismissed for "misconduct or other disciplinary reason", I can only say that if that is a genuine concern, he should simply show that airline this affidavit.' That's not what I am putting to you. It's the next bit: 'If he would prefer' – so he is giving you the option – 'I am authorised by the defendants to say they would be happy to supply on request letters for any of the plaintiffs confirming that their employment was not terminated on the ground of any or any alleged 'misconduct or disciplinary offence.' Do you see that offer having been made?

A. I do see that, but I have to say, in the light of what was said in the press about us, providing this affidavit would hardly endear us to a prospective employer.

Q. Did you form that view? Did you actually think about that?

A. In the light of the experience of the group of 49ers trying to get employment and being turned down everywhere they went.

Q. Mr Warham, can you confine yourself to your own experience, because I don't want you slipping in . . .

HIS LORDSHIP: He was getting to that because he says in the light – you said did he form that view.

MR HUGGINS: He and others.

HIS LORDSHIP: I think what he is saying is in the light of the experience of others and himself, he formed that view. At what point he formed that view you may want to debate with him, but he says, I think, that he formed that view, or he was getting to that until you interrupted him.

Thank you, umpire. Four more.

MR HUGGINS: I'm so sorry, again, my Lord. Carry on, Mr Warham. I interrupted you, and again I apologise.

A. I'm sorry, I have forgotten what the question was now.

Q. That is, I am sure, my fault, and I will do it again. I am interested in your indication on oath, '. . . I will not seek alternative employment unless and until [Cathay Pacific] confirms that I have a clear record . . .' Right? One of the things it did offer, through Mr Barley, in this paragraph, was to give you a letter, on request, if you wanted [paraphrased]: 'We will give you this letter that you can show to any prospective employer, making it perfectly clear that you have not been terminated on the ground of any or any alleged "misconduct or disciplinary offence".' What I am suggesting to you is that that is an offer which you chose not to take up. Do you agree or disagree?

A. I didn't take it up because I don't believe that what Mr Barley is offering here would undo the damage from the defamatory statements made in the press about us.

Four penn'orth.

Q. But again I come back to the fact that at the stage you were saying all this, you weren't complaining in these proceedings about any defamatory statements at all. No complaint is made about that until 2005.

A. Right. I could give you the reason for that, but his Lordship has said I shouldn't.

HIS LORDSHIP: I didn't say you shouldn't. It is normally unwise to undo legal and professional privilege. It's your choice, but you are not the only one involved here; there are other plaintiffs, and I'm not sure that you can waive legal and professional privilege of advice to them insofar as the case concerns them. I would simply state the outcome, that you decided not to take up this offer because, in 2002, in your particular circumstance – what, Mr Warham?

A. Because in my particular circumstance, with the experience of my peers and my colleagues, this would not be sufficient to restore our reputations. We were effectively pariahs in the business.

HIS LORDSHIP: So your evidence is this: in 2002, knowing what you knew about the experiences of your colleagues, you didn't believe that this type of offer would undo the stigma that would be attaching to you and others?

A. That is correct.

MR HUGGINS: When you finally did come to add defamation as a cause of action in these proceedings in 2005, of course at that stage your statements began to say, 'Oh, well, it's the defamatory statements that have been causing me all this distress and difficulties with – or would have caused difficulties with employers'; is that right?

A. Yes. It's the statements they made in the media about us that stigmatised us.

Keep it coming. Boundaries flowing thick and fast now. Must be past the half century by now. Don't look at the scoreboard. Just keep your head down and play the next delivery.

Q. But before then, when it was still only the contract claim, the distress you were referring to was the distress of having been unlawfully terminated?

MR GROSSMAN: My Lord, I'm sorry, I think my learned friend, to be fair, should show the witness the statement that he had made to which Captain Barley was replying, because that indicates my learned friend's question is on a wrong basis. If you would look . . .

HIS LORDSHIP: You can bring out whatever you want to bring out in re-examination. Thank you very much, Mr Grossman.

MR GROSSMAN: Very well. I am simply saying the witness is not being given correct information.

HIS LORDSHIP: I will just say this, Mr Huggins: I'm not stopping you but I'm not sure where this is going to go to. It seems to me to be a point you can simply make by way of submission. I'm not sure there is any point of fact here which we need to elicit from Mr Warham. If you want to make a submission as to the quantum of damages or whatever in relation to the defamation claim, I think that's open to you.

Did he signal a couple of byes then? Not sure. Bowler's running in again. Concentrate.

MR HUGGINS: As your Lordship pleases. Let me go on to something quite different then, in the same general context but a different point. As I understand it from your statements, you've had no income at all, since when?

A. Since 2001, I've had no earned income.

Q. So what have you been living on?

A. When I was terminated, I received my provident fund, which I had been paying 10 per cent of my salary into for 17 years, so I received that sum of money. I have sold my house and I've been living on investment income. I have also started a company, making electronic devices for the hearing impaired, but that's only been going for two years and we are not in profit there yet. So basically I've been living on the proceeds of my provident fund, the proceeds of selling my house and investment income.

Q. During the two years you've just been telling us about, would you have been receiving money out of the company, though, whether or not it was in profit or not – would they have been paying you any moneys?

A. No.

Q. And you weren't taking any moneys at all out of the company?

A. That's correct.

Q. Now can I move to another subject. I'm certainly not, for a moment, going to debate with you the meanings of the statements of Mr Tony Tyler and Mr Philip Chen that you complain about in these proceedings, that would not be appropriate and his Lordship will deal with that in due course. But in relation to what you say is the distress caused to you, I hope I will be permitted to at least ask you one or two questions. When you have described in your various witness statements the distress you say was caused by those particular statements, what was it, can you put in your own words, that you felt was giving you this distress and grief? What was it that you thought they were saying about you that led to the grief and distress?

Oh look at this one. Slow full toss. Take your time, let it come onto the bat and knock it out of the ground.

A. There's a famous phrase that it takes a lifetime to build a reputation and seconds to destroy it. We were all professional pilots. I started – my father was a pilot during the war and so was my uncle.

Q. I'm not asking you for your life history.

HIS LORDSHIP: Mr Huggins, you have brought it upon yourself. You asked him 'in his own words'.

MR HUGGINS: I meant to the question, my Lord.

HIS LORDSHIP: There we are, Mr Huggins. It's normally a bad idea for a cross-examiner to ask an open-ended question, as opposed to a 'yes' or 'no' question or a leading question.

MR HUGGINS: Forgive me, I of course take any stricture that comes from your Lordship, but I hope the question was directed to what was the meaning that you understood gave you the distress.

HIS LORDSHIP: Perhaps then we will answer that question directly.

A. Mr Tyler and Mr Chen made statements in the media which reflected on my professional reputation and effectively – they said that I was not acting in the best interests of the company, and in particular Mr Tyler was quoted as saying that I was unprofessional. Now, for a senior airline pilot, who has spent 30-odd years building his reputation, for somebody to come out and say that in the media, we immediately became pariahs in our own business. Aviation is a very, very small community. There are only 120,000 airline pilots in the world. We all know each other. As soon as these statements come out, we were immediately excluded from that brotherhood. We were blacklisted, we were pariahs in our own business.

Six.

HIS LORDSHIP: Perhaps I'll stop you there. I think we have an idea of the meaning.

MR HUGGINS: It was the meaning I was asking, not what you say is the consequences.

HIS LORDSHIP: We have the idea of the meaning.

MR HUGGINS: We have the idea of what it was you say caused you the distress. Can I ask you about this: the seniority system. If you had been able to have remedial surgery, and if you had been able to get your licence back, when do you say that would have happened?

A. I had the remedial surgery. It would have taken me another year after that surgery, so that would have been July 2003.

Q. So it's the period after – is it the period after 2003 which you say prevented you getting a new job with a new airline, for reasons other than your health?

Another dolly. Four more. Play the stroke.

A. No. I say, Mr Huggins, that it started as soon as I was dismissed. Had we not been defamed, I would have been able to go to another airline and get myself a job, as has recently happened to Captain Wilkinson after he was fired. He is now a senior captain in Qatar Airways. I would have been able to go to Qatar or to Emirates and got myself a job as a senior captain.

Q. Do you not agree that within most international airlines there's a seniority and promotion structure whereby new entrants are generally required to start at the bottom, at the lowest rank, and/or the lowest point on the applicable salary scale, regardless of their rank and seniority with the previous employer?

A. There are some airlines that operate a strict system like that, yes. Some airlines. A lot of other airlines employ direct entry captains.

Q. You see, you are probably now aware that you have made two completely inconsistent statements about this, are you not? Are you not, in your statements?

The seniority Yorker. You knew this was coming at some point. Just keep your toes out of the way and dig it out.

MR GROSSMAN: About what?

MR HUGGINS: About the seniority system. Let me take it in stages. Let's look at your latest statement on this issue, in response to Mr Nick Rhodes. Let's start at paragraph 2.4 on page 1330-6: 'Mr Rhodes also makes the statement that, because of the seniority system and promotion structure within "career airlines", only jobs in lower ranks would have been available to the plaintiffs. This is not correct. In fact many career airlines recruit direct entry captains straight into senior ranking positions.' Do you see that?

A. Yes, that's correct.

Q. And then you give Cathay as the only example of that, do you not, in this statement?

A. The only example in this statement, yes.

Q. Let us try and understand what you are saying, because I'm going to put to you, and it may be you are not qualified to answer this, but Mr Rhodes will be so Mr Grossman can cross-examine him about it, but I'm going to put to you that as far as Cathay is concerned, although they do employ captains, when they come in, they go to the bottom of the pile and have to work their way up. Are you . . .

A. I agree with you, Mr Huggins. They come in as captains and they are at the bottom of the seniority list, and they are employed as captains.

Q. They are in terms of seniority and so on right at the bottom of the pile?

A. In terms of seniority they are at the bottom of the pile but they are captains, they are not first officers, so they actually join the captains in a senior rank, albeit at the bottom of the seniority list.

HIS LORDSHIP: Are you saying they come in as first officers, Mr Huggins?

MR HUGGINS: They come in as first officers and then they are made up to captain.

HIS LORDSHIP: So he disagrees with you on that. He says they come in as captain but they are most junior at the captain level; they don't have the same . . .

MR HUGGINS: They come in as first officers and then they are promoted.

HIS LORDSHIP: Let me just clarify. What do you say, Mr Warham?

A. My Lord, there are some airlines that operate the way Mr Huggins is saying, that you come in at the bottom as a first officer. There are some airlines that do that. Also there are some other airlines, first tier airlines, that employ people as captains directly in, they don't have to start as first officers. But Mr Huggins is right, they will still be at the bottom of seniority list.

MR HUGGINS: Even below second officers?

A. They would be below second officers but they'll be in the rank of captain. Seniority doesn't just rule promotion, it also rules rostering, it rules – seniority rules an airline pilot's career, when you bid for leave, when you bid for trips, your seniority . . .

HIS LORDSHIP: You have the title of captain but in terms of seniority you may be junior to someone who is, say, a second officer?

A. That is correct.

MR HUGGINS: Mr Warham, I don't know whether you recall now that when you were before the Labour Tribunal, you, together with Mr Heron, who will be coming later to give evidence – he is also a co-plaintiff – you and Mr Heron made a joint statement on behalf of all the then plaintiffs, did you not? This was in 2002.

A. If you say so. It's a long time ago, Mr Huggins.

Q. I will hand you a copy. First of all I will see if you can recall. In one of your paragraphs – I will read it to you and then I can show it to you if there is any doubt about it.

HIS LORDSHIP: It's not in the bundle?

MR HUGGINS: It's not in the bundle although another statement in similar terms is, and I will come to that.

HIS LORDSHIP: A copy has been provided to Mr Grossman? Normally one doesn't want to surprise parties, one normally has the document in the bundle, or one has handed it to the other side before one refers to it, and one hands a copy to the court normally, as a matter of courtesy.

MR HUGGINS: In my respectful submission, on issues of credibility, even discovery doesn't require documents to be disclosed.

No balled and now he's arguing with the umpire. This should be good. Take a breather.

HIS LORDSHIP: In my court it does. This is not Perry Mason, Mr Huggins. Normally good practice requires disclosure of documents that one's going to refer to with sufficient time. It may be short notice because you didn't come to the document until recently, but as soon as you can, you show it to the other side. That's normal practice in my court and I believe normal practice in these civil courts.

Oh dear. Strayed much too far down the leg side. Four wides. He tried some more deliveries down the seniority line but got nowhere with it. The umpire had clearly got the message when he intervened:

HIS LORDSHIP: As I understood it earlier, you were making a distinction: you can come in with the same rank as captain in some reputable airlines but you would not have the same seniority.

A. That is correct.

HIS LORDSHIP: So you wouldn't be coming in with the same rank and seniority. You may come in with the same rank but not necessarily the same seniority.

A. That is correct, my Lord.

HIS LORDSHIP: Some airlines, you couldn't even come in in the same rank, you couldn't come in either with the same rank or seniority, you would have to stay at a lower rank and bottom seniority; is that right?

A. That's correct, my Lord.

Another change in line coming up.

MR HUGGINS: Can I turn to another subject: global downturn after 9/11. Do you not accept that there was a global downturn in international airline passenger traffic following the events of 11 September 2001?

A. I do accept it, certainly.

Q. Have you not produced that same statement on 18 September in which you are in effect disputing what Nick Rhodes says about the global downturn?

A. No, Mr Huggins. Nick Rhodes has said that the reason – he has put forward reasons why we couldn't get jobs, such as 9/11, global downturn, SARS. I am saying the airline business is cyclical anyway, yes, it may have had a minor effect, but the reason we couldn't get jobs is not because of the global downturn, it is because we were defamed and our reputations have been destroyed.

Cover drive. I just love that shot. Send me another one.

Q. Forgive me, I'm not interested in any submission Mr Rhodes may or may not have indicated as to why you couldn't get jobs. I am interested in the objective issue and objective fact as to whether or not the global downturn did lead to global, international airline traffic diminishing.

HIS LORDSHIP: I think he said yes to that.

MR HUGGINS: He has and I am therefore moving on. Nevertheless, are you still adhering to your dispute in your latest statement with what Nick Rhodes has said about it?

HIS LORDSHIP: Perhaps just focus – tell us what that dispute is so I am clear what that dispute is and we are all clear what the parameters of the question are. My understanding at the moment is that he accepts that the factors identified by Mr Rhodes would lead to a downturn in the number of passengers internationally, but he says those are temporary blips; the overarching reason why he says he and others would not have found jobs would be because of the alleged defamatory statements.

MR HUGGINS: Can I just look, then, so that I don't put any words in your mouth, at what you have actually said in your latest statement. You say this: 'In his supplemental witness statement, Mr Rhodes postulates that the reason none of the plaintiffs were able to obtain

418

employment' – that's your interpretation of what he is saying – 'subsequent to their dismissal was not because of the defamatory statements . . . but rather because of various events in the airline industry such as 9/11, the SARS epidemic and the global financial downturn.' You then say: 'Since the events affected air carriers worldwide, one would expect this to be reflected in employment statistics, including Cathay's.' I may have misread this and his Lordship has read it correctly, I don't know, but I had understood this as you in effect saying that you don't accept what Rhodes is saying because if he were right you would expect to see it reflected in Cathay's employment statistics; is that what you are saying?

A. I think his Lordship summed up my reply very succinctly in that, that yes, those things like 9/11 and SARS, et cetera, would have had an effect but . . .

Q. For how long? Are you qualified to say?

HIS LORDSHIP: I don't think anyone is qualified to say, Mr Huggins. I just deal with the evidence here. This is a matter of submission. I'm not really sure Mr Warham can take it any further.

Thank you, umpire. Four more.

MR HUGGINS: I have now had two indications from your Lordship and I'm not going to now attempt a third. Your Lordship has indicated that this is a matter for submission. I accept that and I will move on. Then we come to another matter: publicity created by the union. Do you agree that a great deal of publicity has been given by the union to the termination of the 49ers' employment?

HIS LORDSHIP: By the union, you mean Cathay Pacific's union or the pilots' union or the international . . .

MR HUGGINS: The HKAOA, one way or another, through publications and through their own announcements, have given wide public coverage to the termination of the 49ers.

Put this for six straight over his head.

A. I would say, Mr Huggins, the wider public coverage came from your clients' reports in the media on their websites. Certainly the AOA has responded to press enquiries, there was a large amount of interest, but the initial publication of this took place when your clients gave press conferences and put things on their website at the beginning of July 2001.

Q. Mr Warham, it's not only unseemly but it's inappropriate for us to argue about what inferences are to be drawn from this, and as to whether one or the other was a greater cause. His Lordship will determine that. My question, purely objectively, is focusing for a moment upon the publicity given by the HKAOA.

Ho ho ho. Didn't like that one. He's giving me the bowler's stare. Walk past him and do a bit of gardening.

HIS LORDSHIP: If it helps you, Mr Huggins, I think it cannot be denied that the union itself gave publicity to this event. In fact they requested the international union to blacklist Cathay Pacific. So however one looks at it, there was a lot of publicity attached to this generated by the union itself.

MR HUGGINS: But the IFALPA publicity was prompted, was it not, by the HKAOA?

HIS LORDSHIP: I think that's a matter I can just infer from the documents.

MR HUGGINS: As your Lordship pleases.

HIS LORDSHIP: Mr Warham has repeatedly stressed that at the relevant time he wasn't part of the managing committee of the union, so I can read the documents and I can draw inferences, aided by your submissions.

MR HUGGINS: My Lord, if you are to take the earlier answer, 'I was merely a negotiator' as meaning 'I don't know anything about what the union is doing', obviously that is right, but I rather ...

HIS LORDSHIP: I don't think that is what he was saying. He was a negotiator, he cannot deny that he knew what things were going on in the union, because he had access, for instance, to the union newsletters, which you have taken him through.

MR HUGGINS: Do you agree that the union and IFALPA were playing a central role in internationalising the issues in relation to this dispute and drawing attention worldwide to the dispute?

Put it over his head again. When's he going learn I've got that delivery covered?

A. The issues were already internationalised by Cathay's statements in the international media.

Q. That's a matter for his Lordship to decide.

HIS LORDSHIP: Again, as I have said, I don't know how many more indications you want on this. It is a matter for submission. You can argue it with Mr Grossman. I'm not going to be assisted too much by what Mr Warham says on this.

MR HUGGINS: My Lord, that's an indication you have now given on this issue, and I will therefore move on. Let me ask you this. In your earlier witness statements you seek to say that both your dismissal and the defamatory statements led to stress, anxiety and deterioration in your health, leading to the myocardial infarction. That's part of the evidence which you have now given by affirming to the earlier documents. Have I understood that correctly?

A. That is correct, yes.

Q. It is your opinion, which you are giving to this court, that your myocardial infarction was actually caused or contributed to by, one, the dismissal and, two, the statements of Tony Tyler and Philip Chen; is that what you are saying?

A. I am saying that the stress I was put under contributed to my MI.

Q. And have you sought to adduce any medical evidence to support that opinion of yours, in this case?

HIS LORDSHIP: I think there is obviously no medical evidence in the bundle, Mr Huggins, so the answer there is self-evident.

MR HUGGINS: I know, my Lord, but I respectfully submit, and perhaps this isn't the time to do it, but that might call in question the credibility of a witness who expresses that view, but that's a matter again for your Lordship, and you have given me another indication.

HIS LORDSHIP: Given his view that in his opinion it was brought upon or contributed to by stress, whether I can come to any conclusion on that on the evidence available, that's a matter for submission.

MR HUGGINS: Thank you, my Lord. Can I now move on, and at this rate if these are all matters for submission I won't be very much longer, but can I ask you this in relation – you have referred to a statement which I have tried to have ruled inadmissible but at the moment it's not, it's in and so I don't know whether to cross-examine about it or not, but you have expressed certain views in . . .

HIS LORDSHIP: I'm not quite sure how to take that statement, Mr Huggins, because the court expects that you use your judgment in matters of examination, cross-examination, and as we proceed, if I think we are going on something that I don't need cross-examination or examination on, I will tell you.

Some more byes coming here. Take a breather.

MR HUGGINS: My Lord, perhaps . . .

HIS LORDSHIP: I'm not sure if there is a criticism of the court.

MR HUGGINS: Oh, good heavens, no. Your Lordship must know me for long enough to know that there is no way that I would publicly criticise the court.

HIS LORDSHIP: I just want to make it clear, Mr Huggins, that we are proceeding in the way we are proceeding. Whether you like it or not, we will proceed in this way.

MR HUGGINS: I will do whatever your Lordship tells me to do. You have my assurance and I had hoped . . .

HIS LORDSHIP: If that puts you in difficulties, that's the job of senior counsel, to deal with such difficulties.

MR HUGGINS: It is your Lordship that rules this court, and I will without fail . . .

HIS LORDSHIP: If you don't like it, Mr Huggins, you can go to another court . . .

MR HUGGINS: My Lord, there is no question of referring . . .

HIS LORDSHIP: Right. Shall we continue, Mr Huggins?

Bloody hell. Byes and overthrows as well. Must be a ton on the scoreboard by now.

MR HUGGINS: As your Lordship pleases. I really am trying to assist your Lordship. If your Lordship is giving me another indication that the DGP affirmation of this witness is not something that needs to be . . .

HIS LORDSHIP: I don't know what the question is that you are going to put, Mr Huggins.

MR HUGGINS: If the DGP had been applied in this case, you, John Simpson Warham, would have done everything in your power, would you not, to have engaged in that procedure as economically and expeditiously as possible?

A. I would have . . .

HIS LORDSHIP: I'm not sure I will be assisted by this, Mr Huggins. Again, I think one can make submissions on both sides as to the length of the DGP, if that's what you are after.

MR HUGGINS: My Lord, certainly. At the moment I am faced – and obviously I have to deal with it as best I can – with the possibility that the court might have regard, I know not what weight . . .

HIS LORDSHIP: I know in Mr Crofts' English proceedings there was expert evidence on the length of time taken, but I'm not sure to what extent that expert evidence would have been helpful.

MR HUGGINS: In my respectful submission . . .

HIS LORDSHIP: I think it's a matter of submission, Mr Huggins.

MR HUGGINS: That is all I need to pass on. Forgive me, my Lord, but may I just say, without asking for any assistance from the court, which I wouldn't dream, that this is one of the difficulties one has if one doesn't know . . .

HIS LORDSHIP: Just deal with that difficulty, Mr Huggins. Plough on and then I react accordingly.

MR HUGGINS: I will, my Lord. In that case, I am not going to ask you about the details of that affidavit at all, in the light of the very helpful indication given to me by this court. Again, can I just ask one or two questions, because I don't know whether this is going to help his Lordship or not: in relation to what you have sought to say about what Ian Wilkinson told you, what steps, if any, have you taken to get Mr Wilkinson to come and give that evidence?

HIS LORDSHIP: I don't think I am helped by that, Mr Huggins.

MR HUGGINS: As your Lordship pleases. My Lord, I think what I am going to do – I hope it is consonant with all the indications your Lordship has given me – is ask your Lordship now to break for lunch, and I hope that I am going to come back and ask no more than half a dozen questions, if any.

HIS LORDSHIP: We will resume at 2.30. Mr Warham, you are still giving evidence, so again you can't discuss the matter with anybody else during the break. Thank you.

We knocked off for lunch and, when we came back to resume the innings, they gave up. No more questions. Now for some gentle net practice with Clive in re-examination.

MR GROSSMAN: Mr Warham, would you look, please, at bundle X, page 157. . . This is the letter . . . when there were references to people going off sick. Would you tell his Lordship, please, what was the procedure if you were sick or you wanted to take days off because you were sick?

A. First, you would have to visit – first, you would confirm to crew control and report unfit for duty, and I believe at the time, if the period of unfitness was more than two days, you had to go and see a doctor and get a certified sick note. The company also had its own principal medical officer, Dr John Merritt, and generally speaking the pilots would go and see him. Then you would file a sick note with Cathay Pacific, crew control, to let them know.

Q. This was in February 2001?

A. That's correct, yes.

Q. So was it possible to take off more than two days without getting a sick note?

A. No, it wasn't.

Q. Who was Mr Findlay at this stage?

A. He was the general secretary of the AOA.

Q. I see. Was he one of the 49ers?

A. No. He was an employee of the AOA.

Q. I see. What about Mr Demery? Was he one of the 49ers?

A. No, he wasn't. He was the union president at the time.

Q. Would you look now at page 221. You were taken to this letter from Mr Demery, and your attention was drawn to the third paragraph. I want to go through it with you; 'We must emphasise at this time we are not asking for heroes. This next logical step of incremental pressure can be performed without placing undue risk on any union member. Management will undoubtedly continue their attempts to intimidate you and may be looking for victims, so it is essential during this dispute that you fully comply with all company policies and procedures.' Just pause there. As far as you were concerned, was it always necessary to comply with company policies and procedures?

A. Yes, it was. As a professional airline pilot, the profession is very highly regulated, and all the procedures, operational procedures, standard operational procedures, are laid down in the company's operations manuals, and you are required to comply with the terms of those operations manuals whilst operating the aircraft.

Q. It goes on to say: 'Union policy will remain not to disobey any company order.' As far as you are aware, was that complied with?

A. I can only speak for myself, but certainly I did not disobey any company order.

Q. Then it says: 'Ensure that you are fully conversant with all the latest company procedures.' Was this something you were expected to do?

A. Yes. We would get, as well as the operations manuals, from time to time we would have notices to aircrew which would be issued by management, which would deal with operational matters that would come up from time to time that perhaps weren't covered fully in the manuals or needed clarification.

Q. It then goes on to say: 'We will be judged not only by management, but by the media and public, so remain professional both on and off the flight deck.' As far as you are concerned, did you try to maintain that standard?

A. Absolutely. I tried to maintain that standard throughout the whole of my career as a professional pilot.

Q. As far as you are aware, did this limited industrial action have any effect on the professional behaviour of the pilots?

A. Not in my experience, no.

Q. Was it ever part of the union plan that anyone should act unprofessionally?

A. Absolutely not.

Q. Now, you mentioned, during the course of some of your answers to my learned friend Mr Huggins, that you wanted to get the company back to the negotiating table. He suggested to you that the whole plan was to cause maximum commercial disruption. I'd like you to explain, please, what the purpose was of, first of all, the . . . limited industrial action.

A. As I saw it, I was not the author of this but as I saw it, it was a means to apply some more pressure to management to come back to the table and sort out the rostering practices which had been ongoing, the negotiations had been ongoing for two years, with no resolution in sight.

Q. You said you wanted to get them back to the negotiating table. Were you prepared to negotiate?

A. Yes, we were.

Q. Was management?

A. Well, at the last rostering negotiating meeting, management took a position which was unacceptable to the union, to the pilots, specifically with regard to an issue that's called commander's discretion. In commander's discretion, the captain of the aircraft has discretion to operate outside normal procedures under certain circumstances, but the decision to do that is the captain's and the captain's alone, and it's traditionally always been that way, and what the company were asking for was, anathema to us, for a clerk, rostering controller, to be able to order the captain to exercise that discretion. In exercising discretion, it would usually be in unusual circumstances, so there would be a lot of issues for the captain to consider before he decided whether or not to exercise such discretion, and there is no way that a person on the ground or a guy in the office can take all those factors into consideration, and it's traditionally, and always has been, the captain's decision alone, because if something goes wrong, he carries the can. So they were looking for a variation to this, to be able to order a captain to be able to exercise such discretion, and that professionally, to us, was completely unacceptable. That was one of the major stumbling blocks in the rostering practices negotiations.

Q. Thank you. Would you look now, please, at bundle III, and go to page 471. . . Captain Barley in this statement says: 'If he would prefer, I am authorised by the defendants to say they would be happy to supply on request letters for any of the plaintiffs confirming that their employment was not terminated on the ground of any or any alleged "misconduct or disciplinary offence".' Do you see that?

A. Yes.

Q. He refers in the first line to your paragraph 23 . . . [which] says: 'To emphasise the damaging and prejudicial effect of the defendants' actions, if I were now to apply to another airline for employment, that airline would undoubtedly know about my dismissal and the statements of Mr Tyler and Mr Chen (the airline industry is very close knit and matters such as this would be followed throughout the industry). The other airline would, therefore, regard me as someone who had been dismissed for misconduct or other disciplinary reason and my employment prospects would be damaged.' In that case, what you refer to is the statements from Mr Tyler and Mr Chen?

A. That's correct.

Q. These are the basis of your defamation case?

A. That's correct.

Q. Incidentally, do you know whether, notwithstanding this offer, any such letter was ever supplied to any plaintiff?

A. Not to my knowledge.

Q. Was it to you?

A. No, it wasn't.

Q. You can put that away. I want to ask you a general question, please, in addition to something you have already said. You were asked by Mr Huggins about the distress you felt, and I think you were elaborating on that perhaps when he interrupted you. I'd like you to tell the court, please, the effect that it had on you, as a senior captain, an alpha male, if I can put it that way, one day, and an unemployed, unemployable, airline pilot the next day.

A. Pilots are generally alpha male type characters. We are leaders. We are also very unforgiving of each other, and to have the reputation as I had at that time as a senior professional and to suddenly have that reputation taken away and excluded from the brotherhood that I had spent 32 years in was just a completely devastating blow. To have your reputation – I was internationally known through IFALPA, my peers and colleagues, and to have that suddenly destroyed was devastating. Being the sort of people we are, our peers and colleagues would say to me, 'You must have done something; they wouldn't have just done this to you, you must have done something', and we live in a sort of blame culture, in a way. Being an airline pilot is a very prestigious occupation. You . . .

HIS LORDSHIP: I think I've got the idea.

A. So for that, for 32 years to be taken away in a matter of seconds, it affected me professionally, it affected my home life, it affected me financially, it affected my health, and it affected every aspect of my life. We went from being, if you like, the alpha male leader of the pack to being the scraggy dog around the dustbins scavenging for food. It was a complete destruction of everything that we had worked for . . .

MR GROSSMAN: What do you put that down to?

A. I put it down to the defamation. Had the defendants merely sacked us and said nothing, we could have gone and got alternative employment, as did, for instance, just recently, Mr Wilkinson, as he was quite publicly fired by the defendants, three months later he has got a job as a senior captain in Qatar Airways. Because of what the defendant said about us in the public media we became unemployable, we became blacklisted throughout the aviation world. I put it down to the remarks that the defendants made about us in the media.

Q. Just one other question. If you had not been dismissed, for whatever reason, if you had had the heart problem that eventually developed, what would have been the position with your employment with Cathay?

A. My employment would have remained. There are very clear sickness provisions in the contract of employment. I would have had the surgery, I would have been on sick leave until I could regain my licence and my employment would have continued.

MR GROSSMAN: Thank you.

HIS LORDSHIP: Thank you very much. Mr Warham, thank you very much for coming this morning to give evidence. You are discharged.

THE WITNESS: Thank you, my Lord.

And that's how it went in direct and cross examination for all of us. No questions on supposed misconduct that they had tried to bring up in their last minute witness statements. Nothing in defence of their defamatory statements. No attempt to show justification. Just repeated attempts to paint us as a bunch of hard line unionists bent on deliberately causing maximum disruption to the airline's operations. Each of us played the bowling in different ways but we all told the same story. It wasn't rehearsed. The advantage we had over our opponents was that we were just telling the truth. We didn't need to hide under a cover of half truths and deceit.

Quentin Heron played an innings that was worthy of Geoff Boycott. He dead batted and stonewalled and didn't let a single ball through his guard. His forward defensive game was so good that at one point the bowler's frustration showed through when, in reply to one of Quentin's answers he exploded with:

MR HUGGINS: Mr Heron, I regret to tell you, but I am a blunt man, that is a bare-faced lie, I suggest to you.
A. I can only put it to your Lordship that I am giving you as much information as I possibly can, and I am being as truthful as I possibly can. I must admit that making that sort of accusation, without any foundation, I am sorry, I find offensive.

Four more to the boundary.

Mike Fitz-Costa's stroke play was reminiscent of David Gower. His shots were exquisitely timed and looked effortless. He used the pace of the ball and hardly worked up a sweat as he progressed rapidly to a century.

MR HUGGINS: 'I'll do my best. That is the answer you should give to any and all questions regarding your travel time to Cathay City after a Hong Kong reserve call-out.' 'When will you arrive?' 'I'll do my best', and so on. The spirit of that, did you follow that?
A. I don't need the union to tell me how to handle myself on the telephone and how to handle myself with crew control. If you are asking me whether I sat there and said those words, no, I did not. They knew where I lived, they knew that I had a bus schedule to get to work, they knew I had limited transportation. They asked me several times which bus I could take and I would tell them which bus I would take so to answer your question, no, I did not follow those regulations that were published in what I perceive to be a communication tool.
Q. Pages 196 to 197, please. This is a document sent on 16 May about the meeting on 20 June. Paragraph three on page 196: 'Your committee has selected "limited" industrial action with the aim of increasing the pressure incrementally . . .' Do you see that?
A. Yes, I do.

Q. What did you understand by that?

A. It has no meaning to me whatsoever.

Q. What does the word 'industrial action' mean to you, Mr Fitz-Costa?

A. 'Industrial action' can imply many issues. There was no – it was just purely limited industrial action. They had not stated at that stage what they were trying to imply.

Q. Mr Fitz-Costa, I'm not asking you in what circumstances, different circumstances it might be applied. I'm asking you, as a concept, what do you understand 'industrial action' to be, in the context of employers and employees?

HIS LORDSHIP: I'm not going to be too helped by whatever he answers to that question. I think what you're asking is what he understood the limited industrial action in this particular case to be. I think he's replied he had no idea – I think, if I understood you correctly.

A. That's correct. I had no idea. It was a statement that was put in there. I don't think at the time they knew what they were going to do. It was just – I keep coming back to this and this is my perception of this, there is a communication war that's going on between the company and the union, they were raising issues here. I was happy to watch and let it go along.

MR HUGGINS: Pages 217 to 220, the letter to the public; you would have seen that, would you not?

A. Yes, indeed.

Q. And you would have seen the clear statement to the travelling public of Hong Kong that the union was proposing limited industrial action and that inconvenience would be caused to them.

A. I never issued this letter.

Q. I know that.

A. Yes, I'm aware of this letter.

Q. And its contents.

A. I was aware of this letter after it was issued.

Q. You are hardly likely to have been aware of it before it was issued.

A. Then how do I – sorry, I'm not too sure where we're going with this, whether I'm asked to–

Q. Never mind where we're going. Just answer the question. The question is – you have told us you were aware of this, you were therefore aware that whatever form the limited industrial action was going to take, it was going to cause inconvenience to the travelling public, your union was telling them that, and anyone who saw this letter.

HIS LORDSHIP: The question, Mr Huggins?

A. The question, sorry?

MR HUGGINS: Did you appreciate that? I want to know your appreciation and understanding of that, that that was going to be the consequence.

A. My appreciation, as I said before, limited industrial action was very, very restricted to what the union could actually do. We were staying within contract compliance. There was nothing which we could actually do to actually – in my opinion, that would actually have breached our contracts. So our contracts were firmly in place, to operate the contract as I would do as a captain. What their rhetoric, what they were putting out there in public, what they wanted to say was up to them. I did not have any control over that documentation at all.

Q. But you were going to be asked yourself to support a resolution which was going to have that effect, which was designed to have that effect, were you not?

A. What we're asked to support and what we actually do are two different things. So I can quite distinctly, by myself, work out that if the union wants to bring up the tension a little bit, a little bit more pressure on the management, I can easily identify what is pressure and what is not pressure, what's reality, what's the reality of the situation and how I actually perceive the question to be.

Q. Did you vote on the particular resolution?

A. Yes, I did.

Q. In favour of it?

A. In favour.

Q. So when you voted in favour of it, the only thing, as I understand you to be saying, that you knew was that you were voting in favour of a form of limited industrial action, the precise nature of which you did not know at that stage.

A. Correct.

Q. But you did know that it was going to – it was designed to cause – it was going to be designed to cause . . .

A. To cause what?

Q. Inconvenience to the travelling public, and you were endorsing that, were you not?

A. I voted for limited industrial action. At the time I did not know what would be the outcome of that.

Q. So therefore you were in effect voting for something which you knew was going to be inconvenient to the travelling public, and the only way that could happen would be by disrupting the operations of the airline; is that not right?

A. No. I still disagree with you, because . . .

Q. How else was the travelling public going to be inconvenienced? If the airline's operations were running smoothly ...

HIS LORDSHIP: He was about to explain, because he started with the word 'because'; usually there are other words that are going to come in ...

MR HUGGINS: Sorry, I didn't hear that.

HIS LORDSHIP: I heard it quite clearly. He did say 'because'. You jumped right in and cut that off. I think he is entitled to say why he disagrees, because that would help me.

MR HUGGINS: Of course he is, my Lord. Mr Fitz-Costa?

A. We took a vote for limited industrial action. We did not know at the time what that implied. As my Lord said previously, it's like writing a blank cheque. I did that on the understanding that there's another phase in this situation as well, that we would be advised of what that industrial action could be or take place. As an individual and the captain of an aircraft, I would take it upon my own judgment whether I apply any industrial action or any safety management system they put in place. Again, I saw this more as rhetoric towards the public and towards the management.

Doug Gage played a cheeky innings and pinched a naughty single off the first ball:

MR HUGGINS: Mr Gage, I am going to try and finish you by lunch.
A. Are you really? Be gentle; I bruise easily.

Another little exchange about job applications led to some titters in the stand.

Q. Did you feel that was perhaps more important than getting – applying for a new job yourself?

A. Well, it doesn't say I didn't – we were in a situation where I think in the early days all of us were rather hoping that this situation would have been resolved in a rather more amicable fashion than it has turned out to be, and my home was in Hong Kong, this is where I live, and the Association had an enormous amount of work that needed to be done and I felt that I could best spend my time helping them sort out distressed families and all that kind of thing, as best I could.

Q. The only reason I ask, Mr Gage, is that of course the longer you choose to be off flying, as a pilot, the more difficult it's going to be for you to get another job as a pilot; is that not right, in general terms?

A. Potentially, that's true, yes.

Q. Nevertheless, it's your choice: you put, perhaps commendably, the union activities before your own well-being in that regard?

A. To be frank, Mr Huggins, a number of people, a number of my 49er colleagues, shall we say, dived straight in, as soon as the all-clear was given by our lawyers, and started applying for jobs. They were all being stonewalled, and I don't like banging my head against a brick wall, basically.

Q. Mr Gage, what I'd like you to do, if you would, is to focus on your own position.

A. Sure.

Q. The others are all being given a chance to speak.

HIS LORDSHIP: I think he was going to focus on his own position. Had he been allowed to speak a little bit more, he would have said I think, possibly, that on the basis of the stonewalling that he saw his colleagues encountering, then that affected the decisions that he took.

A. I couldn't put it better myself, my Lord.

Henry Van Keulen came in at end of the order. If the bowler was expecting to finish off the tail quickly he was in for a big surprise. Henry played a one-day innings and knocked up a quick 50 off very few balls. He concentrated on the flight safety issues and the bowler gave him huge opening when he opened the door on fatigue and tried the sick-out line.

MR HUGGINS: So that where it says, for example, that you were deeply concerned about the ever-eroding safety margins, were you personally?

A. Yes, I was.

Q. You were? So you would have felt pretty strongly, wouldn't you, that something needed to be done to put that right, if that was your feeling?

A. Yes, I would.

Q. Can I then go back in time. You would help me if you go back to page 101. You will see there reference to a – it's really a reminder by the union to its members about a resolution on contract compliance which became effective on 11 July 2000. We see that in paragraph 3. Can you just remind yourself of that? You have probably seen questions about this in the transcripts.

A. Yes, I have.

Q. Over the page, they set out a number of things which the union is encouraging its members about. Did you notice me asking questions about this in the transcript?

A. Yes, I recall that.

Q. Good. Can I now ask you, perhaps: some of the things it's reminding the aircrew that they are not required to do – let's go down six bullet points. For example, you are not required 'to discuss any matter of a medical nature with members of crew control or flight operations management. Specifically, you are not required: To give reasons for being unfit for duty beyond stating whether you were "ill" or "injured".' Do you remember that sort of indication being given, encouragement being given?

A. I would have most likely read this document, yes, this newsletter.

Q. So that in relation to your own experience, where I have suggested to you that there were a number of occasions when you called in sick on your reserve days, would you have felt that perhaps it might be of assistance to actually ring the management and explain the difficulties you were having, or did you think, 'Oh no, I don't have to do that, I'm not required to do that'?

A. No, I never thought that that was not a requirement. My relaying my own personal situation and well-being to the company was done through the company medical doctor. I recall at least two of my medicals prior to my dismissal, that would take me back to a year beforehand or almost a year, where I expressed concern with our company medical doctor that I was experiencing these fatigue cycles and, you know, the stress associated with those and other things like AMP and whatnot. He asked me at the time, 'Would you like some time off? In other words, do you want me to write you a chit for three weeks off or something like that?', and I told him I didn't want to do that because that would withdraw my services from the company over a period of time. I said what I would rather do is take it on a situation-by-situation basis, so that my services would be available for the company when I was feeling well or considered myself fit to fly, but when that was not the case then I would notify the company that I wasn't. I always did that. I never did that in a way that I left the company hanging. In other words, I wouldn't call up an hour before the flight and say, 'Sorry, I'm unfit for duty'. If I felt that I was going to be unfit for an upcoming duty period, be it reserve or flying duty, I would, if possible – obviously there are cases when you do become physically sick at the last moment, but whenever possible, if my feeling was that I would be unfit for a duty period, I would let crew control know in such a way that they were able to roster someone else, find a replacement with the least amount of disruption.

Q. Mr Van Keulen, it may be that I'm not getting through to you the precise point that I'm making, and I know that's my fault. Can I perhaps approach it this way: can we go to your own statement on this subject. In paragraph 24, you say, 'I became sick quite often. I had to recover to a normal standard of health. I was sick about once every three months. The time to recover was usually 10 to 12 days.' Then this: 'I discussed this situation at length with the company doctor during each six month medical.' So, yes, you spoke to your doctor.

A. Yes.

Q. But of course a doctor would have obligations of confidentiality in relation to you. Even though he may have been the company doctor, he couldn't speak to the company about this. Do you agree with that?

A. I agree, yes.

Q. 'He normally asked if I needed a period of time off to recover' – this is what you are telling us – 'and I replied that I would handle it on a trip by trip basis.'

A. That's right.

Q. 'In this manner', you say, 'the company was aware of the effect the roster was having on my personal health and ability to operate [Cathay] flights safely.' That's the bit I don't follow. That's your statement, isn't it?

A. That's correct.

Q. Can you help me with that, because of course the doctor couldn't have a word with Cathay . . .

A. Yes, he could.

Q. Forgive me, how?

A. He couldn't discuss with Cathay management directly my medical situation, but on an overview, if he has, let's say, a number of pilots coming to him with this same problem, he could then very well go to the company and say, 'There is a problem here. I have numerous people coming to me and saying that they're tired, they're fatigued, their roster is doing this to them. You need to do something'. So in that manner I feel that, yes, he did have a way of making the company aware of these fatigue problems.

Their whole defence seemed to us to be a very leaky boat. It seemed the judge agreed with us when the following exchange took place during the cross examination of Matt Rogers as he responded to a question about a job interview he went to at Emirates.

A. During the course of the interview they have a cocktail party, which is a gathering of all the people who are being interviewed and generally management or the people who are doing the employing. All the candidates are issued with a card name tag which had my name on it, and written 'Employer: Cathay Pacific', so that obviously they didn't know that I was no longer working for Cathay Pacific. The first person came up to me asked me, 'So why does a person want to leave Cathay Pacific and come and work for Emirates?' And it was at that point that I said, 'Are you familiar with the 49ers?' He said, 'Yes, I know exactly who the 49ers are', and then left the room.

MR HUGGINS: This is just the sort of . . .

MR GROSSMAN: I wonder if he could finish this. This is important.

MR HUGGINS: My Lord, my learned friend is saying it's important and this is one of the issues this morning that we weren't able to deal with.

HIS LORDSHIP: He is simply answering your question.

MR HUGGINS: In my respectful submission – and I will make it again — this kind of hearsay evidence is inadmissible.

HIS LORDSHIP: I can't really tell people how to answer your question, Mr Huggins. You control how you ask the question. You asked, how did the issue of his being terminated in 2001 arise. That was the thrust of your question that he is answering.

MR HUGGINS: I asked him whether or not he told them. He said no. Then he went on to embark on what in my respectful submission is the inadmissible area.

HIS LORDSHIP: He is elaborating on this. He is answering your question. Witnesses do this all the time, Mr Huggins. I am not going to cut him off.

MR HUGGINS: I am already feeling embarrassed that I even for a moment am appearing to debate with your Lordship and I should not. I should immediately . . .

HIS LORDSHIP: I am surprised at the way in which you are conducting this matter today, which to a certain extent I believe is not your usual style. I am somewhat surprised.

Things were going well for us. The case was being conducted in a businesslike and professional manner as we expected it would be given the judge's reputation. On the fifth day of the trial, however, a very unsavoury incident occurred that sickened me to my stomach and changed the whole nature of the thing for me. One of our number had been ill for quite some time and we were very concerned about him. It became obvious that Mr Huggins had realised this as, during cross examination, he was far less aggressive than he had been with some of us and we were all very grateful for his considerate treatment. Despite that, it soon became clear that our friend and colleague was in considerable distress as he began to break down emotionally under questioning. What followed next I can only liken to an experience I had some years earlier when I visited an 'animal park' in China with my wife to get some undercover film footage of abuse that was going on in one of their exhibits.

The 'show' consisted of a small arena in the centre of which a domestic cow was tethered. Two tigers were let into the arena and they attacked the cow. The tigers were fat and well fed and did not bring down the animal with a quick kill by suffocating it as they would normally do in the wild. Instead they just took bites out of it, gnawed at its legs and ripped at its hide with their claws. This went on for some time before the tigers were removed from the arena. The cow was still alive and bellowing pathetically but, even then, the 'keepers' did not dispatch the poor, wretched animal. Instead they tied ropes to its legs and dragged it out of the arena behind a lorry. It was one of the most sickening and disgusting spectacles of animal cruelty that I have ever witnessed and, throughout the whole thing, the audience of men, women and children was sitting there eating ice creams, laughing and pointing at what was happening in front of them. It made me ashamed to be a part of the human race.

What happened in court on the fifth day put me right back in that animal park. As my friend and colleague broke down on the witness stand, just like the disgusting crowd at the park, some of the people from Cathay in the public gallery started laughing and pointing and making fun of him. Of course, they couldn't laugh out loud because Caesar was watching. Instead they sat there nudging each other, snickering and giggling behind their hands. I have been told that some people cover up their discomfort by such behaviour. I don't buy it. These are supposed to be educated men. I am ashamed to say that I was ever involved with them in a professional capacity. I will neither forgive nor forget what they did.

29

Trial 3

*'The truth is incontrovertible. Panic may resent it, ignorance
may deride it, malice may distort it, but there it is.'*
                                                Winston Churchill

On the evening of the third day of the trial, something very significant
happened. The opposition filed two new witness statements from Tyler
and Chen. They were going to put them on the stand. Why would they
change their position? We could only speculate. Things were going badly
for them and maybe they thought it would bolster their defence. Maybe
the Swires in London had told them to get in there and fix it. They had
made the defamatory statements so they had better sort it out. We didn't
care either way. It would be good to get the mouthpieces up there to try
to defend themselves. The judge gave us an opportunity to object to their
late statements but we declined his invitation. Bring them on. The more
the merrier. It's not often you can get the CEO of the biggest Hong in
Hong Kong under cross examination. We licked our lips and looked
forward to taking the new ball.

On the fourth day of the trial, something else happened. As we were
getting though our witnesses so quickly, we had to re-jig our batting
order again because of the logistical problems of getting our overseas
players in from abroad. The judge brought up some housekeeping matters
as a suggestion.

HIS LORDSHIP: I am just going to make a few more suggestions,
    possibly more radical suggestions, but they are just suggestions . . .

There are only two witnesses on Monday, so is there some way that we can make better use of Monday by having some, possibly the less consequential of Cathay's witnesses cross-examined on that day? I will in a moment indicate who those witnesses – who might be considered that type of witness. We have three witnesses on Tuesday, and if Tuesday is going to go anything like this, there is the possibility, let's say, that Tuesday afternoon might be free. Can we have other Cathay witnesses on that day? And then Wednesday, Thursday, proceeding along the lines discussed earlier. Which witnesses might be considered? I am just going to give some names that, having had a quick look through their witness statements, might be considered, but these are just suggestions. Mr Huggins, you might feel that you don't want to put them in until after you have heard certain witnesses: Mr Nipperess, Mr Hau, Mr Davies, Mr Hall, Mr Lam, Mr Dennis Leung, Ms Christina Wong, Mr Hoyland and Mr Maddox. Now, some of them give a list of names of pilots and say, "This one, we, crew control, thought uncooperative; we thought this one argumentative; we thought this one obstructive", whatever. But their witness statements don't really give any particulars about that; they are vague on particulars, so I can't really make any findings on that. So even if those witness statements came in without cross-examination, it's not really going to be very helpful to me if that's all they are going to be saying, because without specific particulars I just couldn't make any particular finding at all. I think Mr Huggins, from the way he has been conducting the case, I think implicitly he recognises that. That's reading between the lines, the way the cross-examination has taken place. Mr Grossman might consider that because certain witnesses, particularly in light of my remarks, you might think there is really no point in cross-examining them because even if their witness statements go in it gets no one any further, and we may save time that way. Or we may interpose them briefly, quickly, and Mr Grossman deals with them as he thinks fit. Those are just suggestions. You don't have to respond right now.

MR GROSSMAN: My Lord, I can say this. Actually, it is a matter for my learned friend. I have no objection whatsoever whether any of the defence witnesses are interposed, let me say that immediately. Subject to my learned friend of course telling me the order, I don't care. Your Lordship will understand from my point of view, I have 18 different cases to put. I'm not saying it will be a long time. Most of them will be a sentence or two. I am very wary, not in front of your Lordship, but I am wary of having allegations made against individual pilots – like some of them say Mr Gage was difficult to contact, for instance

– and I just leave it. Unless your Lordship indicates to me that you are not going to make a finding in that regard.

HIS LORDSHIP: I have given an indication, I think, that unless we have specific matters, "This and this event", then I'm not really sure how I can make findings. The individual pilots are actually going up and giving evidence now on behalf of the plaintiffs. We have seen what Mr Huggins puts and what Mr Huggins doesn't put, so that — it seems to me it will be hard, if he hasn't put any particulars that "you didn't answer the phone on such and such an occasion", I don't see how I can suddenly allow further and better particulars suddenly to materialise in the defendants' witness statements when such a case hasn't been put forward in cross-examination. Just reflect on that, Mr Grossman.

MR GROSSMAN: I understand that but of course – I am really thinking aloud here – when these statements are put in at the last minute, put in the bundle, I have to assume some use will be made of them by my learned friend.

HIS LORDSHIP: Some fair use will be made of them, because the court will not allow unfair use to be made of them.

MR GROSSMAN: I have to assume my learned friend . . .

HIS LORDSHIP: I'm not going to tell you how to do your job, Mr Grossman. You just think about it, and you take whatever decision you feel – you run it the way you think you ought to. There are risks, Mr Grossman, in yourself over, how do you say – like Mr Huggins at times, when Mr Huggins asks the question, he gets an unexpected answer which then sometimes surprises him, possibly annoys. You would face the same risk, Mr Grossman.

MR GROSSMAN: Very well.

In other words, all the anecdotal 'evidence' submitted in witness statements authored by Hoyland and his crew controllers wasn't worth the paper it was written on. There was no documentary evidence to back up any of their claims and, since we hadn't been cross-examined on any of the content, it was worthless to the judge in his deliberations. Result. They were down to four witnesses, Rhodes, Kroutil, Tyler and Chen.

Rhodes was first up in the afternoon of Tuesday 13 October 2009, the sixth day of the trial. Oh, how we had waited for this day. Clive got stuck straight in with a full-on pace attack.

MR GROSSMAN: Mr Rhodes, I have read your statements and I have listened to the case that has been put by Mr Huggins to the witnesses.

You have been in court all the way through, I think. Tell me, why were these 49 dismissed?

A. Because, after very careful review, we felt that they weren't working in the best interests of the company.

Q. What did that have to do with the contract compliance scheme?

A. It was a combination – the assessment was a combination of attitude during the contract compliance period, helpfulness and level of co-operation with the company, and attendance. It was a combination of attendance and attitude was really how we assessed the plaintiffs.

Q. What about the maximum safety scheme? Was that a contributing factor?

A. No. The introduction of the MSS was really the trigger for us to conduct the review, but it wasn't a factor in itself.

Q. Is it the position that any of these 49 were dismissed because of their union activities concerning the contract compliance scheme or not?

A. That was purely their individual attitude and attendance. That's all we could assess.

Q. It had nothing to do with the contract compliance scheme?

A. Well, their behaviour during the contract compliance scheme was reflected in their level of co-operation with the company and their level of helpfulness.

Q. Yes?

A. But we couldn't have any way of knowing whether they voted for contract compliance. We just could see their actions, and all we were assessing was the actions in their day-to-day duties, and whether they were helpful/unhelpful, cooperative/uncooperative, pro-company/anti-company. All we could do was assess the actions. We don't know where they lie in any other union matters.

Q. Would it be right to say, then, that your evidence is that union matters had nothing to do with the decision to dismiss any of these individuals?

A. Well, the decision to dismiss the individuals was based purely on the actions we were witnessing. Now, I mean, I was aware that the union was promoting contract compliance, was promoting crew to be uncon-tactable. We believe the union was involved in the sick-out campaign, based on that email I had received. I know the union was involved in that, but all we could judge was which crew members were acting in an unhelpful fashion that we felt was against the company's interest. That was all we could assess.

Q. So, as far as the individuals are concerned – I want to make sure that I do understand it – these 49 are concerned, none of them was dismissed because of specifically taking part in union activities?

A. No, I think I'm quite clear they were specifically dismissed because of their actions and their attitude and their attendance issues.

Q. I see. You've heard the case that was put by your counsel, and I think it's true to say to every single one of them, the suggestion was they were participating in union activities. Didn't you hear that?

A. I . . .

Q. That was the case that was put.

A. I've been in court, yes.

Q. First of all, would you look at bundle IX, page 2907? This is a letter dated 27 June 2001. We haven't looked at it yet. It's from Captain Barley. It's written on Cathay Pacific letterhead, and can I take it that it would have been written with some kind of official sanction?

A. If it was written by Captain Barley, yes.

Q. All right. Let's see what it says. 27 June 2001, we understand the chronological context: 'Dear Crew Member, I thought it was important to update you personally on current negotiations and to clearly state the company's intentions in the event of disruption.' Do you see that?

A. Yes.

Q. 'Let me begin by strongly stating the company's hope that an agreement can still be achieved and that we are prepared to continue nonstop talks toward that end.' Would it be fair to say that that was the company's attitude at that stage?

A. Yes, we were still in talks.

Q. 'As you may be aware, I delivered a letter to the HKAOA on Monday setting a firm deadline to conclude negotiations by midnight Thursday 28 June unless the HKAOA withdrew their intention to distribute their disruption plan to members the following day.' Do you see that?

A. I see that.

Q. It goes on to say, '. . . we are committed to reaching a negotiated settlement . . .', et cetera. If you turn to page 2, it says: 'I realise that the month ahead may be a difficult one. Sadly there are some militant members of the HKAOA who will put pressure on the rest of our pilots to disrupt our operations. Some of this pressure may also be directed against families and loved ones and so I would like to offer our unconditional support to help all pilots and their families who feel they are subjected to this sort of pressure.' I want to pause there. Is any of the 49 included in these militants that are referred to?

A. I haven't referred to any of the 49 as militant, no.

Q. Captain Barley does. I just want to know if he is representing individual people, you understand.

441

A. I don't think he was referring to anyone specifically, no.

HIS LORDSHIP: Did you help in the drafting of this letter?

A. I can't recall.

HIS LORDSHIP: You can't recall whether you helped in the drafting of this letter?

A. I can't recall specifically, my Lord.

HIS LORDSHIP: Did you discuss the letter with him?

A. Most likely.

MR GROSSMAN: Very well. The last paragraph says: 'Let me stress once again that we will do all we can to help reach a comprehensive settlement with the HKAOA and put this current dispute behind us. Then we can work together once more to concentrate on making Cathay Pacific the world's most admired airline.' If you had reached a settlement, which everybody was striving for, it says, would these 49 have been dismissed?

HIS LORDSHIP: I think that's speculative, Mr Grossman.

MR GROSSMAN: No, I want to know what his intention was. Was it still the intention, on the 29th – when this document was signed, 27 June, was it the intention at that stage to sack people, to dismiss people?

A. No.

Q. It wasn't?

A. We had no intention at this stage to sack people.

Q. All right. So, can we assume . . .

HIS LORDSHIP: That wasn't quite the question. The question was if negotiations had succeeded, would anyone be sacked?

A. Again a hypothetical. I'm not certain what would have happened.

HIS LORDSHIP: I think the way Mr Grossman wishes it to be put: if the negotiations had succeeded, was the intention on 27 June 2001 that anyone would be sacked?

A. My wish, my desire, was to reach a negotiated settlement round the table, in which case the threat of industrial action would be lifted, contract compliance would be lifted, and we'd return to normal. That was our hope.

MR GROSSMAN: That was your hope?

A. That was my hope.

Q. So it was your hope, was it, that everybody could get round the table, everything would be sorted out, nobody would need to be dismissed?

A. Absolutely. That was my wish.

Q. These 49 people, then, were dismissed because you didn't get around the table and come to an agreement?

442

A. Well, I think once we failed to reach an agreement and the limited industrial action was launched, and we started to lose those hundreds of millions of dollars, that's when the patience of my seniors ended. I'd been under a lot of pressure for the past 18 months from some of my seniors, who couldn't believe how patient we were being in trying to reach a deal, while all of the increased sickness was going on, and I said, 'Look, give me time, give me time. When we reach a deal, the sickness levels will come down. If we reach a deal, the crew will start co-operating', and I pushed and pushed for time to reach an agreement. I think once the limited industrial action started and we failed to reach an agreement, that was the catalyst for the senior management to say, 'No more time. We don't wish to employ crew working against our interests'.

Q. 49 people were dismissed because you didn't reach an agreement?

A. No, 49 people were dismissed because of their actions over the previous 30 months.

Q. What did that have to do with whether you reached an agreement or not?

A. Well, if we'd reached an agreement, the hope was they would stop the sickness and stop the contract compliance and everything would return to normal and we'd be able to crew our flights and passengers would stop cancelling bookings.

Q. Those 49 people, those 49 would stop their misbehaviour, as it were?

A. Well, all – yeah, all crew members who were participating in contract compliance or the sick-out campaign would stop and come back to normal behaviour. That would be the hope.

Q. I'm talking about the 49 people.

A. Well, the 49 people are the ones during the review on 5/6/7 July who we thought were the most active participants in the contract compliance and the . . .

Q. They were the most active participants in the contract compliance scheme?

A. In being uncooperative and unhelpful and poor attendance, those were the ones who we assessed as being the most unhelpful to the company during that period.

Q. But they would not have been dismissed had you reached an agreement with the union?

A. If we'd reached an agreement that day and limited industrial action was called off, and contract compliance was lifted, of course there would have been no further action.

Q. I see. Thank you. You can put that away for a moment . . .

MR GROSSMAN: His Lordship is not going to make a ruling one way or another whether you were under-crewed or over-crewed one way or whatever, but would you accept that there was a real concern, justified or not, amongst the pilots, that Cathay Pacific was under-crewed?

A. I can't comment whether it was a real concern. That was the line the union was using, and I believe that was the line that many of the AOA members believed, but it wasn't the situation. I think that was part of the communication campaign or propaganda campaign or rallying the troops. That was why the roster was so unstable, because we were short of crew, whereas the truth is the roster was unstable because of that heightened level of sickness.

Q. Would you accept that the pilots themselves were in a better position than the management to know if they were flying too much, if they were stressed from overflying?

A. No – well, two questions there, but we had the data as to how many hours the pilots were flying, how many days the pilots have off, and we don't believe that that was beyond the norm in terms of hours flown and days off.

MR GROSSMAN: We will continue this tomorrow, with his Lordship's permission.

HIS LORDSHIP: Unfortunately, Mr Rhodes, apparently we will be interposing a few witnesses before you resume. During the time that you are giving evidence, during the adjournment, you may not discuss the case with anyone. So until you resume, which may be sometime tomorrow morning, or perhaps tomorrow afternoon, you may not be able to discuss the case with anyone. That may make you very happy. You have been living with the case for a little while . . . So we will start with Mr Tyler . . . Thank you very much.

It was a good start from our bowler. Four maiden overs to end the day, the night watchman ducking and weaving as the bouncers sprayed around his head and he hadn't managed to get bat on ball. He was in for a lonely time until he could resume his innings. Our team repaired off to our de facto office, The Captain's Bar in the Mandarin Oriental Hotel, for a post-match analysis and a few well earned coldies.

Wednesday 14 October, the seventh day of the match, dawned bright and clear. We walked out into the field and Tyler came in to bat. Clive was bowling from his long run up and set five slips and a gully plus silly mid-off with only two men on the leg side at silly mid-on and deep backward square. The batsman was crowded.

MR GROSSMAN: Mr Tyler, I understand from what you have said in your statement that you were not part of the decision-making process as to who to dismiss?

A. That's correct.

Q. You simply understood that you had been told by someone or some people that it was necessary to sack a number of people; is that the position?

A. I wasn't . . .

Q. Perhaps I will put it more clearly. Did you know in advance of being given a list of 49 people that a number of people were going to be dismissed?

A. I knew that the decision had been taken to review the records of the aircrew workforce, to identify those who were – who the company had lost confidence in and in whom we couldn't rely. So I knew that the outcome of this process was likely to be the decision to terminate people, but I had no idea who it would be or how many.

Q. What did you understand the reason for the sacking of these 49 people was?

A. The company had been subjected to, over the past few years, indeed, an escalating amount of pressure from the union, exhibited by behaviour of pilots to attempt to disrupt the company's operations. Just prior to this particular episode, if you like, the union had announced a significant stepping-up of the pressure, and we in the company believed that we couldn't allow this to go on, in the interests of the company, and indeed the travelling public of Hong Kong, so therefore, as I think we said, some firm and resolute action was necessary.

Q. But why these 49?

A. I don't know why – I wasn't involved in the process of identifying the particular pilots who were selected for contract termination, so I don't know why each individual one was selected, but I was aware there was a process of reviewing all the records.

Q. What did you understand was the reason for the sacking of these 49 people? Not talking about the individual but the group.

A. I think I have already explained that, that we felt some firm action was necessary on the part of the company to make sure that those pilots who we could not rely on to basically do their jobs and who we could not rely on to – in whom we had lost confidence, to leave the company.

Q. I see. What did this have to do, if anything, with their union activities?

A. It had nothing to do with their union activities.

Q. Nothing whatsoever to do with their union activities?

A. We had selected them based on their behaviour, and as far as I was aware – and I wasn't involved, as I say, personally in the process – the union activities had nothing to do with this.

Q. Nothing to do with this? So these 49, then, would they have been dismissed anyway, irrespective of whether there was contract compliance, whether there were any union activities?

A. We don't, as I believe I've said in my witness statement, we don't as a matter of routine examine the files with a view to terminating contracts of employment. I think we've got to remember, this was in the middle of, if you like, a culmination of a long and escalating campaign of industrial action, disruption by some pilots.

Q. But I understand you said industrial action had nothing to do with the sackings?

Beautiful. Brought him out of his crease and then stuck one right in the block hole.

A. These individuals were selected – my understanding was these individuals were selected on the grounds based on their individual behaviour, as pilots for Cathay Pacific.

Q. Would they have been dismissed whether or not there was industrial action?

A. Well, it's a hypothetical question. As I've said, we don't, as a rule, just review, as a matter of routine, the files.

HIS LORDSHIP: I think, Mr Tyler, it's a 'yes' or 'no' question or 'I don't know'.

Whoops. Careful now. Don't get the umpire tetchy.

A. In that case, I don't know.

MR GROSSMAN: All right. I will take it from there. You were satisfied, were you, that these 49 were deserving of being dismissed and publicly vilified?

Reverse swing and right on his toes. Let's see how he plays this one.

A. Well, if I may, there are two questions in that.

Q. Yes, that's true.

A. The first one, was I satisfied that these 49 – it was appropriate to terminate these contracts? I was satisfied that the process that had been gone through was thorough and was fair, and I trusted the individuals involved in that process. So yes.

Q. Did you think that the behaviour of these 49 was such that they deserved that a person like you and Mr Chen and Captain Barley would say to the aviation world and the world at large that they were troublemakers, unprofessional?

A. I don't believe I used those words. In fact I didn't use those words. We had a responsibility and a requirement to tell our staff, tell the travelling public what was going on and why we had taken various actions. As everybody knows, there was massive interest among the public, and of course our staff, in what was happening. So we had to give an explanation of what was going on.

Q. But if these people were dismissed because of nothing to do with their union activities, why was it necessary to even mention it to the public? Why not simply say to the public, 'Well, we have taken internal measures and we're satisfied that there are not going to be any problems with delays', et cetera?

That's it, keep him on the back foot.

A. Because the public – it was not realistic to expect, in the interest – to expect that one could satisfy the public interest in this with such an explanation. One had to say more than that.

Q. So, correct me if I am wrong, I don't want to be unfair, but essentially what you're saying is that you thought that these 49 people were not working in the interests of the company, or didn't have the interests of the company at heart?

A. That's correct.

Q. That would be a fair way of putting it, would it?

A. Yes.

Q. I just want to ask you about one particular aspect. Are you familiar with the Sunnyside Club?

Nice change of pace. See if he picks it.

A. Yes.

Q. What is it?

A. It is a club which exists to raise funds and assist in other ways; a home, called the Sunnyside Home, for severely disabled children.

Q. This is done from the point of view of goodwill from Cathay Pacific?

A. Cathay Pacific supports the club in a number of ways. The members of the club are either all or mostly Cathay Pacific staff.

Q. Yes. They do a fair amount, do they, to bring good public relations, put it that way, to Cathay Pacific?

A. Clearly the fact that the Sunnyside Club exists is obviously a good thing for Cathay Pacific and it's something that certainly internally everybody knows about, yes.

Q. And the people who run it presumably are doing so in the best interests of Cathay Pacific?

A. I think they're doing it actually in the best interests of the children who they are benefiting, and I support the club myself, so I mean . . .

Played and missed.

Q. That's something you applaud, presumably?

A. Indeed.

Q. Are you aware that of these 49 the chairman and vice-chairman of the Sunnyside Club were sacked?

A. I am aware of that, they had their contracts terminated.

Q. You said they weren't acting in the best interests of Cathay Pacific?

A. I think their prime – I think they were – certainly, what they were doing for the Sunnyside Club was a very worthy activity. But their duties as far as their responsibilities to Cathay Pacific were concerned were to operate as pilots, and that was the grounds upon which we were evaluating their performance.

Straight past the bat again.

Q. Would you consider that doing that at least indicates they have the interests of the company at heart?

A. I believe what it indicates is that they have the interests of the children of that school at heart, and as you've said, that's a very merit-worthy thing.

Owzat umpire? Plumb LBW.

HIS LORDSHIP: That's not quite an answer to Mr Grossman's question.

A. Sorry.

HIS LORDSHIP: He asked whether you believed whether they had, in working for the club, the interests of Cathay Pacific at heart as well as the interests of the children.

A. I don't believe that working for the club demonstrates necessarily that they had the interests of Cathay Pacific at heart, no.

Oh really? Thick edge surely? We'll check the replay later.

MR GROSSMAN: Aren't you being a little unkind? Surely, if they are spending their spare time working on a matter which obviously they thought was worthwhile, the good publicity going to Cathay Pacific would indicate goodwill on their part towards the company?

A. I don't believe I'm being unkind. I think the people involved, clearly what they were doing for the Sunnyside Club was a very good thing, but they weren't doing it for Cathay Pacific, and what we needed from our pilots was behaviour as pilots which supported – their prime job, obviously, was not to do PR for Cathay Pacific, it was to act as pilots, and it was therefore on those grounds that their performance was assessed.

Q. In fact, one of the people who was dismissed used to fly the Cathay balloon, take it around the world, in his spare time, on vacation, showing a huge amount of Cathay Pacific publicity. Don't you think that was showing goodwill to . . .

Beauty. He didn't see that coming.

A. Well, I think of course it was a good thing for the company, but it was also – and I'm not aware who you're talking about, but generally speaking several pilots over the years have done this, it was a hobby of theirs, and of course the company assisted them in their hobby, indeed you might say funded it, by providing the resources to do it, and probably some time off to assist. And certainly the company benefited from the PR, so I think it was something that benefited everybody.

Right on the helmet. Didn't manage to get out of the way of that one. Stick the next one in his box.

Q. Come on, Mr Tyler. You've got a situation here where one of the persons, who also happened to be the chairman of the Sunnyside Club, was going around the world, in his spare time, not on Cathay Pacific's time, and flying this balloon which had 'Cathay Pacific'

449

circled round it; huge publicity for Cathay Pacific. Is that not showing interest, goodwill, towards the company?

Perfect. Right on target.

A. Well, I'm sure that these things were taken into account by the group of people who were – I mean, everybody will have known that. I can only assume that that sort of thing would have been known by the gentlemen and others in the flight operations department who were largely involved with the process.

Yep, he'll have a nice bruise there later.

Q. Well, we have seen a lot of documentation here. I haven't seen anybody here saying Mr Gage and Mr Fitz-Costa, for instance, were doing a lot of good work for the company. Does that surprise you?

A. Does it surprise me that . . . ?

Q. That there is nothing in writing, no document, in all these thousands of documents we have seen, that indicates that that was taken into account, that anybody thought about it?

A. Well, I haven't reviewed – I don't know what is in all these many documents. I don't have any view on it.

Q. Does it surprise you that there's no record of it?

A. In these documents?

Q. Yes.

A. No, it doesn't.

Q. It doesn't? All right. Now I want to ask you about some of the things that were said. Look at bundle I, page 6. You see it says [Mr Tyler] stated that the dismissals of the aircrew officers were the result of a review of pilots' records begun 'a few days ago when the union made it clear it was going to escalate industrial action'.

A. Yes.

Q. Just pausing there for the moment, the review was specifically consequent upon the industrial action that the union said it was going to escalate?

A. That's right.

Q. So would it be right to say, therefore, that the dismissals did have something to do with the industrial action?

Beamer. Look out.

450

A. Well, yes. Clearly, as I've said, we wouldn't have been undertaking this if we weren't in a position where the company was under great stress and pressure as a result of the actions being taken by the pilots, and those actions were, as we all understood, instructed by the union.

Q. All right. You then go on to say: 'Hong Kong is tired of being held to ransom.' Held to ransom by whom? Who did you have in mind?

A. What was happening was that the pilots who were disrupting our operations were – it's, if you like, a colourful turn of phrase – but to imply that travel in and out of Hong Kong was being disrupted by the pilots taking this action.

Q. I'm not concerned so much about being held to ransom. There is no criticism of that. One understands. I want to know, who was holding Hong Kong to ransom?

A. The pilots who were seeking to disrupt company operations.

Q. Those are the 49 who were dismissed?

A. It certainly included those people, as I understood it.

Q. It included the 49?

A. As I – yes.

Q. So we can assume, therefore – this was what you were told, was it?

A. Yes.

Q. That these 49 people were holding the company to ransom?

A. Yes.

Q. Or were amongst those?

A. Amongst them, yes.

Q. 'We believe it was time for some form of resolute action.' This resolute action was to dismiss these people, or 49 of them, anyway?

A. Yes.

Q. All right. Then at (9A) is set out the press release, which I think Mr Huggins showed you. Do you see that?

A. I do.

Q. All right. That was on your website – until when, Mr Tyler?

Oh good ball.

A. I don't know.

Q. I can tell you. It was on your website until 12 September 2009. That's the evidence. Why?

A. I don't know, but I imagine that when the things are put on the website, they stay there unless they are specifically taken off. I imagine that they're gradually, as it were, buried by other press releases that

451

come along later on. But I would imagine that is why it remained there: nobody thought to take it off.

Straight past the bat to the keeper.

Q. These 49ers, as they became known, famously, throughout the world, are still referred to, or they were referred to until a couple of weeks ago, on your website. Don't you think that's appalling? Anybody who wanted to find out about them, what was going on, if they applied for a job and looked up the Cathay Pacific website, could see your statement.

A. I'm not denying that they can do that. The statement doesn't, of course, mention anyone by name.

Q. Of course not, but I think you know perfectly well that the word '49ers' became notorious in the aviation world?

A. It was not the name the company used ever, certainly in public.

Q. Mr Tyler, you know perfectly well that the word '49ers' became notorious in the aviation world; is that right?

Yorker. Mind your toes.

A. I don't know. It certainly was well known in Hong Kong. How notorious it is around the aviation world, I don't know.

Q. All right. Well, we have heard evidence about that anyway. Let's have a look at what you said: "Cathay Pacific cannot simply stand by and allow the [union's] selfish action to cause such damage." All right? So your complaint here, the first line is about the union, not the 49ers, not the 49 people, but about the union?

A. That's what it says, yes.

Q. "Nor is Hong Kong prepared to tolerate such disruptions by the [union] on what seems to be a repeated basis." Do you see that?

A. Yes.

Q. Did you have in mind when you were saying that, or did you have in mind – when you talked of the union, you were talking about these 49 people?

A. We were talking about all the pilots who were participating in this disruption.

Q. All the pilots, which includes the 49, and the 18 that I represent?

A. I did not, of course, have in mind specific individuals.

Q. No. Then it says: "Under the circumstances, we need to take prompt and firm action to resolve the situation for the good of all our employees, our customers, our shareholders, the tourism industry and the whole of Hong Kong ... We were frustrated that union leadership blocked our earlier proposal." So your complaints here still, it seems to me, were about the union, all right?

A. Yes. There is a sort of gap there, so ...

Q. All right.

A. But certainly, clearly I said these words.

No really? Talk about stating the bleedin' obvious.

Q. "Sadly, we have also taken the very painful decision to terminate the employment of 49 of our pilots. This is in addition to the three cases previously announced. Thus, today, we have issued letters of termination to these pilots." It is perfectly clear, is it not, that you linked the sacking, the dismissal of these pilots to the union action, the actions taken by the union?

A. It's certainly clear that if there wasn't this action going on, this would not have happened.

Q. No, no, no. What you say is, and I'm summarising, "These people are holding us to ransom, the union is holding us to ransom, there's a body of people holding us to ransom, thus we have decided to dismiss them"?

Good straight fast ball. Right on line and length.

A. We decided to review the records. Because of the union action we decided to review the records of all pilots, and we didn't know whether they were union members or non-union members – really that was not a consideration – and terminate the contracts of those whom we felt we could not rely on and in whom we had lost confidence.

Past the bat again. I don't think he's even off the mark yet is he?

Q. Mr Tyler, what you are saying in this press release, which from the evidence had very wide circulation, is, "There was union activity which we believed was going to cause disruption, and thus we decided to sack the 49 pilots"?

A. Well, the press release says what it says.

Yes it does. Umpire?

HIS LORDSHIP: If you feel like it, Mr Grossman, just point to the actual words . . . I think what you are after, Mr Grossman, is the sixth bullet point from the bottom of the page: "Therefore, after extremely careful consideration we have decided on two courses of action."

MR GROSSMAN: Thank you very much. Mr Tyler I simply will suggest to you that it is perfectly clear here that what you are saying is, "Because of the union disruption, we have decided to sack 49 people".

A. Well, if you like . . . As I say, the rest of the words really – I mean, the words say what we honestly and truthfully meant them to say.

Umpire? Please . . .

HIS LORDSHIP: But the answer to Mr Grossman's question, Mr Tyler – he says, because of the union's action, you did two things: you point out, first, there was the pay rise; and then second, there was also the sacking of the 49 pilots. Is that a correct reading by Mr Grossman? Do you say that's a wrong reading?

A. It's putting it into different words, but it's essentially correct.

HIS LORDSHIP: Right. Mr Grossman?

MR GROSSMAN: Thank you. I'm just going to continue. If we could turn to page 7 it says: "We have taken this serious step only after extremely careful consideration. We have undertaken a detailed review of the employment history of all our pilots and identified those who, we feel, cannot be relied upon to act in the best interests of the company in the future." Pause there. Is that right?

A. Yes.

Q. That's correct, is it? So we can take it, then – and we will look at some of them – that on the basis of their history, those 49 people, you couldn't rely upon to act in the best interests of the company in the future?

A. Yes.

Q. "We have, essentially, lost confidence in those employees who have been terminated and decided their continued employment by the company is no longer in the best interests of the company as a whole." Yes?

A. (Witness nodded).

Q. "Hong Kong is tired of being held to ransom. The time has come for prompt and resolute action. This is what we have done."

A. Yes. I can't see it here, but . . .

Q. If what is said here is not in context, I am sure that Mr Huggins, if he thinks it necessary, will ask you . . . Mr Tyler, you're making it clear, are you not, here – I think you have agreed but I'm just reading it through here: "Hong Kong is tired of being held to ransom." What you are saying is these 49 people were holding Hong Kong to ransom.

A. I think I have said this a few minutes ago. The pilots who were participating in this campaign were holding Hong Kong to ransom and I believe that these 49 were included in that number.

Q. But the 49 were the ones specifically you were referring to here, because you had been talking about the 49 who were dismissed.

A. I'd like to see where it is in the press release, because . . .

Q. By all means.

HIS LORDSHIP: The second page, 1477, the third bullet point from the bottom of the article.

A. I think – no, I'd like to – in the construction – and I don't want to get into the detailed phrasing, this whole thing, but in the construction there, I was talking there about generally the situation. I said, "Look, we have done these two things". I described what they were. "We have taken the step after a lot of consideration". Then I, if you like, at the end of the thing, and this is near the end, if you like, have generalised the situation and just said, "Hong Kong is tired of being held to ransom." I wasn't in my mind specifically referring to the pilots whose contracts had been terminated that day. It was the general situation that was going on.

MR GROSSMAN: But it says here specifically, both at page 1477 and what is set out in page 7 of volume I . . .

HIS LORDSHIP: I think he has given his answer, Mr Grossman. I can read the article and I can decide what a fair-minded person reading it would decide.

Thank you, umpire. Another maiden. Let's try him from the other end again.

MR GROSSMAN: Please continue at page 7 at (9B). I just want to go through this with you. On 9 July, an article in the *South China Morning Post* quoted you as saying: "'The review, which started a few days ago, was prompted by the union making it clear industrial action could last as long as a year'." I think this is in accord with what you have told us. So the review was tied up with the industrial action? That's simply the point I am making.

A. Yes.

Bit of movement off the seam again.

Q. Then at (9C), you are quoted as saying: "The reason why we made these decisions yesterday ... we decided we were not prepared to accept what the union was saying, that the dispute would go on until the company's resources were drained ... we felt that firm and resolute steps were necessary." What you are saying here perfectly clearly is, "We were fed up with the union, so we sacked these 49 people". That's what you said.

More reverse swing. Good ball. Let's see how he plays that one.

A. That's putting words in my mouth that I didn't say, but that's ...
Q. Is there any other way to describe it?
A. We were not prepared, as a company, to see the future of our company threatened by what we believed to be unreasonable actions by a number of our staff. That is why we took the decision to terminate the contracts of a number of staff who we believed we couldn't rely on in future to support the company.
Q. They were acting unreasonably?
A. I believe they were.
Q. We'll look at some of them and you can explain what was unreasonable about what it was alleged they did. Then the second part, which you deny; I understand that. ". . . the sackings had nothing to do with the labour action, that they would have happened anyway because of an examination of the pilots' records." You say you didn't say that?
A. Those are not my words. I didn't say that.
Q. Did you ask them to correct it?
A. No. I don't – but I can't remember. I doubt it. There was so much going on and I personally would not necessarily have even read the thing when it happened, when it came out.
Q. Before we look at your statement, I just want to ask you this: would it be right to say that the resolute action that you were taking was a warning – put it that way – to the other pilots not to engage in the industrial action that was being planned?
A. That was not the intention of what we were doing. I've explained why we did it.

He's all over the place. Give him some more of the same.

Q. Surely that was the intention. You were saying, "We've got to take resolute action, we've got to get rid of the troublemakers and we are saying to everybody else, 'If you carry on doing what you are doing, you are going to be sacked also'." Isn't that effectively what you are saying?

A. Effectively it operated as a warning, of course,

Owzat, umpire?

... but the prime concern that we had was to try to stop this industrial – sorry, stop this disruption that was going on through the – by a number of pilots.

Q. Yes, by complying with the contract?

A. Indeed.

Q. Was it the unreasonable actions that were causing delays or was it the industrial action that was causing delays?

A. What was causing delays and damage to the company was the actions of individual pilots. That's what was causing the delays.

Q. Was it the industrial action or was it the unreasonable behaviour of these 49 people?

A. Well, of course it's behaviour by individuals which causes problems.

Q. Was it the industrial action that they were engaging in, or not? Can you answer that?

A. If they were doing these – if the industrial action was intended to tell them what to do, how to disrupt the flights – but what was actually causing delays, of course, is action by individuals.

Q. Is what, sorry? I didn't hear the last ...

A. Is the action by the individuals or the inaction by individuals.

Q. The reason I ask you this, it's not simply out of context, but if you turn to page 9 and what Captain Barley said: "The shareholders of this private Company, in this part of China are concerned about the preservation of the [airline's] ... travel rights. If the company had adopted a 'do nothing' strategy and simply allowed the industrial action to delay or cancel flights, for an indefinite period, we could have found our routes being taken up by other airlines ..." Captain Barley apparently had no concerns about that. He seemed to think clearly it was the industrial action that was causing the problems. Do you disagree with what he said?

A. I think it's a way of putting it.

Q. But do you disagree with what he said?

A. No, I don't.

Beautiful, you've got him tied up in knots. He's playing all around the ball. Give him some more.

Q. You don't. All right. If you would go to page 10, there's a quotation, 28 September 2001, entitled "Bulletin – Talks about Talks", by Captain Barley. Look at the last paragraph. "We have a great many pilots whose loyalty to Cathay Pacific is above question. Unfortunately, there are those whose commitment does give cause for concern." Pausing there, I think you probably would agree with that because that's what you've been saying.

A. Yes.

Q. "From this point forward we have little choice but to demonstrate far less tolerance towards any pilot who undertakes industrial action that is contrary to the company's interests." Do you agree with that?

A. Yes.

Q. That was the purpose of sacking these 49, dismissing these 49 people, wasn't it?

A. The purpose of dismissing these particular pilots was because we'd lost confidence in them, we couldn't rely on them in future, we didn't want to have staff in the workforce on whom we could not rely and in whom we had lost confidence.

Q. Mr Tyler, basically what is being said here, under the rubric of Cathay Pacific, is, "Look, you do anything that Cathay Pacific doesn't like and you're going to get sacked". That is what Captain Barley is saying; I've put it in cruder terms, but that is exactly what he is saying, is it not?

Play that one if you can.

A. It's not exactly what he's saying. He is saying that we will be less tolerant towards pilots who disrupt the airline. We had been putting up with it for several years, and we were just announcing that in future we were going to be less tolerant.

Q. Then he says: "If you have any trouble interpreting company's interest, then my advice is really simple. Do your job in accordance with normal custom and practice, and to the best of your ability." Of course you didn't write this, I understand, but it reflects, let me say, the Cathay philosophy about this incident?

HIS LORDSHIP: Just explain what you say that philosophy is.

MR GROSSMAN: All right. Let me put it a different way, my Lord. Thank you very much. Do you agree, first of all, with what Captain Barley was saying?

A. Yes.

Q. I suggest to you that you know perfectly well that what he was saying

458

was, "You do what we want, or else you're going to go the same way as the other 49ers".

A. He's saying – and he says it in his words, his advice is very simple; "Just do your job in accordance with normal custom and practice, to the best of your ability". That's what he is saying. People will interpret it however they wish, but that's what he is saying and I agree with what he is saying. That's his advice to his pilot workforce, "Please get on with the job and do it properly".

Q. We have had 16 witnesses so far, all of whom have said without challenge, "I was just doing my job". Did you know that?

Right in the block hole again.

A. I haven't followed this . . .

MR HUGGINS: I don't think it is appropriate for my learned friend to comment on what I have said and where I am coming from. Submissions will be made in due course about that.

Appeal for no ball from the pavilion. Is that allowed?

HIS LORDSHIP: Mr Grossman.

MR GROSSMAN: Would it be true to say that whatever criticism you have of these *49ers*, you would accept that they were fully professional in their jobs as pilots? You don't have a complaint about their professionalism?

Bloody hell. He's just bowled him a googly straight off a pace attack.

A. I – let me first of all say, I have not personally – I'm not personally acquainted with the performance in their jobs of these individuals, so I'm not sure I can answer that question.

Q. All right. Let me put it this way: would it be fair to say that it's never been a suggestion to you, and you have no reason to think that these 49 people were anything other than fully professional in their job?

A. I am confident because I know that Cathay Pacific takes very seriously its training, its management of the technical aspects of flying aircraft and other operational issues, that they were technically very professional and proficient, in the technical sense.

LBW surely?

Q. Thank you . . . one thing I just want to ask you about: when you made these various statements we have been looking at, do they refer to these 49 people, amongst others?

A. I think I would have to know which statements.

Q. Well, all of them. All the statements.

A. In some senses they are referring to individuals, or the collection of individuals known as the *49ers*. In other cases it refers more generally to the pilot body, and in other cases more generally to those pilots who were seeking to disrupt the company operations. I . . .

Q. When you're talking about those who were seeking to interrupt the company's operations, I think we have already established that we are talking about the *49ers*, the 49 that were dismissed.

A. Well, they were among those. There may have been others.

Q. When you were being critical of the people who were disrupting Cathay's performance . . .

A. Would I have been critical?

Q. No. When you were being critical of those people who were disrupting Cathay Pacific, did you include those 49 people?

A. I didn't have in my mind those particular people. I was – generally all those who were disrupting Cathay's operations.

Q. All those did, of course, include *The 49ers*?

A. Yes.

Q. You have told us, and you say in your statement also, that you were starting to lose millions a day, or a lot of money, anyway. You did say in your evidence that you were losing a large amount of money.

A. Sorry, where did I say that?

Q. You said it in court yesterday. Were you losing money?

A. Sorry, I didn't say it, but we were losing . . .

Q. Of course you didn't. My apologies. It was Mr Rhodes.

Sorry, batsman, the ball just slipped out of my hand there.

A. Well, the company was losing a lot of revenue, yes, because of this campaign.

Q. Yes. Quite right. I wonder if you would look, please, in bundle X at page 211 . . . This is one of a series of letters that were being put out by the union, all signed by Captain Demery. I just want to ask you about one thing here, under the heading "Contract compliance"; do you see that?

A. Yes.

Q. The date you will see at the bottom, and that is 12 June?

A. 12 June, yes.

Q. So contextually, you understand when this was being sent out?

A. Sure.

Q. What it says is: "Contract compliance continues to apply added pressure to the commercial operation. Management would love you to believe that it is having no effect, so that you release the pressure." I want to ask you about that. Were you, was management telling the staff, "Look, it's having no effect"?

A. I don't remember what we were saying at the time.

Q. It's true, I think, and I think others have said it, that there was a lot of – some people called it propaganda – being distributed by both sides, union and management, and what has been produced here are the letters from the union. Do you remember if management were also sending out letters to their crew and to staff?

A. Certainly to the crew.

Q. But you don't recall them saying, "Look, it's not working, so don't do it because we are not losing any money"?

A. I don't remember what the content was or whatever it was.

Q. Look at paragraph 7 of your statement, please . . . This is the paragraph that starts, "I was not personally involved". Do you see that?

A. Yes.

Q. Five lines down, I want to read this: "From my own perspective, anyone who had been ready and willing to support and implement the industrial actions proposed and encouraged by the union, including the contract compliance campaign and the go-slow campaign through the maximum safety strategy in order to pressurise the airline in furtherance of the union's demands, could not be relied on to have the best interests of the airline at heart." That's correct, is it?

A. Yes.

Q. Do you know 92 per cent of the people voted to participate in this limited industrial action?

Good delivery. Bet he plays right across the line.

A. I didn't. I mean, I may have known that number once. I've forgotten if that was the number.

Q. You knew it was extremely high?

A. I knew that the vote was very high for supporting the contract compliance.

Q. You can take it from me, I don't think there is any dispute, that 92 per cent voted in favour of the resolution to take limited industrial action. Do you say that not one of those persons could be relied on to have the best interests of the airline at heart?

A. I believe – not – of course, voting is one thing. Taking part in the thing is a bit different, and certainly I doubt if as many as that actually took part. But certainly it would raise questions in my mind, if somebody was taking part and supporting and implementing the industrial actions, it raises the question: can this person be relied on to have the best interests of the airline at heart?

Q. So if the 92 per cent who voted in favour of it, all decided, to one degree or another, to participate in MSS, do you say that 92 per cent of your pilots didn't have the interests of the airline at heart? That's what I'm trying to . . .

A. I'm saying, because we could not rely on those who participated to have the best interests of the airline at heart.

Q. And are you satisfied in your mind, from what you've been told, that the 49 who were dismissed all participated in contract compliance and maximum safety strategy?

A. I am satisfied that the 49 who we identified and had their contracts terminated could not be relied on to have the best interests of the airline at heart, and I am satisfied that the thorough process of the review of their performance had taken place. I don't know specifically whether individuals did or did not take part in these particular campaigns.

Q. I'm just a bit surprised at your statement, then. What's the relevance of it in your statement? We are talking here about why these people were dismissed, and you say: "From my perspective, anybody who is ready and willing to support and implement the industrial actions could not be relied on." You have no idea whether these 49ers participated or not.

A. Well, I think I have answered in my statement–

HIS LORDSHIP: I think he said he doesn't have any particular idea in respect of any particular pilot.

MR GROSSMAN: Thank you, my Lord.

HIS LORDSHIP: He was satisfied about the process, the integrity of the process, but he has no particular knowledge about any particular pilot.

A. That's correct, my Lord.

Umpire's seen enough. Finish him off. Give him another wrong un.

Q. Mr Tyler, have you ever suggested – I'm going back to something I asked you before – that any of these pilots who were dismissed were unprofessional?

HIS LORDSHIP: I think you have asked that previously. It is a slightly different question. You said "have you ever suggested". You asked whether he thought that they were professional, and he said, to his mind, given Cathay Pacific's training, he was confident they were technically professional, but this is slightly different.

MR GROSSMAN: Thank you. Have you ever suggested that they were unprofessional?

A. I don't believe I've ever used that word.

MR GROSSMAN: Thank you.

Well bowled. Umpire's finger's up. Batsman's on his way back to the pavilion. Next lamb to the slaughter please.

Chen walked out to the crease looking very uncomfortable in his gear. His pads were flapping about, he was missing a glove and holding his bat upside down. After a bit of adjustment, he took a guard that looked like somewhere outside off stump. Definitely unorthodox but in these days of reverse sweep and switch hitting, perhaps we were going to learn something new about the game.

Clive opened with some gentle right arm leg spin.

MR GROSSMAN: Mr Chen, just a few questions. When you are ready, Mr Chen, look at page 5. These are the matters about which we complain. I don't think it's denied that you said these things. At subparagraph (8) – do you see that?

A. Yes.

Q. Mr Philip Chen stated about the dismissed aircrew that 'we cannot allow this crew to disrupt the airline . . .' Pause there. Was that your belief, that this group of 49 was disrupting the airline?

A. I think the individuals with their action would be disrupting the airline.

Q. But were you talking about a group together or were you talking about individuals?

A. I think a group of individuals.

It's in the keeper's gloves. Did he get some bat on that? Was that an edge?

Q. A group of individuals?

A. Yes.

Q. Was it your belief at the time that this group was a coherent group, a group that had got together to disrupt the airline?

463

A. I mean, the disruption happened at that time.

Q. What was your belief at the time? There were 49 people who got together to disrupt the procedures?

A. Well, I think there were individuals, a lot of individuals involved, yes.

Q. Yes, but was it your belief that there was some kind of coherent group that had got together, they were planning – those 49 were planning to disrupt the operations of Cathay Pacific?

A. I think with the information we have got, definitely there was communication leading to these disruptions.

Good over. He can't play spin. Give him another over of the same.

Q. Oh yes, but that was from Captain Demery. He's not one of *The 49ers*. Are you saying these 49 got together and said, "Let's do the utmost we can to disrupt . . ."

A. I don't think I said that here.

Q. But what do you mean by "this group were going to disrupt the airline"?

A. Well, the people who were actually disrupting the airline.

Q. I know, but are you saying that they were acting together in concert, as it were, or just 49 happened not to . . .

A. I do not have a number here, and I think it's – that's what I am referring to. There are people . . .

Umpire???

HIS LORDSHIP: Mr Grossman's question is this, Mr Chen: are you saying there was some sort of conspiracy among these 49 people to act as a group to disrupt the airline, or are you simply saying this group of persons individually were acting in a way which disrupted the operations of the airline?

A. I think my impression was there were efforts, not just individual initiatives, to disrupt the airline.

MR GROSSMAN: Sorry, I didn't hear the first part. I don't know if Mr Huggins did. I didn't hear the answer – the first part of the answer to his Lordship.

HIS LORDSHIP: His impression was that it was not just individual initiatives, that there was actually a group, that is, concerted effort.

MR GROSSMAN: Where did you get this impression from?

A. There are obviously communication letters and whatnot that we have understood.

Q. Yes, that's how this conspiracy took part, but where did you get the impression from there was a kind of conspiracy among these 49?

A. I am not referring specifically to the 49 people.

Q. Well, you are, actually. You're talking about "this group", the group are *The 49ers*.

A. I am saying the group of people were disrupting the airline.

Q. Yes, *The 49ers*, the ones who . . .

A. That includes *The 49ers*, yes.

Q. Where did you get the impression from that this group had some kind of conspiracy going between them?

A. Because there are disruptions and constant disruptions of the airline at that time, not happening in individual cases but there are general disruptions.

Q. So people based overseas, people in Hong Kong, were getting together and saying, "Let's see what we can do to disrupt the airline"?

A. Well, that is beyond me, but I mean . . .

The whole bowling attack's beyond this bloke. Has he played this game before? If he has, it doesn't look like he's had a net in years.

Q. I am asking you, Mr Chen. What did you believe?

A. The consequence was that we had flight cancellations, we had flight delays, and obviously these happened at the same time, around that period.

Q. Yes. So that's the reason why you thought there was a conspiracy, I understand.

A. I didn't use the word "conspiracy" but I am saying, yes, there were a lot of disruptions of the airline, to the eye, at that time.

Q. I want to make sure – I understood you to say, in answer to his Lordship, "Yes, I wouldn't use the word 'conspiracy' but, yes, a group of them together were doing their best to disrupt the airline".

A. There are a group of people disrupting the airline, yes, I agree with that, yes.

Q. And they were acting together?

A. Well, it's a matter of how you put it, but yes, there are – there is a group of people disrupting the airline, yes.

Q. Thank you. That was the impression you were trying to convey?

A. Yes.

Another maiden. He hasn't got off the mark yet. Keep at him.

Q. Thank you. "We cannot allow this group to disrupt the airline, employees, our customers or the reputation of Hong Kong. Nor can we allow this group to let the much larger numbers of flight crews who are showing total professionalism we require – suffer." I want to ask you this: this is an extremely serious allegation to make, that these people weren't acting professionally, that these pilots were unprofessional. Do you adhere to what you said there, they weren't acting professionally?

A. I must honestly say, I do not actually remember making such a statement.

Q. All right. Would you now publicly then say, as Mr Tyler was good enough to do, "We do not make any allegation of unprofessionalism against these 49 people"?

A. I really do not think I would make allegations of unprofessionalism, and everything I said – I mean, I would not deviate from carefully considered written scripts.

Q. But it is very important for people to know, and for future employers to know, that there is no allegation by Cathay Pacific that they were unprofessional. Do you understand that, Mr Chen?

A. I listened to Mr Tyler and agreed with Mr Tyler that on the technical side we have definitely no questions about it.

Plumb LBW. Hope the umpire saw that.

Q. Thank you very much. On 9 July you said: "The company and the Hong Kong community are unable to acquiesce to such tactics." These are the tactics you have been talking about, Mr Chen. "We cannot be held to ransom indefinitely . . ." Pause there. How were these 49 people holding you to ransom?

A. I do believe if the airline, other staff members and the travelling public, in fact the whole of Hong Kong, faces such disruptions and uncertainty, it is definitely not to the benefit of the airline. This is . . .

Q. But how were these 49 holding Cathay to ransom? What were these 49 doing, or any of them, or all of them doing, that was holding Cathay to ransom?

A. The disruptions.

Q. Disruptions?

A. Yes. And the uncertainty looking to the future.

Q. The disruptions in the context of contract compliance?

Oh good ball again. Almost unplayable. Let's see what he does.

A. The actions that have been taken, yes.
Q. In the context of contract compliance?
A. I think that's part of it, yes.

What? Owzat, umpire? Give him another delivery just like the last one.

Q. So you're satisfied, are you, that these 49 people were dismissed at least in part because of their participation in an industrial activity?
A. No, I don't think so.
Q. You don't think so?
A. I don't think so.
Q. Then how do you square that with your suggestion a moment ago that it was in part – part of the reason was because they were involved in contract compliance, which was an industrial action?
A. It is the behaviour and the – well, the behaviour, basically, that has been considered, I think.
Q. What behaviour?
A. The attitude and the behaviour.
Q. Mr Chen, were these people sacked – dismissed, your words – as a result of a participation in a union activity or not?
A. I do not think so.
Q. You don't think so?
A. I don't think so.
Q. So the fact that they were engaged in what's been called contract compliance, and some of them in MSS, has absolutely nothing to do
. . .
A. No, not entirely so, I should say.

What? He just said it again. Umpire? Umpire??

Q. Not entirely . . . ?
A. Not entirely so.
Q. Perhaps you would like to explain. I'm told that people at the back can't hear. You will understand there is a lot of interest here. I wonder if you wouldn't mind speaking up.
A. Yes, I will. Sorry, Mr Grossman, you were saying?
Q. You were about to say they were not dismissed entirely because of contract compliance. I think that's what you were going to say.
A. Yes.

Q. What do you mean?

A. I think the flight operations review team had a thorough review of all the employees and they looked at the attitude and the behaviour, and I think they have looked at everybody with full knowledge, full considerations.

Q. Speak up.

A. Yes. And I think there are many other factors they have taken into consideration.

Q. Other factors, but included in those factors was there the factor that they were taking part in the union activities, which you didn't agree with.

He's got to play at this one, it's right on middle stump.

A. Well, in disruption, shall we say.

Q. Disruption. What you call disruptions, and they were saying is contract compliance.

A. I think it's really – I mean, that's your interpretation, Mr Grossman.

Q. No, no, no. Yours. I'm asking you, Mr Chen.

A. Yes.

Q. They were taking part in contract compliance. Nobody said that they weren't. And you say that this has nothing to do with their dismissals, or not? I've lost track.

A. No. The termination basically is based on our confidence with the employees in question.

Q. I see. So it's not to do with their contract compliance?

A. It's not entirely, as I said.

He said it again. Pin him down, bowler. Umpire, are you listening?

Q. But partly?

A. Well, it's a behaviour, shall I say.

Q. Sorry, I must pin you down on this: was it partly to do with contract compliance or not? You can say "yes", "no" or "I don't know".

A. It's whether they are disrupting the airline. That's the behaviour.

Umpire. Out surely?

HIS LORDSHIP: That's not an answer to Mr Grossman's question, Mr Chen. The question is: was it partly due to contract compliance? My understanding of what you have just been saying is that the answer is "yes". Is my understanding right or wrong?

A. I think my point is . . .
HIS LORDSHIP: <*LOUDLY*> Sorry, is my understanding right or wrong?
A. Yes, my Lord.
HIS LORDSHIP: It's right?
A. (Witness nodded).

Clean bowled!!!! Middle stump's gone ten yards back to the keeper!!! Look he's walking on the rest of his stumps as well!! He's just given us the match! Hope the stumpcam's not damaged. We're going to want to watch that replay over and over. We looked round the main stand. Tyler had turned grey and was holding his head in hands. Do we need to trouble the batsman further? Give him another over for fun.

HIS LORDSHIP: Mr Grossman?
MR GROSSMAN: Thank you. If you turn to page 6, you say: "This has been a very painful decision and one that has not been entered into lightly. However, we are only prepared to take this airline forward with pilots who we believe will have the best interests of the company at heart." Do you see that?
A. Yes.
Q. Mr Chen, does that mean you then had complete confidence in the other – the rest of the other 1,500-odd pilots?
A. We always have confidence in our staff, except the fact when there are disruptions to the airline.
Q. Mr Chen, you didn't have confidence, you said, in 49 of them. Does this statement here mean that you then had confidence in the other 1,500-odd?
A. Yes.
Q. Notwithstanding the fact that they had been involved, or most of them had been involved in contract compliance one way or another?
A. Well, we have confidence, yes.
Q. I beg your pardon?
A. We have confidence taking the airline forward with the rest of the – with . . .
Q. Notwithstanding that they had been involved in the same union activity that you were criticising the 49 for?

He's not going to fall for that one again surely?

A. As I said before, I think this is really – I mean, there are a whole host of considerations that we have undertaken, so what you just high-lighted is just part of the consideration.

Clean bowled again!!! Send him back to the pavilion. I can't watch anymore.

MR GROSSMAN: Give me a moment, please ... I propose to allow Mr Chen to go. I'm not going to ask any more questions.
HIS LORDSHIP: You have concluded?
MR GROSSMAN: Yes.
HIS LORDSHIP: Thank you very much, Mr Grossman.

And thank you very much Mr Chen. He'd just admitted that they sacked us for our union activities. And both he and Tyler retracted their "unprofessional" remarks. Under direct examination from Mr Huggins, Chen said he couldn't remember saying that, even though it was right there in the evidence. It was game over as far as they were concerned. We'd got it won! Time to send the tail end back to the pavilion. After the drinks break, Rhodes came back on to resume his innings.

The full transcripts of the court proceedings amount to almost 1,300 pages and are available for download from the CPU website at:

www.cathaypilotsunion.org/proceedings/transcripts.htm

The second part of Rhodes' testimony is contained in Day 7 and, if one was looking for an object lesson in innuendo, evasion and half truths, this would be as good a place as any to start. Space constraints prevent reproduction of the transcripts in full. However, the following excerpts from Rhodes' cross examination relating to the Star Chamber proceedings are worthy of note.

MR GROSSMAN. Now I would like you to look, please, in bundle III, at page 740. This is an affidavit you swore; do you see that?
A. Yes. On what date?
Q. It's dated 21 June 2007. You see that on page 741. Do you see that?
A. Yes, I do see that.
Q. If you go to paragraph 3, what that says is: "By a letter dated 27th April 2007 from [the solicitors] to [my solicitors], the plaintiffs indicated an intention to apply for an order requiring the directors or executives of your company to make affidavits stating that [CPA and Veta]

do not have the agenda and minutes or record of the review team meetings." Do you see that?

A. I do see that.

Q. JSM replied. Then in paragraph 4: "On behalf of the defendants, and as a member of the review team (in my then capacity as General Manager Aircrew), I confirm the defendants have never produced any documents such as agendas, circulars, memoranda, notices, notes, minutes or a transcript for and/or during the review meetings." Is that true?

A. That's true, correct.

Q. Is it? Well, I've heard what you said ... Do you remember Mr Wilkinson then produced a document?

A. I remember Mr Wilkinson produced a list of the crew, yes.

Q. He did, which was handed out or dealt with at that meeting?

A. Yes. We had two lists of crew at the meeting, that list Mr Wilkinson produced and the seniority list.

Q. How does that gel with what you said in your affidavit, that there was nothing ...

A. Well, we only had one agenda item for the meeting, which was to review every crew member in Cathay Pacific and look at their employment records, attendance, attitude, et cetera. That was the only agenda item. So there wasn't an agenda produced, a circular to announce the meeting. There were notices or memorandums. We just had a list of crew, two lists of crew, to review.

Q. Why didn't you say so? Why did you swear an affidavit that said, "We didn't have any documents", to put it in a general sense?

A. Well, I thought that the plaintiffs were looking for agendas, notes, circulars. I mean, a list of crew – we have a list of crew.

Q. Why didn't you say so?

A. I didn't think it was – it was irrelevant. I thought they were looking for notes from the meeting, minutes of the meeting, transcripts of the meeting, an agenda for the meeting. We didn't have any such documents.

Q. I will read it to you again: "On behalf of the defendants, and as a member of the review team ... I confirm the defendants have never produced any documents such as agendas, circulars, memoranda, notices, notes, minutes or a transcript ...", et cetera.

A. I – we weren't trying to be evasive. We didn't produce documents such as agendas, notes, minutes and transcripts. There were no documents attached at the meeting. But we had to work through every crew member in Cathay Pacific. So we had various lists of crew. The only agenda item was to review whether they were working in our best interests. So we had lists of crew.

Q. Mr Rhodes, I think you will accept that this affidavit is not wholly correct, is it?

Too damned right it wasn't 'wholly correct'. He swore under oath that they, "... *never produced any documents such as agendas, circulars, memoranda, notices, notes, minutes or a transcript **for and/or during** the review meetings*." If the hit list that was distributed to each and every person in the room wasn't a document, what was it? They tried to suppress the document because it showed conclusively that they targeted union members. It was only when Ian Wilkinson came forward that they were forced to admit that this document was produced for use during the meeting and were caught out in a lie. And, given Rhodes' continued insistence under oath that no notes were taken during the meeting, presumably we must assume that Barley suddenly acquired the powers of Marvo the Memory Man and kept the names of *The 49ers* stored in his head. Not that they were 'trying to be evasive' you understand.

After Rhodes was finally sent back to the pavilion having failed to trouble the scorer to any great extent, Clive finished off our day in the field with a few questions for Kroutil on the Star Chamber records.

MR GROSSMAN: Mr Kroutil, I just have a few questions. Were you present at the review meeting for all three days?

A. Yes, I was.

Q. What was the nature of your participation?

A. I had compiled the short master crew list, which was used. Unfortunately, I had only been there four or five months prior to that and my direct knowledge of any of the crew members was either non-existent or very limited.

Q. The crew list that you refer to I think we can see on page 257. This is the one you are referring to, going right up to about page two nine something?

A. Yes. That's the long one. That was not used during the meeting.

Q. That wasn't used?

HIS LORDSHIP: That's the long one. What is the short one?

MR GROSSMAN: ... page 1831-93. This is the one actually produced by Mr Wilkinson.

HIS LORDSHIP: Is that the short list that you are referring to?

A. Yes, it is.

MR GROSSMAN: The one we are looking at now is the short list?

A. Yes.

Q. Did you keep a copy of this?

A. Not following the meeting, no.

Q. You didn't? Why not?

A. We were advised to delete them.

Q. To do what?

A. To destroy them, delete them.

Q. Why?

A. As I understand, they contain personal information which, once we completed the task for which it was compiled, we were obliged to delete.

MR HUGGINS: It's data privacy.

MR GROSSMAN: What about the long list? Was that deleted, the master list?

A. I believe I provided a copy to our solicitors, and then I deleted it.

Q. When did you – you wouldn't have provided it immediately, would you? I'm just trying to find out what was destroyed and what wasn't.

HIS LORDSHIP: So the question is: when did he provide the list to his solicitors?

MR GROSSMAN: Yes. It must have been after the proceedings started?

A. It would have been after the proceedings, yes.

Q. So you kept a copy of that long list?

A. For possibly a few days, yes.

Q. Why didn't you destroy it immediately?

A. Because I wanted to make sure that the solicitors had a copy of it.

Q. So you sent it to the solicitors immediately, within days of the decision being taken to get rid of the 49 people?

A. That's the advice that I received and I complied with that.

Q. That's what happened?

A. I believe so, yes.

That little exchange was destined to come back and bite Kroutil later.

And so that was it as far as direct and cross examination of witnesses was concerned. The ninth and last day of the trial, Friday 23 October, was held a week after all the oral evidence had been completed. It was taken up with final submissions by counsel and Judge Reyes reserved his judgment. After knocking up a record bar bill in the Captain's Bar, we all went home to await the outcome of his deliberations.

30

Judgment

'*A man does what he must in spite of personal consequences, in spite of obstacles and dangers and pressures, and that is the basis of all human morality.*'

John F. Kennedy

'*You have enemies? Good. That means you've stood up for something, sometime in your life.*'

Winston Churchill

We had to wait almost four weeks from the end of the evidential stage of the trial until the morning of 11 November 2009 when the Hon Justice Reyes handed down his judgment under HCMP 4400/2001. Despite the fact that he was very efficient in delivering his verdict so quickly, it was the longest four weeks of the eight and a half years we had been waiting for justice. The actual process was something of an anticlimax. Of course, we would have preferred it if all parties were required to attend, the judge to enter the court, don the black cap and sentence the miscreants to be taken down from this place to a lawful place of execution and so on. Unfortunately, that is not the way things are done. The judgment is not delivered to a full court. Rather, you just turn up at the court at the appointed time, the door opens and the judge's clerk hands out printed copies of the judgment. Like the court transcripts, the full text of the judgment is available for download on the CPU website at:

www.cathaypilotsunion.org

In his summary, Judge Reyes stated the following:

(1) Unfair dismissal:
  (a) The predominant reason for the Plaintiffs' termination by Cathay was their perceived participation in union activities.
  (b) The Plaintiffs were unfairly dismissed.
  (c) HK$150,000 is awarded to each Plaintiff (with the exception of Mr Crofts) for unfair dismissal.
(2) Wrongful termination:
  (a) The reasons which Cathay publicly gave when dismissing the Plaintiffs in July 2001 amounted to accusations of 'gross misconduct' within the terms of the DGP.
  (b) The Plaintiffs' employments with Cathay were wrongly terminated since the procedures mandated by the DGP were not followed.
  (c) A month's pay is awarded to each Plaintiff (with the exception of Mr Crofts) as damages for wrongful termination of their contracts.
(3) Defamation:
  (a) The statements were defamatory.
  (b) Cathay has no defence of justification or qualified privilege.
  (c) General damages of HK$3 million and aggravated damages of HK$300,000 are awarded to each Plaintiff (with the exception of Mr England).

The judge also made an order for costs in full in our favour. We had won everything: the lot. George did not get damages for the first two legs of the case because he had already received damages in the UK. We made a mistake with Greg England's estate. A complaint for defamation dies with the plaintiff if he becomes deceased. We did not know that at the time. We do now. We should have filed a cause of action for malicious falsehood, which is similar to defamation but survives the death of the plaintiff. We made alternative arrangements to ensure that Greg's estate would receive the same compensation as the rest of us. We leave no one behind.

The judge made various remarks in his judgment about the credibility of the opposition's testimony and other matters. In referring to a witness statement by one of the crew controllers he stated:

Mr Lam's statement amounts to no more than embarrassing assertion and name-calling. No specific details are mentioned, so that it was impossible for the Plaintiffs concerned to rebut the same at trial. The statement was of no help to the Court at all.

On the main reason for the dismissals he opined as follows:

> . . . how (one asks oneself rhetorically) could the 'conduct' of *The 49ers* be the underlying or true reason for their dismissal?
>
> Management had no real idea whether any of them were genuinely malingerers or troublemakers. There was merely the probability that they were. That was deemed a sufficient basis for management despite the strictures of the DGP. That could only have been because **the real target behind the mass dismissals was not the individuals concerned, but the union** . . .
>
> . . . I am fortified in this conclusion by Mr Chen's grudging admission in the course of his cross-examination that at least 'part' of the reason for the Plaintiffs' dismissal had to do with contract compliance.

On the opposition's 'multiple defence' strategy, he had this to say:

> Cathay has maintained that the Plaintiffs were dismissed without cause. But, in the same breath, Cathay says that it could not rely on them to act in its best interests. Through Mr Tyler's statement, Cathay has accused the Plaintiffs of showing a lack of professionalism in their conduct. By this is plainly implied that the Plaintiffs have not discharged their duties at Cathay in the manner in which they should.
>
> **I do not think that Cathay can have it both ways**, on the one hand to say 'no cause' and on the other to make serious allegations of professional failings on the part of the Plaintiffs . . .

As for us holding Hong Kong to ransom, he remarked:

> Nor is it apparent how such reasoning could justify characterising someone as 'not having Hong Kong's best interests at heart'. It is true that Cathay Pacific is a Hong Kong airline. But it does not logically follow from a pilot voting for contract compliance or for limited industrial action within the bounds of his contract with Cathay, that such pilot does not care about Hong Kong. **There is more to**

Hong Kong than just Cathay. A pilot may sincerely vote for what he believes to be right in the context of his union's dispute with management and still care deeply about Hong Kong.

Finally, on the subject of contract compliance, he had this to say:

On contract compliance, those Plaintiffs who voted in favour of the campaign did so because that was what they believed they were supposed to do in any case, namely, comply with their contracts. Even in relation to limited industrial action, the pilots were assured by the union membership at the 20 June 2001 EGM that, whatever the industrial action might be, it would be within the bounds of the pilots' contracts. **A desire to abide by the terms of one's contract can by no stretch of the imagination be treated as equivalent to an anti-company attitude**.

So there we were. It was a rout. The opposition had lost by an innings and several wickets. Presumably now they would accept the judgment, learn the lessons of the last nine years and try to move on to rebuild a proper working relationship with their employees. Not a bit of it. They filed an appeal against the judgment and also made applications to the court to have execution of the damages and costs awards stayed pending outcome of the appeal. Their applications to stay the payments were heard on 15 December before Judge Reyes. Their junior counsel was in attendance and, in support of their applications, stated, 'We believe that we have strong grounds for appeal.'

The judge responded, 'I do not for one minute agree that you have grounds for appeal. Application denied.'

They took it further, to the Court of Appeal. Their application was heard on 18 December but the judge delivered a closed ruling and, therefore, I cannot disclose what took place.

Even with all this going on, Rhodes still could not keep his mouth shut. Despite everything that Judge Reyes had said in his judgment about the true reasons for *The 49ers'* dismissals and the veracity or otherwise of the opposition's testimony, on 11 December 2009 he published a newsletter in which he stated:

The Company had been tracking attendance records, in great detail, for 30 months prior to July 2001 and The 49ers were selected, primarily, on the basis of their attendance records, i.e. their level of participation in the so-called 'Sick-Out' campaign.

Despite the fact that this was supposedly an internal company newsletter, it was available to more than 20,000 employees and Rhodes knew full well that it was likely to get out into public circulation, which indeed it did. He knew this because in a previous newsletter, dated 27 November 2009, he stated:

There is little to report on the Ops front this week. This is good news as I am no longer able to share too much information with you about the technical difficulties or operational challenges that we face each week as the news keeps ending up in the press!

Evidently somebody forwarded last week's Update to a journalist at the *South China Morning Post* which [led] to a front page story about blocked toilets on the Airbus. This may sound like a fun sport (and I'm the first to accept that it was a good story) but it doesn't do much for the airline's reputation.

It is a great pity that he doesn't have the same concern for *The 49ers'* reputations as he clearly does for the company's. It typifies the whole management attitude that prevails in Cathay. Despite everything, it appears that they still believe they are above the law and can do whatever they wish. Well they can't. Whether or not Rhodes' latest outburst was sanctioned, he was still speaking on behalf of the company in his position as a senior director. In response to this repeated defamation, new law suits have been filed in Australia, Canada, Hong Kong, the UK and US. These new lawsuits are not just coming from the Band of Brothers either. Some of the original *49ers* who took 'the offer' have also joined them. So here they are, nine years on and they haven't learned a thing. They are right back where they started, facing multiple lawsuits in multiple jurisdictions worldwide.

Rhodes and Kroutil faced another problem as well. As a result of their testimony under oath, an officer of the court was so incensed by their behaviour that he filed complaints of perjury against them with the Hong Kong police. Kroutil dropped himself in it when he stated under oath that all company records of the crew lists were destroyed in 2001 after they had given them to their solicitors. Presumably this was to help out Rhodes with his obvious porkies about there being no records, documents, etc. One of the crew lists that Kroutil provided in his evidence, which he said was used in the 'Star Chamber' meeting, was dated 22 November 2004 on each page, so clearly they had not destroyed the data as he testified. Lack of attention to detail will get you every time. The 6P rule. In another newsletter Rhodes stated that the perjury complaints had been filed by one of the plaintiffs. He couldn't even get that right.

As mentioned earlier, they were initiated by an officer of the court. On 28 September 2010 this officer received a letter from the Hong Kong police informing him that the Department of Justice had decided not to launch a prosecution at this stage because of 'insufficient evidence'. However, should any additional information become available, 'then the case will be considered further'. In the letter, the Commissioner of Police thanked the complainant 'for being a responsible citizen and fulfilling [his] obligations as a member of the community by reporting this serious crime'. One wonders how big a lie one has to tell under oath before the authorities are prepared to institute a prosecution.

The main appeal proper against Judge Reyes' ruling was heard in the Hong Kong Court of Appeal from 27 to 29 July 2010 before a panel of three judges. In many ways the appeal hearing was more stressful than the main court case itself. At least during the case we had a speaking part and were able to put forward our point of view. Not so during the appeal, which consisted of counsel making their submissions to the panel of judges without any witnesses being called. We had to just sit in court and listen to the opposition's arguments being regurgitated all over again.

They again tried to drown us in paperwork, with their initial skeleton arguments amounting to some 40 pages with appendices. If this was a skeleton, the whole body must be morbidly obese. There is a maxim in legal circles that if a counsel can't summarise his case in 12 pages, either he is incompetent or he hasn't got a case. It certainly applied here. Their submissions can be summarised quite easily. In their view, Justice Reyes simply 'got it wrong' on just about all the points of law and the damages awarded were grossly excessive and out of all proportion.

They tried some dirty tricks as well. During oral submissions at appeal, they tried to bring up matters which were not even part of their original pleaded case and slip them in through the back door. This is very naughty and disrespectful to the court. They tried to argue that we were fired without cause for no reason under Clause 35.3 and that the public comments made by Tyler and Chen, only four hours after the dismissal notices were sent out via by DHL, were irrelevant to the actual dismissals themselves since they took place after the fact. They tried to argue that Brian Keene was not one of *The 49ers* because his dismissal took place two days after the rest of us and, therefore, that the defamatory statements did not apply to him. This argument of course, skated over the fact that Brian was selected for dismissal at the Star Chamber meeting a week earlier. They even tried to argue that voting at a union meeting during one's own time and away from the workplace should *not* be a protected activity under the terms of the EO Clause S21B. What precisely *would* be protected under his proposition, Mr. Huggins failed to explain.

We were also treated to some histrionics by their counsel. At one point, whilst fixing the judges with one of his beadiest of stares, he propounded on the 'I'll do my best' response advocated by the AOA in response to enquiries from crew control.

'I'll do my best? I'll do my best?? At the school I attended such a response to a question would have been considered to be grossly impertinent and, at least in my day, would have led to a severe thrashing!!!'

After the appeal hearing was completed, just like the main case, all we could do was sit back and wait for the judges to hand down their ruling. The waiting was interminable. In the meantime, perhaps someone somewhere would have to take responsibility for the mess our company was now in. As a shareholder in Cathay, I would certainly hope so.

On 19 April 2010, it was announced that Philip Chen, director of John Swire & Sons (HK) Ltd, chairman of John Swire & Sons (China) Ltd, executive director of Swire Pacific Ltd, deputy chairman and non-executive director of Cathay Pacific Airways Ltd, had decided to leave the Swire Group at the end of June 2010 after a career spanning 33 years. He had apparently expressed a 'desire to pursue other interests'. With responsibility comes accountability.

On 20 May 2010, it was also announced that Rhodes would be moving from his position as DFO to the post of director cargo. The announcement was all wrapped up in a statement about routine annual management changes but it remains to be seen whether or not, like Turnbull's departure, this sideways move is a precursor to a face-saving exit. With responsibility comes accountability.

At least one good thing may come out of this from the Flight Ops point of view. The new DFO is actually going to be a pilot so perhaps they are admitting that the non-operational DFO experiment has failed. I don't envy him his task. He was a member of the 'Star Chamber' so he carries that baggage with the pilots and potentially is picking up a very poisoned chalice.

But what of the pilots' flight safety concerns and the Flight Ops ethos dating back to the 1990s? Have any of those issues been addressed?

On 13 April 2010, Cathay flight CX780, an A330, got airborne from Surabaya, Indonesia *en route* for Hong Kong. During the flight it encountered repeated engine malfunctions on both engines, which resulted in a Mayday distress call being put out by the crew on the approach to CLK.

The aircraft landed at a ground speed of 230 kt, almost double the normal landing speed. During the landing and roll out, the number one engine pod struck the runway, five of the main wheel tyres deflated and there were brake fires. The tyre deflation and brake fires were to be expected because of the very high energy landing. The crew managed to bring the aircraft to a halt within the available runway length and evacuate the passengers, during which 57 of them were injured. Clearly the pilots did an outstanding job to land the aircraft safely in such difficult circumstances and the cabin crew were similarly adept at evacuating all the passengers safely. So what is the point of relating the events of this flight other than to congratulate the crew?

The engine problems first became apparent early on in the more than four hour flight and the accident has resulted in a lot of speculation in the media about whether or not the decision to continue the flight to Hong Kong after the initial fault indications was the correct one. This speculation led to the ridiculous quote from a Cathay source mentioned earlier that:

'Even with both engines dead, our planes still have a backup power supply that should allow it to glide for up to [an] hour, with the help of flaps and spoilers.'

It also prompted both Tyler and the head of the Cathay Corporate Safety Department, Richard Howell, to write letters to the *South China Morning Post* in an attempt to quell the speculation. The full facts of the case will not be known until the CAD accident investigation is complete. However, the following question will have to be answered: was it the correct decision to continue the flight to CLK when the indications of engine problems first manifested themselves and, if not, what prompted the Captain to continue the flight instead of landing at the nearest suitable airport? From reports published so far we know that the Captain contacted Cathay's Engineering Department for advice and that 'after consultation with engineers and other specialists in [Cathay's] Integrated Operations Control Centre in Hong Kong, it was decided that the flight should continue its onward journey to Hong Kong airport.' So, clearly, there was a number of people involved in the decision making process.

Perhaps a better question to be asked is: with the benefit of hindsight, knowing what we know now, if faced with a similar situation and circumstances, would we make the same decision again? If the investigation concludes that the answer to this question is no and that the safest course would have been to land back at Surabaya, or another *en route* alternate airfield, who will carry the can? In this event, it is essential that the motivation and role of everyone in the decision-making chain, especially where commercial considerations were involved, be fully considered by the investigators in making their recommendations.

At the present time, the pilots are being hailed as heroes and, like Captain Chesley Sullenburger who successfully ditched his stricken A320 in the Hudson River on 15 January 2009 saving the lives of all on board, let us hope it stays that way. Experience shows us that, should events take a different course, there will be a lot of arse covering going on, especially from those who have made public statements in the media. When you are up on a pedestal, the only place to go is down.

We saw this only too clearly with Captain Peter Burkill, the commander of British Airways flight BA038, a B777 that landed short of the runway at Heathrow on 17 January 2008 after a double engine failure. The cause of the accident was determined to have been ice crystals in the fuel clogging the fuel-oil heat exchanger on each engine. Basically, a design fault in the fuel system. Subsequent investigation ultimately revealed that Peter's decision to retract the flaps to 25 degrees at the last moment had extended the aircraft's glide and meant that it came to rest within the airport boundary instead of crashing into buildings and other obstacles on the approach. His instinctive airmanship prevented a much more serious accident and probably saved the lives of many on board. The day after the accident, Captain Burkill appeared at a very public press conference alongside the BA CEO, Willie Walsh. It appeared then that Peter was the hero of the day and that he had the full backing and support of BA management. Subsequent events revealed a very different story and, as a result of misinformation and management failures, his career in professional aviation effectively is now over.

Perhaps the outcome of the investigation into the CX780 accident and the subsequent treatment of its crew will give us a good indication whether or not the Cathay pilots' flight safety and Flight Ops ethos concerns of the 1990s *have* been addressed or not.

We can similarly ask whether or not anything has been learned from the experiences of *The 49ers*. Let us start with an examination from my own perspective. Let us apply the same acid test and ask the question: given the same circumstances, would I do the same thing again? My answer is in two parts.

Would I stand up again and defend myself and my colleagues against a bullying management ethos? Unequivocally, yes. Bullies, corporate or otherwise, must not be permitted to prevail. If those who have the knowledge, the resources and the strength do nothing to combat this, then who will? History teaches us that appeasement in the face of bullying is doomed to failure. The only way to defeat bullies is to confront them. So, yes, I would do it again.

Would I use the same strategy and tactics against the bullies? The strategy, yes, but the tactics, probably no. Had we known at the outset what the ultimate cost was going to be in terms of ruined lives, marriages and careers, not to mention the three people who are no longer with us, we would probably have chosen a different road to travel. What those alternative tactics would have been I cannot say. We can only assess each situation on its merits at the time and make our decisions accordingly. What we can learn from our experience, however, is that if we are faced with a similar situation in the future, there are now more options and consequences to consider before coming to a decision.

One thing we know for certain is that bullying is alive and well in airline management. We have only to look at BA management's treatment of its cabin crew in their recent dispute. Whatever stance one may take regarding the core issues of the dispute, management pursued a course of victimisation and attempted to penalise the union leaders in its aftermath. This is precisely what Cathay management did back in 1993 after the cabin crew strike. Seventeen years on and we are still seeing the same tactics from the Sutch, Eddington and Walsh school of management. This is not just restricted to airlines, however. We see it in many other industries. So what is the answer? The answer is to continue to stand up to the bullies and not to give in to their tactics. The time may come one day when management teams genuinely do want to forge new working relationships with their employees in the aftermath of industrial disputes rather than just paying lip service to such noble principles. Until that day dawns, to use a Churchill maxim, we must KBO – keep buggering on!

Of course, no analysis of *The 49ers* story can be complete without considering the financial implications. The courts awarded us around HK$4 million each. Does that compensate us for our financial loss? Of course not. Nowhere near it. I lost around eight times that amount in career earnings and pension benefits alone as a result of my enforced retirement at the age of 49, not to mention other losses.

So, the simple conclusion is that the nine-year fight for justice wasn't worth it then? On the contrary. Yes it was. My name and my reputation are important to me. Our fight for justice has cleared the names and the reputations of all *The 49ers* and, on that basis alone, it was worth the fight. There is no denying, however, that we have all paid a high price, some more than others, and our lives have been changed forever.

Everything in life that is worth having comes with a price. The only question is whether or not we are prepared to pay it.

And what of the price that Cathay and the Swires have paid? We know that they value their reputation, otherwise why spend so much money on PR? Faced with a similar situation with their pilots, would they do the same thing again? I would like to think not, but I am not convinced attitudes have changed that much. It has recently been reported that their pilots based in North America are attempting to form a union there under the protection of the local labour laws, but management is doing its best to find legal means of preventing them from doing so. At the time of writing, Cathay management is once again embroiled in an increasingly bitter dispute with its pilots over similar issues that led to the events of 2001. Almost ten years on and it seems that the lessons that could be learned have been either ignored or forgotten.

But probably a more direct measure is to look at how much this has cost them in financial terms since this seems to be their main motivation. In the UK alone, the investigation by HM Revenue & Customs (HMRC) has probably cost them over £100 million, and resulted in significantly increased costs of employment, not just in the UK but in other overseas bases as well. Their total legal costs in the UK probably approach something in the region of £400,000. Estimates of the total legal costs of the case in Hong Kong come in at around HK$100 million.

As a Cathay shareholder, I seriously question a management ethos that allows these sorts of sums to be spent on litigation involving our own employees. At the time of writing, Cathay is currently involved in at least ten similar ongoing legal cases. Wouldn't our money be far better spent actually addressing the worries and concerns of our employees and building a workplace where people genuinely want to spend their time and give 110 per cent effort to the company? As it is, many of the Cathay pilots with whom I am still in contact tell me that morale is at rock bottom. Cathay City, their headquarters building at CLK, is variously nicknamed 'Shitty City' and 'The Lubyanka' after the old KGB headquarters in Moscow. People want to spend as little time as possible in that building.

The directors point to the profitability of the company as an indication of its success; that is when they are not pleading poverty and asking our employees to take unpaid leave to help out with the latest 'financial crisis'. As Judge Reyes remarked, they can't have it both ways. The point is that any company, no matter how it is managed, should be able to make a profit when it operates in a monopoly such as Cathay enjoys in Hong Kong. Yes, the company is profitable except when its managers cost its employees and shareholders hundreds of millions of dollars when they take a wrong punt on the fuel price as they did in 2008.

Also in 2008 Cathay paid a fine of US$60 million to the US authorities in settlement of criminal charges arising from its participation in a cargo price-fixing cartel. This was followed by another swingeing €57.1 million fine by the European Commission in November 2010 for similar price-fixing on cargo rates to and from Europe. These rulings now leave our company open to damages suits by customers who became victims of the cartels. Currently Cathay is being investigated for similar allegations in several other jurisdictions worldwide, and the Office of Fair Trading in the UK recently announced another investigation for price-fixing on the passenger network. An investigation reportedly is also underway by the Internal Revenue Service for non-compliance with withholding tax regulations in respect of employees based in the US. Like the HMRC investigation, this has the potential to cost us millions of dollars.

How is it that Cathay's directors and managers have got our company into this position? In the global marketplace, we must comply with both local and international legislation. The 'Well we can do it in Hong Kong' defence is disingenuous at best and negligent at worst.

The buck must stop somewhere. Like the Captain of an aircraft, someone has to take ultimate responsibility for the operation. Who is it? As a shareholder, I want managers who are competent, managers who have the qualifications and ability to do the job. I do not want managers who have to hire outside consultants to tell them how to run our company. If our managers do not know how to do that themselves, then let's get rid of them and employ those who do. If we stopped attacking our employees and instead returned to the ethos that used to prevail before the hatchet men were brought in, we could be even more profitable than we are now. Cathay could once again be a company that the rest of the industry looks up to as a role model and aspires to emulate rather than a case study in how not to do things. Fundamental changes were made to how Cathay conducts its business back in 1993. We live with the aftermath of those changes today; some good, but some bad and some very, very bad. There is no reason why we cannot make fundamental changes again, but this time learn from previous mistakes, get it right and correct past errors. It is this type of thinking that has made aviation safety what it is today and we should draw on that experience.

Perhaps there is a change in the air. In December 2010 it was announced that Tyler will 'step down' from the position of CEO of Cathay Pacific with effect from 31 March 2011, ending a career spanning 32 years with the Swire Group, to take up the position of director general and chief executive of IATA. The announcement cited his looming retirement age as one of the reasons for his decision. Ignoring for the moment the fact that three of the directors on the board of Cathay in 2009 were well over the normal retirement age of 57, the question might be asked, why would anyone want to resign the highest paid job in the company that yielded remuneration of HK$15.1 million and 12.1 million in 2008 and 2009 respectively, especially with record profits being forecast for the future? Whatever the reasons, let us hope that his departure might herald a new and more enlightened approach towards industrial relations within our company. With responsibility comes accountability.

As the press deadline for publication of this book approached, the judgment by the Court of Appeal still had not been handed down. I wanted very much to be able to finish the story but, on the timeline that had been set, it seemed it was not to be. I was in Australia over the Christmas period in 2010 to fulfil one of my bucket list ambitions: to attend the opening day of the Boxing Day Ashes Test Match at the Melbourne Cricket Ground. On 22 December, I received notification that the judgment would be handed down by the court at 09:30 on Christmas Eve. The next 48 hours were unbearable. I went through the whole gamut of emotions from unbridled optimism to a sickening fear of the unknown. One thing was for certain; whatever the judgment, one side or the other was going to receive an unexpected Christmas present. It turned out to be a double-edged sword.

Firstly, the Court of Appeal upheld Judge Reyes' judgment that *The 49ers* were dismissed for taking part in the legitimate and protected activities of their trade union. The court also declined to disturb the damages award in this leg of the case. In other words, Cathay management had acted in breach of the E.O. S21B(2)(b), a criminal offence in some cases.

Secondly, the court also upheld the judgment that Cathay had defamed *The 49ers*. So far so good. Having found in our favour, however, the court decided to reduce the damages award for defamation from HK$3.3 million to HK$700,000 per plaintiff. Part of the reasoning behind this swingeing reduction was that we had failed to show a causal link between the defamation and our subsequent inability to obtain equivalent alternative employment which occasioned our financial losses. In other words, we had not been able to field a witness in the form of a prospective employer who was prepared to testify words to the effect that, 'Because of the malicious and untrue statements made about you by Cathay Pacific, I refused to give you a job'. Well of course we couldn't. In these litigious times, it is difficult enough to get a past employer to give a character reference in any more than the blandest of terms for fear of being subject to a law suit by a new employer if the employee subsequently fails to live up to expectations. To get a prospective employer to make a statement that would lay him open to a discrimination suit borders on the impossible. Many confirmed the situation off the record but would not make sworn statements. We offered anecdotal evidence in abundance on the treatment of *The 49ers* in their search for employment. Naturally, the opposition tried to have this excluded as inadmissible hearsay and it seems that the Court of Appeal had some sympathy for this view. But how are we supposed to provide proof of a causal link when no one is prepared to testify? How do you obtain a conviction against the Godfather when witnesses are too afraid of reprisals to give evidence? That is precisely why we asked the court to assess damages 'at large' and adopt a common sense approach. What would a reasonable person think to be appropriate damages in such circumstances? One year's pay? Two years' pay? Maybe even three or more years' pay. Certainly not less than three *months'* remuneration, which is what the reduced award amounts to in my particular case.

On top of this, Judge Reyes' aggravated damages award was struck out altogether. It appears the court felt that, despite the fact that Cathay left their defamatory statements on their website for more than eight years, despite the fact that they repeated their defamatory statements in public both after George Crofts' success in the House of Lords and again in December 2009, despite the fact that they refused to apologise or show any contrition whatsoever, despite the fact that they forced us to sit though two court cases where their malicious defamation was aired all over again in their attempts at justification, despite all this the court did not consider such behaviour to merit aggravated damages. In summary, in assessing damages for defamation, it seems that Justice Reyes took our points whereas the Court of Appeal did not. We will have to see what the highest arbiter in Hong Kong, the Court of Final Appeal, has to say on the matter.

The last part of the judgment by the Court of Appeal is perhaps the most worrying. It overturned Judge Reyes' ruling on the breach of contract leg of our case. In doing so, it also held that the answers to the first two questions posed at the hearing on preliminary issues should be 'yes'. To refresh ourselves, the questions posed were:

(1) As a matter of law ... by virtue of Clause 35.3 of Cathay's Conditions [of Service] . . . whether the Defendants had an unfet-

tered contractual right to terminate the Plaintiffs' contracts of employment . . . without invoking the DGP.

(2) In the event of misconduct and/or alleged misconduct by the Plaintiffs, whether the Defendants had a contractual right to terminate the Plaintiffs' contracts of employment . . . without first invoking . . . the DGP.

Judge Reyes answered 'no' to both questions. He held that Cathay did *not* have such a contractual right. He held that the DGP cannot simply be ignored in the event of dismissal for misconduct. That was precisely the intent of those who drafted the DGP. I can say that for certain as I was the leader of the team that drafted the DGP. The Court of Appeal not only overturned that judgment, but it went further than that. It held that, under the terms of the Employment Ordinance, there is a statutory right conferred on the employer to be able to terminate the contract unilaterally without cause at any time. In other words, irrespective of *any* provisions included in the contract of employment intended to provide the employee with job security, the employer still has a statutory right to terminate the contract on notice any time he feels like it.

So, it doesn't matter how carefully you write your contract of employment; in Hong Kong it provides you with no protection against dismissal whatsoever. It doesn't matter if your contract expressly provides for a career path and a seniority structure. It doesn't matter if your contract is clearly designed to form a permanent and lasting relationship between the parties to a normal retirement age of 55. It doesn't matter if the provident fund only provides you with a means of supporting your family in retirement after many years of service. It doesn't matter that you have dragged your wife and children halfway across the world to pursue a long term career with a supposedly 'caring' employer. All of this apparently counts for nothing. According to the judgment by the Court of Appeal, your employer can simply dismiss you on a whim any time he feels like it, no questions asked, no reasons given and no remedy available to you. Actually the last part of that statement is not quite correct. According to the judgment, if your employer is silly enough to make public statements about you after the fact, you have the remedy of suing him for defamation; that is if you can afford expensive and lengthy litigation and are prepared to take the risk that the damages award may leave you considerably out of pocket.

It is hard to see how this can be right. It goes against all the mores of natural justice and common sense. It certainly goes against the intent of those who drafted the DGP in the Cathay pilots' contract. Surely it must also go against the intent of those who drafted the Employment Ordinance. Not even the most cynical, pro-employer legislators would intentionally draft such one-sided and toothless legislation would they? One thing is for certain: as things stand now, the contracts of employment of every man and woman working in Hong Kong are worth no more than lavatory paper. They provide no job security whatsoever against unscrupulous employers. Unless and until the judgment is reversed, or the law is changed, rather than being 'Asia's world city' as Tung Chee Hwa branded it at the Fortune Global Forum in May 2001, Hong Kong will remain just another Asian third world city, at least as far as employment legislation is concerned.

As a final aside, in a press statement dated 24 December 2010, a Cathay spokeswoman stated that, 'We welcome the court's ruling'. Presumably this means that, as well as welcoming the reduction in damages, they are also pleased to have been found guilty of breaching the Employment Ordinance and defaming their employees.

So, after almost ten years, the story still is not over. There is one more act in the drama yet to be played out. We will take this to the Court of Final Appeal and see if we can find a remedy there. This time it is not just about *The 49ers*; it is about the employment rights of all working people in Hong Kong. In the meantime, until that final act is completed, we will continue to stand together and KBO.

In the original manuscript of this book, I had written that my career in professional aviation is now over. It did not end the way I had either planned or hoped. I still remain proud that I was a Captain with what was once one of the most prestigious airlines in the world. I am proud that I stood up for the principles that my father instilled in me when he brought me up. I am extremely proud to have stood alongside the Band of Brothers, travelled the road and left no one behind along the way. Together we formed a bond between us that can never be broken.

Aviation is indeed a great way to earn a living and I have been privileged to be part of that select brotherhood. I hope that I have lived up to Tony Dodd's advice all those years ago and managed to put as much back into it as I derived from it. I hope I have left our profession in a better condition than when I entered it.

To those who are still active members of our brotherhood, I can do no better than to pass on that same advice. If this book helps in any way to assist you, then I have achieved one of my objectives in writing it. Sometimes it may be difficult to follow that advice and it may come at a cost, but it is worth it in the end.

Having written those words, life has a way of delivering surprises when we least expect them. After more than nine years in the wilderness, in October 2010 I was approached by a colleague. He offered me an opportunity once again to put something back into our profession. I accepted his invitation and am now employed as a flight simulator instructor on the Airbus A330. It is an opportunity I do not intend to waste. It is good once more to be part of our brotherhood.

Sources

1   The Arab Oil Embargo of 1973-74 Brian Trumbore
2   www.measuringworth.com
3   Housing Finance, Compendium of Housing Finance Statistics,
    Council of Mortgage Lenders
4   UK AAIB Report 1/1981
5   UK AAIB Report 4/1973
6   FLIGHT International 28 February 1976
7   SCMP 11th September 1986
8   UK AAIB Report 7/1981
9   SCMP 14th Feb 1993
10 SCMP 6th June 1993
11 SCMP 28th May 1993
12 SCMP 27th May 1993
13 SCMP 23rd Feb 1993
14 SCMP 18th Aug 1994
15 SCMP 21st Dec 1997
16 Listener, 6/10/01; 'Crash Landing', Bruce Ansley"
17 SCMP 23rd May 1997
18 UK AAIB Report 2/1987
19 Regina v P & O European Ferries (Dover) Ltd (1991) 93 Cr App
    R 72 (CCA)
20 HKCAD Accident Report 1/2004

Appendix 1

The Demise of Philippine Airlines

'Would you buy a used car from this man?'

Mort Sahl

Over the past four years we have witnessed the demise and closure of the oldest airline in our region; Philippine Airlines (PAL). As usual, much of the world's media have laid the blame for the failure of PAL at the door of the pilots' strike initiated earlier this year. Once again we are told that the greedy pilots ignored the commercial realities that PAL faced and by their selfish actions caused the closure of the company with the loss of thousands of jobs and immeasurable damage to the economy of their country.

What is the true story? What is the truth behind the media hype, the propaganda and the smoke and mirrors? Who is truly responsible for the demise of PAL and just who is it that has been greedy and self serving?

Perhaps the following information, which has been gathered from reputable sources, will help to answer these questions.

A Short History of PAL

Philippine Airlines, Asia's first airline, has a 57-year history. On 15th March 1941, it first took to the skies in a twin-engined Beech 18 carrying five passengers the 212 km from Manila to Baguio. Upon the outbreak of the Pacific war, PAL's two aircraft were pressed into service with the US Army Air Corps. Post-war operations began on 14th February 1946 with five ex-military DC3s. In July 1946 PAL chartered DC4s to carry American servicemen home to Oakland, making it the first Asian airline to cross the Pacific. Regular services to San Francisco began in December 1946 and in May 1947 PAL opened a route to Europe. By 1952, PAL's international route network covered two-thirds of the world and the Philippine government had become PAL's majority stockholder. This remained the situation until 1992 when PAL underwent privatisation and, in 1994, the Lucio Tan Group of companies obtained controlling interest following a share issue and increase in equity from P5 billion to P10 billion.

The Equity Issue

The table below shows the change in shareholding and equity after 1994[1]. At the time of the equity issue, 12 Senators in the Philippine Government wrote to the then President, Fidel Ramos, spelling out the dangers of surrendering control of their national flag carrier to one man, Lucio Tan. Under the proposed deal, which eventually went through despite their concerns and action in the Supreme Court, the Government and GFIs waived their pre-emptive rights over a total of 463 million shares in PAL, thus allowing Lucio Tan to gain majority control of PAL. In their letter to their President, the Senators stated:

> "We cannot close our eyes to the preponderant issue that underlies the PAL controversy; from the standpoint of public interest and national security, can government institutions rightfully enter into a compromise agreement that will yield majority control over the country's national airline to one man and his group? Is not PAL a strategic national asset that the government rather than one man should control? Should the government under your administration allow Filipino passengers and shippers to be at the mercy of this one man? Is it in the interest of GFI stakeholders for the GFIs to waive their pre-emptive rights to PAL shares as provided [for] in the proposed compromise agreement? What will the government secure in return for yielding its clear majority over the national airline?

Philippine Airlines Ownership Structure						
Owners	Before 1994			After Increase in Equity		
	PhP (m)	%	Stock (m)	PhP (m)	%	Stock (m)
Philippine Government & Government Financial Institutions (GFIs)						
Government	525	10.50	105.0	525	5.25	105.0
Philippine National Bank	250	5.00	50.0	250	2.50	50.0
DBP[1]	250	5.00	50.0	250	2.50	50.0
AFP-RSBS[2]	165	3.30	33.0	165	1.65	33.0
GSIS[3]	750	15.00	150.0	750	7.50	150.0
Land Bank	375	7.50	75.0	375	3.75	75.0
Total	**2,315**	**46.30**	**463.0**	**2,315**	**23.15**	**463.0**
BPI Group & Others						
Cumulus Holdings	545	10.90	109.0	545	5.45	109.0
Aeropartners/Foreign	465	9.30	93.0	465	4.65	93.0
Others				1,012	10.12	202.4
Total	**1,010**	**20.20**	**202.0**	**2,022**	**20.22**	**404.4**
Lucio Tan Group						
Ascot Holdings Inc				788	7.88	157.6
Cube Factor Holdings Inc				1,104	11.04	220.8
Network Holding & Equities				552	5.52	110.4
Pol Holdings Inc				756	7.56	151.2
Sierra Holdings & Equities				788	7.88	157.6
Lucio Tan Group	1,675	33.50	335.0	1,675	16.75	335.0
Total	**1,675**	**33.50**	**335.0**	**5,663**	**56.63**	**1,132.6**
Total Ownership						
Total	**5,000**	**100.00**	**1,000.0**	**10,000**	**100.00**	**2,000.0**
Total Shares Waived						
Government				1,650		330.0
GFIs				665		133.0
Total				**2,315**		**463.0**

Notes:
1 Development Bank of the Philippines
2 Armed Forces of the Philippines
3 Government Service Insurance System

At most, Tan promises, under the proposed compromise deal, to save the GFIs from loss if the value of PAL shares deteriorate within the next six years. Tan then commits to buy PAL shares at the par value of P5.00 per share, for which GFIs paid P14.00 per share four years ago in the public bidding. But for this to happen PAL shares must have deteriorated under a Tan management. And the purchase price is not something the GFIs can crow about; it is not even half of what the GFIs paid for their PAL shares.

Our experience has been that when private parties do not succeed in PAL, the Government ends up picking up the pieces in the interest of national security. Why allow for this contingency once again after the sad experience of the past?

To preserve this control and the financial viability of PAL, the government may be called upon to invest P2.3 billion through the government financial institutions. This amount is a pittance when compared with the P300 billion AFP modernisation program and the PNP's P48 billion modernization plan; which investment is equivalent to less than 1% of the aforesaid modernization budgets.

Mr. President, your action on this request will establish the falsity of claims that your administration has been following an ambivalent policy towards Mr. Lucio Tan and his business interests, on one hand running after him on tax evasion charges and, on the other hand, coddling his monopolistic control of the national airline.

We strongly urge you to act now before it is too late."

Despite the concerns raised at high levels of government, despite action in the Supreme Court and despite the fact that Lucio Tan was under investigation for tax irregularities, the deal went ahead. The Government and GFIs waived their pre-emptive rights over the equity issue and Lucio Tan was permitted to buy 463 million shares in PAL, which had a market value of P14 per share, at the bargain basement issue price of P5 per share, a net income opportunity loss of P4.167 billion. Tan paid P2.315 billion and obtained a 56.63% holding in PAL. In return, the government received nothing other than a promise that Tan would buy back shares at P5 per share from the GFIs if the value of PAL shares deteriorated within the next six years.

Since Lucio Tan took over the reins of the national airline, PAL has lost P14.8 billion.

The MacroAsia Connection[2]

MacroAsia is a medium-sized Manila-based airline support services provider with subsidiaries engaged in catering services, property development and aircraft chartering. It started as a subsidiary of PAL's Catering Division. PAL even provided for its initial capital by pumping into MacroAsia 70% of its capital stock requirement.

MacroAsia's subsidiary structure is shown in the following table:

Subsidiaries	Lucio Tan's Ownership
MacroAsia – Eurest Catering Services	64%
MacroAsia Air Taxi Services	100%
MacroAsia Property Development Corporation	100%
Cebu Pacific Catering Services	40%
MacroAsia Airport Services Corporation	100%

MacroAsia-Eurest Catering Services
This is a joint venture between MacroAsia, Eurest International BV and Singapore Airport Terminal Services. The facility employs 50 people and is the only in-flight kitchen in Manila which has state-of-the-art equipment. Its kitchen has the capacity to produce 5,000 meals per day.

MacroAsia Air Taxi Services
This wholly owned subsidiary of MacroAsia is engaged in the charter business with a licence to operate a domestic non-scheduled airline. It plans to enter into a wet lease agreement with Lucio Tan by which MacroAsia will lease five-seater helicopters.

MacroAsia Properties
MAPDC is involved in property development to support its logistical support business. It was the key division of MacroAsia, contributing 97% of operating revenues, but with the company's

increased focus on airline-related services, its contribution fell to 71% in 1997.

Cebu Pacific Catering
This is a joint venture between MacroAsia (40%), MGO Pacific Resources (20%) and **Cathay Pacific** (40%) with the latter acting as the managing partner. It is the only in-flight kitchen based in Mactan and has the capacity to produce 3,000 meals a day.

In June 1997, Lucio Tan controlled Philippines Airlines bought a 70% share in MacroAsia. The purchase, which the PAL management hailed as a *'logical and strategic investment for PAL'*, was done supposedly to transfer some of PAL's non-direct operations to MacroAsia.

The question arises, however, **why did PAL effectively set up a subsidiary company that not only duplicates, but also challenges, one of its most profitable service centres – Catering?**

Perhaps the answer is to be found in subsequent dealings on the stock exchange.

On 20th February 1998, the Securities and Exchange Commission approved the listing application of MacroAsia to trade 700 million common shares to cover the private placement of PAL. The issue was listed on 2nd March 1998.

On 9th June 1998, just three months after its listing and four days after the pilots' strike began, MacroAsia traded 686 million shares which comprised 68% of its outstanding capital stock. The haste with which the shares were gobbled up by an unknown investor created wild rumours in the market. It was speculated that PAL owner and shareholder of 700 million shares of MacroAsia, Lucio Tan, had unloaded PAL's 686 million shares in MacroAsia to himself. MacroAsia tried to squelch the speculation by claiming in newspaper reports on 15th & 16th June 1998 that the company was not aware of the alleged sale by PAL of its equity stake to the Tan family.

On 26th June 1998, a report in the business journal *PJB Pacific* stated that: "*Last year, MacroAsia issued 700m shares to cover the purchase by PAL of a 70% controlling stake. On 9th June 1998, PAL sold the shares through a block sale to Lucio Tan who is the owner of PAL.*"

If these reports are correct, a number of questions are raised:

- Has MacroAsia been designed to take over PAL's profit centres, leaving the airline with only cost centres – clearly a losing proposition – and if so why?
- How much did PAL pay to provide MacroAsia with its 70% start-up capital?
- How much did Lucio Tan pay PAL for the purchase of its MacroAsia shares?
- Is there a conflict of interest?

At the present time, MacroAsia is debt free. On the other hand, PAL, after four years of Lucio Tan management has the following debts:

Creditor	PhP (m)
Philippine National Bank	*3,000.00
Bureau of Treasury	*210.00
Land Bank	*140.00
Government Service Insurance System	*50.00
Banks and suppliers abroad	*81,600.00
Mobil Philippines Inc.	351.10
Petron (40% government owned)	201.77
Caltex (Philippines) Inc	27.16
Philippine Aviation & Security Services Corp.	7.02
Filipino Society of Composers, Authors and Publishers	3.85
Total	85,590.90
Japan Energy Corporation	US$208,083

* As at PAL's application to the Securities & Exchange Commission to suspend payments on its debts and liabilities.

It is also interesting to review PAL's financial performance over the last eleven years, and in particular, since Lucio Tan gained control of the airline.

Year	Profit/(Loss) PhP (m)	Majority Shareholder
1987	318.128	Philippine Government
1988	(70.115)	Philippine Government
1989	304.606	Philippine Government
1990	(3.020)	Philippine Government
1991	(3,334.611)	Philippine Government
1992	1,113.478	Antonio Cojuangco
1993	1,025.665	Antonio Cojuangco
Total	**(645.869)**	
1994	(451.397)	Lucio Tan
1995	(1,716.914)	Lucio Tan
1996	(2,182.280)	Lucio Tan
1997	(2,501.677)	Lucio Tan
1998 1st Quarter	(8,000.000)	Lucio Tan
Total	**(14,852.268)**	

Under Lucio Tan's management, PAL has lost P14.85 billion in five years of operation.

In July 1997 when PAL was already in financial difficulty, P40-60 million was spent on new uniforms and matching luggage ordered by PAL's manager of corporate development, one Vivienne Tan who also happens to be Lucio Tan's daughter. Describing the uniforms in detail, PAL's official publication, *PALiner* reported that Vivienne Tan commissioned a '*technologically advanced foreign textile company to manufacture the fabric. Shoes, belts, bags and other accessories were carefully chosen as much for their style as for their quality, practicality and comfort. A favourite among the crew are the Italian-made shoes with special features like gum inserts and arch supports . . .*'

At the time when PAL asked the Securities and Exchange Commission for permission to suspend payments on its debts, GFIs in the Philippines were owed P3.4 billion by PAL. This is not counting their respective investments in PAL, the largest of which is the Philippine National Bank (PNB). As it stands, of PNB's original equity investment of P752 million, Lucio Tan now recognises only P350 million.

But what has caused these losses, where has the money gone and how can Tan sustain such an operation? Surely, as the major shareholder, this must be impacting on his own personal wealth? Perhaps if we dig deeper into the web of companies, more of the picture will be revealed.

Aircraft Leases[3]

Despite its ailing financial condition, PAL management entered into a number of contracts for capital leases of Airbus aircraft between August and December 1997. Based on the standards of PAL's Corporate Code, the question might be asked, were these fair and reasonable under the circumstances?

Analysis of debts and liabilities incurred by PAL shows that 56% fall under capital leases as a result of a fleet acquisition programme initiated by Tan. The following table shows some of the major contracts and the amounts owed by PAL:

Alleged Lessor	Address	US$ (m)	Date
Paladin Aviation Ltd	c/o Credit Agricole Indosuez Asian Aerospace Group, 3-29-1 Kanda-Jimbocho Chiyoda-ku Tokyo 101	84.018	27 Aug 97
Pert Aviation Ltd		83.970	24 Sep 97
Peloras Aviation Ltd		96.873	29 Sep 97
Pacer Aviation Ltd		84.105	29 Sep 97
Princely Aviation Ltd		96.852	22 Oct 97
Platinum Aviation Ltd		86.000	3 Nov 97
Prestige Aircraft Leasing	c/o Marubeni Corporation 4-2 Ohtemachi 1-chome Chiyoda-ku, Tokyo 101	34.252	05 Aug 97
Paramount Aviation Ltd		34.800	25 Nov 97
SPR Acacia Air Lease Co Ltd	c/o Sanwa Business Credit Co Ltd Shinjuku-ku, Tokyo 101	76.261	30 Jul 97
Total		**677.131**	

This raises a number of issues:

- Why do almost all the capital lessors bear the same initials as PAL and many share the same address?

- Credit Agricole Indosuez Asian Aerospace Group is **not listed** in the NTT telephone directory. Why not?

- A company called Indosuez Guardmore Management Japan, a credit company, is listed at the same address in Kanda Jimbocho but all attempts to contact the listed number have proved fruitless. Is there a connection?

- When contacted for comment, Toshio Kagaya of Marubeni Corporation said officials in charge were not available.

- Sanwa Business Credit declined to comment when contacted but Hirofumi Kanai, an official in the finance section of Sanwa Bank (the parent company of Sanwa Business Credit), stated that the company could not discuss anything about SPR Acacia Air Lease and PAL. He stated that it is the company's duty to protect classified information.

So, who actually owns these companies?

An article by Teddy Casiño published in an August issue of Business World[4] offered the following:

"Is it possible to lose money and yet make a profit, lots of it?

Yes especially if you're Lucio Tan. Not only that, you can even run your company into the ground, make millions and then position yourself for more.

The scheme is very simple.

First, buy an ailing government asset like Philippine Airlines for a song. Then embark on a US$4 billion refleeting program involving the purchase of 36 new jets.

But don't use your own money. Or if you do, just put in enough to make people think you've put out a lot.

The trick is to borrow US$850 million from European creditors, US$230 million from local banks including one you own, and billions more from other local and international sources.

After pocketing the commissions from the planes, you can even form some dummy corporations to lease the planes to your newly acquired airline at 40% more than normal rates."

Subsidiary Companies[5]

PAL Training Centre
The PAL Training Centre building on Padre Faura in Manila was reported to have been purchased from Caltex by PAL. Investigation has shown that it was not purchased by PAL, it was purchased by the Tan Yan Kee Foundation, a foundation owned by Lucio Tan. PAL pays the Tan Yan Kee foundation P1.775 million a month in rental.

Absolute
PAL offices and buildings do not have any water fountains. PAL employees and PAL passengers drink water supplied by Absolute. Absolute is a Lucio Tan owned company.

Asia Brewery
Only Carlsberg beer, supplied by Asia Brewery, is sold on PAL flights. Asia Brewery is a Lucio Tan owned company.

Fortune Tobacco
Only Winston and Hope cigarettes, supplied by Fortune Tobacco, are sold on board PAL flights. Fortune Tobacco is a Lucio Tan owned company.

DPSI
DPSI is a Macintosh computer company. It has been stated that Macintosh computers have been brought into the country on a tax-free basis by listing them as 'PAL company materials' and that PAL also bore the freight costs. DPSI is a Lucio Tan owned company.

The Allied Bank Connection

The following article recently appeared in Business World[6]:

"Fifteen days before seeking the regulators' nod on its planned suspension of debt payments, PAL moved to substantially reduce its debt exposure to Allied Banking Corp. by transferring several real estate holdings.

Industry sources said the move may be in violation of provisions under the Insolvency Law which prevents the disposition of assets of a firm seeking debt relief with the SEC at least within a month before filing an application.

The sources said PAL may have acted in 'bad faith' when it trans-ferred the assets to Allied Bank knowing it will later run to regula-tors to seek debt relief. This prejudices its other creditors, the sources said.

Allied Bank, owned by Lucio Tan, *is one of the biggest creditors of the airline, along with the Philippine National Bank and foreign banks. A total of 30 creditors piled up debt exposures amounting to more than US$2 billion (or P85 billion) to PAL.*

The troubled airline has announced plans to close its operations by midnight tomorrow.

Officials of the Airline Pilots Association of the Philippines (ALPAP), in a news conference yesterday, said the transfer of certificate of titles of PAL's real estate holdings amounted to US$30 million and covered four parcels of land in Bacolod, Bulacan, Iloilo and Parañaque.

These properties were mortgaged to Allied Bank on June 8, documents provided to BusinessWorld show.

"These holdings were earmarked for mortgage in a PAL board resolu-tion on May 18, 1998, a week after ALPAP declared its serious inten-tion to go on strike and backed this up by requesting its members to submit their travel documentation,' the PAL pilots" group said.

According to its petition filed with the SEC last June 23, PAL declared the properties as security for its US$6.019-million short-term loan to Allied Bank, along with rotables and reparables, and flight equipment.

Allied Bank also has US$25.34 million in outstanding loans to PAL, backed by spare engines and 'class A' rotables. In addition, another US$6.6-million long-term loan to the airline was backed by aircraft and 'assignment of rights to the relevant Airbus purchase agreement,' its SEC petition stated.

ALPAP officials said PAL transferred the assets 'to arrange for Allied Bank's foreclosure of these prime properties in the event of PAL's failure to meet its obligation in a strike situation.'

This will facilitate the closure of a strike-bound company while trans-

ferring its assets effectively to another company which are both owned by the same person."

A top Allied Bank official, speaking on condition of anonymity, yesterday contended the bank still has US$42.8 million in outstanding exposure to PAL.

He said PAL's total loans are US$37.6 million while its letters of credit (LCs) stood at US$5.2 million. Of the total loans, he said US$6 million were obtained 'in-house' or outside of a loan syndication.

The official denied any knowledge about the transfer of PAL's assets last June."

Financial Summary

The International Monetary Fund has expressed concern that the P85 billion debt of PAL (which has since ballooned to P90 million) could adversely impact the Philippine banking system. Salvador Enriquez, in his last days as Finance Secretary, noted that the government stands to lose billions from its investments in PAL, as it already has, leaving government financial institutions – ultimately the Filipino people – to pick up the tab; P90 billion in liabilities not to mention their original investments in the national carrier.

The Pilots' Strike[7]

So where does the pilots' strike fit into all this? After all, some press reports have stated that it was the pilots' strike that brought PAL down. Weren't they just on strike for more money, being greedy as usual at a time when the company needed their help? Or was the labour situation manipulated to precipitate a strike so that this could be used as a smokescreen to blame the company's woes on the work-force?

The pilots of the Airline Pilots Association of the Philippines (ALPAP) did not go on strike for more money. The strike came about partly as a result of the intimidation, persecution and, ultimately in one case, sacking of Captains Albino Collantes and Florendo Umali, both long-serving PAL Captains.

Captain Collantes had recently completed an Airbus A330 conversion course at a cost to PAL of around P2 million. He was scheduled to operate a flight Manila-Laoag-Hong Kong. However, his Chinese visa had expired and his passport was with the PAL office for processing. Unfortunately, PAL had not renewed Captain Collantes' visa in time for the flight. Instead he was assigned to another flight via a dispatched message. PAL claimed that the said message was delivered yet a copy of the message does not show any proof of receipt by Captain Collantes who maintained that he did not receive the message. His supervisor, Captain Lorenzo Lim, filed administrative charges against Captain Collantes alleging that he had refused to operate the reassigned flight. At the subsequent enquiry, the Chief Pilot – Turbo Prop Division cleared Captain Collantes of all charges whereupon he filed a suit for damages against Captain Lim in court. PAL management, having failed to dissuade Captain Collantes from pursuing his case against Lim, handed him a letter advising him of his enforced retirement, invoking an outdated provision in the PAL-ALPAP Retirement Plan of 1967. This stated that:

> "Section 2. _Late Retirement_. Any member who remains in the service of the Company after his normal retirement date may retire either at his option or _at the option of the company_ and when so retired he shall be entitled either (a) to a lump sum payment of P5,000 for each year of completed service as a pilot or (b) to such termination benefits to which he may be entitled under existing laws, whichever is the greater amount."

Captain Collantes, at age 45, had not yet reached his normal retirement date and, in any case, this agreement had been superceded by a new retirement plan agreed in 1971 which states that:

> "Section 1. Normal Retirement Date. The Normal Retirement Date of a participant shall be his 60th birthday, provided he has then rendered at least ten (10) years of service with the Company.
>
> Section 2. Early Retirement Date. The Early Retirement Date of a participant shall be when he shall have completed at least ten (10) years of service with the Company and has attained the age of 50 years."

ALPAP's position was that PAL cannot 'retire' a pilot under the age of 60 years because:

- Provisions in the 1971 Retirement Plan override those stipulated in the 1967 Retirement Plan; and

- The company's option to retire pilots before the mandatory age of 60 violates the Labour Code, specifically on the aspect of security of tenure; and

- This interpretation by management, if allowed to prosper, will become a tool for coercion by management and could seriously hamper the decision making ability of a pilot in the exercise of his profession.

ALPAP's view is that this was being used purely as a tool to intimidate the pilots as, had PAL management intended retiring Captain Collantes, they would not have sent him on the A330 conversion course.

On 9th December 1997, ALPAP filed a first notice of strike based on the retirement issue of Captain Collantes among other issues.

The Department of Labour & Employment (DOLE) Secretary, then Leonardo Quisumbing, assumed jurisdiction on 23rd December 1997. Quisumbing was later appointed to the Supreme Court and was replaced by Cresenciano Trajano in February 1998.

New DOLE Secretary **Trajano did not call for the first conciliation meeting until 20th May 1998** after a five-month hiatus since assumption of jurisdiction.

Two more conciliation meetings were held but yielded negative results.

In the meantime, a further case of victimisation arose. Captain Florendo Umali, a 23 year veteran of PAL with a clean record, was charged by PAL management with '*serious misconduct deliberately causing damage to or disruption to the Company.*' His supposed infraction occurred on a flight from Manila to Dubai on 19th January 1998. After extensive delays on the taxiway prior to take off due to heavy traffic, his taxi fuel had been consumed. After consultation with his crew, it was decided to return to the ramp for refuelling. As a result of his decision, he faced dismissal for refusing to take off because his aircraft's fuel load was now below the minimum required for the proposed flight. That Captain Umali is also a Principal Officer of ALPAP was, no doubt, not considered by management when bringing these charges against him.

ALPAP's view is that management was now using retrenchment and disciplinary action as a ruse to mask its union-busting activities. Retrenchment and/or disciplinary action were being used as justification to selectively dismiss pilots who are perceived to be 'undesirable' to the company, as in the cases of Captains Collantes and Umali.

Faced with this situation, and the fact that for the last seven months, PAL had not been remitting union dues or assessment deducted from the salaries of ALPAP members, **on 5th June 1998, ALPAP filed a second notice of strike**.

The following events then took place:

1. Termination and Return to Work Order

- ALPAP went on strike on 5th June 1998.

- In a 6th June 1998 press release, PAL management declared that '*all 29 officers of ALPAP have lost their employment status.*'

- PAL management, usurping the DOLE's authority, gave striking pilots until noon of 7th June 1998 to return to work otherwise, '*the pilots have lost their jobs.*'

- In a 7th June press release, management fired all pilots who did not return to work as of noon on 7th June 1998.

- On 7th June 1998, DOLE issued a return to work order after PAL management had terminated all ALPAP officers and members. **The order was not served to ALPAP's legal counsel until 25th June 1998**.

- ALPAP officers and members marched to PAL on 26th June 1998 in compliance with the DOLE's order.

- PAL management insisted on accepting strikers as new applicants to serve a 6-month probationary period and not as returning workers.

- **To date, no ALPAP member has received an official termination letter from management.** "Termination" was made only through press releases.

The DOLE has neither declared the strike as illegal nor has it authorised the termination of the ALPAP officers and members.

2. Retrenchment of Ground Employees and Cabin Crew

On 15th June 1998, 3,600 ground employees and 1,400 cabin crew personnel were served termination papers stating the following:

> "*We regret therefore to inform you that your employment will be terminated effective after one (1) month from receipt hereof. You will be given all the benefits that you may be entitled to **as soon as the company is in a position to do so**.*"

On 19th June 1998, the union of ground employees, PAL Employees Association (PALEA), filed a notice of strike. On 22nd July 1998 at 03:30, PALEA went on strike.

The President of the Philippines, Joseph Estrada, intervened in the dispute and a settlement agreement was reached on 26th July 1998. However, at least 1,800 ground employees will still be retrenched effective thirty (30) days from the signing of the agreement.

The Flight Attendants and Stewards Association of the Philippines (FASAP), the cabin crew union, filed a class suit before the National Labour Relations Court (NLRC) for illegal dismissal.

NLRC has asked PAL to reinstate the 1,400 flight attendants but PAL management has refused.

3. Conciliation Meetings

DOLE has held regular conciliation meetings since day one of the strike. Most of the ALPAP officers attended, while PAL was represented only by middle-management lawyers.

At all meetings, management reiterated its position that '*as far as we are concerned, all pilots are terminated and any returning pilot will be deemed a new applicant.*'

4. Complaint for Illegal Lockout

A complaint for illegal lock out was filed on 29th June 1998 at the NLRC.

The complaint demands that:

- PAL be declared guilty of illegal lockout; and

- PAL unconditionally accepts all officers and members of ALPAP without any loss of pay or seniority status; and

- PAL pays all the salaries and benefits of all locked out officers and members pursuant to existing contracts of employment and pertinent collective bargaining agreement (CBA) provisions effective 26th June 1998.

The case was assigned to Labour Arbiter Voltaire A. Balitaan on 28th July 1998.

On 21st August 1998, Arbiter Balitaan ordered that the case be consolidated with the First Notice of Strike filed on 9th December 1997. **It took the arbiter almost two months to decide that he is not the proper person to resolve the case.**

5. Petition for Injunction

A Petition for Injunction was filed on 29th June 1998 to seek the issuance of a Temporary Restraining Order (TRO) which will prevent PAL from hiring new pilots after 26th June 1998 and that a permanent injunction be issued after due hearing.

The case was assigned to the First Division of the NLRC.

On 26th August 1998, two out of the member commissioners dismissed the case for lack of jurisdiction. **One filed his dissenting opinion but, just like the complaint for illegal lock out, it took the NLRC almost two months to decide that it is not the proper body to resolve the case.**

6. Rehabilitation Program

PAL filed a petition to the SEC for approval of a rehabilitation plan, appointment of a receiver and a petition for debt relief.

Under its plan, management intends downsizing the existing fleet of 51 aircraft to 14.

SEC has approved the creation of an interim receiver composed of **3 high ranking PAL executives**, 1 representative from SGV and Mr. Roman Cruz Jr. to finalize the rehabilitation program for submission on 24th July 1998.

SEC granted an extension for the submission of the rehabilitation program. The new deadline was set for 21st September 1998.

ALPAP has filed a motion to intervene as a creditor.

7. Government Inter-Agency Task Force

On 28th August 1998, President Joseph Estrada signed an administrative order creating an inter-agency task force to solve the problems at PAL.

The task force is composed of the Department of Finance, Department of Labour, Department of Transportation & Communication, Department of Foreign Affairs, Department of Tourism and the SEC. The Chairman is Finance Secretary Edgardo Espiritu.

The task force commenced conciliation meetings between management and labour. During these meetings, management presented Lucio Tan's offer as follows:

- From the issued share of stocks of Lucio Tan, 60,000 PAL shares will be transferred in favour of each PAL employee on the active payroll as of 15th September 1998

- The aggregate shares of stock will permit the employees 3 seats on the PAL Board of Directors

- The Collective Bargaining Agreements (CBAs) will be suspended for 10 years.

12 members of the PALEA board reportedly voted to accept the offer but this has yet to be ratified by the membership.

The FASAP board rejected the offer.

ALPAP has written to Tan to inform him that its board cannot recommend a decision to its membership until the ongoing labour dispute is first resolved.

The Pilots' Position[8]

The 600 'dismissed' ALPAP pilots, 230 of whom have served the airline for over 20 years, are unable to obtain other employment simply because PAL has not issued their termination papers.

If the dismissal of the pilots is held to be legal by the courts, this would save PAL from paying them their claims for benefits which include:

- Accumulated vacation leave of 60,000 days

- Separation pay in excess of P281 million

- Productivity income of 6,000 hours.

ALPAP's view is that the non-issuance of the pilots' termination papers is an obvious ruse designed to:

- Prevent pilots from seeking employment in other airlines

- Force pilots to return to work as new applicants because they cannot find work elsewhere

- Cause pilots to lose all accrued benefits

Pilots seeking employment with other airlines will not be accepted there unless they can produce their termination papers. PAL claims that it will take a longer time to process the pilots' termination papers yet, just 4 days after the pilots' strike began, PAL was able to process the termination of 5,000 ground employees and flight attendants.

The message is obvious – 'if you do not want to work for PAL under Tan, you cannot work elsewhere'.

Comment

So whose fault is it that Asia's oldest airline has shut up shop with the loss of thousands of jobs and billions of Pesos to the country and the

Filipino people? Should the blame be laid at the door of the pilots who were only asking that their contractual and constitutional rights be upheld? Or should the blame more correctly be attributed to financial misman-agement? And what of the government's role in this episode? Teddy Casiño[9] again:

"Next spin off the company's money-making operations – like training and in-flight catering – to your other companies. Buy spare parts and equipment, not from the manufacturers themselves which sell them cheap, but through your own distributorship which allows bigger commissions.

In other words, milk all you can from the company. That's right, suck it to the marrow.

If you do everything correctly, your company will have lost P451 million in the first year and P8.08 billion in the fifth, the biggest loss in the airline's 57 year history.

With your company now severely in the red, you will have a convenient excuse to lay off thousands and, in the process, bust the unions. Tell your workers you have no choice. Blame the Asian currency crisis, the liberaliza-tion of the aviation industry, the down-grading of the Philippines to a category 2 destination by the US Federal Aviation Administration, the high cost of plane maintenance and the 'grossly unprofitable missionary domestic routes.'

But never, never blame yourself or your mismanagement of the company.

When your airline finally crashes, file for insolvency at the Securities and Exchange Commission and save your-self the trouble of paying P85 billion worth of debts, including billions worth of separation pay and retirement bene-fits due thousands of workers you have laid off with impunity.

In the end you will be left with a bankrupt company but with millions more in your pocket. By this time you will have succeeded in turning your workforce into a horde of servile commercial labourers without a union to protect them.

Now you can reorganise the company the way you want it with the minimum of opposition. Now you can really make money.

That is how the picture looks to the workers of PAL, many of whom are still smarting from their recent stand-off with the management of Lucio Tan. For clearly their woes are far from over.

Things are worse for the pilots, the original strikers whose 500 or so members remain jobless. Ironically, the PAL management refuses to give them their termination papers, proof that the company still needs them and, in fact, wants them to re-apply; of course as second-class probationary or contrac-tual workers As far as ALPAP is concerned, Mr. Tan's plans are to break the union, prevent the pilots from getting jobs in other airlines and starve them into submission.

It should be made clear that the issue here is not merely job security. Even the unions admit that these lay-offs are actually part of management's plan to restructure the corporation and were here long before the strike and long before the massive losses.

In fact it seems that the severe losses were actually stage-managed to justify lay-offs and will be further used to justify whatever sweeping changes may be made at PAL.

What we see here is a kind of corporate restructuring that preys on its own workers. What we see here is plain and simple greed taking precedence over the livelihood and rights of thousands of workers. And what we see here is a government that condones such actions.

In the meantime, Mr. Tan gets away scot-free. Capitalism does work doesn't it?"

Summary

Perhaps the following article which appeared in the Philippine Daily Enquirer[10] on September 22nd 1998 best summarises the whole situation:

'Tantarado' (Stupid Fool) – It's a breathtaking exercise in deceit.

"We are deeply saddened," said the Philippine Airlines management's 'Notice of Closure' in the Inquirer last week, "to announce that at midnight of September 23, 1998, PAL will close following the breakdown of negotiations between management and the labor unions in PAL to forge an acceptable arrangement to ensure continuing industrial peace.

"Management has exhausted all efforts to keep the company operational pending the outcome of its negotiations with the labor unions. Management's offer was aimed at guaranteeing long-term industrial peace and harmony in PAL, which is a key requirement for any rehabilitation plan to succeed.

"It is not easy to preside over the demise of a great Filipino institution.

Sadly, our sincere efforts to keep PAL flying and serve the riding public have not been matched by a similar commitment from our employees' union."

Look at the gall of these people. After having wrecked a truly great Filipino institution (why it was given to them to run in the first place, only God and government know), they now blame the workers for its closure.

PAL in fact had been haemorrhaging long before Palea, Fasap and Alpap, the ground crew union, the flight attendants union and the pilots union staged strikes over the last few years. It was haemorrhaging because Lucio Tan, its new owner, went into a refleeting binge that buried the company in debt but allowed Tan himself to profit from the commissions on the purchase of airplanes and the servicing – by his companies – of PAL's needs. That the unions became restive in the course of his stewardship (they were not so before his time) by itself should say something about the quality of his management, such as his way of running things may be called that. It was symptomatic of the rot there. To blame the unions now for PAL closing shop – that is deceitfulness of epic proportions.

Why should PAL's employees bear the cost of management's monumental ineptitude or avarice? Why should they agree to prostitute themselves, or wear the metal collars and chains of bonded slaves, just because their employers pillaged the company coffers? Which was what Tan's offer of giving the unions some seats in the board in exchange for their giving up their right to bargain collectively – a right enshrined in the Constitution – amounted to. After driving the airline literally to the ground, he now wanted the workers to give up their working rights so they could bail him out. And failing that, he went on to blame the workers for not sharing his depth of commitment to his company. What commitment? The only commitment he has shown is the commitment to commit perfidy. He should be committed to another truly great Filipino institution, which is the one located in Muntinlupa. Who's being unreasonable? None of the strikes the unions have taken over the years has had to do with a raise in pay, which PAL employees are well

within their rights to ask. They have merely asked that management respect the country's labor laws. Before retrenching, exhaust all options. If retrenchment is unavoidable, follow the procedures set by the labor department. What is unreasonable about those things?

How reasonable those demands are you see clearly in comparison to the demands of the pilots of Northwest Airlines, who have been on strike for several days now. Like PAL, Northwest has been absorbing huge losses over the years, though unlike PAL for reasons other than bad management. But entirely unlike PAL, the Northwest pilots are asking for a raise, which they feel is commensurate to the worth of their skills in the open market.

Yet look at the way the strike has been reported in the American media. Look at the way the American public has viewed the strike. Nobody says the striking pilots are acting irresponsibly. Nobody says the pilots are subverting democracy. Nobody says the pilots are driving their company to the brink of disaster. For good reason: People there take their labor laws seriously. People there find it completely just that a worker should exert himself to get his due. People there find it completely normal that a worker should press management to get his due. By going on strike, if necessary.

Certainly, you will not find people there calling a proposal for airline workers *to junk collective bargaining for 10 years to save their premier airline a wise and compassionate one. What they will call it will not be fit to print. What does that proposal mean but that the unions agree to commit suicide? What is a union without collective bargaining? That is its heart and soul. That is what the framers of the Constitution, following democratic tradition all over the world, put it in the fundamental law of land for. You want a social club, form a social club, not a union.*

It is not PAL management that has bent over backwards to accommodate the unions, it is the PAL unions that have bent over backwards to accommodate management. The unions were not beyond negotiating Tan's proposal, notwithstanding its patent anti-union thrust. It was PAL management that took a take-it-or-leave-it attitude. You're a self-respecting union, you leave it. No, more than that, you're a responsible union, you trash it. Never mind yourself, think of what that proposal will mean to the terms of employment in the rest of the country.

It will set a precedent for the wholesale slaughter of labor.

Everywhere, employers need only threaten to close shop to force workers to dissolve their unions and stop complaining about abuses. Everywhere, employers need only threaten to close shop to fire anyone, to rob anyone, to flog anyone.

Why we call ourselves a democracy, I'll never know. The feeblest democratic instinct should compel anyone to find that proposal an outrage. That is not industrial peace, that is the peace of the dead. That is not industrial harmony, that is the silence of the terrorized. Times are hard, true. But why should that be an excuse to repress labor? Whoever decreed that labor should be the last to profit in good times and the first to suffer in bad times? Times are hard, and that should be a reason to indict the people who make the times harder. That should be a reason only to convict the people who make themselves richer.

That should be a reason only to jail the tantarados of this world.

Footnote

As a result of ALPAP releasing certain information at a recent press conference, Lucio Tan has filed a suit for libel against ALPAP and its President, Captain Sotico Lloren. At a recent IFALPA regional meeting, Captain Lloren informed HKALPA that both he and ALPAP will be defending the suit. It will be interesting to follow the testimony and, perhaps, to find out more of the truth behind the demise of PAL.

It was also interesting to hear Captain Lloren's response to a journalist who was present at the meeting when he asked, now that PAL has closed down, has the strike been worth it? Captain Lloren replied, yes, most definitely. With no contract and no collective bargaining agreement, it is better not to work at all than to work as a slave.

References

1   ALPAP Fact Sheet – PAL: A Failed Privatization
2   ALPAP Fact Sheet – MacroAsia: PAL Profit Centre Divested in Favour of Lucio Tan
3   ALPAP Fact Sheet – PAL: Lucio Tan's Milking Cow
4   Teddy Casiño © BusinessWorld Publishing Corporation
5   ALPAP Fact Sheet – PAL: Lucio Tan's Milking Cow
6   Sheila A. Samonte and Reena J. Villamor © BusinessWorld Publishing Corporation.
7   ALPAP Fact Sheet – The PAL-ALPAP Labour Dispute
8   ALPAP Fact Sheet – The Pilots Plight
9   Teddy Casiño © BusinessWorld Publishing Corporation
10 © Philippine Daily Enquirer

Appendix 2

APPENDIX 2

From: MEMO.CX.FOPRBD
To: CXHKGCLK1.CLKPO3(FOPRBD)
Date: Sat, Oct 3, 1998 9:21 AM
Subject: Minutes

--- Received from CX.FOPRBD RON DAVIES   * 03/10/98 09.21
 -> CX.FOPDER   DAVE ROBERTS   (FLT) HKGOFCX
 -> GRPWISE.FOPRBD   RON DAVIES   HKGWECX
Ack/Ron

--- Received from CX.FOPDER DAVE ROBERTS   * 02/10/98 09.11
 -> CX.FOPJPC   PADDY CAVANAGH
 -> CX.FOPRBD   RON DAVIES   (FOP) HKGWECX
 -> CX.FOPHKH   DENLY HAU (X8581)   (CRW) HKGOPCX
CC:
 -> CX.FOPCGA   *> Being forwarded by receiver
 -> CX.FOPTTL   *> Being forwarded by receiver
Gentlemen: Would like to get together at 09:00 on Wednesday the 07th.

Corinne: Any thoughts/suggestions. Cheers, Dave

--- Received from CX.FOPWJC JOYCE WONG (FOP)   29/09/98 15.31

       Minutes for the "Sick Leave" Meeting
       29 September 1998 10AM 3/F Conference Rm CLK

Attendees :

Nick Rhodes (Chairman)	Netsson Wu
Corinne Aldis	KM Chan
Chris Hoyland	Richard Hall
Greg Gibbins	Paddy Cavanagh
Denly Hau	Dave Roberts
K.Y. Cheng	Dennis Leung
Joyce Wong (Secretary)	

1. A summary table re sick leaves for the year 1997 & 1998 will be created for each cockpit crew. This will serve as a tool for the annual interview. It's been proposed that the report will be updated annually or as required.
2. A separate chart will be provided for the "black listed" crew. Proposed to be updated every 3 months or before the Chief Pilot signs the annual increment for the particular individual.
3. A list of all cockpit crew sick leave reports will be updated quarterly.
4. Incentives & Dis-incentives

a) Incentives   Action parties
===========   ===============

- leave points	DER / DH
- request G days	CH / KM
- request trips	X
- temp bases / swaps	DER RD
- more reserves / less G	CH / KM
- roster "in bin"	X

12

- O days after ULH vs G days   CH / DL
- repeat rosters - including X'mas   KM
- staff travel (annual FOC, UGSA)   DER / DH
- work from age 55 - 60

b) Dis-incentives
===========

- loss of training
- loss of job
- loss of increment
- loss of base
- loss of command / delay in promotion

5. Sick note

It has been agreed that with good measures to tackle the sick leave problems, there should not be a need for submitting sick notes in the future.

6. PMO

If a particular cockpit crew has been sick for several occassions in a year, he may be asked to see the PMO for body check.

```
-> CX.FOPNPR      *> Being forwarded by receiver
-> CX.FOPCGA      *> Being forwarded by receiver
-> CX.FOPHCH      CHRISTOPHER HOYLAND        HKGWQCX
-> CX.FOPGAG      *> Being forwarded by receiver
-> CX.FOPHKH      DENLY HAU (X8581)     (CRW) HKGOPCX
-> CX.FOPKYC      K. Y. CHENG (X8569)   (ADM) HKGOACX
-> CX.FOPWYK      NELSSON WU            (CRW) HKGOCCX
.> CX.FOPKMC      *> Being forwarded by receiver
-> CX.FOPRJH      *> Being forwarded by receiver
-> CX.FOPJPC      PADDY CAVANAGH
-> CX.FOPDER      DAVE ROBERTS          (FLT) HKGOFCX
-> CX.FOPLWH      *> Being forwarded by receiver
```

02 November 1998

Our Ref: 4009/pj/98/143

Mr P D A Sutch
Chairman
Cathay Pacific Airways Limited
35/F, 2 Pacific Place
88 Queensway
Hong Kong

**Hong Kong
Aircrew Officers
Association**

14

Dear Mr Sutch

AIRCREW SICK LEAVE

I am compelled to write to you on a subject of extreme gravity.

It has been brought to the attention of the Association that, at a meeting held on 29th September 1998, chaired by Mr. N. Rhodes, General Manager Aircrew, and attended by a number of managers from the Flight Operations Department, the subject of aircrew sickness was discussed.

At that meeting it was decided that a "blacklist" of aircrew who are deemed to be taking too much sick leave is to be compiled. Furthermore, aircrew are to be subjected to "incentive and disincentive" treatment.

The recently initiated annual aircrew interviews are to be used as a tool to apply subtle intimidation to aircrew and "incentives and disincentives" are to include:

- leave points
- request G days
- temp bases/swaps
- more reserves/less G
- O days after ULH vs G days
- repeat rosters - including X'mas
- staff travel (annual FOC, UGSA)

- loss of training
- loss of job
- loss of increment
- loss of base
- loss of command / delay in promotion
- full body check by PMO

Additionally, at the meeting, responsibility for implementing these policies was assigned to various individual managers.

Disregarding the fact that those assigned such responsibilities have no qualifications whatsoever to determine the fitness, or otherwise, of aircrew to undertake their assigned duties, any attempt to coerce aircrew, either by reward, intimidation or threat, into reporting for duty in contravention of Article 20(8)(a) of the Air Navigation (Hong Kong) Order 1995 constitutes a criminal offence and such actions can only be described as both negligent and reckless.

In the past when senior Flight Operations managers have attempted to coerce or intimidate Officers as a result of their reporting unfit for duty, the Association has viewed these cases as isolated incidents and treated them as such. This can no longer be the case.

5/F Daily House, 35-37 Haiphong Road, Tsim Sha Tsui, Kowloon, Hong Kong
Tel: (852) 2736 0823   Fax: (852) 2736 0903   E-mail: hkaoa@hkaipa.org
Member of International Federation of Airline Pilots Associations.   Member of International Flight Engineers Organization.

The actions of these managers constitute an immediate threat to the operational safety of Cathay Pacific Airways and call into serious question not only their suitability to hold positions of responsibility within Flight Operations management, but also the integrity and competence of the Flight Operations management structure as a whole to hold an Air Operator's Certificate.

The aircrew of Cathay Pacific view this matter most seriously and urgently request that you give an assurance that the implementation of such policies will cease with immediate effect and that appropriate action will be taken against those responsible.

In view of the seriousness of the situation, this matter has also been referred to the Director Civil Aviation Department, the Principal Medical Officer and Manager Corporate Safety Department.

I await your urgent reply.

Yours sincerely

Captain A E Pleavin
President

526

FAXED
DATE: ___2 NOV 1998

02 November 1998

Our Ref: 4009/pj/98/144

Mr R A Siegel
Director of Civil Aviation
Civil Aviation Department
46/F Queensway Government Offices
66 Queensway
Hong Kong

**Hong Kong
Aircrew Officers
Association**

Dear Mr Siegel

AIRCREW SICK LEAVE

Information of a very serious nature has come to the attention of the Association.

Enclosed is a copy of a letter which I have sent today to the Chairman of Cathay Pacific Airways Ltd., the contents of which I believe are self-explanatory.

The Association believes that any attempt, either through threat or reward, to influence aircrew to operate a flight if he knows or suspects that he is unfit to do so, cannot be allowed. Indeed, we view such action as clearly in contravention of the law.

We feel that it is our duty as a Professional Association to bring this matter to your attention, together with a request that you take such action as you deem appropriate to ensure that Cathay Pacific Airways are not permitted to introduce such policies.

Please deal with this matter as one of great urgency. I look forward to hearing from you.

Yours sincerely

Captain A E Pleavin
President

Encl.

5/F Daily House, 35-37 Haiphong Road, Tsim Sha Tsui, Kowloon, Hong Kong
Tel: (852) 2736 0823   Fax: (852) 2736 0903   E-mail: hkaoa@hkalpa.org
Member of International Federation of Airline Pilots Associations. Member of International Flight Engineers Organization.

_5 NOV 1998

民航處 Civil Aviation Department
飛行標準及適航部 Flight Standards and Airworthiness Division

香港啟德國際機場協調道五十二號停機坪大廈 261 室
ROOM 261 APRON SERVICES COMPLEX 52 CONCORDE ROAD HONG KONG INTERNATIONAL AIRPORT HONG KONG

檔案編號 OUR REF.	來函編號 YOUR REF.	電話 TEL.	圖文傳真 FAX.	專用電訊 TELEX:	航空專用電訊 AFTN
(2) in A/OPS/AOA/1		2769 7641	2362 4250	39524 CFSHK HX	VHHHYAYC

3 November 1998

Captain A E Pleavin
President
Hong Kong Aircrew Officers Association
5/F Daily House
35-37 Haiphong Road
Tsim Sha Tsui
Kowloon

pls faxed

File No:	4009
P	VPs
PCs	GS
Clie	TS
Day	Co
Inc	Pers
Dir:	CAD
REPLY:	Y / N

Dear Captain Pleavin,

Aircrew Sick Leave

Your letter 4009/pj/98/144 dated 2 November 1998 to the Director of Civil Aviation has been passed to this Division for further action. In view of the nature of the allegations contained therein, we have asked Cathay Pacific Airways for their comments thereon.

Please be advised that Mr Albert K Y Lam assumed the position of Director of Civil Aviation on 2 October 1998.

Yours sincerely,

(Captain J H A Adams)
Chief, Flight Standards
for Director of Civil Aviation

JHAA/al

1 1 NOV 1998

Cathay Pacific Airways Limited
35/F, Two Pacific Place
88 Queensway, Hong Kong.

Telephone: (852) 2747 5112, 2747 5115
Fax: (852) 2810 4893

Peter Sutch
Chairman

Ref : SC22/231

Captain A E Pleavin,
President - HKAOA,
5/F Daily House,
35-37 Haiphong Road,
Tsimshatsui, Kowloon,
Hong Kong.

File No:	4009	
P		VPs
	POs	GS
	Ctte.	TS
	Day	Co
	Inc	Pers
Dir:		
REPLY:		Y / N

10th November 1998

Dear Captain Pleavin,

Thank you for your letter reference 4009/pj/98/143 dated 2nd November 1998 concerning Aircrew Sick Leave.

I have checked with Flight Operations Department Management who have confirmed that this issue has been discussed but that no policy changes have been formulated, let alone implemented. I believe it would have been more appropriate for you to raise any concerns you may have had with the Management team rather than write direct to me with unsubstantiated allegations.

You will need to understand that employee sickness absence rates among some Cathay aircrew are extremely high and it would be irresponsible of any Management group to simply ignore the issue. All Companies within the Group adopt the philosophy of monitoring employee sickness absence rates and I expect the same of Cathay Pacific Airways Flight Operations Department.

Yours sincerely,

Peter Sutch
Chairman

PDAS/spt

Swire Group

民航處 **Civil Aviation Department**

飛行標準及適航部 Flight Standards and Airworthiness Division

2 3 NOV 1998

香港啟德協調道五十二號停機坪服務大廈261室
Room 261 Apron Services Complex 52 Concorde Road Kai Tak Hong Kong

檔案編號 OUR REF.	來函編號 YOUR REF.	電話 TEL.	圖文傳真 FAX.	專用電訊 TELEX:	航空專用電訊 AFTN
(6) in A/OPS/AOA/1	Your Ref	(852)2769 8896	(852)2382 4577	39524 CFSHK HX	VHHHYAYC

BY FAX & POST

19 November 1998

Captain A E Pleavin
President
Hong Kong Aircrew Officers Association
Daily House
35-37 Haiphong Road
Tsim Sha Tsui
Kowloon

Dear Captain Pleavin,

Aircrew Sick Leave

Thank you for your letter of 2 November 1998 on the above subject.

In the interest of an unbiased and balanced view, we have requested Cathay Pacific Airways to comment on this issue. In their response, they stated that they have been reviewing and monitoring sickness absence levels amongst Cathay Pacific crew, but at the time of writing, had not implemented any new measures in this area. They also advised that they are well aware of their legal obligations under the AN(HK)O 1995, and have assured us that they will always operate within the spirit and intent of that document.

We note your concern. However, we have no evidence to hand to suggest that Cathay Pacific had exceeded the normal management prerogatives in this area.

Thank you for bringing this matter to our attention. Please rest assured that we always attach great importance to issues of flight safety.

Yours sincerely,

(Norman LO)
for Director of Civil Aviation

致力於安全及有效率的航空系統 Committed to a Safe and Efficient Air Transport System

DCA 155 (8/98)

530

FAXED
DATE: 2 6 NOV. 1998

9

26 November 1998

Our Ref: 4009/cmp/98/18

Mr P D A Sutch
Chairman
Cathay Pacific Airways Limited
35/F, 2 Pacific Place
88 Queensway
Hong Kong

**Hong Kong
Aircrew Officers
Association**

Dear Mr Sutch

AIRCREW SICK LEAVE

Thank you for your letter of 19th November, Ref: SC22/231, concerning Aircrew Sick Leave.

I wrote to you directly on this matter because of concerns, which I believe will become apparent to you after reading the attached copy of the minutes of a meeting held within Flight Operations Department on 29th September 1998.

From the minutes, it appears that several items will be, or have been actioned.

Specifically:

1   Sick leave tables will be created for each cockpit crew and these "will serve as a tool for the annual interview."

2   A separate chart "will be provided for the 'black listed' crew."

3   Incentives and disincentives are listed, and a number of items are allocated to individual management personnel for action.

In the light of the conflicting information the Association has received on this issue, I remain gravely concerned for the operational safety of Cathay Pacific Airways. I would be most grateful if you would give an undertaking that no section of these minutes will be implemented.

Furthermore, on behalf of the aircrew body, I would welcome your assurance that all Flight Operation's managers will cease and desist with actions of this nature, which are only deteriorating an already poor climate of trust between the aircrew and management.

5/F Daily House, 35-37 Haiphong Road, Tsim Sha Tsui, Kowloon, Hong Kong
Tel: (852) 2736 0823   Fax: (852) 2736 0903   E-mail: hkaoa@hkalpa.org
Member of International Federation of Airline Pilots Associations.   Member of International Flight Engineers Organization.

P.10   2736 0903   Administrator   11:35e 01 Nov 15

I have copied this letter and the attachment to the Director of the Civil Aviation Department, the Principal Medical Officer and the Corporate Safety Manager for their information.

Yours sincerely

Captain A E Pleavin
President

cc   Mr A K Y Lam – Director of Civil Aviation
Dr John Merritt – Principal Medical Officer, Cathay Pacific Airways
Mr D Mawdsley - Corporate Safety Manager, Cathay Pacific Airways

01 December 1998

Our Ref: 4009/pj/98/147

Mr Norman Lo
Assistant Director (Flight Standards)
Civil Aviation Department
Flight Standards and Airworthiness Division
Room 261 Apron Services Complex
52 Concorde Road
Kowloon
Hong Kong

**Hong Kong
Aircrew Officers
Association**

Dear Mr Lo

AIRCREW SICK LEAVE

Thank you for your letter dated 19 November 1998 regarding Aircrew Sick Leave.

I have attached for your information a copy of a second letter to the Chairman of Cathay Pacific Airways (CPA) and a copy of the minutes of a meeting held within Flight Operations on 29 September 1998. As you can see from the minutes a number of incentive and disincentive items were discussed and management personnel assigned action items. The items discussed directly effect an Officer's ability to objectively assess whether his physical or mental condition renders him temporarily or permanently unfit to perform as a member of the flight crew of an aircraft registered in Hong Kong. The Association does not see how CPA can be aware of their obligations under the AN(HK)O 1995, or indeed operate within the spirit and intent of that document, whilst intending to action the items listed in the minutes.

The tracking of sickness rates is an acceptable management practice, however the "black listing" of crew and the implementation of incentives and disincentives is well beyond reasonable. It is pertinent to note that one of the reference works on Human Factors for Pilots, which is included as part of the ATPL examination syllabus, contains the following statement:

"If a management consistently exerts pressure on its employees to operate in ways that are more consistent with the short-term economic health of the company than with safety and good practice, the company is likely to develop symptoms of 'organisational stress'. These symptoms include poor industrial relations, antagonism at work, high labour turnover and absenteeism, and, most importantly for the aviation industry, a high accident rate."

The Association believes that CPA is now exhibiting the first four symptoms listed and, as a result, views the increase in sickness rates as a very serious indicator.

Although the Association has repeatedly attempted to engage CPA management in meaningful dialogue to address the 'organisational stress', to date we have been unsuccessful. The Association views Management attempts to pressure aircrew with

5/F Daily House, 35-37 Haiphong Road, Tsim Sha Tsui, Kowloon, Hong Kong
Tel: (852) 2736 0823   Fax: (852) 2736 0903   E-mail: hkaoa@hkalpa.org
Member of International Federation of Airline Pilots Associations.   Member of International Flight Engineers Organization.

regard to sickness, together with their subsequent unconditional denials, as a grave
threat to the operational safety of CPA.

Yours sincerely

PP *Lung Tsui*

Captain A E Pleavin
President

民航處 **Civil Aviation Department**
飛行標準及適航部 Flight Standards and Airworthiness Division

– 9 DEC 1998

香港啟德協調道五十二號停機坪事務大廈261室
Room 261 Apron Services Complex 52 Concorde Road Kai Tak Hong Kong

檔案編號 OUR REF.	來函編號 YOUR REF.	電話 TEL.	圖文傳真 FAX.	專用電訊 TELEX:	航空專用電訊 AFTN
(10) in A/OPS/AOA/1		2769 7641	2362 4250	39524 CFSHK HX	VHHHYAYC

8 December 1998

Captain A E Pleavin
President
Hong Kong Aircrew Officers Association
5/F Daily House
35-37 Haiphong Road
Tsim Sha Tsui
Kowloon
Hong Kong

FAXED

File No: 4009/CAD	
Γ	VPs
POs	GS
Ctio	TS
Dy	Co
Inc	Pers
Ι ::	
REPLY:	Y / N

Dear Captain Pleavin

Aircrew Sick Leave

I acknowledge receipt of your letter 4009/pj/98/147 of 1 December 1998.

Having carefully studied your letter, and the attachments thereto, I do not believe that there is any material change to the position to which I responded in my letter of 19 November 1998. I am pleased to note that you acknowledge that 'tracking of sickness rates is an acceptable management practice'. As previously stated, we have no evidence to suggest that the operator concerned has exceeded normal management prerogatives in this area.

I can assure you that any evidence confirming the imposition of measures likely to result in 'organisation stress' will be effectively addressed. I do not believe that any such evidence exists at the present time.

Yours sincerely,

Norman Lo

(Norman LO)
for Director of Civil Aviation

致力於安全及有效率的航空系統 Committed to a Safe and Efficient Air Transport System

DCA 155 (8/98)

535

W

Peter Sutch
Chairman

faxed

CATHAY PACIFIC

Cathay Pacific Airways Limited
35/F, Two Pacific Place
88 Queensway, Hong Kong.
Telephone: (852) 2747 5112, 2747 5115
Fax: (852) 2810 4893

16 DEC 1998

File No:	4009	
P		VPs
POs		GS
Ctte		TS
Day		Co
Inc		Pers
Dir:		
REPLY:		Y / N

14th December 1998

Captain A.E. Pleavin
President - HKAOA
5/F, Daily House
35-37 Haiphong Road
Tsim Sha Tsui
Kowloon

Dear Captain Pleavin,

Aircrew Sick Leave

This is to acknowledge receipt of your letter dated 26th November 1998.

In my previous reply I invited you to contact Flight Operations Department if you had concerns. I still believe this to be the most appropriate course of action. Nick Rhodes has also covered the issue very openly and frankly in the last edition of Crews News giving, I would have thought, re-assurance to all concerned.

Yours sincerely,

PDAS/mi

◄H Swire Group

536

FAXED
2 1 MAR 2001

21 March 2001

Our Ref: 9009/01/sh/041

24/4/01

**Hong Kong
Aircrew Officers
Association**

Mr Philip Chen
Director and Chief Operating Officer
Cathay Pacific Airways Limited
CX City, 8 Scenic Road
Hong Kong International Airport
Lantau
Hong Kong

Dear Mr Chen

FLIGHT SAFETY

The Association has Objectives in its Rules pertaining to professional interests and Members' interests. I wish to assure you that I am writing to you purely about professional matters and flight safety in particular.

In the last 6 months, the communications between the Association and the Company have fallen into two broad categories: industrial and safety. The former category of communications is part of the normal day-to-day relations in any company and I do not wish to comment on those here. However, unlike most unions, the Association also has a specific safety function because its members are the last line of defence in preventing an accident. Although some may find the line between safety and industrial matters to be blurred, we have striven in our communications to maintain that distinction. I reiterate that this letter is solely about flight safety and has nothing to do with industrial issues.

Attached is a series of correspondence with the Flight Operations Department concerning operational matters and their effect on flight safety. For ease of reference, I have also attached a summary.

Our main concern is the declining margin of safety as our airline expands. The Association has serious misgivings that our requests concerning this problem have not received the appropriate attention or urgency. In the interests of the flight safety both of our members and of the travelling public, we can no longer tolerate the non-committal replies. The latest response, dated 12th March, typifies the problem. Vague statements about being *"mindful of responsibilities"* and being *"guided accordingly"* are dismissive at best and negligent at worst. However, avoiding this issue will not solve the problem.

We are all aware of the difficulties created by expansion. There is no doubt that the Flight Operations Department's resources are stretched to meet the task. Unfortunately, those closest to the problem, through no fault of their own, often cannot perceive the risks; it is the responsibility of senior management to maintain overall corporate safety. The Association shares that responsibility. Accordingly, we

5/F Dally House, 35-37 Haiphong Road, Tsim Sha Tsui, Kowloon, Hong Kong
Tel: (852) 2736 0823   Fax: (852) 2736 0903   E-mail: hkaoa@hkalpa.org
Member of International Federation of Airline Pilots Associations. Member of International Flight Engineers Organization.

have copied this letter to the Chairman and the Chief Executive Officer as well as the Corporate Safety Department for their information.

The Association is, therefore, making a final in-house approach to you, as Chief Operating Officer, to request that you take action to address the safety concerns highlighted in our letters.

Yours sincerely

Nigel Demery
President

Copy:

Mr James Hughes-Hallett, Chairman
Mr David Turnbull, Deputy Chairman and Chief Executive
Mr Peter Wigens, Head of Corporate Safety

Enclosures:

Annex A – Summary of Issues
Annex B – Series of Letters

16

02 April 2001

Our Ref: 9017/sh/01/048

Captain K R Barley
Director Flight Operations
Cathay Pacific Airways Ltd
3/F South Tower, Cathay City
8 Scenic Road
Hong Kong International Airport
Lantau, Hong Kong

**Hong Kong
Aircrew Officers
Association**

Dear Captain Barley

AIRCREW HEALTH

It has been brought to our attention that pilots are being denied temporary basings on the basis of their medical history. I refer to our previous correspondence 4009/pj/98/143 dated 2nd November 1998. It is disappointing that a policy, which affects corporate safety and crew morale, has again been implemented without prior consultation.

Members have informed us that they have been contacted by Flight Operations managers and advised that, due to their previous year's health history, they will be denied a temporary basing. Disturbingly, managers also stated that, should they avoid calling in sick for a specified period, they would re-qualify for temporary basings. Members were also informed that the provision of doctor's certificates during the past year was irrelevant.

A Captain recently described how his First Officer, obviously ill and unfit for duty, came to work because he feared he would lose his eligibility for a temporary basing. This policy is not a responsible way in which to address inadequate manning levels and has already negatively impacted flight safety. Accident investigations clearly show that corporate stress and roster instability are major contributory factors in the "accident chain". This policy adds yet another link to that chain.

I understand that recent health history may now be a criteria in judging a pilot's potential for Command. Aircrew health (referred to erroneously by your department as "absenteeism") should not be used as a basis for eligibility for aircrew bases, benefits, appointments or upgrades. Pilots have a legal responsibility to report if they are unfit for duty. It would be illegal to incite them to do otherwise. May I suggest that a responsible course of action would be to withdraw this new policy?

I ask that you treat this matter with the urgency it deserves. Notwithstanding the safety issues, this policy is adding to the continuing decline in management-crew relations. Reviewing this policy may help to reverse this trend. I look forward to discussing how we might work together to responsibly implement an Absence Management Programme as you suggested in your previous letter.

Yours sincerely

Captain N J Demery
President

c.c. Mr Sten Kroutil - IRM

5/F Daily House, 35-37 Haiphong Road, Tsim Sha Tsui, Kowloon, Hong Kong
Tel: (852) 2736 0823   Fax: (852) 2736 0903   E-mail: hkaoa@hkalpa.org
Member of International Federation of Airline Pilots Associations.   Member of International Flight Engineers Organization.

24 APR

Cathay Pacific Airways Limited
Flight Operations Department
Cathay Pacific City, 8 Scenic Road
Hong Kong International Airport
Lantau, Hong Kong

Ref: FOP-AOA-6-01027

ᒃ E D
20-4-2001

20th April, 2001

Captain N.J. Demery
President - HKAOA
c/o Mailbox No. 001
CX-CLK

Dear Captain Demery,

ABSENCE MANAGEMENT

Thank you for your letter of 2nd April which refers to the above subject.

Over the past six months the Company has collated a body of evidence to suggest that a number of individual crew members are using absenteeism as a means of disrupting the commercial operation of the airline.

Whilst this remains the case the Company has little option but to attempt to manage absence as best it can. This is not to suggest that all crew members are acting irresponsibly or that the HKAOA is co-ordinating such activity.

I am encouraged to learn that the HKAOA is willing to discuss implementation of an Absence Management Programme and I look forward to receiving the names of Association members willing to undertake this responsibility. I will be happy to co-ordinate such a series of meetings at the earliest opportunity.

Yours sincerely,

Captain K.R. Barley
Director Flight Operations

a member of **oneworld**

Swire Group

Registered office: 35th Floor, Two Pacific Place, 88 Queensway, Hong Kong

p.17   2736 0903   Administrator   12 Nov 01 11:17a

540

2 6 APR 2001

 **CATHAY PACIFIC**

Cathay Pacific Airways Limited
9/F, Central Tower
Cathay Pacific City, 8 Scenic Road
Hong Kong International Airport
Lantau, Hong Kong
Telephone: (852) 2747 5000

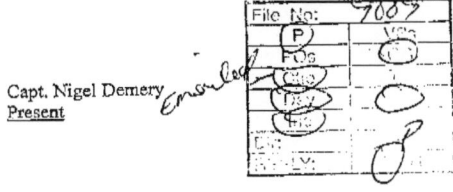

Capt. Nigel Demery
Present

24th April 2001

Dear Captain Demery,

<u>Flight Safety</u>

Thank you for your letter, ref: 9009/01/sh/041, dated 21st March 2001.

Let me say in the first instance that we always welcome constructive suggestions on many issues, including safety. However the Company has final responsibility in this area and, in this case, does not accept your claim that we are experiencing a declining margin of safety as we expand. Cathay Pacific Airways has always had, and continues to have, a vigorous commitment to Safety and Security, and we can find no evidence that this commitment has diminished.

You are, we hope, aware of some of the safety factors we take into account as a responsible operator:

- We have, for many years, invested significant resources in personnel, systems and equipment to ensure that the recruiting, training and operational standards of our personnel are of industry leading quality.

- Our regulator, the Hong Kong Civil Aviation Department, maintains a rigorous safety oversight programme of our Flight Operations, Engineering and other relevant departments. These Company departments are audited throughout the year by the CAD, and the findings and recommendations contained in the annual report are carefully analysed and implemented.

- Both Flight Operations and Engineering departments maintain Quality Audit sections with the aim of proactively managing compliance with regulatory requirements and industry best practice.

- We have a committed Corporate Safety Department with a direct reporting line to the Deputy Chairman and Chief Executive.

- We comply with possibly the most restrictive Flight Time Limitations requirements in the world.

- We operate one of the best-maintained and youngest aircraft fleets in the world.

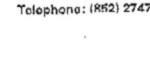 member of **oneworld**

Swire Group   Registered office: 35th Floor, Two Pacific Place, 00 Queensway, Hong Kong

1

All of these factors were taken into account last year when the business environment changed and the Company considered expanding in the wake of earlier difficult business conditions.

We are committed to ensuring that the Company is operating in a safe and secure manner.

There are many challenges facing Cathay Pacific, which will affect all of us. Let us use our energies and resources to positively and constructively ensure our future together.

Yours sincerely,

PHILIP N L CHEN

Copy Capt. Ken Barley
Mr Nick Rhodes

2

02 May 2001

Our Ref: 4009/cmp/01/10

6

Captain M S Davis
Chief Flight Standards for Director of Civil Aviation
Civil Aviation Department Flight Standards and Airworthiness Division
10/F Commercial Building
Airport Freight Forwarding Centre
2 Chun Wan Road, Chek Lap Kok
Hong Kong

**Hong Kong
Aircrew Officers
Association**

Dear Captain Davis

CPA ABSENCE MANAGEMENT PROGRAMME

It is with great frustration that we have come to seek your assistance on an important matter of flight safety.

As the instability of the Cathay Pacific roster increases beyond the dramatic levels audited in December 2000, aircrew sickness rates also continue to rise. The correlation between the two is well documented and is certainly not an "industrial action" as Cathay Pacific management would have the public believe. Instead of reducing its flying schedule to a manageable level, Cathay Pacific management have embarked on a dangerous course of action, under the guise of an Absence Management Program (AMP).

The concept of an AMP was originally broached with the Association as a method of reaching out to pilots in need, by identifying those who were unfit for duty on about 15 or more occasions per year. These pilots would be contacted and offered assistance by a caring management concerned for the employees' welfare. As a professional Association, we agreed with the advantages of such a benign system.

Unfortunately, this system quickly degenerated into a policy of intimidation, targeting aircrew with 6 or more occasions of sickness per year and denying them benefits, for example, temporary basings. The provision of valid doctors' certificates for the occasions of sickness was dismissed as irrelevant. Furthermore, managers are even advising pilots that they will be able to obtain currently denied basings by not reporting sick for a specified period.

A recent incident highlights just how dangerous this situation has become. A Captain advised the Association how his First Officer, arrived late on the flight deck due to a roster disruption. In flight, it became apparent that he was obviously ill and unfit for duty. The First Officer explained that he did not want to call in sick because he feared management repercussions.

I am sure that a system of rewarding good "attendance" may have a place amongst Cathay Pacific's clerical staff. However, the AMP as instituted by Cathay Pacific's Flight Operations Department is an unsafe attempt to solve insufficient manning levels by inciting crew to breach the ANOs by operating while unfit. This AMP has no place in professional Hong Kong aviation.

Despite correspondence and face-to-face meetings requesting Cathay Pacific to desist from this policy, management have steadfastly refused to address this dangerous approach to sickness. Accordingly, we ask you, as one of the primary lines of defence in Hong Kong aviation safety, to intervene. May I remind you of previous correspondence on the subject *Aircrew Sick Leave* dated November/December 1998, attached for ease of reference. Please be advised that this is one item that we shall raise with DGCA on 11th May.

Yours sincerely

Captain N J Demery
President

5/F Daily House, 35-37 Haiphong Road, Tsim Sha Tsui, Kowloon, Hong Kong
Tel: (852) 2736 0823   Fax: (852) 2736 0903   E-mail: hkaoa@hkalpa.org
Member of International Federation of Airline Pilots Associations.   Member of International Flight Engineers Organization.

5

民航處 Civil Aviation Department
飛行標準及適航部 Flight Standards and Airworthiness Division

香港赤鱲角駿運路 2 號機場空運中心商業大樓十樓
10th Floor, Commercial Building, Airport Freight Forwarding Centre, 2 Chun Wan Road, Chek Lap Kok, Hong Kong.

檔案編號 OUR REF.	來函編號 YOUR REF.	電話 TEL.	圖文傳真 FAX.	專用電訊 TELEX:	航空專用電訊 AFTN
(4) in A/OPS/ALP/1 II	4009/cmp/01/10	2769 7230	2362 4250	39524 CFSHK HX	VHHHYAYC

Lord Copy
3 May 2004

– 8 MAY

Captain N J Demery
President
Hong Kong Aircrew Officers' Association
5/F Daily House
35-37 Haiphong Road
Tsim Sha Tsui
Kowloon
Hong Kong

BY FAX and BY POST

Dear Sir,

CPA Attendance Management Programme (AMP)

I have today requested Cathay Pacific to forward to my office all information regarding their proposed Attendance Management Programme (AMP). In the meantime you may wish to re-emphasise to your members their responsibility regarding Article 55 of the AN(HK)O 1995.

I would sincerely hope that the alleged 'practices' outlined in the 1998 dated attachments to your letter are not in force. In any event this matter will be discussed with Cathay Pacific upon receipt of their proposed AMP programme, and you may rest assured that any Flight Safety matters will be addressed accordingly.

Yours faithfully,

(Captain M S Davis)
Chief, Flight Standards
for Director-General of Civil Aviation

MSD/al

FAXED
16 MAY

12

16 May 2001

Ref: 9017/pmw/01/064

Captain K R Barley
Director Flight Operations
Cathay Pacific Airways Ltd
3/F South Tower, Cathay City
8 Scenic Road
Hong Kong International Airport
Lantau, Hong Kong

**Hong Kong
Aircrew Officers
Association**

Dear Captain Barley

AIRCREW HEALTH

Thank you for your letter, FOP-AOA-6-01027, dated 20th April that refers to the above subject. We remain seriously concerned about any system that penalises crew who may be exercising their legal duty *not* to operate a flight.

The true reason for a rise in the number of pilots reporting sick is that the current rostering system is failing, which is compounded by incorrect crewing levels. I must observe that attendance and health records are a measure of the efficiency and morale of a team.

We have previously agreed that it is best to institute a new rostering system first to isolate one area of influence. In the meantime we will continue studying the British Airways system.

Once these steps have been taken, we look forward to supplying you with a team to assist in your management of aircrew health.

Yours sincerely

Captain N J Demery
President

cc: Captain MS Davis   Chief, Flight Standards, CAD
        Mr Sten Kroutil   Industrial Relations Manager

5/F Daily House, 35-37 Haiphong Road, Tsim Sha Tsui, Kowloon, Hong Kong
Tel: (852) 2736 0823   Fax: (852) 2736 0903   E-mail: hkaoa@hkalpa.org
Member of International Federation of Airline Pilots Associations. Member of International Flight Engineers Organization.

17th May 2001

Ref: 9009/pmw/01/066

Mr Philip Chen
Director & Chief Operating Officer
Cathay Pacific Airways Ltd
Cathay City
8 Scenic Road
Hong Kong International Airport
Lantau, Hong Kong

**Hong Kong
Aircrew Officers
Association**

Dear Mr Chen

FLIGHT SAFETY

Thank you for your letter, which we received by fax on 25th April.

The Association has never doubted the Company's or its employees' commitment to Flight Safety and we do not believe that the commitment is diminishing. The purpose of our previous correspondence is to attempt to maximise *"our energies and resources positively and constructively to ensure a safe future"*.

Unfortunately, your letter does nothing to address the specific issues we raised. Accordingly, the Association again requests:

1. A system for the Commander to monitor cabin crew FDPs

2. An assurance that managers will not use the threat of disciplinary action if a pilot exercises his obligations under the Air Navigation Order

3. A transparent system that monitors Mixed Duties and cumulative Duty Hours

4. An audit of the last 3 months' duty hours of Check and Training and management personnel

5. That no pilot is given less than 12 hours' notice involving a change of duty from a non-Ultra Long Range Operation (ULRO) duty to either a ULRO duty or a Window Of Circadian Low (WOCL) operation

6. That if a pilot is given a change of duty to a ULRO or a WOCL operation, following the completion of a reserve duty, then he/she is given prior rest in accordance AFTLS sub-paras 22.2.C.a or 22.2.C.b or 22.2.C.c

7. An assurance from you that no commander will be questioned about any Commander's Discretion decision

8. Access to and discussion on the results and findings on the internal audit on roster instability

5/F Daily House, 35-37 Haiphong Road, Tsim Sha Tsui, Kowloon, Hong Kong
Tel: (852) 2736 0823   Fax: (852) 2736 0903   E-mail: hkaoa@hkalpa.org
Member of International Federation of Airline Pilots Associations.   Member of International Flight Engineers Organization.

9. That the Company desists from using an "O" Day as a defined Domestic Day Off or legal Day Off

10. The Company definition of the minimum notification requirement for duty and for days off in accordance with CAD 371

11. That no Hong Kong based crew are scheduled for less than 12 hours' rest in Hong Kong

Subsequent to our initial letter, despite our strong objections to the contrary, Flight Operations has introduced a punitive programme that incites pilots to work when they are unfit. This is a resurgence of a similar attempt in 1998 and is similar to the system that has been employed on cabin crew for a number of years. We have already conditionally agreed with the Flight Operations management that, if the Company feels that an officer's sickness record is excessive, then we should work together to assess and address the problem. The sickness management program in its present form is unacceptable and detrimental to flight safety.

Finally, I must address the issue of the declining safety margin. We agree that Cathay Pacific Airways *is* a safe airline. However, what concerns the Association is that the *margin* of safety is reducing. Obviously, our airline will only continue to be safe as long as that margin exists. We are concerned that:

- Some C&T captains are:

  - o Experiencing an unacceptable level of roster changes
  - o Adversely affected in their training task

- Some C&T captains believe flight safety risks have increased due to:

  - o Rostering to the limits
  - o Reduced training quality
  - o Reduced experience levels
  - o Increased fatigue and stress
  - o High roster disruption

- An undermanning situation exists

- An audit showed that the level of roster instability produces a risk to flight safety

- Simulator training is being reduced to meet the flying task

11

- An Association Survey found that:

  o >94% of pilots feel more fatigued
  o Nearly 20% pilots are *frequently worried* about safety
  o Nearly 30% of Check and Training (C&T) captains feel more fatigued *and* frequently worried about safety

The data (Surveys and Company publications) on which the above statements are based is available on request. The point is that the Company *must* listen to and act on the feedback from the professionals it employs to ensure that we *remain* a safe airline. In particular, the C&T pilots are one of the airline's greatest assets and it would be perilous for you not to listen to them.

In conclusion, the Association is attempting to work with management towards a safer operation. Indeed we participate in many Company flight safety programs, such as Crew Resource Management (CRM), Line Operations Safety Audit (LOSA) and the Flight Data Analysis Programme (FDAP), I therefore remain concerned that our current flight safety concerns remain unaddressed.

Yours sincerely

Captain N J Demery
President

cc: Mr James Hughes-Hallett Chairman
     Mr Albert Lam   Director-General of Civil Aviation
     Mr David Turnbull   Deputy Chairman and Chief Executive
     Captain Ken Barley   Director Flight Operations
     Mr Peter Wigens   Head of Corporate Safety
     Mr Sten Kroutil   Industrial Relations Manager

13th June 2001

4009/pmw/01/081

**Hong Kong
Aircrew Officers
Association**

Mr Philip Chen
Director & chief Operating Officer
Cathay Pacific Airways Ltd
Cathay City
8 Scenic Road
Hong Kong International Airport
Lantau, Hong Kong

Dear Mr Chen

SICKNESS MANAGEMENT

I am writing to express our concern over the recent introduction of an Absence Management Programme by Cathay Pacific administration staff. This programme includes non-medical staff "counselling" pilots over their recent medical history.

This "counselling" appears to follow a discredited 1980's North American initiative that was designed to "pressure" pilots to report for duty when unfit, in order to achieve the commercial task.

As you are aware, it is a legal and Company requirement for all aircrew to be medically and mentally fit to undertake their assigned duties. In effect, this Company policy will induce some crew to report for duties when not fit to do so in order to avoid real or implied repercussions. As such the Absence Management Programme in its present form is not a responsible management initiative and is prejudicial to flight safety.

It is in the best interests of the Company, the travelling public and the employees that this policy ceases immediately.

Yours sincerely

Captain N J Demery
President

  cc: Captain K R Barley   Director Flight Operations
       Mr Sten Kroutil   Industrial Relations Manager

5/F Daily House, 35-37 Haiphong Road, Tsim Sha Tsui, Kowloon, Hong Kong
Tel: (852) 2736 0823   Fax: (852) 2736 0903   E-mail: hkaoa@hkalpa.org
Member of International Federation of Airline Pilots Associations. Member of International Flight Engineers Organization

FAXED
15 JUN 2001

15th June 2001

Ref: 9017/pmw/01/082

Mr Albert K Y Lam, JP
Director-General of Civil Aviation
Civil Aviation Department
46/F Queensway Government Offices
66 Queensway
Hong Kong

**Hong Kong
Aircrew Officers
Association**

Dear Mr Lam

SICKNESS PROGRAM – CATHAY PACIFIC AIRWAYS

Further to our meeting on 11th May, I refer to the sickness management program currently being initiated by Cathay Pacific Airways. This letter amplifies some of our previous points.

We expressed our grave concerns that aircrew are being incited to operate commercial transport aircraft whilst unfit. This is contrary to the Air Navigation Order and is a hazard to flight safety.

Subsequent to our discussions, the operator has sent further letters to crew, which refer to periods of sickness as "absences", inviting them to attend an interview. This follows previous letters on the subject and increases the pressure on crew to operate whilst unfit. Sample letters are attached. Additionally, punitive measures are taken on crew who reach the arbitrary level of 6 occasions within one year. Combined, these measures incite crew to operate whilst unfit.

I should point out that our work contract specifically permits Cathay Pacific Airways to order unfit crew to perform other duties, such as simulator crew-up etc, however this practice is not the norm. The intimidatory measures are directed towards crew unfit for flying duties. Furthermore, the current system of rostering practices, introduced forcefully in 1994, was designed to permit excess flying pay after 700 hours annually. One of the "advantages" proclaimed by management at the time was that the Company could still achieve its productivity targets, even if a pilot reports sick during the month, by increasing the flying rate the following months. Therefore, there is negligible contractual impediment to the operator.

Despite repeated written requests to the operator, attached, to desist from introducing this scheme, we now have sufficient confidential reports to indicate that crew are indeed flying when they should not. This is cause for serious concern. A deidentified message to the Association is also attached that explains some of the problems we are facing. The original can be produced for viewing although we are unable to breach the pilots' confidentialities.

The Association acknowledges that the actual sickness rates have increased dramatically in the past few years. We believe this is due to a very low level of morale, which is induced by poor leadership and man-management, combined with

5/F Daity House, 35-37 Haiphong Road, Tsim Sha Tsui, Kowloon, Hong Kong
Tel: (852) 2736 0823   Fax: (852) 2736 0903   E-mail: hkaoa@hkalpa.org
Member of International Federation of Airline Pilots Associations. Member of International Flight Engineers Organization.

18-JUN-2001 10:37   HKAOA   + 852 2736 0903   P.02

roster instability that precludes a long-term stable family life. Nonetheless, the current program affects *all* crew. That is unsafe.

We repeat our request for the Department's assistance as our only other alternative involves legal remedies, which would involve the public domain.

Yours sincerely

Captain N J Demery
President

Encl:

TOTAL P.02

5

ATTACHMENT TO CAD LETTER

This message was originally addressed to HKAOA
and was forwarded to you by HKAOA.

To whom it may concern,

I wish to you inform you of an event yesterday which I am at a loss as to how to proceed with. Having discussed the matter on the phone with the Office this morning I wish to outline the events for your info.

Yesterday I showed up at work for CX xxx to yyy. On sign on the JFO stated that he was not feeling 100% and should probably not be at work, but that it should be OK. Not being a doctor I am in no position to make a judgement as to fitness to operate.

During the flights it was discussed why he was at work. He said that he had felt quite badly in the morning before coming to work and had thought very seriously about calling in sick. When questioned as to why the decision had been made to go to work versus calling in the answer was chilling.

It seems that he had been on sick leave for another reason and was very concerned about the "sick record". He was rostered G days starting from immediately after the trip and was then proceeding on leave. Anecdotal information led her to believe that this was an "alarm" for the "absence management program". In addition he cited to me another anecdote of a JFO who had done well throughout his upgrade to FO but then was turned down due to the number/frequency of sick days. Being in a position of upgrading shortly this seemed to be a major factor in the decision to go to work. As I am sure you are aware, there are significant financial advantages to being upgraded.

In the latter part of the flight into Hong Kong, especially on descent frequent valsalva's were used by the JFO to equalize pressures. To me, problems clearing ears is an immediate "unfit". The consequences of being unable to properly clear ears are impressed upon us from very early in our careers and could result in permanent damage. That someone would both operate a commercial airliner in this condition and risk permanent damage deeply concerns me.

On arrival last night I looked for some way to deal with this event. Filing an ASR would be one answer, but the obvious response is that a) if one suspects they are unfit for duty they have a legal obligation to not operate, and b) the only result would be the JFO being put in a position that he was so desperately trying to avoid. I thought of calling the CAD directly but thought that the consequences would be the same as above.

I have now seen first hand the result of this "program". It is a dangerous, illegal and ill-conceived series of actions which must be dealt with. It is easy to say, "don't fly sick" but when faced with censure it is easier to say then do, especially for the younger of our peers.

I write this missive to you as I see no point in pursuing it through official channels. These JFOs have been put in a lose/lose position. Not to go sick risks their health and licence and going sick risks their careers. I am reminiscent of flying bush planes in zzz where pilots routinely flew overloaded, unmaintained aircraft because if they didn't they "would never work again in this business". This type of coercion has no place in a professional organization.

If I seem to have overreacted that may be true. On the other hand I have been put in a position where I can either tacitly accept the proceedings or put someone's licence and/or career in jeopardy. I find neither of these palatable. It may be possible that you may know of some way in which to deal with this matter. I would appreciate any assistance and if nothing else I am willing to take action as you see fit, without endangering the JFO involved.

One thought I have had is the ICAC. They are tasked with overseeing the activities of companies and government departments. The CAD must be aware of this program and its consequences. To ignore it can only be described as at best a dereliction of their mandate to ensure safety and at worst criminal negligence of their duties.

I am not intimidated and if you require any further action from me I am willing and able. My concern is that the JFO involved is not identified. To do so and cause exposure to action from any party would negate the purpose of this letter.

I thank you for your attention in this matter.

Sincerely,

AAA
Captain

Cathay Pacific Airways Limited
9/F, Central Tower
Cathay Pacific City, 8 Scenic Road
Hong Kong International Airport
Lantau, Hong Kong
Telephone: (852) 2747 5000

– 5 JUL 2001

20th June, 2001

Captain N.J. Demery
President · HKAOA,
c/o HKAOA Mail Box,
CX CLK

Dear Captain Demery,

ABSENCE MANAGEMENT PROGRAMME

Thank you for your letter of 13th June, 2001.

We are disappointed that the Hong Kong Aircrew Officers Association has chosen not to support this important initiative. Programmes of this nature are in use by many companies including the Hong Kong SAR Government and demonstrate that employers are aware of their responsibilities in relation to duty of care to employees.

We do not agree that we will induce some crew to fly when not fit, but it may be of use for crew members who may need help to carry out the inherent requirements of their employment.

We are sorry that you do not see this programme as being positive, we believe it is of value to employee and company alike.

With regards,

Yours sincerely

PHILIP N L CHEN
Director & Chief Operating Officer

Copy   Capt Ken Barley
        Mr Nick Rhodes
        Mr William Chau

Swire Group   Registered office: 35th Floor, Two Pacific Place, 88 Queensway, Hong Kong   member of oneworld

p. 9   2736 0903   Administrator   11:14 01 NOV 21

FAXED
2 2 JUN 2001

Pages 1 - 18

**Hong Kong
Aircrew Officers
Association**

22 June 2001

Ref: 9017/pmw/01/085

Mr Philip Chen
Director & Chief Operating Officer
Cathay Pacific Airways Limited
8 Scenic Road
Hong Kong International Airport
Lantau, Hong Kong

Dear Mr Chen

ABSENCE MANAGEMENT PROGRAM

We refer to our previous letters of 13 June 2001 and 17 May 2001 wherein the Association expressed our strong objection to the introduction of an Absence Management Program.

It appears to the Association that the company has undertaken a deliberate campaign to exert pressure on flight crew with the object of influencing a pilot's decision concerning their statutory obligations under the *Air Navigation (Hong Kong) Order 1995* ("AN(HK)O").

In particular, the company has issued a series of letters to pilots who have been unable to undertake flying duties for medical reasons.

The first letter from the company sets out the number of "absences" during the past twelve months, which the pilot is recorded to have had, notes that the "level of absence" is higher than the norm, and describes the "level of absence" as a "cause for concern." In addition to asking for corrections to the company's records, the letter asks whether the company can do anything to assist the pilot to "return to full flying duties." The letter then offers medical and non-medical contacts to discuss "the situation" and comments that a quiet informal chat can sometimes help. The letter concludes by advising the pilot that the company will "continue to monitor the situation."

If additional "absences" arise, the company then sends out a second letter. Again, it describes the "level of absence" as continuing to be of "concern." The letter then requests a meeting with non-medical officers to discuss "your attendance."

It is apparent from these and other letters that the company's interest is in attendance, not the medical reasons for the inability to undertake flying duties. In both letters, it is the "level of absence" which is of "concern." The first letter includes a medical officer as a contact but the second does not. The second letter, in particular, makes clear that it is "your attendance" which is the company's primary reason for writing.

Although "a quiet, informal chat" is suggested, it is worth noting that the company chose not to initiate this subject by first speaking informally with the pilot. Instead,

5/F Daily House, 35-37 Haiphong Road, Tsim Sha Tsui, Kowloon, Hong Kong
Tel: (852) 2736 0823   Fax: (852) 2736 0903   E-mail: hkaoa@hkalpa.org
Member of International Federation of Airline Pilots Associations.   Member of International Flight Engineers Organization.

2

the company chose to write to the pilot with the clear notation that a copy of the letter would be inserted into the pilot's personnel file. Of the range of options the company had at its disposal for communicating its concerns, the company has chosen the heaviest.

In response, the Association wrote to express its concern that the company's policy is directly inducing crew to report to duty in breach of the AN(HK)O. The Association describes the company's program as prejudicial to flight safety. An example is attached to illustrate the problem caused by the company's heavy approach which led to a junior Officer undergoing upgrade reporting for duty even though unfit. Of equal concern is the anecdote of a junior flight officer said to have been turned down for upgrade due to his "level of absence."

Now the parties are locked in dispute, with the company stressing its concern regarding "attendance levels" and the Association stressing its concern regarding the impact this policy is having on flight safety.

The allegation that the company would be using a carrot (smoother upgrade prospects) and stick (letters, personnel file record and advancement refusals) approach to achieve its ends toward increasing "attendance levels" is a matter of concern. That the company would adopt a policy which invariably requires the pilot (whilst sick) to weigh the risk to flight safety against the risk to the pilot's own career advancement can only be described as the first step down a steep and slippery slope.

Needless to say, section 20(8) of the AN(HK)O is relevant:

> 20(8)(a) A person shall not be entitled to act as a member of the flight crew of an aircraft registered in Hong Kong if he knows or suspects that his physical or mental condition renders him temporarily or permanently unfit to perform such functions or to act in such capacity.

Under section 98, "flight crew" are defined:

> "Flight crew" in relation to an aircraft means those members of the crew of the aircraft who respectively undertake to act as pilot, flight navigator, flight engineer and flight radio operator of the aircraft;

Section 20(8)(a) is mandatory. It prohibits a person from acting as a member of the flight crew if that person knows or suspects that his physical or mental condition renders him unfit to perform the functions he is required to perform as a member of the flight crew. The standard is subjective in that it is the pilot who must determine if he knows or suspects that he is unfit to perform his functions as a member of the flight crew.

3

If the pilot has obtained a medical certificate which states that he is unfit, he can be said to know that he is unfit as it is reasonable to defer to a medical expert with the relevant expertise to make this determination. However, section 20(8) does not require proof, knowledge beyond a reasonable doubt or even above the balance of probabilities. The requirement is not that the pilot must be more inclined on balance to conclude he is unfit. Instead, the standard is that he must not suspect he is unfit.

The term "suspects" is used again in section 55 of the AN(HK)O in connection with fatigue. It is worthwhile contrasting its use with section 54. Section 54 requires the operator not to "cause or permit any person to fly therein as a member of its crew if he knows or has reason to believe that that person is suffering from, or, having regard ... is likely to suffer from, such fatigue ... as may endanger the safety of the aircraft or of its occupants." Thus, whilst the operator is required to have reason to believe, the pilot is required merely to suspect.

The term "suspects" is not defined in the AN(HK)O. The ordinary meaning of the term describes a belief specified on little or no evidence. Thus, if the pilot, even in the absence of evidence thinks, imagines, or supposes or surmises that he is unfit, he is prohibited from acting as a member of the flight crew. If the pilot is debating internally about whether he is or is not unfit, he has already exceeded the threshold of suspicion. If a thought flashes through his mind that he is unfit, already he has suspected that he is unfit.

Although the term "unfit" is also not defined in the AN(HK)O, the ordinary meaning of the term is that one is incapable of meeting requirements or qualifications, or not being physically fit or sound. Thus, if the pilot suspects he is incapable of meeting the requirements of his capacity or function, he should not act as a member of the flight crew. Given the very high standards imposed upon flight crew, and the very low threshold that suspicion represents, even in the presence of little or no evidence the pilot may be prohibited from acting as a member of the flight crew.

A contravention of this provision is an offence and liable on summary conviction to a fine not exceeding $5,000 (section 91(5)). Given the extremely low threshold suspicion represents, if the pilot is asked after an incident whether he thought he might be unfit and replies that he thought about it and dismissed it or thought about it but concluded he wasn't, there is a danger that he has already exceeded the threshold. It is only if the pilot can reply that the possibility did not cross his mind that he can be said not to have suspected that his physical or mental condition would render him unfit.

In light of this low threshold, the company's actions are not helpful in ensuring compliance with the AN(HK)O. By the time the pilot considers weighing the risk of sanction by the company in regard to his "level of absence" he has already crossed the threshold of suspicion.

557

The unacceptable decision then becomes one of weighing the risk of consequences from contravening AN(HK)O against the risk of sanction by the company. Instead of taking steps to ensure compliance with the AN(HK)O, the company's actions can only be seen as an attempt to override the pilot's duties under section 20(8) in an effort to improve the "level of absence." Unfortunately, this conclusion arises because by the time the pilot needs to consider the Absence Management Program, and the company's communications sent to him, he has already passed the threshold of suspicion mandated under section 20(8).

The implication arising from the company's continued pursuit of the Absence Management Program is that notwithstanding that the company is aware of the requirements under the AN(HK)O, it values "level of absence" above compliance with section 20(8) of the AN(HK)O.

We look forward to the company's confirmation that it has ceased its Absence Management Program, failing which we can only conclude that it has deliberately or recklessly pursued a program which will likely lead to breach of section 20(8) of the AN(HK)O and the commitment of an offence under section 91(5). Such a conclusion will unfortunately require the Association to pursue this matter further with the consequential legal fees and costs that would entail. We look forward to the company's reply by 29 June 2001.

Yours sincerely

Captain N J Demery
President

Encl:

APPENDIX 2

民航處 **Civil Aviation Department**

飛行標準及適航部 Flight Standards and Airworthiness Division

香港大嶼山駿坊路 2 號機場麥運中心商業大樓十樓
10th Floor, Commercial Building, Airport Freight Forwarding Centre, 2 Chun Wan Road, Lantau, Hong Kong.

檔案編號 OUR REF.	來函編號 YOUR REF.	電話 TEL.	圖文傳真 FAX.	專用電訊 TELEX:	航空專用電訊 AFTN
(17) in A/OPS/ALP/1 II	9017/pmw/01/082	852-2769 8896	852-2382 4577	39524 CFSHK HX	VHHHYAYC

27 June 2001

Captain N J Demery
President
Hong Kong Aircrew Officers Association
5/F., Daily House
35-37 Haiphong Road
Tsim Sha Tsui
Kowloon

Dear Sir,

Sickness Program – Cathay Pacific Airways

Thank you for your letter of 15th June 2001. The matter is receiving our attention and we will revert to you later.

Yours faithfully,

(Y K Leung)
for Director-General of Civil Aviation

THE 49ERS

FAXED

2 8 JUN 2001

28 June 2001

Our Ref: 9017/pmw/01/086

Your Ref: (17) in A/OPS/ALP/1 11

Mr Y K Leung
Civil Aviation Department
46/F Queensway Government Offices
66 Queensway
Hong Kong

**Hong Kong
Aircrew Officers
Association**

Dear Mr Leung

SICKNESS PROGRAM – CATHAY PACIFIC AIRWAYS

Thank you for your letter dated 27 June 2001.

For your information, please refer to the attached letter, dated 22 June 2001, sent to the company on this matter.

Yours sincerely

Captain N J Demery
President

Encl:

5/F Daily House, 35-37 Haiphong Road, Tsim Sha Tsui, Kowloon, Hong Kong
Tel: (852) 2736 0823   Fax: (852) 2736 0903   E-mail: hkaoa@hkalpa.org
Member of International Federation of Airline Pilots Associations. Member of International Flight Engineers Organization.

民航處 **Civil Aviation Department**
飛行標準及適航部 Flight Standards and Airworthiness Division

香港赤鱲角駿運路 2 號機場空運中心商業大樓十樓
10th Floor, Commercial Building, Airport Freight Forwarding Centre, 2 Chun Wan Road, Chek Lap Kok, Hong Kong.

檔案編號 OUR REF.	來函編號 YOUR REF.	電話 TEL.	圖文傳真 FAX.	專用電訊 TELEX:	航空專用電訊 AFTN
(19) in A/OPS/ALP/1 II	9017/pmw/01/086	2769 7230	2362 4250	39524 CFSHK HX	VHHHYAYC

29 June 2001

Captain N J Demery
President
Hong Kong Aircrew Officers' Association
5/F Daily House
35-37 Haiphong Road
Tsim Sha Tsui
Kowloon
Hong Kong

BY FAX and BY POST

Dear Sir,

Absence Management Programme (AMP)

Your facsimile dated 28th June 2001 refers.

I will be having a further meeting with Cathay Pacific Airways regarding the overall influence the AMP may have on Flight Safety, and in particular, the methodology currently in place for the operation of their AMP.

Yours faithfully,

(Captain M S Davis)
Acting Assistant Director-General of Civil Aviation (Flight Standards)
for Director-General of Civil Aviation

MSD/al

致力於安全及有效率的航空系統 *Committed to a Safe and Efficient Air Transport System*

20 July 2001

Fax to JSW
This page then pages 1–15.

Ref: 9017/pmw/01/099

Mr Y K Leung
For Director-General of Civil Aviation
Civil Aviation Department
10/F Commercial Building
Airport Freight Forwarding Centre
2 Chun Wan Road
Lantau. Hong Kong

**Hong Kong
Aircrew Officers
Association**

Dear Mr Leung

CATHAY PACIFIC AIRWAYS – ABSENCE MANAGEMENT PROGRAM

Thank you for the informal meeting on 18th July 2001 where we discussed our concerns concerning the Cathay Pacific Absence Management Program.

As you know Cathay Pacific terminated 49 officers on 9th July 2001 with 3 months' pay in lieu of notice citing a "loss of confidence" in those officers. Initial analysis reveals that approximately 80% of those officers had received one or more letters from Cathay Pacific management referring to the Absence Management Program. The program does not distinguish between absence or certified sickness. We believe that 6 "instances" of either absence or sickness within a specified period results in an officer attracting the attention of this Program.

We are currently determining the percentage of all Cathay Pacific officers who have come to the attention of the Program however it is fair to say it will be far less than 80%. We believe that there is an established link between an officer being involved in the Absence Management Program and likelihood of termination or other disciplinary action.

It is reasonable to assume that if an officer suffers genuine sickness prior to flight but has recorded 5 absence or sickness events within the specified period, that there is then a dangerous inducement to report fit for flight in contravention of the ANO for fear of the consequences of doing otherwise. Anecdotal evidence suggests that some officers are indeed undertaking flight duties when they are not fit to do so.

We believe that situation is producing a real rather than potential flight safety hazard at Cathay Pacific Airways and requires the urgent attention of the Hong Kong Civil Aviation Department.

Yours sincerely

Captain N J Demery
President

5/F Daily House, 35-37 Haiphong Road, Tsim Sha Tsui, Kowloon, Hong Kong
Tel: (852) 2736 0823   Fax: (852) 2736 0903   E-mail: hkaoa@hkalpa.org
Member of International Federation of Airline Pilots Associations. Member of International Flight Engineers Organization.

p. 1   2736 0903   Administrator   15 Nov 01 11:333

民航處 Civil Aviation Department
飛行標準及適航部 Flight Standards and Airworthiness Division

2 6 JUL

香港大嶼山駿盛路 2 號機場空運中心商業大樓十樓
10th Floor, Commercial Building, Airport Freight Forwarding Centre, 2 Chun Wan Road, Lantau, Hong Kong.

檔案編號 OUR REF.	來函編號 YOUR REF.	電話 TEL.	圖文傳真 FAX.	專用電訊 TELEX:	航空專用電訊 AFTN
(34) in A/OPS/ALP/1 II	9017/pmw/01/082	852-2769 8896	852-2382 4577	39524 CFSHK HX	VHHHYAYC

23 July 2001

Captain N J Demery
President
Hong Kong Aircrew Officers Association
5/F., Daily House
35-37 Haiphong Road
Tsim Sha Tsui
Kowloon

Dear Sir,

Cathay Pacific Airways – Absence Management Program

Thank you for your letter of 20th July 2001, the conents of which are duly noted.

Yours faithfully,

(Capt M S Davis)
for Director-General of Civil Aviation

致力於安全及有效率的航空系統 Committed to a Safe and Efficient Air Transport System

Appendix 3

Monday February 4th 2002

Eulogy to Greg England – Corey Bousen:

When I first met Greg England less than a year ago during last year's Rugby Sevens celebrations he was wearing a blue T-shirt with a Superman logo on the front. Within the first few minutes of his talking I was quickly impressed with his calm, assured aura. Already knowing that he was a pilot, I could tell that if there was anyone you wanted sitting in the front of an airplane in an emergency situation it was this cool character before me. As the evening continued I quickly gained an appreciation of Greg's fun-loving nature. Somewhere along the line he managed to acquire a red, rectangular piece of cloth which he tied around his neck to make a cape. Among the mad Rugby Sevens throngs I could still picture Greg in Lan Kwai Fong; he was Superman and he was indestructible. Over the following weeks and months I quickly formed a strong bond with Greg and he became my best friend in Hong Kong.

We spent much time together, talking about life, its many challenges but, most of all, its many opportunities and its countless joys. I grew to know and understand Greg as I know and understand very few people; I grew to know and understand him as a brother. He had become an essential part of my Hong Kong life and my Hong Kong family. While his many friends here today knew Greg to be a generous and trusting man with an open heart who always accepted people into his life and home without judgment or discrimination, he was quick to lend friends money when asked and to offer his house to those who needed a place to stay 'cause they had nowhere else to go.

I wasn't surprised to hear from Greg's dad the other night that, at home growing up in Canada, Greg was known in his home town for often protecting the weak. When bullies threatened bodily harm to a physically weak child, unable to defend themselves, it was always Greg that was quick to step in to protect them, physically if need be. As he became an adult, Greg matured to learn that he didn't need to resort to his superior physical stature to protect those unable to protect themselves. Instead of growing his muscles, Greg actively grew his mind and quickly became the calm individual that I first met and he carried with him an impressive, sharp intellect. He was a person who taught himself to speak Cantonese fluently because he loved Hong Kong and he loved its people. He was a fiercely proud Canadian but he called Hong Kong his home and he intended to stay here and continue to build his life and his successful career.

This plan was thrown into chaos one tragic day last August when I received a short e-mail from Greg while I was on vacation in Tokyo. *"Call me as soon as you get this message,"* was all it read. I called him at home and asked what was up. He told me that he had been fired from his job. A job where he was only one test flight away from being promoted to First Officer; an impressive feat for a man who was only thirty years of age. I was extremely saddened that I couldn't be with Greg to help him at greatest time of need. Prior to this, I knew Greg as a strong, independent individual. He looked out for those who couldn't look out for themselves. He'd been put in a situation beyond his control where he now felt helpless to protect his livelihood and the career which he had tirelessly spent thousands and thousands of hours to build. The weeks that followed I believe were the toughest of Greg's life. I do know that he soon found comfort and hope amongst many of you here today, his pilot colleagues and particularly the people at the pilot union. Greg then devoted his energies to the fight for *The 49ers* to get their jobs back and he worked tirelessly to achieve this end. It was true that Greg sometimes had his down days since the sometimes vicious industrial dispute began, just as I'm sure did his fellow *49ers* and their families.

But I do know that in the days following the tragic event of last Monday night there has been a lot of speculation about Greg's fall to his death and some people speculated that it was an outcome of his own free will. To all of you gathered here today I feel obliged to clear the air and put forward the facts as best as they can be pieced together by his close friends that had contact with Greg in the days and hours prior to his death.

Two weeks ago Greg went to hospital complaining of severe stomach pains and received treatment. I saw Greg the Friday before his death and he spoke of having a stomach ulcer although we understand this might be Greg's own description of what were severe stomach cramps for which, on that same Friday, Greg had been prescribed various medications for the stomach cramps and stress etc. Three days later, last Monday morning, he called me and he asked if I had a VCD player on which he wanted to test a video disc that he'd made for the pilots' union. I asked him how he was going and he said his medication was making him hallucinate. I told him to take care and said to call me that evening if he wanted to come over to test the disc but he said he couldn't because he had ice hockey practice on. Gerard, a good friend of both Greg and I, tells me that Greg had called him over on Sunday night to talk about some urgent matter. As I was late, Gerard, also a staunch and giving friend of many of us here today, went over to Greg's place to discover that all was not well and to find that Greg was behaving abnormally. He was seeing visions of God; he was having a terrible reaction to his medication Gerard was so concerned he spent the rest of the night at Greg's asleep on the couch. Greg and Gerard also researched his medication on the Internet and found that in some cases it can cause hallucinations. Gerard said to Greg that he would help find some alternative natural medication that did not provide the terrible stomach cramps that were plaguing him.

That Monday night Greg, who last year led his team of Cathay Pacific colleagues to win a world ice hockey championship, went to practice at a local ice hockey league. His good friends on the team report that Greg was in high spirits at practice, joking about and having a good time generally. Subsequently he enjoyed a couple of drinks with his team mates in Wan Chai until around 1 am when he returned home still sort of located in Wan Chai. He spoke to a friend on the phone and organised to go out with him the following evening. His friend says that Greg sounded very tired and his speech was a bit erratic, but also that he didn't seem to be talking like someone who, only one and a half hours later, would voluntarily throw himself out of his bathroom window. Greg's beautiful girlfriend Vicki dropped in after work to see Greg at around 2.30 in the morning. She works as a professional singer so doesn't finish 'til that time. She found he wasn't there although his mobile phone which Greg never leaves home without was in his office. What happened before Vicki's arrival I don't think will ever really be known although I can only conclude that the alcohol may have further exacerbated Greg's allergic reaction to the stage where he was again hallucinating and this ended with his tragic fall from his bathroom window.

But even for me to conclude that Greg did not intentionally kill himself, no less reduces the tragedy of his death. He was taking that medication because he was repressing a massive amount of stress in his life. But I know that the only stress he had was his on-going struggle to get his job back with Cathay Pacific.

As I speak there continues legal battles between *The 49ers* and Cathay Pacific in various jurisdictions around the world. But I distinctly remember Greg once telling me that even if one of these cases saw him receive say a million US dollars in compensation he wouldn't give a damn. He'd trade in any money if he could just fly again for the airline that he respected and loved and he could stay in his adopted home of Hong Kong which he really believed was the best city in the world and the only place he wanted to be. Greg wasn't a political guy. He didn't want to see any harm come to Cathay Pacific. I know some of you here today have intense feelings of anger at Cathay Pacific management. Greg could never even bother disparaging the airline management who put him in this position. All he wanted was his job back. He didn't want to be caught up in this bitter dispute that harmed Cathay Pacific and profoundly damaged the lives and livelihood of *The 49ers* and their families.

It is for this reason that on Greg's behalf that I urge this dispute to end. Cathay Pacific's management I ask to not let Greg's tragic death be for nothing. To Swire's chairman, James Hughes-Hallett, who I've had some dealings with in a previous time as chairman of Hong Kong's shipowners association. I know you to be a good-hearted and extremely intelligent man. Show the world that you understand that this dispute is no longer about dollars. This dispute is about people's lives and it has gone on for far too long. To the pilots of Cathay Pacific I urge you all to make unwavering your support of the union and *The 49ers*. To the parties on both sides I remind you that this dispute should be one where those involved are able to rise above the hatred and vitriol and conduct themselves like the highly trained professionals that all of you are.

To both sides, let's honour Greg's memory, let's bring this dispute to an end, let *The 49ers* return to work.

To conclude, I would like to try and put some perspective on the apparent senselessness of Greg's death. To do so I want to tell you about the New Year's Eve just passed. I dropped over to Greg's place in the evening after work. We thought about going downtown but we both agreed that we couldn't give a damn about the hype that surrounded New Year's Eve. Both of us struggled to garner any real excitement for the so-called big event. In fact Greg said that it wasn't any different from any other night. And having had a late night the previous evening, Greg was always a bit of a late night-owl, around 10.30 he said he was going to bed to get some sleep and wait for Vikki to drop by. I subsequently caught up with both of them later that morning but at that stage, not particularly fussed myself, I went home and at quarter to midnight

I finished the book that I was reading, *The Fifth Mountain* by Paulo Coelho. I remember a line I found in that book particularly on the issues of God and death. The book talks about why God usually meets with his prophets on mountain tops.

But while re-reading the following words I think of Greg sitting on his own movable mountain top, the cockpit of an Airbus wide-bodied jet. To see photos of Greg in the cockpit is to see him where he was happiest and where he found the peace and contentedness that he carried with him to his day-to-day life before he lost his job. The following are Paulo's words:

"From these great heights both our glories and follies lose their importance. Whatever we have conquered and whatever we have lost remains below. From these heights you see just how large and beautiful this world is, and how far are its horizons."

As the book concludes, the central character, Elijah the prophet, is talking to a boy about tragedy and why God allows what humans perceive as tragedy to occur in the first place. The boy says to Elijah, *"Couldn't God have chosen a better way of showing us his lessons? There was a time when I thought he was evil." "God is all powerful,"* replied Elijah. *"He can do anything and nothing is forbidden to him. For if anything were forbidden to God there would have to be someone more powerful and this someone more powerful is who we would worship."*

Elijah continued to explain that God, because of his infinite powers, has chosen only to do good. If you clearly see and truly understand God's plan you would see that often good is disguised as evil. But it goes on being good and it is part of the plan that God created for humanity.

Upon finishing this book, at the stroke of midnight, I listened to the first time the Marvin Gaye *What's Going On?* CD that Greg had loaned me that evening. A remake of that song has been put in the wake of the tragic events of last September 11. But Greg, who was of the most passionate lovers of music on this planet, preferred what he described as the old school version of Marvin Gaye's. And we'll listen to this song shortly. It was also this same CD that was in Greg's CD-player the night that he died so it was probably the last music he ever heard. And so to this question Greg, *"What's going on?"* I can't provide the answers. I guess that in the end you weren't Superman at all. You lost your powers to fly and then you tragically came crashing to the ground. Greg, I love you as do many of your friends here today. Peace to you my brother. Your memory and your spirit continue to fly with us always in our hearts.

Words of thanks from Greg's father:

My wife and my son would like to join me in personally thanking the union and the membership for their amazing show of care and concern over the week since Greg's death. The union was quick to contact us and we were truly overwhelmed at the efforts of all involved. Needless to say, the past seven days have been both painful and tiring, but the stress was alleviated by the generous assistance of many of you. I would like to make a special note of thanks to *49ers* Pat Doherty, Cam Blakeney-Williams, and Bruce Schoettler who patiently escorted me around Hong Kong and assisted me in the daunting administration task associated with Greg's passing.

Greg truly loved life as no other and I believe the memorial address given by Greg's friend Corey provided a wonderful reflection of his attitude toward life. Those who had the opportunity to know Greg will surely agree.

I am not an emotional man by nature and during the memorial, I sat facing the photographs of Greg who seemed to stare back, reminding me, *'Dad, be strong and don't break down.'* Throughout the service I was afraid to look behind me and count how many had decided to appear to remember Greg. But I was emotionally overwhelmed when, at the conclusion to the service, I turned around to see the great Cathedral without a single empty seat. The camaraderie shown by his friends and peers that day was something I will never forget.

I would like to join Corey in voicing my wish that my son will not have died in vain. I hope that a resolution for all of the other *49er* officers and their families can be born from the grief surrounding Greg's death. I know Greg would certainly share those thoughts.

Yours sincerely,
Stephen England

Greg England

November 20, 2006

Regarding Greg England

To Whom It May Concern:

I have been thinking about how to write this letter for months, have written it in my mind a hundred times and realize that it may be impossible to do and achieve the desired result. How on earth do you express in writing the value of someone else's life? How the loss of that person affects your own life every day, every breath, every dream, on and on. It's been said many times that children are not supposed to precede their parents in death. It's just wrong, just too hard to bear. So here I am, trying to do the impossible, knowing that I cannot do justice to the task, and typing through the tears.

The main point of all this, I suppose, is that I truly believe that had it not been for the abrupt and unjust end to Greg's job as a Pilot with Cathay Pacific, the end to his career and the life that he loved immensely in Hong Kong, he would still be with us today. Greg was completely involved in his career and in the life that rushed around him in Hong Kong. He spoke the language so well that strangers thought he was born there. He had many friends that were indeed born there. He was actively involved with all aspects of life in HK, and his job was the focal point of it all. He also loved sports, and was extremely fit and active always. And, like his father, he loved to fly! Greg had a zest for life that knew no bounds! He was up and running before he was even 1 year old and just never stopped! Until that day. God only knows what happened. One thing I am very sure of is that he did not want to die. He was very much in love and planning on marriage and a family.

We communicated with Greg constantly, via email, messenger, telephone. He often called me when he was out with friends, or just walking down the street, to share an idea, or a beautiful day, and crazy conversations half in Cantonese – half in English! His loss is unbearable. I feel him standing beside me as I write this, I see him coming around a corner, saying 'Hi Mumsy', I feel him hugging me. I look at his picture, and miss him. I look at my younger son Brad, and know that he has lost his only brother, his only sibling, and know that his life will be different, less than what it should be and that his grief is different from mine, but equally deep. I look at my husband, and realize that we can never recover what we lost, and never share all of our pain, because it would overwhelm both of us.

Coroner's reports and police documents explain very little to me. All we are left with is pain and a huge question mark. Language barriers made it even more difficult to deal with the realities of the situation, to get answers to our questions. The police even managed to disable Greg's computer, where he kept a daily journal, and returned to us a useless hulk. Whatever drove Greg to his death that night, I know that he was still hoping to return to the job he loved. I know that he was having terrible problems with stress, the stomach ulcers that resulted from it and just dealing with the uncertainty of his future. We wanted him to come home, start again in Canada, just be here where we could help him through this, but he was steadfast in his resolve to remain in Hong Kong. He loved life there. He loved life. Hong Kong had become his home.

We all live in a space just above the pain of past experiences, the losses in our lives, so that we can function and get through every new day. It is hard to focus on the events that so devastate our lives and bring all of the emotions to the surface.

Greg's CD player had the last song that he listened to on it, a Marvin Gaye tune called 'What's going on?' I guess that's what he wanted to know. What is going on? How can employees be treated so badly? How can their lives be toyed with in such a fashion? How despicable! How unjust! Appalling? Yes. Illegal? Probably. Immoral? Yes, but so much more than that. Our son only wanted to get back to work. He just wanted a fair deal. Greg was smart, talented, handsome and on the brink of his adult life. He should have had everything to live for. He was concerned about the other *49ers*, the men with families to support, the ones who were worse off than he was, and he made efforts to be of help. He was an admirable man. Perhaps the decision makers of Cathay Pacific are not?

Sincerely,

Terry England
Greg's Mom

Appendix 4

	No.	Svc Type	Full Name	Total	Letter on file	Attnd Ltr 1	Attnd Ltr 2	No rep to Ltr 2	Attnd Ltr 3	No rep to Ltr 3	No AEP	High RSV bk-off	Short Notice bk-off	Crew Control Assist
B –1	1	P x	WILSON, BRETT ALEXANDER (MR) B Fo	7		X	X	X	X		X		3	X
B ~2	2	P x	BULTEEL, STEVE JAMES (MR) B Fo	5		X	X	X					2	X
A –3	3	P x	DOHERTY, PATRICK JAMES (MR) A Fo	5	PF0501 & F0898	X					X		2	X
B –4	4	P x	GAGE, DOUGLAS (MR) B CAPT	5	WR1298	X					X	57		X
B ~5	5	P x	GRIBBLE, TREVOR CRAIG (MR) B Fo	5		X	X				X		2	X
B –6	6	P x	HONNER, DAVID MICHAEL (MR) B Fo	5	WR1099	X					X	57		X
B –7	7	P x	MACNEIL, GERARD SIDNEY (MR) B Fo	5		X					X	86		X
B –8	8	P x	SHAW, MICHAEL STEVEN (MR) B Fo	5		X	X	X					2	X
B –9	9	P x	VAN POELGEEST, CRAIG DIRK (MR) B Fo	5		X	X				X	56		X
	10	P ok	CAVILL, MALCOLM LINDSAY (MR) A Fo	4		X	X						2	X
	11	P ok	COOK, BENJAMIN IAN JAMES (MR) A	4		X	X						3	X
	12	P ok	D'ALTERIO, FRANCIS BERNARD (MR) A	4		X	X				X			X
	13	P ok	DAVIS, LANCE PAUL (MR) B	4		X	X						2	X
A –14	14	P x	ENGLAND, GREGORY STEPHEN (MR) A	4		X	X					50	2	X
A –15	15	P x	FITZ-COSTA, MICHAEL JOHN (MR) A CAPT	4		X	X				X		2	X
A –16	16	P x	GERHARDS, KENNETH WOLFGANG (MR) A	4 CAPT		X	X	X			X			X
	17	P x	HUGHES, NIGEL JOHN (MR) A	4 CAPT		X	X						2	X
	18	P ok	JACKSON, MARK WILLIAM (MR) A	4		X	X				X		2	X
B –19	19	P x	KEENE, BRIAN DAVID (MR) B Fo	4		X	X				X			X
	20	P ok	KLUBI, STEPHEN PATRICK (MR) A	4		X						63	2	X
	21	P ok	MUGFORD, JAMES MATTHEW (MR) B	4		X	X	X	X					X
A –22	22	P x	O'TOOLE, MARK LANE (MR) A Fo	4		X						67	3	X
B –23	23	P x	ROTHE, TEVA PIERRE HERMANN (MR) B Fo	4		X	X				X			X
	24	P ok	SCANLON, SIMON NOEL (MR) A	4		X	X					50	2	X
A –25	25	P x	SCHOETTLER, BRUCE MICHAEL (MR) A Fo	4		X	X				X			X
	26	P ok	SHAW, LAURIE JAMES (MR) B	4		X						60	2	X
B –27	27	P x	VAN KEULEN, HENDRIK (MR) B CAPT	4		X					X	58		X
	28	P ok	VINNA, PETER JAROSLAV (MR) B	4		X	X				X	50		
A –29	29	P xx	WONG, LAWRENCE YING FAN (MR) A Fo	4		X	X				X	63		X
	30	P ok	ADKIN, PHILIP GEORGE (MR) B	3		X					X		2	
	31	P ok	BARCLAY, GLENN ANDREW (MR) B CAPT	3		X						67		X
	32	P ok	BEGG, ALAN RAYMOND (MR) B	3		X	X							X
A –33	33	P x	BENNETT, RICHARD DAVID (MR) A Flo	3		X	X						3	
	34	P ok	BERLIE, RONALD JOHN (MR)	3		X					X	75		
	35	P ok	BOWERS, JASON KAI (MR) A	3		X							3	X
	36	P ok	BRADY, BRENDAN JAMES (MR) B	3		X					X	88	3	
A –37	37	P x	CHUNG, KAIWAN (MR) A Fo	3		X	X					50	2	
	38	P ok	COLLINS, PETER JAMES WINDSOR (MR) A	3		X						50	2	X
	39	P ok	DEMERY, NIGEL JONATHAN (MR) B	3	U0895 & U0396								2	X
A –40	40	P x	EVANS, MARK ANDREW (MR) A Fo	3		X						80	5	X
	41	P ok	FISHER, CHRISTOPHER JOHN RICHARD A	3	UR0797						X		2	
	42	P ok	GORDON, PETER ALAN (MR) A	3		X	X				X			
	43	P ok	HOLLIDAY, LEE GAVIN (MR) A	3		X					X	56	2	
	44	P ok	HOLMES, THOMAS FREDERICK (MR) B	3	U0198						X			X
	45	P ok	JACOBSON, JOSEPH BRADLEY (MR) B	3		X	X						2	X
	46	P ok	KIERNANDER, SIMON KEITH (MR)	3		X						50		X
	47	P ok	LAM, MARK TZE FUNG (MR) A	3		X					X		2	
29 B –48	48	P x	LANG, STEVEN (MR) B CAPT	3		X					X			X
	49	P ok	LANGLEY, DEAN NIELS (MR) A	3		X							2	X
	50	P ok	LAU, CHUN FAI (MR) A	3		X					X		2	X
	51	P ok	LAWRENCE, CHRISTOPHER HOWARD (MR) A	3		X	X							X
	52	P ok	LO, AUGUSTINE HIN CHI (MR) A	3		X	X				X			
B –53	53	P x	MACLEOD, IAN DOUGLAS (MR) B CAPT	3		X					X	53		X
	54	P ok	MACPHAIL, CALLUM CAMPBELL (MR) A	3		X	X							X
B –55	55	P x	MUNRO, KEITH IAN (MR) B CAPT	3		X					X			X
B –56	56	P x	PALMER, MICHAEL GORDON (MR) B	3	U0800 & U0599	X					X	57		X
	57	P ok	PSHEBYLO, WESLEY RONALD WAYNE (MR) A	3							X		2	X
	58	P ok	SAUNDERS, DAVID ALLEN (MR) B	3							X	83	2	X
A –59	59	P x	SEARLE, ANDREW DAVID (MR) A Fo	3		X					X			X
A –60	60	P x	SIMPSON, ST. JON FRASER (MR) A CAPT	3	U0800						X			X
A –61	61	P x	SPONG, DAVID BRUCE (MR) A CAPT	3		X					X			X
A –62	62	P x	ST. HILL, PHILIP FRASER (MR) A CAPT	3		X					X			X
	63	P ok	SULLIVAN, MICHAEL PATRICK (MR) A	3	FR1100	X					X			
B –64	64	P x	SWEENEY, CHRISTOPHER LEO (MR) B Fo	3		X							4	X
	65	P ok	TAYLOR, DAVID MICHAEL (MR) A	3		X					X			X
	66	P ok	TONG, EDMOND KA CHUEN (MR) B *	3		X							5	X
	67	P ok	TSANG, EDDY YIU CHUNG (MR) B *	3		X							6	X
B –68	68	P x	URQUHART, STEVEN AUBREY (MR) B Fo	3		X					X		2	X
	69	P ok	WILSON, ANDREW JOSEPH (MR) B	3		X					X	50		
	70	P ok	WONG, DAVID TAI WAI (MR) B	3		X						67	3	
	71	P ok	WORRELL, JASON GLYN (MR) B	3		X	X					57		
B –72	72	P x	YIASOUMI, PHILIP ANDREAS (MR) B CAPT	3	U0200	X								X
B –73	73	P x	YOUNG, CRAIG MICHAEL (MR) B CAPT	3		X	X							X
	74	P ok	AMBLER, JOHN RICHARD (MR) B	2		X								X
	75	P ok	ARMSTRONG, IAN CUNNINGHAM (MR) A	2		X						50		
	76	P ok	ASHFORD, JOHN WARWICK (MR) A	2		X	X							
	77	P ok	ATACK, MATTHEW JOHN (MR)	2								50	2	
	78	P ok	BAKER, MATTHEW DAVID (MR) A	2								71	2	
	79	P ok	BALMAN, DAVID STANLEY (MR) B-SICK	2							X		2	
	80	P ok	BEAUCHESNE, DENIS ERNEST (MR) A	2		X					X			
	81	P ok	BJORGAN, DAVID WAYNE ERLING (MR)	2		X						50		
A –82	82	P x	BLAKENEY-WILLIAMS, CAMPBELL RICHA A Fo	2		X							2	

575

SB 19/16 [handwritten] | B/H 10/2 [handwritten]

	Svc Type	Full Name	Total	Letter on file	Attnd Ltr 1	Attnd Ltr 2	No rep to Ltr 2	Attnd Ltr 3	No rep to Ltr 3	No AEP	High RSV bk-off	Short Notice bk-off	Crew Control Assist
83	P OK	BOYD, TIMOTHY JOHN (MR) B	2							X			X
84	P OK	BOYENS, ALAN ROSS (MR)	2		X					X			
A-85	P X	BOYLE, RON (MR) A CANT	2		X					X			
86	P OK	BROWN, GREGORY PHILLIP (MR) B	2		X					X	50		
87	P OK	BURNS, DONALD BRUCE (MR) A	2		X					X			
B-88	P X	BURTON, CHARLES BRUCE (MR) B FO	2	WR0401								3	
89	P?OK	CALLANDER, PHILIP STEPHEN (MR)A	2										
90	P OK	CARR, JAMES ANTHONY (MR) B	2		X					X			X
B-91	P X	CARVER, KENNETH GORDON (MR) B CANT	2		X								X
92	P OK	CASHEL, DAVID GEORGE (MR) A	2		X	X							
93	P OK	CHESTER, THOMAS ROBERT (MR) B	2							X			X
B-94	P X	CLAPSON, DAVID BRIAN (MR) B FO	2	PF1100									X
95	P OK	COCHRANE, ANNABELLE KATE (MS) B	2		X	X							
96	P OK	CREIGHTON, PAUL HARTLEY (MR) A	2	U0899									X
97	P OK	CVITAN, GREGORY JOHN (MR) A	2							X			X
98	P OK	DEMPSEY, DANIEL VANCE (MR) B	2									2	X
99	P OK	DICKS, MICHAEL RICHARD (MR) A	2		X					X			
100	P OK	DOWLING, ROBERT JOHN (MR) A	2							X			X
101	P OK	DUCKHAM, ANTHONY JOHN (MR) A	2							X			X
102	P OK	ELLIS, STEPHEN MARK (MR) B	2								50		X
103	P OK	EMPEY, KEITH RANDALL (MR) B	2		X					X			X
104	P OK	EVANS, LAWRENCE JAMES (MR) A	2		X					X			X
105	P OK	EVES, CHRISTOPHER JOHN (MR) A	2		X							2	
106	P OK	FARREL, MALCOLM HARCOURT (MR) A	2		X								X
107	P OK	FINDLAY, DANIEL WILLIAM (MR) B	2								100	2	
108	F OK	FOWLER, JEFFREY ALLEN (MR) B	2	PF0400						X			
109	P OK	FRASER, MAXWELL CHARLES (MR) A	2	WC0393 & U0999	X					X			
110	P OK	FREDERICK, WILLANS JOHN (MR) B	2		X					X			
B-111	P X	GARLICK, PHILIP JOHN (MR) B FO	2							X			X
112	P OK	GIBBS, CAMERON CHARLES (MR) A	2							X	60		
113	P OK	GREEN, LAINE HOWARD (MR) B	2								80	3	
114	P OK	GREEVES, BRIAN JOHNSTONE (MR) A	2		X								X
115	P OK	GUINEA, DONALD TAUVIRAATEA (MR) B	2								63	2	
116	P OK	HANCOCK, LESLIE DAVID (MR) B	2		X								X
B-117	P X	HARRIS, BRADFORD DEAN (MR) B CANT	2		X								X
118	P OK	HASKETT, BRADLEY LIONEL (MR) B	2		X							2	
119	P OK	HASLEMORE, PHILIP NEIL (MR) B	2								50	2	
120	P OK	HAZELTON, THOMAS JENKINS (MR) A	2		X						50		
B-121	P X	HERON, QUENTIN JAMES LEE (MR) B FO	2							X			X
122	P OK	HEYES, TERENCE ANTHONY (MR) B	2	PF0100									X
123	P OK	HOWELL, MALCOLM DAVID (MR) B	2		X					X			
124	P O	KHOY, KENNETH COLIN (MR) A	2		X								X
125	P OK	JERDAN, IAN STUART (MR) A	2		X								X
126	P OK	JONES, TREVOR JULIAN FAIRBRASS (MF	2		X								X
127	P OK	KALADE, POVILAS DARIUS (MR) A	2							X			X
128	P OK	KALMAR, JOSEPH LESLIE (MR) A	2								80	2	
B-129	P X	KELLY, CHRISTOPHER JOHN (MR) B CANT	2		X							2	
130	P OK	LANGLEY, ROSS FRANCIS (MR) A	2		X							2	
131	P OK	LARSEN, KIM PHILLIP (MR) A	2		X								X
132	P OK	LAW, KENNETH SIU WING (MR) A	2		X							2	
B-133	P X	LEE, NICHOLAS PAUL (MR) B CANT	2	U0599	X					X			
134	P OK	LEE, PETER YUEN MAN (MR) B	2							X			X
135	P OK	LI, KIN CHUNG (MR) B	2		X	X				X			
136	P OK	LUCAS, KARL ERIC (MR) B	2							X	69		
137	P OK	MA, KELVIN YEE HIM (MR) A	2		X						67		
138	P OK	MARSHALL, SIMON JAMES (MR) B	2									3	
139	P OK	MASON, PATRICK ERNEST (MR) B	2	C0100						X			
140	P OK	MCLAUGHLIN, ADAM MATTHEW (MR) B TFO	2	W1100						X			
141	P OK	MCPHERSON, DARREN NEIL (MR) B	2								50	3	
A-142	P X	MIDDLEMASS, DUNCAN RAYMOND (MR) A CAPT	2	U1000									X
143	P OK	MOORE, DAVID THOMAS (MR) B	2							X	55		
B-144	P X	MORISSETTE, PIERRE JOSEPH ROGER (B P/O	2							X			X
145	P OK	MOXHAM, TREVOR JOHN (MR) B	2							X			X
146	P OK	MRAD, SAM (MR) B	2	WR1100						X			
147	P OK?	NELSON, MARK ANTHONY (MR) B	2		X					X			
148	P OK	NICHOLLS, JOHN (MR) B	2								67		X
149	P OK	NUTTALL, LAWRENCE JAMES (MR) B	2		X					X			
150	P OK	OBORNE, GEOFFREY ALAN (MR) A	2		X					X			
151	P OK	O'DONOGHUE, CHRISTOPHER (MR) B	2		X					X			
152	P OK	O'SHAUGHNESSY, DARYL MARK (MR) A	2	W0399									X
153	P OK	PAU, JEFFREY CHI HONG (MR) A	2		X					X			
154	P OK	POXON, LAWRENCE JOHN (MR) A	2							X		2	
155	P OK	RATTIGAN, STEPHEN MATTHEW (MR) A	2		X					X			
156	P OK	RATTIGAN, STUART ANDREW (MR) A	2		X								X
157	P OK	ROBINSON, JASON MARK (MR) B	2		X							2	
158	P OK	ROBSON, JUSTIN SIMEON (MR) B	2									2	X
159	P OK	ROGERS, AARON WAYNE (MR) B	2								50	2	
160	P OK	ROONEY, GILES LACHLAN (MR) A	2		X	X							
B-161	P X	ROSEWALL, BRETT KENNETH (MR) B FO	2		X						69		
162	P OK	ROWLAND, MICHAEL JOHN (MR) B	2		X							2	
163	P OK	RUTLEDGE, WILLIAM FORSTER (MR) A	2		X							2	
164	P OK	SALAM, OWAIS MICHAEL (MR) B	2								83	2	

	Svc Type	Full Name	Total	Letter on file	Attnd Ltr 1	Attnd Ltr 2	No rep to Ltr 2	Attnd Ltr 3	No rep to Ltr 3	No AEP	High RSV bk-off	Short Notice bk-off	Crew Control Assist
165	P OK	SCOFFOM, ANDREW JONATHAN (MR) B	2							X			X
166	P OK	SCOTT, JAMES GARY (MR) B	2								56	3	
167	P OK	SCOTT, SIMON CHRISTIAN MARTIN (MR) A	2		X					X			
168	P OK	SIGSON, SKULI MARK (MR) B	2		X					X			
169	P OK	STEPHANSON, GREGORY ALEXANDER (IA	2		X							2	
170	P OK	SYCAMORE, GLEN LESLIE (MR) A	2							X			X
171	P OK	TAYLOR, ROBIN CAMERON (MR) B	2							X			X
172	P OK	THOMAS, NICHOLAS (MR) B	2		X							4	
173	P OK	THOMAS, PHILLIP WILLIAM (MR) B	2		X						67		
174	P OK	TORLOF, CHRISTER HANS OLA (MR) B	2		X					X			
175	P OK	TRACY, ANDREW JOHN (MR) A	2							X			X
176	P OK	TSE, CLEMENT CHI YIN (MR) A	2		X					X			
177	P OK	VASIL, JOHN PAUL DEWAR (MR) B	2		X						60		
178	P OK	WAN, DUNCAN WAI YEUNG (MR) A	2		X							3	
179	P OK	WARD, IAN MARTIN (MR) A	2		X					X			
A— 180	P X	WARHAM, JOHN SIMPSON (MR) A CAPT	2							X			X
181	P OK	WIEBE, SHELDON HENRY (MR) B	2		X							3	
182	P OK	WINDLE, GEOFFREY LLOYD (MR) B	2							X	71		
183	P OK	WONG, ALBERT HO YIN (MR)	2		X					X			
184	P OK	WONG, REX PAK FOO (MR)	2		X					X			

F/O | CAPT
26 | 21

	CAPT 400	A 400
	14 42	8 10
	FO 400	A BUS
	18 12	9
	29	18

(56)

CAPT 400 | CAPT A

FO 400 | FO A

CREW CONTROL LIST

1. ✓ DICKIE JW.   B 744 CAPT.
       A CAPT A
2. ✓ HALL RC
3. ✓ ROBINSON   P B CAPT 744
4. ✓ ACORN   DC   B744 F/O.
5. ✓ HETHERINGTON G · B744 CAPT
6. ✓ ROGERS RD   A F/O.
7. ✓ NEICH- BUCKLEY. B F/O.
8.   — CROFT GA   B CAPT 744
9.   BRADLEY S   B747 CAPT.   } ? F
(9) 7 PARROCK SJ   B744 FO
10. 7 DONAVAN   JP   B744 F

577

Glossary of Terms

Abbrev	Full Form	Explanation
A/C	Air conditioning	
AAIB	Air Accident Investigation Board	
AC	Alternating current	
ACM	Air combat manoeuvring	
ADC	Aide de Camp	
ADD	Acceptable Deferred Defect	U/S items that are permitted to be carried in accordance with the MEL
AEA	Atomic Energy Authority	
AFAP	Australian Federation of Air Pilots	
AFTLS	Approved Flight Time Limitations Scheme	
AGL	Above ground level	
AHK	Air Hong Kong	
AI	Accident Investigator	
AIPA	Australian and International Pilots Association	
AK47		Russian assault rifle
ALPA-K	Air Line Pilots' Association of Korea	
ALPAP	Airline Pilots' Association of the Philippines	
ANO	Air Navigation Order	
ANZ	Air New Zealand	
AOC	Air Operator's Certificate	Certification required to operate public transport aircraft

AOG	Aircraft on ground	An aircraft that is grounded pending repair due to unserviceability
APC	Armoured personnel carriers	
APD	Anti personnel department	
APU	Auxilliary Power Unit	A small engine used to provide electrical power and A/C to an aircraft on the ground
ARB	Air Registration Board	
ASI	Airspeed indicator	
ASL	Aircrew Services Limited	
ATC	Air traffic control	
ATK	Available Tonne Kilometre	A measure of capacity used in airline analysis
BA	British Airways	
BAF	British Air Ferries	
BALPA	British Airline Pilots Association	
Barbers pole		Maximum operating speed indicator on the ASI
BCal	British Caledonian Airways	
BEA	British European Airways	The short haul arm of BA before its merger with BOAC to form BA in 1974
BGA	British Gliding Association	
Bingo fuel		Lowest fuel level allowable before diverting
Black Star		IFALPA airport rating as 'critically deficient'
Blood wagons		Airfield emergency services vehicles
BMA	Britsh Midland Airways	
BOAC	British Overseas Airways Corporation	The long haul arm of BA before its merger with BEA to form BA in 1974
Bowser		Fuel tanker
Bundu		South African slang for a remote uninhabited region

580

c/b	Circuit breaker	
CAA	Civil Aviation Authority	
CAAC	Civil Aviation Administration of China	
CAD	Civil Aviation Department	
CAR	Commanders Administrative Report	
Casevac		Casualty evacuation
Cb	Cumulonimbus cloud	
CBA	Cost Benefit Analysis	
CCF	Combined Cadet Force	
CDG	Paris Charles DeGaulle	
CFI	Chief Flying Instructor	
CFP	Computer flight plan	
CG	Centre of Gravity	
Chop rate		Failure rate in flying training
CLK	Chek Lap Kok	The international airport at Hong Kong which replaced Kai Tak
CofA	Certificate of Airworthiness	
CoL	Cost of Living	
Combi		Part passenger part cargo aircraft
Comms	Communications	
Contrail	Condensation trail	
CoS	Conditions of Service	
CPL	Commercial Pilot's Licence	
CPU	Cathay Pilots Union	
CRS	Compagnies Républicaines de Sécurité	French police riot squad
CVR	Cockpit voice recorder	
DBR	Damaged beyond repair	
DDFO	Deputy DFO	
DDO	Design Deviation Order	A modification which varies from the standard design
DDO	Domestic Day Off	A period of 34 consecutive hours including 2 local nights
DFO	Director Flight Operations	
DGP	Discipline & Grievance Procedure	
DH	Decision height	The miniumum permissible descent height on an instrument approach without visual reference

Dingbat		US slang for a missile
DOC	Direct Operating Costs	
DPGFD	Delay, prevarication & general foot dragging	
DPS	Denpassar	The main international airport at Bali
DT	Duty Travel	
DUI	Driving under the influence	
EAT	Employment Appeal Tribunal	
ECAM	Electronic Centralised Aircraft Monitor	
EFP	Excess Flying Pay	
EGM	Extraordinary General Meeting	
EGT	Exhaust gas temperature	The temperature of the air leaving a jet engine exhaust
EIU	Economist Intelligence Unit	
EO	Employment Ordinance	
EPR	Engine pressure ratio	A measure of the power output used on Rolls Royes aero-engines
ERA	Employment Rights Act	
ET	Employment Tribunal	
ETOPS	Extended-range Twin-engine Operational	Performance Standards
F/E	Flight Engineer	
F/O	First Officer	
FAA	Federal Aviation Administration	
FCMC	Fuel Control & Monitoring Computers	
FCOM	Flight Crew Operating Manual	
FDP	Flight Duty Period	
FDR	Flight Data Recorder	The so called 'black box' which is actually orange
FIR	Flight Information Region	A designated ATC area
Fire walled		At maximum power
Fish Head		Slang for surface warfare personnel used by Navy aircrew
FM	Fleet Manager	
FMV	Fuel metering valve	
FNC	*Forum non conveniens*	
FOC	Free of charge	
FOCC	Flight Operations Control Centre	
FOD	Foreign Object Debris	

FOI	Flight Operations Inspector	
Four bars		Captain's epaulette badges of rank
FRA	Frankfurt	
FSD	Flight Safety Department	
FTL	Flight Time Limitations	
FTLWG	Flight Time Limitations Working Group	
FTM	Flying Training Manager	
GAPAN	Guild of Air Pilots and Navigators	
GC	General Committee	
Gen Sec	General Secretary	
Glideslope		The vertical guidance part of an ILS
GMA	General Manager Aircrew	
GMFC	General Manager Flight Crew	
GNP	Gross National Product	
Go around		An aborted landing
GPU	Ground power unit	A generator providing electrical power on the ground
Gweilo		A Cantonese term for foreigners
HSI	Hang Seng Index	
HAECO	Hong Kong Aircraft Engineering Co Ltd	
Hamster		Graduate of the College of Air Training, Hamble
HF	High frequency	A method of radio communication
HKALPA	Hong Kong Airline Pilots Association	
HKAOA	Hong Kong Aircrew Officers Association	
HKMA	Hong Kong Monetary Authority	
HMY	Her Majesty's Yacht	
howgozit		A graphical representation of fuel consumption used in flight to compare actual vs planned consumption
IATA	International Air Transport Association	
iaw	in accordance with	
ICAO	International Civil Aviation Organisation	
ICI	Imperial Chemical Industries	
IFALPA	International Federation of Air Line Pilots' Associations	
IFE	In flight entertainment	

IFR	Instrument Flight Rules	Flight solely by reference to aircraft instruments
IGS	Instrument Guidance System	
ILS	Instrument Landing System	
IMC	Instrument Meteorological Conditions	Low visibility flight conditions with no external visual reference
Inop	Inoperative	
INS	Inertial Navigation System	
Inversion		Atmospheric condition where the air temperature increases with altitude instead of decreasing
IOCC	Integrated Operations Control Centre	
IRC	Industrial Relations Commission	
IT	Inclusive tours	
KaDeWe	Kaufhaus des Westens	A large department store in Berlin
Kai Tak		The name of the old city centre airport in Kowloon, Hong Kong
KAL	Korean Air Lines	
KAL FCU	Korean Air Flight Crew Union	
KBO	Keep buggering on	
KT	Knots	Speed in nautical miles per hour
LBA	Leeds/Bradford Airport	
LBW	Leg before wicket	
Legco		Hong Kong Government Legislative Council
LHR	London Heathrow	
LIA	Limited industrial action	
LMC	Last Minute Change	Minor changes to the aircraft loadsheet just prior to departure
Localiser		The lateral guidance part of an ILS

Lower 41		A compartment under the flight deck floor on the 707
Luqa		The main airport in Malta
MAEL	Monarch Airline Engineering Limited	
MAUW	Maximum All Up Weight	
Max Diff	Maximum differential	The maximum permitted differential pressure between the inside and the outside of an aircraft
MAYDAY		Distress radio call
MCFA	Mixed Crew Flying Agreement	
MEL	Minimum Equipment List	A list of aircraft components that may be U/S under certain circumstances yet still permit flight
MI	Myocardial infarction	
MiG		Russian made Mikoyan fighter aircraft
MLO	Manager Line Operations	
MMO	Maximum operating Mach number	The maximum permitted aircraft speed at high level
MO	Modus operandi	
MoD	Ministry of Defence	
MSF	Médecins Sans Frontières	
MSS	Maximum safety strategy	
MTOW	Maximum Take Off Weight	
N1		The rotational speed of the first stage turbine on a jet engine
Narita		Tokyo's international airport
Nav	Navigator/navigation	
Nav Bag		A pilot's flight case
Navaid	Navigation aid	

NBC kit	Nuclear Biological & Chemical Protection kit	
NCO	Non Commissioned Officer	
Nil Further		No further defects noted
Nitromors		Paint stripper
NM	Nautical miles	
NOPAC	North Pacific Routing	
NPV	Net present value	
NTC	Notice to Crew	
NTSB	National Transportation Safety Board	
Nullah		Storm water course
NUM	National Union of Mineworkers	
OCCC	Oneworld Cockpit Crew Coalition	
OEB	Operational Engineering Bulletin	A notice affecting the 'normal' operation of the aircraft
Oleo		Hydraulic undercarriage strut
OPEC	Organisation of Petroleum Exporting Countries	
Ops manager	Operations Manager	
Orly		The regional airport serving Paris
OTP	On Time Performance	
P1	Pilot in command	The Captain of the aircraft
PA	Public address	
PADD	Performance Acceptable Deferred Defect	An ADD which directly affects the performance of the aircraft
PAL	Philippine Airlines	
PAN		Emercency radio call one level below MAYDAY
PanAm	Pan American World Airways	
pcm	per calendar month	
PIA	Pakistan International Airlines	
PIO	Pilot induced oscillation	Divergent flight caused by over controlling by the pilot
PLA	People's Liberation Army	
PMO	Principal Medical Officer	
PO	Principal Officer	
Positioning		An empty flight with no passengers or cargo

PPL	Private Pilot's Licence	
QFI	Qualified Flying Instructor	
QNH		Altimeter pressure setting relating to height above mean sea level
QRA	Quick reaction alert	
R/W	Runway	
RA	Radio altitude	
Rad Alt	Radio Altimeter	
RCAF	Royal Canadian Air Force	
Recency	Recency flying	Just sufficient flying to maintain currency of one's flying licence – e.g. one T/O & landing every 28 days
Redcap		Ground handling agent so-called because of the colour of his hat
Redux		An adhesive used in aircraft construction
REM	Rapid eye movement	
RLWG	Roster Liaison Working Group	
RPI	Retail Price Index	
RPM	Revolutions per minute	
RPs	Rostering Practices	
RT	Radio telephony	
RTOW	Regulated take-off weight	
Russian Bear	Tupolev Tu-95	A 4 engine turboprop powered strategic bomber
RVP	Rendezvous point	
S/O	Second Officer	
SADD	Significant Acceptable Deferred Defect	An ADD which is considered to be more significant than a 'normal' ADD
SARPS	Standards and Recognised Practices	
SCMP	South China Morning Post	
SF/O	Senior First Officer	
SG	Specific Gravity	
Sim	Simulator	
Skydrol		Hydraulic fluid

SOP	Standard Operating Procedure	
STA	Scheduled Time of Arrival	
STD	Sexually transmitted disease	
STD	Scheduled Time of Departure	
TAECO	Taikoo (Xiamen) Engineering Company Limited	
TAT	Total air temperature	
Tech Log	Aircraft technical log	Completed after each sector recording sector times and any defects that occurred
Tit	The RT transmit button	
TM	Transcendental Meditation	
TMAC	Transmeridian Air Cargo	
TOGA	Takeoff go around	Maximum engine power for takeoff or go around
TWA	Trans World Airlines	
U/S	Unserviceable	
ULR	Ultra Long Range	
UPAS	Universal Pilot Application Service	An employment agency run/sponsored by USALPA
USAF	United States Air Force	
USALPA	United States Airline Pilots Association	
V1		Take off decision speed
VASIs	Visual Approach Slope Indicator	A system of lights to assist pilots in assessing their vertical position on approach
VFC	Very fucking close	
VFL	Very fucking low	
VHF	Very high frequency	
VIGV	Variable Inlet Guide Vane	
VMC	Visual Meteorological Conditions	Flight conditions with exterior visual reference
Vol 1		Volume 1 of the Flight Operations Manual
VOR	VHF Omni-directional Range	A radio navigation aid which indicates bearing to or from the beacon
VPA	Vice President Admin	
VPP	Vice President Professional	
VR		Take off rotation speed
VSV	Variable Stator Vane	

Water/meth	Water/methanol	A means of increasing power output on a turbo-prop engine on takeoff
WHO	World Health Organisation	
Wide-body		Multi aisle 'Jumbo' aircraft
wie	with immediate effect	
WOCL	Window of Circadian Low	